*School Children*

*in the*

*Urban Slum*

# School Children in the Urban Slum

*Readings in*

SOCIAL SCIENCE RESEARCH

EDITED BY

## JOAN I. ROBERTS

THE FREE PRESS, *New York*
COLLIER-MACMILLAN LIMITED, *London*

*To Mother and Dad*
*—with gratitude*

# ACKNOWLEDGEMENTS

This book is produced through Project TRUE (Teacher Resources for Urban Education) at Hunter College under Grant Numbers 64227 and 65320 of the United States Office of Juvenile Delinquency and Youth Development. Project Director, Dr. Marjorie Smiley, Professor of Education, and Research Director, Dr. Elizabeth M. Eddy, social scientist, carefully examined this collection of readings from their own disciplinary vantage points. Since this volume is an effort to apply social scientific findings to urban education, their combined criticisms have proved invaluable.

To Dr. Eddy, I am further indebted for numerous discussions from which were derived ideas that clarified my thinking and support that sustained my efforts. I am also grateful to Mrs. Helen Randolph, Research Assistant, who has provided initial bibliographic material and Project research observations for my perusal.

In the production of this book there have been a number of tasks such as obtaining publishers' permissions that required organizational skill and perseverance which Mrs. Susan Stein, Research Assistant, has provided. To her, I am particularly grateful for assumption of responsibility for the technical problems of production. Working with Mrs. Stein, Mr. Norman Bailey has provided typing skills necessary for various manuscripts for the experimental version. In addition, Mr. Bailey and Miss Carol Bryant have assumed responsibility for obtaining permissions for this commercial edition. To these people, my appreciation is also extended.

And last, Miss Thetis M. Group has provided encouragement and editorial advice which has contributed much to this book.

# Contents

ix

*i*

---

# General Introduction

## PURPOSE

> There was a child went forth every day;
> And the first object he looked upon and received
>     with wonder, pity, love or dread,
>     that object he became.
> And that object became part of him for the day,
>     or a certain part of the day,
> Or for many years or stretching cycles of years.
>
> —Walt Whitman, "There Was a Child Went Forth"

This book is about children who go forth in the slums of our big cities. It is about children whose first objects, first encounters in their own worlds—the neighborhoods and schools of the inner-city—shape them for the day or, perhaps, for their lifetimes. This book is for you, the teacher or teacher-in-training in our urban centers, for it is you who encounter the great diversity of backgrounds that forms groups of children differently. The basic assumption of this volume is that children are influenced in many different ways according to the nature of prevailing conditions by what they look upon and incorporate in their social and physical environments. These readings are, therefore, presented to you, the teacher, with one purpose: to help you understand the differences that children from various backgrounds bring to the classroom in order that you may respect and help each individual child in terms of his own world. The readings do not, however, apply to every child in every school in a slum neighborhood in exactly the same way. Rather this collection is presented to help you examine the trends from social scientific research that indicate differences in broad groupings of children.

Educators and social scientists have long accepted the idea that one should teach with constant awareness of and consistent provision for individual differences among children. It is axiomatic to say that children differ in personality, intelligence, motivation, and interests. It is not yet axiomatic to say that groups of children may differ because of widely varied environments that include their family positions in the social structure, their membership in minority groups, their racial identification, and their cultural heritage. A child does not go forth into a vacuum nor does he come from one. Our concern with characteristics of the individual child has, unfortunately, led to limited concern with the worlds in which different children live, worlds which become part of them.

Perhaps our interest in the internal aspects of the individual child is partially derived from our democratic concern for equal rights of individual citizens. We Americans, educators and laymen alike, believe in the necessity for equality. We have said that we are at base the same no matter where we come from and no matter what conditions we live in. This principle of equal justice and respect for all, has ironically obscured the reality of life in our own society. Our belief in "equality" has allowed us to overlook the fact that groups of children live in very different environments across the 3,000-mile span of our continent and across the ten-block span from upper Park Avenue in Harlem to lower Park Avenue in the wealthy East Side of New York or in any other major city where people are invariably separated by income or color.

The brilliance of the democratic ideal as embodied in the phrase, "All men are created equal," has blinded our eyes to the inequality of conditions into which some men are born. A skeptic once said, "But some men are created more equal than others." Americans are just beginning to realize that this may indeed be the case. You are asked in reading this book to keep in mind that, much as we proclaim our classless society, it does not in fact exist. Groups of children do, in fact, differ as a result of the varied environments in which they are raised. Acceptance of this idea does not, in the long run, negate the principle of equality; rather, it allows us to make educational opportunities more nearly equal for all children by providing the teacher with information that can help improve the learning of school children in urban slums.

This book of readings, therefore, presents materials that show differences by social class and ethnic group memberhip of young people. Research studies are drawn from three social sciences—anthropology, sociology, and psychology—in the belief that a cross-disciplinary approach is most profitable when dealing with the diverse problems a teacher faces in urban schools. In addition, a fairly broad coverage of topics is attempted since the multiplicity of challenges before the teacher requires a wide acquaintance with information and ideas.

Each part is concerned with concepts that relate to teaching problems you may have in your urban classroom. The introduction that precedes each part presents the major idea of each reading and unifies the readings for you. Numbers within these introductory texts refer to a list of references at the end of the book on pages 611 through 613 that you may wish to examine for additional reading. The excerpts and articles are chosen to provide information to help you understand ideas that are pertinent to the educational difficulties evident in urban slum schools. Thus, readings in the second part on cognitive factors should enable you to understand the intellectual potential, learning differences, and problems of inner-city children. The third part presents materials on non-intellectual or affective factors that are related to personal attributes, self-concepts, and motivation of children from low socioeconomic areas and different subcultural groups. In the fourth part, readings are concerned with family influences on the urban child's behavior in terms of different forms of family organization and of various methods of child-rearing. The fifth part focuses on the question of the influence of school and teacher on children and, to some extent, the effect of urban school life on the teacher.

It is hoped that, in reading each subsection, you will gain a feeling for the topic from the first short selection which is taken from case studies, interviews, or literature. From the remaining readings you should (1) be able to acquire an understanding of the major ideas in each area, (2) obtain a range of information from the data and theories currently under consideration, and (3) develop an understanding of the research methods used in social science. In addition, extensive references are available with many excerpts; these should prove very valuable for any further study you may wish to do. And most important, it is hoped that you will gain insight into the social situation and resulting characteristics of the children you teach.

Keep in mind, however, that research on poor children is lacking in many crucial areas. For example, the classroom behavior of children from low socioeconomic areas viewed in terms of small group theory is almost totally lacking in the literature reviewed for the period 1958–1965. Despite these kinds of limitations, the readings selected should provide you with new ways of looking at the worlds of your children and should sensitize you to the problems and strengths they have.

## SOCIAL SCIENCE CONCEPTS

Basic to the selections in this volume are orientations and concepts derived from three social scientific disciplines. In order to comprehend the studies in this collection of readings, we will analyze an educational problem from all three disciplinary vantage points so that you can become acquainted with fundamental social scientific concepts used in the book.

Often teachers in slum areas find teaching difficult; therefore, we will focus on this educational problem. A description of different aspects of this problem is followed by social scientific explanations in which various concepts and terms are used to familiarize you with each disciplinary approach.

Frequently, teachers feel their work is difficult because they must deal with academically retarded children who, they feel, cannot or do not learn and who are seen as disciplinary problems. One research study has found that very negative reactions to such children can occur. In schools observed in a large metropolitan area, examples of teachers' attitudes included one teacher who referred to her second graders as animals; a second who called her pupils hoodlums; and a third who said her children were brats.(47) Obviously, these extreme reactions exemplify an educational problem of importance to both teachers and students.

There are many differences between children and teachers in slum areas that may contribute to some of these negative reactions. In general, urban teachers are white, and middle class by birth or aspiration.(21) The children, on the other hand, are often of a different skin color and from lower-income situations. Some are from poverty-stricken families while their teachers are probably from families that have never been on welfare or known the pinch of extreme economic deprivation. In addition, teachers are frequently from the "better" areas of the metropolis or from suburbs where citizens know how to organize and demand at least a few of the services needed in humane societies to maintain the decency of a civilized existence. In contrast, the children frequently live in decaying neighborhoods where influential parents are rare and in cities that allow these children to grow up in squalid, ugly conditions with streets or small cement parks for playgrounds.

What happens when teachers and children from different backgrounds face each other in the school? Perhaps we can best understand what transpires by following Miss Jones, a hypothetical teacher, whose experience is typical of other beginning teachers in slum neighborhoods.

Miss Jones has been sent to a school in a poor section of town that might also be called a ghetto because it is one of many semi-enclosed communities containing people whose economic or racial status force them to congregate together with others equally deprived.

Miss Jones enters a school in this neighborhood as a beginning teacher.

Because many of the older teachers have long since been transferred to "better" schools by their own request, there are other young and inexperienced teachers who, along with Miss Jones, are beginning their careers in this school.

Our first-year teacher walks into a school building that is older than schools elsewhere and which she sees as inadequate for her modern training in educational methods.(55) It is a school in which outside doors are locked to keep out the public and in which some teachers even lock their classroom doors during class.(47) It is a school that has neither trees nor grass, but only a high meshwire fence surrounding a gray playground.

She talks to the older teachers in the lunch room and finds that "these children" aren't interested in learning and are "impossible" to handle. She walks into her classroom and finds that her training doesn't seem to help her keep control. She hears language she thinks she shouldn't hear and watches apathy corrode and hostility explode in pockets of the room as she struggles on with her lesson. She begins to feel that the children of this environment, with a few exceptions, are really just what that teacher down the hall says they are—animals. So with all her good intentions and her belief that she can do something to help, that she can teach, she finally gives up and becomes a custodian: a warden whose purpose is to keep order. If incidental learning occurs, it is a lucky happening in her view. After two years, she transfers to a "nice" school in the suburbs. This is the process by which the feelings between the adult and child become hostile and helplessly hopeless.

But need this happen? Some teachers enjoy their work in the big city schools. Some children succeed in school and are not categorized as animals. Some schools do not need to lock out the public. But, unfortunately, the process of alienation between teacher and the taught is all too common.

What causes this alienation? What research or practical knowledge do we have about urban children and their environments that can help a teacher enjoy her work in the metropolis? What do social scientists have to offer from their research that can account for the learning and teaching difficulties in metropolitan schools? What is the cause, according to scientists, of the chain of events leading the teacher to resign after her brief career in a slum school? Let us analyze this educational problem of teaching difficulty with the concomitant alienation of teachers and pupils from the perspectives of anthropology, sociology, and psychology.

Anthropologists say that one cause of difficulties in urban schools is to be found in the contact between members of different subcultures. They have learned that every group of human beings develops distinctive ways of living, objects of use, myths and beliefs to support a particular view of the world and a distinctive way of relating objects, people, and ideas together. This distinctive ethos is called the culture. In large societies where separate national, racial, and social status groups maintain different ways of life that contribute to the general culture, the term subculture is used. When people of these different groups meet there are sometimes a number of problems that arise. The most difficult of these is the feeling that we are right and the other people are wrong. Certain ways of doing things in each group are so deeply engrained that they are considered the natural state of affairs. For example, "Of course you can eat with chopsticks, but who wants to when it's more convenient and efficient to eat with a fork?" Or, "A man and his wife should live alone, not with all those parents and grandparents around like those people do." Or, on a very basic level, "Our Bible is right and your Koran is wrong."

When teachers of different backgrounds meet with children of the slum school, they are, in effect, involved in contact with members of different subcultures within the American culture. Teacher and students are all Americans and thus share distinctive traits which can be easily recognized by foreigners; however, they will differ in certain ways of behaving. Our country is composed of a wide variety of different ethnic groups, some of which are assimilated, that is, adapted to the prevalent ethos and some of which maintain—either because of desire or of exclusion by others—a different cultural identity. Teachers in the slum seldom have been raised in the slum. Very frequently, they are at least second-generation members of different ethnic groups and of different social strata in the society. When the teacher meets her students, she engages in a form of culture contact.

Difficulty in accepting or adapting oneself to the situation of being in another group is frequently a reaction to culture contact. Culture shock is the term used to denote the process of adaptation with its concomitant disturbances. "How can these people live this way?" "The language they use is terrible—poor grammar and vulgar words!" "Why can't they sit quietly in class? When I was a child, the children didn't jump up and run around." If the kids don't behave as the teacher was raised to behave or as she has been trained to believe children do behave, the other group, the children are different. And when they don't adapt to the teacher's model, they are not only different, they are wrong. Finally, after sufficient frustration on both sides, they are drastically wrong, even subhuman.

Today, with decreased immigration and increased mass communication, nationality groupings are not the major source of subculture conflict. It is in those subgroups where skin color bars the way to complete assimilation that problems are still paramount. And, it is in this area where problems of subcultural contact are most enmeshed with the complexities of racial prejudice.

A second way to view the cause of the process leading to hostility and discouragement between teacher and pupil in the slum school is suggested by sociologists who propose that differences among people raised in varied strata of a society may cause conflict when interaction occurs. They theorize that human societies have been characterized throughout the centuries by division of people into roles that mark their positions in society, telling them who they are and what is expected of them by others. A society is organized into different strata that are known roughly to the members. These strata are called social classes or socioeconomic levels. In some societies these classes or groups have been rigidly controlled so that some people are considered untouchable or unworthy of any social intercourse outside their own level. Where rigid standards of movement or change are set, the level is called a caste. In a caste system, a man's destiny is set by birth and there is little hope for upward mobility.

Various objective factors form the basis of assignment to any one class, among which are educational level, financial status, area of residence, and length of residence in a community. All of these serve as indicators of who is who and how one should regard and behave toward another person. In thinking of New York City, for example, even the most naive observer could classify the following three children into lower, middle, and upper classes:

John Jones lives in a tenement on the lower East Side of Manhattan. He lives with his mother, grandmother, and three brothers and sisters in a two-room apartment on the fourth floor of a walk-up building. His father, who was a laborer, is now absent from the home; his mother works as a waitress. Neither his father nor his mother graduated from high school. The family has lived in New York for five years.

James Jones lives in a suburb of New York in a house that his parents own. His father is an engineer and his mother is a school teacher, both having college degrees. He has one sister who is three years younger than he. His grandparents live in the same town in a home they have lived in since their marriage about forty years ago.

Paul Jones lives in a penthouse apartment on Park Avenue. His father is a financier on Wall Street and his mother is active in the Symphony Guild. They own an estate on Long Island that has been in the family for three generations. His father graduated from Harvard and his mother completed two years at a private women's college before marriage.

The sociologist proposes that people who come from different classes have different experiences, thus learning to behave differently in various activities of life and forming a kind of subculture in anthropological terms. Others perceive a person according to his approximate location in the social hierarchy and behave toward him according to their perceptions of his position. In large metropolitan areas, lines can be blurred more often, but external factors such as race and location of residence, for example, are still used—sometimes incorrectly—as indicators of social class position.

When teachers work with children in slum schools, they are frequently dealing with members of a lower-class group. At the same time, the teacher is most likely a member of the middle class by birth or by the process of movement up the ladder of social class structure. The behaviors expected of middle-class children are often those the teacher desires. When those behaviors are not in evidence, the teacher tries to reinforce her original expectations by making the children comply with her own expectations. On the other hand, the children feel that they are being pushed into ways of behaving they may not find comfortable or even necessary. After all, why is it necessary to wear a tie to school? Why does a child have to stand up every time he has something to say? Why does silence in the classroom indicate good discipline? Can't noise indicate involved learning? When behaviors do not change to fit the teacher's expectations based on her own training as a child and her training as a college student, then the children are seen as different. And again, from this difference, they are often judged to be wrong: not wrong by the time they are in high school, but by the time they are in the second grade.

We can say, to summarize and qualify the concepts of anthropology and sociology, that societies are structured vertically in layers of social classes of which people are members. Societies are structured horizontally in collections of subcultural groups that are derived from ethnic or racial origins. This, however, is a highly simplified statement. Membership in social classes is constantly shifting through a process of upward and downward mobility. Membership in ethnic subcultures is also constantly changing through the process of acculturation and assimilation. Thus, it is important that when such entities are spoken of, they are seen not as static, but as always in flux.

It is equally important to understand clearly that the vertical structure of social strata cuts through each subcultural grouping in the United States today. A Northern Negro community, for example, may appear to the naive observer as lower class. But to the knowledgeable person, the Negro community has upper-, middle-, and lower-class divisions, although the number of persons in each may not correspond to those in another, all-white community. Further, our knowledge of metropolitan status systems is largely derived from studies of smaller communities. Therefore, any picture of urban social class is still far too simplified to adequately represent the complexity of the metropolis. Anthropologists, who were early pioneers in the investigation of American communities, have suggested that the conception of social class as a vertical arrangement of subcultural systems must in the future also take account of the parallel of public and private social grouping. The separation of work and non-work activities is more sharply demarcated in urban centers where organizational superstructures of the public world are separate from the private world of nuclear families. Thus, our picture of social status and urban organization becomes more complex.

Although we increasingly recognize the complexity of urban centers, there is the tendency to lump together all children who come from different environments under presently voguish terms such as the "culturally deprived" or the "socially disadvantaged" child. These terms can be and sometimes are used in place of the clearer though sometimes prejudicial words of the layman, and can thus perpetuate toward children from different backgrounds an attitude of condescension or even disdain. The term "culturally deprived" is an extraordinary example of cloaked, and, in most cases, unknowing middle-class superiority. Culture, as indicated earlier, is a term used by anthropologists to describe the total ethos of any group of people: the way they live, the beliefs they have, the values that guide their behavior. Of what, then, are poor children—whether white, brown, or black—deprived? They are most certainly not deprived of a culture. Such children are clearly members of their own subcultures. They are deprived only if one believes that they lack some other culture. In this case, it can only be the middle-class culture that is missing. The term "culturally different" respects the values and behaviors of a child's own world. The only sense in which such children are deprived is in the absence of opportunities or material objects of the children of wealthier parents. Even the old-fashioned word "poor" would at least be clear and avoid the pseudo-sophistication of euphemisms that may cover the inadequacies of schools, teachers, and communities to help these children. In addition, an old term such as "slum" should be used with qualification because the vertical structure described above creates areas and groups within each slum that are middle class and do not fit the stereotype. Therefore, it is important to keep in mind the changing and complex phenomenon to which we apply words to describe society and the people who occupy positions in it. Regardless of the terms we use, our first and foremost concern is with the individual child in terms of the experiences he has had in his own world.

Such an emphasis on the individual is stressed by a third discipline, psychology. Historically, psychologists have studied the personality, intelligence, motivation, and other attributes and processes of the individual. However, psychologists have also increasingly recognized the interrelationship of individual and environment. Accordingly, they, especially through the work of social psychology—a sub-division in the profession, have used the concepts developed in anthropology and sociology that describe the organization of societies to clarify and refine their findings concerning the individual.

Psychologists, for example, have, for many years, amassed data concerning the relationship between social class and intelligence test scores. Considerable work with ethnic groups and intelligence testing has been done. In all cases, the scores on intelligence tests show that there are effects on children that are related to their location in society. Others

in the field have studied the attitudes and relations among members of
different ethnic groups and among different social classes. Still others have
researched the problems of juvenile delinquency to determine the social
factors correlated with personal difficulties of young people.

More recently, research on the culturally different child has gained
increased attention. Findings suggest that the deprivation of certain
early learning experiences—or more broadly, environmental stimuli—may
cause learning difficulties for the child in slum schools.(17) Data of this
kind lead the psychologist to explain problems in urban schools as coming
from various kinds of deprivation that lead to learning and emotional
inadequacies and/or differences in children from certain strata and certain
ethnic groups. The cause, then, of the teacher's difficulties can be traced
to her inadequate understanding of the difficulties and variations in learning
that some groups of children share. With increased knowledge of the
problems that the slum children bring to class, the teacher should be able
to work more effectively with each student in her class.

Though the stress is still on the individual, the psychologists share
analytical concepts with anthropologists and sociologists. And the findings
from research in all three disciplines strongly affirm the complex interrelationship between environment and the individual. This interaction is
the one concept basic to our analysis of an urban education problem. We
have, in this section, looked at teaching difficulty in slum schools from
different perspectives involving ideas and terms that will help you understand the readings in this volume.

## BACKGROUND ENVIRONMENTAL
## CHARACTERISTICS

With an understanding of the purpose of this book and a knowledge of
social scientific concepts used, we turn to a consideration of some background characteristics of slum areas in big cities. In this section, you are
given information that should provide a backdrop against which the
readings are studied.

What characterizes the urban world of the child in your classroom?
Unfortunately, the word poverty describes one aspect of the world that
many urban children come to know too well. Many of their parents
migrated to the metropolis with the hope of a better life. Let Mrs. Martin
tell you: "We come from McCrory, Arkansas. We'd been born there an'
we was croppin'. . . . It was pretty bad. We had two kids and they wasn't
nothing to eat. . . ."(5) Mrs. Martin, a Southern Negro migrant to Chicago,
speaks for the millions who have joined the exodus from rural to urban
centers of our nation. Today, one sixth of the population of the entire
nation resides in our fourteen largest cities. From 1950 to 1957, 97 per cent

of the national growth occurred in these same areas.(49) The rate of movement of Negroes is indicative of the trend. In 1910, eight out of ten Negroes lived in the Southern states. By 1960, 48 per cent of all Negroes lived in the the South; thus, only one out of two Negroes still remained in the Southern states. Today, 31 per cent of the total population of Negroes in America live in our twelve largest cities.(57)

The majority of new city dwellers have come looking for better jobs, better living conditions, more equal opportunities, and justice. But a great number of them exchanged rural poverty for the more depressing destitution of the city. The poor in America constitute about 25 to 30 per cent of our total population, or from 40,000,000 to 50,000,000 individuals, depending on the criterion of low income used.(29, 42) Today, it is estimated that one child out of every three in the classrooms of our fourteen largest cities is from deprived circumstances.(48)

As the poor have moved into the cities, urbanites with better incomes have retreated to the suburbs; thus, the segregation of the poor has increased to the point where they are often invisible to many middle-class suburbanites. In addition, invisibility is increased by the segregation of non-white people who represent a disproportionately large number of the poor.(29)

Ironically, as our capacity to increase national productivity grows, the possibility of the poor improving their own incomes often decreases. Automation, an increasing necessity for competitive business, continues to reduce the jobs that the poor and uneducated can get.(41) Yet, despite the difficulties they encounter, the vast majority of the poor live on their own efforts. In Spanish Harlem, the lowest-income area in New York City, 79 to 87 per cent of the inhabitants in different housing projects are not on welfare.(56) It is said by some people that those who are on welfare really don't want to work, that they are lazy and don't want to get ahead. Yet the Moreland Commission Report on public welfare in New York State concludes, after a carefully conducted sociological survey of welfare recipients, that from one-quarter to one-half, depending on the district, have no alternative but to live on welfare. These people include those who are physically handicapped and those whose age precludes job-hunting. Of those temporarily unable to work, the report shows that the majority are dissatisfied with living on welfare.(43) This group includes, for example, mothers with young children and no breadwinners in the family, and partially or temporarily disabled persons.

What kinds of living conditions do the children of the poor have? Miller says, "For the country as a whole, nearly half of the non-white families live in homes that are either already so run down that they are hazardous to live in or are badly in need of repair."(42) Schoor reviews research on housing for parents and children of all races and concludes, "Poor housing correlates to a high degree with rates of illness and death, with the rate of mental illness, with juvenile and adult delinquency, and

with other social problems such as chronic drinking and illegitimacy."(51)
For the privilege of obtaining slum housing, the tenants pay proportionately
more for what they get. For, example, the slum tenants on the West Side
of New York City pay $2.10 per square foot while the inhabitants of
elevator apartments off Central Park West average $1.02.(54) The rich
may pay more rent, but they get more for what they pay.

Some say that the poor who live in slums don't really want to improve
or to get out of their tenements. Here is an excerpt from the diary of a
Puerto Rican mother whose landlord seemed unable to provide heat for his
tenement. After several winter days without heat, she writes, "I got up at
five and light the oven and put some water to heat. At seven, I called the
two oldest girls for school. I didn't send the little one, because she was
coughing too much and with a running nose. I gave some baby aspirin
and I put some Vick in her nose and chest and I gave some hot tea. I leaved
her in bed . . . later on I fixed dinner . . . I was not feeling good. . . . It
is really hard to believe that this happens here in New York and richest
city in the world. But such is Harlem and hope. Is this the way to live?
I rather go to the Moon in the next trip."(56)

The child in your classroom in the inner city is familiar with poverty
and with the consequences of this fact. Like the mother above, many
parents and their children are afflicted with poor health because of bad
living conditions and inadequate funds for medical bills. These problems
affect the school. Listen to one teacher from a big city school: "I explained
that Jose also needed dental care, that the doctor in the school said that
his teeth were terrible and that this was one reason he had started crying
in class one time—because of a toothache."(47)

Jose, a poor child from an urban center, is not alone in having problems
of health. Statistics from public health sources indicate that the poor
family is plagued with a greater number of health problems including
hearing, visual, and dental disorders. Not only are more organic defects
found among the poor, but there is also a higher prevalence of such
diseases as tuberculosis.(6)

Jose's teacher is also not alone with learning problems related to poor
health; teachers in slum areas frequently face the learning problems that
result from health difficulties. Studies, though sparse, indicate that
nutritional deficiencies lead to a loss of energy, lack of ability to concentrate, loss of self-control, and increased irritability.(7) Volunteers for
starvation experiments, for example, have found it difficult to concentrate
on reading or to maintain their usual social relations because excessive food
imagery interrupts their normal thinking patterns.(32, 25) Dick Gregory,
the popular Negro comedian, tells of eating paste in school to assuage
hunger pangs and of inability to focus on learning tasks which eventuated
in his teacher considering him a "dunce."(24) His personal experience is a
practical example of the theory of Maslow, a psychologist who postulates a

need-hierarchy by which he refers to the ordering of basic needs of human beings. It is his contention that basic physiological needs must be met before higher needs, as the acquisition of knowledge through curiosity, can emerge.(40) In short, the child in your class is not free to explore the intellectual aspects of his world until he has adequate food, sleep, exercise, and medical attention to fulfill his basic physiological needs.

The best indicators of the general health of any population are mortality rates. Lerner states, "The time lag between white and non-white mortality is now about 20 years, i.e., the mortality of non-whites in 1958 was roughly equivalent in the white population in 1937."(37) In 1961, the infant mortality rate in Harlem was 45.2 per 1,000 live births as compared to New York City as a whole in which there were only 25.7 deaths per 1,000.(11) Excluding non-whites, Anderson finds that infant mortality rates are higher for lower-class Caucasians, historically and currently, in European countries and in America.(4)

To be sure, the general improvement in health standards and medical knowledge has decreased the health problems of all classes and colors of people. But it has done so differentially. The effects of environment, as determined to a great extent by finances, still may decide whether or not a child lives, how long he is likely to live, and the kinds and numbers of illnesses he will have while he is alive.

Less obvious, but equally important to the teacher, is the influence of the child's world on his attitude toward medical care, sickness, and health. Perhaps the most important mediator of such attitudes is the child's family. The poor family is less likely to have access to and knowledge of medical practices. For instance, Clausen reports that children in polio vaccine trials were less likely to be vaccinated if they were from poor families.(13) Other psychological attitudes toward health and sickness are often developed through membership in a particular ethnic group. Medical folk remedies are usually handed down from parents or grandparents to children. The educated person regards such beliefs as "old wives tales." But the medical folk lore can seriously affect the attitudes of the impressionable child and the uneducated adult toward getting medical treatment and their cooperation in the course of treatment. A hospital may be a terrifying place to a young Mexican-American mother whose parents and grandparents have always delivered children at home with the aid of a midwife.(12) Children of the poor in our urban centers learn the meaning of poverty and poor health early in their encounter with their own world. They also learn the importance of the ethnic group into which they are born. What we call American society today is, in reality, a blend of many subgroups into which each new generation comes. The urban child enters a public school populated by children whose families came from different nations and races throughout the world. As the generations pass by, many of these ethnic groups take on more of the characteristics of the general culture that is primarily Protestant, Anglo-Saxon in origin. This process of change takes place gradually, with the non-English mother tongue and other external features fading with time, followed by changes in the deeper orientations to and styles of life. Though changes occur, it appears that, ". . . ethnic groups already established before 1930 continue to retain their identity. . . . The character of some groups has changed and there is some loss by intermarriage and by passing, that is, by the unobtrusive movement of individuals from one identification to another. But these shifts have not been of such magnitude as radically to alter the distribution [of the population] with which New York City was left after the great migrations of the nineteenth century."(28) If other large cities across the nation also retain consistency of ethnic composition, it would seem that subcultures are still somewhat influential in the lives of American parents and their children.

The process of migration has brought to our shores 41,411,600 people from different ethnic groups since 1776.(54) But this process has not, of course, stopped. Mass migration from the West Indies and the southern United States continues. Together the Negroes and Puerto Ricans in the metropolitan area of New York total 2,000,000. This number represents an increase in about a quarter century of 250 per cent. The magnitude of this migration is comparable to the large movements of Irish and Germans between 1840 and 1860 and of Jews and Italians between 1890 and 1915.(28) Although the movement to cities, as indicated earlier, has affected all subcultural groups, Negro migration has been greater proportionately. There are, in addition, striking differences associated with the recent migrations, chief among them being that the migrants are already Americans, in many cases of several generations; that they are often non-whites; and that the nature of the cities to which they move is very different from that which awaited foreign immigrants of earlier years.

From the viewpoint of people already here, there has always been something wrong with each new ethnic group. "In 1819, the Society for the Prevention of Pauperism said, 'This inlet of pauperism threatens us with the most overwhelming consequences. From various causes, the city of New York is doomed to be the landing place of a great portion of the European population, who are flocking to our country for a place of permanent abode. . . .'"(28) Very recently a report from Chicago of new migrants there said, "They are satisfied with poor living conditions. . . . They don't want modern facilities. . . . They won't use bathtubs. . . . They don't want to change their standards. . . ."(54) The writer is referring to the Southern mountaineers, some of the earliest white arrivals in the United States. Though the process of rejection of recent arrivals is common, those of different skin color have received the worst rejection, thus making it much more difficult for them to adapt to the general culture. An 18-year-old Puerto Rican boy expresses this rejection in the following excerpt from an interview: "There was this white woman from downtown who sometimes came into the neighborhood to help my mother when she was sick. One day, this woman said to me, 'Now, I don't have anything against the Irish or the Italians, but I just don't like most Negroes and I don't like most Puerto Ricans.'"(27)

Every child in your class has been born into a world in part defined by the ethnic group to which his parents belong. Depending on the generations that have preceded his birth, the family will exhibit certain behaviors which reflect their ethnic heritage. The kinds of food served, the religion preferred, the roles of male and female may all be affected by this ethnic group membership. There will be children in your class who are newcomers to the school and city who may be in different stages of adaptation to the over-all ethos of this country. These children and their parents will exhibit some of the strains and stresses that accompany change from one environment to another.

Ethnic groups are sometimes associated with racial characteristics. Many inner-city children belong to ethnic groups of non-white color. Research shows that such children are aware of the negative evaluations of their racial groups at as early an age as three. The world into which these children venture is too often marked by negative relations between racial groups. Unfortunately, the child frequently incorporates the prevalent attitudes around him.

The concept of race, however, is a vague one at best. Very roughly it denotes a group of persons connected by common descent or heredity. To the layman, races are explained in a variety of ways, including organic through blood differences. Giles presents the scientific evidence on race, saying, "Blood is human rather than racial in its character. All races tested so far have the same blood types. . . . Furthermore, no 'pure' races have been found. American Negroes, for example, are a 'mixed' race, coming from intermarriage among many parts of Africa and from different strains of white people originally from Europe. . . . Mixing of ancestral genes has been going on for thousands of years. In this country, it is reliably estimated that nearly 80 per cent of those whom we call Negroes have some white ancestry."(23) Thus, race must be seen as a continuum with various color and physical characteristics overlapping different categories which have been used for rough classification.

Despite the fallacies commonly believed about racial groups and despite the scientific difficulties in the use of such a concept as race, physical characteristics of children in your classroom are commonly grouped by race categories. If you have a very fair, mulatto child in the third desk in the second row of your classroom, she will be classified as Negro, regardless of the fact that her ancestry is dominantly white. As long as people continue to use the word "race" to define others, the process of prejudice must be considered.

Race relations in this country have long been dominated by over-generalized emotional reactions to other people. The non-white children you teach learn very early in life that they are the objects of negative emotional generalizations. They learn that others look at them as groups, not as individuals. Listen to little Victoria in a slum school explain why she is black, and you will understand how deeply these learnings are incorporated in children and adults. "Victoria shook the silence with, 'That ain't true. My mother told us that the reason we is black is that Adam and Eve had two sons, Cain and Abel—Cain was black and Abel white. Because Cain kill Abel, all the Black folks like us are bad, and the darker we are, the badder we are.'"(8)

How do we explain and understand the process of prejudice that Victoria has internalized so well? People can be prejudiced toward people of their own race as indicated before; however, the prejudice toward people of another race is usually a much more pervasive and deeply-held attitude. We must look at this phenomenon from various vantage points in order to achieve understanding. For example, we now know that the personal dynamics of the prejudiced person can be a cause of distorted perceptions. Research shows that insecure personalities are much more likely to exhibit prejudicial attitudes. Socialization is another significant way of explaining this process. For example, it is now known that first-hand contact of children with others of another race is not necessary for the development of prejudice to occur. This simply means that the transmission of attitudes from parents to child in the process of child-rearing is a dominant factor in the learning of prejudice. Or we can study this process situationally. Findings from studies of integrated housing, for example, show that prejudice is diminished best in situations where members of different racial groups are from a common social strata in the society.(1)

Prejudice affects the non-white child in your class in a wide variety of ways. Today, the emphasis on desegregated schools places great importance on the intergroup relations between children in educational institutions in metropolitan areas.

Poverty, poor health, ethnic and racial prejudice are some of the characteristics of the world in which the urban child goes forth. These four aspects of urban slum-living may help you place the readings in this volume in wider perspective, and thus enable you to interpret and use information in relation to other environmental factors of importance.

# *ii*

---

# *Cognitive Factors and Environment*

## INTELLECTUAL FUNCTIONING

"So, they want a lot of books to carry, to make it look as though they are smart. Of course, they know they aren't 'smart,' that they aren't in a bright class, but even carrying books they can't read helps a little." The teacher in the first article in this section goes on to say that both she and the children feel "It's a Disgrace to be Behind . . .".

These ten-year-olds are obviously aware of the importance of "being smart" in school, trying pathetically to overcome the stigma of stupidity placed on them. However, they already label themselves as "dumb." The school has effectively given them their label by publicly segregating them into a "slow" class. The school, the teacher, and the children know that, right or wrong, the most valued commodity in the educational enterprise is intelligence, which is usually defined by academic achievement.

Today, the current stress on the "gifted child" often leads teachers to

17

believe that it is not rewarding or prestigeful to work with children who aren't considered "bright." Unfortunately, many urban slum children are described as "slow" and considerably less as very intelligent. Too often the assumption that children from the slums are unable to learn has been supported by measurements of learning potential that have given erroneous estimates of the lower class child's real intellectual possibilities. If you, as a teacher of children from lower socioeconomic areas, really want to help them learn, it is vitally important to begin your efforts with this question: What is their *real* potential for learning?

For years, the schools have used I.Q., measured by intelligence tests of a wide variety, as the best single indicator of basic capacity to learn. Historically, the early concept underlying these measurements was that intelligence was innate and fixed by inheritance. If I.Q. scores changed for any individual, it was believed due to the insufficiency of the test; with time and better tests, such fluctuations wouldn't occur. When research in the earlier part of this century showed Negroes scoring lower than whites, it was considered proof of inborn racial inferiority. Similarly, the low scores of lower-class children, whether white or black, were considered evidence that these children were products of parents too unintelligent to rise in the social structure.

Within the last three decades, these assumptions have been proved wrong. Starting with the work of Klineberg(34), who found that with the better environment of the North, Southern Negro migrants' I.Q. scores improved markedly, more and more evidence has been amassed that strongly negates the idea that I.Q. scores are inherent and unchangeable.(35) As Pettigrew in "Negro American Intelligence" points out, the learning potential of any child in your classroom is a result of the interaction of *both* heredity and environment. Where the environment does not contain the objects and opportunities necessary for maximum learning, measures of intelligence will reflect this lack in lowered scores, thus giving inaccurate estimates of the child's true capacity to learn.

A recent example of research that pinpoints environmental influences on intelligence is Deutsch and Brown's "Social Influences in Negro-White Intelligence Differences." This study shows the typically depressed scores of children from lower-class environments, regardless of race. In addition, it indicates the typically lower scores of Negro children when compared with those of white children, regardless of class level. However, it also shows a considerable number of Negro children who achieve higher scores than most of the white children, again a typical finding from research studies. In addition, it documents the increase in both Negro and white children's scores with middle-class status and presumably a better environment. All these findings are similar to those in other studies.(45) The importance of this investigation is that it goes beyond the delineation of these social factors and isolates other environmental influences that affect intelligence. The investigators found that the absence of the father in the home is a negative factor associated with lower scores, while early child training in a nursery is a positive factor increasing intelligence scores. In short, family composition and early learning experiences are crucial to the development of learning potential in the children you teach.

Pettigrew concludes from his review of studies of this kind, "Thus, the severely deprived surroundings of the average Negro child can lower his measured I.Q. in two basic ways. First, it can act to deter his actual intellectual development by presenting him with such a constricted encounter with the world that his innate potential is barely tapped. And, second, it can act to mask his actual functioning intelligence in the test situation by not preparing him culturally and motivationally for such a middle-class task."

The idea of an intelligence test defined as a middle-class task is one attested to by Charters in "Social Class and Intelligence Tests," in which he traces the history of protest against the middle-class bias found in such instruments when administered to lower-class children of any race. Charters sums up the arguments of those who claimed that children from poorer economic levels were penalized on such tests by saying that they believed ". . . the general intelligence tests in common use were culturally loaded against the lower class. They tested only those mental abilities favoring the cultural experiences of the middle class; they were couched in language and linguistic forms unfamiliar to the lower class; and they called for kinds of work habits and motivation which were not valued or taught in the lower-class culture . . . intelligence tests were products of the middle class and incorporated the bias of the middle-class culture."

We move, then, in this article, from an emphasis on environmentally defined intelligence to consideration of the construction of the measurements themselves. Not only are the outcomes—the scores—of tests affected by social influences, but also the very instruments used to assess learning potential favor one environment more than another. Since these reactions against tests constructed by middle-class adults and standardized on middle-class children, there have been attempts to construct culture-free tests that do not discriminate against lower-class children. These have not been too successful.(2, 61) On the whole, tests that are used to assess your children's learning potential are still subject to problems of interpretation because of bias in their construction.

You can see that the concept of intelligence and the ways of measuring it have been changing over the years. As research continues, it is also becoming apparent that intelligent behavior is not a single entity, but is rather a complex multiplicity. Intelligence, defined as the number of correct responses to a test, yields a single score which is used to indicate learning potential. It is increasingly clear that this single score of global intelligence, whether culturally biased or not, does not adequately describe the multiple abilities that are involved in intelligent behavior, nor does it allow you, as a teacher, to analyze the different intellectual capabilities of your children. There has been a trend toward test batteries that try to measure various specific mental processes and different aptitudes for particular tasks.(2)

Lesser's "Mental Abilities of Children in Different Social and Cultural Groups" is a recent example of research that obtains information on a variety of capacities and that, at the same time, avoids cultural bias by using test items common to all middle- and lower-class children of four subculture groups—Chinese, Jewish, Negro, and Puerto Rican. The investigators discovered that "Social class and ethnic group membership . . . have strong effects upon the level of each of four mental abilities. . . . Ethnic group affiliation also affects strongly the pattern or organization of mental abilities . . . once the pattern specific to the ethnic group emerges, social class variations within the ethnic group do not alter this basic organization."

In short, a lower-class child of any ethnic group is likely to score lower than a middle-class child. But the child's membership in one ethnic group is likely to determine which of the mental abilities will probably be higher and which lower. As you can see, testing specific abilities, such as reasoning and numerical facility, in relationship to both social class and ethnicity provides you with a better understanding of the learning potential of each child in your classroom. On the basis of this research, for example, it is possible for you to expect that a Chinese boy of average intelligence in your classroom will probably have less difficulty with problems of space conceptualization than a child from a different ethnic group. In short, you, as his teacher, should be able to develop the strengths and eliminate the weaknesses of children from various ethnic groups based on the knowledge you have of the different organization of abilities fostered in the groups from which they come.

Even though you have a more complete picture of learning potential from tests of specific abilities, you still, however, do not know how or why such abilities came to be. You know some of the environmental factors that affect learning potential differentially, but there is still considerable information missing. Guilford has tried to present a fuller explanation by correlating basic intellectual operations—such as cognition, memory, evaluation, convergent thinking, and divergent thinking—with the kinds of materials or content involved—such as figural, symbolic, semantic, and behavioral. When different intellectual operations are applied to problems differing in content, six products may result including units, classes, relations, systems, transformations, and implications. Guilford views intellect, therefore, three-dimensionally, as a cube with one face named operations, another content, and another products. It is possible to locate in this cube, using all three faces as coordinates, as many as 120 distinct abilities derived from a combination of the operation, the content, and the product involved in the task.(26) This gives you some indication of the complexity of intelligence in comparison to the one or two scores usually derived from I.Q. tests of global intelligence. This view of intelligence also provides more information as to how any one score came to be.

Probably the intellectual operation that has aroused most interest is that which Guilford calls divergent thinking. Normally, schools demand a different operation called convergent thinking. For example, a problem is given and the student is asked to converge on the right one of four multiple-choice answers given. In divergent thinking, the task is to arrive at a large number of original solutions to a single problem for which no right answers are given. This process is called creativity by some, and is of great concern to educators who have been criticized for teaching children to think convergently at the expense of divergent thinking or creativity. It is, therefore, appropriate to examine Torrance's "Cultural Discontinuities and the Development of Originality," a research study which is closely related to Guilford's work on divergent thinking.

Torrance is particularly interested in how different cultures and educational procedures used in these cultures affect the process of creative thought. Using non-verbal tasks requiring original responses, he tested Australian, German, Indian, Samoan, and American white and Negro children. Data were obtained on children at each grade level from kindergarten through the twelfth grade. Torrance finds that there are distinct periods of decline in originality in children in the American culture at ages five, nine, thirteen, and seventeen. He shows that these discontinuities in the development of original thinking are peculiar to the American culture, thus establishing the differential impact of cultural and educational training on this mental ability.

Not only were there differences between national cultures, but also between subcultures of Negro and white children in America. Though Negro children scored lower than white youngsters, both groups of American children showed considerable originality when compared with young people from other cultures. This finding is particularly interesting since the Negro children tested in this study were from segregated schools in Georgia where, presumably, they were exposed to inferior educational opportunities.

Possibly the most important finding from this research for you, the teacher, is the effect of certain educational procedures in contributing to the decreased use of creative potential in children at certain ages. In regard to decline of originality at age nine, for example. Torrance says, "In the fourth grade they had to begin sitting in orderly rows in the classroom, keeping their feet on the floor. Classroom activity became more organized and formal. Credit was given only for what they put on paper. The animals in their stories did not talk. . . . They had to start doing homework and their papers were expected to be neat with no smudges." These changes at school were associated with "the inhibiting influence of their preoccupation with prevention and fear of making mental leaps." As pressures for conformity in school increased, the children's ability to think creatively decreased. It is interesting to note that research conducted by Davidson and her associates in Harlem schools showed "non-achieving" Negro children obtained higher scores on tests of creativity than those scores of children who were "achieving"—by the school's standards.(15)

What does this say to you, the teacher? Simply this: Potential to learn is affected not only by the culture in which the child is raised, by the ethnic subculture to which he was born, by the socioeconomic position of his family in the social structure, by his early experience in learning activity; it is also affected by the school and the teacher who may, through inhibiting procedures, decrease the child's capacity to use his learning potential.

The readings presented indicate many correlations between environmental factors and intelligence. You have been able to see that the test scores of children from poor districts in the metropolis are influenced by the situations into which they were born. However, much of the research has focused on the association of social influences with the *outcomes* of tests, the total scores from tests, rather than with the *processes* of intellect that caused these outcomes. Piaget says, "A test only gives us results on efficiency of mental activity without grasping the psychological operations in themselves . . . the test provides the sum of successes and failures, which is the actual result of past activities and attainments, but it leaves untouched the way in which these have been reached."(46) With tests of specific mental abilities, we begin to obtain a better understanding of different outcomes that are related to processes. In Guilford's study, there is an attempt to put together content, operation, and result. But we are still left with the problem of processes underlying operation and resultant scores.

Let's consider how Piaget, through a lifetime of observing children, explains the psychological processes that develop over time in children. Piaget sees intelligence as an increasingly more complex product of the interaction between the organism and the environment. The child's intellectual performance moves through stages that include first, the intuitive recognition of vague properties; next, the isolation of one relational concept from another and the ability to carry out an action mentally with anticipation, reversal, and conservation; and finally, the representation of mental operations in a formal symbolic system. The forms of organization developed at one stage become incorporated in subsequent ones. At each stage new competencies arise, but these are founded on a few basic generic operations.

During the first two years of life the child learns to distinguish fields of color that move together as objects. He learns in this sensori-motor phase to coordinate sense impressions and movements. From roughly the second to the beginning of the fourth year, language aids the development of concepts. At this stage, the child begins to understand ideas that relate objects together. He may understand the word "ball" and attach the word to the proper object, but he must learn that a ball when put in a box and brought out the other side is the same ball. The idea of sameness must develop. From the fourth year until the beginning of the seventh, the child establishes inexact relational concepts. He is able to compare one ball with another in terms of their similarities if they are both before him. But he is not able to hold information in his mind and rearrange it mentally. He thinks, for example, that many small pieces of candy are more than one unbroken piece. The concept of quantity is still inexact.

From the age of seven to the beginning of the eleventh year, he develops concrete operational thought, which means that he can reason successfully about things that are or have been concretely before him. He is able to understand the conservation principle: that breaking up a piece of candy does not change its amount. He is also able to grasp the idea of reversibility: that adding and taking away are part of a common relational concept. In early adolescence, from about eleven on, the child is able to use formal operational thought. He can hold in his mind abstract propositions, considering more than that which is concretely before him. He can systematically consider a variety of solutions and possibilities in his mind, deriving theories and logical inferences about a problem.(31)

How do these processes in intellectual development relate to the problems of teaching children in slum schools in our big cities? Though the stages described above are considered by many as rough approximations of a general trend, they, nevertheless, provide us with a way in which to link outcomes—intelligence and mental ability test scores—with processes leading to these outcomes.

We know that children of lower-class and non-white backgrounds start school with roughly similar potential to learn as white middle-class children. Their scores on I.Q. tests are approximately equivalent when social class differences are controlled.(3, 39) Yet, test scores of children from low-income areas decrease over time until, when the children are about eleven, they are often seriously behind on most achievement tests, sometimes from two to four years behind in reading, and exhibit losses in I.Q. scores of as much as ten points or more.(44, 60)

This increasing loss over time has been accounted for by deprivation theories. Earlier, we discussed Deutsch's finding that nursery school experience of lower-class children was correlated with higher I.Q.'s in the fifth grade. On the basis of research of this kind, the cumulative deficit idea is advanced. This term means that the incomplete acquisition of bits of elemental knowledge in early life may cause serious damage in the child's later learning ability.(15)

The problem, of course, is *which* bits of knowledge? In order for you, as a teacher in the urban schools, to overcome this cumulative deficit, you must know which processes have been affected. It is not enough to know, for example, that verbal ability is retarded. You must be able to understand how and in what ways this retardation has occurred.

It is proposed that the time at which the greatest decrease in achievement and intelligence occurs is the *same* time at which Piaget postulates the transition from concrete to abstract operational thought. We know that abstract thought requires verbal competence, which is exactly the mental ability most depressed at this time. We also know that this period is marked by two major declines in creativity related to pressures in school and in the culture.

In short, it is suggested that the intellectual process most affected among children born and raised in slum environments is that involving abstract operations. What the child needs, then, in order to overcome cumulative deficit is help in identifying and developing conceptual operations that are inadequately formed in stages over time. The child needs assistance in making the transition from concrete to abstract thought necessary for the rational thought processes that are increasingly stressed in the later years of his education. In addition, it is suggested that the schools, through different procedures and teaching practices, must provide ways for reducing the pressures for conformity on the child that accelerate in fourth grade and continue during his junior-high years, for this is the important point of transition from one mode of thought to another.

You, as his teacher, must assess more than his grasp of facts or knowledge in your classroom. More important, you must be able to assess the child's ability to deal with concepts that *relate* facts to one another. It is possible that the transition from concrete to abstract thought is the major stumbling block in the slum child's use of his potential. It is possible that the stages of intellectual growth are retarded in such children because of environmental deprivation in family situations and neighborhoods and because the school and teachers have focused on the outcomes—the achievement scores and I.Q.'s—more than on the actual processes of intellectual development.

## LEARNING DIFFERENCES

Ashton-Warner, a white woman teaching Maori children in New Zealand, is one teacher who understands the importance of words as they represent concepts. She also knows how to make new words—new ideas—make sense to children from a cultural group far different from her own. She says, "Back to these first words. To these first books. They must be made out of the stuff of the child itself. I reach a hand into the mind of the child, bring out a handful of the stuff I find there, and use that as our first working material. Whether it is good or bad stuff, violent or placid stuff, coloured or dun. To effect an unbroken beginning. And in this dynamic material, within the familiarity and security of it, the Maori finds that words have intense meaning to him which cannot help but arise a love of reading." Note also her concern for the continuity between the child's own home and the school to which he comes. She, in effect, reduces cultural discontinuities as Torrance suggested in the reading presented earlier.

With these excerpts from the introductory article to Section B of this part, we move more deeply into the problem of Learning Differences. Here we are concerned with the different problems and styles of learning among children from the inner city. Obviously, if environmental factors affect potential for learning, they must also influence the particular problems and ways of learning that children evidence. Again, we know more about the fact that Negro children, for example, differ more widely in I.Q. scores than in the ways their learning styles differ from or are the same as those of Caucasians. Though the research is limited, let us consider some of the ideas about learning that have been proposed.

Just as a white teacher in New Zealand must consider the problems of movement from one culture to another among her children, so the urban teacher must understand and deal with the problems of culture contact in the metropolitan school. Elam in "Acculturation and Learning Problems of Puerto Rican Children" deals with the difficulties this newest wave of migrants experience in the schools. She emphasizes the importance of learning new cues, saying, "Language is one of the tools for learning which the emigrant child lacks. He is left with only the cues he can obtain from nonverbal communication; the expressive gestures which may convey some meaning for him. Here too, however, a facial expression or a gesture may mean something else to him, since gestures are also a language and are richly colored by each culture with specific meanings. Meanwhile he must manage without the necessary cues for directing his behavior. . . .

"How does it feel to be unable to comprehend the cues in this new setting? How does it feel not to understand what people are saying? How do anxiety and insecurity affect a child's readiness to learn?" These are questions you, the teacher, must face if you are to help the children who move to cities where they encounter new language, new values, and new ways of behaving. It is important to remember that a white child from the Ozarks in Chicago or a Southern Negro child in Los Angeles will also experience many similar adjustment difficulties that will affect his rate of learning.

For example, Southern Negro children have more difficulty in verbal communication and comprehension than Northern Negro children.

Carsons and Rabin in "Verbal Comprehension and Communication in Negro and White Children" also find that both Northern and Southern Negroes, compared with white children, tend to have different response patterns when an analysis of definitions given by them is made. The white children tend to give abstract definitions; whereas the Negro children give more concrete ones. This finding is in line with our earlier discussion of Piaget's stages of learning and indicates that Negro children may need help in forming concepts that relate objects together in abstract categories.

In addition, the authors point out, ". . . verbal comprehension and verbal communication seem to be two different functions. Although the groups were equated on comprehension, they showed marked differences with respect to communication. It would appear that differences on conventional intelligence tests, and especially on vocabulary subtests, may be primarily due to failure in verbal communication rather than in comprehension."

Bernstein, in "Social Structure, Language, and Learning" develops a theory to account for these verbal difficulties that children from lower-class groups have. He states that the social form of a relationship acts selectively on the mode and content of communication. For example, we know that children's speech when with other children is different from that used when they are with adults. We also know that groups of army men, or of families or of different sexes develop different vocabularies and styles of communication.

Bernstein therefore proposes that "What is made relevant by the form of lower working-class speech is markedly different from that which is made relevant by the form of middle-class speech. The experience of children from these gross strata follows different paths from the very beginnings of speech. The type of learning and the dimensions of relevance initiated and sustained by the spoken language are completely different."

The two linguistic forms that develop from early social training in different socioeconomic levels he calls public and formal. Public language is a form of communication in which certain meanings are restricted and the possibility of elaboration of meaning reduced. A formal language allows for highly individual selection of meanings and for complete expression of relational ideas. The lower-class child is more likely to have learned only the public or restricted linguistic form while the middle-class child has learned to use both forms.

Therefore, when the lower-class child comes to school, problems in learning are accentuated since the teacher as a middle-class representative uses a formal language system. The child may be able to comprehend, but how can he communicate if he has not learned the mode of language being used? Thus, we can see that just as the Puerto Rican child has difficulty making the transition to another language, so may the nativeborn speaker of English from the lower class have difficulty in the middle-class dominated institution of the school.

In addition, the child of the lower-class culture is most likely to have learned a linguistic form favoring concrete word usage while the middle-class child is more likely to have developed a form that supports abstract word usage. This contributes to the problem of movement through stages of conceptual development discussed earlier. If the lower-class child has learned to use a system of language that favors concrete words, then the transition to abstract conceptual thought will be much more difficult for him than it is for the middle-class child whose language system has trained him for such thought. However, and this should be stressed, the use of concrete language is a most potent tool in expressive English. The use of abstract rather than concrete images may be more common to the middle-class child while the lower-class child may be able to use the real-life images around him to convey his emotions and ideas in powerful, if not necessarily grammatical, ways. For a good example of this use of concrete words, read in the final section of this book the first selection written by a young Puerto Rican girl.

Various other explanations of learning styles in different classes have been suggested. Moving to a quite different approach, we encounter the idea that children from lower socioeconomic groups work best for tangible rewards. This is, in one sense, an extension of reinforcement theory that is concerned with the type, frequency, and presentation of rewards necessary for learning in different situations. Rewards reinforce the likelihood that correct responses will be given in learning a new behavior. Terrell, Durkin, and Wiesley in "Social Class and the Nature of the Incentive in Discrimination Learning" find that the kind of reward or the reinforcement that produces the best learning in lower-class children is one that is tangible. Middle-class children seem to learn best with rewards that are not tangible.

This finding is particularly important when related to the idea of lower tolerance for delayed gratification in lower-class children. Research indicates that these children are more likely to want an immediate reward for the work they do; that they are less able to wait a long time for the results of their efforts.(36, 50, 58) It appears, therefore, that children in schools in poor areas of big cities will be more likely to learn if reinforcement for their learning is achieved immediately, and if that reinforcement is tangible or physically concrete. This fact has obvious implications for you, the urban teacher. When you work with children who have never had very many tangible objects they could call their own, you can be fairly sure that concrete results attainable within a short span of time are more likely to bring about satisfactory learning in your children.

Finally, let's consider another explanation of learning differences in children from different backgrounds. Swanson and Miller in "Social

Class and Motoric Orientation" find that boys from lower-class families are more likely to do better in tasks involving physical or motoric activity. The young boys in their study were much less inhibited in using their bodies expressively in different test situations than were their middle-class counterparts. On the basis of this research, Riessman and others have stressed the importance of a motoric style of learning, advising teachers to use learning situations that encourage their children to physical activity.(48)

Certainly it is a good idea to allow children much more expressiveness in classrooms in which teachers are too often obsessed with keeping order at the expense of involved learning. However, there is the danger that the idea of motoric orientation in lower-class children will be seen by some as an extension of the very old notion that children from the slums are better at physical things and should therefore receive vocational curriculum to prepare them to work with their hands. It is probably true that the conformity and passive silence demanded in many of the classrooms of our big cities is particularly uncongenial to lower-class children. But it is *not* true that the old idea of vocational training for kids who are better at physical tasks than mental ones is what such children need. Further research is needed before we can say, at this time, that physically-oriented tasks will give the child from the slums a better chance of using his learning potential in urban schools.

These then are some of the current explanations of the differences in learning patterns among children of the inner city. There is need for more research on every topic discussed in this introduction. We are only beginning to apply scientific inquiry to the problems of the poor in our society. However, these readings are presented to acquaint you with what has been researched to date. We have considered many of the crucial ideas necessary for a grasp of the problems related to a child's real potential to learn. And we have covered a few of the problems and styles of learning that are found among children from different backgrounds. As you read the articles in this part, look for the information that can help you in dealing with children in your own classroom. Remember, however, that the information given describes, in general, trends for groups of children and may not adequately represent the child who varies from the central tendencies found in the research reported.

*A. Intellectual Functioning*

# IT'S A DISGRACE TO BE BEHIND . . .

*Dorothy M. McGeoch, Carol R. Bloomgarden, Ellen O. Furedi,*
*Lynne W. Randolph, and Eugene D. Ruth, Jr.*

Last summer I went with my parents to see my sister, who lives in a nice, middle-class community. When people heard where I was going to teach, they immediately got this horrible, nightmare-like picture—pure black— and they thought I was so brave. It was really funny.

I didn't even think about teaching during those five weeks of traveling, but, when we got home, I bought the courses of study in every subject area, from arithmetic to writing, and read through every one of them. I couldn't do any planning because I didn't know yet what kind of children would be in my class. I had been told that I'd probably have the second grade. Then I got a letter saying that I would have a fifth grade. There was no information about the type of group, so I still couldn't do very much planning. I spent the remainder of the summer finding an apartment near the school so that the traveling experiences of my graduate school year would not be repeated. I was very happy and very excited.

But then school started and I had the lowest section on the grade. Do you know what that means? Over half of them are repeaters; they all know that they are in the "dumb" group, that they are "failures," and that everyone looks down on them.

I looked up their records and they were all reading at second- or third-grade level. I tried to start them in with third-grade texts when I finally got some books. But they wouldn't have them. They wouldn't even try. Some of them had had the same books before and they hated them. They hated to be reminded that they were failures, and I couldn't really blame them.

Reprinted with permission from *Learning to Teach in Urban Schools* by Dorothy M. McGeoch, Carol R. Bloomgarden, Ellen O. Furedi, Lynne W. Randolph, and Eugene D. Ruth, Jr. (New York: Teachers College Press, 1965), pp. 67–70. © 1965 by Teachers College, Columbia University.

The simplest—the very simplest—words were impossible for them. Everything was impossible, it seemed. If I put an assignment on the board, I had to have every word of it read aloud. There was a boy in the back of the room who copied things perfectly but when I asked him to read it back to me he couldn't read it. I had to have it read aloud and even then some of them couldn't understand it.

I needed help during those first days of school, but I didn't get it. All I got were interruptions—people coming in and handing me things and asking me to fill out things when I was trying to keep the class in order. We had three days of orientation, but in all that time we spent only twenty minutes meeting with the principal. He gave us the key to the book room and told us to take what we wanted, but I didn't know enough about my group and their needs to know what to get.

The other teachers were wonderful. They were very sympathetic and if I asked them anything they would tell me, but the trouble was that I didn't find out what I needed until I was in front of the class, and by that time it was too late. I put a sentence on the board and realized that half the class couldn't read cursive writing and the other half resisted manuscript writing because they thought it was childish. I thought I knew what to expect in a school like this—I had been here for a year as a student teacher and I had seen lots of classes. But nothing seemed to help. My class was so unruly and so impossible to discipline that I didn't sit down even for a minute for weeks. I was exhausted, and I didn't know how to help them or myself.

I remember sitting down with the curriculum bulletins, my college texts, and the children's books and almost crying every night. I didn't know how to plan for a class like mine and when I went to the curriculum bulletins they were just mountains. They were such insurmountable hills to climb that I would want to just give up, because I knew I could never teach what they said I should to the group I had. It is very hard because as a new teacher you want to do everything the right way, and it takes such a long time to know what you can and can't do.

I think you should really know your grade curriculum, but trying to plan the year ahead of time and trying to do just certain things is so ridiculous. After all, you have to start where the children are and go through to the end of the year, not to the end of the bulletin. At least, that was what I tried to believe.

Social studies was the hardest subject. There was a lot of material and a thousand ways to organize it. To find the best way for a particular class is the difficulty, and the textbook was *not* the best way for my class.

These kids needed to know something about their own city and state and country, and how these related to the rest of the world. They needed lots of mapwork and help in physically imagining their own city in relation to the rest of the world. They have such narrow concepts. They ride around on their bicycles, and they know something of their own surroundings, but they think that New York State is the United States; when I showed them a map of the world and tried to talk about continents and hemispheres, they got all mixed up. Something had been left out somewhere. To get these children to relate their city to their state and their country was practically an impossibility, and these are very important concepts. For a long time, I didn't do much with social studies because they couldn't read the books, but now I use maps and try to tell stories. I make the stories very dramatic and then ask questions. It helps, but it is slow work.

One of the very worst experiences is to have a child from another class come into the room on an errand when you are teaching social studies and say, "Oh, we did that three weeks ago. We finished that already." And it's true. Sometimes I walk up to another teacher and ask her where she is in the book. If she's as slow as I am, I feel good. And if I find someone who is fourteen chapters ahead, I feel sick to my stomach. I'm confused and I'm afraid that next year's teacher will think the children don't know what they should. She will try to start with what she is supposed to be teaching instead of where they are; there will be a big gap, and they won't be able to bridge it.

The class feels that it is disgrace to be behind, too. They realize that there is a schedule to be met, and other people are meeting it and they're not. They think it is terribly important. Of course, they are doing all they can, but they feel it, nevertheless. The pressure to be doing what the others do is enormous.

It shows in their feelings about taking books home. One of my youngsters remarked that, the more books you have for homework, the brighter you are. So, they want a lot of books to carry, to make it look as though they are smart. Of course, they know they aren't "smart," that they aren't in a bright class, but even carrying books they can't read helps a little. They're insulted because they don't have more homework and frustrated because they can't do what they have. So, I just let them take as many books as they wish, as long as they bring them back the next morning. . . .

# NEGRO AMERICAN INTELLIGENCE

*Thomas Pettigrew*

White supremacists maintain that Negroes are innately less intelligent than Caucasians. In a statement remarkably comparable to those made two centuries ago by advocates of the theory of American degeneration, one modern-day racist phrases the claim in these words:

Any man with two eyes in his head can observe a Negro settlement in the Congo, can study the pure-blooded African in his native habitat as he exists when left on his own resources, can compare this settlement with London or Paris, and can draw his own conclusions regarding relative levels of character and intelligence. . . . Finally, he can inquire as to the number of pure-blooded blacks who have made their contributions to great literature or engineering or medicine or philosophy or abstract science.(94, p. 7)*

Such claims assumed special importance among the opponents of the Supreme Court's school desegregation ruling in 1954. Interracial education simply will not work, contended many segregationists; Negro children are too retarded innately to benefit and will only act to drag down the standards of the white children.

Americans are far less receptive to such reasoning now than they were a generation ago. Public opinion poll data reveal that, while only two out of five white Americans regarded Negroes as their intellectual equals in 1942, almost four out of five did by 1956—including a substantial majority of white Southerners.(55a) Much of this change is due to the thorough repudiation of racist assertions by the vast majority of modern psychologists and other behavioral scientists. Indeed, the latest research in this area lends

* Numerals in parentheses denote references at end of article.

From *A Profile of the Negro American* by Thomas Pettigrew (Princeton, New Jersey: D. Van Nostrand, Inc., Copyright 1964), pp. 100–135. Reprinted by permission of D. Van Nostrand, Inc.

the strongest evidence yet available for this repudiation. This chapter takes a new look at this old controversy and presents a summary of the relevant research.[1]

## THE "SCIENTIFIC RACIST" POSITION

The dominant scientific position on this subject has been termed an "equalitarian dogma" and described as "the scientific hoax of the century" by one psychologist, Professor-Emeritus Henry Garrett.(39a) He charges that other psychologists have prematurely closed the issue for ideological, not scientific, reasons.

Garrett is publicly joined by two other psychologists, out of the roughly twenty-one thousand who belong to the American Psychological Association. Frank McGurk, of Villanova University, has conducted research with an unvalidated intelligence test of his own design and concluded that "Negroes as a group do not possess as much [capacity for education] as whites as a group."[2] In 1956 this work gained wide attention when the *U.S. News and World Report* featured an article under the imposing title of "A Scientist's Report on Race Differences," in which McGurk surveyed six investigations that he claimed to be "the only existing studies that relate to the problem." (77b, p. 96)

The crowning production of this small band is Audrey Shuey's *The Testing of Negro Intelligence*.(102) Shuey, a psychologist at Randolph-Macon Woman's College in Lynchburg, Virginia, provides a large, though carefully selected, review of over two hundred studies bearing on racial differences in intelligence.[3] She ignores the newer conceptions of intelligence and instead relies heavily upon the earlier, less sophisticated investigations, with over half of her references dated prior to World War II. She also concentrates on research performed in the South, with three fourths of her studies on students coming from tightly segregated Southern and border communities. The great bulk of this research found most Negroes scoring lower on I.Q. tests than most whites. Shuey unhesitatingly interprets this fact as pointing "to the presence of some native differences between Negroes and whites as determined by intelligence tests."(102, p. 318)

[1] An earlier draft of this chapter by the author appeared in 1964 in the *Journal of Negro Education*, under the title of "Negro American Intelligence: A New Look at an Old Controversy."
[2] For a critical discussion of McGurk's work, see Anastasi.(3, pp. 557–558 and 562–563)
[3] Garrett claims that Shuey's book examined "*all* of the comparative studies of Negro-white performance on mental tests over the past 40 years."(39b, p. 1) This is not the case. Even papers by Garrett and McGurk are missing.(39c, 77a) But more critical is the exclusion of numerous and important publications which appeared prior to Shuey's work and run directly counter to its conclusion.(17, 27, 41, 51, 57, 64, 86, 88, 96, 112, 116, 131)

In addition to this "sheer weight of uncontrolled data" argument, these three psychologists attempt to show that the impoverished environment of the typical Negro cannot account for the observed test differences. One favorite example, prominently cited by all three, is H. A. Tanser's 1939 investigation of intelligence among the Negro and white children of Kent County, Ontario, Canada.(115a) Tanser found that his white sample obtained a higher average I.Q. than his Negro sample; and the "scientific racists" maintain that this is convincing evidence for their position, since in Kent County "the social and economic conditions of the whites and Negroes were substantially the same."(39d)

## THE MODERN PSYCHOLOGICAL POSITION

These arguments have not altered the dominant opinion of modern psychology on this topic. In the first place, the studies repeatedly cited by the "scientific racists" in defense of their position are not, upon closer scrutiny, critical tests of their contentions. Consider the Tanser work in Canada.[4] As in investigations in the United States, the "social and economic conditions" of the two groups were *not* equal. One psychologist, Mollie Smart, was born and raised in Kent County at approximately the time Tanser conducted his study there. She candidly describes the condition of the Negroes in this period:

... Nearly all of [the Negroes'] houses were small wood buildings, often lacking paint and tending towards dilapidation. The theaters had a policy of seating Negroes in certain areas. The all-Negro school had been abandoned by my day. My elementary school classes always included Negro children, but I remember none during the last 3 years of high school. My Negro classmates were usually poorly clothed and badly groomed. Negroes held the low-status jobs. They were the servants, garbage collectors, and odd-job men. People called them "Nigger" more often than "Negro." I did not know until I grew up that a Negro could be a doctor, lawyer, teacher, member of Parliament, or even a clerk in a store. . . . I cannot conceive of any social advantages which Negroes enjoyed in Kent County at the time of the Tanser study.(103a, p. 621)

Tanser himself admitted that his sample of Negro children had not attended school as regularly as the white children. Moreover, it cannot be said that Southern Ontario is free of racial prejudice and discrimination. Ever since the close of the American Civil War, the position of the Negro Canadian has steadily declined, with violent outbursts against Negroes occurring in Kent County itself.(16a, 36a, 77a) The racial differences in I.Q. observed by Tanser, then, cannot be interpreted apart from the area's racial situation.

These difficulties point up the severely limiting methodological problems which confront this research realm. Any test of native intelligence

[4] For similar analyses of other investigations of so-called "equal groups" commonly cited by white supremacists see Anastasi.(3, pp. 556–558)

must of necessity assume equivalent backgrounds of the individuals and groups under study. But until conditions entirely free from segregation and discrimination are achieved and the floor of Negro poverty is raised to the level of whites, the definitive research on racial differences in intelligence cannot be performed. Meanwhile, psychologists must conduct their work in a culture when training and opportunity for the two groups are never completely equal.

Other fundamental problems complicate the issue. The very concept of "race" injects special issues. Since Negro Americans do not even approach the status of a genetically pure "race," they are a singularly inappropriate group upon whom to test racist theories of inherent intellectual inferiority of the Negroid subspecies. In addition, confusion is introduced by the ambiguity of the phrase "race differences." To find that many descriptive investigations using intelligence tests elicit differences between the "races" does not necessarily mean that these differences *result* from race.

Empirical efforts are also hampered by the operation of selective factors in sampling. That is, Negroes and whites in the same situation— such as those inducted into the armed forces—may have been selected differently on intelligence, thus biasing the comparison of test scores between the two groups. For instance, Hunt found that the Navy during World War II did not employ the same screening and selection standards for the two groups, permitting a far higher proportion of mental defectives among Negro than among white acceptances.(54a) Such a finding renders any comparisons in test scores between Negro and white sailors of dubious value. Much has been made of the intelligence test performances of the two "races" in both World Wars I and II, but such selective factors make these data difficult to interpret.

Despite these limitations, however, modern psychology has managed to achieve significant theoretical and empirical advances in this realm. These advances strongly favor a non-genetic interpretation of the typically lower intelligence test score averages of Negro groups. This work can be conveniently summarized under four general rubrics: (1) new theoretical conceptions; (2) the mediators of intellectual underdevelopment; (3) varying opportunities and group results; and (4) the individual versus the group.

## NEW THEORETICAL CONCEPTIONS

Since World War II, psychologists and other scientists have seriously reviewed earlier notions about such basic concepts as "the environment," "heredity," and "intelligence." Instead of the older nature versus nurture conception, the emphasis is placed on nature and nurture.[5] Rather than

[5] Much of the following discussion is based on Gottesman's review.(44)

asking which set of factors—environmental or hereditary—contributes more to a particular trait or ability like intelligence, investigators ask how the environment and heredity combine to form the observed characteristic. Genes not only set broad limits on the range of development, but also enter into highly complex interactions with the environment, interactions which have not been emphasized enough in the past.

An ingenious animal experiment by Cooper and Zubek illustrates this genetic-environmental interaction.(21) These investigators employed two genetically distinct strains of rats, carefully bred for thirteen generations as

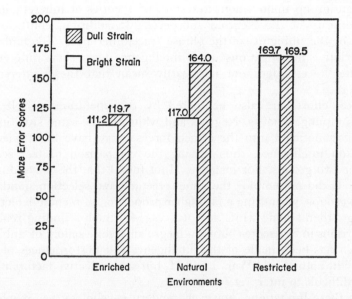

Figure 1—Maze Error Scores for Genetically Bright and Dull Rats Reared in Three Contrasting Environments

Data from: R. M. Cooper and J. P. Zubek, "Effects of Enriched and Restricted Early Environments on the Learning Ability of Bright and Dull Rats," *Canadian Journal of Psychology*, 1958, **12,** 159–164.

either "bright" or "dull." Separate groups of the two strains grew up after weaning in three contrasting environments: a restricted environment, consisting of only a food box, water pan, and otherwise barren cage; a natural environment, consisting of the usual habitat of a laboratory rat; and an enriched environment, consisting of such objects as ramps, swings, slides, polished balls, tunnels, and teeter-totters plus a decorated wall beside their cages. Figure 1 shows the maze learning performances of the six groups of rats (the fewer the errors, the more "intelligent" the behavior). Note that the two genetically diverse groups did almost equally well in the enriched and restricted environments, sharply differing only in the natural situation. In fact, the environment masks genetic potential to the point where it is impossible to distinguish the enriched dulls from the natural brights or the natural dulls from the restricted brights.

The data of Figure 1 bear important implications. "Genotypes," the true genetic potential, often do not coincide with "phenotypes," the actual, expressed trait. Similar genotypes may have different phenotypes (e.g., the bright rats in the restricted and enriched environments), and similar phenotypes may have different genotypes (e.g., the restricted bright and dull rats). Any phenotype is the composite product of the genotype and the environment in which the genetic potential must be realized. Relevant nature-nurture questions thus become: how environmentally modifiable is the phenotypic intelligence of each genotype? And what is the contribution of heredity to the intelligence score differences among a group of individuals on a specific test in a specified environment?

This newer view of the nature-nurture controversy and a mounting accumulation of new developmental evidence has resulted in a revised conception of the nature of intelligence. J. McV. Hunt presents this modern thinking in his volume, *Intelligence and Experience*.(54) Taking his cue from the strategies for information-processing that are currently programmed for electronic computers, Hunt defines intelligence as central neural processes which develop in the brain to mediate between the information coming into the individual via the senses and the return signals for motor reaction. Moreover, he maintains that the initial establishment and subsequent capacity of these processes are probably rooted in the child's earliest encounters with the world around him. Intelligence, then, is not merely an inherited capacity, genetically fixed and destined to unfold in a biologically predetermined manner. It is a dynamic, on-going set of processes that within wide hereditary limits is subject to innumerable experiential factors.

Hunt's view upsets two long-unquestioned dogmas about intelligence, dogmas critical in the area of race differences. He terms them the assumptions of "fixed intelligence" and "predetermined development." The first of these has its roots in Darwin's theory of natural selection. It accepts intelligence as a static, innately-given quantity, and it long influenced psychological thought and the design of I.Q. tests. Indeed, the assumption of fixed intelligence became so established before World War II that many psychologists regarded all evidence of substantial shifts in I.Q. as merely the product of poor testing procedures. But, objected Stoddard in 1943, "to regard all changes in mental status as an artifact is to shut one's eyes to the most significant and dramatic phenomenon in human growth." (114, p. 281)

The second assumption of "predetermined development" refers to the idea that, barring extreme interference from the environment, intelligence will unfold "naturally" with gene-determined anatomical maturation.

Classic work on salamanders and Hopi Indian children was cited to demonstrate this maturational effect and that prior experience was unnecessary for normal development.(15, 20, 25) In this era, mothers were told to avoid overstimulating their children, to allow their children simply to grow "on their own." Hunt considers such advice "highly unfortunate," for it now appears that a proper matching of a child's development with challenging encounters with his environment is a critical requisite for increasing ability.

Notice this new outlook in no way denies an hereditary influence on intelligence, an influence well established by twin studies.(44) Rather, it views intelligence in much the same way longevity is now regarded. A strong hereditary component is recognized in longevity; consistently long or short life spans typify many families. Yet, despite this component, the life expectancies at birth of Americans have almost doubled in the past century.(79) Better medical care, better diets, and a host of other environmental factors converge to enable Americans to make fuller use of their longevity potential. Likewise, the modern view of intelligence holds that we have not begun to expand our genotypic intelligences even close to our genotypic potentials. From this vantage point, it appears our society has placed too much emphasis on personnel selection and eugenics at the expense of effective training programs and euthenics.

Some of the most imaginative experimentation behind this new thinking is that of the eminent Swiss psychologist, Jean Piaget.(54, 92) His ingenious and detailed studies with children of all ages provide abundant evidence that intelligence is the very antithesis of a fixed, predetermined capacity. And a wide range of other types of investigations amply bears out this conclusion. Even animal intelligence seems to be importantly affected by environmental opportunities. The previously-cited rat work of Cooper and Zubek shows how diverse cage environments affect later learning. In addition, pet-reared rats and dogs, with backgrounds of richly variegated experience, later evidence considerably more intelligent behavior than their cage-reared counterparts.(117, 118) And Harlow has demonstrated that monkeys can "learn to learn"; that is, they can develop learning sets which enable them to solve general classes of problems almost at a glance.(49)

Similar effects of early environmental enrichment on the intelligence of young children have been noted. Kirk has shown that early educational procedures can often produce sharp increments in intellectual functioning among mentally retarded children, sometimes even among those diagnosed as organically impaired.(61) Other studies on normal children, both white and Negro, suggest that preschool training in nursery and kindergarten classes may act to raise I.Q.'s.(29; 3, pp. 200–205; 54, pp. 27–34; 68) Among criticisms of this research is the contention that a selection factor could be operating. The natively brighter children may be those who tend to have preschool education. But among deprived children in an orphanage, the beneficial results of early schooling have been noted in a situation where selection factors did not operate.(127) Also relevant is the tendency for orphans to gain in I.Q. after adoption into superior foster homes, the gain being greatest for those adopted youngest.(37)

After reviewing research on cognitive learning in these early years, Fowler concludes that this is the period of human "apprenticeship."(35) The infant is acquiring the most elementary and basic discriminations needed for later learning; like Harlow's monkeys, the infant is "learning to learn." Fowler speculates that conceptual learning sets, interest areas, and habit patterns may be more favorably established at these early stages than at later stages of the developmental cycle. Indeed, emphasis on "practical," concrete, gross motor learning in these early years may even inhibit later abstract learning.

In any event, research has documented the intellectually damaging consequences of deprived environments. An English study found that the children of such isolated groups as canal-boat and gypsy families achieved exceptionally low intelligence test scores, scores considerably below those typically found among Negro American children.(43) Interesting, too, is the fact that as these children grow older their I.Q.'s generally decline, though this is not the case for children of more privileged groups. In a similar fashion, children in orphanages and other institutions tend to have lower I.Q.'s and more retarded motor and linguistic development than children in stimulating home environments. Once again selection factors may operate, with the brighter, more developed children being more often chosen for adoption. However, studies which overcome much of this difficulty still note this institutional retardation.(12, 26, 40, 42)

A related finding concerns the trend toward lower I.Q.'s of children raised in large families.(2) One common explanation of this phenomenon is simply that parents who have large families are natively less intelligent. Yet, as Hunt points out, other findings strongly suggest that it is partly because parents of large families have less time to spend with each child.(54) Thus, twins and doubles born close together in otherwise small families reveal a similar tendency toward lower I.Q.'s. And the negative relationship between family size and intelligence does not appear among wealthy families who can afford servants to provide stimulating attention for each child.

Finally, the extreme effects that can ensue from an impoverished environment are dramatically illustrated in a series of sensory-deprivation experiments.(9) These investigations reveal that normal people respond with marked psychological disturbances when severely restricted in activity and stimulation. They typically experience temporal and spatial distortions and pronounced hallucinations; and they evidence sharply impaired thinking and reasoning both during and after their isolation.

## THE MEDIATORS OF INTELLECTUAL UNDERDEVELOPMENT

Within this new perspective on intelligence as a relatively plastic quality, a series of environmental mediators of the individual Negro child's intellectual underdevelopment has been determined. In fact, these mediators exert their effects even upon the Negro fetus. One study found that dietary supplementation by vitamins supplied during the last half of pregnancy had directly beneficial effects on I.Q. scores of the children later.(51) In a sample of mothers from the lowest socioeconomic level, 80 per cent of whom were Negro, the group fortified with iron and Vitamin B complex had children whose mean I.Q. at three years of age averaged five full points above the children of the unfortified control group, 103.4 to 98.4. One year later, the mean difference had enlarged to eight points, 101.7 to 93.6. The same researchers failed to find a similar effect among white mothers and their children from a mountain area. Presumably, the largely Negro sample was even poorer and more malnourished than the white sample from the mountains. Dire poverty, through the mother's inadequate diet, can thus impair intelligence before the lower-class Negro child is born.

Economic problems also hamper intelligence through the mediation of premature births.(66, 89) Premature children of all races reveal not only a heightened incidence of neurologic abnormalities and greater susceptibility to disease, but also a considerably larger percentage of mental defectives. (50, 67) A further organic factor in intelligence is brain injury in the newborn. And both of these conditions have higher incidences among Negroes because of their greater frequency in the most economically depressed sectors of the population.

Later complications are introduced by the impoverished environments in which most Negro children grow up. At the youngest, preschool ages, race differences in I.Q. means are minimal. Repeated research shows that in the first two years of life there are no significant racial differences in either psychomotor development or intelligence.(41, 64, 86) Racist theorists discount these findings on two conflicting grounds.(39, 102) They either claim that infant tests have no predictive value whatsoever for later I.Q. scores, or cite an older study by McGraw that found Negro infants retarded in comparison with white infants. Neither argument is adequate. Three recent investigations provide convincing evidence that properly administered infant tests *do* predict later scores.(31, 55, 65) And the 1931 McGraw study is no longer regarded as a decisive experiment—not even by Myrtle McGraw herself.(75, 76, 87) It was a pioneer effort that compared white infants with Negro infants of markedly smaller stature on an unvalidated adaptation of a European test. Furthermore, later Northern investigations show little or no Negro lag in intellectual development through kindergarten and five years of age when thorough socio-economic controls are applied.(4, 13)

It is only after a few years of inferior schooling have passed that many Negro children drop noticeably in measured I.Q.(85, 121) Part of this drop is due to the heavier reliance placed by intelligence tests at these ages upon verbal skills, skills that are particularly influenced by a constricted environment. One Southern study of "verbal destitution" discovered that Negro college students most retarded in a reading clinic came from small, segregated high schools and exhibited language patterns typical of the only adult models they had encountered—poorly educated parents, teachers, and ministers.(84)

Another factor in the declining test averages over the school years is simply the nature of the schools themselves. Deutsch gives the example of an assignment to write a page on 'The Trip I Took,' given to lower-class youngsters in a ghetto school who had never been more than twenty-five city blocks from home. Psychologist Deutsch maintains: "The school represents a foreign outpost in an encapsulated community which is surrounded by what, for the child, is unknown and foreign."(28, p. 3)

This tendency of the measured I.Q.'s of Negro children to diminish with increasing age is interpreted by racists not as evidence of the eroding effects of ghetto living, but as proof that Negroes mature more rapidly and begin to decline earlier than whites.(39, 102, 94) Such an idea, based on the belief that Negroes as a "race" are less evolved, is seriously challenged by the often demonstrated fact that environmentally-deprived Caucasian groups reveal precisely the same phenomenon—mountain and other rural children in America and the canal-boat and gypsy children in England.(3) Furthermore, the positive relationship between socio-economic status and tested I.Q. among Negroes increases with age, again suggesting that environmental factors become ever more vital as the child matures.(121)

The nature of the disrupted family life of many lower-status Negro youths decreases further the slum's environmental stimulation. Most of these youngsters are reared in large families, with reduced parental contact. And many of them are in fatherless homes. Deutsch and Stetler have both demonstrated that Negro children raised in such broken homes score significantly below comparable Negro children from intact homes on intelligence measures.(28, 29, 113)

Other research pinpoints the tasks tested by intelligence tests which are most impaired by this restriction of stimulation. Woods and Toal matched two groups of Negro and white adolescents on I.Q. and noted sub-test differences.(132) While superior to the whites on some tests, the Negroes were noticeably deficient on tasks such as detection of errors and drawing pictorial completions which required spatial visualization. And other similar studies reach the same conclusion.(8, 19, 24, 27, 36, 47, 53,

70, 82) One demonstrated that this difficulty with perceptual and spatial relations was considerably more marked in a Southern-reared Negro sample than in an I.Q.-matched Northern-reared Negro sample.(70) This breakdown of spatial performance among otherwise intelligent Negro children, especially in the more restrictive South, offers a suggestive parallel with the comparable spatial breakdown noted in the sensory-deprivation research. In any event, two additional studies provide evidence that this disability is correctable.(10, 32) Both studies gave groups of Negro and white children special training in spatial perception and found that the Negro subjects benefited more from the practice. Intelligence quotient test scores were markedly higher for the Negro subjects five months after the training.(10) Test authority Anne Anastasi believes this work supports the idea that the Negroes tested suffered from an unusually barren perceptual experience in early life.(3)

Organic complications and environmental impoverishment are not the only mediators depressing Negro American intelligence. Both the "functioning intelligence" and the measured I.Q. of an individual are inseparably intertwined with his personality.(45, 59, 106, 115, 122, 126) Edith Weiss-kopf has given case evidence of the greatest variety of ways personality problems can deter normal intellectual development.(126) A child may do poorly in learning situations in a conscious or unconscious desire to punish his parents, to inflict self-punishment, or to avoid self-evaluation. And Roen has demonstrated that such personality problems are more highly related to intelligence test scores among Negroes than among whites.(98) He equated two racial groups of soldiers on a wide range of social variables and found that a series of personality measures were more closely correlated with intelligence for the Negroes than for the whites. In particular, he noted that Negro soldiers who had low intelligence scores rated especially low on a self-confidence questionnaire.

Racist claims of Caucasian superiority contribute to the Negro's lack of intellectual self-confidence. This insecurity is especially provoked by any direct comparison with white performance. One investigation administered a task to Southern Negro college students with two different sets of in-structions.(60) One set told how other students at their college did on the task, while the second told how whites throughout the nation did. Those subjects who anticipated white comparison performed significantly more poorly on the task and indicated stronger concern and anxiety about their performance.

The role of "Negro" is again a critical factor. Put simply, the Negro is not expected to be bright. To reveal high intelligence is to risk seeming "uppity" to a white supremacist. And once more the self-fulfilling prophecy begins to operate, for the Negro who assumes a façade of stupidity as a defense mechanism against oppression is very likely to grow into the role. He will not be eager to learn, and he will not strive to do well in the testing situation. After all, an intelligence test is a middle-class white man's instrument; it is a device whites use to prove their capacities and get ahead in the white world. Achieving a high test score does not have the same meaning for a lower-status Negro child, and it may even carry a definite connotation of personal threat. In this sense, scoring low on intelligence measures may for some talented Negro children be a rational response to perceived danger.

In addition to stupidity, the role of "Negro" prescribes both passivity and lack of ambition as central traits. And these traits are crucial personality correlates of I.Q. changes in white children. The Fels Research Institute found that aggressiveness and intense need for achievement differentiate those children whose scores rise between six and ten years of age from those whose scores recede.(59)

Another protective device is slowness. This trait assumes major importance in the speed instruments typically employed to estimate intelligence. In the Negro lower class there is no premium on speed, for work is generally paid by the hour and there are realistically few goals that fast, hard endeavor can attain. One experiment noted that differences in speed of response are primarily responsible for racial differences in I.Q. estimated by timed performance tests.(24)

Playing "Negro" is made especially critical when the examiner is white. Even two-year-old Negroes seem verbally inhibited when tested by a white.[6](88) In fact, this verbal inhibition may be the principal factor underlying the common observation that Negro children generally evidence verbal comprehension superior to their verbal communication.(16) One investigation had students of both races tested alternately by Negro and white examiners.(14) For both groups, the mean I.Q. was approximately six points higher when the test was administered by an examiner of their own race.

Adult Negroes evidence a similar reaction. A public opinion poll in North Carolina asked Negro respondents for the names of the men who had just run for governor in a primary election.(93) Three out of five Negroes questioned by Negro interviewers knew at least two correct names and gave no incorrect names, compared with only two out of five of a similar sample questioned by whites. A Boston survey replicated these results with two measures tapping intelligence.(91) The first consisted of six informational items; each respondent was asked to identify six famous men: two Africans (Kwame Nkrumah and Haile Selassie) and the rest Negro Americans (Louis Armstrong, Martin Luther King, Adam Clayton Powell, and Elijah Muhammad). The other test required synonyms for ten words, ranging in difficulty from "space" to "emanate." Negro interviewers questioned half of the respondents, and white interviewers the

---

[6] Shuey (102, p. 316) concludes that race of examiner is not important by omitting this key investigation (88) and not mentioning the full results of another.(14)

other half. The two samples were equivalent in income, age, education, and region of birth. Figure 2 presents the results. Note that on both tests the Boston Negro adults rendered more correct answers when interviewed by a Negro.

Apart from the role of "Negro," the middle-class bias of intelligence testing situations operates to hinder a disproportionate share of Negro examinees. Children perform best in situations familiar to them, but the conditions best suited for lower-status children are seldom attained.

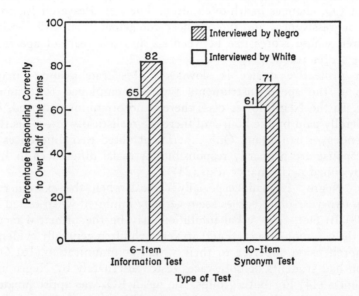

Figure 2—Race of Interviewer and Negro Test Performance

Data from: T. F. Pettigrew, "The Negro Respondent: New data on old problems," unpublished paper.

Most I.Q. tests are strictly urban middle-class instruments, with numerous references to objects and situations unfamiliar to rural and lower-class people. Haggard showed that a less middle-class-oriented test led to significant increases in the performances of lower-class children.(46)

Tests are only one aspect of class bias, however. Middle-class students have generally internalized their need to excel at such tasks; a high test score is itself a reward. Moreover, they perform most competently in silent testing atmospheres that place heavy reliance upon reading skills. By contrast, lower-class students frequently require tangible, external rewards for motivation. And their typically restricted home environments are overwhelmingly dominated by the spoken, rather than the written, word. It is not surprising, then, that Haggard discovered notable increments in intelligence test scores of lower-class children when there was extra motivation for doing well (e.g., a prize of movie tickets) and when the questions were read aloud as well as written.(46) Sophisticated testing in ghetto schools should follow such guidelines for more adequate estimates of the abilities of disadvantaged children.(105)

## VARYING OPPORTUNITIES AND GROUP RESULTS

If all of these mechanisms are operating to mediate the influence of a lean, hostile, and constricted environment upon the individual Negro's tested intelligence, certain group trends under conditions of varying opportunities can be predicted. These testable hypotheses are: (a) In environments which approach being equally restrictive for children of both races, the intelligence test means of both will be low and will approach equality; (b) In environments which approach being equally stimulating for children of both races, the intelligence test means of both will be high and will approach equality; and (c) When any racial group moves from a restrictive to a comparatively stimulating environment, its measured I.Q. mean will rise.

The first of these hypotheses was tested on an isolated Caribbean island, offering little stimulation to its youth. It had:

no regular steamship service, no railroad, motion picture theater, or newspaper. There were very few automobiles and very few telephones. The roads were generally poor. There were no government schools above the elementary level and no private schools above the secondary level. . . . People of all colors, then, were restricted to a rather narrow range of occupational opportunity.(22, p. 14)

Even here, however, complete equality of status between whites and Negroes was not achieved. White skin was "highly respected," whites typically held the better jobs, and, while almost half of the white students attended private schools, nine-tenths of the Negroes attended government schools. Nevertheless, there were no significant color differences on nine of the fourteen intelligence measures. The Negroes did best on tests which were less class-linked, less threatening, and less dependent on uncommon words. Thus, socioeconomic status was a more important factor than race on four of the five instruments which did yield racial discrepancies, and "lack of confidence," as rated independently by teachers, was highly related to three of them. In general, the island youngsters scored rather low on the tests, with race a relatively insignificant consideration. And the selective migration possibility that the brighter whites were leaving the island is not an explanation for these findings, since there was apparently little emigration or immigration. These data, gathered in a locality which approached being equally restrictive for both races, do "not lend support to the conclusion that colored inferiority in intelligence tests has a racial basis."(22, p. 26)

The second hypothesis has also received support from a number of studies. Three investigations, testing young children in Minneapolis, grade-school students in a Nevada city, and adolescents in the Boston area, revealed that, once social-class factors are rigorously controlled, there are only minor black-white mean I.Q. differences.(13, 74, 78) In these relatively stimulating, educationally-desegregated urban communities, both racial groups secured test averages equal to the national norms.

An additional study was conducted in West Germany.(34) A representative sample of 51 *neger-mischlingskinder*—the mulatto children of Negro American soldiers and German women—was administered a number of intelligence tests and their performance contrasted with a comparable group of 25 white German children. There were no significant differences. Two counter-balancing factors complicate the interpretation of this research. The Negro fathers of these children are undoubtedly an intelligent, highly selected group, selected not only in terms of being chosen to serve in the United States Army in Germany but also in terms of having become acculturated enough to establish an intimate relationship with a German woman. But this factor is balanced by the fact that the children are mostly illegitimate and viewed as such in the German culture, almost by virtue of their color. Furthermore, most of their mothers are probably of lower-status backgrounds and as such have not been able to provide them with the cultural enrichment of the typical German home. And, finally, German culture, even in this post-Hitler era, can hardly be described as totally free of racist thinking. All in all, the satisfactory test performance of these mulatto Germans appears quite remarkable.

Thus, I.Q. means of groups are retarded where there are constrictive environmental conditions and elevated where there are at least average conditions. Three ecological projects provide further evidence for this generalization. One project correlated home rentals with the I.Q. averages of the school children in 300 New York City neighborhoods.(71) Moderately high and positive relationships were found; the more expensive the neighborhood, the higher the test scores. Another noted very close and positive associations between such variables as per capita income and the mean I.Q. level of sixth-grade pupils in 30 American cities.(119) The third project discovered that these ecological correlations tend to be higher for intelligence scores than for scholastic achievement, demonstrating again the extreme sensitivity of the measured I.Q. to the total social environment. (120)

This research is confirmed by further investigations conducted exclusively among Negroes.(29, 81, 96, 97) Especially since World War II and its attendant expansion of social class differentiation among Negro Americans, socioeconomic variables correlate highly and positively with

I.Q. means in Negro samples. For example, the I.Q. means of groups of third-graders in Washington, D.C. tended to be highest in areas where radios were most often present in the homes and where rents were highest.

These results suggest the third hypothesis: when any group moves from a restrictive to a comparatively stimulating environment, its measured I.Q. mean will rise. Dramatic evidence for this propositon comes from the unique situation of the Osage Indians. Like many other Indian groups, the Osage were granted land for the establishment of a reservation. Oil was later discovered on their land, and the Osage became relatively prosperous. Since the Osage had not chosen their land, the oil discovery was not an indication of native ingenuity beyond that of Indian groups in general. But now they could afford living standards vastly superior to other Indians, and on both performance and language tests they were found to meet the national norms and to have achieved the level of comparable whites in the area.(99) This finding is all the more impressive when it is remembered that Indian children generally perform considerably below Negro children in I.Q. tests.

Similar improvements are recorded among white mountain children in East Tennessee, public school students in Honolulu, and white enlisted men in World War II. Wheeler gave tests to over three thousand mountain children in 1940, and compared their performance to that of children in the same areas and from virtually the same families in 1930.(128) This ten-year span had witnessed broad economic, social, and educational changes in East Tennessee, and the median I.Q.'s reflected these changes in an increment of 11 points, from 82 to 93. Equally remarkable gains are reported for children of many racial groups in Honolulu after a 14-year period of steady improvement in the city's schools.(104) And, finally, 768 soldiers, representative of white enlisted men in World War II, took the old Army Alpha verbal test of World War I and provided striking evidence of the nation's rising intelligence between the two wars. Tuddenham shows that the typical white World War II enlisted man did better on the test than 83 per cent of the enlisted men of the first war.(123)

This last study, incidentally, refutes reasoning put forward by Frank McGurk concerning the intelligence test performances of Negroes in the two world wars. He has argued that if environmental factors are responsible for racial differences in intelligence scores, then Negro scores should have steadily approached the white scores between the two wars; yet "the various differences in socioeconomic environments of the Negroes, between 1918 and 1950, have not altered the Negro-white test score relationship."(77) Such "logic" assumes that the socioeconomic standards of whites have not changed over these same years. But in fact the prosperity of whites throughout the nation has been increasing in many ways faster than that of Negro Americans. If the old Alpha test had been administered to World War II Negroes, they would have most certainly done significantly better than World War I Negroes. "The Negro-white test score relationship," McGurk refers to, has only remained constant because Negroes have made giant strides in intellectual growth where environmental improvements allowed it. Meanwhile, as the Tuddenham data demonstrate, the white median intelligence has also been climbing with environmental improvements. Intelligence, like longevity, is not a fixed capacity for either Negroes or whites.

Another curious assumption made by racist theorists arises from interpreting regional as well as racial results on the World War I Alpha. A number of social scientists noted that Negro recruits in World War I from such states as Ohio and Illinois had higher median scores than white recruits from such states as Arkansas and Mississippi.(80) These extreme comparisons revealed that the environmental deprivations of some Southern whites clearly exceeded even those of some Northern Negroes. Garrett hesitated to apply his usual explanation for low scores: namely, to conclude that whites in these Southern states were innately inferior intellectually.(38) Instead, he emphasized that Negroes scored below whites within each state; he argued that the low white scores in the South were environmentally induced, but that the even lower Negro scores in the South were a combination of environmental factors and genetic inferiority. To advance this argument, Garrett had to assume that Negroes and whites in the South were *equally* deprived—even before World War I. This assumption, of course, is absurd. The period between 1890 and the First World War was the lowest ebb of Negro fortunes since slavery. Today the last traces of that era insure that Negro Southerners as a group are the most environmentally impoverished of all Southerners. And while there were often no public schools at all for Negroes in some rural areas of the South before World War I, the belatedly-improved facilities of today still lag behind those of the whites.(6, 73, 109n)

Once the Negro American escapes from these inferior conditions, however, his improved performance parallels that of the Osage Indians and the East Tennessee mountain children. Service in the armed forces is one of the most important sources of wider experience and opportunities for Negroes, including those who are illiterate. The Army in the Second World War operated Special Training Units and provided a basic fourth-grade education in eight weeks for 254,000 previously illiterate soldiers—roughly half of them Negroes and the great majority Southerners. A slightly higher percentage of the Negroes than whites successfully completed the intensive course, though how this bears on larger questions of Negro intelligence is a matter of debate, since the men given this special training were selected. There is no debate, however, over the fact that the success of these units proves the educability of many apparently retarded men of both races.(5, 11, 33, 129, 130)

Another mode of improvement for many Negroes is migrating North. Negro Northerners routinely achieve higher test medians than comparable Negro Southerners.(1, 23, 90, 95, 96) And Negro children born in the North achieve higher medians than those who come to the North from the South.[7](63, 68, 69, 100, 113) But do the Negro children who migrate improve their group performance as they remain in the North? This was the central question the eminent psychologist, Otto Klineberg, set out to answer in 1935; and it led to perhaps the best known research in the field of race differences.(63) Over three thousand ten-to-twelve-year-old Harlem Negroes took an array of individual and group intelligence instruments. These data clearly indicate that the longer the Southern-born children had resided in New York City, the higher their intelligence scores. Those who had been in the North for a number of years approached the levels attained by the Northern-born Negroes. Smaller studies with less elaborate designs obtained parallel results in Cleveland and Washington, D.C.(30, 69)

More recently, Lee replicated these findings in Philadelphia with the most rigorous research on the topic to date.(68) Employing large samples in a variety of different schools, Lee analyzed the test scores of the same children as they progressed through the city's school system. Though never quite catching up with the Philadelphia-born Negro students, the Southern Negro migrants as a group regularly gained in I.Q. with each grade completed in Northern schools. And the younger they were when they entered the Philadelphia school system, the greater their mean increase and final I.Q. The effects of the more stimulating and somewhat less discriminatory North, then, are directly reflected in the measured intelligence of the youngest of Negro migrants.

The majority complication in interpreting the Klineberg and Lee work is again introduced by possible selection biases. Those Negro Southerners who migrate North in search of a better life may be selectively brighter and rear brighter children. Such a possibility is emphasized by the "scientific racists," though Shuey concedes this factor could reasonably account for only one-third to one-half of the I.Q. increases observed.(102) But other possibilities also exist. Many of the more intelligent Negroes in the South gain some measure of success and establish roots that are more difficult to break than those of the less intelligent. This phenomenon would operate to make the Klineberg and Lee data all the more impressive. Or, perhaps, intelligence has little or nothing to do with the decision to migrate; personality traits, such as aggressiveness or inability to control hostility over racial frustrations, may be more decisive. In any event, Klineberg found the Southern school grades of 562 Negro youths who had since

[7] In a reanalysis of her New Haven I.Q. data (100), Nancy St. John found that the presence of at least one Northern-born parent was an even more critical variable than the region of birth of the child. (Private communication)

gone North were typical of the entire Negro school populations from which they migrated.(63) More research is needed, but it seems that selective migration cannot begin to account for the dramatic improvement in test performance demonstrated by Negro children who move to the North.

Further evidence that Negro ability goes up when environmental opportunities expand derives from the many diverse educational-enrichment programs current in our major cities. The best known of these is New York City's "Higher Horizons" project.(72) This effort provides a selected and largely Negro student body with an expensive saturation of skilled specialists: remedial-reading teachers, guidance counselors, psychologists, and social workers. Its results have been striking; in the first year, the program cut third graders' retardation in reading from six months down to a single month. Backed by major foundation grants, other cities have also begun to experiment. Detroit and Philadelphia tried sending "school-community agents" into ghetto schools in an attempt to win parental support for education. Kansas City's Central High School and Tucson's Pueblo High School initiated imaginative new programs.(72) And Washington, D.C., launched in 1959 a "talent search" project for 200 deprived seventh graders, 92 per cent of whom were Negro.(109j) Similar to Higher Horizons in its concentration of staff and exposure of students to new cultural experiences, the "talent search" was soon declared a success. Contrasted with a matched control group, the students of the program showed a sharply reduced scholastic failure rate and notable instances of I.Q. increments.

Perhaps the most remarkable demonstration of all is Samuel Shepard's "Banneker Group" work in St. Louis.(7, 103, 109b, 109e, 109h, 109i, 109m, 109n, 109p) A forceful educator, Shepard performs his "miracles" on the most underprivileged school children in the city without the vast expenditures of other efforts. The Banneker group consists of 23 elementary schools with over sixteen thousand slum and public housing children, more than 95 per cent of them Negro. A Negro who overcame serious economic disadvantages himself, Shepard adamantly rejects the old dogma that sub-standard school work is all you can realistically expect from ghetto children. He bluntly challenges the pupils, parents, principals, and teachers of the district to perform up to national standards; he appeals to race pride and resorts to continuous exhortations, rallies, contests, posters, and meetings with teachers and parents. Students who make good grades are asked to stand in assemblies for the applause of their classmates. Teachers are asked to visit the homes of their charges. And parents are asked to provide their offspring with encouragement, study space, a library card, a dictionary, and other books as gifts. As a concrete incentive, Shepard points out the new and better jobs now open to Negroes in St. Louis and the lack of qualified Negroes to fill them.

The results of the Banneker effort speak for themselves. Despite an unending stream of poorly educated migrants into the area from the South, all test indicators have risen. In the first four years of the program, the median I.Q. increased from the middle 80's to the 90's; median reading, language, and arithmetic levels all climbed; and the percentage of Banneker graduates accepted for the top-ability program in St. Louis's desegregated high schools tripled.

The striking results of these imaginative demonstrations may not be due directly to the exact procedures introduced. Given their vast variety of techniques and their uniform success, the demonstrations probably achieve most of their gains because of the sheer fact of intervention—any kind of thoughtful intervention. Often the rate of initial progress slows once the beginning enthusiasm cools. But this is irrelevant to the larger issue of Negro American intelligence. Dramatic improvement in Negro performance for whatever reason is evidence of the underlying potential for learning heretofore stifled by lack of opportunity and attention. This potential for learning is also evident in the findings of a recent experiment at the University of Texas.(101) Negro children learned series of paired material as rapidly and well as white children, even though they came from lower socioeconomic backgrounds and had significantly lower I.Q.'s.

Such demonstrations arouse speculation concerning the effects of desegregation of public school systems. Segregationists have long voiced the unsubstantiated opinion that "school mixing" would mean educational chaos, with the Negroes dragging down the higher white standards. But the experience of a great diversity of communities indicates that these fears are unjustified. Administrators of 17 desegregated school systems appeared before the United States Civil Rights Commission in March, 1959, and candidly discussed their problems.(108) Twelve of the educators dealt with the question of academic standards. Ranging from Logan County, Kentucky, and Muskogee, Oklahoma, to Baltimore and Nashville, all twelve reported unequivocally that their academic standards had not been lowered—in fact, many maintained that their standards had improved for both races.

Washington, D.C. provided the acid test. It embarked upon a sweeping process of educational desegregation in 1954 with Negroes comprising three-fifths of the students, many of them from the South with limited backgrounds. The *U.S. News and World Report* soon published articles claiming that the District of Columbia's public school system was well on its way to ruin, and these tracts were widely quoted by segregationists.(125a, 125b, 125c, 125d) But such dire consequences never materialized. A four-track system of ability grouping and other innovations were adopted. Five years later, in 1959, a factual assessment of the changes was made. (48, 109c, 109d, 109f, 109g, 109k, 109l, 111) Though Negro students, swelled by migrants, now comprised three-fourths of the student body, achievement test scores had risen significantly for each grade level sampled and each subject area tested approached or equaled national norms. Furthermore, both Negro and white students shared in these increments.[8] Such results are not unique to Washington. Louisville reported substantial gains in Negro performance and slight gains in white performance after only one year of desegregation.(107, 110)

Clearly, desegregation *per se* does not accomplish these feats. The Banneker demonstration in St. Louis took place in virtually all-Negro schools; Washington and Louisville witnessed sharply improved test medians among their Negro students, whether in biracial or uniracial schools. The principal factor seems to be the new and healthier self-image Negroes acquire in the process. The act of community desegregation bolsters and encourages Negro pupils, parents, and teachers alike. Combining with this heightening of morale is the entrenched Negro desire for education. *Newsweek's* 1963 national poll revealed that 97 per cent of the nation's Negroes want their children at least to graduate from high school.(83)

Also important is the sudden interest Negro education finally wins from the whole community. As long as Negro education is a racially separate system, dominant white interests can and do forget it. But once desegregation forces the community to handle the education of its youth in one package, to consider Negro education as an integral part of the whole process, new attention is given to the schools. Indeed, the rise in white test scores after desegregation suggests that public education as a whole benefits from the greater public interest. Washington offers an illustration. Prior to desegregation, survey testing was only done with the white pupils; Negroes were ignored.(108) But immediately after desegregation, testing throughout the system was instituted, and the same standards were applied at last to both races. Certainly, desegregation is no panacea for the immense problems faced by public school systems with large percentages of environmentally impoverished children, but it does prepare the way for tackling the *real* problems of modern education.

Thus, an array of stimulating circumstances—service in the armed forces, migration to the North, and participation in revitalized school systems—all act to lift substantially the intelligence and achievement levels of Negroes. Often these improvements still do not bring the average Negro performance completely up to white norms, but this cannot be considered as evidence for genetic racial differences until *all* racial discrimination is abolished.

[8] This is not to say that school difficulties no longer exist in Washington. They continue not because of desegregation, however, but because certain Southern members of the House of Representatives insist on treating the District's "children as pawns in a wicked game designed to prove that desegregation cannot succeed." (*Washington Post* editorial, March 2, 1963)

## THE INDIVIDUAL VERSUS THE GROUP

The discussion so far has concentrated on group results, yet many of the most important considerations involving Negro American intelligence concern the individual. Not even racists deny the existence of outstanding Negro Americans. Usually, however, the same individuals are cited— Marian Anderson, Ralph Bunche, George Washington Carver—and are considered "exceptions" and special "credits to their race." The truth is that a surprising number of such "exceptional" Negroes have somehow managed to overcome the formidable obstacles of discrimination. Many have naturally entered the struggle for equal rights. But others achieve such stature in non-stereotyped work that they are no longer thought of as Negro. For instance, the originator of the Hinton test for syphilis, the late Professor William A. Hinton, was well known as a bacteriologist and immunologist at Harvard Medical School but not as a Negro.

Superior intelligence comes in all skin colors. While the intelligence test means of the two races are still divergent, the range of performance— from the most retarded idiot to the most brilliant genius—is much the same in the two groups. Some Negro children score I.Q.'s into the gifted range (130 or over) and right up to the testable limit of 200.(56, 57, 116, 131) To be sure, the frequency of such bright Negroes is less than that of whites, but this, too, can be explained by differential environmental factors. The great majority of these superior Negroes are located in biracial schools in the urban North and West, which suggests that many potentially gifted Negroes go either undiscovered or undeveloped in the segregated schools of the South.(56, 58) Proof that such children do exist in the South comes from programs which intensively seek talented Negro Southerners. (17, 112) Once found, they receive scholarships and attend a variety of desegregated high schools and colleges in the North, and the great majority of them accommodate well to their new and challenging situations. Indeed, a recent study of Negro scholarship applicants from the South who have attended integrated colleges reveals that they have a far smaller drop-out rate than white students at the same colleges.(18)

A further embarrassment to racist theories is created by the fact that the degree of white ancestry does not relate to Negro I.Q. scores.(52, 62, 90, 131) Among intellectually superior Negroes, for example, the propor- tions of those with varying degrees of white ancestry correspond closely with those of the total Negro American population.(131) Indeed, the brightest Negro child yet reported—with a tested I.Q. of 200—had no traceable Caucasian heritage whatsoever.(116, 131) "Race *per se*," con- cludes Martin Jenkins, "is not a limiting factor in psychometric intelli- gence."(56, p. 401)

There exists, then, a considerable overlap in the I.Q. distributions of the two groups. A few Negroes will score higher than almost all Caucasians.

Figure 3 shows two typical intelligence test distributions with an overlap of 25 per cent, that is, 25 per cent of the Negroes tested (shaded area) surpass the performance of half of the whites tested. Notice how the ranges of the two distributions are virtually the same, even though the means are somewhat different. This figure illustrates one of the most important facts about "race" and measured intelligence: individual differences in I.Q. *within* any one race greatly exceed differences *between* races.

There are two practical consequences of this phenomenon for desegregated education. First, when a school system institutes a track program of ability grouping, there will be Negroes and whites at all levels. Second, some gifted Negroes will actually lead their biracial classes even during the

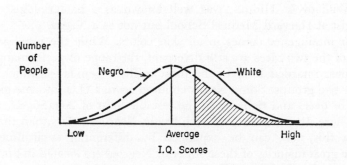

Figure 3—Typical Test Distributions With "25 Per Cent Overlap"

initial stages of desegregation. Thus, Janice Bell, a seventeen-year-old Negro girl, led the first graduating class of superior students at Beaumont High in St. Louis (109q); Julius Chambers, a twenty-four-year-old Negro Southerner, became the 1961–1962 editor of the University of North Carolina's *Law Review* in recognition of his leadership of his law school class (109o); and Charles Christian, a thirty-seven-year-old Negro Virginian, led his Medical College of Virginia senior class academically in 1962.(109r) "In the study of individuals," summarizes Anastasi, "the only proper unit is the individual."(3)

## THE CURRENT CONCLUSION

Intelligence is a plastic product of inherited structure developed by environmental stimulation and opportunity, an alloy of endowment and experience. It can be measured and studied only by inference, through observing behavior defined as "intelligent" in terms of particular cultural content and values. Thus, the severely deprived surroundings of the average Negro child can lower his measured I.Q. in two basic ways. First, it can act to deter his actual intellectual development by presenting him with such a constricted encounter with the world that his innate potential is barely tapped. And, second, it can act to mask his actual functioning intelligence in the test situation by not preparing him culturally and motivationally for such a middle-class task. "Only a very uncritical psychologist would offer sweeping generalizations about the intellectual superiority or inferiority of particular racial or ethnic groups," comments Tuddenham, "despite the not very surprising fact that members of the dominant racial and cultural group in our society ordinarily score higher than others on tests of socially relevant accomplishments invented by and for members of that group."(124, pp. 499–500)

The principal mechanisms for mediating these environmental effects vary from the poor nutrition of the pregnant mother to meeting the expectations of the social role of "Negro." Some of these mechanisms, like fetal brain injuries, can leave permanent intellectual impairments. Consequently, the permanency and irreversibility of these effects are not, as some claim, certain indicators of genetically low capacity. Fortunately, many of these effects are correctable. Moving North to better schools, taking part in special programs of environmental enrichment, and benefiting from challenging new situations of educational desegregation can all stimulate Negro children to raise their I.Q. levels dramatically.

From this array of data, the overwhelming opinion of modern psychology concludes that the mean differences often observed between Negro and white children are largely the result of environmental, rather than genetic, factors. This is *not* to assert that psychologists deny altogether the possibility of inherited racial differences in intellectual structure. There may be a small residual mean difference—small not only because of the demonstrably sweeping influence of experience, but also because the two "races" are by no means genetically "pure" and separate.

Psychology is joined in this conclusion by its sister behavioral sciences: sociology and anthropology. Witness the following professional statements.

The Society for the Psychological Study of Social Issues, a division of the American Psychological Association, concluded in 1961:

There are differences in intelligence test scores when one compares a random sample of whites and Negroes. What is equally clear is that no evidence exists that leads to the conclusion that such differences are innate. Quite to the contrary, the evidence points overwhelmingly to the fact that when one compares Negroes and whites of comparable cultural and educational background, differences in intelligence diminish markedly; the more comparable the background, the less the difference. There is no direct evidence that supports the view that there is an innate difference between members of different racial groups. . . . We regret that Professor Garrett feels that his colleagues are foisting an "equalitarian dogma" on the public. There is no question of dogma involved. Evidence speaks for itself and it casts serious doubt on the conclusion that there is any innate inequality in intelligence in different racial groups . . .

The Society for the Study of Social Problems, a section of the American Sociological Association, concurred in the same year:

. . . the great preponderance of scientific opinion has favored the conclusion that there is little or no ground on which to assume that the racial groups in question are innately different in any important human capacity . . . the conclusion of scientists is that the differences in test performance by members of so-called racial groups are due not to racial but to environmental factors. This is the operating assumption today of the vast majority of the competent scientists in the field . . .

The American Anthropological Association passed a resolution by a unanimous vote (192 to 0) in 1961:

The American Anthropological Association repudiates statements now appearing in the United States that Negroes are biologically and in innate mental ability inferior to whites, and reaffirms the fact that there is no scientifically established evidence to justify the exclusion of any race from the rights guaranteed by the Constitution of the United States. The basic principles of equality of opportunity and equality before the law are compatible with all that is known about human biology. All races possess the abilities needed to participate fully in the democratic way of life and in modern technological civilization.

The final, definitive research must await a racially integrated America in which opportunities are the same for both races. But, ironically, by that future time the question of racial differences in intelligence will have lost its salience; scholars will wonder why we generated so much heat over such an irrelevant topic. Yet the results of this belated research should prove interesting. Even if small inherent differences are found, their direction cannot be taken for granted. Racists have never considered the possibility that the "true" Negro capacity might actually average somewhat above that of the white. Certainly, there are enough environmental barriers operating in the present situation to mask any such Negro superiority. If this possibility should actually be demonstrated, one wonders if white racists would be thoroughly consistent and insist that white children be given separate and inferior education.

The important conclusion for the present, however, is that if there are any inherent distinctions they are inconsequential. Even now, differences in I.Q. within any one race greatly exceed differences between races. Race as such is simply not an accurate way to judge an individual's intelligence. The *real* problems in this area concern ways to overcome the many serious environmental deprivations that handicap Negro youth. To return to the analogy with longevity, the problem is akin to that which faced medicine in the nineteenth century. Automatized America needs to expand the intelligence level of its underprivileged citizens in much the same way it has expanded the life potential of its citizens in the past one hundred years. The success of such programs as the Banneker group in St. Louis demonstrates this job can be accomplished when American society decides to put enough of its resources into it. "The U. S. must learn," writes Charles Silberman in *Fortune,* "to look upon the Negro community as if it were an underdeveloped country."(103, p. 151)

### References to *Negro American Intelligence*

1. Thelma G. Alper and E. G. Boring, "Intelligence Test Scores of Northern and Southern White and Negro Recruits in 1918," *Journal of Abnormal and Social Psychology,* 1944, **39,** 471–474.
2. Anne Anastasi, "Intelligence and Family Size," *Psychological Bulletin,* 1956, **53,** 187–209.
3. Anne Anastasi, *Differential Psychology,* Third edition, New York, Macmillan, 1958.
4. Anne Anastasi and Rita D'Angelo, "A Comparison of Negro and White Pre-School Children in Language Development and Goodenough Draw-a-Man I.Q.," *Journal of Genetic Psychology,* 1952, **81,** 147–165.
5. H. Aptheker, "Literacy, and the Negro and World War II," *Journal of Negro Education,* 1946, **15,** 595–602.
6. H. S. Ashmore, *The Negro and the Schools,* Chapel Hill, University of North Carolina Press, 1954.
7. H. Baron, "Samuel Shepard and the Banneker Project," *Integrated Education,* April, 1963, **1,** 25–27.
8. K. L. Bean, "Negro Responses to Verbal and Non-verbal Test Material," *Journal of Psychology,* 1942, **13,** 343–353.
9. W. H. Bexton, W. Heron, and T. H. Scott, "Effects of Decreased Variation in the Sensory Environment," *Canadian Journal of Psychology,* 1954, **8,** 70–76.
10. J. H. Boer, "An Experimental Study of the Effects of Perceptual Training on Group I.Q. Test Scores of Elementary Pupils in Rural Ungraded Schools," *Journal of Educational Research,* 1952, **46,** 43–52.
11. Gladyce Bradley, "A Review of Educational Problems Based on Military Selection and Classification Data in World War II," *Journal of Educational Research,* 1949, **43,** 161–174.
12. A. J. Brodbeck and O. C. Irwin, "The Speech Behavior of Infants without Families," *Child Development,* 1946, **17,** 145–156.
13. F. Brown, "An Experimental and Critical Study of the Intelligence of Negro and White Kindergarten Children," *Journal of Genetic Pyschology,* 1944, **65,** 161–175.
14. H. G. Canady, "The Effect of 'Rapport' on the I.Q.: A New Approach to the Problem of Racial Psychology," *Journal of Negro Education,* 1936, **5,** 209–219.
15. L. Carmichael, "A Further Study of the Development of Behavior in Vertebrates Experimentally Removed from the Influence of Environmental Stimulation," *Psychological Review,* 1927, **34,** 34–47.
16. A. S. Carson and A. I. Rabin, "Verbal Comprehension and Communication in Negro and White Children," *Journal of Educational Psychology,* 1960, **51,** 47–51.
16a. S. N. Chant and S. S. Freedman, "A Quantitative Comparison of the Nationality Preferences of Two Groups," *Journal of Social Psychology,* 1934, **5,** 116-120.
17. K. B. Clark, "The Most Valuable Hidden Resource," *College Board Review,* 1956, **29,** 23–26.

18. K. B. Clark and L. Plotkin, *The Negro Student at Integrated Colleges*, New York, National Scholarship Service and Fund for Negro Students, 1963.
19. D. P. Clarke, "Stanford-Binet Scale L Response Patterns in Matched Racial Groups," *Journal of Negro Education*, 1941, **10**, 230–238.
20. G. E. Coghill, *Anatomy and the Problem of Behavior*, New York, Macmillan, 1929.
21. R. M. Cooper and J. M. Zubek, "Effects of Enriched and Constricted Early Environments on the Learning Ability of Bright and Dull Rats," *Canadian Journal of Psychology*, 1958, **12**, 159–164.
22. Margaret W. Curti, "Intelligence Tests of White and Colored School Children in Grand Cayman," *Journal of Psychology*, 1960, **49**, 13–27.
23. R. K. Davenport, "Implications of Military Selection and Classification in Relation to Universal Military Training," *Journal of Negro Education*, 1946, **15**, 585–594.
24. K. S. Davidson, R. G. Gibby, E. B. McNeil, S. J. Segal, and H. Silverman, "A Preliminary Study of Negro and White Differences in Form I of the Wechsler-Bellevue Scale," *Journal of Consulting Psychology*, 1950, **14**, 489–492.
25. W. Dennis, "The Effect of Cradling Practices upon the Onset of Walking in Hopi Children," *Journal of Genetic Psychology*, 1940, **56**, 77–86.
26. W. Dennis, "Causes of Retardation among Institutional Children: Iran," *Journal of Genetic Psychology*, 1960, **96**, 47–59.
27. W. P. De Stephens, "Are Criminals Morons?" *Journal of Social Psychology*, 1953, **38**, 187–199.
28. M. Deutsch, "Minority Group and Class Status as Related to Social and Personality Factors in Scholastic Achievement," *Monograph of the Society for Applied Anthropology*, 1960, **2**, 1–32.
29. M. Deutsch and B. Brown, "Social Influences in Negro-White Intelligence Differences," *Journal of Social Issues*, 1964, **20**(2), 24–35.
30. E. H. Dombey, "A Comparison of the Intelligence Test Scores of Southern and Northern Born Negroes Residing in Cleveland." Unpublished Master's thesis, Western Reserve University, 1933.
31. C. M. Drillien, "Physical and Mental Handicap in Prematurely Born," *Journal of Obstetrics and Gynaecology* (British), 1959, **66**, 721–728.
32. O. W. Eagleson, "Comparative Studies of White and Negro Subjects in Learning to Discriminate Visual Magnitude," *Journal of Psychology*, 1937, **4**, 167–197.
33. R. W. Erickson, "On Special-Training-Unit Performance as an Index of Negro Ability," *Journal of Abnormal and Social Psychology*, 1946, **41**, 481.
34. K. Eyferth, "Eine Untersuchung der Neger-Mischlingskinder in Westdeutschland," *Vita Humana*, 1959, **2**, 102–114.
35. W. Fowler, "Cognitive Learning in Infancy and Early Childhood," *Psychological Bulletin*, 1962, **59**, 116–152.
36. J. C. Franklin, "Discriminative Value and Patterns of the Wechsler-Bellevue Scales in the Examination of Delinquent Negro Boys," *Educational and Psychological Measurement*, 1945, **5**, 71–85.
36a. J. H. Franklin, *From Slavery to Freedom*, Second Edition, New York, Knopf, 1961.
37. F. N. Freeman, K. J. Holzinger, and B. C. Mitchell, "The Influence of Environment on the Intelligence, School Achievement, and Conduct of Foster Children," *27th Yearbook, National Society of Social Science Education*, 1928, Part **I**, 103–217.

38. H. E. Garrett, "A Note on the Intelligence Scores of Negroes, and Whites in 1918," *Journal of Abnormal and Social Psychology*, 1945, **40,** 344–346.
39. H. E. Garrett, "Klineberg's Chapter on Race and Psychology: A Review," *The Mankind Quarterly*, 1960, **1,** 15–22.
39a. H. E. Garrett, "The Equalitarian Dogma" *Mankind Quarterly*, 1961, **1,** 253-257.
39b. H. E. Garrett, "Rejoinder by Garrett," *Newsletter of the Society for the Psychological Study of Social Issues*, May, 1962, 1-2.
39c. H. E. Garrett, "Psychological Differences as among Races," *Science*, 1945, **101,** 16-17.
39d. H. E. Garrett, "The SPSSI and Racial Differences," *American Psychologist*, 1962, **17,** 260-263.
40. A. R. Gilliland, "Environmental Influences on Infant Intelligence Test Scores," *Harvard Educational Review*, 1949, **19,** 142–146.
41. A. R. Gilliland, "Socioeconomic Status and Race as Factors in Infant Intelligence Test Scores," *Child Development*, 1951, **22,** 271–273.
42. W. Goldfarb, "Emotional and Intellectual Consequences of Psychologic Deprivation in Infancy: A Reevaluation," in P. H. Hoch and J. Zubin (eds.), *Psychopathology of Childhood*, New York, Grune and Stratton, 1955.
43. H. Gordon, *Mental and Scholastic Tests Among Retarded Children*, London, Board of Education (Educational Pamphlet no. 44), 1923.
44. I. I. Gottesman, "Genetic Aspects of Intelligent Behavior," in N. Ellis (ed.), *The Handbook of Mental Deficiency*. New York: McGraw-Hill, 1963, 253–296.
45. H. G. Gough, "A Nonintellectual Intelligence Test," *Journal of Consulting Psychology*, 1953, **17,** 242–246.
46. E. A. Haggard, "Social Status and Intelligence: An Experimental Study of Certain Cultural Determinants of Measured Intelligence," *Genetic Psychology Monographs*, 1954, **49,** 141–186.
47. E. F. Hammer, "Comparison of the Performances of Negro Children and Adolescents on Two Tests of Intelligence, One an Emergency Scale," *Journal of Genetic Psychology*, 1954, **84,** 85–93.
48. C. F. Hansen, *Addendum: A Five-Year Report on Desegregation in the Washington, D.C. Schools*, New York, Anti-Defamation League of B'nai B'rith, 1960.
49. H. F. Harlow, "The Formation of Learning Sets," *Psychological Review*, 1949, **56,** 51–65.
50. P. A. Harper, L. K. Fischer, and R. V. Rider, "Neurological and Intellectual Status of Prematures at Three to Five Years of Age," *Journal of Pediatrics*, 1959, **55,** 679–690.
51. R. F. Harrell, E. R. Woodyard, and A. I. Gates, "Influence of Vitamin Supplementation of Diets of Pregnant and Lactating Women on Intelligence of Their Offspring," *Metabolism*, 1956, **5,** 555–562.
52. Melville J. Herskovits, "On the Relation between Negro-White Mixture and Standing in Intelligence Tests," *Pediatrics Sem.*, 1926, **33,** 30–42.
53. C. Higgins and Cathryne Sivers, "A Comparison of Stanford-Binet and Colored Raven Progressive Matrices I.Q.'s for Children with Low Socioeconomic Status," *Journal of Consulting Psychology*, 1958, **22,** 465–468.
54. J. M. Hunt, *Intelligence and Experience*, New York, Ronald, 1951.

54a. W. A. Hunt, "Negro-White Differences in Intelligence in World War II —a Note of Caution," *Journal of Abnormal and Social Psychology*, 1947, **42**, 254-255.

55. J. G. Hurst, "Relationships between Performance on Preschool and Adult Intelligence Measures." Paper presented at the Annual Meeting of the American Psychological Association, held at Philadelphia, August, 1963.

55a. H. H. Hyman and P. B. Sheatsley, "Attitudes toward Desegregation," *Scientific American*, 1956, **195**, 35-39.

56. M. D. Jenkins, "The Upper Limit of Ability among American Negroes," *Scientific Monthly*, 1948, **66**, 399-401.

57. M. D. Jenkins, "Intellectually Superior Negro Youth: Their Problems and Needs," *Journal of Negro Education*, 1950, **19**, 322-332.

58. M. D. Jenkins and Constance M. Randall, "Differential Characteristics of Superior and Unselected Negro College Students," *Journal of Social Psychology*, 1948, **27**, 187-202.

59. J. Kagan, L. W. Sontag, C. T. Baker, and Virginia Nelson, "Personality and I.Q. Change," *Journal of Abnormal and Social Psychology*, 1958, **56**, 261-266.

60. I. Katz, E. G. Epps, and L. J. Axelson, "The Effects of Anticipated Comparison with Whites and with Other Negroes upon the Digit-Symbol Performance of Negro College Students." Unpublished paper.

61. S. A. Kirk, *Early Education of the Mentally Retarded*, Urbana, Ill., University of Illinois Press, 1958.

62. O. Klineberg, "An Experimental Study of Speed and Other Factors in 'Racial' Differences," *Archives of Psychology*, 1928, **15**, no. 93.

63. O. Klineberg, *Negro Intelligence and Selective Migration*, New York, Columbia University Press, 1935.

64. Hilda Knobloch and B. Pasamanick, "Further Observations on the Behavioral Development of Negro Children," *Journal of Genetic Psychology*, 1953, **83**, 137-157.

65. Hilda Knobloch and B. Pasamanick, "Environmental Factors Affecting Human Development before and after Birth," *Pediatrics*, 1960, **26**, 210-218.

66. Hilda Knobloch and B. Pasamanick, "Mental Subnormality," *New England Journal of Medicine*, 1962, **266**, 1092-1097.

67. Hilda Knobloch, R. Rider, P. Harper, and B. Pasamanick, "Effect of Prematurity on Health and Growth," *American Journal of Public Health*, 1959, **49**, 1164-1173.

68. E. S. Lee, "Negro Intelligence and Selective Migration: A Philadelphia Test of the Klineberg Hypothesis," *American Sociological Review*, 1951, **16**, 277-233.

69. H. H. Long, "The Intelligence of Colored Elementary Pupils in Washington, D.C.," *Journal of Negro Education*, 1934, **3**, 205-222.

70. S. Machover, "Cultural and Racial Variations in Patterns of Intellect," *Teachers College Contributions to Education*, 1943, no. **875**.

71. J. B. Maller, "Mental Ability and Its Relation to Physical Health and Social Economic Status," *Psychological Clinic*, 1933, **22**, 101-107.

72. M. Mayer, "The Good Slum Schools," *Harpers*, April 1961, **222**, 46-52.

73. P. McCauley and E. D. Ball (eds.), *Southern Schools: Progress and Problems*, Nashville, Tenn., Southern Education Reporting Service, 1959.

74. W. M. McCord and N. J. Demerath, III, "Negro Versus White Intelligence: A Continuing Controversy," *Harvard Educational Review*, 1958, **28**, 120-135.

75. Myrtle B. McGraw, "A Comparative Study of a Group of Southern White and Negro Infants," *Genetic Psychology Monograph*, 1931, **10**, 1–105.
76. Myrtle B. McGraw, "Need for Denial," *American Psychologist*, 1964, **19**, 56.
77. F. McGurk, "Negro vs. White Intelligence—an Answer," *Harvard Educational Review*, 1959, **29**, 54–62.
77a. F. McGurk, "On White and Negro Test Performance and Socio-Economic Factors," *Journal of Abnormal and Social Psychology*, 1953, **48**, 448-450.
77b. F. McGurk, "Psychological Tests: A Scientist's Report on Race Differences," *U.S. News and World Report*, September 21, 1956, 92-96.
78. R. McQueen and B. Churn,"The Intelligence and Educational Achievement of a Matched Sample of White and Negro Students," *School and Society*, 1960, **88**, 327–329.
79. Metropolitan Life Insurance Company, "Progress in Longevity since 1850," *Statistical Bulletin*, July, 1963, **44**, 1–3.
80. M. F. A. Montagu, "Intelligence of Northern Negroes and Southern Whites in the First World War," *American Journal of Psychology*, 1945, **58**, 161–188.
81. W. I. Murray, "The I.Q. and Social Class in the Negro Caste," *South-Western Journal of Anthropology*, 1949, **4**, 187–201.
82. T. E. Newland and W. C. Lawrence, "Chicago Non-Verbal Examination Results on an East Tennessee Negro Population," *Journal of Clinical Psychology*, 1953, **9**, 44–46.
83. *Newsweek* editors, "The Negro in America," *Newsweek*, July 29, 1963, **62**, 15–34.
84. Eunice Newton, "Verbal Destitution: The Pivotal Barrier to Learning," *Journal of Negro Education*, 1960, **24**, 497–499.
85. R. T. Osborn, "Racial Differences in Mental Growth and School Achievement: A Longitudinal Study," *Psychological Reports*, 1960, **7**, 233–239.
86. B. Pasamanick, "A Comparative Study of the Behavioral Development of Negro Infants," *Journal of Genetic Psychology*, 1946, **69**, 3–44.
87. B. Pasamanick and P. H. Knapp (eds.), *Social Aspects of Psychiatry*, Washington, D.C., American Psychiatric Association, 1958.
88. B. Pasamanick and Hilda Knobloch, "Early Language Behavior in Negro Children and the Testing of Intelligence," *Journal of Abnormal and Social Psychology*, 1955, **50**, 401–402.
89. B. Pasamanick and Hilda Knobloch, "The Contribution of Some Organic Factors to School Retardation in Negro Children," *Journal of Negro Education*, 1958, **27**, 4–9.
90. J. Peterson and L. H. Lanier, "Studies in the Comparative Abilities of Whites and Negroes," *Mental Measurement Monograph*, 1929, no. 5.
91. T. F. Pettigrew, "The Negro Respondent: New Data on Old Problems." Unpublished paper.
92. J. Piaget, *The Psychology of Intelligence*, translated by M. Piercy and D. E. Berlyne, London, Routledge and Kegan Paul, 1947.
93. D. O. Price and Ruth Searles, "Some Effects of Interviewer-Respondent Interaction on Responses in a Survey Situation." Paper presented at the Annual Meeting of the American Statistical Association, held in New York, December 30, 1961.

94. C. Putnam, *Race and Reason: A Yankee View*, Washington, D.C., Public Affairs Press, 1961.

95. D. C. Reitzes, *Negroes and Medicine*, Cambridge, Mass., Harvard University Press, 1958.

96. S. O. Roberts, "Socioeconomic Status and Performance on the ACE of Negro Freshmen College Veterans and Non-Veterans, from the North and South," *American Psychologist*, 1948, **3**, 266.

97. Mary L. Robinson and M. Meenes, "The Relationship between Test Intelligence of Third-Grade Negro Children and the Occupations of Their Parents." *Journal of Negro Education*, 1947, **16**, 136–141.

98. S. R. Roen, "Personality and Negro-White Intelligence," *Journal of Abnormal and Social Psychology*, 1960, **61**, 148–150.

99. J. H. Rohrer, "The Test Intelligence of Osage Indians," *Journal of Social Psychology*, 1942, **16**, 99–105.

100. Nancy St. John, "The Relation of Racial Segregation in Early Schooling to the Level of Aspiration and Academic Achievement of Negro Students in a Northern High School." Unpublished doctoral thesis, Harvard University, 1962.

101. I. J. Semler and I. Iscoe, "Comparative and developmental Study of the Learning Abilities of Negro and White Children Under Four Conditions," *Journal of Educational Psychology*, 1963, **54**, 38–44.

102. Audrey Shuey, *The Testing of Negro Intelligence*, Lynchburg, Va., Bell, 1958.

103. C. E. Silberman, "The City and the Negro," *Fortune*, March, 1962, **65**, 89–91, 139–154.

103a. Mollie S. Smart, "Confirming Klineberg's Suspicion," *American Psychologist*, 1963, **18**, 621.

104. S. Smith, "Language and Non-Verbal Test Performance of Racial Groups before and after a 14-Year Interval," *Journal of Genetic Psychology*, 1942, **26**, 51–93.

105. Society for the Psychological Study of Social Issues, "Guidelines for Testing Minority Group Children." Pamphlet in press.

106. L. W. Sontag, C. T. Baker, and Virginia Nelson, Personality as a Determinant of Performance," *American Journal of Orthopsychiatry*, 1955, **25**, 555–562.

107. Southern Regional Council, "Did you Find That There Was Much Difference in the Ability of Negro Children to Receive and Profit by Instruction?" *Report No. L-13*, December 15, 1959.

108. Southern Regional Council, "Desegregation and Academic Achievement," *Report No. L-17*, March 14, 1960.

109. *Southern School News:* (a) May, 1958, **4**(11); (b) January, 1959, **5**(7); (c) May, 1959, **5**(11); (d) July, 1959, **6**(1); (e) August, 1959, **6**(2); (f) December, 1959, **6**(6); (g) January, 1960, **6**(7); (h) April, 1960, **6**(10); (i) May, 1960, **6**(11); (j) June, 1960, **6**(12); (k) July, 1960, **7**(1); (l) August, 1960, **7**(2); (m) November, 1960, **7**(5); (n) February, 1961, **7**(8); (o) June, 1961, **7**(12); (p) September, 1961, **8**(3); (q) February, 1962, **8**(8); and (r) June, 1962, **8**(12).

110. F. H. Stallings, "A Study of the Immediate Effects of Integration on Scholastic Achievement in the Louisville Public Schools," *Journal of Negro Education*, 1959, **28**, 439–444.

111. F. H. Stallings, "Racial Differences and Academic Achievement," *Southern Regional Council's Report No. L-16*, February 26, 1960.

112. J. M. Stalnaker, "Identification of the Best Southern Negro High School Seniors," *Scientific Monthly*, 1948, **67**, 237–239.

113. H. G. Stetler, *Comparative Study of Negro and White Dropouts in Selected Connecticut High Schools*. Hartford: Connecticut Commission on Civil Rights, 1959.

114. G. D. Stoddard, *The Meaning of Intelligence*, New York, Macmillan, 1943.

115. Lorene A. Stringer, "Academic Progress as an Index of Mental Health," *Journal of Social Issues*, 1959, **15**, 16–29.

115a. H. A. Tanser, *The Settlement of Negroes in Kent County, Ontario, and a Study of the Mental Capacity of their Descendants*. Chatham, Ontario, Shephard, 1939.

116. V. Theman and P. A. Witty, "Case Studies and Genetic Records of Two Gifted Negroes," *Journal of Psychology*, 1943, **15**, 165–181.

117. W. R. Thompson and W. Heron, "The Effects of Restricting Early Experience on the Problem-Solving Capacity of dogs," *Canadian Journal of Psychology*, 1954, **8**, 17–31.

118. W. R. Thompson and R. Melzack, "Early Environment," *Scientific American*, 1956, **194**(1), 38–42.

119. E. L. Thorndike and Ella Woodyard, "Differences within and between Communities in the Intelligence of Children," *Journal of Educational Psychology*, 1942, **33**, 641–656.

120. R. L. Thorndike, "Community Variables as Predictors of Intelligence and Academic Achievement," *Journal of Educational Psychology*, 1951, **42**, 321–338.

121. H. Tomlinson, "Differences between Preschool Negro Children and Their Older Siblings on the Stanford-Benet Scales," *Journal of Negro Education*, 1944, **13**, 474–479.

122. R. Trumbull, "A Study in Relationships between Factors of Personality and Intelligence," *Journal of Social Psychology*, 1953, **38**, 161–173.

123. R. D. Tuddenham, "Soldier Intelligence in World Wars I and II," *American Psychologist*, 1948, **3**, 54–56.

124. R. D. Tuddenham, "The Nature and Measurement of Intelligence," in L. Postman (ed.), *Psychology in the Making*, New York, Knopf, 1962.

125. *United States News and World Report:* (a) September 28, 1956, **41**, 98–107; (b) October 5, 1956, **41**, 68–69; (c) October 12, 1956, **41**, 82–88; and (d) January 4, 1957, **42**, 92–100.

126. Edith Weisskopf, "Intellectual Malfunctioning and Personality," *Journal of Abnormal and Social Psychology*, 1951, **46**, 410–423.

127. Beth L. Wellman and Edna L. Pegram, "Benet I.Q. Changes of Orphanage Preschool Children: A Reanalysis," *Journal of Genetic Psychology*, 1944, **65**, 239–263.

128. L. R. Wheeler, "A Comparative Study of the Intelligence of East Tennessee Mountain Children," *Journal of Educational Psychology*, 1942, **33**, 321–334.

129. P. Witty, "New Evidence on the Learning Ability of the Negro," *Journal of Abnormal and Social Psychology*, 1945, **40**, 401–404.

130. P. Witty, "Reply to Mr. Erickson," *Journal of Abnormal and Social Psychology*, 1946, **41**, 482–485.

131. P. Witty and M. D. Jenkins, "Intra-Race Testing and Negro Intelligence," *Journal of Psychology*, 1936, **1**, 179–192.

132. W. A. Woods and R. Toal, "Subtest Disparity of Negro and White Groups Matched for I.Q.'s on the Revised Beta Test," *Journal of Consulting Psychology*, 1957, **21**, 136–138.

# SOCIAL INFLUENCES IN NEGRO-WHITE

# INTELLIGENCE DIFFERENCES

*Martin Deutsch and Bert Brown*

This paper reports on some aspects of experience that influence the development of intellective functions in children. The social experiential variable is often treated in the psychological literature in a most macroscopic manner. It has been one of our purposes to break down the attributes of social experience along what might be called social environmental and developmental dimensions.

As regards the social environmental, the attempt has been to analyze racial group membership by some of its psychological properties, to determine some of the components of social class, and to determine something of the interaction of the two, particularly as it impinges on intellectual achievement and growth.

On what we are calling the developmental dimension, the focus has been on identifying "experience groups" in terms of language, perception, learning, general intellective functioning, and to a lesser extent, self, attitudinal, and motivational variables. These variables, in turn, have been broken down into more specific components for measurement and for evaluation of interrelationships.

The data have been collected on cross-sectional samples, but the work is closely associated with a large-scale longitudinal study which attempts to manipulate mediating environmental variables and to measure any subsequent behavioral modification or facilitation in intellectual growth.

From *Journal of Social Issues*, **20**, 2 (April, 1964), 24–35. Reprinted by permission of the *Journal of Social Issues* and by permission of the authors.

The data reported here were collected as part of studies supported by the Taconic Foundation, by Research Grant No. MH-1098 from the U.S. Department of Health, Education, and Welfare, and by Project #908 of the Cooperative Research Program of the Office of Education. The research was carried out at the Institute for Developmental Studies, Department of Psychiatry, New York Medical College.

The cross-sectional study referred to is a large social class and race analysis, involving first- and fifth-grade children, which we colloquially refer to as "the verbal survey"—a term which is something of a misnomer, as the range goes beyond verbal measures.

This report is concerned with the intellectual test differences between Negro and white first- and fifth-graders of different social classes—though the focus in this report is largely on the lower class. Two more specific independent variables of special significance are presence or absence of father in the home, and whether the child had an organized preschool experience.

The data reported in this paper are from a sample of 543 urban public school children stratified by race, grade level (first- and fifth-graders), and social class, as measured by the Institute's twelve-point SES (socioeconomic status) scale. This scale is derived both from prestige ratings of occupation as well as education of main breadwinners and yields a weighted index of these factors for each subject in the sample. The distribution of index scores is broken down into twelve levels and sub-sequently trichotomized into three socioeconomic strata. SES comparisons reported in this paper are made among three distinguishable social class levels, I, II, and III, where level I represents the lowest group on the continuum and III the highest. Housing condition for these S's was evaluated along a six point continuum from "Sound, with all plumbing facilities" to "Dilapidated" following from the technique suggested by the U.S. Census of Housing.[1] The weighted SES index score correlates .27 with the housing condition index for a sample of 292 children within the larger group of 543. The magnitude of this correlation is low but significant for the sample size on which it was obtained.

The intelligence test used was the Lorge-Thorndike, Level I, Primary Battery for first-graders, and Level 3 for fifth-graders. Both forms, as described by the authors, are essentially non-verbal (Lorge-Thorndike, 1959). Level I uses pictorial items only to measure abstract thinking, pictorial classification and pictorial pairing. Level 3 uses picture classification, pictorial analogies, and numerical relationships. This test was selected because of the inclusion in its standardization population of a much better than usual representation of the lower social class categories. It was given in small groups, during school hours, by trained examiners on the Institute's research staff.

The SES data were gathered by mailed questionnaires and home interviews. The SES items were only a part of the interview schedule. The rest of the items had to do with home conditions, daily routine, and aspirations of both parents and children. The appropriate items here are now being collated into a "deprivation index" for purposes of identifying the sources of inter- and intra-class variation.

[1] U.S. Bureau of the Census, *U.S. Census of Housing*, 1960, 3, City Block, Series HC (3), Nos. 274–276.

Table I presents results of a three-way analysis of variance using Lorge-Thorndike I.Q. scores as the dependent variable. It can readily be seen that fifth-grade I.Q. scores do not differ significantly from scores achieved by first-grade children. Differences between scores of Negro and white children can be seen to be highly significant ($p < .0001$) and are equally strong between SES levels. Examination of the secondary tables

*Table 1*—Analysis of Variance* and Cell Means on Lorge-Thorndike Intelligence Test Performance by Grade, Race and Social Class
(N = 543)

| Source | Sum of squares | d.f. | F | Sig. |
|--------|---------------|------|-----|------|
| Grade | 634.429 | 1 | 3.153 | N.S. |
| Race | 10,119.416 | 1 | 50.296 | $p < .0001$ |
| SES | 14,429.344 | 2 | 35.859 | $p < .0001$ |
| Within | 106,834.966 | 531 | | |
| Total | 137,656.866 | 542 | | |

Mean Lorge-Thorndike I.Q. Scores for SES Groups, Race Groups Within SES Groups and Total Race Groups

| Group | $\bar{X}$ | S.D. | N |
|-------|-----------|------|---|
| SES I | | | |
| White | 97.24 | 15.35 | 104 |
| Negro | 91.24 | 13.25 | 157 |
| Total | 93.63 | 14.43 | 261 |
| SES II | | | |
| White | 105.59 | 14.88 | 68 |
| Negro | 94.87 | 14.70 | 111 |
| Total | 98.94 | 15.67 | 179 |
| SES III | | | |
| White | 114.92 | 12.05 | 52 |
| Negro | 102.57 | 14.53 | 51 |
| Total | 108.81 | 14.70 | 103 |
| Total Race Groups | | | |
| White | 103.88 | 16.12 | 224 |
| Negro | 94.32 | 14.53 | 319 |

\* *Note.*—Interaction terms have been omitted from the table, as none reached significance.

*Note.*—Two-tailed *t*-tests for differences between total race groups and SES levels significant at $p < .01$.

of means and sigmas for subgroups within each of these variables indicates the direction and magnitude of these differences. Clearly, the means for white children are significantly higher than are mean I.Q. scores for their Negro counterparts and the relationship is documented by *t*-test differences between race groups reaching significance at $p < .01$. Similarly, interlevel differences are significant for SES groups at $p < .01$. While the analysis of variance does not indicate a significant race by SES interaction, inspection of the means shows: (1) that Negro children at each SES level score lower than white children, and (2) that Negro-white differences increase at each higher SES level. While children in each racial group show gain in I.Q. with ascending SES level, gains for the white group appear to be considerably greater.

These results are consistent with other data (Kennedy, 1963; Anderson, 1962; Eells, 1951) and could reflect the ascending isomorphism between social class and the item content of intelligence tests. Nevertheless, such results are usually predictive of school achievement, although their meaning with regard to individual potential may be questionable.

It is extremely interesting to note this more sharply defined escalation of the white majority group child's I.Q. through the three social class steps. In the lowest class, where social deprivation is most homogeneous and the influence of race is attenuated by the pervasiveness of poor living conditions, there is somewhat less difference, as has been mentioned, between Negro and white.

To summarize: (1) A linear relationship exists between SES and performance level for both Negro and white groups, and (2) Within this linear relationship the absolute increase in I.Q. is greater for the white group than it is for the Negro.

The interpretation put forth here for these data is that the influence of racial membership tends to become increasingly manifest and crucial as the social class level increases. The hypothesis we would advance has to do with increased participation in the cultural mainstream, and the differing conditions under which Negroes and whites participate (Deutsch, 1963). The weight of color and resulting minority status, it is postulated here, results in much less participation by the Negro, while the lowest class status operates similarly for the white as well as for the Negro. In other words, it is much more difficult for the Negro to attain identical middle- or upper-middle-class status with whites, and the social class gradations are less marked for Negroes because Negro life in a caste society is considerably more homogeneous than is life for the majority group. This makes it extremely difficult ever really to match racial groups meaningfully on class status as the context and history of social experience are so different.

There is support for the "participation" hypothesis in some social background data. These data indicate that there are fewer variegated family activities, such as eating together or taking trips, in the Negro as opposed to the white group. These differences are especially apparent at the lower SES levels. It may well be that such family experiences operate differentially at the higher SES levels, but our current data for the SES III group are incomplete and there is no indication that the differences would reach statistical significance.

This information demands that we probe even more carefully into background variables as possible sources of some of the variation in intelligence scores found in different population groups.

One of the most striking differences between the Negro and white groups is the consistently higher frequency of broken homes and resulting family disorganization in the Negro group. Indeed, Table 2 indicates that this phenomenon varies directly with social class and with race, both at $p < .001$ by $\chi^2$ test.

Table 2—Incidence of Father's Presence in the Home by Race Within SES Group
(N = 543)

|  | SES I | | | | SES II | | | | SES III | | | |
|---|---|---|---|---|---|---|---|---|---|---|---|---|
|  | WHITE | | NEGRO | | WHITE | | NEGRO | | WHITE | | NEGRO | |
| Condition | N | % | N | % | N | % | N | % | N | % | N | % |
| Father present in home | (88) | 84.6 | (88) | 56.1 | (61) | 89.7 | (80) | 72.1 | (52) | 100.0 | (44) | 86.3 |
| Father *not* present in home | (16) | 15.4 | (69) | 43.9 | (7) | 10.3 | (31) | 27.9 | — | 0.0 | (7) | 13.7 |
| N = | (104) | | (157) | | (68) | | (111) | | (52) | | (51) | |

Note.—$\chi^2$ for SES × father condition = 28.01, 2d.f., p = < .001.
$\chi^2$ for Race × father condition = 39.152, 1d.f., p = < .001.

Table 3—Analysis of Variance* on Lorge-Thorndike Intelligence Scores by Sex, Grade, Race, and Presence of Father in the Home
(SES Groups I and II only, N = 440)

| Source | Sum of squares | d.f. | F | Sig. |
|---|---|---|---|---|
| Sex | 8.726 | 1 | <1.000 | N.S. |
| Grade | 404.317 | 1 | 1.882 | N.S. |
| Race | 2,580.069 | 1 | 12.013 | < .01 |
| Father in Home | 954.073 | 1 | 4.442 | < .05 |
| Within | 91,490.127 | 424 | | |
| Total | 101,313.415 | 439 | | |

Means for Race Groups**

| Group | $\overline{X}$ | S.D. | N |
|---|---|---|---|
| Negro | 92.75 | 14.02 | 268 |
| White | 100.72 | 15.91 | 172 |

Means for Father Condition**
(Combined Race Groups)

| Condition | $\overline{X}$ | S.D. | N |
|---|---|---|---|
| Father in Home | 97.83 | 15.25 | 317 |
| No Father in Home | 90.79 | 14.18 | 123 |

* Note.—Interaction terms have been omitted from the table, as none reached significance. The obtained F value in each case was less than 1.00.
** Note.—t-tests for differences between race groups and father condition significant at p < .01.

We are *not* here considering the very real historical, social, and economic antecedents of this condition, but are instead simply making an empirical observation. Since in the vast majority of cases, the home is broken by the absence of the father, this is used as a rough indicator of family cohesiveness. The absence or presence of the father has been shown in other studies to relate to need achievement and aspiration levels, especially of boys (Ausubel, 1963; Deutsch, 1960).

Table 3 presents the results of a four-way analysis of variance of Lorge-Thorndike scores, using sex, grade, race, and presence of father as independent variables.

As can be seen, significant differences are obtained on the race and presence of father variables, with white children scoring higher than Negro, and children coming from homes where fathers are present having significantly higher scores than children from fatherless homes. None of the interaction terms was statistically significant. (SES could not be included

*Table 4*—Performance on the Lorge-Thorndike Intelligence Test Among Lower and Lower Middle (SES I and II) Negro Children with and without Fathers Present in the Home

| | Group | FATHER PRESENT | | | FATHER ABSENT | | |
|---|---|---|---|---|---|---|---|
| | | $\overline{X}$ | S.D. | N | $\overline{X}$ | S.D. | N |
| **SES I** | Grade 1 | | | | | | |
| | Male | 95.55 | 15.74 | 31 | 87.71 | 21.70 | 28 |
| | Female | 94.50 | 10.39 | 10 | 88.20 | 12.19 | 5 |
| | Total | 95.24 | 14.51 | 41 | 87.78 | 20.40 | 33 |
| | Grade 5 | | | | | | |
| | Male | 90.81 | 13.14 | 26 | 83.41 | 9.65 | 17 |
| | Female | 95.19 | 14.73 | 21 | 87.70 | 9.75 | 20 |
| | Total | 92.77 | 13.89 | 47 | 85.73 | 9.81 | 37 |
| **SES II** | Grade 1 | | | | | | |
| | Male | 98.35 | 12.18 | 26 | 92.80 | 18.64 | 10 |
| | Female | 99.27 | 12.99 | 15 | — | — | — |
| | Total | 96.68 | 12.33 | 41 | 92.80 | 18.64 | 10 |
| | Grade 5 | | | | | | |
| | Male | 94.78 | 15.12 | 23 | 91.75 | 15.67 | 16 |
| | Female | 90.25 | 17.19 | 16 | 93.00 | 12.27 | 5 |
| | Total | 92.92 | 15.89 | 39 | 92.05 | 14.65 | 21 |

in the analysis of variance because on our Class III sample there were no white fatherless families. Thus, by dropping SES III's from this analysis, the N here becomes 440.)

To get at the influence of father's presence on intelligence score within groups, several additional comparisons were made. Because the absence of significant interactions in the data might relate to the strong pull exerted on the scores by race differences, the data from the Negro sample were subjected to specific analysis within grade and SES. Special attention was paid to lower SES, as the number of homes without fathers was largest in this group, and the comparisons, thus, were more meaningful.

Table 4 presents the comparisons for first- and fifth-grade Negro children in the lowest two SES groups.

As is seen from Table 4, a consistent trend within both grades at the lower SES level appears, and in no case is there a reversal of this trend: for males, females, and the combined group, the I.Q.'s of children with fathers in the home are always higher than those who have no father in the home. In addition, a constricted range of performance, as reflected in standard deviation units is found among fifth-graders without fathers in the home, as opposed to both first- and fifth-graders in homes where fathers are present.

Differences between first- and fifth-grade children, controlling for father in home, are not significant, and they are not reported here in tabular form. Within the Negro lower-class, there is a consistent decrement in I.Q. level from the first to fifth grade, there again being no reversals in direction in sex or father-in-home categories. (In comparisons made between first- and fifth-graders in the white lower-class sample, there is a nonsignificant increment in score from first to fifth grade.)

While the specific interaction term for this break in the previous four-way analysis of variance did not reach statistical significance, the data in Table 4 are presented for the purpose of identifying cells in which I.Q. differences, as predicted by family stability, are greatest. Also the specific descriptive data are revealing in that there is no reversal of trend even though the analysis of variance did not yield statistically significant results.

Further analysis will reveal if the Negro score decrement from first to fifth grade is accounted for by the great proportion of broken Negro homes. This also might account for some of the differences between Negro and white intelligence scores.

A weakness in these cross-sectional data is that there is no reliable way of knowing how long the fifth-grade children have lived in homes without fathers, or whether this has been a recurrent or a consistent condition. But it is reasonable to assume that on the average the fifth-graders have had more fatherless years than the first-graders. If this is tenable, then what we might be tapping is the cumulative effect of fatherless years, and if so, this might explain why the first grade differences are not significant: they are simply not significant *yet*. This hypothesis is supported by the limited variance reported in Table 4 for fifth-grade children from fatherless homes in contrast to the greater variance shown among children on the same grade level but coming from homes in which fathers are present.

A second, and perhaps more parsimonious, explanation for this finding is that I.Q. tests at the fifth-grade level may tap more responses which directly relate to the role of the father in the family structure for both boys and girls. This might have particular reference to the cohesiveness of the family and the variety of activities in which the family participates, and most specifically simply reflect the quantity of verbal interaction engendered through the medium of family organization and activity.

Another background variable which might relate to intelligence test performance is the amount and timing of schooling the child has had. As with the father variable, it was thought that the more opportunity the child has for adult-child contact, conversation, and experimential variety, the more positive the influence on his performance. Also Fowler's analysis (1962) pointed out the importance for the child of cognitive stimulation and practice in the early years. As was seen in Lee's study (1951) of I.Q. differences between Negro children born in Philadelphia and those who migrated there from the South, consistently higher I.Q. test scores were obtained by children who had the longest residence in the presumably

*Table 5*—Analysis of Variance on Lorge-Thorndike Intelligence Scores by Sex, Race, and Preschool Experience
(Grade 5, SES I and II only, N = 246)

| Source | Sum of squares | d.f. | F | Sig. |
|---|---|---|---|---|
| Sex | 128.204 | 1 | < 1.000 | N.S. |
| Race | 1,785.477 | 1 | 7.873 | < .01 |
| Preschool Experience | 1,619.750 | 1 | 7.143 | < 0.1 |
| Within | 43,083.956 | 238 | | |
| Total | 50,027.132 | 245 | | |

### Means for Race Groups

| Group | $\overline{X}$ | S.D. | N |
|---|---|---|---|
| Negro | 90.90 | 13.89 | 144 |
| White | 99.82 | 16.40 | 102 |

### Means for Preschool Condition*

| Condition | $\overline{X}$ | S.D. | N |
|---|---|---|---|
| Preschool Experience | 97.42 | 15.72 | 152 |
| No Preschool Experience | 90.65 | 14.32 | 53 |

*Note.*—Interaction terms have been omitted from the table, as none were significant. The F value in each case was less than 1.00.
*Note.*—N's for Preschool Condition reduced from total N for fifth grade due to missing data.

more fostering northern environment. Lee's data also show a consistent difference in favor of Negro children who had a kindergarten experience, as compared with those who did not. Therefore, an experiential variable selected for analysis in the present study was whether or not the child had any formal preschool educational experience. Because of the variety of types of preschool experience—some children had nursery and no kindergarten, others reversed—the variable was treated dichotomously as "some preschool experience" or "no preschool experience."

Table 5 reports results of a three-way analysis of variance of Lorge-Thorndike scores for fifth-grade children by sex, race, and preschool experience.

As can be seen, race differences are significant at the $p < .01$ level, and so are preschool experience differences. Those children who have had preschool experience score significantly higher than those without. Again, the interaction terms were not significant.

Table 6 presents the same analysis for the first grade group. Here, while the significant race difference in test performance prevails (p < .05), the difference as predicted by preschool experience is not significant, although *directionality* is still apparent. In other words, presence or lack of preschool experience at grade 5 more highly differentiates intelligence test scores than it does at grade 1. Nevertheless, at grade 1 it is still differentiating (p < .10), though not within the conventional limits of statistical significance.

This finding is consistent with those for the father-in-home variable, and, therefore, lends support to the cumulative deficit hypothesis previously advanced: that deprivational influences have a greater impact at later developmental stages than at earlier ones.

*Table 6*—Analysis of Variance on Lorge-Thorndike Intelligence Scores by Sex, Race, and Preschool Experience
(Grade 1, SES I and II only, N = 194)

| Source | Sum of squares | d.f. | F | Sig. |
|---|---|---|---|---|
| Sex | 17.283 | 1 | < 1.000 | N.S. |
| Race | 1,152.579 | 1 | 5.817 | < .05 |
| Preschool Experience | 609.235 | 1 | 3.074 | < .10 |
| Within | 25,162.214 | 186 | | |
| Total | 27,148.326 | 193 | | |

Means for Race Groups

| Group | X̄ | S.D. | N |
|---|---|---|---|
| Negro | 94.90 | 13.92 | 124 |
| White | 102.01 | 15.27 | 70 |

Means for Preschool Condition*

| Condition | X̄ | S.D. | N |
|---|---|---|---|
| Preschool Experience | 100.03 | 13.99 | 112 |
| No Preschool Experience | 94.48 | 16.24 | 23 |

Note.—Interaction terms have been omitted from the table as none were significant.
* Note.—N's for Preschool Condition reduced from total N due to missing data.

The effect of the father-in-home variable on I.Q. for this sample has been shown in the data presented here. What is less easily measurable, but may nonetheless exist, is the potential systematic lowering of Negro children's I.Q. by the greater prevalence of broken homes in Negro SES groups I and II. In our samples, for example, there is a significantly greater frequency of broken homes among the Negro group, as compared with the white, and it is hard to estimate what the over-all effect may be of this family instability in the development of the Negro child. From these data, it is quite conceivable, if not probable, that one effect would be the systematic lowering with age of I.Q. scores of the children where markedly unfavorable social conditions exist.

The data presented here represent only a small portion of those we have collected on the children in the various samples. When one surveys the entire mass of data, what is striking is the fact that on most of the *social* variables, the Negro group shows greater deprivation. This is true within social class categories, with the possible exception of Social Class II, and even here the factors associated with racial discrimination and caste are still quite operative; the class and caste discussion of Dreger and Miller (1960) is an adequate recognition of this problem. The conclusion is inescapable that the Negro group is a socially deprived one, and that whatever other measures and functions are sensitive to social effects will also reflect this deprivation.

We are now attempting to measure the ingredients of deprivation with the aim of developing a typology of deprivation which organizes experience in developmentally relevant groupings that can be related to sources of socially determined group variation in I.Q. performance. It would seem probable that when behavioral scientists have been able to classify and measure the elements and variables in social deprivation, the observed differential in intelligence test scores between Negro and white samples will be accounted for.

The present data on family cohesion and preschool experience represent two possible environmental modifiers of intelligence test performance that would seem to account for a portion of differences found between ethnic, class or experiential groups. If these are influential variables, a positive implication is that they are amenable to social intervention and change.

References to *Social Influences in Negro-White Intelligence Differences*

A. Anastasi. *Differential Psychology*, Third edition. New York, Macmillan, 1958.
W. F. Anderson. "Relation of Lorge-Thorndike Intelligence Test Scores of Public School Pupils to the Socioeconomic Status of Their Parents," *Journal of Experimental Education*, 1962, **31**(1), 73–76.
D. P. Ausubel and Pearl Ausubel. "Ego Development Among Segregated Negro Children," in A. H. Passow (ed.), *Education in Depressed Areas*, New York, Teachers College Bureau of Publications, Columbia University, 1963, pp. 109–141.
M. Deutsch. "Minority Group and Class Status as Related to Social and Personality Factors in Scholastic Achievement." Society for Applied Anthropology, Monograph 2, 1960.
———— "The Disadvantaged Child and the Learning Process: Some Social, Psychological, and Developmental Considerations," in A. H. Passow (ed.), *Education in Depressed Areas*, New York, Teachers College Bureau of Publications, Columbia University, 1963, pp. 163–179.
R. M. Dreger and K. S. Miller. "Comparative Psychological Studies of Negroes and Whites in the United States," *Psychological Bulletin*, 1960, **57**, 361–402.
K. Eells, et al. *Intelligence and Cultural Differences*, Chicago, University of Chicago Press, 1951.
W. Fowler. Cognitive Learning in Infancy and Early Childhood," *Psychological Bulletin*, 1962, **59**, 116–152.

W. A. Kennedy et. al. *A Normative Sample of Intelligence and Achievement of Negro Elementary School Children in the Southeastern United States.* Society for Research in Child Development, **20**, Monograph 6, 1963.

O. Klineberg. *Negro Intelligence and Selective Migration*, New York, Columbia University Press, 1935.

——— "The Intelligence of Migrants," *American Sociological Review*, 1938, **3**, 218–224.

——— "Negro-White Differences in Intelligence Test Performance: A New Look at an Old Problem," *American Psychologist*, 1963, **18**, 198–203.

E. S. Lee. "Negro Intelligence and Selective Migration: A Philadelphia Test of the Klineberg Hypothesis," *American Sociological Review*, 1951, **16**, 227–233.

I. Lorge and R. I. Thorndike. *Lorge-Thorndike Tests of Intelligence*, Specimen Test Booklet, Boston, Houghton-Mifflin, 1959.

M. Schwebel, "Individual Differences in Learning Abilities," *American Journal of Orthopsychiatry*, 1963, **33**, 60–71.

M. Whiteman, "Intelligence and Learning." Paper presented at the Arden House Conference on Preschool Enrichment of Socially Disadvantaged Children, Arden House, Harriman, N.Y., December 17, 1962.

# SOCIAL CLASS AND INTELLIGENCE TESTS

*W. W. Charters, Jr.*

Few thoughtful people today believe that the Intelligence Quotient reflects purely innate, hereditary ability of humans. Half a century of intelligence testing and research has made it clear that a person's environmental experiences help to determine the I.Q. score he achieves.

In the 1920's and 1930's studies were made of the intelligence of orphanage children before and after they had been placed in foster homes, of Negro children from the Deep South attending public schools in Northern cities to which their families had migrated, and of identical twins separated at an early age and reared under different environmental conditions.[1] These and other studies showed important differences in I.Q. scores which could not be attributed solely to hereditary or constitutional differences among the subjects.

While demonstrations of the contribution of environmental experiences to measured intelligence have been impressive, they have not led psychologists to assume that biological factors play no part. The question of whether it is heredity *or* environment which makes for differences in intelligence was abandoned many years ago as fruitless. Obviously, both

[1] F. N. Freeman, K. J. Holzinger, and B. C. Mitchell, "The Influence of Environment on the Intelligence School Achievement and Conduct of Foster Children," *Twenty-seventh Year-book of the National Society for the Study of Education*, Part 1, 1928, pp. 103–217; H. H. Newman, F. N. Freeman, and K. J. Holzinger, *Twins: A Study of Heredity and Environment*, Chicago: University of Chicago Press, 1957, O. Klineberg, *Negro Intelligence and Selective Migration*, New York: Columbia University Press, 1935.

From Readings in the Social Psychology of Education by W. W. Charters, Jr. and N. L. Gage, eds. (Boston: Allyn and Bacon, Inc., Copyright 1963), pp. 12–21. Reprinted by permission of Allyn and Bacon, Inc. Permission to quote material used in this article has also been obtained from The University of Chicago Press (K. Eells, A. David, R. J. Havighurst, V. E. Herrick, and R. W. Tyler, *Intelligence and Cultural Differences*, Chicago: 1951); Educational Testing Service (I. Lorge, "Difference or Bias in Tests of Intelligence" in *Proceedings of the 1952 Invitational Conference on Testing Problems*, Princeton, N.J.: 1953); Harvard University Press (A. Davis, *Social Class Influences upon Learning*, Cambridge, Mass.: 1948); Annual Reviews, Inc. (A. Anastasi, "Individual Differences," in *Annual Review of Psychology*, Stanford, Calif.: 1953)

are necessary to produce an intelligently functioning human being. Moreover, psychologists today tend to agree that biological and environmental factors interact with one another in intricate and complex ways to produce intelligent behavior. No longer is it fruitful to ask how much is contributed by heredity and how much by environment, as though their contributions to intelligence were entirely independent of one another. Psychologists still disagree, however, in their conceptions of the particular way the various factors interact to determine differences in intelligence and, to a certain extent, in the relative emphasis they attribute to the biological and environmental determinants.[2]

## SOCIAL CLASS DIFFERENCES IN I.Q.

Shortly after World War II a group of scientists at the University of Chicago began an intensive examination of the impact of family social class position on I.Q. scores of children. It had long been known that intelligence test scores of children from the lower classes averaged below those of children from the higher social classes. Indeed, Alfred Binet was acutely aware of the influence of social status on children's responses to test items at the time he was developing his pioneer intelligence measure in the early 1900's.[3] A number of studies had accumulated in the intervening years to show that the correlation between socioeconomic status and intelligence test scores was in the neighborhood of .35 and that scores for children of professional families typically ran from 15 to 25 points higher on the average than for children of unskilled laborers.[4] But the Chicago group, composed predominantly of sociologists and anthropologists, introduced a new perspective regarding the nature of the environmental influence.

Psychologists of the day explained the relationship between social class and intelligence in one of two ways. Some took the position that it was primarily the result of a process of social selection. Those persons with higher levels of intelligence were capable of climbing into and remaining in the upper reaches of the social class structure, leaving behind in the lower

---

[2] The development of the "heredity-environment controversy" with respect to intelligence testing can be traced conveniently through various Yearbooks of the National Society for the Study of Education. See G. M. Whipple (ed.), *Intelligence: Its Nature and Nurture*, Thirty-ninth Yearbook, National Society for the Study of Education, Bloomington, Ill.: Public School Publishing Company, 1940, Parts I and II.

[3] A. Davis, "How Does Cultural Bias in Intelligence Tests Arise?" in K. Eells, A. Davis, R. J. Havighurst, V. E. Herrick, and R. W. Tyler, *Intelligence and Cultural Differences*, Chicago: University of Chicago Press, 1951, Ch. 5.

[4] V. E. Herrick, "What is Already Known About the Relation of the I.Q. to Cultural Background?" in Eells et al., *Intelligence and Cultural Differences*, *ibid.*, p. 12.

ranks the less intelligent members of the society. Other psychologists attributed to the environment a more direct role in shaping the intellectual capacity of individuals. They believed that social environments could be ranked on a continuum of "mental stimulation value"—the extent to which the environment provided experiences necessary for intellectual development. In this view, the important environmental difference between foster homes and orphanages, for example, or between urban schools in the North and the Southern segregated schools, was in the amount of mental stimulation they offered. With respect to social class, the more intellectually nurturant experiences were afforded the child by higher- than by lower-status homes so that the lower-class child was usually deprived of the environmental support vital to the full fruition of his intelligence.

## A CULTURAL POINT OF VIEW

The University of Chicago scientists, too, attributed to the environment an active, direct role in shaping individual intelligence, but they disagreed with the prevailing view that environments differed simply in the amount of mental stimulation they provided. Environmental influences, the Chicago scientists argued, differed not only in degree but in *kind* with the consequence that different kinds of intellectual skills were fostered in various environments. The proper explanation for the relationship between intelligence and social class lay in the *cultural* differences existing among the social classes.

It is not surprising that this cultural point of view arose when and where it did. About 1945, major studies of social class in American communities, under the leadership of W. Lloyd Warner, were underway or had recently been completed.[5] Warner and his colleagues had applied to contemporary society the perspectives and methods of cultural anthropology, theretofore reserved largely for the study of primitive societies. Prominent in the anthropological perspective was the concept of *culture*. This concept referred to the observation that groups of people living in relative isolation from others develop standard, more or less distinctive, ways of doing and thinking about things, of expressing themselves, of raising their children, of deciding what is valuable in life, and so on. As these students investigated the cultural patterns in the various social classes of the American community, they found them to be surprisingly diverse. The social classes, of course, were not entirely isolated from one another: they shared in important cultural patterns and institutions of the

[5] W. B. Brookover and D. Gottlieb, "Social Class and Education," *Readings in the Social Psychology of Education*, by W. W. Charters, Jr., and N. L. Gage, eds. Boston: Allyn and Bacon, 1963.

general American society. But the community studies indicated that the isolation was sufficient to allow the various classes to develop significant variations on the general theme of American society. The variations were sufficiently divergent to warrant regarding them as *subcultures* within the society. And, according to the Chicago research workers, children from the lower classes performed poorly on intelligence tests because the tasks required of them by the tests were either unimportant in or alien to their particular sub-cultures.

## THE ARGUMENT FOR CULTURAL BIAS IN STANDARD INTELLIGENCE TESTS

Implications of the cultural point of view for intelligence testing were extensively developed by Allison Davis, who had been a prominent participant in the early social class studies.[6] These implications were presented at length in his 1948 Inglis Lecture[7] and more compactly in the contributions of Davis and his colleagues to Part I of their subsequent research monograph.[8] Davis's basic argument was that the social class differentials in I.Q. scores resulted from cultural biases in intelligence test construction and not from differences in the reasoning ability of children. In short, intelligence tests were unfair to children of the lower-class culture.

*Problem-solving abilities.* Davis elaborated the argument in several ways. Most fundamental was his position that intelligence tests were designed to measure only one of several kinds of problem-solving ability—the kind associated with scholastic achievement in what he regarded as the typically middle-class educational program of the schools. From the earliest days, intelligence tests had been validated against the scholastic success of pupils. Those test items which could discriminate between "good" and "poor" students were retained in the tests while those which could not were rejected. Consequently, the tests measured only those forms of mental ability which were adaptive for superior achievement in educational institutions. They stressed verbal facility and ability to deal with abstract problems.

In nearly all general intelligence tests, the authors have depended chiefly upon two types of verbal questions to furnish the most difficult problems in their tests, and to screen the "mediocre" and "average" pupils from the "superior" pupils. These two types of questions are based upon (1) verbal relationship and complex

[6] A. Davis, B. B. Gardner, and M. R. Gardner, *Deep South*, Chicago: University of Chicago Press, 1941.
[7] A. Davis, *Social-Class Influences upon Learning*, Cambridge, Mass., Harvard University Press, 1948.
[8] Eells et al., *op. cit.*

academic phrasing (such as verbal "analogies" and "opposites," and "syllo-gisms"); and (2) rare words (used in vocabulary tests and "definitions").[9]

But mental ability—including such things according to Davis as inventive-ness, the analysis and organization of observed experiences, and the draw-ing of inferences—is considerably more than facility with language, and intelligence tests failed to measure these other aspects of problem-solving capacity.

The intensive studies of social class had indicated that it was precisely with respect to an emphasis upon verbal skills and "bookish" abstractions that the cultures of the middle and lower classes departed. Davis illustrated this point in a passage on reading skill.

These low socioeconomic groups fail because their parents themselves have not been trained to read: nor do they regard reading or school curriculums as important. Moreover, neither the parent nor the child's social group urges the child to practice reading or school exercises or sets him an example for attainment in this field. The parents and friends of the average child in the high socio-economic groups, on the other hand, do offer him a powerful example of their skill in reading and in the school type of culture. Furthermore, the latter group of parents consciously and unconsciously reveals an interest in the child's learning this behavior; they likewise afford him practice in such problem-solving.[10]

Middle and lower class cultures differed, too, in the extent of their con-gruency with the educational institution in which verbal intelligence of the kind measured by intelligence tests is nurtured.

School is an extension of home to the average middle-class child. It rewards and punishes him for the same things that the home does. It is familiar ground. On the contrary, school is often a strange place to the lower-class child, with strange expectations. It often contradicts the home in its rewards and punishments.

From school experience are drawn many of the items of current intelligence tests. Hence the child who spends the greatest amount of time in school, and who is most receptive to the school's teaching, prepares himself best for intelligence tests. Middle-class children tend to stay longer in school than lower-class child-ren. In many cities the best-equipped schools and the best-prepared teachers are in the higher-status areas of the community, while the lower-class pupils go to run-down schools with less able teachers. Consequently, the experiences of the lower-class children are less conducive to good performance on intelligence tests. There is also more retardation of lower-class pupils, which means that they are exposed to less advanced school work, with a consequent decreased experience with the materials from which the more difficult test items are drawn.

There is a tendency to place and to keep middle-class children in the most academic or "bookish" curriculums in school. Test items which are drawn from these curriculums will probably favor middle-class children. For example, a test item requiring the pupil to know that geometry, algebra, and trigonometry all belong together, but that botany does not belong closely with them, would more probably be known by a pupil in the college preparatory than in the vocational or general curriculum.

[9] A. Davis, *Social-Class Influences . . . , op. cit.*, pp. 78–79.
[10] A. Davis, "What are Some of the Basic Issues in the Relation of Intelligence Tests to Cultural Background?" in K. Eells et al., *op. cit.*, p. 27.

The sectioning of children by "ability" tends to place the middle-class children in "high" sections and the lower-class children in "low" sections. . . . The higher groups get more verbal and abstract learning experience, which gives them an advantage with intelligence tests of a verbal or abstract character.[11]

Intelligence tests, then, were designed to measure those aspects of mental ability in which middle-class children, by virtue of their culture and by virtue of the orientation of educational methods of the school, were bound to excel and to ignore those other aspects of mental ability in which the lower-class culture would lead its children to perform favorably.

*Language forms.* Following from his cultural perspective of the social classes, Davis added another facet to his argument. Not only the emphasis upon linguistic skills but the very language itself differs from one class to the next. Intelligence test instructions and items frequently contain words and refer to situations which are common-place for the middle-class child but foreign to the lower-class child. An oft-quoted example of this is the test item the correct answer to which depends upon the pupil's familiarity with the word *sonata*—"a word which will clearly be heard more often in a home in the higher socio-economic brackets than in a family from the low socio-economic group."[12] Another illustration is the following analogies question:

A symphony is to a composer as book is to what?
( ) paper
( ) sculptor
( ) author
( ) musician
( ) man

In this version, 81 per cent of higher- as opposed to 51 per cent of lower-class children marked the answer correctly in a trial administration. Not only were the key words culturally loaded but the linguistic form of the question was highly abstract: the form " . . . is to . . . " was hardly a linguistic structure to which lower-class children would be exposed in the normal course of their lives. A second, less "biased" version was drawn up as follows:

A baker goes with bread, like a carpenter goes with what?
( ) a saw
( ) a house
( ) a spoon
( ) a nail
( ) a man

[11] R. J. Havighurst, "What are the Cultural Differences which May Affect Performance on Intelligence Tests?" in K. Eells et al., *op. cit.*, p. 20.
[12] Davis, *Social-Class Influences . . .* , *op. cit.*, p. 45.

In this version an equal proportion of children in the lower and higher classes responded correctly.[13]

One of the major research investigations conducted by the University of Chicago group was designed to illuminate the preceding criticisms of intelligence tests. By means of an exhaustive, item-by-item analysis of social class differences in responses of school pupils to standard tests of intelligence, Eells[14] sought to discover what particular kinds of test items favor high-status as compared with low-status children. Ten widely-used group intelligence tests were administered to 9- and 10-year-old and 13- and 14-year-old school children in Rockford, Illinois, in such a way that each age group responded to five tests on five succeeding days. The 5,000 children tested constituted most of the white pupils at these age levels in the city. When the total I.Q. scores were compared for children in the various social classes, the typical correlations were found—ranging from .20 to .43, depending upon the particular test.

Detailed examination of 650 individual items in the tests showed that social class differences in correct responses appeared on nearly two-thirds of the items among the younger children and on nine out of ten items among the older age group. Eells had hoped to discover the nature of the "bias" in test items by comparing the items which discriminated between the social classes with other items on which social class differences did not appear. But most of the items which showed no social class differences were at the extremes of the difficulty range and were either passed or failed by virtually all children, regardless of their social class. Excluding these, only a small number of items remained on which the lower-status children performed as well as their higher-status peers and which could be used for the purpose of comparison. Hence, Eells could draw no definitive conclusions, but his inferences about these few items followed closely the general arguments advanced by Davis.

It is shown that, when the test item is expressed in terms of strange, academic, or bookish words, the status differences are much greater than when the item is expressed in simple everyday words. Differential opportunity for familiarity with certain objects is also stressed for a number of items. In other items, status differences are related to formal school learning, or to an assumed greater ability of high-status pupils to handle abstract as opposed to concrete terms.

Practically all the items which show unusually small differences either are nonverbal in symbolism or are expressed in relatively simple everyday vocabulary and deal with objects or concepts which are probably equally familiar, or equally unfamiliar, to pupils at both status levels.[15]

But the investigator goes on to warn his readers that on many items there were large status differences for which he could offer no plausible explanation.

[13] A. Davis, "Socio-economic Influences upon Children's Learning," *Understanding the Child*, 1951, **20**, pp. 10–16.
[14] K. Eells, in K. Eells et al., *op. cit.*, Parts II and III.
[15] *Ibid.*, p. 357.

It was possible to analyze the items in another way. Besides comparing the few items showing no class differences with those showing large differences, the investigator could inspect the items as they varied in the *amount* of advantage they gave the higher-status children. From this standpoint, Eels first classified items according to the kind of symbolism they employed and then compared the average status differences in correct responses. He found that the greatest status differences occurred for the verbal items and the least for items employing pictures, geometric designs, and stylized drawings. When the items were classified according to the kinds of intellectual operations they required of children (analogies, opposites, and so on), no consistent or meaningful variations in the amount of status difference could be discovered.

Eells was extremely cautious in drawing conclusions from his study. It was clear that status differences in responses to the test items persisted on virtually all items, regardless of their form. Nevertheless, the analysis yielded certain clues as to how items could be written so as to minimize if not to eliminate social class differences.

*Motivation and work habits.* A third feature of Davis' argument came close to setting a condition which would have made it impossible to *disprove* his argument. He asserted that test-taking itself is alien to the lower-class culture, and that, even if intelligence tests were constructed to measure the I.Q.s of lower-class children fairly, the children still would not have the work habits or motivation in the testing situation sufficient to compete with their middle-class peers. Davis set forth the issue in this passage:

> It is possible that the middle class will also prove superior on all, or nearly all, types of possible test problems, because they have a cultural advantage in habits of work and in test motivation. That is, since *training* is an essential part of all problem-solving, it may be that the superiority of middle-class culture in establishing habits of school work will generalize to all kinds of mental problems, including also those in which the cultural content and symbols are common to all social classes.[16]

If this were true, no empirical evidence could establish the truth or falsity of Davis' overall position. His analysis, however, led to an investigation of the effects of training and motivation on intelligence test scores. The analysis also encouraged Davis and his colleagues, in connection with the intelligence test they eventually developed, to attempt to "relax" the testing situation under which it was administered (by reading test questions to groups of children rather than requiring them to read them for themselves, by encouraging laughter, by fashioning test items to look like comic-strip cartoons) so that the class differences in work habits and test motivation would operate less to the advantage of middle-class children.

In sum, Davis argued that the general intelligence tests in common use

[16] A. Davis, "What are Some of the Basic Issues . . . ?" *op. cit.*, p. 28.

were culturally loaded against the lower class. They tested only those mental abilities favoring the cultural experiences of the middle class; they were couched in language and linguistic forms unfamiliar to the lower class; and they called for kinds of work habits and motivation which were not valued or taught in the lower-class culture. The trouble was, Davis believed, that intelligence tests were products of the middle class and incorporated the bias of the middle-class culture.

[Test-makers and educators] continually make the error of regarding middle-class culture, and even more narrowly, middle-class school culture, as the "true" culture, or the "best" culture. More than 95 per cent of our teachers and professors are middle-class in their socio-economic status. Like all other cultural groups, teachers and professors regard that particular version of culture (those mores, emotional patterns, and social values) which they have learned from their own families, friends, and teachers, as the "best" and only "true" culture. This attitude is powerfully reflected in school curriculums, in intelligence tests, and in teachers' judgments of their pupils.[17]

If Davis' points were true, then social class differences in I.Q. would disappear when children were tested on culturally-fair intelligence measures in a testing situation equally motivating to those of higher and lower status.

*The Haggard experiment.* As mentioned above, another major empirical investigation in the Chicago research program was designed to examine the effects of motivation, training, and certain other conditions on intelligence test scores. Specifically, Haggard[18] predicted that lower-class children would show substantial improvement in their test scores under the following conditions: a) when they were tested on an intelligence test form in which the content was more in keeping with the language and experiences of lower-class children, b) when test items were read aloud to them instead of depending upon them to read the items to themselves, c) when they were given practice in answering questions similar to those which appeared on intelligence tests, and d) when either their practice or their test taking was motivated by the promise of a free pass to a movie for a good performance. Haggard evaluated these predictions by measuring the intelligence of nearly 700 high- and low-status children on a conventional test and then separating them into a variety of experimental groups of 40 to 50 children each. These groups, then, were subjected to different combinations of the experimental conditions. All were retested five days later, some with the conventional test and others with a revised form of the test, some under motivating conditions and some not, some with practice during the intervening days and some without such practice, and so on. Haggard's fundamental question was: Would lower-class

[17] *Ibid.*, p. 26.
[18] E. A. Haggard, "Social-Status and Intelligence: An Experimental Study of Certain Cultural Determinants of Measured Intelligence." *Genetic Psychology Monographs*, 1954, **49**, pp. 141–186.

children *improve more* in their scores than higher-class children under the predicted circumstances?

As one might imagine, the number of comparisons reported from this study was large, and they cannot be itemized in detail here. Generally speaking, the results were mixed and inconsistent. Thus, it was the high-status and not the low-status children who benefited from the practice sessions, particularly when they were retested on the conventional test. In some experimental conditions the investigator's attempts to motivate the children *decreased* the retest scores of high- and low-status children alike, in other conditions the motivation attempts made no difference, and in still others motivation improved the retest scores of low-status children but not high-status children in accordance with Haggard's prediction. The lower status children showed substantial gains when they were retested on the form of the test deliberately revised to make it more suitable for them, but these gains were overshadowed by the fact that higher-status children also showed remarkable gains on the revised form.

In sum, while Haggard's study was unable to demonstrate that social-class differences in intelligence were fully accounted for by such matters as motivation, practice, test forms, and the like, it did show that test scores of children, whether of low or high status, could be influenced by these factors. Test performance, the investigator concluded, depends upon the experience children bring with them and upon psychological factors in the testing situation itself. The mere revision of current intelligence tests to remove their middle-class bias would not be sufficient to measure mental ability adequately.

## AN UNBIASED TEST: CRITICISMS AND DISAPPOINTMENTS

The Chicago scientists culminated their five years and more of intensive work by producing a measure of general intelligence which they believed would not unduly favor children of the upper status levels. In 1953 a series of group tests for elementary-school age levels was commercially published as the Davis-Eells Games.[19] Their anthropological perspective had led the authors to point up limitations in the conventional intelligence tests insofar as these incorporated "biases" which penalized children from the sub-culture of the lower class. Their investigations, in turn, suggested ways in which they might avoid in a new test the shortcomings of their predecessors. Thus, the authors wrote items which required reasoning about everyday events rather than about abstractions, and they avoided language which was academic or bookish in form and content. As the

[19] A. Davis and K. Eells, *Davis-Eells Tests of General Intelligence or Problem-Solving Ability*, Yonkers, N.Y., World Book Company, 1953.

word *Games* in the title implies, the test was to be administered in a relaxed atmosphere. Even the test format, giving it an appearance not unlike a comic strip, attempted to remove the impression that the testing session was an examination. This format, too, was designed to engage motivations more universal than that of simply performing well on a school test. But publication of their own test also provided the opportunity to put their whole approach on trial, and scholars across the country were quick to do so.

*Criticisms of the approach to test construction.* Prior to the appearance of the Davis-Eells Games, however, the academic community had been receiving abridged reports of the work at Chicago. A number of sophisticated criticisms were made concerning the approach and the assumptions on which it was based. Thus, Anastasi wrote:

Perhaps the principal weakness in the approach of these investigators is their inadequate recognition of the extent to which the cultural differences in information, motivation, and work habits manifested in test performance also influence the individual's overall intellectual development. Removing culturally biased items from a test does not eliminate cultural differences in behavior. The criteria against which the tests are validated are themselves culturally loaded, and "intelligence tests" are operationally meaningless unless defined in terms of such criteria. To be sure, it is important to investigate behavior differences between cultural groups. But such differences cannot be studied by eliminating culturally loaded items. They can be explored only by constructing tests which sample the behavior functions fostered by each culture.[20]

Some critics questioned the assumption running through the work of Davis and his colleagues that, since the social classes do not differ fundamentally in problem-solving capacity, any test which shows such differences must be biased. With this assumption Davis took a firm "environmentalist" stand, discounting the possibility that members of the social classes may differ in biological constitution as well as in cultural circumstances. The heredity-environment issue was still capable of evoking well-entrenched sentiments which served to add heat to the criticisms.

One of the more balanced of the early criticisms was that of Lorge.[21] He noted that differences in measured intelligence have been well-established between groups classified by education, occupation of father, geographic origin, personality structure, and so on. As a result, psychologists have become "increasingly aware of the multiplicity and intricacies of factors related to test performance of individuals and of groups."[22]

[20] A. Anastasi, "Individual Differences," in C. P. Stone and D. W. Taylor (eds.), *Annual Review of Psychology*, Stanford, Calif., Annual Reviews, Inc., 1953, vol. 4, p. 151.
[21] I. Lorge, "Difference or Bias in Tests of Intelligence," in *Proceedings of the 1952 Invitational Conference on Testing Problems*, Princeton, N.J., Educational Testing Service, 1953, pp. 76–83.
[22] This and subsequent quotations in the following paragraphs have been taken from Lorge, *ibid., passim.*

Psychologists and test-makers have taken pains to provide "normative data for a variety of groups because they know differences in test performance are related to sex, age, grade-placement, and socioeconomic status," and those who use the tests have been cautioned time and again to interpret test scores in the light of the variety of factors, such as the child's motivations and health, which are known to affect them.

Inevitably some users of tests neglected to profit from the tutelage. They wilfully treated test scores as absolute determinations about individuals, or, even, groups. Others, of course, failed to appreciate fully the range and interaction of circumstances that affect test performance. To overcome such perversity and such ignorance, some psychometricians tried to be quit of the *bias* of the test-user by attempting to eliminate the *differences* from the tests. One procedure long in use is to add items of a certain kind which favor an otherwise unfavored group. In this way, the composite I.Q. score is adjusted until it is "fair" to each group.

For instance, it is well-known that boys and girls (and men and women) perform differently on tests of verbal, and of numerical, content and process. . . . All of us are fully aware that to overcome the obtained verbal superiority of women, the test-maker adds a sufficiency of numerical reasoning items to make the average total score of men equal that of women. *No difference, ergo, no bias.* Fortunately, there still are differences between the sexes.

Lorge pointed out, however, that the description of a person's intelligence by means of a single, composite score is a practice of convenience and compromise, not an ideal to emulate. Current knowledge has made it plain that intelligence is not a single, unitary capacity, and that to express it in a single-index score is to cover up important differences in the mental organization of different individuals and groups. Better that intelligence scores be broken down into their component parts and reported as such, as differential aptitude tests have done in another realm of psychometrics, than to adjust a composite score until it is "fair" to everyone.

Lorge also disagreed with the test-making strategy of Eells and Davis. To select test items principally on the grounds that they do *not* discriminate between groups is to use an extremely restrictive, if not a reversed, approach to the construction of a measure of intelligence. "Some criterion about intellectual functioning, other than the one that the items make for no diversity, seems, at least, a psychological prerequisite." Lorge had no doubt that the Eells method could produce a test, but he, along with other critics of the day, had serious questions as to what such a test would measure. Conventional intelligence tests had been eminently successful in predicting behavior with respect to the wide variety of tasks in our society which call for verbal and linguistic skills. If a test were constructed which minimized verbal processes and favored those requiring the manipulation of numbers, geometric designs, and pictures, what meaningful behavior would it predict? The Eells and Davis approach included no clear provision for behavioral criteria against which the test could be validated.

Throughout Lorge's commentary was the fundamental objection that the removal of systematic group differences from intelligence measures reduces the amount of decision-relevant information yielded by the tests, information useful in guiding children to appropriate educational experiences and vital to the further understanding of intellectual processes in both individuals and groups.

There can be little doubt that among some kinds of groups differences do exist. As a matter of fact, the wide range of general and specific tests of intelligence has made it possible to establish much of the available knowledge of differential psychology. Not only has the awareness of such differences led to the emergence of a more adequate understanding of the relative advantages and limitations of intelligence tests but it also has increased our appreciation of the significance of difference in the understanding of children as individuals, and in groups. In a democracy, such as ours, respect for difference as difference is necessary. There is no virtue in developing instruments so blunted that they decrease the amount of information. Perhaps the best method for reducing bias in tests of intelligence is to use them with the full knowledge that endowment interacting with opportunity produces a wide range of differences. Appraisal of the variation of different kinds of intellectual functioning requires many kinds of tests so that the differences can be utilized for the benefit of the individual and for the good of society. Intellectual functioning certainly does involve the ability to learn to adjust to the environment or to adapt the environment to individual needs and capacities by the process of solving problems either directly or incidentally. Such a concept recognizes a variety of different aptitudes for success with different kinds of problems. The full appreciation of the variety of aptitudes and the development of adequate methods for appraising them, should in the long run, ultimately lead to the production of enough information to eliminate bias.

With this, Lorge returned to the theme with which he started: the *bias* in intelligence tests resides not in the tests themselves—they only show *differences*—but in those who interpret the tests as though the I.Q. scores were an "absolute determination" of the inherent mental capacity of the individual.

*Empirical assessments of the new test.* Once the Davis-Eells test was published, the theoretical discussion of the Chicago group's approach gave way to empirical evaluation of the product. The research findings accumulated rapidly, and by 1956 they indicated unequivocally that the test had fallen short of its goal. In view of the amount of time required for its administration, the test had relatively low reliability. But even more to the point, it had not eliminated the social class differences in I.Q. In five of six grade-levels of children studied in a Southwestern city, for example, high-status children still averaged 5 points higher than low-status children on the Davis-Eells test.[23] Another investigator found the advantage of the high-status pupils to range from 12 to 17 points in three Tennessee cities, and, moreover, the mean scores from the Davis-Eells test looked no

[23] H. Angelino and C. L. Shedd, "An Initial Report of a Validation Study of the Davis-Eells Test of General Intelligence or Problem Solving Ability," *Journal of Psychology*, 1955, **40**, pp. 35–38.

different from mean I.Q.s derived from a conventional intelligence test given at the same time.[24] The Davis-Eells scores still showed a correlation of about .35 with social class among a number of 10-year-olds in the Detroit area—not much different from the correlations obtained with two conventional tests.[25] More recently one investigator found the kind of results initially promised by the test: Among children in a Mid-western suburb the correlations between father's occupation and score on the Davis-Eells Games were close to zero while I.Q.s from a standard test showed the usual correlations with social class.[26] But taken as a whole, these and other studies[27] made it clear that the "culture-fair" test produced by the Chicago workers could not be counted on to equalize the I.Q.s between the classes.

## THE RESIDUE

It may have been unfortunate, in one sense, that Davis and his colleagues attempted to produce an intelligence test. The test's publication and the subsequent efforts to assess its promise seemed to divert scholarly attention away from the fundamental issues posed by Davis in his cultural analysis of environment and intelligence. In some quarters of psychology, at least, the failure of the Davis-Eells test to live up to its promise simply closed the chapter on the Chicago group's excursion into the theory of intelligence; the underlying arguments, it seemed, no longer needed to be met.

Other psychologists viewed the work at Chicago in broad perspective, seeing it as one among many attempts to refine the meaning of intelligence and its relation to experience. Lorge took such a view. He opened his critique of the Eells book with the following paragraphs.

From time to time, scientists need to reappraise the concepts of their science, their methods of measurement, and the application of their knowledges for the general good. Psychologists, during the nature-nurture controversy, have had to reevaluate not only the concept of intelligence but also that of environment. For more than fifty years, they have been revising the *meaning* of intelligence, the various tests and procedures for its estimation, and, more especially, the implica-

[24] W. Coleman and A. W. Ward, "A Comparison of Davis-Eells and Kuhlmann-Finch Scores of Children from High and Low Socio-economic Status," *Journal of Educational Psychology*, 1955, **16**, pp. 465–469.
[25] W. L. Fowler, "A Comparative Analysis of Pupil Performance on Conventional and Culture-controlled Mental Tests," *Yearbook of the National Council on Measurements Used in Education*, 1957, **14**, pp. 8–19.
[26] V. H. Noll, "Relation of Scores on Davis-Eells Games to Socio-economic Status, Intelligence Test Results, and School Achievement," *Educational and Psychological Measurement*, 1960, **20**, pp. 119–130.
[27] W. G. Warrington and J. L. Saupe, "Development and Applications of Tests of General Mental Ability," *Review of Educational Research*, 1959, **29**, p. 19. These authors review several additional studies, but for a more complete bibliography, see O. K. Buros (Ed.), *Fifth Mental Measurements Yearbook* (Highland Park, N.J.: The Gryphon Press, 1959), pp. 459–462.

tion of the evidence from tests for the understanding of children and their achievements. . . .

Psychologists, as well as educators in the fullness of time may feel obligated to the authors for "Intelligence and Cultural Differences." For again, they have asked them to reconsider the meaning of test intelligence. As contemplated, the book has motivated anew serious reexamination of intelligence and of intelligence-tests.[28]

The implication is plain, from this perspective, that the concerns of which Davis wrote represented general movements of thought and work which already existed in the field. For example, there had been a number of efforts, which preceded Davis by many years, to create "culture-free" measures of intelligence and to de-emphasize the verbal and linguistic components of tests. Similarly, the part of Davis' argument suggesting that there were different *kinds* of problem-solving capacity resembled a prominent current of thought among American psychologists, strongly reinforced by the work of Thurstone in the 1930's and epitomized by Guilford's theory of the structure of intelligence.[29] Psychologists of Lorge's perspective, then, found little that was new in the work of the Chicago group and assimilated the underlying arguments largely to ongoing theoretical developments in psychology.

The one relatively novel contribution of Davis and his co-workers—the use of a detailed anthropological-sociological analysis of cultural differences to highlight different kinds of intellectual development—failed to find a foothold in the psychological domain. The main currents of thought among the psychometricians contained little to which it could be assimilated.

In recent years, the research of social psychologists and others has continued to illuminate the bearing of cultural influences upon intellectual functioning and closely allied psychological processes, although quite apart from the rationale and program of Davis and his colleagues. Thus, studies of creativity, studies of the development of talented youth, studies of achievement motivation—all have pointed to the significance of social and cultural factors underlying the psychological attributes.[30] But they have shown, too, that the significant factors are not organized simply and uniquely according to social class variations. Indeed, some scholars believe that the particular cultural differences among the social classes of which Davis spoke a decade or more ago are becoming less distinct.[31]

[28] Lorge, *op. cit.*, p. 76.
[29] J. P. Guilford, *Personality*, New York: McGraw-Hill Book Co., Inc., 1959.
[30] See D. C. McClelland et al., *Talent and Society*, Princeton, N.J., Van Nostrand: 1958; E. P. Torrance (ed.), *Talent and Education*, Minneapolis, University of Minnesota Press, 1960; A. Roe, *The Making of a Scientist*, Dodd, Mead & Co., 1952.
[31] See U. Bronfenbrenner, "Socialization and Social Class through Time and Space," in E. E. Maccoby, T. M. Newcomb, and F. L. Hartley (eds.), *Readings in Social Psychology* (3rd ed. New York, Holt, Rinehart & Winston, Inc., 1958), pp. 400–424; W. B. Brookover and D. Gottlieb, "Social Class and Education," *Reading in the Social Psychology of Education* by W. W. Charters, Jr. and W. L. Page, eds. Boston: Allyn and Bacon, 1963.

In any event, many school people found something of a revelation in the work of the Chicago group. Davis, Warner, Havighurst, and others often addressed themselves to the education audience, already sensitized to their research on social class patterns in the school. This was an audience, also, rarely reached by the academic psychometricians. The fallibilities of the Intelligence Quotient, of which the test-makers and the psychologists were so fully aware, were not recognized by all schoolmen. Numbered among the educators were some who, in Lorge's words, regarded I.Q.s as "absolute determinations" about their pupils. Despite courses in educational psychology, not a few of the nation's teachers believed the I.Q. to mark the innate mental capacity of the child, or at least, to indicate a trait so firmly a part of the child that little help could be held out for the dull.

Such faith in the intelligence test was badly shaken by the charges of "bias" which emanated from Chicago and by the dramatic illustrations of "biased" test items. The possibility that low test scores could be a product of cultural experiences and motivational patterns which were different from those stressed by the school gave pause to many educators. It reinforced the pleas from certain leaders for teachers to review their teaching methods and their curriculums in order to fit the school to children from all walks of life. Quite apart from the technical issues, the work of Davis and his colleagues at the University of Chicago helped to remove the bias, if not from tests, at least from the test-users in the education profession.

# MENTAL ABILITIES OF CHILDREN IN

# DIFFERENT SOCIAL AND CULTURAL GROUPS

*Gerald Lesser, Gordon Fifer, and Donald H. Clark*

## BACKGROUND

This study examines the patterns among various mental abilities in first-grade children from different social class and ethnic backgrounds. The main intent is to extend the empirical analysis of the development of differential mental abilities in children, but the findings of this research also bear directly upon the problems of building valid and precise assessment instruments for children from different cultural groups.

Despite the considerable amount of work in the field of mental abilities in an attempt to create "culture-free" or "culture-fair" tests, little has been shown to yield consistent and valid results. The problem still remains of how to evaluate the intellectual potential of children whose backgrounds necessarily handicap them seriously on the usual tests of mental ability. This study focuses on two major aspects of the problem: First, to devise tests that would be as free as possible of any direct class or cultural bias but that would still be acceptable measures of intellectual traits; Second, to structure a testing situation that would enable each child to be evaluated under optimal conditions.

The problems of identifying differentiated mental abilities and of determining their relationships to social class and cultural group composition challenge us directly in urban centers. The provision of suitable educational programs for all school children presupposes knowledge of the patterns of abilities that children from culturally diverse groups display.

From "Mental Abilities of Children in Different Social and Cultural Groups," by Gerald Lesser, Gordon Fifer, and Donald H. Clark. Unpublished manuscript, 1963. Printed by permission of the authors.

## OBJECTIVES

The goal of this study is to examine various mental abilities in first-grade children from different social-class and ethnic backgrounds. We accepted a definition of intelligence that postulates diverse mental abilities; hence, intelligent behavior can be manifested in a wide variety of forms. This definition provided a basic premise for the study: that social class and ethnic influences differ not only in degree but in kind, with the consequence that different kinds of intellectual skills are fostered or hindered in various environments.

Hypotheses were tested regarding the effects of social class and ethnic group affiliation (and their interaction) upon both the level of each mental ability considered singly and the pattern among mental abilities considered in combination. Four mental abilities (verbal ability, reasoning, number facility, and space conceptualization) were studied in first-grade children from four ethnic groups (Chinese, Jewish, Negro, and Puerto Rican), with each ethnic group divided into middle-class and lower-class groups.

Specific predictions were:

1] Significant differences will exist between the two *social-class* groups in the *level* of scores for each mental ability.

2] Significant differences will exist among the four *ethnic* groups in the *level* of scores for each mental ability.

3] *Social-class* and *ethnicity* will interact significantly in determining the *level* of scores for each mental ability.

4] Significant differences will exist between the two *social-class* groups in the *pattern* of scores from the four mental-ability scales.

5] Significant differences will exist among the four *ethnic* groups in the *pattern* of scores from the four mental-ability scales.

6] *Social-class* and *ethnicity* will interact significantly in determining the *pattern* of scores from the four mental-ability scales.


## PROCEDURE

To test these hypotheses, a $4 \times 2 \times 2$ analysis of covariance design (completely balanced randomized blocks) was used. Four ethnic groups (Chinese, Jewish, Negro, and Puerto Rican) were included, each divided into two social class groups (middle and lower), each in turn divided into equal numbers of boys and girls. A total of 16 subgroups, each composed of 20 children, is represented. The total sample is thus composed of 320 first-grade children.

Three test influences were controlled statistically in the analysis of covariance design: effort and persistence, persuasibility or responsiveness to the tester, and age of the subject.

The following procedural issues were prominent:

1. Perhaps the primary procedural problem was to insure the fact that observed differences among social class and ethnic groups reside in the respondents and not in the test materials themselves (or in the definitions upon which the tests are based). To accomplish this, tests were constructed that presuppose only experiences that are common and familiar within all of the different social class and ethnic groups in New York City. There was no intention to "free" the test materials from cultural influence, but, rather, the tests utilize elements that appear commonly in all cultural groups in New York City.

2. Attempts to study the organization of mental abilities in different groups must elicit group factors reliably and unambiguously. It is thus desirable to have more than one test representing each mental ability to be identified and the tests must have adequate lower and upper limits in order to prevent artificial restriction of range among such young children. They also must be of sufficient length and precision to yield reliable measures with young children. A table follows of scales, subtests, and numbers of items:

| Scale | Subtests | Number of Items | |
|-------|----------|-----------------|---|
| Verbal | Picture Vocabulary | 30 | |
| | Word Vocabulary | 30 | |
| | | | 60 |
| Reasoning | Picture Analogies | 18 | |
| | Picture Arrangement | 16 | |
| | Jump Peg | 12 | |
| | | | 46 |
| Numerical | Enumeration | 6 | |
| | Addition | 10 | |
| | Subtraction | 10 | |
| | Multiplication | 10 | |
| | Division | 10 | |
| | | | 46 |
| Space | Object Completion | 16 | |
| | Estimating Path | 12 | |
| | Jigsaw Puzzles | 16 | |
| | Perspective | 10 | |
| | | | 54 |

The reliabilities of total scale scores were satisfactory, except that the reliability of the Space scale (0.85) was somewhat lower than desired. Intercorrelations among the scales were somewhat higher than desired, but (given the high reliabilities of the scales) considerable unique nonchance variance exists within each scale.

Other general considerations regarding the scales and their administration are (a) The tests required of the subject neither reading nor writing ability; (b) Directions were kept extremely simple; (c) Ample practice material was provided prior to each subtest, and examiners were instructed to proceed with scored items only when certain that the child was familiar with the material and understood the task; (d) There were no formal steps of test administration left to the discretion of the examiner; each step was specified in detail to assure standard procedure; (e) Each child was tested in a room in his own public school during regular school hours; (f) The length of the testing periods varied and were determined primarily by the examiner's judgment regarding degree of rapport and fatigue; most commonly, a child was seen for one session of thirty to forty-five minutes on each of three separate days; (g) Each child was tested by an examiner representing the child's own cultural group in order to maximize chances of establishing constructive rapport and to permit the administration of instructions and test items in the child's primary language, in English, or in the most effective combination of languages for the particular child.

3. Another procedural difficulty was achieving an unambiguous definition and assessment of criteria for social-class and ethnic-group placement. Both variables are obviously multidimensional in nature, and to define and measure the necessary components is a formidable task. Since members of each ethnic group were to be located in both lower- and middle-class categories, additional problems arise in attempting to maintain an equal degree of separation between the social-class categories for each ethnic group.

An Index of Social Position (based upon the Hollingshead and Redlich scale) was derived for each child from ratings of the head of the household's occupation, education, and the dwelling area of the family. Although good social-class separation was obtained for each ethnic group, the degree of separation varied somewhat among ethnic groups. This fact is considered in the interpretation of the results.

The ethnic designation demanded that both parents be known to be of the particular ethnic group. Cases were discarded if verification of ethnic group membership could not be obtained from one of several sources.

4. Additional procedural problems arose from the fact that each child was tested by a psychometrician who shared the child's ethnic identity. Each tester had been trained beyond the Master's Degree level and each had extensive experience administering psychological tests, including the standard tests of intelligence. However, the tendency of the testers to empathize with the children from their own cultural groups demanded careful control of the testing procedures to insure uniform test administration. This was accomplished by the use of extensive video-tape training experiences in which each examiner observed other testers and himself administer the test materials. The capability of video-tape to allow self-viewing and repeated review of test sessions permitted the establishment of uniform test procedures.

## RESULTS

The major findings related to the test of the hypotheses are:

*1*] Differences in *social-class* placement *do* produce significant differences in the absolute *level* of each mental ability but *do not* produce significant differences in the *patterns* among these abilities.

*2]* Differences in *ethnic-group* membership *do* produce significant differences in *both* the absolute *level* of each mental ability and the *patterns* among these abilities.

*3]* *Social class* and *ethnicity do* interact to affect the absolute *level* of each mental ability but *do not* interact to affect the *patterns* among these abilities.

Thus, Hypotheses 1, 2, 3, and 5, listed in the Objectives section of this summary were strongly confirmed. No statistically significant support was found for Hypotheses 4 and 6. Other specific results are:

*1]* Regarding social-class effects upon mental abilities, middle-class children are significantly superior to lower-class children on all scales and subtests.

*2]* Regarding ethnic-group effects upon mental abilities:

a. On Verbal Ability, Jewish children rank first (being significantly better than all other ethnic groups), Negroes second, Chinese third (both being significantly better than Puerto Ricans), Puerto Ricans fourth.

b. On Reasoning, the Chinese rank first, Jews second (both being significantly better than Negroes and Puerto Ricans), Negroes third, Puerto Ricans fourth.

c. On Numerical Ability, Jews rank first, Chinese second (both being significantly better than Puerto Ricans and Negroes), Puerto Ricans third, Negroes fourth.

d. On Space, Chinese rank first (being significantly better than Puerto Ricans and Negroes), Jews second, Puerto Ricans third, Negroes fourth.

*3]* Regarding sex differences, boys are significantly better than girls on the total Space scale, on the Picture Vocabulary subtest (but not on the total Verbal scale), and the Jump Peg subtest (but not on the total Reasoning scale).

*4]* Regarding the interactions of social class and ethnicity, two effects combine to produce the statistically significant interaction effects upon each scale of mental ability:

a. On each mental-ability scale, social-class position produces more of a difference in the mental abilities of the Negro children than for the other groups. That is, the middle-class Negro children are more different in level of mental abilities from the lower-class Negroes than, for example, the middle-class Chinese are from the lower-class Chinese.

b. On each mental ability scale, the scores of the middle-class children from the various ethnic groups resemble each other to a greater extent than do the scores of the lower-class children from the various ethnic groups.

That is, the middle-class Chinese, Jewish, Negro, and Puerto Rican children are more alike in their mental ability scores than are the lower-class Chinese, Jewish, Negro, and Puerto Rican children.

5] Regarding the interactions of sex and ethnicity, the significant interactions for both Verbal and Space reflect higher scores for boys than for girls in all ethnic groups, except for Jewish children; Jewish girls are superior to Jewish boys for both Verbal and Space scales.

## CONCLUSIONS

Social-class and ethnic-group membership (and their interaction) have strong effects upon the level of each of four mental abilities (verbal ability, reasoning, numerical facility, and space conceptualization).

Ethnic-group affiliation also affects strongly the pattern or organization of mental abilities, but once the pattern specific to the ethnic group emerges, social-class variations within the ethnic group do not alter this basic organization. Apparently, different mediators are associated with social-class and ethnic-group conditions. The mediating variables associated with ethnic-group conditions do affect strongly the organization of abilities, while social-class status does not appear to modify further the basic pattern associated with ethnicity.

These findings allow a reassessment of the various proposed explanations of cultural influences upon intellectual performance. The importance of the mediators associated with ethnicity is to provide differential impacts upon the development of mental abilities while the importance of the mediators associated with social class is to provide pervasive (and not differential) effects upon the various mental abilities. This conclusion allows selection among the several explanations offered to interpret cultural influences upon intellectual activity; explanations based upon natural selection, differential reinforcement, motivation, problem-solving tactics, work habits and so forth were re-examined in the light of the present results.

In summary, the findings lend selective support to Anastasi's premise that "Groups differ in their relative standing on different functions. Each . . . fosters the development of a different *pattern* of abilities." It seems true that social-class and ethnic groups do ". . . differ in their relative standing on different functions." However, ethnic groups do ". . . foster the development of a different pattern of abilities," while social-class differences do not modify these basic organizations associated with ethnic-group conditions.

The present effort to construct suitable testing procedures for studying children from culturally diverse groups must now incorporate the broader educational considerations of curriculum development, teacher training, and school organization. We have shown that several mental abilities are

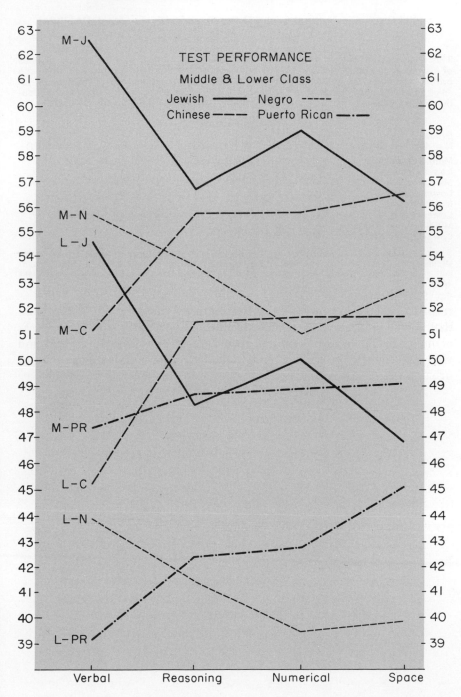

TEST PERFORMANCE
Middle & Lower Class

Jewish ———     Negro - - - - -
Chinese —··—     Puerto Rican —·—·—

## Social Class and Cultural Group Differences in Diverse Mental Abilities

### Classification Analysis

This compares the pattern of scores for each individual subject with the pattern profiles of his group and other groups. It yields data concerning the degree to which a subject's profile resembles the profile of his or the other groups. Reference: Tatsuoka, M. M. *Joint probability of membership and success in a group,* Harvard Graduate School of Education Report 1957.

*Group Patterns*

| Group<br>N = 40, each Group | M Ch | L Ch | M J | L J | M N | L N | M PR | L PR |
|---|---|---|---|---|---|---|---|---|
| Middle Chinese | 13* | 10 | 6 | 1 | 5 | 1 | 2 | 2 |
| Lower Chinese | 6 | 14 | 2 | 4 | 3 | 1 | 1 | 9 |
| Middle Jewish | 4 | 0 | 32 | 4 | 0 | 0 | 0 | 0 |
| Lower Jewish | 0 | 1 | 9 | 18 | 7 | 4 | 0 | 1 |
| Middle Negro | 5 | 1 | 11 | 10 | 11 | 0 | 0 | 2 |
| Lower Negro | 1 | 3 | 0 | 3 | 0 | 28 | 0 | 5 |
| Middle Puerto Rican | 6 | 6 | 3 | 6 | 4 | 0 | 3 | 12 |
| Lower Puerto Rican | 0 | 7 | 1 | 1 | 0 | 8 | 3 | 20 |

* Figures to be read across as follows: The scores of 13 Middle-Class Chinese subjects fit the Middle-Class Chinese pattern and level on the four mental ability scales; 10 Middle-Class Chinese look more like Lower-Class Chinese; 6 look more like Middle-Class Jews, 1 more like Lower-Class Jews, etc.

related to each other in ways that are culturally determined. We propose that the identification of relative intellectual strengths and weaknesses of members of different cultural groups must now become a basic and vital prerequisite to making enlightened decisions about education in urban areas.

# CULTURAL DISCONTINUITIES AND THE

# DEVELOPMENT OF ORIGINALITY

*E. Paul Torrance*

When our staff began to study the development of the creative thinking abilities, first by cross-sectional methods and later by longitudinal ones, we were puzzled by what we discovered. Clearly, the intellectual abilities that we had labeled "creative thinking" did not follow the same course of development as other abilities. For most of our measures of creative thinking, there were distinct periods, of decline rather than growth at about ages five, nine, thirteen, and seventeen. We became particularly interested in the decline that appears at about age nine, or the fourth grade, because it is so acute and is accompanied by so many problems of behavior, learning difficulty, delinquency, and personality disturbance.

Many possible explanations were advanced for the decline in creative thinking and creative activities in the fourth grade—physiological changes, increasing peer pressures for conformity, and many others. Knowing that the need for consensual validation and peer approval becomes tremendously important at about age nine, I placed a great deal of confidence in hypotheses in this area. Since anthropologists maintain that the United States has one of the most peer-oriented cultures in the world, we have attempted to test some of our hypotheses by conducting developmental studies in several cultures outside the United States and in segregated Negro schools in the United States. Now that the developmental curves for the creative thinking abilities of some of these cultures are becoming clear, the idea has been thrust upon us that the declines in the creative thinking abilities that occur at about ages five, nine, thirteen, and seventeen are the result of

From *Education and the Creative Potential* by E. Paul Torrance. No. 5 Modern School Practices Series (Minneapolis: University of Minnesota Press, Copyright © 1963 by the University of Minnesota). Reprinted by permission of the University of Minnesota Press.

the stresses imposed by cultural discontinuities and are accompanied by personality disturbances.

Using the measures of originality on three nonverbal tasks, I should like to discuss some of our findings and thinking concerning this problem. First, I shall describe briefly the tasks used to measure originality of thinking in these cross-cultural studies. Then, I shall present some of the developmental data, review some of the discontinuities in our society, and discuss them in the light of data from five other cultures.

## MEASURING ORIGINALITY OF THINKING

Three nonverbal and six verbal tasks were used for assessing originality of thinking in the cross-cultural studies. Originality has been defined in terms of statistical infrequency of a response within the given culture. In addition, it was required that responses be relevant to the task, show intellectual strength, and represent some break away from the obvious, the commonplace, and the banal. Each of the tasks had undergone considerable developmental work and had yielded satisfactory evidence of test-retest reliability, validity, and ease of administration. From all of the evidence we were able to obtain, the tasks did not seem to favor one sex over the other or one culture over another.

In each of the cultures studied, approximately 1000 pupils in grades one through six were examined. Native examiners were used in all cultures, instructions were given in the native language of the subjects, and the subjects responded in their preferred language. Responses were then translated by expert linguists and afterwards scored by our own staff. Results of the nonverbal tasks are now available for our United States sample (pupils in a school system having a broad range of talent), Australia, Western Samoa, Germany, India, and a sample from segregated Negro schools in Georgia. In Australia we obtained an urban and a rural sample, both in the western part of the continent. The Western Samoan sample included schools in the larger towns and in the remote villages where white men seldom go. In Germany, the samples were from two different sections of Free Berlin. The samples from India included Moslem, Sikh, Christian, and Hindu schools in New Delhi.

*Nonverbal Tasks and Scoring for Originality.* The three nonverbal tasks on which the measures of originality are based were described in the preceding paper, "Creative Students in Our Schools Today."

To obtain data for a scoring guide, a tabulation was made of the frequency of responses made by the subjects, separately for each culture. Weights from 0 to 4 were assigned on the basis of statistical frequency: 0 —12 per cent or greater; 1 —5 per cent to 12 per cent; 2 —2 per cent to 5 per cent; 3 —$\frac{1}{2}$ per cent to 2 per cent; 4 —less than $\frac{1}{2}$ per cent.

Some responses are obvious and unoriginal in all cultures; others are common in two or more cultures; while some are common in only one culture. For example, on the Circles Task the following responses were common or unoriginal in all six of the cultures studied: apple, balloon, ball, clock, coin, design, earth, moon, sun, eggs in some form, flowers, glasses, spectacles (all except Negro), globe, tree, wheel.

The following responses were unoriginal only in the United States samples: baseball, basketball, basketball hoop, door knob, doughnut (fairly unoriginal in Negro and German samples), hole, hoop, steering wheel, sputnik, satellite.

The following were unoriginal only in the United States and Germany: button, clown's face, target, tire.

Responses scored as unoriginal in Samoa, but original in other cultures, include: boat, bowl, breadfruit, cat, leaf, rabbit.

Common among the responses of the sample from India, the following are unoriginal: eggplant, melon, pomegranate, racket, pitcher, table.

Common among the responses of children from Germany are: butterfly, ice cream cone, rabbit, traffic sign, table.

Unoriginal responses among Australian subjects include: decoration (also in U.S.), light bulb (also in U.S.), game, table ware.

Common among the Negro responses are: cat, goat, grapefruit (also other U.S. samples), ice cream cone, lollipop, pumpkin, scissors.

The developmental curves used in this report were obtained by obtaining the sum of the weighted originality scores for the three nonverbal tasks for each subject and then computing the mean for each task for each sample.

## DEVELOPMENTAL CURVES IN OUR CULTURE

The generalized developmental curve that holds for most measures we have devised of the creative thinking abilities shows that beginning at age three there is an increase until a peak is reached at about age four and a half. A drop occurs at about age five, at about the time the child enters the kindergarten, and is followed by increases in the first, second, and third grades. At about age nine, near the end of the third grade or at the beginning of the fourth grade, there is a rather severe decrement in almost all the creative thinking abilities. Then comes a period of recovery, especially for girls in the fifth grade. Recovery, however, is largely in fluency, not in originality. Recovery in originality comes largely in the sixth grade. After this, another decrease in the seventh grade is followed by recovery in the eighth and continued growth until a peak is reached in the eleventh grade. After this, there is a leveling off or slight drop near the end of the high school period. Although I have not charted carefully the course of development for the remainder of the educational stages, almost no group studied has thus far exceeded the performance of eleventh graders. Studies of the performance of many subjects under many different natural and experimental conditions suggest that decrements continue to occur during other crises or discontinuities throughout the life span.

It is interesting to note that each of the generalized drops occurs at an age at which the transition from one developmental stage to another begins. Using Harry Stack Sullivan's (1953) conceptualization of the stages of development of interpersonal skills, the drop at about age five occurs at the end of the childhood stage and the beginning of the juvenile stage with its demands for social accommodation, compromise, and acceptance of authorities outside the home. The second drop occurs with the onset of the preadolescent stage with its increased need for consensual validation, peer approval, identification with peers of the same sex, and conformity to peer norms. The third occurs at the onset of early adolescence with its increased anxieties, striving for approval of the opposite sex, and the like, all of which restrict many areas of awareness and impose new demands for conformity.

## DEVELOPMENTAL CURVES IN OTHER CULTURES

The shape of the developmental curves for originality in other cultures should help us determine whether the various drops we find in our culture are biologically or culturally determined. The mean originality scores for each grade-level for each of the six cultures is shown in Table 1 and Figure 1.

*Table 1*—Mean Originality Scores on Nonverbal Tasks for Grades One through Six for Six Cultural Groups

| Grade | Australia | U.S. Negro | Germany | India | Samoa | U.S.A. |
|-------|-----------|-----------|---------|-------|-------|--------|
| First | 17.37 | 14.58 | 19.50 | 14.88 | 12.72 | 22.95 |
| Second | 17.19 | 22.35 | 16.53 | 13.59 | 15.27 | 28.20 |
| Third | 15.24 | 21.42 | 15.75 | 17.64 | 16.08 | 30.90 |
| Fourth | 20.16 | 26.07 | 19.83 | 15.00 | 18.60 | 26.40 |
| Fifth | 20.76 | | 28.44 | 20.73 | 19.53 | 24.90 |
| Sixth | 19.83 | | 26.07 | 24.42 | 22.50 | 33.30 |

It will be noted that there are no drops in the developmental curve for the Samoan subjects. The level of originality begins in the first grade at the lowest level of any of the cultures but the growth is continuous from year to year. The second greatest continuity in development is shown by the American Negro sample. A slight drop occurs between the second and third grades but there is considerable growth between the third and fourth grades. Through the fourth grade, German and Australian children seem to show about the same level and pattern of development. Pressures toward standardization and conformity apparently occur quite early, especially for the Australian child. German children show tremendous growth between the fourth and fifth grades, but the Australian children remain at about the same level in the fourth, fifth, and sixth grades. The

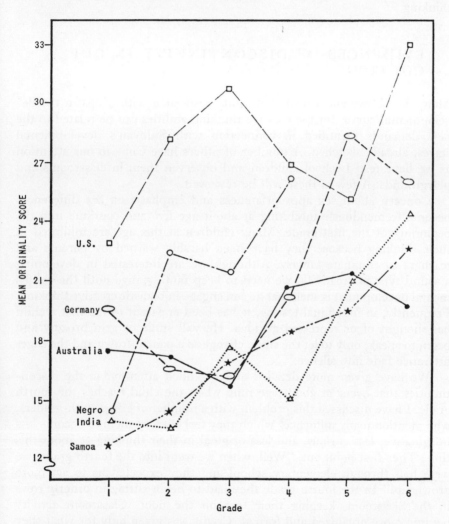

*Figure 1*—Developmental curve for originality on nonverbal tasks for six cultural groups.

pattern of growth among the children in India is much the same as in the United States, though the level is considerably less. (Incidentally, the level of the children in India is comparatively higher on the verbal than on the nonverbal tasks, while the reverse is true of the American Negro sample.)

Now, let us examine some of the evidence concerning the continuities and discontinuities, especially in the United States and Western Samoa, to provide a preliminary test of the hypothesis that cultural discontinuities are accompanied by discontinuities in the development of originality of thinking.

## EVIDENCES OF DISCONTINUITY IN OUR CULTURE

Many of the evidences of discontinuity associated with drops in the developmental curves for the creative thinking abilities can be related to the new demands identified in connection with Sullivan's developmental stages, already sketched. A number of others have come to our attention as we have tested school children and observed them in classrooms and playgrounds. A few of these will be reviewed.

Concern about sex appropriateness and emphasis on sex differences become tremendously inhibiting at about age five and continue into the beginning of the first grade. Many children at this age are inhibited in their thinking because they have been harshly warned by parents and teachers to eliminate fantasy. Although we are interested in developing a sound type of creativity, we need to keep fantasy alive until the child's mental development is such that he can engage in realistic creative thinking. Frequently, in individual testing, it has been apparent to me that a child has thought of or repressed an idea. He will smile or grin broadly and begin to speak, only to let the smile change to a pained frown and the eager utterance fade into silence.

We have given more detailed and extended attention to the discontinuities that occur at about age nine when the child reaches the fourth grade. I have discussed this problem with a number of gifted sixth-graders, who mention many influences which they feel coerced them to become less imaginative, less curious, and less original in their thinking at about this time. They first point out, "Well, when we went into the fourth grade, we were half through elementary school and they expected us to act more grown up." In the fourth grade they had to begin sitting in orderly rows in the classroom, keeping their feet on the floor. Classroom activity became more organized and formal. Credit was given only for what they put on paper. The animals in their stories did not talk. Usually, they had to go to another building or upstairs in a two story building. They had to start doing homework and their papers were expected to be neat with no smudges. The subject matter became different; they began having lessons in geography and history. They began taking part in student government and started serving as monitors of their fellow student's behavior.

As we tested children of this age, we were impressed with the inhibiting influence of their preoccupation with prevention and fear of making mental leaps. The problem, "What are all of the possible things Mother Hubbard could have done when she found no bone in the cupboard for her dog?" was easy for younger children but extremely difficult for the nine-year-old. The nine-year-old was so preoccupied with the notion that Old Mother Hubbard should have prevented this predicament that he could think of no way she might remedy it. These older children also wanted to stick close to the stimuli and resisted making mental leaps. In the Product Improvement Task resistance in many cases seemed to stem from the inhibitions surrounding cost. Uncertainty expressions became frequent. These phenomena have been observed and documented by other investigators. For example, L'Abate (1957) found that nine-year-olds showed a greater use of uncertainty expressions. Professional workers in the field of remedial vision have also observed uncertainty in children of this age. On the Rorschach test, subjects will say they are less imaginative than other children and that they can't make anything out of the ink blots. They will practice visual-training exercises endlessly but fail to make progress, continuing to be uncertain, hesitant, and slow in their perceptions.

Our work with teachers has also shown that many teachers in the intermediate grades live in a world quite different from that of their colleagues who teach in the primary grades. Their training, their attitudes toward children, and their methods of instruction have little in common. Many intermediate teachers admit frankly that they have no idea about what goes on in the primary grades.

In our research we have also found that primary teachers, when working with the creative writing of children, were more willing than intermediate teachers to sacrifice preoccupation with correctness and form for creative values.

When a youngster enters the seventh grade, he usually has to go to another building, frequently in another part of town, in a strange neighborhood. The school is usually larger, with different teachers for each subject. Promptness is strongly emphasized and tardy slips impose penalties. Extremes in dress and appearance, deviations from what all the others are wearing, are discouraged. New pressures and anxieties arise about winning the approval of the opposite sex. Pressures to be well-rounded socially and athletically are intensified.

Apparently the transition from junior high school is marked by greater continuity than that from elementary school. Since our developmental data are based on samples from schools having both junior and senior high schools in the same building, with a continuous organization, this aspect of continuity-discontinuity may be operating. Our data suggest that some discontinuities are introduced into the senior high school about the senior year and may be attributed to the immediacy of the transition to college, work, or military service at that time. New demands for grown-up behavior and sanctions against regression to childish thinking are then being experienced.

## INDICATIONS OF PERSONALITY DISTURBANCE IN OUR CULTURE

A recent experience has strongly reinforced my observation that considerable personality disturbance is associated with the stresses of discontinuity at about ages five, nine, thirteen, and seventeen. I analyzed a sample of one hundred letters written to me by parents whose children fell into some kind of trouble because of their creativity. Figure 2 presents

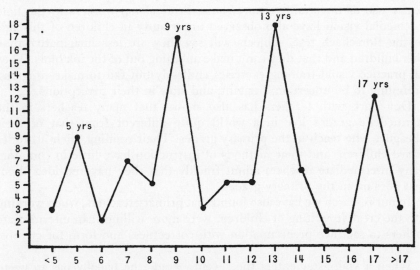

*Figure 2*—Distribution of 100 letters from parents about creative children in difficulty, according to age.

the data derived from this analysis. The greatest frequency of letters corresponds with the drop in the developmental curves, giving a rough indication that many creative children are in trouble at each of these stages. From these data it would seem that parents most frequently tend to be disturbed about their nine- and thirteen-year-olds. The five- and the seventeen-year-olds cause the next greatest concern. For each of these age groups, the following excerpts from the letters illustrate the nature of these personality disturbances.

### Age Five

"In January, the head of the school recommended that Don be removed from school because of his inability to conform."

"Upon arriving at public school, John clung to me and cried bitterly.

He was taken day after day and he remained. His interest span remained short and his hyperactivity persisted."

"To make Carl remain in his chair, his teacher used rope to tie him. A school conference revealed the teacher's opinion that he was heading for the life of a criminal. It was during this period that he reverted to soiling his pants."

One type of school experimentation now growing in popularity is introducing a discontinuity in the first grade, which apparently is associated with personality disturbances for some children and apparent losses in creativity, as described by one mother:

"Charles is in one of the few schools to adopt a new plan of education. He moves from room to room for different subjects. It's sponsored by the local college. His desire to have the teacher single him out if only to scold him makes me wonder if this plan is making him feel insecure. One teacher that Charles likes told me that he asks directions to the next class every few minutes. He is constantly at her side."

### Age Nine

"Each year since the first grade, the teachers have raved about Ray's creative ability, but moaned over his reading development. This year (his fourth in school) has been the first that he hasn't been in the bottom group, but also, since he's learned to conform, his creativity is not as outstanding as formerly. He tries *not* to be different, he says!"

"When Tom was about nine, his teacher was an older woman who returned to teaching after eleven years away from the classroom. His demand for attention resulted in his confinement in the hall coatroom. He took off. He had his special hiding places around the neighborhood, and the school would phone me up to come up. The principal, gym teacher, and I would hunt for him. He was usually found fairly easily by me."

"Asked outright, the school replied that they admit defeat, that they haven't been able to reach Bruce . . . asked for specific diagnosis with reference to the broad term, 'Emotionally Disturbed,' the specific is 'Behavioral Disturbance.' They say he is *not* retarded and that he is *not* psychotic."

"In the fourth grade, George had a disastrous year. He had a rigid teacher who tried to bend him to his will and he would not comply. Needless to say, the war was on . . . After this sad experience, we sent him to a creative art camp during the summer where he bloomed like a filly kicking up its heels at being free. He did some marvelous work."

### Age Thirteen

"When Jerry gets up to make an unorthodox statement he is ridiculed and so I find him becoming more and more introverted. He travels alone though he loves companionship but the boys his age don't know what he is talking about. He prefers the company of men with his interests."

"In the first grade Bob was a happy child who wanted to go to school more than anything . . . And even before he started to school, several friends had noted his unusual questions and answers and asked if he was in the third or fourth grade . . . But today his disposition has changed. He is still a happy boy and a ball of energy when he has time and is left alone to create something seemingly senseless to the adults around him . . . Is he mentally retarded? I cannot believe it."

### Age Seventeen

Many in this group have already left school or are in the process of leaving. School proved to be unchallenging or they were unable in some way to conform to its requirements. Some are described as lonely and mixed up, confused. Others had been unwilling to conform during the first few years of high school but had started making all A's, although their grade-point averages are still so low that they will have difficulty gaining admission to a "respectable" college. Their parents are concerned that these youngsters will not be able to earn a living and will have difficulty surviving.

One seventeen-year-old girl wrote that she no longer considers herself a creative person. During the first two years of high school, she expressed her opinions and ideas and held to the truth as she saw it. As a consequence, she was ridiculed, laughed at, scorned, and given low grades. She then decided that she would keep quiet in class and begin to earn A's. She now feels that she has cheated herself. Her over-all high school average is mediocre, in spite of the high grades earned during the past two years. Furthermore, she feels that she has become less of a person in adopting conformity and surrendering her independence of mind. She feels that she has not taken the courageous course. Boys who have adopted conformity have even greater feelings of guilt, perhaps, and consider themselves effeminate to have given in.

## CONTINUITIES AND DISCONTINUITIES IN OTHER CULTURES

Since the development of originality of thinking shows greater continuity in Western Samoa than in any of the other cultures studied, it seems desirable to examine the Samoan data in considerable detail. Margaret Mead's pioneering work (1939), the reports of modern observers (Johnson, 1962), and the data of this study support a picture of high cultural continuity and suppression of creativity and independence of thought almost from birth.

According to Margaret Mead, "Keep still," "Sit still," "Keep your mouth shut," and "Stop that noise," are thoroughly ingrained into the Samoan child. He is not even permitted to cry. Since the older children are given responsibility for disciplining the younger ones, conformity is taught from birth. Even today, Samoan teachers place an unusually high value upon *quietness* as a desirable characteristic on our "Ideal Pupil Questionnaire." Mead pointed out that Samoans were imitative and reproductive in their crafts rather than creative. Likewise, today we find that Samoan children excel in the craftmanship of their drawings, when administered the Goodenough Human Drawing Test or Buck's House-Tree-Person Test. Their drawings are reproductive rather than creative. The characteristic most valued by Samoan teachers in their pupils is *remembering well*.

Mead and other observers stress the role of the extended family, the participation of all ages in the life of the community, and the mixing of all ages in Samoa. Mead uses these facts and the continuities in regard to sex in explaining why Samoan adolescents do not experience the periods of emotional upset and personality disturbances common among adolescents in the United States. In today's Samoan schools there is no strict age segregation and a wide range of ages is found in a single grade, especially in the remote government schools.

The following three characteristics were ranked highest by Samoan teachers on the Ideal Pupil Checklist: remembers well, is healthy, and is always asking questions. From other data, it is obvious that "always asking questions" means something quite different to the Samoan teacher as opposed to the United States teacher. It was even difficult to administer the test of creative thinking to Samoan pupils, because they continually asked, "Is this all right?" "Is this what you want?" Samoan teachers tended to rank the following characteristics *lower* than the teachers of other cultures: adventurous, a selfstarter, curious, determined, energetic, independent in judgment, industrious, selfconfident, selfsufficient, sincere, thorough and versatile. They tended to place a *higher* value than teachers in other cultures on being a good guesser, competitive, prompt, haughty, physically strong, quiet, and liking to work alone. In general, this pattern of values is likely to support cultural continuity and a low degree of creativity.

Johnson (1962), who directed collection of the data in Western Samoa, identifies three major factors underlying this pattern. First, conformity is deeply embedded in thousands of years of Samoan history. A strong patriarchal family system evolved with emphasis on a chain of command, the highest decisions being made in the village "fono" of chiefs and passed down to submissive subjects. Acceptance of authority relationships was apparently rewarded and regarded as an ideal characteristic. A second influence is attributed to the influx of missionaries and German traders since the early 1830's. Here also the emphasis was on submission, either to God and his "special representatives," or to the traders who needed submissive workers on the plantations. A third influence began with New Zealand's entrance into the government of Samoa in 1914. With this came the idea of an extensive school system, school uniforms, leaving examinations, and uniformity of learning.

Both in the government and in the schools the authoritarian, hierarchal traditions were extended. In other ways, however, the schools introduced by the New Zealanders do not reflect the culture of the people. This is apparently more evident in the remote areas of the island where government educators inspect the schools regularly but are the only contact the people have with the "palagis" (whites). The school is modified somewhat but the culture of the village hardly changes.

Johnson cites the example of Faleolo to show how thoroughly students are imbued with the attitude of doing nothing until told. Faleolo, the housegirl of one of the teachers, satisfactorily performed the tasks assigned her. When the teacher returned from a two-day trip, he discovered that the girl had not eaten during the entire time. When he asked her why, she replied, "You didn't tell me to eat." In the Samoan home, children are told each thing they are to do.

Johnson also remarks upon the excellent memory of Samoan children today. Memory is important in the leaving examinations stressed in the school system. (One question in the 1960 examination: "How many eggs does an earthworm lay in a season?") Mead, about thirty years ago, observed that Samoans were notorious for their poor memory. Although this emphasis on memory for the great mass of Samoan children may have come with the mission and government schools, memory has long been important to Samoan rulers. Written language is a recent innovation in Samoa. Samoan leaders always had to memorize tapa designs, history, legends, songs, and rituals.

It is interesting to note that along with the importance attached to remembering, Samoan teachers regard a "good guesser" with high favor. Johnson relates that on occasion he has written a mathematical formula on the blackboard, had students work out a proof, asked a question about the formula that would necessitate an obvious "no" answer, given deliberate yet subtle "yes" cues with his head, and received incorrect "yes" answers by almost everyone in the class.

Apparently, a number of discontinuities are creeping into Samoan culture, in the more urban mission schools. Many of the Christian taboos are contrary to the traditions of the culture. Johnson recounts one incident in which two adolescent boys came to him as a counselor, requesting that a certain girl be expelled. Johnson recognized the accused girl as one of the school's leading students and a model of circumspect behavior. Puzzled, he sought to learn the reason for the boys' request. They explained simply that whenever they touched her she hit them, behavior approved by the school but disapproved by the culture and upsetting to the cultural continuity governing sex relationships.

These emerging discontinuities are reflected in the development curves, if we separate the more urban mission schools from the more remote government schools. The resulting developmental curves are

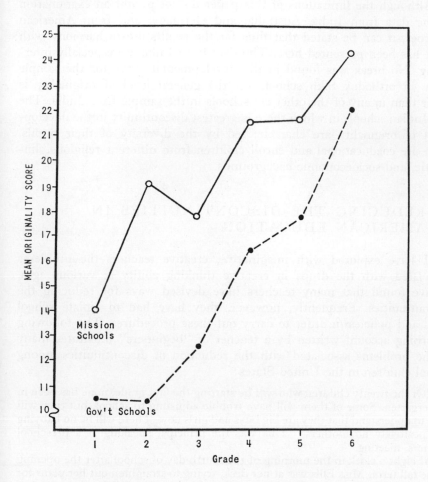

*Figure 3*—Developmental curve for originality on nonverbal tasks for remote government schools and more urban mission schools.

shown in Figure 3. Although the degree of originality is lower in the more remote schools, there is no break in the continuity of development. The introduction of discontinuities seems to be associated with a rise in the level of originality, discontinuity in the development of originality, and personality conflict. In Western Samoa the problem of increasing originality in thinking seems to be one of how to introduce cultural discontinuities without producing undue personality conflicts and disruptions in the development of thinking abilities. In the United States the problem seems to be the reverse: how to reduce the cultural discontinuities without retarding creative development.

Although the limitations of this paper do not permit an examination of the data from India, Australia, and Germany, and from American Negroes, it can be stated that thus far the results are in harmony with what has been presented here. The data from India are especially interesting. No break was found in the developmental curve for the sample from an orthodox Sikh school, yet the general level of originality is lower than in any of the other six schools in the sample from India. The two Indian schools in which there is greatest discontinuity in the development of originality are characterized by the diversity of their pupils. Both are coeducational and enroll children from different religious, linguistic, and socioeconomic backgrounds.

## REDUCING THE DISCONTINUITIES IN AMERICAN EDUCATION

As I have explored with imaginative, creative teachers the problems associated with the drops in creative thinking ability at various ages, I have found that many teachers have devised ways for reducing the discontinuities. Frequently, however, they have had to violate school rules and policies in order to carry out these procedures. The following absorbing account written by a teacher of "beginners" illustrates many of the problems associated with the reduction of discontinuities among school children in the United States:

"Of the twenty children who will be starting the first grade, none has been in kindergarten. Some of them will have trouble adjusting to school, but they will have to understand that they are big boys and girls now. There will be no babying and positively no mothers." This was the principal speaking at a preschool teachers' meeting.

At eight o'clock in the morning of the fourth day of school after the opening of the fall term, Miss Ellis was at her desk, trying to straighten out her plans for the day, before the onslaught of commotion that would announce the arrival of her forty-six pupils, grades one, two, and three. The principal's words rang in her ears. In her room there was work enough for two teachers. How could she handle it alone? And then there was the problem of Jimmy. There always had to be at least one beginner who had trouble "settling in." Would he be like Margie of a previous year who became ill several times a week? On every such occasion her mother had had to be called to take her home. When her mother arrived, Margie always sobbed, "I was so lonesome for you, Mommy," but no one could deny that the child was sick. Her violently upset stomach gave evidence of that. Now there was Jimmy. Would the stress of his first days of school be too great for him, too? The first two days, he had simply followed his sister to her eighth-grade room. There he had been forcibly separated from his sister by the principal and had been carried, kicking and screaming, down the corridor to his own room where he sat, crying and trembling, until time for dismissal. Yesterday he had deliberately missed the bus.

The bell rang, and as the children trooped in, Miss Ellis had a fleeting hope that the fire-inspector—or somebody—would decide that she had too many children—or, at least, that a kind angel would solve the problem of Jimmy. Looking over the sea of faces, she noticed that, once again, Jimmy was not there.

Nevertheless, there was no time to worry. First things first—the Pledge of Allegiance and a verse of the "Star Spangled Banner"; but the Pledge of Allegiance was barely finished when came a rap on the door. It was Jimmy *and* his mother. Both looked a little frightened. "Do you mind if I stay?" whispered Mrs. Lon. "I know it is against the rules but I thought I might help."

"I shall be very glad to have you stay," Miss Ellis replied, and then mentally clapped a hand over her mouth. "What have I said? Now I have broken a rule." However, the words were out, and as the day wore on, she had no feeling of regret. Somehow, everything was going better. Mrs. Lon circulated throughout the room, helping all the children. She paid no particular attention to Jimmy, nor he to her. During intermission he went out to play with the other children and immediately found a "special" friend. When Miss Ellis met the principal in the corridor at noon, he said, "What? A mother already?" She replied, "Yes, and I am so very glad to have her."

Mrs. Lon was in school again the next day. She was very unobtrusive and, somehow, the children gathered that she was there to help their teacher. So ended the first week of school. Thereafter, Jimmy needed no further help in adjusting to his new role. He was a happy child and a good student. As for Miss Ellis, she could not help thinking that the unorthodox procedure may not always work, but that it did this time, and that she might try it again sometime! She felt rather pleased about having been able to alleviate Mrs. Lon's feeling of guilt for being where she knew the head of the school did not want her: "I was deeply wishing for a kind angel to help me with my problems."

Essentially what this teacher did was to reduce in a small degree the discontinuity between home and the beginning of school for Jimmy. Perhaps there are many other ways by which this could have been done, but this case illustrates a number of the problems involved in reducing cultural discontinuities.

One important problem not answered by this case is that of determining whether or not the reduction in cultural discontinuities will reduce the drop observed in the creative thinking abilities as measured by our tests. Positive clues concerning this issue, however, were obtained from studies of the creative development of the pupils of two fourth grade teachers in our project. The pupils of these two teachers did not experience a decline in their creative development during this period. In both cases, the teacher did many things to reduce the discontinuities and their stressfulness. One of them permitted his pupils to continue experimenting in the fourth grade with different seating arrangements, as they had done in the third grade. He did not insist that they sit in rigid rows with their feet flat on the floor. He kept them writing poems, stories, and plays, and their inventions continued to have a place in the classroom. These activities were so exciting that the instructor did not have to make his pupils waste time in writing five hundred times, "I will not whisper in German class" or "I will not run in the hall." Along with their continued creative development, the children also experienced more than the usual growth in reading, language, study skills, and arithmetic. Similar observations could be made about the second teacher and his efforts to encourage creativity.

If we are able to establish more firmly that some of our cultural discontinuities are associated with personality disorganization and decreased mental functioning in certain areas and that some of these discontinuities are unnecessary, imaginative teachers, curriculum workers, and administrators should be able to devise changes, and evaluate the effects of changes, that will reduce these discontinuities.

### References to *Cultural Discontinuities and the Development of Originality*

1. Johnson, R. T., "Unpublished Observations on Western Samoan Culture and Education," Minneapolis; Bureau of Educational Research, University of Minnesota, 1962.
2. Mead, Margaret, *From the South Seas*, New York, William Morrow, 1939.

## B. Learning Differences

# I SEE THE MIND OF A FIVE-YEAR-OLD AS . . .

*Sylvia Ashton-Warner*

I see the mind of a five-year-old as a volcano with two vents; destructiveness and creativeness. And I see that to the extent that we widen the creative channel, we atrophy the destructive one. And it seems to me that since these words of the key vocabulary are no less than the captions of the dynamic life itself, they course out through the creative channel, making their contribution to the drying up of the destructive vent. From all of which I am constrained to see it as creative reading and to count it among the arts.

First words must mean something to a child.

First words must have intense meaning for a child. They must be part of his being.

How much hangs on the love of reading, the instinctive inclination to hold a book! *Instinctive*. That's what it must be. The reaching out for a book needs to become an organic action, which can happen at this yet formative age. Pleasant words won't do. Respectable words won't do. They must be words organically tied up, organically born from the dynamic life itself. They must be words that are already part of the child's being. "A child," reads a recent publication on the approach of the American books, "can be led to feel that Janet and John are friends." *Can be led to feel.* Why lead him to feel or try to lead him to feel that these strangers are friends? What about the passionate feeling he has already for his own friends? To me it is inorganic to overlook this step. To me it is an offence against art. I see it as an interruption in the natural expansion of life of which Erich Fromm speaks. How would New Zealand children get on if

From *Teacher* by Sylvia Ashton-Warner (New York: Simon and Schuster, Copyright 1963 by Sylvia Ashton-Warner) pp. 33–38. Reprinted by permission of Simon and Schuster, Inc.

115

all their reading material were built from the life of African blacks? It's little enough to ask that a Maori child should begin his reading from a book of his own colour and culture. This is the formative age where habits are born and established. An aversion to the written word is a habit I have seen born under my own eyes in my own infant room on occasion.

It's not beauty to abruptly halt the growth of a young mind and to overlay it with the frame of an imposed culture. There are ways of training and grafting young growth. The true conception of beauty is the shape of organic life and that is the very thing at stake in the transition from one culture to another. If this transition took place at a later age when the security of a person was already established, there would not be the same need for care. But in this country it happens that the transition takes place at a tender and vulnerable age, which is the reason why we all try to work delicately.

Back to these first words. To these first books. They must be made out of the stuff of the child itself. I reach a hand into the mind of the child, bring out a handful of the stuff I find there, and use that as our first working material. Whether it is good or bad stuff, violent or placid stuff, coloured or dun. To effect an unbroken beginning. And in this dynamic material, within the familiarity and security of it, the Maori finds that words have intense meaning to him, from which cannot help but rise a love of reading. For it's here, right in this first word, that the love of reading is born, and the longer his reading is organic the stronger it becomes, until by the time he arrives at the books of the new culture, he receives them as another joy rather than as a labour. I know all this because I've done it.

*First words must have an intense meaning.*
*First words must be already part of the dynamic life.*
*First books must be made of the stuff of the child*
  *himself, whatever and wherever the child.*

The words, which I write on large tough cards and give to the children to read, prove to be one-look words if they are accurately enough chosen. And they are plain enough in conversation. It's the conversation that has to be got. However, if it can't be, I find that whatever a child chooses to make in the creative period may quite likely be such a word. But if the vocabulary of a child is still inaccessible, one can always begin him on the general Key Vocabulary, common to any child in any race, a set of words bound up with security that experiments, and later on their creative writing, show to be organically associated with the inner world: "Mummy," "Daddy," "kiss," "frightened," "ghost."

"Mohi," I ask a new five, an undisciplined Maori, "what word do you want?"

"Jet!"

I smile and write it on a strong little card and give it to him. "What is it again?"

"Jet!"

"You can bring it back in the morning. What do you want, Gay?"

Gay is the classic overdisciplined, bullied victim of the respectable mother.

"House," she whispers. So I write that, too, and give it into her eager hand.

"What do you want, Seven?" Seven is a violent Maori.

"Bomb! Bomb! I want bomb!"

So Seven gets his word "bomb" and challenges anyone to take it from him.

And so on through the rest of them. They ask for a new word each morning and never have I to repeat to them what it is. And if you saw the condition of these tough little cards the next morning you'd know why they need to be of tough cardboard or heavy drawing paper rather than thin paper.

When each has the nucleus of a reading vocabulary and I know they are at peace with me I show them the word "frightened" and at once all together they burst out with what they are frightened of. Nearly all the Maoris say "the ghost!" a matter which has a racial and cultural origin, while the Europeans name some animal they have never seen, "tiger" or "alligator," using it symbolically for the unnameable fear that we all have.

"I not frightened of anysing!" shouts my future murderer, Seven.

"Aren't you?"

"No, I stick my knife into it all!"

"What will you stick your knife into?"

"I stick my knife into the tigers!"

"Tigers" is usually a word from the European children but here is a Maori with it. So I give him "tigers" and never have I to repeat this word to him, and in the morning the little card shows the dirt and disrepair of passionate usage.

"Come in," cry the children to a knock at the door, but as no one does come in we all go out. And here we find in the porch, humble with natural dignity, a barefooted tatooed Maori woman.

"I see my little Seven?" she says.

"Is Seven your little boy?"

"I bring him up. Now he five. I bring him home to his real family for school eh. I see my little boy?"

The children willingly produce Seven, and here we have in the porch, within a ring of sympathetic brown and blue eyes, a reunion.

"Where did you bring him up?" I ask over the many heads.

"Way back on those hill. All by heeself. You remember your ol' Mummy?" she begs Seven.

I see.

Later, standing watching Seven grinding his chalk to dust on his blackboard as usual, I do see. "Whom do you want, Seven? Your old Mummy or your new Mummy?"

"My old Mummy."

"What do your brothers do?"

"They all hits me."

"Old Mummy" and "new Mummy" and "hit" and "brothers" are all one-look words added to his vocabulary, and now and again I see some shape breaking through the chalk-ravage. And I wish I could make a good story of it and say he is no longer violent. . . .

"Who's that crying!" I accuse, lifting my nose like an old war horse.

"Seven he breaking Gay's neck."

So the good story, I say to my junior, must stand by for a while. But I can say he is picking up his words now. Fast.

Dennis is a victim of a respectable, money-making, well-dressed mother who thrashes him, and at five he has already had his first nervous breakdown. "I'm not frightened of anything!" he cries.

"Is Dennis afraid of anything?" I asked his young pretty mother in her big car.

"Dennis? He won't even let the chickens come near him."

"Did you have a dream?" I asked Dennis after his afternoon rest.

"Yes I did."

"Well then . . . where's some chalk and a blackboard?"

Later when I walked that way there was a dreadful brown ghost with purple eyes facing a red alligator on a roadway. I know I have failed with Dennis. I've never had his fear words. His mother has defeated me. During the morning output period—when everyone else is painting, claying, dancing, quarrelling, singing, drawing, talking, writing, or building —Dennis is picking up my things from the floor and straightening the mats . . .

# ACCULTURATION AND LEARNING PROBLEMS

## OF PUERTO RICAN CHILDREN

*Sophie L. Elam*

Many studies have been made and much has been said about the Puerto Rican child in cities. Although there are characteristics common to Puerto Rican children, these are by no means very different from those of other minority and emigrant children in the lower economic range. Problems of acculturation of emigrant groups are not new in our society, but invariably there is an urgency about them which is reflected in the many problems in the school and the community.

Perhaps as we look back at other migrations and note how these have been assimilated it is possible to reflect that people who, like the Puerto Ricans, have recently come out of a rural peasant cultural pattern of living find acculturation more difficult than those who come from an urban center. It may well be that rural peoples tend to be tradition-oriented while those from metropolitan communities are more other-directed so that they more readily respond to the cues available to them in our culture.

Acculturation is basically a problem of accommodation to a whole new set of patterns and being. It is actually the change-over from one culture to another. Culture is primarily a learning which is begun at birth and which provides the base for living. It permeates all behavior, from the simple fundamentals of eating and dressing and talking to the more complex and involved patterns of communication, use of symbols, and the development of a value system. Culture is also considered to be a deter-minant of the way one perceives oneself and others. It involves the totality of living from the biological to the social and intellectual. And the greatest

From *Teachers College Record*, **61** (February, 1960), 258–264. Reprinted by permission of the author and *Teachers College Record*.

complexity of the adjustment lies largely on the social sphere. ". . . under situations of stress or strain, of rapid change and consequent disorientation there is likely to be an increase in manifest ill health."[1]

Despite the vast network of our communications in mass media each emigrant group maintains almost intact its social constructs. For the adult who is already completely oriented to a way of life and whose whole gamut of responses is organized around the expected cues in his culture, the transition is difficult enough. He must select from the new what has resemblance to the familiar and add to this repertoire by trial and error the new learnings as they are needed. He tends to remain in his own ethnic and cultural clusters, both in industry and in neighborhood living, as witness the conclaves of Puerto Ricans in our cities.

But for the child who is still in the process of learning his social role and the inherent responses, the transition—often in only a few hours from the known to the unknown; from the simple to the complex environment; from rural areas to the cosmopolitan city—creates an even greater problem. It is the children who manifest the greatest degree of maladjustment.[2]

When the culture process is interrupted or suddenly changed, learning seems to cease. The new setting often destroys the foundations of security. It is, therefore, little wonder that the child who is an emigrant has not completely learned the culture of the land of origin before he is thrust into the new world with a brand-new set of learning conditions to deal with. He is also usually the child of a family that is socially and economically disadvantaged and is therefore heir to all the insecurity, fears, and instabilities of our society to a larger degree than others. Both he and the adults in his family pursue a day-to-day existence with the attendant problems of inadequate housing, clothing, and nourishment. His parents too are caught in the crosscurrents of adjustment: to find jobs though they may be unskilled; to find housing at a cost they can afford when there is little available; to hold onto their own culture in a setting which neither understands nor is able to accept.

The Puerto Rican child is thus caught between the two cultures, that of his people and the one which he must meet every day in the school. Sometimes he must respond to one that contradicts his own. The little girl who has been compliant is now expected to be active and responsive, to take the initiative, to face new people and situations on her own. In the schoolroom she is expected to talk and play with boys and to socialize more freely with her peers. There are rewards in our culture for this, but when she goes home she is forbidden to go out on the street to play. At home there is no reward for enterprising deeds, but rather the awaited and

[1] Margaret Mead, *Cultural Patterns and Technological Change*, New York, Mentor Books, 1955.
[2] *Ibid.*, p. 281.

expected punishment. The emigrant child's age and sex roles and his developmental tasks are not the same as ours. If he adjusts to one, he negates the other, and as a result may lose his sense of identity with his family. The rewards we offer for these "disloyalties" are perhaps not as satisfying, nor can they be easily integrated into the patterns of the home and the other cultures. We do, in fact, tend to create "culture conflict"— the battle of the supremacy of cultures in the family and the clash of roles between parents and children.[3]

Parents play the primary role in transmitting culture to the child. This is part of the socialization process. The child identifies with the parent and internalizes the learnings. In the new environment the parent is no longer in tune with the prevalent culture. He cannot command his child's involvement, since the new society does not value his contribution to the socialization of his own child. The dichotomies and dualisms we create tend to whip the dog we taught to eat.

## I

Such a situation is evident in the story of Ana, the sixth of eight children in a family.[4] She was eight years old when she came to the mainland. Ana's mother is the strong and managing figure in the family—a traditional Puerto Rican mother who holds her daughters in rigid control. They are not allowed out on the streets; they must not talk to other people, particularly boys. Even the older girls are kept in this strict regimen. Ana could perhaps have developed some ease in interchange, but the mother's restrictions were so forceful that the girl's only recourse was to deny all contact. As a result, no one was able to reach out to Ana. She went on to junior high school, where she is barely passing. In addition, she has developed even more reticence and isolates herself. She has frequent headaches and stomach upsets, and is absent from school very often.

This is a rather extreme example of the frequently found conflict in social roles particularly in reference to the upbringing of girls. Since the neighborhoods in which these families settle are often socially disorganized, there is a kind of justification for the fears of the parents which further constrict the life of the girls and the younger children. It is important in working with Puerto Rican parents to help them find ways to protect their children without completely depriving them of social interchange. However, the traditions are so firmly imbedded in the structure of their living that this is difficult to achieve. It is equally difficult to help growing

[3] *Ibid.*, p. 254.
[4] The cases described below are derived from the operation of a training program for undergraduates in Education at the City College of New York. Students serve as leaders for groups of children in a community group work program. The names of all cases described here are fictitious.

children find the channel between outright rebellion and complete submission. Hence they live in an atmosphere of conflict and indecision. It is at this point that they either compliantly submit and lose the ability to relate to their own peer group, or completely leave their families and join the peer group, thereby losing the support which they still need so much.

The language disability which pervades all these problems is very real. It is also a measure of the emotional stability of the person at this time of pressure. The differential rates of language learning are not only the result of age differentials and intelligence levels (the younger child learning more rapidly than the older and the brighter child learning faster than the duller), but also cues to the general level of the individual's emotional adjustment and the resolution of cultural identification and conflicts. Language is one of the tools for learning which the emigrant child lacks. He is left with only the cues he can obtain from nonverbal communication; the expressive gestures which may convey some meaning for him. Here too, however, a facial expression or a gesture may mean something else to him, since gestures are also a language and are richly colored by each culture with specific meanings. Meanwhile he must manage without the necessary cues for directing his behavior.

As a result of these handicaps the child begins to feel inadequate. He cannot solve all the problems of adjustment to a new land, new language, new living, and new culture. He cannot seek support from his parents since they too are faced with the identical problems and with the added responsibility of founding their families in this new land. Therefore, if the child fails he suffers further indignity. He may reason that it is better not to try. Then one has not failed. Or better still, it is possible to remain so indifferent, uninvolved, and apathetic that one evades all responsibility for functioning in a setting fraught with failure and with many demands that one cannot meet.[5] This kind of "culture shock" is frequently found in great or small degree in many of our children and families.

The school is brought face to face with all these problems. There may be some variation in the nature of these difficulties in different families or individuals, but the total problem is present in every child the school works with who has recently arrived from Puerto Rico. Neither the school nor the teacher has been trained to see behavior in the light of these causes. Rather, they tend to meet each situation separately either as a discipline question or as an education problem. Our training practices in education have dealt chiefly with the child who is native to our land and has no outstanding language problem. The child of the lower economic and social strata is also rarely dealt with in our academic courses. Most of our textbooks are written by middle-class professors for middle-class teachers

[5] A. Anastasi and F. A. Cordova, "Some Effects of Bilingualism upon the Intelligence Test Performance of Puerto Rican Children in New York City," *Journal of Educational Psychology*, **44**, 1–19.

of middle-class children. We tend to think of education as primarily establishing literacy and the ability to deal with the daily technics of middle-class living in urban centers.

Education, although drawn from many other disciplines, for a long time tended to ignore the findings in anthropology, social psychology, and clinical psychology. Or at least it has not found a way to integrate these findings into the educational and developmental sequence usually taught in the teacher-preparation courses. We tend to divide sharply our disciplines at the college level, thus making it more difficult to provide an inter-disciplinary approach to problems that the school faces. It seems hardly necessary to point out that if we are to work with a large number of children from a given culture we must, at the very least, learn something of the specifics of that culture, and of how it pervades the entire personality and its perceptions in new situations. Learning how Puerto Rican children dance or play ball or count in Spanish will not make the teacher aware of how Puerto Rican children view their inadequacy in learning the funda-mentals of arithmetic or how and why it is so difficult for them to retain the fact that three and four are seven or remember that our *j* does not sound like *h*. There needs to be rather the concept of *"fundamental education* to cover the whole of living; to teach not only new ways but the need and the incentive for new ways."[6]

How does it feel to be unable to comprehend the cues in this new setting? How does it feel not to understand what people are saying? How do anxiety and insecurity affect a child's readiness to learn? How do people acquire a new culture without stress and destruction to their sense of well-being? The findings and skills of anthropology, sociology, and social and clinical psychology will help us to interpret this kind of defeat and better still to learn to look for these problems. They will perhaps also sharpen our focus and help us find the educational methods which are best employed for reaching these children who really so desperately want to achieve. The individual caught in the maelstrom of conflicting cultures and feelings can be helped to move from inadequacy and near panic (as in "culture shock") to independence and courage.

## II

In our work we encounter many children who reflect these problems. Rafael, a boy of two, saw his father migrate to the States. His mother left when he was three. When he was four his younger sister was sent to the mainland to join the family. He and his grandmother lived in Puerto Rico until he was seven. All these years of separation seemed to have given him the feeling of being unwanted. When he arrived here his mother was again

[6] Margaret Mead, *op cit.*, p. 253.

unavailable to him, since she worked long hours away from home. During his first two years in this country he made few friends, and seemed to his teacher unable to learn. Carmen, his younger sister, was much more competent than he, and carried on much of the interchange for him and other members of the family with the new and strange world. Rafael was frequently sick and remained at home with his old grandmother to care for him. In the third year of his stay he seemed able to come to terms with his new country—to emerge from his chrysalis. Now he is lively and takes an interest in what goes on around him. He greets adults and children alike with warmth and friendliness, and his work at school has begun to show the real potential that he possesses.

Elsa is another child who experienced the privation of her mother's departure. When Elsa was two, her mother left for the United States, leaving her children to the care of their maternal grandmother. At three Elsa was brought to the mainland, but since her mother was working, the children were left in the care of a woman living in the same apartment house. Elsa's initial adjustment to school was so poor that when she was in the second grade the school notified the mother that something had to be done. The child was hyperactive, inattentive, and created too much distraction in the classroom. The mother sent Elsa back to Puerto Rico to live with an aunt for a year. When Elsa returned, her adjustment to school, and her learning achievement were no better. At this time Elsa is being referred to a child guidance clinic.

These are only two cases among the many which we encounter in the schools. The pattern of emigration here depicted is usual in the Puerto Rican family. Early deprivation of the mother creates social and emotional problems which are very difficult to overcome, even with care and concern by the school and other agencies.

Many Puerto Rican children arrive after a period of separation from their mothers or both parents. Thus the emotional concomitants are disabling before the schools in this country even begin to work with the children. Exploration of conditions in each of the new families might alert the schools to the problems and perhaps gear the school situation to help these children. The syndrome of this difficulty has already been fully described by such writers in this field as John Bowlby and Lauretta Bender. It includes a range of behavior: apathy, lack of social responsiveness, depressed intellectual functioning (discussed by William Goldfarb), inability to form meaningful relationships, hyperactivity, aggression, and lowered intellectual potential.

## III

The Alvarez family present a different picture, yet it also has within it all the problems of adjustment to a new environment. There were four children in this family, who lived originally in a rural community on the island. The father worked in the sugar cane fields; they had a small house, a cow, and chickens. Miguel, the father, migrated to the United States eight years ago. Two years later, Rosa, the mother, leaving the children on the island, came to set up the new home. After a few months of separation, all the children were brought to the mainland.

The father had no skills, but he found employment as a dishwasher and has remained in that work. He is always employed but does not earn enough to care fully for his growing family. Two children were born here and the entire family lives in a partly furnished apartment (they have never been able to save enough to buy the requisite furniture). The Department of Public Welfare helps to subsidize the family, but even with this help the budget is too small to provide adequate bed linen, blankets, and warm winter clothing. All the children are slender and the school records indicate poor nutrition for all the school-age children.

Frequently the members of the family are prey to the upper respiratory illnesses so common to Puerto Rican families. Maria, the thirteen-year-old daughter must then remain at home to help care for the mother and children. She had so many absences from school that the teachers complained they could not really help her.

Maria is a tall, stoop-shouldered girl with large dark eyes, pale olive skin, and a slow, hesitant manner. She attended an after-school club program for three years but always remained on the outskirts of the group, although nearly all the club members are of Puerto Rican background. She uttered hardly a word. When she was ten Maria had the first of a series of minor epileptic attacks and is now attending the Seizure Clinic regularly. (This is another common ailment among newly emigrant families, who refer to this illness as "attaques." It may be another manifestation of the somatic effects of the stress in adjustment.)

Maria has repeated the sixth grade and even now has achieved a reading level of only third grade. Her ability in mathematics is even lower than her reading level. This girl saw herself as completely inadequate in every aspect of her living. She never undertook anything for fear of failure. It was only after a year of intensive work with Maria and her family, using nearly every resource in the community, that Maria gained any sense of competence.

There were many health problems in the family for which nursing, nutritional guidance, and hospital care had to be obtained. Fortunately, though the mother speaks no English and is completely illiterate, she is deeply concerned for her children, has much warmth and affection to give, and is eager to help her family adjust to the new environment. She is able to overcome the traditional patterns and encourages Irma to participate in clubs and activities.

The problem of family finances was partially solved by additional funds allotted for special diets for several of the children. The family was encouraged to make application for public housing. The social service resources were made available for Maria by the Catholic Big Sisters, and Maria is now assured of a permanent relationship to meet her emotional needs.

A special program was set up to give Maria opportunities for relationships with children in the group club program, and a special worker was assigned to act in a supportive role for the child as she began to make the transition to active participation. A remedial program in reading was also arranged. From the start it was felt that Maria had much more potential than her low I.Q. indicated. She seemed quite creative with art materials. As all this enrichment was made available she began to awake from her long passive role and to look out and see people. She clamored for help in her school work; she wanted to achieve. She began to take a more active role with her peers. Even her slow, hesitant manner and walk changed. She ran now and jumped; she had a close friend and she had abandoned her role on the periphery of the group.

Although there are still many problems in the Alvarez family and Maria has a long way to go, we have already some sense of the potential of the child and the possibility that she can move more rapidly now toward the achievement of a large part of that potential. She will probably never achieve all that is possible for her. But having studied Maria we can continue with the other children and help each one of them. They are younger and there may be a better chance to bring to fruition more of their potential. Perhaps the second generation of this family will achieve greater self-actualization.

The school has to meet the needs of many children: now it is the Puerto Rican child, as it was once the Irish, the Italian, the Jewish children in other tides of emigration. In each child there will be problems which stand in the way of learning. It is only as the school and the community come to know the family and its needs that these newcomers can be helped. It will be through the school, together with many other agencies and with a view to the totality of the child and his family, that the acculturation will come about.

# VERBAL COMPREHENSION AND COMMUNICATION IN NEGRO AND WHITE CHILDREN

*A. S. Carson and A. I. Rabin*

Comparisons of intellectual functioning in Negroes and whites have been of concern to research workers for some time. The classical review and summary by Klineberg (1935) is not yet outdated. For the most part, the superiority of the whites, especially on verbal tasks, has been demonstrated. However, the improvement in intelligence test scores of Negro children who migrated to the North from Southern states has also been shown. Moreover, the degree of improvement tends to be related to duration of residence in the North.

Performance tasks which correlate highly with "general intelligence", such as the Goodenough Draw-A-Man I.Q. Test, have not yielded significant differences between Negro and white children (Anastasi and D'Angelo, 1952). It would appear that tasks requiring verbal comprehension and verbal expression are the ones that are to a large extent responsible for the significant differences between the groups.

The present study is concerned with the investigation of these two functions, comprehension and expression or communication, in Negro and white children. We propose to study these functions separately, and in relation to each other, in Southern and Northern Negro, and in Northern white, children. Our prediction was, in consonance with previous related findings, that when groups are matched for age, grade placement, sex, and level of verbal comprehension, the white children will be superior to the Southern and Northern Negroes in verbal communication; also, that

From *Journal of Educational Psychology*, **51** (1960), 47–51. Reprinted by permission of the authors and the *Journal of Educational Psychology*. Based on master's thesis (Carson, 1959) submitted to the Department of Psychology, Michigan State University by A. S. Carson and supervised by A. I. Rabin.

the Northern Negro children will be superior to the Southern Negro children on measures of verbal communication.

## METHOD

The Full Range Picture Vocabulary Test (Ammons and Ammons, 1949) was selected as the method of determining the level of verbal comprehension. This test requires no verbal response from the subjects ($S$). It consists of a series of cards with several pictures on each card. The $S$ is merely required to point to the specific picture each time the examiner reads a word from the vocabulary test.

Two measures of verbal communication were employed for comparative purposes. First, the WISC Vocabulary (Weschsler, 1949) was presented in the standard manner and the responses scored as provided in the manual. Second, the words of the Full-Range Picture Vocabulary Test (FRPVT) which were "defined" by gesticulation were presented as a conventional vocabulary test, requiring oral definition.

The conventional scoring of vocabulary tests is an "all or none" affair. No provisions are made for qualitative differences in definitions or in levels of abstraction, precision and communication. This lack of sensitivity in the conventional scoring of vocabulary tests has been pointed out long ago by Yacorzynski (1940).

In order to provide for scoring of levels of communication with the vocabulary of the FRPVT, an adaptation of a method reported in the literature (Rabin, King and Ehrmann, 1955) was utilized. A description of this Qualitative Vocabulary Scale, of the categories of responses and definitions of the word "wagon" as illustrative of the levels of communication appear below.

Class 1. *Categorization and Synonym*

*a. Categorization.* The categorization responses classified by some definite scheme in terms of its universal characteristics.

Response—"a vehicle"

*b. Synonym.* The synonym response may essentially be used to replace the object or idea with no or little change in the denotative aspects of the stimulus word.

Response—"a cart"

Class 2. *Essential Description.* An essential description response must give the characterizing features of the stimulus word. If the stimulus word is abstract, the response must create mental imagery of the relevant situation. If the stimulus word is concrete (physically tangible), the response must differentiate between the stimulus word and members in its class.

> Response—"It's a wooden thing with 4 wheels,
> and it looks like a box."

Class 3. *Essential Function*. An essential function response must describe primary rather than peripheral usage or purpose of an object or an idea.

> Response—"You ride in it out West."

Class 4. *Example*. An example response defines an object or idea in terms of its aspects or members.

> Response—"There's a red wagon kids play with."

Class 5. *Vague Description and Vague Function*

*a. Vague Description*. A vague description is a response that is not totally irrelevant but does not give the characterizing features of the object or idea.

> Response—"Something that has four wheels."

*b. Vague Function*. A vague function response describes the peripheral rather than primary usage or purpose of the object or the idea.

> Response—"It bumps into people."

Class 6. *Error*. The error response is totally irrelevant to the stimulus word.

> Response—"The dog 'wagons' his tail."

Class. 7. *Don't Know*. A "don't know" response is a statement or a lack of statement designating that the S is unable to verbally define a word *which he had previously designated recognition* for by a gesticulation response.

> Response—"Don't know."

## Subjects

The Ss were Southern Negro (SN), Northern Negro (NN) and Northern white (NW) children in the fourth, fifth, and sixth grades. None of the Ss was advanced or behind in his age-grade placement. The SN group comprised all of the Negro children within the age range from 9.5 to 11.5 years who were born and reared in the South and had migrated to Lansing, Michigan within 28 months of the date tested. All of the NW and NN children were born and reared in Ingham County, Michigan. Data was collected on the occupational levels of the NW and NN children in accordance with the *Dictionary of Occupational Titles* (United States Government Printing Office, 1944) classification. Two of the main wage earners in the NW children's families were professional, technical, or managerial workers, 4 were clerical or sales workers, 3 were service employees, 9 were mechanical workers, and 12 were manual laborers; respectively, there were 0, 5, 2, 5, and 18 NN main wage earners. It may be noted that the occupational levels of main wage earners from the two samples are similar. Due to the recent relocation of the SN families, the main wage earners' vocations were unsettled and therefore unavailable as data.

Children were tested with the FRPVT at random from the NW and NN groups in order to acquire Ss whose scores could be individually matched

Table 1—Grade, Sex, Age, and Mean Picture Vocabulary Test Scores of the Three Groups

| GROUP | N | GRADE | | | SEX | | AGES (MONTHS) | | RAW SCORE OF FRPVT | |
|---|---|---|---|---|---|---|---|---|---|---|
| | | 4th | 5th | 6th | Male | Female | Mean | SD | Mean | SD |
| NW | 30 | 16 | 8 | 6 | 16 | 14 | 128 | 10.9 | 43.67 | 4.95 |
| NN | 30 | 16 | 8 | 6 | 15 | 15 | 125 | 10.9 | 43.57 | 5.74 |
| SN | 30 | 16 | 8 | 6 | 14 | 16 | 128 | 13.5 | 43.53 | 5.21 |

with the scores of children in the SN group. Table 1 summarizes relevant data for the three groups of children.

## PROCEDURE

The FRPVT and the two oral vocabulary devices were administered individually to the Ss by the same examiner in single testing sessions. The SN children were tested first, followed by random testing of NN and NW children who would qualify for the respective samples. When each SN child was matched with a NW and NN child in terms of the FRPVT scores, the testing was discontinued.

Two independent scorers tallied verbal responses to the FRPVT. These responses were scored according to the classification system described above. The total percentage of interscorer agreement was .79. Complete agreement between the two scorers was obtained after the debatable responses were discussed.

## RESULTS AND DISCUSSION

As a preliminary step in the treatment of the data, all Ss were classified into "high" and "low" responders. The Ss whose majority of responses were tallied in categories 1, 2 and 3 were placed in the former classification; the predominance of the remaining four categories characterized the second group. Table 2 reports the incidence of members of each sample in the "high" and "low" categories. The differences in the distribution are statistically significant.

As predicted, the white children assume the top position. It is also interesting to note that the NN group place in an intermediate position between the white and SN children.

The responses of the three groups were also compared on each of the seven categories comprising our qualitative (levels of communication) scoring system. Table 3 summarizes the levels of significance of the differences between the groups computed by means of the Wilcoxon matched-pairs signed-rank test (Siegel, 1956). Thirteen of the 21 comparisons were significant in the predicted direction. The table indicates that the general prediction is supported to a considerable degree. This is especially true with the extremes of the qualitative categories.

*Table 2*—A Comparison of the Incidence of High and Low Responders on the Qualitative Vocabulary Scale in the Three Groups

| Group | High | Low | $x^2$ | $p$[1] |
|---|---|---|---|---|
| NW | 25 | 5 | | |
| NN | 18 | 12 | | |
| SN | 7 | 23 | 22.54 | < .001 |

[1] One-tailed test.

*Table 3*—Summary of Levels of Significance Obtained from Comparisons of Ranks on the Qualitative Vocabulary Scale

| | Groups | | | | | | | | | | | |
|---|---|---|---|---|---|---|---|---|---|---|---|---|
| | NW vs. SN (T) (T') | | | | NW vs. NN (T) (T') | | | | NN vs. SN (T) (T') | | | |
| Class | T | T' | g | p | T | T' | g | p | T | T' | g | p |
| 1 | 271.0 | 29.0 | 3.44 | <.0005 | 289.0 | 62.0 | 2.87 | <.0025 | 181.0 | 72.0 | 1.76 | <.05 |
| 2 | 327.5 | 107.5 | 2.36 | <.01 | 283.5 | 122.5 | 1.82 | <.05 | 206.5 | 171.5 | .41 | ns |
| 3 | 350.0 | 85.0 | 2.85 | <.0005 | 233.0 | 118.0 | 1.45 | ns | 326.0 | 139.0 | 1.91 | <.05 |
| 4 | 274.5 | 160.5 | 1.22 | ns | 126.5 | 198.5 | .82 | ns | 301.0 | 105.0 | 2.22 | <.025[1] |
| 5 | 154.5 | 223.5 | .82 | ns | 147.0 | 231.0 | 1.00 | ns | 202.5 | 203.5 | .00 | ns |
| 6 | 34.5 | 316.5 | 3.57 | <.0005 | 57.5 | 218.5 | 2.43 | <.01 | 55.5 | 295.5 | 3.04 | <.0025 |
| 7 | 3.0 | 432.0 | 4.63 | <.0001 | 95.5 | 229.5 | 1.79 | <.05 | 40.5 | 394.5 | 3.82 | <.0005 |

[1] If a two-tailed test were employed, the difference would have been significant in a direction contrary to the current hypothesis.

*Table 4*—Summary of Comparisons of Ranks on the WISC Vocabulary Subtest

| | TOTAL RANKS | | | THEORETICAL | | | |
|---|---|---|---|---|---|---|---|
| Comparisons | NW | NN | SN | Mean | SD | g | Significance |
| NW vs. SN | 432.0 | — | 3.0 | 217.5 | 46.25 | 4.62 | < .0001 |
| NN vs. SN | — | 345.5 | 60.6 | 203.0 | 43.92 | 3.24 | < .001 |
| NW vs. NN | 334.0 | 101.0 | — | 217.5 | 46.25 | 2.51 | < .01 |

The results of the study demonstrated that NW children, of comparable non-verbal word recognition (or comprehension) abilities, manifest higher levels of verbal communication than NN children, and, in turn, the NN children manifest higher levels of verbal communication than SN children.

All comparisons by means of the WISC vocabulary subtest yield significant differences in the predicted direction (using Wilcoxon's test mentioned above).

Again, global vocabulary scores, as in the case of the more refined treatment of the FRPVT, indicate the superiority of the white children compared with the two Negro samples. Also, the NN group is inferior to the NW but superior to the SN children. This finding is consistent with the results in the previous two tables.

The children's pattern of responding is interesting in that it was unique for each of the groups and may therefore be a clue to differences in characteristic thinking among the three groups. The NW children favor the higher levels of verbal communication (Classes 1, 2, 3). Their percentage of responses decreases sharply in the Example classification and after a slight increase in the Vague classification, their percentage of responses continues to decrease lower than that of the two Negro groups in the Error and Don't Know classifications. NN children favor the Vague type response and manifest a greater percentage of Error type responses than white children. The SN children's pattern is the only one which manifests a high peak in the Don't Know classification.

The differences among the groups cannot be consistently explained according to one theoretical viewpoint. Differences between the NW and NN children could lend support to the contention that constitutional racial differences in intelligence exist or to the viewpoint that a difference of cultural opportunities accounts for the variance between racial groups. However, there are sufficient possibilities of differences in the cultural milieu of the two samples to question their equivalence of social opportunities. The two groups remain segregated from each other in activities other than those which revolve around school. The NN sample, for the most part, lives in a section of town which is a homogeneous Negro settlement. Their cultural milieu is definitely not characteristic of white middle-class modes of living.

The comparisons of the NN and SN children lend themselves to a more clear-cut interpretation since the cultural variable of geographical residence was considered in the experimental design. It is contended that the superior educational environment and the greater opportunity for cultural advancement of the NN child over the SN child accounts for the significant differences between the two groups.

The present study supports Klineberg's (1947) research findings that geographical residency of the Negro child is an important determinant of vocabulary performance. Coppinger and Ammons' (1952) contention that different norms should be utilized when making intergroup comparisons involving Negroes where the members of the groups have different cultural backgrounds is also supported.

Finally, it should be pointed out that verbal comprehension and verbal communication seem to be two different functions. Although the groups were equated on comprehension, they showed marked differences with respect to communication. The former task requires recognition within a certain context, which is quite different from verbal communication and definition of a word in isolation, and not in context. It would appear that differences between Negroes and whites on conventional intelligence tests, and especially on vocabulary sub-tests, may be primarily due to failure in verbal communication rather than in comprehension.

## SUMMARY

Three groups (30 in each group) of NW, NN, and SN school children, matched for age, sex, grade placement, and level of verbal comprehension, were compared on two vocabulary tests requiring verbal communication. In accord with the original prediction, the white children were superior to the Negro children, and the NN children were superior to the SN children on these two measures. The results were discussed in relation to the possible racial and cultural geographic factors involved.

References to *Verbal Comprehension and Communication in Negro and White Children*

R. B. Ammons and H. S. Ammons, "The Full-Range Picture Vocabulary Test," *American Psychologist*, 1949, **4**, 267–268.

Ann Anastasi and Rita Y. D'Angelo, "A Comparison of Negro and White Pre-school Children in Language Development and Goodenough Draw-A-Man IQ," *Journal of Genetic Psychology*, 1952, **81**, 147–165.

A. S. Carson, "Verbal Comprehension and Verbal Communication in Negro and White Children." Unpublished master's thesis, Michigan State University, 1959.

N. W. Coppinger and R. B. Ammons, "The Full-Range Picture Vocabulary Test: VIII. A Normative Study of Negro Children," *Journal of Clinical Psychology*, 1952, **8**, 136–140.

O. Klineberg, *Race Differences*, New York, Harper, 1935.

——— "Negro Intelligence and Urban Residence," in T. M. Newcomb and E. L. Hartley (eds.), *Readings in Social Psychology*, New York, Holt, 1947, pp. 24–32.

A. I. Rabin, G. F. King, and J. C. Ehrmann, "Vocabulary Performance of Short-term and Long-term Schizophrenics," *Journal of Abnormal and Social Psychology*, 1955, **50**, 255–258.

S. Siegel, *Nonparametric Statistics for the Behavioral Sciences*. New York: McGraw-Hill, 1956.

United States Government Printing Office, Division of Occupational Analysis. *Dictionary of Occupational Titles*. Part IV. Washington, D.C.: Author, 1944.

D. Wechsler, *Wechsler Intelligence Scale for Children*, New York, Psychological Corp., 1949.

G. K. Yacorzynski, "An Evaluation of the Postulates Underlying the Babcock Deterioration Test," *Psychological Bulletin*, 1940, **37**, 425–426. (Abstract.)

# SOCIAL STRUCTURE, LANGUAGE,

# AND LEARNING

*Basil Bernstein*

No one in his right mind would plan an educational program without taking into account the age of the pupils, their levels of maturity, intellectual and emotional, their interests and, of course, their social background. However, the extent to which we take account of these factors varies, and of equal importance is how we take account of them. It is the contention of this paper that we have failed to think through systematically the relationship between the pupil's background and the educational measures appropriate to successful learning. This is not to say that we have no information. Many researches have shown a relationship between a bit of the child and a bit of education. Often the teacher becomes the same person as the researcher at a later point in time, but it seems that we are still engaged in psychological or sociological matching.

Although training colleges are aware of the importance of the pupil's social background and sociology is accepted as an important part of teacher training, there is little sign that an educational program has been systematically thought through for the pupil whose origins are lower working class—approximately 29 per cent of the population. This does not mean that we do not possess an armory of visual aids, folk dancing, guitar playing, or text books for the slow but "normal" learner. The teacher does not lack advice on problems of discipline, from the suggestion that "louts should teach louts" to "from innocence to experience: without the aid of the cane." Some think it is simply a matter of class size and fail to see that it may be a question of which sized class for which particular

From *Educational Research*, **3** (June 1961), 1–15. Reprinted by permission of the author, the National Foundation for Educational Research, and their publishers, Messrs. Newnes Educational Publishing Co., Ltd.

134

group of normal children. A few pieces of contemporary research have indicated that it is equivocal to suggest that size of class matters; and yet we have no criterion by which to judge what constitutes a significant difference in size. Is it a drop in number from forty to thirty or a reduction to fifteen? Is it perhaps of greater importance whether the pupils come from the middle or lower working-class?

The general problems involved in teaching children from the lower working class relative to those from the middle class, are not necessarily problems of teaching children who differ in an innate capacity to learn, as indicated by tests of intelligence. In fact, the evidence indicates that there must be a greater absolute number of children with very high intelligence in the lower than in the higher social groups.[1] What is of greater interest is that there appears to be in different social groups a particular and different relationship between scores on group verbal and non-verbal tests (for example, the Mill Hill Vocabulary Test and Raven's Progressive Matrices). In lower working-class groups the verbal scores are grossly depressed in relation to the scores at the higher levels of the non-verbal test. The scores on the verbal test of the majority of children from this group tend to fall within the average range of the test while the scores on the non-verbal test tend to yield a normal curve of distribution skewed to the right, that is, in the direction of the highest scores.

Educational performance as judged by attainment in class is related to the scores on the group verbal test. A fairly consistent pattern emerges that reveals that as the boys' scores move towards the highest points possible on the non-verbal test, the gap between the scores on the two types of test widens. As the present writer found, differences here are of the order of 20+ I.Q. points. In a sample of pupils attending a famous public[2] school this relationship, found in the working class, was not present. The depressed scores on the verbal test for those working-class boys who have very high non-verbal scores could be expected in terms of the linguistic deprivation experienced in their social background. This raises the question of the relationships between potential and developed intelligence and education.

In the light of what we know from much research, we can suggest a pattern of difficulties that the lower working-class pupil experiences in trying to cope with education as it is given in our schools. This pattern will not hold in precise detail for every pupil, but we can say that the probability of finding such a pattern is greater if the pupil's origin is lower working class. Such children will experience difficulty in learning to read, in extending their vocabulary, and in learning to use a wide range of

[1] The statement refers to the *total* number of manual workers (the customary working-class group), *not* to the lower working class considered as a sub-group.
[2] In Britain, public school refers to a private institution as we know it in the United States.

formal possibilities for the organization of verbal meaning; their reading and writing will be slow and will tend to be associated with a concrete, activity-dominated, content; their powers of verbal comprehension will be limited; grammar and syntax will pass them by, the propositions they use will suffer from a large measure of dislocation; their verbal planning function will be restricted; their thinking will tend to be rigid—the number of new relationships available to them will be very limited.

In arithmetic they may master the mechanical operations involved in addition, subtraction, and multiplication, provided they have also mastered their tables, but they will have some difficulty with division. However, verbal problems based upon these operations may confuse them. They will have great difficulty in ordering the verbal argument before applying the operations. They will tend to learn a particular set of operations in relation to a discrete context and they will have difficulty in generalizing the operations to a wide range of contexts. Their conception of number will be restricted. As the progression shifts from the mechanical application of fractions and simple percentages to relatively more sophisticated expressions, their lack of understanding of arithmetical processes will be revealed. Ratio may well be a point in the gradient of difficulty that they are unable to pass. As they develop, failure in their basic understanding will limit what they can do despite persistence and application.

Their time-span of attention will be brief, thereby creating the problem of holding and sustaining attention. They are not interested in following the detailed implications of a concept or object and the matrix of relationships that this involves; rather they are disposed toward a cursory examination of a series of different things. Their interest in *processes*, even those linked to their everyday experience, is limited. As soon as the formal dimension of the process is reached they begin to be uneasy. The interval between feeling and doing is short and facilitates the acting out of impulse behavior. Their curiosity is limited, which removes an important dynamic from learning. They tend to require a very clearcut educational experience with little ambiguity in direction and content. They are highly suspicious of anything that does not look like education as they traditionally conceive it. In the short run, democratic appeals are less successful than dictatorial edicts.

Although the pupil may pass the primary stage without a great sense of unease, the discrepancy between what he is called upon to do and what he can do widens considerably at the secondary level. The character of the educational process changes at this level. It becomes increasingly analytic and relies on the progressive exploitation of what Piaget calls *formal* operations, whereas the lower working-class pupils are more likely to be restricted to *concrete* operations. Finally, and with somewhat less confidence, we may say that there is a general flatness in their overall educational achievements in the basic subjects. Although there may be one or two small peaks, in the main such pupils are confined to the average level. It is, I suggest, a peculiarly undifferentiated educational performance.

No mention has been made—deliberately—of the reduced motivation to learn, of the lack of involvement in the means and ends of education, of the standardized reactions, which are an unhappy defense against the despair and failure that school symbolizes, and the problems of discipline that are so generated. The central problem for the lower working-class child is, primarily, that of learning *how* to learn and secondly, that of learning *what* has to be learned. To make the educational experience happy and contented is not necessarily to solve the problems of learning, if this is achieved through by-passing the problem and playing directly into a concrete perceptual set—as is done by much use of concrete and visual material. Sometimes class control is considered as a substitute, instead of a condition, for learning. The problem, however, is not how to get the pupil interested but what to do after his interest has been elicited.

There is, of course, a wide range of individual differences and, it must be expected, such patterns will not be found with all children of the particular social background under discussion; nor are these patterns confined to such pupils. It is suggested, however, that there is a higher expectation of finding this pattern of educational performance with the social group mentioned than with others.

How does this happen? What is the most important single factor in a boy's history, which generates this consistency of emotional and intellectual behavior in the learning situation? It is not good enough to say that he thinks descriptively and is insensitive to abstract formulations, that he is concerned with substance rather than process, or, on a more sociological level, that there exists a clash in values between the school and the home, that the orientation of education is middle-class. These, and many others, are descriptive statements, that describe differences between some part of the boy and some part of the school. The question raised here is a dynamic one. How does the boy become like this and what is the main agency through which this becoming is facilitated and reinforced?

I suggest that forms of spoken language induce in their learning orientations to particular orders of learning and condition different dimensions of relevance. Teachers, research workers, and educationalists have all commented on the limited linguistic skill and vocabulary of lower working-class pupils and the difficulty of sustaining and eliciting adequate communication.

It is therefore not new to focus upon the use of language as judged by educational criteria. Nisbet thought that part of the negative correlation between family size and I.Q. was the result of the type of speech model made available to the child. He considered that this linguistic limitation effected in some way a general cognitive impoverishment. Mitchell (on the basis of an analysis of a battery of tests given to children of high and low social status) found that the verbal meaning and fluency scores for the low-status children could be used to predict their scores on a range of different factors. In this group there was a lack of differentiation among a number of functions, whereas for the high-status group there was considerable differentiation. Studies reported by McCarthy, of children in the special environments of residential institutions, indicate that they suffer a grave language deficiency and that their powers of abstraction are often impaired.

Luria and Yudovitch recently studied identical twins who were grossly retarded in speech for non-organic reasons. The twins were subjected to experimental changes in their environment and the speech changes subsequent to this were noted. It was found that the twin who had received special language training was able to operate more efficiently in his environment through the development of discursive operations that were not available to the twin who had received no training and who acted as a control. These studies and others point to the critical role of the spoken language in the process by which the child achieves selfregulation. Of particular interest is the relationship between forms of spoken language and the mode of selfregulation. It is the nature of this interrelation I want to consider and its educational implications.

There is little doubt that the social form of a relationship acts selectively on the mode and the content of the communication. The language of the child in a group of other children (as shown by the Opies) is very different in structure and content from that he uses when speaking to an adult. Similarly the spoken language of combat units in the armed services is different from that normally used in civilian life. Vigotsky maintained that the more the subject of a dialogue is held in common, the more probable it is that the speech will be condensed and abbreviated. For example, we may think of the communication pattern between a married couple of long standing or that between old friends. In these relationships, meaning does not have to be made fully explicit; a slight shift of pitch and stress, a small gesture can convey a complex meaning. Communication goes forward against a backcloth of closely shared identifications and affective empathy that removes the need for elaborate verbal expression.

This communion of the spirit, which underlies and conditions the form of the communication, may render what is actually said gravely misleading to an observer who does not share the history of the relationship. The how of the communication is heavily burdened with implicit meanings. Some of the verbal meanings are restricted and not elaborated. The observer will be struck by the measure of his own exclusion and this will be reinforced by the expressive intimacy, vitality, and warmth that accompanies what is said. The content is likely to be concrete and descriptive rather than analytical and abstract. The backcloth of closely shared identifications that create empathy gives to the speech sequences, from the point of view of the observer, a large measure of dislocation. The dialogue appears somewhat disjunctive because of the logical breaks which interrupt the flow of information.

What is the effect on behavior if this form of spoken language is the only one that individuals have at their disposal? What are the implications if individuals are unused to signaling meaning unless it is against a background of common and closely held identification whose nature has rarely, if ever, been verbally elaborated and made explicit? What is the result of learning to operate with restricted speech structures where the burden of meaning may lie not so much in what is said, but in how it is said; where language is used not to signal and symbolize fairly and explicitly individual separateness and difference, but to increase consensus? This does not mean that no disagreements will take place. What does it mean in terms of verbal conceptual growth if speech is only, or mainly, used in circumstances where the intent of the other person may be taken for granted and no pressure induces the need to create speech specially to fit the needs of those outside the group who do not share its experience? What happens to verbal development when the number of situations that serve as stimuli for verbalization is restricted by the conditions and form of the social relationships?

It is suggested that this is the situation in which many children of the lower working class grow up. Their society is limited to a form of spoken language in which complex verbal procedures are made irrelevant by the system of non-verbal, closely shared, identifications that serve as a back-cloth to the speech. The form of the social relationship acts selectively on language potential. Verbalization is limited and organized by means of a narrow range of formal possibilities. These restricted formal strategies for the sustained organization of verbal meaning are capable of solving a comparatively small number of linguistic problems, yet, for this social group they are the *only* means of solving every verbal problem requiring a sustained response. It is not a question of *vocabulary*; it is a matter of the *means* available for the organization of meaning, and these means are a function of a *special type of social relationship*. The size of the vocabulary is a function of other variables as will be shown: it is a symptom but not a cause of the speech form, although in its own right it acts as a reinforcing agency.

The linguistic relationship between the lower working-class mother and her child is such that little pressure is placed upon the child to verbalize in a way that signals and symbolizes his unique experience. The *I* of the mother, the way she organizes and qualifies her experience, will be transmitted to the child not through evoking speech which is specially cut for this purpose. Spoken language is not perceived as a major vehicle for presenting to others the inner states of the speaker. What can be said is limited by the rigid possibilities for verbal organization. Such a system is a combination of non-verbal signals with a particular structure of verbal signals that originally elicits, and later reinforces, a preference in the child for a special type of social relationship, which is limited in terms of verbal explicitness and relies heavily on a pattern of non-verbal signals. The *I* of the lower working-class mother is not, relatively, a verbally differentiated *I*.

The shift of emphasis from non-verbal to verbal signals in the middle-class mother–child relationship occurs earlier and the pattern of the verbal signals is far more elaborate (Bernstein 1961). Inherent in the middle-class linguistic relationship is a pressure to verbalize feeling in a relatively individual manner and this process is guided by a speech model that regularly and consistently makes available to the child the formal means whereby this process is facilitated.

It can be said that for the middle-class child there is a progressive development towards verbalizing and making explicit subjective intent, while this is *not* the case for the working-class child. This is not necessarily the result of a deficiency of intelligence, but comes about as a consequence of the social relationship acting through the linguistic medium. It is through this developing medium that the child learns to internalize his social structure. His environment, and what is significant in his environment, is taken into himself to become the substratum of his consciousness by means of linguistic processing. And every time he speaks, his social structure is selectively reinforced. This does not deny the role of non-verbal learning, but I suggest that even here, from an early age, the effects are fed through language and are stabilized by language. As speech marks out a pattern of stimuli to which the child adapts in the learning of this pattern, his perception is organized, structured, and reinforced. The adequacy of his response is rewarded or punished by the adult model until the child is able to regulate his responses independently of the adult. In this way the outside gets into the inside from the very beginnings of speech. The appropriateness of the child's behavior is thus conditioned to a wide variety of contexts by means of the vehicle of communication.

The lower working-class child learns a form of language that symbolizes the normative arrangements of a local group rather than the individuated experience of each of its members. The form of the communication reinforces the pattern of social relationships but fails to induce in the child a need to create speech that uniquely fits his experience. Luria has suggested that speech may be considered as a complex of additional signals that leads to marked changes in the field of stimuli. It isolates, abstracts, and generalizes perceived signals and relates them to certain categories. Speech becomes a major means of selectively reinforcing perceptions. In the context of this discussion, forms of spoken language mark out what is relevant affectively, cognitively, and socially, and experience is transformed by that which is made relevant.

What is made relevant by the form of lower working-class speech is markedly different from that which is made relevant by the form of middle-class speech. The experience of children from these gross strata follows different paths from the very beginnings of speech. The type of learning, the conditions of learning, and the dimensions of relevance initiated and sustained by the spoken language are completely different. In fact, it would not be too much to say that in strategic respects they are antithetical. The behavior of the children is regulated accordingly to separate and distinct principles. They have learned two different forms of spoken language; the only thing they have in common is that the words are English.

At this point a rather more rigorous definition is necessary of the two linguistic forms that, it is suggested, become the major instruments of initiating and sustaining the socialization process. The linguistic forms associated with the lower working-class I shall call a *public* language. Here it should be remembered that there will not be a one-to-one relationship between the lower working-class and this form of spoken language but the probability of its use is certainly very high. With this in mind, we may dispense with social class concepts and refer to types of spoken language and the behavior sustained by them. Operationally, it is more accurate to use the linguistic forms to distinguish the groups than to use a particular class affiliation.

A public language is a form of language use that can be marked off from other forms by the rigidity of its syntax and the restricted use of formal possibilities for verbal organization. It is a form of relatively condensed speech in which certain meanings are restricted and the possibility of elaboration reduced. In this case speech does not become the object of perceptual activity, neither is a theoretical attitude adopted to sentence organization. While it may not be possible to predict any one content of this language, the formal organization and syntax is predictable for any one individual. The class of the content is also predictable. The characteristics of a public language are as follows:

*1]* Short, grammatically simple, often unfinished sentences with a poor syntactical form stressing the active voice.

*2]* Simple and repetitive use of conjunctions (so, then, because).

*3]* Little use of subordinate clauses to break down the initial categories of the dominant subject.

*4]* Inability to hold a formal subject through a speech sequence; thus a dislocated informational content is facilitated.

*5]* Rigid and limited use of adjectives and adverbs.

*6]* Constraint on the self-reference pronoun; frequent use of personal pronoun.

*7]* Frequent use of statements where the reason and conclusion are confounded to produce a categoric statement.

8] A large number of statements/phrases which signal a requirement for the previous speech sequence to be reinforced: "Wouldn't it? You see? You know?" etc. This process is termed "sympathetic circularity."

9] Individual selection from a group of idiomatic phrases or sequences will frequently occur.

10] The individual qualification is implicit in the sentence organization. It is a language of implicit meaning.

A *formal* language is one in which the formal possibilities and syntax are much less predictable for any one individual and the formal possibilities for sentence organization are used to clarify meaning and make it explicit. The person, when he speaks a *public* language, operates within a mode of speech in which individual selection and permutation are grossly restricted. In the case of a formal language, the speaker is able to make highly individual selection and permutation. Of course, a formal-language speaker does not always do this, but the possibility always exists for him. The characteristics of a formal language are:

1] Accurate grammatical order and syntax regulate what is said.

2] Logical modifications and stress are mediated through a grammatically complex sentence construction, especially through the use of a range of conjunctions and subordinate clauses.

3] Frequent use of prepositions that indicate logical relationships as well as prepositions that indicate temporal and spatial contiguity.

4] Frequent use of the personal pronoun *I*.

5] A discriminative selection from a range of adjectives and adverbs.

6] Individual qualification is verbally mediated through the structure and relationships within and between sentences.

7] Expressive symbolism discriminates between meanings within speech sequences rather than reinforcing dominant words or phrases, or accompanying the sequence in a diffuse, generalized manner.

8] It is a language use that points to the possibilities inherent in a complex conceptual hierarchy for the organizing of experience.

These characteristics must be considered to give a direction to the organization of thinking and feeling rather than to the establishing of complex modes of relationships. The characteristics are relative to those of a public language.

Each of these two sets of criteria refers to an ideal linguistic structure, but what will be found empirically is an orientation to this or that form of language use. It is clear that some of these characteristics will occur in most forms of language use, but a public language is a form of usage in which all the relevant characteristics will be found. It is possible to consider approximations to a public language to the extent that other characteristics are not found. Although any one example of a public language will be associated with a particular vocabulary and sequence frequency, it is worthwhile emphasizing that the definition and characterization are independent of content. Here we are concerned with the implications of a general mode, not with the isolated significance of particular words or speech sequences. This is not to suggest that middle-class children are the only ones oriented to a formal language, but the probability is certainly higher for this group. Neither do such children learn only a formal language. The mode of speech used can and does, in most cases, vary according to the type of social relationship involved. The speech behavior of middle-class children, or for that matter children from any class, will in the peer group approximate to a public language, and will tend to release behavior regulated by the form of speech. Middle-class children will have access to both forms, which will be used according to the social context. This will lead to an appropriateness of behavior in a wide range of social contexts. Other children, a goodly proportion of the total population in this and other countries, are likely to be restricted to one form, a public language. This will be the only form known: the only one that can be used.

Some of the implications of this restricted form of linguistic behavior have a bearing on the educational picture described at the beginning of this discussion. Because of the simple, often broken, sentence structure and the rigid range of formal possibilities available, a public language will be one in which logical modification and stress can only be crudely rendered linguistically. This necessarily affects the length and type of the completed thought. Of equal importance, the verbal planning function is shortened. The shortening of this function often creates, in sustained speech sequences, a large measure of dislocation or disjunction. The thoughts are strung together somewhat like beads on a frame rather than following each other in a planned sequence. The restricted verbal planning function also creates a high degree of redundancy, by which is meant a large measure of repetition of information or sequences that add little to what has previously been given. This is vividly illustrated by the two transcripts of tape-recorded discussion which follow:

It's all according like these youths and that if they get into these gangs and that they most have a bit of a nark around and say it goes wrong and that and they probably knock someone off I mean think they just do it to be big getting publicity here and there.
    Age 16. I.Q. Verbal 104; Non-Verbal 100.
Well it should do but it don't seem to nowadays, like there's still murders going on now, any minute now or something like that they get people don't care they might get away with it then they all try it and it might leak out one might tell his mates that he's killed someone it might leak out like it might get around he gets hung for it like that.
    Age 17. I.Q. Verbal 99; Non-verbal 126+.

As there is a limited and rigid use of individual qualifiers, the adjectives and verbs function as social counters through which the individual qualification will be made. This drastically reduces the verbal elaboration of the qualification that is given meaning by expressive signals. This does not mean that the gross number of adjectives and adverbs in speech samples taken from the two linguistic forms will differ very much but that the range will in one case be restricted. The qualifiers will be drawn from a lexicon commonly held, and (as it were) slotted into position, rather than being individually selected for a specific purpose. In this sense the qualification tends to be impersonal. Ongoing research tends to indicate that adjectives and verbs used in formal language speech samples from subjects matched for age and very high non-verbal I.Q. with public language subjects, are only rarely not present in the active or passive vocabulary of the public language speakers. Feeling, then, is differentiated by referents which are the result of shared conditioning.

A public language is a vehicle for expressing and receiving concrete, global, descriptive relationships organized within a relatively low level of conceptualization. The words and speech sequences refer to a broad class of contents rather than to progressive differentiation within a class. The reverse of this is also possible: a range of items within a class may be specified without knowledge of the concept that summarizes the class. The categories referred to tend not to be broken down systematically, and this has critical implications if the reference designated is a subjective state of the speaker. Despite the warmth and vitality, which is an expressive correlate of the language, it tends to be impersonal in the literal sense of the word. The original linguistic relationship between mother and child exerts no pressure on the child to make his experience explicit in a verbally differentiated way. It is perfectly possible, despite a restricted vocabulary, to create speech that fits individuated experience, but the orientation induced by this mode of communication does not make such characterization appropriate.

The mode of speech, itself, will elicit and reinforce a special affective or emotional correlate. The speech delivery within a normal environment outside the classroom tends to be composed of fast, fluent, short, relatively unpaused utterances. Affect (expressive signals) is not used to discriminate finely among meanings carried within a speech sequence; rather it is used to reinforce dominant words or phrases, or it accompanies the utterance in a diffuse manner. The feelings of the child would seem to be, relatively, undifferentiated for two reasons: Feeling is not differentiated, stabilized, and made specific by linkage through language to a wide range of referents; Secondly, feeling that is regulated by the speech is conditioned by the form of the language. It is a vehicle for expressing concrete, direct, activity-dominated verbal sequences. It reinforces a relationship of immediacy with the environment. The gap between feeling and doing may well be brief. It should be unnecessary to add this, but nothing that has been said should be taken to mean that the natural feelings of sympathy, generosity, kindness, and warmth are not to be found, equally present, in all social groups.

A public language focuses upon the inhibiting function of speech by directing (the attention of the observer) towards potential referents that carry no stimulus value for the speaker. Inasmuch as a public language induces in the user a sensitivity towards the concrete here and now— towards the direct, immediate, the descriptive, the global—then the dimensions of relevance will tend to preclude responses to other patterns of stimuli. Thus an orientation toward a particular type of learning under particular conditions is also involved. An example of this inhibiting function would also illustrate the significance of the seventh characteristic of the language. It was suggested that there would be frequent use of statements in which the reason and the conclusion are confounded to produce a categoric sequence.

Imagine the following two conversations on a bus. A mother has a child sitting on her lap:

MOTHER: Hold on tight.
CHILD:   Why?
MOTHER: Hold on tight.
CHILD:   Why?
MOTHER: You'll fall.
CHILD:   Why?
MOTHER: I told you to hold on tight, didn't I?

MOTHER: Hold on tightly, darling.
CHILD:   Why?
MOTHER: If you don't you will be thrown forward and then you'll fall.
CHILD:   Why?
MOTHER: Because if the bus suddenly stops you'll jerk forward onto the seat in front.
CHILD:   Why?
MOTHER: Now hold on tightly darling and don't make such a fuss.

In the first example a whole range of potential learning and connections have been cut out by the categoric statement. The natural curiosity of the child has been blunted. There is no causal chain between the mother's request and the child's expected response. The change in the behavior has been brought about by a process akin to verbal conditioning rather than through instrumental learning. If the child challenges the statement, then in a short period he is challenging the *right* of the mother to issue the request; that is, he is challenging the authority that inheres in the status of the mother. The potential social power in the form of the relation is revealed very quickly.

In the second example the child is exposed to an area of connection and sequence. If this is challenged, then another set of reasons are elicited. Of course, after a time the categoric statement is applied, but an order of learning has been made available in between. It should be noted that as a result of the linguistically elaborated relationship, the initial challenges are of the reasons given to support the request. The challenge of the mother comes much *later* in the relationship and the latent social power is revealed later *and* under different conditions. If the categoric statement is used frequently in a public language, then it limits learning and curiosity and induces a sensitivity towards a particular type of authority in which social power is quickly and nakedly revealed. The categoric statement becomes part of a language that narrows the range of stimuli to which the child responds. The length of this example also indicates how difficult it is to give concrete illustrations in a short paper.

An important psychological correlate of a public language is that it tends to discourage the experience of guilt. However, strong feelings of loyalty and responsibility to and for the local group will exist. Earlier it was suggested that the verbalizing of subjective states, particularly of motivation, is not highly relevant. This implies that the referents of these states are not selectively reinforced by language. Koln has drawn attention to the fact that middle-class parents are more likely to respond in terms of the child's intent in acting as he does, while working-class parents are more likely to respond in terms of the immediate consequence. Thus the working-class parent is responsive to ends directed to inhibiting disobedient or disreputable acts, while the middle-class parent is responsive to intent and acts with reference to individualized standards. Simply, there is little talking through of acts which require disciplinary measures in working-class homes, little verbal investigation of motive.

The rational control and manipulation of induced guilt are major means available to the middle-class mother for disciplining the child. These means reinforce the individualizing process in the child and transfer attention from consequence, or result, to intent; from the act to the processes underlying the act. This is not the case for a child whose mother speaks a public language. In this case behavior is more likely to be made subordinate to shame. Shame indicates a diminution of respect accorded to conduct by a group. Of course, the middle-class child is sensitive to feelings of shame; the point is that he is also sensitive to guilt.

A public language-user will be aware that an act is wrong or that punishment is just, but feelings of guilt will tend to be divorced from the notion of wrongness. This would seem to make more likely the reoccurrence of the behavior and to create a particular attitude to the punishment. It is not for one moment suggested that because motivational processes are verbally available to an individual, they, in themselves, will always inhibit an action, only that the action would be accompanied by psychological states that might not be present if a child spoke a public language. There is a tendency for this to be recognized. Punishment of a public language-user in a school will frequently tend to be corporal, threatened or actual, because it is hard to elicit a sense of guilt or a sense of personal involvement in the act. Though caning, etc., does exist in public schools where a formal language is spoken, other methods are also used to modify behavior. With a formal language-user, punishment can involve a temporary rejection, or talking through of the misdemeanor aimed at increasing the experience of guilt responsibility, and so of personal involvement. Attempts to interchange the means of social control may lead at first to many difficulties. This is *not* to be taken to mean that corporal punishment is necessarily an effective means of social control. Where it is used as a substitute for the real difficulty of making a social relationship, it is rarely effective.

This rather difficult argument has tried to make clear how learning may be conditioned where the only language of the child is public. In the learning of this linguistic form, the child is progressively oriented to a relatively low level of conceptualization. It induces a lack of interest in processes, a preference to be aroused by and respond to that which is immediately given, rather than responding to the implications of a matrix of relationships. Such an orientation partly conditions the intensity and extent of curiosity, as well as the mode of establishing relationships. In turn, this will affect what is learned and how it is learned and so influence future learning. There will be a tendency to accept and respond to an authority that inheres in the form of the social relationship rather than in reasoned principles. It fosters a form of social relationship that maximizes identifications with the aims and principles of a local group rather than with the complex differentiated aims of the wider society. Finally and of the greatest importance, it is a language of implicit meaning in which it becomes progressively more difficult to make explicit, and to elaborate verbally, subjective intent.

This behavior is all of one piece and is maintained as a relatively "steady state" by protective devices built into the language system. Perhaps the most important of these protective devices is that a formal language (as used, for example, by the teachers) will be mediated through the public language. In the process of mediation, any alternative orientation that would sensitize the listener to a different dimension of significance is neutralized. Where a translation cannot be made, there is no communication. The public language tends to inhibit the verbal expression—and hence the learning attendant on such expression—of those experiences of separateness and difference that would isolate the speaker from his group. It channels cognitive and affective states which, if expressed, might constitute a threat to the equilibrium. For example, curiosity is limited and focused by the relatively low level of conceptualization. The restricted planning function and the concern with the immediate, tend to make difficult the development of a reflective experience. There is a tendency, too, to shift responsibility from self to the environment and this further reinforces the rigidity of the behavior.

## CONCLUSION

It can be seen that attempts to change the system of spoken language of children from certain environments will meet with great resistance, passive and active. It represents an attempt to change a pattern of learning, a system of orientation, which language originally elicited and progressively reinforced. To ask the pupil to use language differently, to qualify verbally his individual experience, to expand his vocabulary—to increase the length of his verbal planning function, to generalize, to be sensitive to the implications of number, to order a verbally presented arithmetic problem—these requests when made to a public language-user are very different from when they are made to a formal language-user. For the latter it is a situation of linguistic development while for the former it is one of linguistic change. Two different psychological states underlie these situations. The public language speaker is called upon to make responses to which he is neither oriented nor sensitized. His natural responses are unacceptable. It is a bewildering, perplexing, isolated, and utterly defenseless position that ensures almost certain failure unless the teacher is very sensitive to the child's fundamental predicament.

This is by no means to say that a public language-speaking pupil cannot learn. He can, but it tends to be mechanical learning and once the stimuli cease to be regularly enforced, there is a high probability of the pupil forgetting. In a sense, it is as if the learning never really gets inside to become integrated into pre-existing schemata. In fact, it looks as if this is so, for unlike the formal language-oriented pupil, the public language pupil lacks these receptive schemata or, if he possesses them, they are weakly organized and unstable.

The very conditions of the classroom situation often make effective education impossible. Large classes reduce the possibility of individual teaching and increase the probability of impersonal authoritarian methods of class control, which in turn increase the passivity of the pupil. If the teacher avoids this by small group techniques, inevitably he adds to his fatigue and in the long run may reduce his efficiency. There is a case for a general rule: the lower the status of the pupil, the smaller should be the number in the class. Expensive as this may seem at first sight, it might be economical in the long run. A small class is the basic condition for a close psychological relationship (interpersonal rather than intergroup) between teacher and pupil. The social organization must enable the person, as well as the function, of the teacher to be felt and perceived. In an important sense, the teacher of a class of public language speakers is much more exposed, psychologically, if he is to teach efficiently. He cannot retreat into his formal role and impersonalize his communication. This does not mean that the appropriate teaching situation is one of "all pals together." Nor does it require teachers who can "speak the language." In this respect there are only two types of teachers: those who can and those who cannot.

This is not the time to discuss techniques, but perhaps it might be possible to seek agreement about the nature and ramifications of the educational problem. Although it appears very similar, the backwardness presented by the public language pupil is different in its dynamic form from that of the pupil whose backwardness is the result of psychological factors. That of the former is a culturally induced backwardness transmitted and sustained through the effects of linguistic processing. The relationship, it is suggested, between potential and developed intelligence is mediated through a language system that encourages insensitivity to the *means* whereby the pupil's dimensions of relevance may be expanded and enhanced. It follows also that the condition progressively worsens over the years. As the educational process becomes more analytic and relatively abstract at the secondary level, the discrepancy between what the pupil can do and what he is called upon to do is painfully revealed.

A public language speaker has at his disposal a vast range of potential responses. His behavior is by no means standardized. The general cognitive impoverishment is an impoverishment only from the point of view of the educator and, of course, it deprives society of potential talent. However, it is a form of language that symbolizes a tradition where the individual is treated as an end in himself, not as a means to a further end. It psychologically unites the speaker to his kin and, on a sociological level, to his group. It should not be undervalued. Under the most hopeful circumstances, the educational process increases the risk of the speaker's alienation from his origins. The task would seem to be to preserve for the speaker the dignity that inheres in his language, its powerful forthrightness and vitality, but to make available also the possibilities inherent in a formal language. We must be very sure that the new dimensions of relevance made available do not also include the measuring of human worth on a scale of purely occupational achievement.

References to *Social Structure, Language, and Learning*

B. Bernstein, "Some Sociological Determinants of Perception," *British Journal of Sociology*, **9** (1958), 159–174.
——— "Language and Social Class," *British Journal of Sociology*, **11** (1960), 271–276.
——— "Social Class and Linguistic Development: a Theory of Social Learning," in J. Floud, A. H. Halsey, and A. Anderson (eds.), *Education, Economy, and Society*, New York, Free Press, 1961.
M. L. Koln, "Social Class and Parental Authority," *American Sociological Review*, **24** (1959), 352–366.
——— "Social Class and Parental Values," *American Journal of Sociology*, **64** (1959), 337–351.

A. R. Luria and Ia Yudovitch, *Speech and the Development of Mental Processes in the Child*, London, Staples Press, 1959.
———— *Speech and Regulation of Behaviour*, London, Pergamon Press, 1961.
D. McCarthy, "Language Development in Children," in *Manual of Child Psychology*, L. Carmichael (ed.), New York, Wiley and Sons; London, Chapman and Hall Ltd., 1954.
J. V. Mitchell, Jr., "A Comparison of the Factorial Structure of Cognitive Functions for a High and Low Status Group," *Journal of Educational Research*, **47** (1956), 397–414.
J. D. Nisbet, "Family Environment," in *Occasional Papers on Eugenics*, No. 8. London Eugenics Society.
I. Opie and P. Opie, *The Lore and Language of School Children*, Oxford, Clare, 1959.
L. S. Vigotsky, "Thought and Speech," *Psychiatry*, **2** (1939), 29–54.

## POSTSCRIPT, SEPTEMBER 1961

### *Elaborated and Restricted Codes: A Note on Verbal Planning*

I think it is possible to present the ideas developed in previous papers in a more economic and general manner. The concepts *public* and *formal* are not good analytic distinctions, they operate at too low a level of abstraction and they are probably semantically confusing. They will be replaced by the terms *elaborated* and *restricted* codes.

The two codes may be distinguished on the linguistic level in terms of the probabilities of predicting for any one speaker which structural elements will be used to organize meaning. In the case of an elaborated code, the speaker will select from a relatively extensive range of alternatives, therefore the probability of predicting the pattern of organizing elements is considerably reduced. If the speaker is using a restricted code then the number of these alternatives is severely limited and the probability of predicting the pattern is greatly increased.

On a psychological level the codes may be distinguished in terms of the extent to which each facilitates or inhibits the orientation to symbolize intent in a verbally explicit form. Behavior processed by these codes will develop different modes of self-regulation and thus different forms of orientation.

The codes themselves are functions of particular forms of social relationships, or more generally, qualities of social structures.

The *pure* form of a restricted code would be one where the lexicon is wholly predictable and, therefore, also the organizing structure. Examples of this pure form would be ritualistic modes of communication. An actor, also, would be using a pure form of a restricted code, although from the point of view of the audience it would be an elaborated code. In fact his success in the role would depend on maintaining these two definitions. It is clear that in the pure form of the restricted code individual intent can

only be signalled through the non-verbal components of the communication, i.e., intonation, stress, expressive features, etc.

In contemporary society what is found more often is a restricted code
where prediction is only possible on the structural level. The simplification
of structural alternatives is a function of the shared identifications that
create the form of the social relationship. This reduces the tension to
verbalize intent and make it explicit. Expressive features again will carry
much of the burden of changes in meaning.

A limiting case of a restricted code is one where the user is linguistically
wholly constrained by the code. This is the condition that corresponds to
the analysis of a public language.

The following model and a brief analysis may be helpful in drawing
attention to the relationships between these codes and to verbal plannings
and modes of orientation.

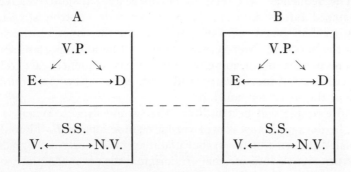

In this model, below the line represents the signal store in which
interrelated verbal and non-verbal signals are contained. Above the line,
$E$ and $D$ represent the usual encoding and decoding processes controlled
and integrated by the verbal planning function ($V.P.$).

When $A$ signals to $B$ I suggest that at least the following takes place:

*Orientation:*     $B$ scans the incoming message for a pattern of dominant
signals. (This is the beginning of the verbal planning
sequence.)

*Association:*     Associations to the pattern of dominant signals control
↑           selection from the signal store ($V.$ plus $N.V.$).

*Selection*
↓

*Organization:* Organization and integration of signals ($V.$ plus $N.V.$)
to produce a sequential reply.

The term code as I use it implies the principles which regulate these
three processes. It follows that restricted and elaborate codes will establish

different kinds of control which crystallise in the nature of verbal planning. The latter is a resultant of the conditions that establish the patterns of orientation, association, and organisation. The originating determinants of this trio would be the form of the social relationship or, more generally, the quality of the social structure. This would allow the following postulate: The form of the social relationship acts selectively on the type of code which then becomes a symbolic expression of the relationship *and* proceeds to regulate the nature of the interaction. Simply, the *consequences* of the form of the social relationship are transmitted and sustained by the code on a psychological level. Strategic learning would be elicited, sustained and generalised by the code which would mark out *what* has to be learned and would constrain the *conditions* of successful learning.

I should like to indicate very briefly four aspects of verbal planning control where the code is restricted.

(1) The sequences will tend to be dislocated, disjunctive, relatively well-organized but with relatively poor syntactic control, stressing the active rather than the passive voice, and point to the concrete, the descriptive, and the narrative. Non-verbal signals will be an important source of significant changes in meaning as the verbal sequences are relatively impersonal, i.e., not individuated and serve as social symbols reinforcing the form of the social relationship.

(2) An example will best indicate the second aspect. When $A$ meets $B$ whom he does not know $A$ will yet have some idea of $B$. This idea will be translated in terms of the verbal planning of $A$'s original signals to $B$. If $B$'s return signals indicate that $A$'s original idea is inadequate, or, perhaps, inappropriate, $A$ will modify his idea and through verbal planning control send different signals and note $B$'s response. After an interval some type of equilibrium regulating the relationship will have become established with occasional fluctuations damped down by feed-back achieved via verbal planning control, $V.P.$—transmission—return signals—check—verbal planning—transmission. By this process $A$ will have internalised the "requirements" of $B$ via speech. If the code is restricted, by definition, so is verbal planning consequently the range and type of others who can be so internalised is limited. By implication the social tie to those who can be so becomes a very powerful bond which is both positively and negatively strengthened by the code.

(3) The third aspect relates to problem solving and the role of speech in orientating and thus changing the quality of the environment for the speaker.

As the problem to be solved moves in the direction of the relatively abstract it is likely that inner verbal sequences will be evolved (not necessarily throat movements, perhaps below the threshold of incipient articulation) which will proceed to orient the thinker and change the quality of the signals responded to in the environment. When the thinker is limited to a restricted code the verbal sequences evoked may direct perception to the more gross aspects of the environment and so his solution will become more and more inappropriate in direct relation to the degree of abstraction of the problem. This verbal feedback in some problem solving activities will be continuously reinforced. The bond relating the thinker to the concrete and descriptive will becomes progressively tighter with the cumulative effect of the use of the restricted code.

(4) The fourth aspect refers to the time dimension of verbal planning; that is to the delay between impulse and signalling.*

If the speaker can use, or is oriented to, an elaborate code he can tolerate the tension associated with delay in selection. Subsequent signalling is likely to be more appropriate and the tension will be reduced by the appropriateness of the signals. In this way (delay→tension→appropriate signalling→reduction in tension↔reinforcement of the total sequence), a channel for the reduction of tension through verbal control is facilitated with the continued use of an elaborate code.

In a restricted code the delay between impulse and signal will be shorter in a normal environment. Raising the level of coding difficulty, thus increasing the delay potential, may lead to a break-down in signalling or the signalling may not adjust to the new demands. The first solution results in a total drop in output; the second *avoids* increasing the delay between impulse and signal. Either way the code does not facilitate the toleration of tension and the reduction of tension by appropriate signalling. In a restricted code the channel for the release of tension will tend to be through changes in somato-motor and expressive sets.

* The measures for this are the mean pause duration per word per utterance and the frequency of pauses greater than 0.25 seconds.

### Further References to *Social Structure, Language and Learning*

B. Bernstein, "Linguistic Codes, Hesitation Phenomena, and Intelligence," *Language and Speech*, **5** (1962), 31–46.
—— "Social Class, Linguistic Codes, and Grammatical Elements," *Language and Speech*, **5** (1962), 221–240.
—— "A Socio-Linguistic Approach to Social Learning," in J. Gould (ed.), *Penguin Survey of the Social Sciences*, Baltimore, Penguin Books, 1964.
E. Goldman-Eisler, "Hesitation and Information in Speech," in C. Cherry (ed)., *Speech in Information Theory*, London, 1961.
K. Lashley, "The Problem of Serial Order in Behaviour," in *Cerebral Mechanisms in Behaviour*, New York, 1951.
D. Lawton, "Social Class Differences in Language Development," *Language and Speech*, **6** (1963), 120–143.
—— "Social Class Language Differences in Group Discussions," *Language and Speech*, **7** (1964).
F. Reissman, *The Culturally Deprived Child*, New York, Harper and Row, 1962.

# SOCIAL CLASS AND THE NATURE OF THE

# INCENTIVE IN DISCRIMINATION LEARNING

*Glenn Terrell, Jr., Kathryn Durkin, and Melvyn Wiesley*

Previous research has suggested interesting differences in the relative effectiveness of material and nonmaterial incentives for children of different social-class backgrounds. In an experiment involving the solution of a series of tasks, Douvan (1956) found that middle-class subjects (*S*s) maintained approximately the same level of achievement motivation when told they had reached a norm as when they were promised a sum of money. The motivation of lower-class *S*s, on the other hand, dropped significantly when the material reward was absent. Terrell and Kennedy (1957) found that children, a preponderance of whom were from a rural background, require significantly more trials to learn a "larger-than" response when given only a light flash as an indication of a correct response than when given a series of material incentives, including candy, praise, token, and reproof. In a similar experiment performed with middle-class children, Terrell (1958) found that children assigned to the light flash condition learned somewhat faster than those who received candy.

From the foregoing, it would be predicted that an interaction exists between social class and the nature of the incentive. Specifically, it was believed that a nonmaterial incentive is as effective as a material incentive for middle-class *S*s, whereas, for lower-class *S*s a material incentive is more effective than a nonmaterial one. The present experiment was designed to test this belief. It is important to note that while Douvan studied the relationship between these variables using a measure of motivation as a criterion variable, this paper is a report of a discrimination learning experiment, involving an acquisition measure as a dependent variable.

From *Journal of Abnormal and Social Psychology*, **59** (1959), 270–272. Reprinted by permission of the authors and the *Journal of Abnormal and Social Psychology*.

154

METHOD

*Subjects.* There were 12 *S*s in each of the following age categories: 5-, 6-, 10-, and 11-year-olds, with an equal number of boys and girls in each age group. The school from which *S*s for this experiment were drawn very appropriately contains children from a wide variety of social-class backgrounds. Warner's Index of Status Characteristics (Warner, Meeker and Eels, 1949) was the measure used to define class position. In the present study, all *S*s designated as middle class fell into either the upper-middle or the lower-middle classes of Warner's schema, while *S*s with scores placing them in Warner's upper-lower and lower-lower classes constituted the lower class.

*Materials.* The apparatus for the problem has been described in detail elsewhere (Terrell, 1957). There were three pairs of three-dimensional geometric figures in the shape of cubes, cones, and cylinders. The small members of each stimulus set had a basal area of 4 square inches, while the large number had a basal area of 8 square inches. These stimuli are hereafter referred to as the training stimulus sets. A third cube with a basal area of 16 square inches was used in a transposition test, along with the 8 square inch cube. These stimuli are hereafter referred to as the test stimuli. The order of presenting the stimuli and the position of the positive, large-size, stimulus were randomized alike for each *S*.

Additional apparatus consisted of a $16 \times 24 \times 4$ inch box which contained the batteries and circuits necessary to operate a signal light. Two jacks and two push button mounts were on top of the box. The stimuli were placed into the jacks on each trial. Locked onto the rear edge of the box was a $10 \times 16 \times \frac{1}{4}$ inch panel board which contained the signal light. The circuits were arranged so that a correct response, pushing the button at the base of the large stimulus, caused the light to go on.

*Design.* There were two experimental groups. Following each correct response, one group of *S*s received a nonmaterial reward, a light flash, while the *S*s of the other group received a material reward, a small piece of candy in addition to the light flash. Within each of the two levels of social class, *S*s were randomly assigned to the two incentive conditions, making a total of 12 *S*s in each treatment-level combination.

*Procedure.* The *S*s were tested individually. Each *S* received the following instructions:

This is a game where I want you to try to choose one of these (*E* points to the training stimulus sets), and push the button in front of the one you choose. If you are right, this little light will go on. If you are wrong, the light will not go on. Now remember, the game is to see how quickly you can learn to choose the one that makes the light go on.

The last sentence was repeated after every tenth trial. Immediately after reaching a criterion of 9 of 10 correct responses, each *S* was given a four-trial transposition test on the test stimuli. The same differential incentive conditions employed during the acquisition trials were continued during the test trials.


## RESULTS AND DISCUSSION

The original design called for an analysis of variance of the mean number of trials to the criterion and mean number of transposition responses. All *S*s except one transposed on every trial, making an analysis of transposition data useless. In the case of the number of trials to the criterion, the homogeneity and normality assumptions were far from met. Also, the criterial means and variances were correlated. For these reasons, it seemed advisable to subject these data to a nonparametric test. Wilson's (1956) chi-square technique makes possible the test of hypotheses concerning main and interaction effects ordinarily tested by a two-way analysis of variance.

*Table 1*—Means and *SD*s of Trials to Criterion in Training
(Each treatment group *N* = 20)

|  | MATERIAL INCENTIVE | | | | | |
|  | PRESENT | | ABSENT | | TOTAL | |
| Class | Mean | SD | M | SD | M | SD |
| Middle | 7.91 | 8.33 | 3.50 | 2.58 | 5.70 | 6.72 |
| Lower | 3.41 | 3.02 | 8.00 | 5.15 | 5.70 | 4.80 |
| Total | 5.66 | 6.66 | 5.75 | 4.65 | | |

*Table 2*—Frequencies Above and Below the Median in Numbers of Trials to Criterion for Each Incentive-Class Combination

|  | INCENTIVE | | | |
|  | MIDDLE CLASS | | LOWER CLASS | |
|  | Material | Non-material | Material | Non-material |
| Above Median | 6 | 7 | 5 | 12 |
| Below Median | 6 | 5 | 7 | 0 |

Table 1 contains the training means and *SD*s. As can be seen from this table, a striking interaction exists between social class and the type of incentive. Middle-class children learn more quickly when given a non-material incentive than when given a material incentive, while the reverse is true of lower-class children. The over-all means for social class are identical, while the difference between over-all incentive means is negligible.

Table 2 contains frequencies above and below the median for each of the incentive-class combinations in number of trials to the criterion. All analyses and subsequent discussion are based on the data of Table 2. The predicted interaction is apparent in this table, and to a significant degree. The chi-square value for interaction is 5.17, which with one degree of freedom reaches significance at about the .03 significance level.[1] The direction of the interaction is the same for ages 5 and 6 as well as for ages 10 and 11. No analyses of interaction effects were made for these ages independently, since the frequencies were very small. The chi-square test for main effects of class was nonsignificant, while the test of main effects of incentive was significant at the .05 level. There was a significant tendency for *S*s assigned to the material incentive condition to learn more quickly than those *S*s assigned to the nonmaterial incentive treatment. This finding is rendered rather meaningless in view of the significant interaction present in this experiment.

Several interesting implications arise from this experiment. There is evidence to indicate that parents of middle-class children place a greater emphasis on learning for learning's sake than do parents of lower-class children (Davis, 1944; Erickson, 1947). Additional evidence in support of this hypothesis was found in the aforementioned experiment by Terrell (1958), in which middle-class *S*s indicated in a questionnaire given to them following the experiment that they would rather "do something for the fun of it" than to be "promised or given something for doing it." It would appear that the most important feature in the learning of middle-class *S*s is merely some indication that they are progressing. It is strikingly apparent in Table 2, however, that the presence of a material incentive is very important to lower-class *S*s. It is possible that the lower-class child is too preoccupied with obtaining the material, day-to-day necessities of life to have the opportunity to learn the value of less material, symbolic incentives. Davis (1941, 1943) suggests such a possibility. Additionally, since it is likely that the lower-class child generally is more deprived of the specific material incentive, candy, used in the present study, this deprivation may result in an intensification of his desire for candy. It would be interesting to know whether or not the same results would be obtained in experiments employing other material incentives such as toys, clothing, movie tickets, and the like.

Finally, there is a possibility that the middle-class child is more adept than the lower-class child at engaging in effective imaginative activity during learning.[2] If this be the case, it would seem that the middle-class child would learn more effectively under a symbolic, nonmaterial type incentive than lower-class children. Research bearing on this point is currently being conducted by the senior author.

---

[1] Yates' correction was applied to the computation of the main effects of social class and incentive conditions.

[2] The writers are indebted to Howard E. Gruber for this interesting suggestion.

References to *Social Class and the Nature of the Incentive in Discrimination Learning*

A. Davis, "American Status Systems and the Socialization of the Child," *American Sociological Review*, **6**, 1941, 345–354.

—— "Child Training and Social Class," in R. G. Barker, J. S. Kounin, and H. F. Wright (eds.), *Child Behavior and Development*, New York, McGraw-Hill, 1943.

—— "Socialization and Adolescent Personality," *Adolescence, Forty-third Yearbook, Part I*, Chicago, National Society for Study of Education, 1944.

E. Douvan, "Social Status and Success Striving," *Journal of Abnormal and Social Psychology*, 1956, **52**, 219–223.

Martha C. Erickson, "Social Status and Child Rearing Practices," in T. M. Newcomb and E. L. Hartley (eds.), *Readings in Social Psychology*, New York, Holt, 1947, pp. 494–501.

G. Terrell, "The Role of Incentive in Discrimination Learning in Children," *Child Development*, 1958, **29**, 231–236.

G. Terrell and W. A. Kennedy, "Discrimination Learning and Transposition in Children as a Function of the Nature of the Reward," *Journal of Experimental Psychology*, 1957, **53**, 257–260.

W. L. Warner, M. Meeker, and K. Eells, *Social Class in America*, Chicago, Science Research Associates, 1949.

K. V. A. Wilson, "Distribution-Free Test of Analysis of Variance Hypotheses," *Psychological Bulletin*, 1956, **53**, 96–101.

# SOCIAL CLASS AND MOTORIC ORIENTATION

*Daniel R. Miller and Guy E. Swanson*

In general, we predicted that boys from the working class would convey ideas most naturally by means of their bodies, but be comparatively inept when asked to express the same ideas conceptually. We thought that middle-class subjects would use conceptual approaches very comfortably, but be relatively inept when required to communicate by physical means.

### The Game of Statues

*Instructions.* To create a natural situation requiring motoric communication, we first saw each boy individually and asked him to play a modified version of the children's game of "statues." First the boy would be turned around. Then he would "freeze" in a pose that depicted an assigned theme. IIe was not to move outside a circle that had been drawn on the floor. We asked him to hold each pose until his picture had been taken.

In a practice session the child was asked to freeze like the statue of a policeman directing traffic. For the experiment proper he portrayed four emotional states: happiness, fear, anger, and sorrow.[1] To make sure that he understood the meaning of each emotion, we illustrated it in terms of a concrete situation. First the boy was told to act "as if you are very, very happy: as if you had just won a million dollars or got the one thing in the world you have always wanted." Next, he was instructed to behave "as if

[1] We chose these emotional states, rather than concrete jobs like swimmer, dancer, or carpenter, because we feared that the latter might be much more familiar to, or have different meanings for, boys in different social classes. Emotional states are well known to everyone.

From *Inner Conflict and Defense* by Daniel R. Miller and Guy E. Swanson (New York: Henry Holt and Co., Inc., Copyright 1960 by Holt, Rinehart, and Winston, Inc.), pp. 341–352. Reprinted by permission.

you are very, very frightened: as if the wall of a building is falling over on you or a tiger is just jumping at you." Then he was told to freeze "as if you were very, very angry: as if you see a boy beating up your little dog, or as if a reckless driver has just missed you with his car." Finally, he was instructed to "behave as if you are in a great deal of sorrow—very, very sad: as if you saved a long time for something you wanted very badly and then lost the money, or as if you just lost your best friend."

*Analyzing Shifts in Position.* We tabulated the frequencies of dilated movements in each child's photographs. Such movements were inferred from shifts from the original position in which he stood upright, facing forward, with his hands at his sides and his feet together. The signs of dilation included a raising of either hand to the height of the waist, both hands to the waist, or one hand to the shoulder. In addition, we tabulated a spreading of the legs, a shifting of the trunk from the vertical position, or a turning from the camera.[2]

*Results.* A person who was unacquainted with our theory and predictions rated each photograph in terms of the six criteria. An analysis of our data reveals that all the differences between middle- and working-class children are in the anticipated direction, and, with one exception, are significant for all criteria of dilation. The exception, which is very close to significant, involves the criterion of vertical position of the body. Table 1, which contains a summary of the major findings concerning social status, reveals that the boys in the two classes also differ on an over-all index of a motoric tendency.[3] There is little question that in the game of statues boys from the working class are more motorically dilated than are our middle-class subjects.

## SOCIAL CLASS AND CONCEPTUAL ORIENTATION

We predicted that a task requiring a conceptual approach would produce a reversal of the previous results. We thought that boys in the middle class would manipulate concepts more easily than would boys in the working class. Before we could test this hypothesis, we had to solve a difficult methodological problem. Most concepts are expressed by means of verbal

---

[2] In the order in which the last three were presented, they were identified by the following criteria: Spread is greater than that required for normal stance and balance; the line perpendicular to the floor does not divide the subject into symmetrical halves; greater parts of top and bottom halves of body are turned from the camera.

[3] To construct the over-all index, we first obtained a distribution of subjects in terms of the number of signs of motoric dilation. Then we divided the boys into three groups. Criteria for membership in the different groups were five signs or more, between two and four signs, and one or no signs.

symbols, but we could not use a verbal test because of the superiority of the middle-class subjects on such instruments. After examining many tasks, we chose two different types. We shall describe the first task, painting,[4] in this section; the second, manual problem-solving, is described in the next section.

### The Painting of Abstractions

*Instructions.* We assembled the children in groups of ten or less in special testing rooms. Each boy sat at a desk on which there were five pots of poster paint—red, orange, blue, green, and black, five sheets of $11\frac{1}{2} \times 16\frac{1}{2}$-inch newsprint, some paint brushes, heavy drawing pencils, a box of crayons, some toothpicks, a toothbrush, and a cup of water. First, we gave him five minutes to paint or draw a theme of his choice. This practice session was intended to familiarize him with the materials and to show him that we would not object to noise or free play during the painting period. After the introductory five-minute period he was told:

Now we are going to do something a little bit different. We are going to do some painting, but you can use the other materials in addition to the paint if you feel like it. I am going to name some things I would like you to paint for me. Paint what you *think* and *feel* about these things. Just use the materials to express the idea or feeling behind the topic. It is not important whether or not anyone will be able to recognize what's in your paintings. It will be like an abstract painting. You don't have to paint the thing the way it may actually look to people. Use the materials to express the feeling or idea behind it.

Then he was asked to portray the same four emotional themes he had expressed in the game of statues.

In what sense can we claim that such a task requires a conceptual orientation? We thought that such an orientation was elicited by the instructions to express the ideas or feelings abstractly. Before the subjects would portray the assigned theme, they had to develop a pictorial concept.

*Analysis.* Guided by literature on the interpretation of artistic productions, we developed six criteria of dilation and constriction. We

---

[4] The choice of painting raised four difficult problems concerning the interpretation of results. First, the middle-class boys might have been trained to paint in nursery school, or they might have had some special instruction elsewhere. Second, we were concerned about the extent to which painting is a motoric act. Upon investigating these two possibilities, we were inclined to dismiss them. We found no differences in training, and observations of the boys during the painting session revealed that almost all movement was confined to digital manipulation of the artistic materials.

It was also possible that boys in the two social classes differed in their information about abstract art. Finally, it could be claimed that middle-class boys have had previous experience with abstraction, so that even if they do not think conceptually, they can grasp the instructions to draw abstractly more readily than can working-class boys. All information pertinent to these interpretations tended to refute them, but we could not reject them with confidence. This is one reason why we later used an additional technique for eliciting a conceptual approach.

assumed that an unconstricted person would employ paint only, portray unrecognizable objects, use four or more colors, and cover most of the paper.[5] If he were constricted, we thought he would outline his shapes with black paint, and that his composition would occupy a small area.[6] A judge with no knowledge of our theory or predictions rated all paintings.

*Results.* With one exception, the differences are in the predicted directions, although the trends are not so marked as those obtained for motoric expression. Two of the six differences are significant, and one is close to significance. Contrary to the prediction, the association between expressive style and the criterion of *paint only* is in the opposite direction from the one predicted. It would have been significant if we had not predicted direction and made two-tailed tests. Whether this result reflects a poor criterion or a contradiction of our hypothesis we cannot say at this point. Boys in the two classes differ very significantly on an over-all index of conceptual orientation.[7]

*Table 1*—Social Class and Expressive Styles of Children and Parents

| Expressive style | Trends: Boxes with greatest frequencies | N | Relation | Probability |
|---|---|---|---|---|
| Over-all motoric tendency in game of statues | WC & most motoric | 99 | .29 ($\tau$) | < .01 (1t) |
| Over-all conceptual tendency in paintings | MC & most conceptual | 99 | .26 ($\tau$) | < .01 (1t) |
| Conceptual tendency in spatial problem | MC & most conceptual | 85 | 8.61 ($\chi^2$) | < .001 (1t) |
| Over-all conceptual-motoric tendency | WC & most motoric; MC & most conceptual | 83 | .37 ($\tau$) | < .001 (1t) |
| Conceptual and motoric tendencies in mothers' reasons for leisure activities | WC & intermediate; MC & conceptual | 117 | .19 ($\tau$) | .02 (1t) |
| Conceptual and motoric tendencies in mothers' lists of satisfactions in jobs | WC & motoric; MC & conceptual | 102 | .37 ($\tau$) | < .001 (1t) |

While the statistics reveal marked differences in motoric and conceptual style, they do not convey the extent of the contrasts observed by members of our staff. In the game of statues the typical working-class boy threw himself into the task with great spontaneity. The middle-class subject, even when his pose was muscular, was often self-conscious. His halting gestures conveyed the impression that he was not accustomed to communicating with his body. Yet once he began to paint, his motoric hesitancy and

[5] The minimal size involved a vertical dimension of at least eight inches and a horizontal dimension of at least ten inches.
[6] The maximal size involved a vertical dimension of five inches and a horizontal dimension of six inches.
[7] To construct this index, we first obtained a distribution of subjects based on the number of signs of conceptual orientation. Then we assigned each boy to one of the three groups. Criteria for membership in these groups were five signs or more, between two and four signs, and one or no signs.

awkwardness usually vanished. When the working-class boy painted he became tentative or complained that he just could not get started.

### A Spatial Problem[8]

We decided to construct one other conceptual instrument, because we felt that the painting test did not have the apparent validity of the game of statues. We also sought another kind of activity, so that we could test the generality of the conceptual orientation. Spatial problems seemed to be the most promising, and we finally decided on a modified version of the Carl Hollow Square Test, an instrument for measuring the subject's speed in fitting three or four blocks into a square frame. There are several problems, each requiring its own combination of blocks. The blocks are triangular, and two of their three dimensions are cut at either 45- or 90-degree angles. Even when given the correct blocks, most boys find them much harder to fit together than they seem at first glance. We increased their difficulty by asking each boy to choose the blocks from a larger group of sixteen.

In giving instructions for the Carl Hollow Square Test, we emphasized the goal of solving the problem: "Now, let's see if you can put the blocks into the square correctly." The score was the total number of different patterns a boy attempted in fifteen minutes. We tabulated an attempt at a pattern if the subject first combined two or more blocks and then inserted them together in the square. We expected that boys from the middle class would assemble more patterns than would boys from the working class.

The results parallel those obtained from the paintings. As indicated in Table 1, boys in the middle class are significantly more conceptual than are boys in the working class. The difference does not result simply from the greater activity of the middle-class subjects. The groups do not differ in the number of blocks picked up. However, in approaching the problem, working-class subjects are likely to fit one block at a time, while middle-class boys are more inclined to work with combinations of two or three.[9]

---

[8] This part of the study was done with the second sample of subjects.

[9] While we were conducting this part of the study we became curious about the extent to which styles of expressive behavior can be deliberately controlled. We anticipated that class differences might disappear if the boys were directed to orient themselves either conceptually or motorically. We used two sets of instructions. One encouraged the subjects to take a conceptual approach: ". . . it helps to work these problems if you spend some time trying to figure out what is the best way to do them . . . this time as long as you are not actually touching the blocks the time won't be up as fast." Another set of instructions encouraged the subjects to be motoric: ". . . you can solve the problem better by trying all the possible ways to fit these together that you can in the time allowed."

On the first trial all the subjects took the test under the goal-oriented condition. On the second trial one half received the instructions emphasizing a conceptual orientation and the other half received the instructions emphasizing a motoric

## SOCIAL CLASS AND INTERESTS

We had to obtain class differences in many different kinds of activities to test the generality of expressive styles. In addition to statues, painting, and problem solving, we chose interests in hobbies, games, and occupations as our final topics.

### Interviews

We gathered our information by interviewing each child in the initial sample. First, we asked him to name his most preferred activities and hobbies and then to pick from a list of reasons regarding leisure-time activity the three he thought were most important. There were eight reasons, four conceptual and four motoric, and they were placed in alternating order. Examples of reasons are: "gives me plenty of exercise" and "develops my mind."

In a second part of the interview the subject chose from a list of ten hobbies the three he preferred most, and then picked the three most attractive games from a list of ten. Equal numbers of conceptual and motoric items were arranged in alternating order. Some of the choices among the hobbies and games were "collecting stamps," "body-building club," "guessing games," and "tug of war."

Next, the subject selected from a group of eight job characteristics the three he deemed most important about the job he would like to have in adulthood. Half of the list was motoric and half conceptual. Among the alternatives were "involves writing at a desk," "keeps me in good physical shape," and "gives me complex problems to solve." He was instructed to evaluate each job, not in terms of its status or the level of income provided but rather in terms of those aspects that seemed most important. Then we showed him a list of jobs that had been judged by a national sample of adolescents as being very similar to each other in status and income. Half of the jobs were motoric and half conceptual.[10] From the list of jobs he chose three that he would most like to have if he could have any job he wanted. We inserted this question as a control. We did not expect any differences between social classes in the ideal jobs boys dream about. Finally, he selected the three jobs in the list that were most like the ones he would probably get.

[10] Questions in the interview required a number of preliminary revisions before we were confident that the alternatives were approximately equal in attractiveness. We discarded Automobile Repairman from the list of jobs, for example, because we found that most parents disapproved of it and nearly all the children chose it first or second.

orientation. The results confirm our predictions. When all the subjects attempted to figure out solutions, and when they were trying every combination manually, the differences between classes were no longer significant.

### Analysis and Results

On the basis of his response to each item, a subject was classified as being predominantly conceptual, intermediate, or motoric. In order to be labeled as *conceptual* or *motoric* within a particular category, it was necessary that he make the choice both first and most frequently. He was classified as *intermediate* if he selected an equal number of conceptual and motoric items, or if the majority of his selections did not agree with his first choice.

On all five comparisons, boys from the working class express more motoric preferences than do boys in the middle class. Only three of the five results have a probability of less than 5 per cent. In both classes the motoric reasons for leisure activities and games outweigh the conceptual ones. This makes sense in view of the subjects' ages. In early adolescence, boys are very concerned with developing physical prowess because it establishes their masculine status. But when the boys list the jobs they expect, or describe reasons for choosing occupations, they make judgments in terms of actual probabilities.[11]

## SOCIAL CLASS, PARENTAL REACTIONS, AND EXPRESSIVE STYLES

Thus far we have found the anticipated differences between boys in the two social classes when they played statues, painted pictures, took a block test, and expressed attitudes toward leisure activities and jobs. Furthermore, the association between social class and expressive styles is the same as the type that we observed in published reports concerning the symptoms of psychiatric patients. Participants from the middle class tend to express themselves conceptually, those from the working class motorically. Because expressive styles are probably established in the first few years of a persons' life, we now examine differences in parental reactions which might contribute to divergent styles. We shall focus on the activities and occupations that parents prefer for their sons, and such child-rearing practices as discipline, reward, and mothers' self-control.

### Mothers' Preferences

*Interviews.* An introductory question called for a listing of activities that the mother would prefer her son to cultivate in his free time and the reasons for her preferences. The interviewer then asked her to choose the

---

[11] As we anticipated, there is no significant difference between the classes with regard to the most desired jobs: the conceptual ones are chosen by boys in both classes.

three most important reasons for an activity from a list of seven. Some
were conceptual and some motoric. The list included: "It involves
planning and organization," "It builds a sound mind and a strong body,"[12]
and "It gives him plenty of exercise."

Next, the mother was questioned about the advice she would give her
son about nonfinancial considerations in selecting a job. After this question
she was asked to pick from a list of seven characteristics of any job, the
three that she thought were most important.[13] We predicted that middle-
class mothers would select activities permitting conceptual expression
and that working-class mothers would select activities permitting motoric
expression.

*Results.* Unlike their offspring, mothers from the two social classes
differ significantly in their reasons for favoring a leisure activity for their
sons. Table 1 reveals that the greatest contrast is in the choice of jobs.
The differences between adults may reflect the long experience that they
have had in their particular socioeconomic positions. They are probably
better able than their offspring to appreciate the satisfactions that are
inherent in these class positions. As for the conceptual and motoric aspects
of a job that the mothers consider most important, the differences between
classes are significant and in the anticipated directions.

### Child-Rearing Practices

It would be difficult to understand the origins of motoric expression
without considering the methods used by parents to train and restrict
children in muscular expression and locomotion. When a baby first
crawls and then walks, he requires considerable supervision, if only to
protect his safety. He cannot be allowed to run into the street; he must
be kept from the medicine cabinet; if he lives in the cramped quarters of a
small city apartment, he must frequently restrict his movements.

The child also learns many incidental lessons in the course of his
training. From his parents' methods of regulating his physical expression
and locomotion, he may conclude that they require impossibly high
standards of performance, that he can manipulate adults by the adequacy
of his performance in front of strangers, or that uninhibited physical
expression is dangerous. We were particularly impressed by the incidental
learning that occurs when the child patterns himself after his mother. He
may consciously copy her behavior or unconsciously identify with her.

---

[12] Before we inserted this item we found that most parents mentioned it spontaneously and found it hard to choose from the remainder. By including it, we allowed
them to make the spontaneous choice, which we did not count. Then they had no
difficulty in making the next selections, which we did count.
[13] Here again we had to insert an item that many parents mentioned spontaneously:
"The child should be happy whatever he does." Almost all the women voted for
the happy child. Then they expressed their next preferences with little hesitation.

When he identifies, he internalizes her most potent child-rearing methods in their identical form in order to convince himself that he really wants to do what she urges.

Applying these premises to our research, we judged that the split by class in the sons' motoric and conceptual styles would be paralleled by a similar split by class in the techniques favored by parents. On the assumption that sons would pattern themselves after their mothers, we predicted that boys whose parents favored corporal punishment would be most motoric and that boys whose parents manipulated behavior psychologically would be most conceptual. We also anticipated that parental use of concrete rewards would be associated with a motoric orientation in the sons, and that psychological rewards would be associated with a conceptual orientation. If mothers retained emotional control while disciplining their children, we predicted that such children would be conceptually oriented.[14] Otherwise, we assumed, the children would be more motoric.

*Table 2*—Child-Rearing Practices and Over-All Conceptual and Motoric Styles

| Parental practice | Trends: Boxes with greatest frequencies | N | Tau | Probability |
|---|---|---|---|---|
| Discipline | Psychological & most conceptual; corporal and most motoric | 83 | .37 | < .001 (1t) |
| Type of reward | Symbolic & most conceptual; concrete and intermediate | 57 | .36 | < .01 (1t) |
| Mothers' affective control | Controlled & most conceptual; uncontrolled & intermediate | 83 | .25 | < .01 (1t) |

*Analysis.* We did not think it necessary to relate parental child-rearing practices to each index of conceptual and motoric orientation; we had no interest in the origins of any particular behavior. We consequently developed a single over-all index of expressive style. In constructing this index we arbitrarily decided to use the first tests, *statues* and *paintings*. They seemed as representative of expressive style as any method we had developed. We classified subjects as most conceptual if they were most conceptual in their paintings and least motoric in the game of statues. We classified subjects as most motoric if they were most motoric in the game of statues and least conceptual in their paintings. A middle group consisted of children who were high in neither motoric nor conceptual scores.[15]

*Results.* As indicated in Table 2, expressive style is significantly related to each of the background variables. Mothers of motorically oriented boys are most likely to employ corporal discipline and concrete reward, to

---

[14] The data were collected from the first sample of mothers. At the time they were seen we had not yet developed the questions on obedience, frequency of reward, weaning time, and harshness of toilet training, so we could not relate these conditions to expressive style.

[15] In this analysis we lost a number of subjects. A few were high on both conceptual and motoric tests, some were absent when one of the tests was being given, and a few could not be used because the mothers' descriptions of their child-rearing methods were too vague to be classified.

lose control of themselves, and to come from the working class. Mothers of the conceptually oriented are most likely to employ psychological discipline and symbolic reward, to retain self-control, and to come from the middle class.

These results are so consistent as to suggest a patterning of the parents' child-rearing practices. Possibly, a motoric orientation, membership in the working class, corporal discipline, and poor control are all characteristic of the same group of people. And, possibly, a conceptual orientation, psychological discipline, and good control are all characteristic of another group of people. If these conjectures are true, the association between expressive style and any parental method or socio-economic status should no longer be significant if we hold another background variable constant. We find the kinds of results we anticipate when we recompute a heretofore significant relation between expressive style and one background variable, such as social class, within the categories of another background variable, such as concrete and abstract reward. The significance vanishes for every association but one.

There is only one variable, effective control, which when held constant does not eliminate the significance of associations between child-rearing and expressive styles. In fact, they all remain significant. In retrospect, this finding seems reasonable when we remember that the parents were normal adults, most of whom were relatively controlled. Even those labeled as uncontrolled had only occasional lapses. Thus, while the difference between classes is significant, it is not very great.

From the findings just cited, we conclude that parents in the working class with motoric sons are generally the same people who use corporal discipline and concrete rewards. And parents in the middle class with conceptual sons are generally the same people who use psychological discipline and abstract rewards. However, most parents in the middle class who use psychological discipline do not necessarily retain control, nor are most parents in the working class who use corporal discipline necessarily prone to the occasional loss of control.

# *iii*

---

# *Affective Factors and Environment*

## INTRODUCTION

### PERSONAL ATTRIBUTES AND SELF CONCEPT

"So I told them, 'If your behavior doesn't improve, you are not getting a Christmas party.' And their behavior didn't improve, so I said, 'I am sorry, we are not going to have anything.' And they knew it and they said that they didn't care. They would have a party when they got home." The teacher in this classroom is resorting to a phrase that is not uncommon in slum schools and which serves as the title of the first reading in this part. "If Your Behavior Doesn't Improve."

Understanding student behavior is necessary in any schoolroom for good teaching to occur. It is, however, crucial to you as a teacher in the metropolis. The pressing need for better understanding is attested to by Deutsch, whose research shows that some teachers in urban schools spend as much as 80 per cent of their time in the classroom attempting to exert control and trying to deal with non-academic tasks. This compares with 30 per cent of teaching time usually devoted to control of students and to non-academic problems in middle-class schools.(18)

What causes these difficulties for some teachers in the slum neighborhoods? Why do some teachers spend as little as 20 per cent of their time teaching and 80 per cent in efforts to direct behavior? Perhaps the frustrations of some teachers in understanding student behavior are partially caused by insufficient knowledge of the ways in which environment shapes children's personalities and motivation. It is probable that some educators tend to view behavioral problems among children as solely individual problems, and to be unaware of the social context in which they occur.

Further, if teacher training has been devoted to an examination of the psychological characteristics of middle-class children or if expectations of behavior are based on teacher's experiences as youngsters in middle-class schools, the image of children of low socioeconomic neighborhoods is not based on the reality of their own backgrounds. It is, therefore, necessary to look at the children you are *really* teaching and ask yourself: What are *their* personal characteristics and self concepts? In short, how does their own social environment shape them and how do they see themselves and their behavior in their own worlds?

When teachers do not understand the social context of behavior, it is possible for them to perceive many if not most of the children as maladjusted in one way or another. Though some children from the slums *are* maladjusted, high estimates of abnormal behavior given by some professionals leads the intelligent listener to ask, "Whose concept of abnormality is being used?" Surely, such large groups of children cannot be maladjusted. Is it possible instead, that such beliefs about children are based on the fact that middle-class ways of doing things are viewed as "normal" and that lower-class ways of behaving are seen as different or "abnormal"? In short, is it possible that the social context of behavior is not seen, thus leading the observer to perceive individual actions from his own frame of reference?

It is not unusual for one culture or subculture to view the members of another as "abnormal" in their behavior. For example, you probably believe that monogamy—marrying one woman at a time—is the normal thing to do and that polygamy is abnormal. Yet, the majority of the societies in the world practice polygamy and see us as abnormal.(19) What, then, we define as normal or abnormal behavior is, to a considerable extent, conditioned by the groups in which we were raised. When we deal with people from different backgrounds, we are prone to see their behavior as unusual or in some ways abnormal.

It may be very abnormal for the child of the lower classes to refuse to fight someone who has offended him. The teacher may tell him not to fight, but the child knows that fighting is necessary at times to obtain his rights in his own world. In short, behavior of any child from another background must be viewed in terms of the meaning it has for him in his *own* world.

Is it more abnormal, for example, for a child to hang on to his possessions and expect an even exchange of favors given and received or to give generously of what he has with no thought of immediate repayment of favors given? On the basis of research, it is the lower-class child who is more likely to behave in the generous way. One must understand the value of objects stressed by the middle class to appreciate the equal exchange demanded by a child from that strata of society.

Lower-class children of the Italian ethnic group often have strong ties of loyalty to friendship and family groups.(22) It is possible that these positive values are not used effectively in urban schools because they are not necessary in the middle-class world of huge bureaucracies, whether industrial or educational, in which the private world of the individual is not crucial to the functioning of such institutions. Is it more normal, for example, for the middle-class father to spend ten hours of work a day in the public world of a commercial institution or for the lower-class man to work seven hours a day and then enjoy his family and friends in the private world of his home and neighborhood?

It is important to remember that you, the teacher, have been raised in a certain strata of society with an ethnic heritage just as your children have, and that your definition of their behaviors as right or wrong is influenced by your group membership, as is their definition of your behavior. However, stressing ethnocentric attitudes about the validity of another group's behavior does not negate the fact that cultural influences of social class and ethnicity have differential effects on personality and create stresses in various environments that foster different emotional upsets.

An example of a well-conducted research study that focuses on personality characteristics and maladaptive behavior in relation to social environment is Langner's excerpt, "Socioeconomic Status and Personality Characteristics." Langner conducted a survey in which interviews were held with a random sample of the non-hospitalized residents of a metropolitan community. He summarizes his findings by saying, "persons of low socioeconomic status are more prone to have organic brain damage, psychoses, and character disorders and are less likely to have neuroses. In particular, they are more rigid, suspicious, and have a fatalistic outlook on life. They do not plan ahead, a characteristic associated with their fatalism. They are prone to depression, have feelings of futility, lack of belongingness, friendlessness and lack of trust in others."

What are some of the causes of these lower-class characteristics and illnesses? It can readily be seen that fatalism and lack of planning are associated reactions to poverty or bare subsistence living. If you don't have enough money to make many of your plans come true, why plan?

Langner points out that apathy and depression in adult life are associated with poverty in childhood. In addition, if you belong to a group that has no power in society, why not feel fatalistic about life? Perhaps, too, feelings of friendlessness and lack of belongingness and trust are reality-oriented responses to the impersonal masses of the metropolis.

People from lower socioeconomic levels are more likely to have stresses in their lives, causing them to worry about the cost of living, their work, and other aspects of their daily lives. What does this say to you the teacher? The behavior of children in your classroom is environmentally conditioned, and many children in the slum schools of our cities will carry a heavy burden of problems in their home lives. It is probable that little John in the fourth row in your class incorporates the personality characteristics common to the adults in his world and that his contact with adults who have the characteristics and feelings described above will affect his behavior in your classroom.

It is necessary to understand, however, that middle-class children also have their troubles. Langner says that it is important to remember at all times that while those in the upper economic strata suffer less severe impairment, persons at all points on the socioeconomic scale exhibit maladaptive behavior and that for every sociopath or psychotic among those in the lower economic strata, there is probably a neurotic among those in higher income groups.

Not only is it important to look at both ends of the scale, one must also question the meaning of different rates of mental illness in terms of how they were determined. Accurate assessment of prevalence of personal attributes or disturbances is difficult. For example, the incidence of juvenile delinquency in lower-class children is reported by some authorities to be higher than among middle-class children.(10) But it is quite possible that such rates are overestimations, because children in the upper strata are more frequently protected by influential parents who keep them out of the court records which are used to determine prevalence of delinquency. Qualifications of this kind may enable you as a teacher to remember that most children from slum neighborhoods are not maladapted and that generalizations about maladjustment must be made with care.

One reason for the tendency of the teacher of middle-class origin to generalize about children in slum schools is that she is more likely to understand and sympathize individually with children with behavior problems from her same stratum because their problems are more likely to be similar in kind, if not in severity, to the difficulties she herself may have had.

Davidson and Lang, for example, show that teachers' attitudes toward children are related to social class. In their study, 58 per cent of the lower-class children were rated as having undesirable behavior by their teachers, while only 20 per cent of the upper class children were rated unfavorably. In addition, children in the upper- and middle- social class groups perceived their teachers' feelings toward them more favorably than did the children in the lower-class group. Even those lower-class children who were rated as high achievers perceived their teachers' feelings as less positive than upper-class high achievers. The researchers found, in addition, that "The more positive the children's perceptions of their teachers' feelings, the better was their academic achievement and the more desirable their classroom behavior as rated by the teachers."

It is apparent that a child's view of himself is highly influential in his functioning at school. The attitudes, feelings, perceptions, and evaluations of the child's self as an object is, in turn, dependent on what others think of him. It is probable that environmentally determined factors such as social class will, in part, influence his teacher's perceptions and consequently his own. If low evaluation of self is reinforced by the teacher's attitude, achievement will be reduced and behavior will be more deviant in the classroom.

Racial identification as well as lower-class derivation affects the self-image of the child. Race awareness begins at an early age; preschool children know the unfavorable ramifications of their racial membership. Perhaps the most damaging effect of race prejudice is the negative attitude toward the self development in non-white children. David and Pearl Ausubel, in "Ego Development in Young Negro Children," state: "The Negro child perceives himself as an object of derision and disparagement, as socially rejected by the prestigeful elements of society, and as unworthy of succorance and affection; and having no compelling reason for not accepting this officially sanctioned negative evaluation of himself, he develops a deeply ingrained negative self-image."

As indicated earlier, ethnic groups, regardless of race, develop distinctive ways of dealing with the world that may result in different personality characteristics. The important point is that some groups, because of different skin color, are exposed to added stresses that result in derogatory self-attitudes. The damaging effects of negative attitudes incorporated from others is amply pointed out by Katz in "The Effects of Desegregation on the Performance of Negroes." The author presents the results of a series of experiments and finds, for example, that " . . . in work teams composed of Negro and white students of similar intellectual ability, Negroes are passively compliant, rate their own performance as inferior *even when it is not*, and express less satisfaction with the team experience..."

It is clear that children from different ethnic groups and socioeconomic levels may have problems of learning that are not primarily associated with their potential to learn nor with their styles of learning, but with the images they hold of themselves. You as their teacher can help each child gain a more positive evaluation of himself. Through respect for the child in terms of his own world it may be possible to alter not only his attitude but your own as well.

## MOTIVATIONAL CHARACTERISTICS

How a young person evaluates himself is intertwined with where he wants to go in school and later life. Certainly, the basis of behavior is the motivation that leads to any action. Human beings do not act at random; they behave in relation to a goal. Human behavior, whether intellectual or emotional, is directed and purposive. Obviously, learning in school cannot proceed if the child is not motivated to learn. If he sees his educational life goals as requiring little formal training, the value of any one course of study in school may be nil for him. To teach, you must understand the purposes of youngsters' behavior, where they see themselves going in school and in life, and why they choose to move toward this goal rather than that one.

In the first selection in the second part of this section, six-year-old Harry says, "I'm going to be a lawyer." Yet an examination of his environment says that, in all likelihood, young Harry will never get to be a lawyer when he grows up. The nature of the situation into which a child is born affects his chances of reaching a goal and also affects the goal he sets for himself. One of the basic assumptions of our culture, however, is that education and willpower can take any child anywhere he wants to go: "Any child can be president if he wants to be." Not only is it assumed that effort will be rewarded, it is also accepted that education will get one to his goal. In the American society, it is expected that each father will want his son to have a better life than his, to move up the status scale to a better job, to more money, to a better home. This process of movement whether upward or downward is called mobility. The school's job can be conceived of as preparation for upward movement. This, however, requires academic motivation and goals that can be reached intellectually and financially; this also presupposes that the goal is worth reaching.

For Negro children, the types of jobs available have historically been so limited by segregation that academic achievement made little sense. Even today, the average white man with an eighth-grade education makes more money than the average Negro with a college education.(42) Our American dream of unlimited opportunities for anyone who will work for them is open to some question. Three separate researchers, for example, have discovered that the clear majority of American business leaders come from relatively well-to-do families. This is not such a surprising statistic until we consider the added finding that this has been the case since 1771, the date of the earliest examination of records.(39) The child of poor parents who works his way up to be president of the company may be a much rarer person than most Americans expect. To explode further the idea that American opportunities are greater, another research study indicates that the rate of mobility for most industrial countries including Germany, Sweden, Japan, France, and Switzerland is much the same as that in America.(39) The children you teach may understand the limited opportunities open to them better than you realize. The "American Dream" is attainable for many of them only if you understand and offset the discouragement some of them may feel in planning for futures they don't really believe are possible. Your realistic encouragement may be more appreciated than glib restatements of glowing generalities.

Motivation of children in your class is closely linked with their eventual mobility beyond school. A fairly large number of studies have been conducted to determine the goals that motivate children in different ethnic and socioeconomic groups. Some of these have found that lower-class parents and children place greater stress on school and career success, while other studies report that middle-class parents and children are more concerned with the achievement of these goals. Weiner and Murray suggest that these contradictions can be explained in terms of the difference between the reality and the ideal of these goals. Many parents and children from both groups have internalized the value of high-school and college education, but the more affluent parent sees his child's goals as a fact while the poor parent sees his child's goals as a wish. The means to obtain the end have not been internalized in the parents and children of lower socioeconomic status.

The influence of the family on children's motivation in school is of extreme importance as Kahl indicates in "Educational and Occupational Aspirations of 'Common Man' Boys." The families and boys studied could be divided into those who believed in just "getting by" and those who were concerned with "getting ahead." The sons of the latter parents, though from the same social status, were college-bound youngsters who were doing well in school. The sons of families that were "getting by," though in some cases of superior intelligence, were, on the whole, less interested in school and planning a job after graduation. On the other hand, individual differences of children in families "getting by" were better accepted with less pressure on the children. In this study, the psychological attributes of parents, such as the father's dissatisfaction with his own accomplishments, were crucial to the motivation and mobility of the children.

Psychological attributes of parents are in part a function of social position, but are also a result of the ethnic group to which the family belongs. Caudill and de Vos in "Achievement, Culture and Personality: The Case of the Japanese-Americans," account for the phenomenal mobility in two generations of this Oriental group in terms of congruence between Japanese and American middle-class values. The achievement drive of both groups is very high, with American middle-class scores on projective tests showing greater similarity to Japanese rather than lower-class white scores. The authors conclude, "The Japanese-Americans provide us, then, with the case of a group who, despite racial visibility and culture traditionally thought of as alien, achieved a remarkable adjustment to middle-class American life because certain compatibilities in the value systems of the immigrant and host cultures operated strongly enough to override the more obvious difficulties."

Rosen in "Race, Ethnicity, and the Achievement Syndrome," presents research evidence on differences in motivation, values, and aspirations of six racial and ethnic groups with dissimilar mobility rates. His data show "that the groups place different emphases upon independence and achievement training in the rearing of children. As a consequence, achievement motivation is more characteristic of Greeks, Jews, and white Protestants than of Italians, French-Canadians, and Negroes." Rosen shows that Negro educational aspirations and values are comparable to the first three groups, but that their vocational aspirations are the lowest of all groups.

The Lotts, however, came to a different conclusion in their study of Negro and white high school students' plans for their futures. They found that Negro teenagers' career goals were in keeping with the type of training chosen and that neither Negro nor white youngsters expected to do unskilled work. When comparing college-bound groups, no differences in educational or career aspirations were found between races. There were, however, fewer selections among Negro boys for "glamour" jobs such as advertising and politics and more choices of service jobs among the total group.

The readings in this section have been selected to give you a grasp of the complexities involved in assessing the goals of urban children. You can, however, be quite sure that environment through family, social position, and ethnicity will influence different means and goals of achievement. Assuming low aspirations for all poor children will most assuredly be erroneous, because different ethnic and racial backgrounds are involved. And, in addition, expectations of low educational and occupational motivations may simply act as a deterrent to the hopes of students in your class. Certainly, high educational goals are valued; but your opportunity as a teacher is to help the children of the poor, internalize and value the *means* to reach their goals.

From the readings on personal attributes and motivational characteristics in both subsections, your understanding of student behavior in a social context will hopefully be enlarged. In addition, the complex interaction of intellectual factors considered in the previous section, combined with the emotional factors dealt with in this section, should enable you to better understand the learning difficulties of children from slum areas.

The personal characteristics found to be common among people in low-income groups; the attitudes and feelings about the self developed in children of limited means and of different races; the motives to achieve seen as the incorporation of means as well as ends are all prominent affective aspects that influence the learning process. The research presented, however, suggests general findings and is not necessarily representative of *every* child in your classroom. Consequently, your reading will be most helpful if you look for those particular facts that seem to apply best to each child in your own situation.

*A. Personal Attributes and Self Concept*

# IF YOUR BEHAVIOR DOESN'T IMPROVE ...

I guess the most important sequence of events is that my class was getting terrible, and I just couldn't wait for vacation to come, because I figured that if I didn't get out of that room soon, that was going to be the end of me. All the teachers were having Christmas parties and I didn't think that I wanted to have my Christmas party because I just didn't think that the kids deserved it, and I didn't want them to think that they could behave any way they want, and still I would turn around and say, "OK, kiddies, I don't mind either, and I'll make your Christmas party anyway." So I told them, "If your behavior doesn't improve you are not getting any Christmas party." And their behavior didn't improve, so I said, "I am sorry, we are not going to have anything." And they knew it and they said they don't care, they will have a party when they go home, but they could see that they were the only class that was not having a party, so they were sort of upset. So the Friday before the end of school I see all the kids walking in with little presents, and I just wanted to die, I felt so badly, and I was glad that the night before I had bought just some little candies and some candy canes, and little dolls like decorations for Christmas presents, and I had just made a little package for each one of them, and I figured that at three o'clock I would walk around and put one at each desk to show that I still thought about them, to get them something for Christmas, so when I saw them walking in with all their little presents, I was glad that I had made this. And they gave me—I got about seven or eight presents and I was very surprised and I felt bad they had brought them, because I didn't appreciate the things that they gave me and took

"If Your Behavior Doesn't Improve..." One teacher interviewed for Project TRUE (Teacher Resources for Urban Education), Hunter College of the City University of New York.

178

their money to buy. But so when it was about a quarter to three, of course, they were very wild in the afternoon because they were the only class that was doing any work. Every other class was having Christmas parties and we could hear the music and dancing, and here I am trying to teach a reading lesson, so that wasn't going too well. At about a quarter to three I walked around and I put this little package on each child's desk and when I came to Rodrigo's desk he said, "I don't want it." So I left it there anyway, and he said, "I don't want it." And then I went around and I came to Wilfredo and he said, "I don't want it." And I walked away and he said, "No, I don't want it." So I took it away from him. So that was that, so we are sort of mutual enemies, and the presents that they gave me, I got two half slips that were really nice, and bath soap, and one girl gave me perfume, 49 cents, Woolworth's original, and it was so terrible but I guess I will have to wear it just one time. Bertha Jones, I don't think I mentioned her too much in the course of the year because she's not any special problem. She's not a bad girl and she's not an exceptionally good girl, and she's not very smart, but she tries hard and she studies, and she had said that she was getting me a present, and she came in in the morning and she didn't have anything. Most of the other girls put their presents on the desk, and obviously she felt bad or she felt funny that she didn't bring a present. Of course, I didn't want anybody to feel bad so I didn't open the presents while the kids were there or anything, so that afternoon Bertha comes walking in and she puts a paper bag on my desk tied with a ribbon, and I put it away, and when I was going home I opened it up, and it was one of her blouses. A blouse that she had worn. I could tell, it was dirty and creased, and I looked at it and I almost cried. I felt very terrible. She had felt badly that she didn't have a present and she had given me one of her own blouses, and it just so happens that I have the same exact blouse. It's my own, so I brought the blouse back and I will give it back to her. I have it in my closet and I keep forgetting to give it to her, but besides that, she gave me about two yards of material neatly folded up with a rough edge, sort of green and blue printed patterned material. And then she had like a card, and I looked at it, and I could tell that it was from a large card or a game or something. She had cut half of it, and it had a picture of a reindeer, it's Christmasy, and she gave this to me. And I really felt terrible. So these are the things that I remember about that week.

# SOCIOECONOMIC STATUS AND

# PERSONALITY CHARACTERISTICS

*Thomas S. Langner*

## A PICTURE OF CLASS AND PERSONALITY

Our methods cannot yield conclusive data, but we can sketch the outlines of the social character of the various social classes. Most important, we can develop hypotheses about the class differences in experience that may possibly be sources of particular types of mental disorder. But first a review of our findings and mention of some other studies which have been able to say something about class differences in type of mental disturbance, personality structure, social character, and the like.

Much of the literature utilizes the term "social class" and divides it into upper, middle, and lower. Therefore, we must relate the Midtown SES categories to the class terminology. This will enable us to compare our data with such findings as those of Ruesch ". . . the lower class culture . . ." and Hollingshead and Redlich ". . . dominance . . . in middle class families. . . ."

The Midtown low SES is roughly equivalent to the "lower class" in most references and to classes IV and V in the Hollingshead and Redlich studies. The Midtown middle and most of the high SES are equivalent to the "middle class" in much of the literature on stratification and to Hollingshead and Redlich's classes II and III. There are very few people in Midtown who could be considered strictly "upper class" in its original sense of landed gentry or nobility. However, according to the current American sociological usage of this term, "old families" and those of extremely high SES should be included.

According to our data, persons of low SES are more prone to have organic brain damage, psychoses, and character disorders, and are less likely to have neuroses. In particular, they are more rigid, suspicious, and have a fatalistic outlook on life. They do not plan ahead, a characteristic associated with their fatalism. They are prone to depression, have feelings of futility, lack of belongingness, friendlessness, and lack of trust in others. They are more authoritarian in their attitudes, stressing obedience, power, and hierarchical relations.

The tendency to "act out" problems in the lower class has been often noted, as well as the preponderance of lower-class psychotics and upper-class neurotics. Although he disagrees with our findings about psychosomatic reactions and omits the preponderance of lower-class schizophrenia, Ruesch is in essential agreement with our data:

... the lower class culture favors conduct disorders and rebellion, the middle class culture physical symptom formations and psychosomatic reactions, and the upper class culture psychoneurosis and psychosis of the manic depressive type.[1]

Although the psychiatrist (who bases his observations chiefly upon the preselected types of patients he sees in his clinic) is at the mercy of the biases of self-selection in the upper class and police selection in the lower class, his views are nevertheless corroborative of and tend to illuminate our nonpatient findings.

We may indulge in the following generalizations as viewed by the psychiatrist: the class V neurotic behaves badly, the class IV neurotic aches physically, the class III patient defends fearfully and the class I-II patient is dissatisfied with himself.[2]

Of course, it is possible that lower-class patients who do not act out their problems and are merely dissatisfied with themselves neither seek treatment nor are referred by the police, since they are not in "trouble." This criticism does not seem to hold, for our nonpatient study shows a much greater proportion of the acting-out personality trait type in the low SES. In this respect at least, the tiny patient population resembles the "parent" nonpatient population.

Only a few observational studies have compared the personality structure of the different social classes. This is quite unbelievable, particularly in view of the hundreds of detailed clinically oriented anthropological studies of cultures other than ours. One study which, although small in scale, actually tries to pin down personality dynamics of lower and upper class was conducted in England by B. M. Spinley, a clinical psychologist. Participant observation, structured interviews with selected informants, life histories, and Rorschach Tests were used to compare slum dwellers with public or boarding school level (high SES) individuals. The findings

[1] Jurgen Ruesch, "Social Technique, Social Status, and Social Change in Illness," in Clyde Kluckhohn and Henry A. Murray (eds.), *Personality in Nature, Society, and Culture,* New York, Knopf, 1949, p. 125.
[2] August B. Hollingshead and Frederick C. Redlich, *Social Class and Mental Illness,* New York, Wiley, 1958, p. 240.

are so crucial to further work in the field of social psychiatry that it would seem best to quote them at length.

The (slum) individual shows a marked absence of a strict and efficient conscience, an unwillingness and inability to deal with disturbing or unpleasant situations, and a flight from these. He is unable to postpone satisfactions. He is seriously disturbed in the sexual areas of his development with predominantly feminine identifications which interfere with his adoption of the masculine sexual role. He has narcissistic trends. (The girl is also disturbed in spite of her feminine identifications, since she feels uneasiness in, or fear of, her feminine sexual role.) Relations with other people are colored by negativism, distrust, suspicion, and excessive fear of ridicule, this last so strong that feelings of inferiority are indicated. He has marked aggressiveness, which is permitted violent expression, and his attitude towards authority is one of hostility and rebellion. Emotional response and fantasy production are constricted and intellectual discrimination poor. His response to failure, frustration, or mishap of any kind is extrapunitive.

The (public school) individual has a strict, effective conscience; he faces disturbing situations and attempts to deal adequately with them. Present satisfactions are postponed for the sake of greater ones in the future. He does not show any serious sexual disturbance. . . . Insecurity is present but few or no indications of inferiority feelings. Aggression is inhibited or even at a deeper level, repressed, and his response to frustration tends to be intropunitive. He is characterized by an internalization of the standards of his own group. . . . In most situations he accepts authority, but may discard rules and commands if they conflict with the standards of his own social group (his own conscience). . . . He has a spontaneous, rich and creative fantasy and good powers of intellectual discrimination. He is more mature than a number of the slum group of corresponding age.[3]

The major points of congruence between these findings and those of other authors are that the low SES has (1) a weak super-ego, (2) a weak ego, with lack of control or frustration tolerance, (3) a negative, distrustful, suspicious character with poor interpersonal relations, (4) strong feelings of inferiority, low self-esteem, fear of ridicule, and (5) a tendency to act out problems, with violent expression of hostility and extrapunitive tendencies.

With some important omissions, such as the predominance of depressive and passive-dependent tendencies in the lower class, these findings agree with the Midtown data. They leave no doubt that social class levels have specific psychological characteristics or basic personality types of their own, even though there is a good deal of overlapping between classes. This character structure is closely related to the types of mental disturbance that we find most prevalent at each level.

## LIFE EXPERIENCES OF THE CLASSES

Now that we have reviewed the social character of the lower and upper classes, we can look at what we and others have learned about the difference

[3] B. M. Spinley, *The Deprived and the Privileged: Personality Development in English Society*, London, Routledge and Kegan Paul, 1953, pp. 129–130.

in the life experiences of the classes. We know that mental disturbance varies in degree of impairment and type with social class and social mobility. It is only reasonable to assume that, over and above hereditary influences, there may be some sources of particular types of illness in the differential class environment. The detailed specification of the class environments and their relation to mental disorder is a task we must initiate at this time, if only in scant detail, and with little actual research data to test our hypotheses. Our goal is to find out how social class might be conducive to differential rates of impairment and different types of disturbances. What aspects of the classes can we consider as potential sources of class differences in personality and mental disorder?

## CHILD-REARING

*Permissiveness; the Channeling of Drives and Needs.* One very likely source is the class differences in child-rearing practices and child-rearing atmosphere. For instance, Hollingshead and Redlich feel that the lower-class infant is less apt to receive affection.[4]

There are experts who feel that the middle-class child is more apt to be rejected, and they point to the lax toilet training and lengthier breast feeding which has been reported in the lower class. In England Spinley found the lower-class first year one of indulgence, ending abruptly with the birth of the next child, particularly with working mothers who probably could afford only brief breast feeding.[5] Bronfenbrenner,[6] however, has shown rather conclusively that while the middle class in the United States was more severe in its socialization and infant care from 1930 to just after World War II, it has become progressively milder in its practices, so that it is now more "permissive" than the lower class. During the last quarter century the middle and lower classes have traded places, so to speak. Middle-class mothers are more apt to feed their children on demand and to wean late, even though they still are less likely to breast feed. They are also more permissive in other areas of oral behavior, toilet accidents, dependency, some types of sexual expression, aggressiveness (in young but not preadolescent children), and freedom of movement outside the home. The middle-class child, however, is given responsibility (even for household chores) earlier, and more demands are made on him, particularly in relation to success in school.

These rather sweeping generalizations tend to conceal a multitude of apparently major disagreements in data and their interpretation by various

[4] A. B. Hollingshead and F. C. Redlich, *op. cit.*, p. 361.
[5] B. M. Spinley, *op. cit.*, p. 131.
[6] Urie Bronfenbrenner, "Socialization and Social Class Through Time and Space," in Eleanor E. Maccoby, T. M. Newcomb, and E. L. Hartley, *Readings in Social Psychology*, New York, Holt, Rinehart and Co., 1958, pp. 400–425.

investigators. To label one social stratum as more permissive than another does a great injustice to the actual findings, for permissiveness is a sponge term. One author may use it to describe late, as opposed to early, toilet training or weaning. The age at which potentially frustrating training practices are initiated or completed is assumed to indicate mildness or permissiveness. The term is also used to describe the degree of freedom allowed by the parents. The direction the behavior takes, the type of behavior, its intensity, and the objects of that behavior may be so important that they should be specified in each study. This is a necessary step before over-all estimates of differential permissiveness according to social class are possible.

An interesting example is that of aggression. Maccoby and Gibbs,[7] after interviewing 198 white upper-middle and 178 upper-lower-class mothers of kindergarten children, concluded that the higher SES parents allowed more expression of aggression toward other children and toward themselves. Davis[8] found that middle-class parents were *less* tolerant of aggression. Even though Davis studied older preadolescent children rather than those in kindergarten, the disagreement can be explained in terms of the *target* of the aggression. Midtown data show that few low SES children disagreed or argued with their parents, compared to the Middles and Highs. If we say that aggression against parents is more often permitted at higher social levels, and aggression against nonfamily members is condoned or even encouraged at lower levels, the contradiction is partially solved. In fact, the stern *paterfamilias* of the immigrant low-status household, by discouraging any verbal or physical expression against himself, is all the more likely to create a need for substitute targets for hostility outside the home. The apparent permissiveness of the higher strata with regard to aggression does not extend to groups outside the family. The Highs probably encourage verbal rather than physical expression, and probably dampen physical expression in both sexes against the parents and siblings at an earlier age, though they are more permissive with the preschool and kindergarten child.

Indeed, which is more permissive: demand bottle feeding with late weaning among the upper strata, or the recently shorter breast feeding of the lower stratum? Some authors are impressed by the harsh physical punishment of the lower class; others bemoan the quashing of instinctual drives and the strict and early demands made on the middle- and upper-class child. Which is more harsh, which more permissive? If our concern is, instead, with the psychodynamic consequences of physical punishment,

[7] E. E. Maccoby, P. K. Gibbs, and the Staff of the Laboratory of Human Development, Harvard University, "Methods of Child-Rearing in Two Social Classes," in W. E. Martin and C. B. Stendler (eds.), *Reading in Child Development*, New York, Harcourt, Brace, & World, 1954, pp. 380–396.
[8] Allison Davis, "American Status, Systems and the Socialization of The Child," *American Sociological Review*, 6(3) 1941, 345–354.

on one hand, and control through the threat of withdrawal of love on the other, no such problem of defining harshness or permissiveness need arise. Ideally we might measure the consequences of such methods with detailed scales of social and psychological impairment, but little research has been done along such lines. While we cannot cite research on the results of these methods of control in terms of impairment or type of disorder, we can make careful guesses based on the child development literature and our knowledge of Midtown's SES distribution of diagnostic entities.

Despite the problems of definition, let us assume that Bronfenbrenner is justified in using the blanket term "permissiveness," especially since he goes into great detail about the individual items or indices of permissiveness. Since the Midtown respondents were at least twenty years old in 1953, they were all children well before the end of World War II, in other words, they were children when the lower-class child-training practices were more permissive than those of the middle class. One-third of the sample, the immigrants, were European-born, and these class characterizations of child-training practices may not apply equally well to them. By and large, however, the middle-class respondents (who are now adults) should have been raised somewhat more "strictly" than the lower-class respondents. Although we tend to think of strict rather than permissive upbringing as damaging to mental health, it is probably more accurate to say that both extremes are damaging and produce different types of disorder.

*Inconsistency.* Furthermore, it was pointed out some years ago that demands on the adult which are inconsistent with childhood training may be quite damaging to the adult personality.[9] Another aspect of inconsistency is the conflicting methods of child-rearing to which the lower-class child is exposed, since the values and methods of his middle-class schoolteachers are bound to differ from those of his parents. Inconsistency is found not only in the demands made by one parent, or the differing values of the father and mother, but also in the parents' or peer-group values as against those of the schoolteacher, clergyman, judge, social worker, and court psychiatrist. There is much less of this latter type of value conflict in the life of the middle-class individual, for parental and larger societal values are more likely to be in accord.

The middle-class respondents, who are roughly equivalent to the middle and high SES groups, show considerably better mental health than the lower-class respondents, despite their (presumed) stricter upbringing in the 1930s. However, it is doubtful that child-training practices *alone* could produce impairment in adult functioning, and evidence in this volume points to the importance of many factors outside of childhood entirely.

[9] Ruth Benedict, "Continuities and Discontinuities in Cultural Conditioning," *Psychiatry*, **I**, (2) 1938, 161–167, in C. Kluckhohn and H. Murray, *op. cit.*, pp. 414–423.

*Civilizing, Taming, and Redirection Related to Type of Disorder.* A more profitable question is, "What types of mental disturbances are engendered by class differences in child-training?" Having no observational data on the child-training to which our respondents were exposed, we can only make guesses about the association of training and disturbance. We also cannot assume that a particular type of child-training causes the development of a particular type of mental disturbance.

Our data show that the middle and upper SES groups are more prone to neurosis (that is, symptoms of anxiety without concomitant psychosomatic manifestations), while the low SES (or lower class, roughly speaking) is more likely to exhibit psychosis or character disorders (suspiciousness, rigidity, dependency). Our tentative hypothesis is that the anxiety found in the middle and upper levels may be due to the relatively severe suppression and accompanying repression and redirection of sexual and aggressive instincts; a sort of "oversocialization." On the other hand, the lower class may be "undersocialized" in certain areas, resulting in an acting-out of problems which we label "character disorders." Hollingshead and Redlich suggest:

Most young people in classes IV and V pass directly from childhood to the occupational, social, and marital responsibilities of adulthood. In doing so, they miss, in varying degrees, what we have come to refer to as sublimation. Their sexual, aggressive, and dependent impulses remain much more pronounced and more primitive than those of classes I and II.[10]

It doesn't really matter whether we use the term sublimation, socialization, or repression as long as we recognize that this is one element which is sometimes missing, in less abundance, or somehow different in the lower class. It is not the age at which the child of each social class identifies with and enters into the adult role, nor is it the lack of an interim period such as our "adolescence" which is crucial for the development of adult personality. It is, rather, the type of adult role he has internalized and the degree (and areas) of repression it involves which determine the kind of adaptation or disturbance he will manifest. That the age of socialization is not crucial to personality development was neatly pointed out by Baldwin.

. . . you find so many so-called primitive societies in which presumably you have so many different cultural patterns and different personalities, but all of the children in all of these societies are identified with adult roles very early.[11]

The adult role at which the middle-class child-training has been aimed can be summed up by the phrase "The Protestant Work Ethic." This ethic,

[10] A. B. Hollingshead and F. C. Redlich, *op. cit.*, p. 364.
[11] See Alfred L. Baldwin's discussion of M. Kuhn, "Family Impact on Personality," in J. E. Hulett, Jr., and Ross Stagner (eds.), *Problems in Social Psychology*, Papers and Proceedings of the Allerton Conference on Social Psychology, Monticello, Illinois, December 1950, University of Illinois, Urbana, Illinois, 1952, p. 54.

with its emphasis on tangible success and initiative, is being slowly eroded by a new emphasis on "inner success," on "psychological income," and social rather than occupational skills, which the author hopes to analyze in a future volume. For the present, a description of middle-class norms given by Cohen[12] is adequate for our purposes, even though strong counternorms have been growing in both the middle and lower class independently. Cohen's list has been summarized by Simpson[13] and shortened by us, as follows: (1) ambition, (2) individual responsibility, (3) skills and achievements, (4) worldly asceticism (postponing immediate satisfaction for long-term goals), (5) rationality, (6) getting along with people (manners, courtesy, personability), (7) control of physical aggression, (8) constructive leisure, (9) respect for property; one "is" what one has; don't take other's property. This list of norms, values, and goals of the middle class is not merely an impression; it has been documented by previous studies. Davis and Havighurst, for example, on the basis of interviews with 200 white and Negro lower-class and middle-class mothers, stated that "middle-class children are subjected earlier and more consistently to the influences which make a child an orderly, conscientious, responsible, and tame person."[14]

The "taming" of the socioeconomic strata may be different in degree, the middle stratum possibly being more tamed. However, the taming is different *in kind* as well as in degree. We have talked about training for aggression within the family and to outsiders. While the middle- and upper-class child is surely weaned away from physical expression of aggression, he is encouraged to develop his capacity for oral combat. Verbal skills may win many more battles in our legalistic society and are rewarded more on the job and at the conference table than a ready fist. People can be destroyed by a quick tongue, a slander campaign, and by legal maneuvers. Thus the child of the higher strata learns other techniques for gaining power, legitimate types of violence, and one could hardly call him completely tamed. As we shall note, premarital sexuality is not exactly "tamed" in the middle class, but is redirected more into masturbation and petting rather than coitus. When we talk of under- or oversocialization, then, we are taking as our standard of socialization the middle-class norms, which is a convenient but hardly objective or scientific basis for our terminology. These prefixes tend to ignore the specific content of socialization at different status levels, which we shall emphasize.

What clues do we have so far about child-training practices conducive to the development of class differences in psychosis and character disorders as opposed to neurosis? Widespread training for orderliness suggests

[12] Albert K. Cohen, *Delinquent Boys*, New York, The Free Press, 1955, pp. 88–93.
[13] George Simpson, *People in Families*, New York, Crowell, 1960, pp. 291–792.
[14] Allison Davis and Robert J. Havighurst, "Social Class and Color Differences in Child-Rearing," *American Sociological Review*, 11(6), 1946, 698–710.

obsessional behavior and repetition compulsion amounting to a socially patterned defect in the middle class. Here, perhaps, is a potential pool of middle-class neurotics, which may help to account for our increasing rates in the higher SES groups. Moreover, taming, even when it involves not total blocking but merely rechanneling of sexual or aggressive behavior, is likely to result in anxiety and guilt. This is typical of neurosis, and the mechanisms are discussed below in terms of the rechanneling of middle-class premarital sexual expression into noncoital forms in favor of prolonged education.

The equating of psychoses and character disorders with the "untamed" nature of the lower class is an attractive but highly oversimplified explanation of the greater rates of such disturbances at lower status levels. Aside from hereditary tendencies to schizophrenia, which may play some part in this phenomenon, there are numerous aspects of family structure and interaction that might promote the development of the psychoses and character disorders. Some of these are the differential development of the superego and ego, middle-class training for a sense of identity and individuality, middle-class emphasis on expression and communication within the family, and the often severe adult-life conditions of the lower class.

*Training for a Sense of Identity.* While it represses and redirects the sexual and aggressive behavior of its children, the middle class also attempts to inculcate a sense of individuality and identity which often seems lacking at lower social levels. This sense of identity we choose to treat separately from the problem of the negative self-image in the lower class. The identity of the middle-class child is enhanced and established in many ways. Not the least of these may be the lower birthrate of the middle class. The only child, or the child with few siblings, may well tend to feel more of an individual. He does not need to share his toys or wear hand-me-down clothing. His parents are less apt to relate to "the children" as a group. The expression "two's company, three's a crowd" might apply to children as well. A certain impersonality almost inevitably develops when there is a large group involved, be it guests or family members. The equanimity of the group, and not its individual members, becomes paramount. The lower the status, the greater the family size in Midtown, as might be expected. Individual identity, therefore, may be enhanced by smaller families typical of the higher strata.

A study of underprivileged children in New York City[15] uncovered an illuminating fact: some of these third- to sixth-grade children had never been to a birthday party, and very few of them knew their own birth dates. Perhaps no single act of the parents symbolizes the identity of the

[15] Judith I. Krugman, "Cultural Deprivation and Child Development," *Strengthening Democracy*, 9(25), May 1957, Board of Education of the City of New York, Brooklyn, New York.

child more clearly than the celebration of his birthday. This is a formal recognition of his growth and development, and a reaffirmation of his membership and acceptance in the family as an individual.

Other middle-class practices seem to have a latent function of feeding the child back his own image and developing in him a sense of growth and accomplishment. The individual scrapbook, the baby book, and the family photo album all help develop the child's sense of identity. Again, individual clothing is emphasized in the upper strata. A girl must not be "caught dead" in the same party dress as her sister or friend. The idea of a uniform style of dress, or working uniform, so common among poorer and especially peasant peoples of the world is repugnant, excepting the higher-status "gray flannel suit." The strength of the repugnance, it is suggested, may stem from its discouragement of individuality. The romantic-love complex, limited mostly to the upper classes of the middle ages, and later to the middle and upper classes stemming from Western Europe, stresses the "one and only love of a lifetime." Among other things, this represents a highly individual approach to marriage, with the choice of partner taken away from the family group. The idea of indispensability is fostered in many ways for the high-status person, and the low-status person is constantly reminded of his replaceability, whether in the family or the factory. In the higher strata the smaller classes in private schools and individual tutoring of lessons (an upper-class phenomenon rapidly dying out) make for a greater sense of identity and perhaps concern with self. The somewhat surprising finding that middle-class parents make demands for individual responsibility earlier than lower-class parents is further evidence of this subtle training. The busy lower-class mother does not have time to train children to set the table, feed the dog, or make the beds when they are not really old enough to help.

Perhaps a sense of identity, although a false sense, so to speak, comes from the possession of material objects in the middle and upper classes. A widely accepted tenet of the Protestant Ethic is "One is what one has." Originally, a person might point to his possessions as evidence that he had worked hard in the occupation to which God had "called" him. Tangible evidence (material possessions) of hard work made one at least an eligible candidate for a state of grace. If we still believe, by and large, that one is what one has, then the "have-not" individual "is not." The expression "He's a nobody" does not refer to a disembodied spirit, but rather to a dispirited person of low status. The middle-class child is trained to want to be "somebody." In a very basic sense, then, one does not *gain* identity unless one has possessions. Conversely, if one loses possessions, one loses identity. This equation is certainly limited to particular segments of particular cultures, and runs almost counter to much Oriental philosophy, which maintains that until one is stripped of earthly possessions one cannot find oneself.

Identity based upon possessions is certainly unstable and impermanent. The fear of losing possessions, then prestige, and finally identity may very well enter into the formation of neurotic anxiety. Nevertheless, possessions may help to foster a sense of identity in a middle-class environment, and as long as this identity is not based *solely* on possessions, it will be relatively stable. Thus the struggle for possessions may encourage neurosis and the lack of possessions encourage loss of identity and perhaps psychosis, especially in the pervasive middle-class atmosphere of pecuniary emulation found in the metropolis. In all probability, the rate of neurosis increases as the rate of individualism increases; perhaps a worthwhile compromise.

The relation of neurosis to identity is certainly not clear. Hollingshead and Redlich feel that identity based on sex and dominance is better developed in the middle class. "We also think that the identity formation covering sex, and possibly also dominance, emerges more clearly defined in the middle-class families where the dissolution of the oedipal conflict is more apt to take its classical course than in lower-class families."[16]

Ivy Bennett,[17] comparing delinquent and neurotic children, comes to somewhat different conclusions. The delinquents are predominantly lower class, the neurotics, half lower and half middle class. The sexual identification of the neurotics was often confused; this was not evident among the delinquents. While this finding is based on patient data, so is the New Haven Study. Our own feeling is that the oedipal resolution of middle-class *girls* is relatively poor. Moreover, the middle-class resolution of dominance seems to be more complete, since in Midtown there are fewer passive, dependent, and submissive persons in this social group and a greater proportion of aggressive ones. Interestingly enough, Midtown women who say they "take after father" are predominantly of higher status, and have a substantially reduced mental health risk. Perhaps some masculine identification is an asset among these younger unmarried women who are often holding more prestigeful jobs than their fathers.

The pathology of excessive concern with identity (as opposed to loss or lack of identity) is given detailed treatment by Hans Syz. What he describes is the neurotic self-destructiveness involved in continual concern with the self-image, a problem more typical of the higher-status individual.

I use the term autistic image dependence to characterize the dynamic trend in self-structure as well as in social interaction that is intensively preoccupied with and dependent upon the defense of the self-image, experienced as a detached entity which is potentially opposed or hostile to other humans and the outside world.[18]

[16] A. B. Hollingshead and F. C. Redlich, *op. cit.*, p. 362.
[17] Ivy Bennett, *Delinquent and Neurotic Children*, New York, Basic Books, 1960.
[18] Hans Syz, "Problems of Perspective Against the Background of Trigant Burrow's Group-Analytic Researches," *International Journal of Group Psychotherapy*, **9**(2), April 1961, 151.

The dynamics of autistic image-bondage are expressed in the prevailing forms of education and social conditioning in which each child is trained to respond to right-wrong signals which are used for parental convenience, as a promise of love and protection, and as mutual defense of personal advantage and distinction. These educational techniques tend to perpetuate a dynamic structure in individual and society through which the *appearance* of social interest is employed for unacknowledged competitive interests and self-centered defenses.[19]

Identity, whether absent, blurred, or excessive, creates a problem for all the social strata. The Lows, however, may have too little identity and the Highs too much, so to speak.

*Training for Communication.* The establishment of channels for communication emotions and expressing feelings might be considered one of the primary eugenic functions of the family. Where such communication is blocked, the feelings, whether of love or of hate, must be focused outside the family or released in fantasy. Strong peer-group formation and high rates of juvenile delinquency suggest that low SES children must focus love and hate to a great degree outside the family. Again, the high rates of psychosis and schizoid symptoms among the Lows might support the hypothesis that withdrawal and fantasy are important alternative modes of adaptation to this stress, blocked communication.

What evidence have we that there are class differentials in communication? On the most general level, middle-class children show much earlier language development, which in itself enables them to tell others how they feel and to understand how their parents feel. Infants under a year old who come from professional and business families vocalize more and employ more different sounds than children from lower-class homes.[20] Another study showed that children with delayed speech came more from lower-class homes than those who spoke at a normal age.[21] Twins of the upper three occupational classes were found superior in language development to twins of the lower three occupational classes.[22] Ella Day, in summarizing previous work, tells us that Descoeudres,[23] Drever,[24] Gesell and Lord,[25] Hetzer and Rcindorf,[26] Smith,[27] and McCarthy[28] have

[19] *Ibid.*, pp. 151–152.

[20] O. C. Irwin, "Infant Speech: The Effect of Family Occupational Status and Age on Use of Sound Types," *Journal of Speech Hearing Disorders*, **13**(3), 1948, 224–226.

[21] R. E. Beckey, "A Study of Certain Factors Related to Retardation of Speech," *Journal of Speech Disorders*, **7**(3), 1942, 223–249.

[22] Ella J. Day, "Language Development in Twins," in Wayne Dennis (ed.), *Readings in Child Psychology*, Prentice-Hall, Englewood Cliffs, New Jersey, 1958.

[23] A. Descoeudres, *Le Développement de L'Enfant de Deux à Sept Ans*, Delachaux et Niestle, Neuchâtel and Paris, 1921.

[24] J. Drever, "The Vocabulary of a Free Kindergarten Child," *Journal of Experimental Pedagogy*, **5**(1), 1919, 28–37.

[25] A. Gesell and E. Lord, "A Psychological Comparison of Nursery-School Children, from Homes of Low and High Economic Status," *Pedagogical Seminary*, **34**(3), Sept. 1927, 339–356.

all found a positive relationship between socioeconomic status and language development.[29]

The higher-status child not only is better equipped to say how he feels but also is allowed to express those feelings more frequently to his parents than the low-status child.

Other evidence from our research substantiates this SES difference. For example, 36.9 per cent of the Lows compared with 23.5 per cent of the Highs said they did not have teenage disagreements with their parents. More high status men disagreed with their fathers, and more high-status women disagreed with their mothers, when compared to the low-status half of the sample. The Highs consistently showed a larger proportion disagreeing where only 7.7 per cent of the Lows, compared with about twice the percentage of Highs (13.8 per cent) said they disagreed with both parents.

These data are in apparent contradiction to some of Davis' generalizations concerning lower-class aggression. The lower-class "girls and boys at adolescence may curse their father to his face or even attack him with fists, sticks, or axes in free-for-all family encounters."[30]

The direction of verbal or physical aggression toward the parent, particularly the father, in the lower-class home is perhaps less frequent than we have been led to believe. That there is more aggressive expression outside the low SES home can be accepted as fact. However, other research seems to corroborate the Midtown data just mentioned. For example, Maccoby and Gibbs[31] found that high SES parents gave their children greater freedom to be aggressive toward them. Perhaps these findings are not truly contradictory, for long-suppressed anger which has been given no vent by very strict low SES parents may burst the dam with greater frequency than in higher SES families, which have a type of safety valve in more frequent verbal battles.

We can only suggest that this lack of emotional communication makes the low SES family a breeding ground for delinquency, when hostile feelings are acted out chiefly beyond the confines of the home, and for withdrawal into fantasy when extrafamilial expression is also forbidden.

[29] E. J. Day, op. cit., p. 300.
[30] Allison Davis, "Child Rearing in the Class Structure of American Society," in Community Service Society of New York, The Family in Democratic Society, Columbia University Press, New York, 1949, pp. 49–69.
[31] E. E. Maccoby and P. K. Gibbs, op. cit.

[26] H. Hetzer and B. Reindorf, "Sprachentwicklung und Soziales Milieu," Zeitschrift für Angewandte Psychologie, 29, 1928, 449–462.
[27] M. E. Smith, "An Investigation of the Development of the Sentence and the Extent of Vocabulary in Young Children," University of Iowa Studies in Child Welfare, 3(5), 1926.
[28] D. A. McCarthy, The Language Development of the Preschool Child, Institute of Child Welfare Monograph Series No. 4, University of Minnesota Press, Minneapolis, 1930.

Perhaps the low communication also fosters the development of character disorders and the personality traits of suspiciousness and rigidity. Suspicion is bred when conflicts are not aired, rigidity is encouraged as a defense against unexpressed hostile feelings (as well as sexual feelings which are more directly expressed at the lower SES levels). The Lows' greater rate of sociopathy, of psychosis (particularly paranoid schizophrenia, which involves the projection of hostile and often homosexual feelings onto others), and character disorders may all be partly related to poor emotional communication in the lower-class family.

Communication is a double-edged sword, however. The improved communication in the higher SES family may also communicate the status anxiety, the competitiveness, the obsession with self that seem more typical of the neurotic. While reducing overt aggression to acceptable levels, the middle-class family's communicative and rechanneling efforts may be less effective in the sexual area. Some data might be construed as casting doubt on the sexual identification of higher SES Midtowners. As we move from the immigrant to the fourth generation (which is almost 100 per cent high SES), there is a steady increase in the number of boys who "take after" their mothers, and girls who "take after" their fathers in "character, personality, and temperament." Bennett[32] found evidence of confused sexual identification in neurotic children, who came half from middle-class and half from lower-class homes. She did not find such evidence of inversion among delinquents, two-thirds of whom came from lower-class homes.

We found in many of the neurotic children trends in their behavior, interests and activities contrary to their biological role and sexual disposition, and indicative of confused identification patterns within their characters. This finding offers indirect support for Freud's theory of the sexual aetiology of the neuroses and of the tendency towards inversion that lies behind many adult neuroses.[33]

The association of both higher rates of neurosis and evidence of a greater proportion of cross-sex identification with higher SES in Midtown seems to have a curious consonance with Bennett's findings. At all times it is important to remember that while the Highs suffer less impairment, persons at both ends of the socioeconomic scale exhibit maladaptive behavior, and that for every sociopath or psychotic among the Lows there is probably a neurotic among the Highs.

## SEX AND EDUCATION

Closely related to the problem of child-rearing is the area of sex and education, in which the greater contrast between the behavior of the

[32] I. Bennett, *op. cit.*
[33] *Ibid.*, pp. 216–217.

social classes occurs. The sexual training of the child seems selected
to produce the correct social type desired in each class. For instance, we
find masturbation still frowned upon in the lower class, whereas early
intercourse is condoned, if not encouraged. To reiterate, Kinsey found that
males who had not had sexual intercourse by age seventeen were either
mentally deficient or on their way to college. The nonacceptance of
masturbation and the condoning of early intercourse tends to channel the
lower-class adolescent into early marriage. By age fifteen, almost 50 per
cent of lower-class males and only 10 per cent of higher SES males have
had sexual intercourse.[34] The parents of the middle-class child certainly
condone and may encourage masturbation, but they frown on early
intercourse. The chance of a pregnancy may mean an early marriage, thus
interfering with college education. This education will provide the
technical and social skills that will allow the young person to maintain a
status equal to or better than that of his parents. Masturbation and petting
are thus socially sanctioned premarital sexual outlets for the middle class.

The girlhood of Herman Wouk's Marjorie Morningstar is a good
example of the redirection of middle-class premarital sexual expression
away from intercourse. After almost 200 pages of constant dating, her
boyfriend, Noel, complains,

"Look—I'm not a college boy. Necking disgusts me. I can have all the sex I want,
when I want it, with the pleasantest of partners—"
"Not with me you can't," she broke in without thinking.[35]

Three hundred and fifty pages later she is still weighing the question
of virginity.

Twentieth century or not, good Jewish girls were supposed to be virgins when
they married. . . . For that matter good Christian girls are supposed to be virgins
too; that was why brides wore white.[36]

It is the middle-class adolescent to whom the terms "stretched puberty"
and "psychosexual moratorium" apply, for they are forced to delay or
rechannel their sexual gratifications. The relationship between higher
education (part of the index of socioeconomic status) and neurosis, so
obvious in our data, was foreshadowed by Freud, who felt that neurosis is
the price we pay for civilization.

If the evolution of civilization has such a far-reaching similarity with the development of an individual, and if the same methods are employed in both, would not
the diagnosis be justified that many systems of civilization—or epochs of it—
possibly even the whole of humanity—have become "neurotic" under the
pressure of civilizing trends?[37]

[34] A. C. Kinsey, W. B. Pomeroy, and C. E. Martin, op. cit.
[35] Herman Wouk, Marjorie Morningstar, Doubleday, New York, 1955, p. 170.
[36] Ibid., p. 552.
[37] Sigmund Freud, Civilization and Its Discontents, translated by Joan Riviere,
Fourth impression, London, The Hogarth Press, 1949, p. 141.

. . . the price of progress in civilization is paid in forfeiting happiness through the heightening of the sense of guilt.[38]

Neurosis is inevitably bound up with the general asceticism necessary to complete a course of higher education. Our educational system is, indeed, the transmitter of our culture and civilization and the source of our growing knowledge and skills. It is the civilizing of sexual and aggressive impulses that enables us to have "civilization," but at the price of neurotic anxiety. Hollingshead and Redlich feel that "It is also possible that more intensive sexualization plays a role in the class V child's inhibition to learn in school."[39] This seems to be putting things backwards, for it is more likely that the *de*sexualization of the middle-class child enables him to continue on the rigorous program of prolonged schooling (or more properly, the channeling of the sexual drives into masturbation, petting, and necking rather than intercourse). These authors also point out that identification with role models (people with higher education and "good manners," or people with lower education given to physical as well as verbal expression of their feelings) has a major part in determining the development and career of the child.

The importance of the channeling of the sexual drive in creating class differences in personality must not be underemphasized. Kinsey[40] found that the sexual history invariably predicts where the individual will end up in the status system. Boys destined for a higher education have later and less frequent intercourse, are more prone to masturbate, neck, or pet, will have less frequent intercourse during their lives, and will cease having intercourse earlier. These patterns are already laid down early in life, therefore preceding the social mobility of the individual. There is good reason to believe that they may be causally related to the mobility patterns that follow. This is all the more true at this stage in our country's development where education is the primary means of achieving upward social mobility. Formerly, fortunes were made quickly in exploiting the raw materials of an expanding frontier, but many of these sources have been exploited, and the man with technical and professional skills is now most likely to "make good." Thus, the parents who can train their children to develop the frustration tolerance necessary to put off such major pleasures as sexual intercourse, marriage, and having children until one is "earning a good living" (i.e., $10,000 to $15,000 a year) will not have downward mobile children.

We have found that the Obsessive-Compulsives are more numerous among the middle and high SES strata and particularly among the upwardly mobile. (The rigid types, associated with the rigid-hostile-suspicious syndrome, are more common in the low SES, however.) The obsessives

---

[38] *Ibid.*, p. 123.
[39] A. B. Hollingshead and F. C. Redlich, *op. cit.*, p. 363.
[40] A. C. Kinsey, W. B. Pomeroy, and C. E. Martin, *op. cit.*, p. 419.

are more punctual, orderly, and perfectionistic. These characteristics enable them to climb in the social system, for it is this type of organization and punctuality that is necessary for most white-collar and many managerial jobs. This type of personality and the obsessional neurosis are usually assumed to be linked to fairly severe toilet training and anal fixation. Certainly our middle class used to have more severe toilet training than did the lower class. This may be causally related to obsessive-compulsive characteristics, or it may be due merely to the fact that parents who want their children to "do better" also tend to be fairly strict in their toilet training, since they want them to be better in that area also. The desire for early speech, early weaning, early toilet training, and rapid advancement in school may well be part of a general desire to achieve and/or maintain status through the child. This desire for early development is coupled, of course, with an apparently inconsistent desire for *late* development in sexual activity. The early or severe toilet training in itself may not be significant, although it may be an index of a parent's general desire for the child to mature rapidly and excel others. It is also not unbelievable that the frustration of sexual and eliminatory pleasures builds up a frustration tolerance that makes it possible for the middle-class child to hold back from forbidden heterosexual activities and develop a general retentiveness that will aid the educational and, later, the financial processes.

Of course, the development of obsessive-compulsive characteristics may eventually interfere with functioning and with advancement, even in a bureaucratic setting. Such writers as Merton[41] and Burke[42] have shown how the bureaucratic personality may eventually interfere with the functions of the individual and the organization. At higher levels, where decision-making and a certain ability to break the rules are necessary, the obsessive bureaucrat is "fit in an unfit fitness." He has become unfitted for advancement, just by fitting so well into his punctual, perfectionist, and rule-abiding role at the lower positions he has held.

The large number of factors—as indicated by the low SES elevated average Stress Score—shows us that persons of low status get more hard knocks in adulthood, but about the same number as the middle class in childhood. It should be remembered, however, that our low SES is chiefly an older and immigrant group. They are no more likely to report broken homes or parental rejection than the middle class (middle and high SES), and only in the sphere of economic deprivation does their childhood seem more severe than that of the middle class. In New Haven, the impression of the research team is that the lower class has a worse time emotionally as well as financially.

Lifelong dependency and characterological states of dejection, apathy, and lack of trust in others may be related to damage in this phase of the life cycle (early

[41] R. K. Merton, *op. cit.*
[42] Kenneth Burke, "Permanence and Change," *New Republic*, New York, 1935.

infancy). We postulate that the presence or absence of these characteristics is related to the child-rearing practices associated with families in the different social classes. For instance, a loveless infancy is more likely in a class V family than in a class II family.[43]

While depression and suspiciousness are certainly more numerous in our lower class (of nonpatients), the respondents' reports of rejecting or domineering parents (Parents' Character Negatively Perceived) do not vary proportionally between the classes. It may be that the dejection, apathy, and suspicion that are part of every infancy are more strongly fostered by childhood, adolescent, and adult experiences of the lower-class individual who finds himself rejected by society, so to speak. Thus, any lower-class parental rejection will be reinforced by societal rejection in adult life, while the compensations of status, power, and other gratifications may be accorded the wealthier individual, thereby counteracting his earlier rejection.

## ADULT LIFE EXPERIENCES

The low SES has more than its share of adult factors. A much larger proportion of the Lows than of the Middle or Highs report Adult Poor Physical Health, Poor Interpersonal Affiliations, and Parental Worries. The physical health factor, it will be remembered, was twice as powerful as any other factor because it was always associated with greater impairment. The high SES is more given to Work Worries (associated with less impairment) and Marital Worries. We already know that a larger proportion of the low than the high SES worry about the cost of living, feel that life is futile (according to the Anomie Scale), are friendless, and worry about loneliness (see Table 1). They also tend to dislike their jobs. They are worse off in terms of physical health, interpersonal relations, and work. The high SES, however, are more apt to worry about a variety of problems that are actually more prevalent at lower SES levels. The most important difference between the classes is that the Lows have, on the average, a greater number of adult stresses than the Highs. Add to this the fact that the low SES stresses seem to involve more mental health risk than the typically high SES stresses, and you have some substantiation of the hypothesis suggested by the New Haven research team.

Lower-class living appears to stimulate the development of psychotic disorders. We infer that the excess of psychoses from the poorer area is a product of the life conditions entailed in the lower socioeconomic strata of the society.[44]

We can even go further, and suggest that it is the adult life conditions in particular that stimulate the development of high rates of psychosis in

[43] A. B. Hollingshead and F. C. Redlich, *op. cit.*, p. 361.
[44] *Ibid.*, p. 242.

the lower class; for the childhood conditions, at least as reported by our respondents, do not vary substantially between the classes.

## SELF-ESTEEM AND EGO-STRENGTH

This brings us to another possible source of class differences in type of mental disturbance: the self-image, self-esteem, and ego-strength. In our country there is a general stigmatization of manual labor. The laborer is looked down upon, and successive waves of immigrants have provided the unskilled labor necessary. Manual labor has not lost its stigma as immigration decreased.

The doctrine of luck is used to preserve the self-esteem of the lower class. Luck, fate, and God's will are often invoked to explain one's poverty and poor health, when these ills may be the result of technological unemployment, poor education, or bad diet. Or, the system may be blamed, so that such expressions as, "It's not what you know, but whom you know" are also more accepted at lower-class levels.[45] The Midtown questionnaire statement, "There are no right and wrong ways, only easy and hard ways to make money," and similar items are invariably agreed with more in the low stratum than among the Middles or Highs. The phrase, "It's all a racket," is the lower-class way of looking at the chancy American Dream, the success pattern that depends not on your skill and stick-to-itiveness but rather on some freak and irrational accident. Life is just a series of hardships or "breaks."[46]

Typically, the lower-class person reduces his status anxiety by lowering his sights, by "dreaming in second gear," as Russell Lynes[47] put it. Surveys have shown that the lower class wants safe jobs in preference to jobs with a chance of advancement. Security quite naturally comes first in the value system of the have-not. "A bird in the hand is worth two in the bush." The lower-class individual doesn't stick his neck out, because he knows the odds are that he'll get it cut off. The middle- and upper-class individual, whose life has been easier, is willing to take a chance, and he has some capital or cushioning behind him in case of failure.

The reduction of aspiration level is seen vividly in studies of high school seniors. Those from lower-class backgrounds reduce their aspirations in their senior year, as they get nearer to graduation and to the reality of their social class position.

The self-esteem of a child is based, to a large degree, on the status of the parents, and the parents' self-esteem. The son of a laborer is more

[45] R. K. Merton, *op. cit.*, pp. 136–140.
[46] Leo Lowenthal, "Biographies in Popular Magazines," in Paul F. Lazarsfeld and Frank Stanton (eds.), *Radio Research, 1942–3*, Duell, Sloan & Pearce, New York, 1944, pp. 507–549.
[47] Russell Lynes, *A Surfeit of Honey*, New York, Harper, 1953.

likely to internalize a self-rejecting father, a father who judges himself in the same way society judges him. This lowers the self-esteem of the son. Perhaps he is also a member of a minority or immigrant group. This, in turn, lowers his liking of himself and he is apt to develop a negative self-image. A good example of how society produces poor self-esteem is this complaint by the son of an Italian immigrant.

You don't know how it feels to grow up in a district like this. You go to the first grade—Miss O'Rouke. Second grade—Miss Casey. Third grade—Miss Chalmers. Fourth grade—Miss Mooney. And so on. At the fire station it is the same. None of them are Italians. The police lieutenant is an Italian, and there are a couple of Italian sergeants, but they have never made an Italian captain in Cornerville. In the settlement houses, none of the people with authority are Italians.

Now you must know that the old-timers here have a great respect for schoolteachers and anybody like that. When an Italian boy sees that none of his own people have the good jobs, why should he think he is as good as the Irish or the Yankees? It makes him feel inferior.[48]

There is a somewhat academic yet interesting distinction between the dynamics of the first- and second-generation identification. The child of the immigrant identifies with a parent who still thinks highly of the ways and values of the "old country," and of himself since he behaves in accordance with those values. The grandchild of the immigrant identifies with a parent who has become partially acculturated, and perhaps thinks less of himself because he is not totally acculturated. Thus the grandchild of the immigrant internalizes a parent with a negative self-image. The child of the immigrant internalizes a parent whose ways are more openly at odds with the new culture and whose self-image may be more positive. These differences, even if valid, do not seem to be associated with broad generation differences in psychiatric impairment, as noted before. Immigrants of low SES exhibit more impairment than immigrants of high SES, and the same is true for their children. What really hurts, as the street-corner boy tells us, is that not one of the Italians has the good job, the job with authority.

The fact that one's parents (particularly one's father) hold inferior positions may do more than create feelings of inferiority or shame. It may lead to social isolation from peer-groups. The feelings of shame may cause the child to withdraw for fear of ridicule, or rejection by children of higher status may produce the same result. Another possible result is the intensification of the normal conflict with the like-sex parent. The son may focus his hostility to his father on the father's menial occupation. He will find that the neighbors or his teacher support his negative perception of his father, which only adds fuel to the fire. The acceptance of the denigration of their fathers is seen in these cases quoted by Simpson:

[48] William Foote Whyte, *Street Corner Society*, Chicago, University of Chicago Press, 1943, p. 276.

When I was in the sixth grade a neighboring woman told me that she considered my father's occupation rather scummy and that she did not want her children contaminated by association with me. It dawned on me that not everybody regarded my father like I did when I was a child, *so that I came not to tell what my father did....*

I seem to have gotten an increasing awareness of the lack of prestige that was associated with my father's occupation. It came to a point where, if I could avoid it, *I never mentioned him.*

I came to feel a sense of *shame* and *embarrassment* about my father's job, not because of the lack of money, but because of the lack of status. I recall being very impressed with the status of occupations of other parents and *secretly wishing that my father could achieve that status* so that I could impress other boys and girls.[49]

Ego-strength and the self-image arise primarily from the strength of the ego-ideal, the internalized parents (in their positive, rather than restrictive, aspects). Recently, several investigators have noted that the lower class suffers from poor ego-strength.

Such future work might explore systematically our impression that members of the lower classes, particularly of class V, have a weaker ego than members of the higher classes. Many of them seem to be less able to check their own impulses, and they are more passive in their attempts to master the harsh reality aspects of their lives.[50]

Other authors consider ego-strength and self-esteem part of the same system. They feel that the individual's self-image is to a large extent an incorporation or introjection of what others think of him. Public definitions of the self tend to be accepted as correct.

Our theory is that the whole network of prerogatives, attitudes, and expectations surrounding any class position has important consequences for the individual ego-structure which, in turn, is an important factor in determining resistance to mental illness. By ego-structure is meant the complex of factors concerning the ego—the self picture, self-esteem, feelings of adequacy, and most important of all, the ego-strength which prescribes, on one hand, the amount of impulse control and, on the other hand, the degree of successful management of the environment.[51]

As kind, generous, and loving as a lower-class father may be, he still does not make a good role-model or identification figure as long as he, like the majority of his class, accepts what society thinks of him. Economic achievement, in our culture, is considered to be ultimate proof of individual superiority. The roots of this belief have been traced from the "state of grace" that hard work in a "calling" gave to the Protestant individual after the Reformation. The Protestant Ethic was important in

[49] George Simpson, *op. cit.*, pp. 304–305.
[50] A. B. Hollingshead and F. C. Redlich, *op. cit.*, p. 366.
[51] Bert Kaplan, Robert B. Reed, and Wyman Richardson, "Comparison of the Incidence of Hospitalized and Non-Hospitalized Cases of Psychosis in Two Communities," *Americal Sociological Review*, **21**(4), August 1956, 479.

laying the groundwork for the pecuniary emulation and invidious comparisons based on money, leisure, and consumption described by Thorstein
Veblen. The American male who is not earning a good living is not
considered to be "a man," and his morality, as well as his virility and
mental health, is open to question.

Since "worldly asceticism" (the denial of instinctual drives in favor
of long-term occupational goals) is assumed to be a social value, and
vertical mobility and advancement are only "natural," it follows that
everyone must have a function, i.e., the performance of useful work, in
order to maintain his mental health. By the same token, those who are
not working or having difficulty in their work are "mentally disturbed."

The psychiatrist, in accord with the conventions of his culture, which sanction
work and condemn idleness, assumes as a rule, that the person who does not
work is ill and that the ability to work once more is evidence of the recovery of
mental health.[52]

Not only is unemployment or work difficulty considered to be a *result*
of mental disturbance, but sometimes the striving for economic security
is written off as a mere displacement, as just a symbol of a "deeper"
emotional insecurity. While this may in part be true of the wealthier
neurotic (who is more likely to be analyzed in these terms), the emotional
insecurity of the lower-class individual may very well arise from an even
more basic economic insecurity, perhaps starting with food deprivation
in infancy or childhood.

Suffice it to say that work as a value pervades our culture and hence
our clinics. Although economic striving dominates our lives, as Davis
points out, case histories seldom give the full details of the effects of our
system of striving and stratification.

Much attention has perforce been devoted to guilt feelings, inferiority complexes,
anxiety states, and emotional conflicts. Yet, though these clearly reflect the
power of invidious comparison, they are hardly seen to be social at all.[53]

Certainly future research should not neglect the investigation of the
exact mechanisms by which status differentials, "relative deprivation,"
class reference and class membership, and particularly status disequi-
libration aid in the production of mental disturbance. How often has the
individual (or patient) been compared to or compared himself to a superior
individual or group? Have emotionally significant people made these
comparisons? Have parents denigrated their own economic achievements,
lack of education, or taste? Have teachers held the parents' ideals up to
ridicule? Have the parents come from different social classes, or different

[52] Stanley A. Leavy and Lawrence Z. Freedman, "Psychoneurosis and Economic
Life," *Social Problems*, **4**(1), July, 1956, 59.
[53] Kingsley Davis, "Mental Hygiene and the Class Structure," in Arnold M. Rose
(ed.), *Mental Health and Mental Disorder*, New York, Norton, 1955, pp. 590–591.

generations with respect to immigration? How meaningful is achievement for a particular lower-class individual? How does he define achievement, and in these terms, has he "achieved," is he "successful?" (Dr. Abraham Kardiner, the psychoanalyst, once told of a patient who was a trigger man and whose trigger finger was paralyzed. He didn't want to be analyzed out of killing, he just wanted to continue to be a success in what he considered a promising career.)

The internalization of socially-disapproved low-status parents, or inability to identify with them, the recurring rejections suffered outside the family by the minority group member and the lower-class individual, the constant reminders of status differentials carried by the mass media, particularly television, all make for reinforcement of a negative self-image. The ability to meet stress and the normal disaster, to fight back and to master life comes, in large part, from self-confidence. This self-confidence, in turn, comes largely from experiencing the love of parents who love and accept themselves.

## THE SUPEREGO AND RELATED ATTITUDES

Directly related to ego-strength is impulse control, for the ego and the superego both take a part. The lower-class person is more likely to have a poorly internalized superego. This may be, in part, because the physical punishment to which he is subjected by parents is more direct and external. Principally, however, the development of a superego is contingent on a strong bond of love between parent and child. The child who is physically punished without the threat of loss of love will play according to the rules only as long as the policeman is watching. The middle-class child, on the contrary, has internalized the policemen, and will stick to the rules even if nobody is looking. This quality in itself is necessary for success, as defined by the middle class in our culture. The development of guilt, the anxiety over loss of love necessary to make an individual sacrifice or redirect both sexual and aggressive activities—these are the mechanisms by which children are prepared to maintain or achieve high social status.

The love bond between parent and child is a key to why the process of civilization or taming results primarily in neurosis rather than in any other variety of mental disorder. First, the middle and upper classes, inasmuch as they bring about greater repression and redirection of the sexual instincts, are more "civilizing." Now if the upper class simply suppressed sexual activity, their children would be covertly rebellious and would engage in coitus whenever they were not being watched. Through the medium of love and the close emotional attachments of parent and child in the middle and upper classes, the sexual prohibitions are deeply internalized by the child. The unconscious desire to circumvent these internalized rules and the hostility aroused against the parent for curtailing sexual activities (as well as aggressive behavior) lead to severe guilt feelings. No guilt is associated with suppression alone. The class differences, then, may find some origins in the strong and demanding child-parent bond in the middle and upper classes. This bond produces a deeply internalized superego and anxiety over possibly losing the parents' love. The low SES child may tend more toward a fear of physical punishment and, due to a less intense relationship with the parents, will probably develop less guilt. As Freud pointed out, the severity of the child's superego does not correspond to the severity of the treatment it has received.[54]

One reason for this is that the kind, loving, intense relationship between parent and child appears to be mild rather than severe treatment. But it is this very "mild" treatment that results (because of the strength of the love bond) in the more "severe" superego formation. The "severe" treatment of the lower-class child by violent and sporadic outbursts of temper and physical punishment punctuating long periods of almost no parental supervision whatsoever results in a "mild" superego. If, from another viewpoint, we examine the mildness or severity of instinctual repression and of emotional and behavioral demands made on the child, then the upper classes are more "severe," and this severity coincides with the severity of the child's superego formation.

The very fact that there is such a strong love bond in the higher stratum makes us feel that there will be closer identification of child with parent. We previously suggested that identification with the low-status father or mother is difficult for the lower-class child surrounded by higher status models (teachers), and this status problem further weakens their supergo formation. If the parent is not in authority by virtue of his skill and knowledge ("rational authority")[55] he must rely on the use of "irrational authority," that is, "Obey me simply because I am your parent." This is more typical of the lower-class parent, who has little "rational authority" because of his low status in the community at large.

Of course, we may be misled through case histories reported by high-status clinicians into believing that only a weak or superficial superego is developed in the low SES. Certainly the lower class has deeply internalized the success goals of the American Dream. They want to get ahead as badly as anybody else. In fact, they want to get ahead so badly that they will use means that are not acceptable to the middle class in order to attain success. As Merton has pointed out, they have internalized the goals, but not the means to those goals.[56] Thus, we find many lower-class persons

[54] S. Freud, *op. cit.*, p. 116.
[55] Erich Fromm, "Individual and Social Origins of Neurosis," *American Sociological Review*, **9**(3), 1944, 380–384.
[56] R. K. Merton, *op. cit.*, p. 146.

with a strongly internalized success drive becoming gangsters or going into ward politics. These channels to success are not socially acceptable to the middle class. It is perhaps not the degree of internalization as much as the integration of the superego that the lower classes lack. Integration involves the incorporation of the "thou shalt nots" as well as the "thou shalts," the acceptance of the middle-class rules of the game as well as the goal of winning.

## EGO-IDEAL AND PLANNING

We can differentiate between the internalized restrictions, or superego, and the internalized positive goals, which we shall call the ego-ideal. The lower class is found to be lacking only in the area of restrictions. They possess a more primitive superego, not the internalized mature conscience we expect in the middle class. They internalize less of the social inhibitions but, on the other hand, they seem perfectly capable of internalizing most of the social goals, such as success. It therefore seems plausible that their ego-ideal is not so impaired as we have been led to believe. Such phenomena as psychopathy, "acting out," dyssocial behavior, and delinquency do not stem perhaps so much from poor internalization of goals as from poor internalization of socially accepted means to those goals. One questionnaire item attempted to assess this very same emphasis on the goals without a corresponding emphasis on the appropriate means to those goals. A much larger proportion of Lows than Highs agreed that, "To make money there are no right and wrong ways any more, only easy ways and hard ways" (see Table 1). This weakness of the inhibitory functions, coupled with what appears to be strong goal striving, makes for an increase of antisocial behavior in the lower class.[57]

It would be logical to expect that along with a disregard for the legitimate means to achieving goals, the immature superego of the lower class would create infantile demands for immediate goal fulfillment. On the contrary, the low SES did not agree more than the middle or upper SES with the statement "When I want something very much, I want it right away" (Lows 28.5 per cent, Middles 22.1 per cent, Highs 34.8 per cent). While these results do not seem to corroborate the hypothesis that the Lows have an immature superego, the following points should be noted.

Approximately one-fourth of the low SES agreed there were only "easy and hard ways to make money" and that they want things "right away." Further analysis may indicate that these are the same individuals, which would tend to corroborate the hypothesis. A type of adaptation

[57] It was suspected that the emphasis on luck and fate in the lower class is bound up with the spirit of gambling (not that the Middles and Highs don't gamble on horses and the stock market). The data make this assumption questionable, since about 22 per cent of all three SES levels said, "I suppose I'm a gambler at heart."

that may be reducing the prevalence of immature acting-out types in the low SES is a widespread lowering of aspiration level. The lowering of ambition and the curtailing of the fantasy life of children found among Lows is better calculated to produce agreement with an imaginary statement such as "When I want something very much, I just try to forget about it." The lower-class individual is less likely to plan ahead for something he wants very much. A somewhat larger proportion of the Lows agreed that "Nowadays, a person has to live pretty much for today and let tomorrow take care of itself" (see Table 1). A larger proportion of the Lows, then, may exhibit a short-term approach to their lives and avoidance of planning. The abandonment of goals is more typical of persons of low frustration tolerance, while the long-range planner chooses the calculated risk of long-term frustration in order to achieve his goals. At the risk of oversimplifying, it still seems probable that the constant postponement of eliminatory drives until it is "time to sit on the potty," the postponement of hunger until it is "mealtime," and of heterosexual relations until one is "ready to support a family" trains the middle- and upper-class individual to wait for the things he wants. The knowledge that he will probably get what he wants aids him during the waiting period. The knowledge, based on past experience, that he often doesn't get what he wants leads the lower-class person to "eat, drink, and be merry" while he can.

The depressive quality of the lower SES outlook has been established in previous chapters by their high Frustration-Depression Score and by their predominance in the psychiatrists' category of "depressed" (Lows 36.2 per cent, Middles 23.9 per cent, Highs 11.1 per cent). This category is typified by the item, "I am in low, or very low, spirits most of the time." Along with depression, the Lows exhibit pervasive feelings of futility as indicated by the "anomie" items.[58] (See Table 1). More Lows felt that "It's hardly fair to bring a child into the world with the way things look for the future." They also agreed that "In spite of what some people say, the lot (situation, condition) of the average man is getting worse, not better." Their alienation from others and political apathy are reflected in their strong agreement with such statements as "These days a person doesn't really know whom he can count on" and "Most public officials are not really interested in the problems of the average man." Another item indicating their feelings of futility and social isolation is "Most people don't really care what happens to the next fellow." Thus, the complex of depression and futility, political apathy and lack of trust in others and oneself is more typical of the lower class. When Fromm labeled the German lower middle class "sadomasochistic,"[59] he might just as well have been describing the low SES in our metropolitan setting.

[58] Leo Srole, "Social Integration and Certain Corollaries, An Exploratory Study," *American Sociological Review*, **21**(6), 1956, p. 709.
[59] Erich Fromm, *Escape from Freedom*, New York, Farrar and Rinehart, 1941.

It seems that Erich Fromm's use of the term lower middle class is more equivalent to the Midtown Lows than to the Midtown Middles. The German *Kleinbeamte*, or small official, such as streetcar conductors or post-office personnel derived some prestige from the fact that they were appointed officials. Such occupations can be classified as either Low, if manual, or Middle, if clerical, in the Midtown job hierarchy which is based on American prestige rankings. Since the *Kleinbeamte* made up a large part of the lower middle class in Germany, Fromm's "lower middles" fall mostly in the low and to some extent in the middle SES groups in Midtown.

*Table 1*—Proportion of Respondents Agreeing With "Anomie" Statements According to Respondents' Socioeconomic Status

| | Respondents' socioeconomic status | | |
| | LOW | MIDDLE | HIGH |
| "Anomie" statements | per cent | per cent | per cent |
|---|---|---|---|
| It's hardly fair to bring a child into the world with the way things look for the future. | 32.0 | 17.8 | 5.9 |
| In spite of what some people say, the lot (situation, condition) of the average man is getting worse, not better. | 48.0 | 28.6 | 11.6 |
| These days a person doesn't really know whom he can count on. | 64.5 | 52.0 | 26.4 |
| Most public officials (people in public office) are not really interested in the problems of the average man. | 60.8 | 54.3 | 40.9 |
| Most people don't really care what happens to the next fellow. | 53.5 | 40.1 | 23.4 |
| To make money there are no right or wrong ways any more, only easy and hard ways. | 24.1 | 14.0 | 4.3 |
| Nowadays a person has to live pretty much for today and let tomorrow take care of itself. | 50.7 | 36.7 | 29.6 |
| Total Number of Cases (*N* = 100 per cent) | 544 | 556 | 560 |

The feeling of impending doom and disaster, the fatalism and resignation, seem similar to Hollingshead and Redlich's picture of the downwardly mobile individual. The Lows and the downward mobile are both given to alcoholism and character disorders. Whether the crime and drug addiction rates are greater in the Midtown low SES cannot be said, but it is quite likely.

Indeed, even authoritarianism is prevalent in the low SES (see Table 2), again pointing to an association with sadomasochism. Such items as "Prison is too good for sex criminals: they should be publicly whipped, or worse," indicate the sadistic component of authoritarianism. The projection of hostile and sexual impulses onto others and the punishment of others for one's own real or imagined misdeeds is typical of persons with an externalized superego. The middle-class person feels guilt, and often punishes himself. The lower-class person is more apt to punish others and to project his motives onto others, such as minority groups, hidden Communists, and Martians, thus avoiding guilt feelings. The interdependence of sadism and masochism is seen in the other four authoritarian items. The Lows agree overwhelmingly with each of these items, "There are two kinds of people in this world: the weak and the strong." "Any good leader should be strict with people under him in order to gain their respect," "The most important thing to teach children is absolute obedience to their parents," and "What young people need most of all is strict discipline." It is unlikely that the large SES differences in agreeing with these questions are due entirely to response biases, such as acquiescence. The latter characteristic is in itself part of the masochistic component of the authoritarian complex, and doubtless is more typical of the low SES.

*Table 2*—Proportion of Respondents Agreeing with "Authoritarian" Statements According to the Respondents' Socioeconomic Status

| | Respondents' socioeconomic status | | |
| | LOW | MIDDLE | HIGH |
| *"Authoritarian" statements* | *per cent* | *per cent* | *per cent* |
|---|---|---|---|
| Prison is too good for sex criminals: they should be publicly whipped, or worse. | 46.3 | 36.5 | 8.0 |
| There are two kinds of people in this world: the weak and the strong. | 72.4 | 50.4 | 30.9 |
| Any good leader should be strict with people under him in order to gain their respect. | 64.9 | 46.6 | 27.7 |
| The most important thing to teach children is absolute obedience to their parents. | 74.8 | 52.3 | 14.5 |
| What young people need most of all is strict discipline. | 63.6 | 49.1 | 24.8 |
| Total Number of Cases (*N* = 100 per cent) | 544 | 556 | 560 |

The authoritarian statements reflect the hypothesized relationship between the lower-class parent and child. The parent is strong, the child weak. When the child becomes strong, he can get away with behavior that was formerly avoided because of fear of physical punishment by the parents. By the same reasoning, a good leader (or parent) should be strict in order to gain respect. The respect for authority is irrational, in the sense that it is based upon strictness and punishment. The upper-class parent, on the contrary, does not demand automatic "respect for elders," but gains such respect, for example, through the occupational sphere, through signs of deference given by subordinates (such as doormen and other servants), and through the threat of withdrawal of love.

The emphasis on discipline and obedience in the lower class seems paramilitary. This is not just a superficial resemblance. The army drains off hostility through war and hatred of the common enemy. The lower class expresses similar hostility in delinquency, crime, alcoholism, and outbreaks of physical violence. This is the essence of the externalized superego, or immature conscience. Strangely, it is the inability to externalize, to stop feeling guilty, to stop punishing themselves, that leads many upper-status neurotics to the psychoanalyst's couch. The acting-out disorder of the lower class is often a major therapeutic goal for the upper-status patient.

While the lower-class parental and societal authority is not supposed to be questioned, it is something that can be "gotten around" when nobody is watching. Authoritarianism indicates an underlying disrespect for all constituted authority, and only a thin shell of superficial conformity hides the violent impulses that sporadically break through.

The complex of rigidity, suspicion, and depression best characterizes the low SES. Tied to this complex is authoritarianism, sadomasochism, anomie, and futility, and social and emotional isolation stemming from distrust and hostility. A poor self-image and weak ego-strength abet this picture. This, together with a poorly internalized superego, results in inability to meet crises, to rise in the status system, and to inhibit socially unacceptable impulses in favor of striving toward approved long-term middle-class goals. A fear of failure in the pursuit of these approved goals, a realistic fear based on past rebuffs, eventually results in a lowering of the aspiration level or a shift in the means used to attain those goals.

The above data and hypotheses enable us to formulate further guesses about the nature and formation of the social classes. We should not view class as a static phenomenon, but see that certain passive-dependents, alcoholics, and rigid or suspicious people are always filtering from the upper down to the lower levels. Similarly, rather anxious and obsessive-compulsive types are climbing up the social ladder. Thus, the social class into which we are born does not completely determine where we are going to end up. Social mobility allows the classes to select certain types that are best suited to rise or fall in the system. People tend to migrate toward the social level that best fits their personality structure. While the middle and upper class generally try to imprint the repressed or "civilized" character on their children, and while the lower class seems to imprint the acting-out character on its children, there are many "misses," and a wide range of types develops in each class. This makes for a rotation of types, a circulation of emotional elites and non-elites which tends to keep the class system somewhat open. We can only hope that intensive studies will soon be available to spell out the methods by which the children of the various classes are imprinted with the social character of their class. These studies will perhaps also tell us how the class deviants develop; how the repressed "college boy" evolves in a slum environment of "corner boys." Perhaps future research will also indicate ways of preparing the low SES individual to meet the stress of his environment with less impairing adaptive devices, and perhaps of alleviating the very conditions that seem to plague his adult life.

### Summary

The differences between the socioeconomic strata can be summarized in tabular form (see Table 3). Those differences based upon data from the Midtown sample appear in roman type. Hypotheses based upon other research or impressions based upon the literature appear in italic type. Although this table does not summarize the complete findings of our research, it can act as a guide to the major socioeconomic differences in experience and adaptive behavior.

*Table 3*—Comparison of Experience and Behaviour of Lower and Higher Status Groups: Findings and Hypotheses

|  | Lower status | Higher status |
|---|---|---|
| CHILDHOOD STRESSES | Slightly more broken homes before age seven. | Disagreed with parents more frequently. |
|  | Greater proportion reporting economic deprivation in childhood. | |
| ADULT STRESSES | Report worse adult physical health. | More likely to worry about work. |
|  | More persons with poor interpersonal affiliation—especially lack of friends. | More likely to worry about marriage. |
|  | Tend to feel children are more trouble than they are worth, to worry about them, and to have problems with them. | |
| STRESS AND IMPAIRMENT | More adult stress. | Less adult stress. |
|  | Greater impairment per stress unit. | Less impairment per stress unit. |
|  | *No financial or other reserves.* | *Financial reserves, cushioning.* |
|  | *Less resilience, less resistance.* | *Greater resilience and resistance.* |
| TYPE OF ADAPTATION TO STRESS | Exhibit increasingly greater proportion of psychotics with increasing stress. | Exhibit a constant low proportion of psychotics, regardless of stress. |
|  | Show moderate increase in proportion of neurotics with increase of stress, ending in a plateau. | Show sharp increase in proportion of neurotics with increase of stress. |
|  | Greater proportion of following gross types: | Greater proportion of following gross types: |
|  | 1. Probable psychotic type. 2. Probable organic type. 3. Probable personality trait type (character disorder). | 1. Probable wells. 2. Probable neurotic type. |
|  | Greater proportion of following symptom groups and diagnostic types: | Greater proportion of following symptom group: |
|  | Alcoholic, brain disease, dyssocial, psychosomatic, hypochondriacal, passive-dependent, depressed, rigid, schizoid suspicious, schizophrenic. | Aggressive (in interview situation, primarily). |

## Table 3 (cont.)

| | *Lower status* | *Higher status* |
|---|---|---|
| MOBILITY | Passive-dependent, rigid, and suspicious individuals as well as alcoholics are moving downward from the high into the low stratum. | Anxious and obsessive-compulsive persons are moving upward from the low into the high stratum. |
| ANOMIE | Greater proportion agree with "anomie" items, *suggesting feelings of futility, alienation from group and society, depression, resignation, social isolation, and concomitant distrust of others.* | Greater proportion disagree with "anomie" items, *suggesting that effort will be rewarded, integration with the group and society, absence of depression, determination, social integration, and confidence that others can be counted on.* |
| AUTHORITARIANISM | Greater proportion agree with authoritarian items, *suggesting strong authoritarian attitudes.* | Greater proportion disagree with authoritarian items, *suggesting moderate or antiauthoritarian attitudes.* |
| | *Sadistic or punitive attitudes toward the weak.* *Masochistic or submissive attitudes toward the strong.* | *Less sadomasochism, possibly more egalitarian.* |
| | *Belief in strict discipline.* *Stronger moralistic trend.* | *Belief in rewards and conditional love for child training.* |
| | *Greater projection of hostile and societally disapproved sexual impulses onto others.* | *Less projection, possibly more intropunitive.* *More guilt and self-blame.* |
| SUPEREGO | *Tendency to externalized, superficial, or "immature" superego.* | *Internalized strict conscience.* |
| | *Social control is by shame, ridicule, or threat of punishment.* | *Social control primarily by creation of guilt; less shaming or disparagement, less physical punishment.* |
| | *Underlying disrespect for, but inability to question established authority, combined with superficial and sporadic conformity to middle-class norms (corresponding more to Piaget's state of "moral realism").* | *Some ability to question established authority if necessary, with generally internalized and consistent conformity to middle-class norms (corresponding more to Piaget's state of "moral relevance").* |
| | *Rigid adherence to the rules in judging morality, with emphasis on "natural" (hence external) law.* | *Emphasis on individual judgment, taking account of extenuating circumstances, motivation and intention of the individual.* |
| | *Authoritarian quality of control system also suggested by high agreement with Authoritarian Scale statements.* | |

*Table 3 (cont.)*

| Lower status | Higher status |
|---|---|
| Authority is not to be questioned but can be circumvented. Acting on impulse, or the "spur of the moment" legitimates the circumvention. | Repression of impulses and redirection ("sublimation"). |
| May encourage: Inability to postpone gratification; more irritability and explosiveness in the face of frustration, less apparent self-control. | May encourage: Inhibition of socially unacceptable impulses in favor of striving toward long-term goals, greater frustration tolerance; tendency to extreme self-control |
| Possibly predisposes to: Psychopathy (lack of conscience and improper internalization of norms). Sociopathy (internalization of middle-class goals, but use of disapproved means to achieve those goals. | Possibly predisposes to: Neurosis—establishment of internal conflict, signified by guilt, compulsions. |

**GENERAL CHILD TRAINING**

| | |
|---|---|
| Irrational authority exerted by parents; "Respect for elders," "Do as I say, not as I do." | Rational authority. Parents must earn the child's respect through their behavior and occupational achievements; teaching by example. |
| Methods of social control (see above). | Methods of social control (see above). |
| The authority and control methods may lead to: an externalized superego. | The authority and control methods may lead to: an internalized superego. |
| Later abrupt responsibility is thrust on the child. | Early individual responsibility training in household chores and school work. |
| Current mothers more likely to breast feed, but with abrupt weaning, especially full-time working mothers. | Current mothers feed on demand, wean later, toilet train later, allow more freedom of movement outside home. Formerly (1930s) were less "permissive" in these areas. |
| Less consistent, more sporadic training. | More consistent training, less a function of parental mood. |
| Discourage expression of hostility against parents. Encourage or accept hostile expression or behavior outside the family and toward siblings. | Accept expression of hostility, particularly in younger male child, toward parents and siblings, but not outside the family. |
| Training by teachers and others conflicts with parents' values. | Teachers' values coincide with parents' values. |

*Table 3 (cont.)*

| | Lower status | Higher status |
|---|---|---|
| **IDENTITY TRAINING** | Less identity training. | Identity training through scrapbooks, baby books, family albums, birthday parties. |
| | Interchangeability of function emphasized, clothes and toys (if any) handed down, large school classes. Expendability of individual reinforced by job experience of parents. | Individuality emphasized — in clothing, love, school work, possession of own toys rather than sharing. |
| | Identity formation concerning dominance may be poor, reflecting low status of parents. Parental sex roles, however, are distinct. A man does not do a woman's job in the house. However, more women work full time outside the home. | Sexual identity may be more confused, one possible basis for increased rates of neurosis. Parental sex roles are less distinct and may promote diffuse or cross-sex identification. |
| | Inadequate concern with identity may result. | Excessive concern with identity or self-image may be promoted. |
| | Internalization of middle-class norm, "One is what one has," may result in the feeling that one is "nobody." Lack of possessions may promote lack of identity. | Possessions and property promote the feeling that one is "somebody," or will "grow up to be somebody." |
| **COMMUNICATION TRAINING** | Slower development of verbal communication. | Rapid development of verbal skills. |
| | Less room for expression of disagreements with parents; "Children should be seen but not heard." | Greater permission to argue or disagree with parents. |
| | Either no expression of hostility to parents, or sporadic physical violence toward parents—an "all or none" expression. | Verbal expression of hostility to parents, providing a "safety valve." |
| **SEX AND EDUCATIONAL TRAINING** | Masturbation, petting tabooed. Early intercourse condoned, especially for boys. | Masturbation, petting condoned. Early intercourse tabooed. |
| | Shorter adolescence. | "Stretched puberty." Sexual union and marriage deferred in favor of higher education, attainment of occupational and social skills. |
| | | Development of sexual "frustration tolerance," or a rechanneling of sexual behavior away from coitus. |

## Table 3 (cont.)

| | Lower status | Higher status |
|---|---|---|
| TRAINING FOR GRATIFICATION AND PLANNING | *Little training for retentiveness or compulsive trends.* | *"Holding back" and other training in sex, eating (at meals only), and elimination may promote educational and financial retentiveness. Ability to memorize, to save money, to be punctual, excessive concern with personal cleanliness, and a bureaucratic personality may all stem in part from this type of training.* |
| | *Less planning and a present orientation—"Live for today and let tomorrow take care of itself."* | *Emphasis on planning is related to "holding back," and to a future orientation.* |
| POVERTY AND PLANNING | *Poverty reduces planning, promotes the immediate gratification pattern. Poverty in childhood seems associated with depression or apathy in adults. Being poor may also have effects through inadequate diet or malnutrition, for example, which might promote depression, apathy, and lack of trust in others. Poverty, or its lack, is part of the child-training complex.* | *Plenty creates an atmosphere more conducive to planning— one has time to consider the future, one has been rewarded, and plans toward the next reward.* |
| SELF-ESTEEM AND EGO-STRENGTH | *Parents' occupation despised or causes shame and embarrassment leading to disidentification.* | *Parents' occupation respected, leading to strong identification.* |
| | *Negative self-image due to acceptance of negative stereotypes of the low status person or to internalization of low status parent.* | *Generally a more positive self-image.* *Those in prestigeful occupations or families are in a "state of grace."* *Emphasis on maintaining the self-image may be conducive to neurosis: "I'm not living up to myself—to my family name."* |
| | *Pecuniary emulation results in relative deprivation, shame, and hostility which is often expressed physically, resulting in lowered status.* | *Pecuniary emulation may produce some anxiety, but this often maintains the status, if it is channeled into work anxiety and competition.* |
| NORMS | *Limited ambition.* | *Greater ambition—high aspiration. (Recently the middle-class college student has started "dreaming in second gear," showing lower aspiration levels.)* |

## Table 3 (cont.)

| Lower status | Higher status |
|---|---|
| Group responsibility. | Individual responsibility. |
| Less emphasis on technical skills. School of "hard knocks" is the best teacher; "It's not what you know, it's whom you know." | Development of skills and achievements—through education. |
| Less postponement of satisfaction; experience teaches that postponement of gratification seldom brings rewards; Doctrine of luck replaces doctrine of hard work. | Worldly asceticism; work hard, postponing pleasures for future goals. Planning pays off. |
| Emotional expression. | Rationality. |
| Individual expression—content of relationship with others rather than form. | Getting along with people—manners, courtesy. |
| Expression through physical aggression when called for. | Control of physical aggression. Use of verbal or legal aggression ("White Collar Crime"). |
| Enjoyment of leisure. | Constructive leisure, self-improvement, develop a hobby outside your work. |
| Less emphasis on property values and/or individual ownership. | Respect for property; One is what one has. |

# CHILDREN'S PERCEPTIONS OF THEIR TEACHERS' FEELINGS TOWARD THEM RELATED TO SELF-PERCEPTION, SCHOOL ACHIEVEMENT, AND BEHAVIOR

*Helen H. Davidson and Gerhard Lang*

## INTRODUCTION

The child's self-concept arises and develops in an interpersonal setting (30).* Feelings about the self are established early in life and are modified by subsequent experiences. Among the significant people believed to affect the child's feelings about himself are first, his parents, and, later, his teachers. Ausubel (2) and Jourard and Remy (16) are among the few investigators who have reported results which support these theoretical contentions.

Rogers (24), Snygg and Combs (27), among others, assign the self-concept a central place in their personality theories and suggest that the individual's self-concept is a major factor influencing his behavior. Vigorous research in this area by Martire (17) and Steiner (28) has produced corroborative evidence for these views.

Only recently has the concept of the self been introduced into the school setting. Typical studies are those by Jersild (15), Reeder (23), and Stevens (29). Jersild demonstrated the value of the self-concept theory in making the educative process more valuable. Reeder, using grade school children and Stevens, working with college students, explored the relation between self-concept and school achievement. Both of these investigators found that positive feelings about the self are associated with good academic achievement.

A series of studies dealing with teacher-pupil relations have sought to determine a) How children see and feel about their teachers (11); b) How

---

* Numerals in parentheses denote references at end of article.

From *Journal of Experimental Education*, **29**(2), December 1960, 107–118. Reprinted by permission of the authors and DERS. This study was supported by a grant from the James McKeen Cattell Fund.

teachers see and feel about their pupils (5, 20); and c) How teachers think their pupils see themselves (22).

It has been widely recognized that teachers influence the personality development of their pupils (21). Perkins, for example, found that teachers who had completed several years of child study were able to promote healthier personality growth in children, defined in terms of congruency between the self and the ideal self. For this reason, many researchers, among them, Barr and Jones (3), and Symonds (31), are engaged in the study of personality development of the teacher herself.

Despite the abundance of research on these aspects of the school setting, an important dimension, not previously investigated, is how the child perceives his teacher's feelings toward him. In an investigation of this interaction, we not only may gain insight into the question of what qualities make for an effective teacher, but also an understanding of how the child's perception of his teacher's feelings, irrespective of its accuracy, relates to his self-concept, school achievement, and classroom behavior.

It is the purpose of this investigation to determine what the relation is between children's perception of their teachers' feelings toward them and the variables: self-perception, academic achievement, and classroom behavior.

Specifically, three hypotheses were tested:

1] there exists a positive correlation between children's perception of their teachers' feelings toward them and children's perception of themselves. In behavioral terms it is predicted that the more favorable the child's perception of himself, the more positive will be his perception of teachers' feelings towards him.

2] There exists a positive relationship between favorable perception of teachers' feelings and good academic achievement.

3] There exists a positive relationship between favorable perception of teachers' feelings and desirable classroom behavior.

## THE INSTRUMENT

To test the hypotheses proposed, it was necessary to develop an instrument to measure self-perception and the perception of the feelings of others. It was decided to use an adjective checking method, since it is direct and simple. Adjective checklists have been used to measure adjustment (18), self-acceptance (4), empathy (9), character traits (13), and to distinguish the self-perceptions of persons classified according to some social and psychological variables (26). In the main these lists have been used with adults.

In developing the checklist with children, words and phrases to be included were selected on the basis of the following three criteria:

1] The words should be those commonly used to describe how people feel toward and how people think of others, especially how teachers feel toward and think of children. An attempt was made to cover varied aspects of behavior and personality. For this purpose, lists already developed, like those of Allport (1), Gough (12), and Hartshorne and May (13), were scanned for appropriate words.

2] The words should be easy enough for children in approximately the 10–16 year age range to read and comprehend. The Thorndike-Lorge Frequency Count (33) was used to eliminate words that would be too difficult.

3] The list should contain about an equal number of words connoting positive and negative feelings.

From an initial pool of 200 trait names, 135 remained after the application of criteria 1 and 2. The next step was to determine the feeling tone of the 135 words. Each of the words was then rated by 35 teachers and 50 junior high school pupils as *favorable, unfavorable,* or *neutral.* Only those words were retained that were judged by more than 80 per cent of the teachers and 80 per cent of the pupils as being favorable or unfavorable. The words judged neutral were eliminated.

Fifty words remained after the teachers and students judged them as favorable or unfavorable. The 35 words finally used are listed below along with the *F* or *U* rating received. Fifteen words were dropped either because of the level of difficulty or because of some duplication in meaning.

| | | | |
|---|---|---|---|
| Fair | (F) | A hard worker | (F) |
| A nuisance | (U) | Bad | (U) |
| Afraid | (U) | A good sport | (F) |
| Cheerful | (F) | Considerate | (F) |
| A time waster | (U) | Not eager to study | (U) |
| Neat | (F) | Helpful | (F) |
| Not eager to learn | (U) | Careless | (U) |
| A leader | (F) | Sociable | (F) |
| Unhappy | (U) | Clever | (F) |
| Loving | (F) | Not alert | (U) |
| Outstanding | (F) | Smart | (F) |
| Loud | (U) | Silly | (U) |
| Generous | (F) | Kind | (F) |
| Nervous | (U) | Shy | (U) |
| Sensible | (F) | A sloppy worker | (U) |
| Polite | (F) | Dependable | (F) |
| Lazy | (U) | A day dreamer | (U) |
| Forgetful | (U) | | |

*Administration and Scoring of the Checklist.* The children are instructed to decide how the teacher feels toward them with respect to each trait name, and then to rate it on a three-point rating scale: *most of the time, half of the time, seldom or almost never.* A favorable word is assigned a score of 3 when it is checked in the most of the time column; a score of 2 for half of the time, and 1 for seldom or almost never. For an unfavorable word the scoring is reversed.

The total score, the Index of Favorability, is obtained by adding the scores of all the words and dividing the total by the number of words checked. The higher the index, the more favorable is the child's perception of the teacher's feelings toward him. Theoretically, the index can range from 1.00 to 3.00.

*Reliability and Validity.* The Checklist of Trait Names was administered twice to four classes comprising 105 junior high-school children. The interval between the two administrations was from four to six weeks. A correlation of .85 was obtained (rank difference, $p < .001$).

The Checklist may be considered to have logical validity. However, it was desired to obtain a measure of empirical and concurrent validity. This was done by correlating the child's own perception of his teacher's appraisal of him with his classmates' perceptions of the teachers' feelings toward him. For this purpose, a modified version of the de Groat and Thompson *Teacher Approval and Disapproval Scale* (7) was administered along with Checklist to 93 children (3 classes). The de Groat and Thompson scale, as modified, consisted of 8 positive statements, such as, "Here is someone whom the teacher praises for trying hard," and 8 negative statements, such as, "Here is someone whom the teacher often points out as wasting too much time." For each statement, pupils were asked to name one to four of their classmates to whom these characteristics applied. They could also name themselves, if they so desired. Of the 93 children, 56 received 5 or more votes on one of the teacher approval and disapproval statements. For these 56 children, a teacher approval score was determined by subtracting the number of unfavorable statements on which five or more votes were received from the number of favorable statements on which five or more votes were received. A correlation of .51 was obtained (rank difference, $p < .001$) between the Index of Favorability and the teacher approval score.

The Checklist developed to assess children's perception of their teachers' feelings toward them appears to have satisfactory reliability and validity. Although the estimate of reliability and validity was based on a sample of junior high-school students, the list was considered appropriate also for the upper grades of the elementary school because of the way the words were chosen.

## EXPERIMENTAL DESIGN

*Subjects.* The subjects of this study were 89 boys and 114 girls, attending 4th, 5th, and 6th grades of a New York City public school. These children were distributed in 10 different classrooms. In terms of reading ability the classes selected were in the upper half of their respective grade level. Originally, it was planned to test all 4th, 5th, and 6th grade children, but after preliminary experimentation, it was found that several words were too difficult for children of limited language ability. It was therefore decided to test children in those classes which were known to have the better readers.

The children represented a wide range in socioeconomic status. It was possible to divide them into three distinct groups on the basis of their fathers' and mothers' occupation. The upper group, consisting of 63 children, came from families of professional people, white collar workers, and business men; the middle social class group of 57 children had parents who were skilled workers, policemen, and firemen; the low group contained 83 children of semi-skilled and unskilled workers and a number of unemployed.

Table 1 presents the background information for the 203 children

*Table 1*—Distribution of Subjects in the Ten Classrooms by Sex and Social Class Status

| | Socio-economic status | | | | | | | |
|---|---|---|---|---|---|---|---|---|
| | UPPER | | MIDDLE | | LOWER | | TOTAL | |
| Classroom | Boys | Girls | Boys | Girls | Boys | Girls | Boys | Girls |
| 4-1 | 8 | 5 | 3 | 8 | — | 2 | 11 | 15 |
| 5-1 | 1 | — | — | 2 | 7 | 8 | 8 | 10 |
| 5-2 | — | — | — | — | 3 | 5 | 3 | 5 |
| 5-3 | 7 | 10 | 7 | 2 | — | 1 | 14 | 13 |
| 5-4 | — | 2 | 3 | 1 | 9 | 8 | 12 | 11 |
| 5-5 | 2 | 4 | 6 | 3 | 3 | 7 | 11 | 14 |
| 6-1 | 5 | 5 | 4 | 3 | — | — | 9 | 8 |
| 6-2 | 2 | 5 | 4 | 2 | 1 | 6 | 7 | 13 |
| 6-3 | 3 | 3 | 5 | 3 | — | 9 | 8 | 15 |
| 6-4 | — | 1 | — | 1 | 6 | 8 | 6 | 10 |
| Total | 28 | 35 | 32 | 25 | 29 | 54 | 89 | 114 |

involved in the study.

*Procedure.* The Checklist of Trait Names was administered twice to the children. At the first administration, the children were instructed to respond to the 35 adjectives comprising the list in terms of "My teacher thinks I am," and at the second testing, in terms of "I think I am." The first testing was done in the morning, the second in the afternoon. The "My teacher thinks I am" scale yields a measure of perceived teacher feelings, referred to henceforth as the Index of Favorability; the "I think I am" scale yields a measure of self-perception.

The teachers, nine women and one man, rated their pupils on academic achievement, on a four-point scale: Very Well, Adequately, Below Average, and Very Poorly. In the analysis of data, the last two categories were combined due to the paucity of cases in the category Very Poorly. At the same time, the teacher also rated each child on 10 behavioral or personality characteristics. A weight of +1 was assigned to each of the traits judged to be desirable. The four desirable traits were: eager, obedient, cooperative, assertive. A weight of $-1$ was given to the characteristics judged to be undesirable: disorderly, destructive, hostile, defiant, unfriendly, and troublesome. The sum of the weights yielded a behavior rating score ranging theoretically, from $+4$ (very desirable) to $-6$ (very undesirable). Subjects who received the 0 and minus behavioral ratings were combined into one group due to the small number of cases in these categories.

## RESULTS AND DISCUSSION

*Hypothesis 1.* There exists a positive correlation between children's perception of their teachers' feelings toward them and children's perception of themselves.

The two perceptual favorability indexes correlated .82 (product–moment, $p < .001$). The children who had a more favorable or a more adequate self-concept, that is, those who achieved a higher self-perception score also perceived their teachers' feelings toward them more favorably.

The finding of a significant correlation between the two kinds of perception lends support to the view that a child's assessment of himself is related to the assessment "significant people" make of him (30). In two previous research investigations, a close relationship was found between self-appraisal and children's perception of their parents' feelings toward them (2, 16). The present study for the first time has shown that a child's self-appraisal is significantly related to his perception of his teacher's feelings as well. Such a finding was anticipated in view of the fact that one role of the teacher, at least at the elementary level, is that of a "parent substitute." Several interesting questions may be raised: To what extent does a child's perception of his teacher's feelings resemble his perception of his mother's or father's feelings toward him? Does the child's perception of his present teacher differ from his perception of his previous teacher? Does favorability or perception decrease or increase with years in school?

*Hypothesis 2.* There exists a positive relationship between favorable perception of teachers' feelings and academic achievement. Table 2 presents the mean favorability scores and their standard deviations for the three levels of estimated achievement. The $F$ ratio of 15.61 was significant at less than the .001 level. The three $t$ tests were also significant at better than the .01 level.

*Hypothesis 3.* There exists a positive relationship between favorable perception of teachers' feelings and desirable classroom behavior. The findings pertaining to the relationship between children's perception and their classroom behavior are shown in Table 3.

The overall $F$ ratio of 7.38 was significant at less than the .001 level. The only significant $t$ tests were those between the lowest category (0 and less) and all the other categories. In other words, the children who were rated as being disorderly, defiant, unfriendly, or troublesome, perceived their teachers' feelings toward them as being less favorable than the children who were rated as being eager, cooperative, assertive and the like.

One of the axioms of educational psychology is the statement that a child learns only when he is motivated to learn. Furthermore, the basic incentives which a teacher can furnish are her acceptance of the child on the one hand, and approval on the other. The findings of the present study furnish supporting evidence. The teacher's feelings of acceptance and approval are communicated to the child and perceived by him as positive appraisals. It is likely that these appraisals encourage the child to seek further teacher approval by achieving well and behaving in a manner acceptable to his teacher. We may also begin this cycle with the child's behavior. The child who achieves well and behaves satisfactorily is bound to please his teacher. She, in turn, communicates positive feelings toward the child, thus reinforcing his desire to be a good pupil. Which of these variables serves as the primary determiner is a fact difficult to ascertain. It seems rather that they reinforce each other. The implication is clear. It is essential that teachers communicate positive feelings to their children and thus not only strengthen their positive self-appraisals but stimulate their growth, academically as well as inter-personally.

*Table 2*—Index of Favorability as Related to Three Levels of Estimated Achievement

|  | ACHIEVEMENT CATEGORY | | |
|  | Very Well | Adequately | Below average |
|---|---|---|---|
| Mean Favorability Score | 2.68* | 2.57 | 2.40 |
|  | (N = 53) | (N = 111) | (N = 39) |
| S. D. | .22 | .24 | .25 |

* The higher the score, the more favorable the child's perception of his teacher's feelings toward him.

*Table 3*—Index of Favorability as Related to Five Levels of Rated Behavior

|  | BEHAVIOR RATING CATEGORY | | | | |
|  | Very desirable | | Desirable | | Undesirable (0 and |
|  | (+4 | +3) | (+2 | +1) | minus scores) |
|---|---|---|---|---|---|
| Mean Favorability Score | 2.62* | 2.65 | 2.58 | 2.53 | 2.39 |
|  | (N = 40) | (N = 54) | (N = 46) | (N = 23) | (N = 40) |
| S. D. | .26 | .19 | .27 | .27 | .28 |

* The higher the score, the more favorable the child's perception of his teacher's feelings toward him.

It should be emphasized that these findings do not imply causality but rather suggest that certain pupil characteristics, such as self-perception, perceived teacher feelings, achievement, and behavior in school are interrelated.

In addition to the results relevant to the tested hypotheses, other findings will now be reported.

*Sex Differences.* Sex differences were observed with regard to the three variables studied: index of favorability,[1] achievement, and behavior in school. Girls perceived their teachers' feelings toward them more favorably than did the boys (girls mean = 2.60; boys mean = 2.52; $t = 2.41$, $p < .02$). The behavior ratings of the girls were more favorable than those of the boys ($\chi^2 = 10.72$, df = 4, $p < .05$); the girls were likewise rated more favorably in achievement, although this difference was not significant ($\chi^2 = 3.41$, df = 2, $.10 < p < .20$).

Past research has consistently shown that teachers report more problem behavior among boys (32). One explanation, though not widely accepted, is that boys are naturally more aggressive. Another view, more plausible, holds that our society encourages aggressive behavior in men (and men to be) and submissive behavior in women. Teachers, most of whom are women, especially in the primary grades, therefore regard boys' classroom behavior as disturbingly different from the norms of behavior appropriate to their own female sex. The temptation is great to reward children of one's own sex. Meyer and Thompson's study (19) is pertinent here. Teacher-pupil interaction of sixth-grade pupils were studied over a one-year period and analyzed in terms of "approval" and "disapproval" contacts. In addition, children were asked to nominate by the "Guess Who" technique which of their classmates receive their teacher's approval and disapproval. Both approaches yielded the same finding. Classroom observers, as well as the children themselves, noted that teachers expressed greater approval of girls and greater disapproval of boys. The findings of the present investigation, which ascertained directly children's perceptions of their teachers' feelings, are in accord with the results of prior research. The suggestion has been frequently made that more men should be urged to teach at the primary level. Findings such as those discussed above suggest the urgency to establish a sexual balance in the teaching staff at the primary grades. Not only is it desirable for boys to have a male model with whom to identify, but conditions may then be created which may assure greater teacher approval for boys and reduce teacher disapproval for behavior which is, to a large extent, culturally instigated.

*Social Class Differences.* Because of the distinct differences found in social class status in this group of children, it was decided to investigate the relation of social class to the index of favorability, achievement and behavior in school. All three variables are related to social class in the direction one would predict. These data are shown in Table 4.

It may be observed from Table 4 that there is a decline in mean favorability index from the upper to the lower social class. Two of the three $t$ tests were significant at better than the .01 level; $t$ was not significant between the upper and middle social class groups. Children in the two

---

[1] The index used in this and subsequent analyses is based on the Checklist score of the child's perception of his teacher's feelings toward him.

advantaged social class groups perceive their teachers' feelings toward them more favorably than do the children in the lower class group.

Social class and achievement in school are significantly related ($\chi^2 =$ 18.38, 4df, p <.01). The differences in the percentage of children in the several categories may be pointed out, especially the differences between the two extremes: in the upper social class 43 per cent of the children were rated by their teachers as doing very well in school while only 15 per cent were rated as doing below average work.

*Table 4*—Social Class Status Related to Favorability Index, Achievement and Behavior

|  | Upper social class (N = 63) | Middle social class (N = 57) | Lower social class (N = 83) |
|---|---|---|---|
| Mean Favorability Index | 2.63 | 2.60 | 2.49 |
| S.D. | .26 | .22 | .26 |
| **Achievement Rating Category:** | | | |
| Very Well (N = 53) | 43% | 34% | 23% |
| Adequately (N = 111) | 31% | 22% | 47% |
| Below Average (N = 39) | 15% | 36% | 49% |
| **Behavioral Rating Category:** | | | |
| Very Desirable (N = 94) | 41% | 29% | 30% |
| Desirable (N = 69) | 23% | 30% | 46% |
| Undesirable (N = 40) | 20% | 22% | 58% |

* These percentages are based on the *N*'s of the Achievement and Behavior categories.

Social class and behavior in school as rated by the teachers were not significantly related ($\chi^2 =$ 14.97, 8df, .05 <p <.10). However, the distribution of children in the several categories reveal interesting differences. While the great majority of the children in the group were rated favorably by their teachers, there were 58 per cent of the children in the lower class whose behavior was rated as undesirable while only 20 per cent of the upper class children were so rated.

It has been suggested that teachers, as surrogates of middle-class values, tend to give preferential treatment to the middle- and upper-socioeconomic class pupils, and to withhold rewards from pupils who belong to the lower socioeconomic class (6, 8). Furthermore, previous research has shown that lower class children do not achieve as well as middle and upper class children (10, 14), in part due to lower motivation (25). The data obtained in the present study corroborate these observations.

The interrelations found between children's perception of teachers' feelings, school achievement, behavior and socioeconomic status are particularly significant since the majority of children in the public schools throughout the country come from families of low social class status. It is therefore likely that a lower class child, especially if he is not doing well in school, will have a negative perception of his teachers' feelings toward him. These negative perceptions will in turn tend to lower his efforts to achieve in school and/or increase the probability that he will misbehave. His poor school achievement will aggravate the negative attitudes of his teachers toward him, which in turn will affect his self-confidence, and so on. This vicious entanglement must be interrupted at some point. The point of attack may well be the teacher whose capacity to reflect feelings conducive to the child's growth should be of concern to educators.

*Table 5*—Mean Indexes of Favorability for the Three Achievement Categories and for the Three Social Class Groups

|  | ACHIEVEMENT CATEGORY | | |
|  | Very well | Adequately | Below average |
| --- | --- | --- | --- |
| Upper Social Class | 2.71* | 2.61 | 2.51 |
|  | (N = 23) | (N = 34) | (N = 6) |
| Middle Social Class | 2.71 | 2.60 | 2.44 |
|  | (N = 18) | (N = 25) | (N = 14) |
| Lower Social Class | 2.59 | 2.52 | 2.34 |
|  | (N = 12) | (N = 52) | (N = 19) |

\* The higher the score, the more favorable the child's perception of his teacher's feelings toward him.

*Analysis of Variance of Favorability Scores.* It was found that the index of favorability was positively related to achievement in school as well as to social class position. It is also evident from this and other studies that achievement in school is correlated with social class position. In order to study the influence of each of these factors on index of favorability, the favorability scores were re-analyzed first, for the three achievement levels within each social class and second, for the three social class groups within each achievement category. The mean favorability indexes for these separate groups are presented in Table 5.

Reading Table 5 vertically, it may be observed that the mean favorability score declines from the upper social class to the lowest social class for each of the achievement categories; this decline is most noticeable between the two highest social class groups and the lowest social class group. It is apparent that the social class variable plays a part in the way a child perceives his teacher's feelings toward him regardless of his achievement in school. Similarly, reading Table 5 horizontally, the mean favorability score is observed to decrease from the highest achievement level to the lowest within each social class group. The evidence here suggests that achievement in school colors the child's perception of his teacher's feelings, regardless of his social class position. Analysis of variance of the data yielded two significant $F$ ratios. These results indicate that both the factors of social class position and achievement are operating independently in affecting the way a child will perceive his teacher's feelings toward him.

These findings should arouse the educator for they imply that a teacher's reaction to a child is not solely influenced by the individuality of the child but also by his social class and achievement characteristics.

*Differences Among Teachers.* It may be assumed that teachers reflect a variety of feelings toward children, either because of their own personality needs, or because of the way they use punishment or praise or for any other reason. These differences from teacher to teacher should be observable in the perceptions of the children affected by them. Table 6 presents the mean favorability indexes for the 10 teachers in this study.

*Table 6*—The Index of Favorability for the Ten Classrooms

| Class | N | Mean | S.D. |
|-------|-----|--------|------|
| 4-1 | 26 | 2.61* | .26 |
| 5-1 | 18 | 2.25 | .21 |
| 5-2 | 8 | 2.45 | .29 |
| 5-3 | 27 | 2.62 | .17 |
| 5-4 | 23 | 2.45 | .23 |
| 5-5 | 25 | 2.62 | .22 |
| 6-1 | 17 | 2.57 | .08 |
| 6-2 | 20 | 2.64 | .23 |
| 6-3 | 23 | 2.64 | .19 |
| 6-4 | 16 | 2.70 | .10 |

* The higher the score, the more favorable
the child's perception of his teacher's feelings
toward him.

It may be observed that the range in mean favorability score is from 2.25 to 2.70. Although the children generally perceived their teachers' feelings more favorably than otherwise, and the actual differences among the classrooms were not large, there were 3 or 4 classrooms with markedly low mean scores. The overall $F$ ratio of 2.95 is significant at less than the .01 level. It should be remembered, at this point, that the classes were selected for better than average ability in reading, which makes the finding of significant differences even more compelling. Teachers do seem to vary in their inclination and/or their capacity to communicate favorable feelings. It seems urgent that teachers be helped to recognize the significance of the feelings which they express toward children, consciously or unconsciously. Some teachers, in addition, may need the help which can only come through a process of self-understanding, in order to avoid or to minimize the expression of negatively-toned feelings toward children, because of their sex, their socioeconomic status, their behavior or achievement in school.

*Possible Uses of the Checklist.* The Checklist of Trait Names, in addition to its use as a research tool, may be adapted to practical school situations. Conceivably, it can be employed for the purpose of teacher selection and guidance. For instance, a principal might wish to select a teacher for a class comprised of underprivileged or troublesome children who are very much in need of acceptance and approval. A good candidate for such a class would be a teacher who can easily project positive feelings. Supervisors of student teachers may find the checklist useful in evaluating the quality of teacher-student relations.

Teachers who are found to communicate largely negative feelings may be advised to participate in some kind of counseling or therapy. Similarly, children whose perceptions are primarily negative and/or distorted can be identified for personality diagnosis and thus be helped in self-understanding or in obtaining a more accurate perception of reality.

## SUMMARY

The purpose of the study was to relate children's perception of their teachers' feelings toward them to self-perception, academic achievement, and classroom behavior. A Checklist of Trait Names, consisting of 35 descriptive terms, was administered to 89 boys and 114 girls in grades 4, 5, and 6 in a New York City public school. The children were rated by their teachers for achievement and on a number of behavioral characteristics.

The major findings were: 1) The children's perception of their teachers' feelings toward them correlated positively and significantly with self-perception. The child with the more favorable self image was the one who more likely than not perceived his teacher's feelings toward him more favorably. 2) The more positive the children's perception of their teachers' feelings, the better was their academic achievement and the more desirable their classroom behavior as rated by the teachers. 3) Further, children in the upper and middle social class groups perceived their teachers' feelings toward them more favorably than did the children in the lower social class group. 4) Social class position was also found to be positively related with achievement in school. 5) However, even when the favorability index data were re-analyzed separately for each social class and for each achievement category, the mean favorability index declined with decline in achievement level, regardless of social class position and, similarly, the mean favorability index declined with social class regardless of achievement level. 6) Girls generally perceived their teachers' feelings more favorably than did the boys. 7) Finally, there were some significant classroom differences in the favorability of the children's perception of their teachers' feelings. These findings must be considered in light of the non-random selection of the sample. Nevertheless, it is reasonable to assume that these subjects are representative of the population of New York City elementary school children at these grade levels.

Possible uses of the Checklist were suggested. As a result of this investigation, a number of changes in the Checklist were indicated. The new form along with instructions, used in a study at the junior high school level, is given below.

## CHECKLIST (New Form)

We are asking your cooperation in a study being conducted at_____ Our interest is in the way you think your_____teacher feels toward you.

Now read the following and do the example:

On the next page are pairs of words. In each pair, one is the opposite of the other. There are five steps between the pairs of words, as shown below.

A    B    C    D    E

PLEASANT·———·———·———·———·———·UNPLEASANT

Consider the words PLEASANT and UNPLEASANT. Here is what you are supposed to do. If you feel your teacher judges you as being pleasant most of the time, put an X in the "A" box. If you feel your teacher considers you to be unpleasant most of the time, place an X in the "E" box. If you feel your teacher considers you to be pleasant sometimes and unpleasant sometimes, mark the "C" box. If you feel your teacher considers you to be somewhat more pleasant than unpleasant, put an X in the "B" box. If you feel your teacher considers you to be somewhat more unpleasant than pleasant, place an X in the box marked "D".

Now do the example. Be sure to place an X in the middle of the box which describes most nearly how your teacher feels about you. Do not worry or puzzle over any one word. It is your immediate feeling that we want. Do not omit any word.

Be as honest as you can. Neither your teacher nor your principal will see your paper.

If you do not understand a word, please raise your hand, and the Examiner will come to your seat and explain it to you.

TURN THE PAGE AND BEGIN.

*Name*...........................................

...........................................　　　　...........................................

| | A | B | C | D | E | | | | A | B | C | D | E | |
|---|---|---|---|---|---|---|---|---|---|---|---|---|---|---|
| Selfish | | | | | | Unselfish | Wise | | | | | | Foolish |
| Obedient | | | | | | Disobedient | Rude | | | | | | Polite |
| Intelligent | | | | | | Unintelligent | Alert | | | | | | Lazy |
| Good | | | | | | Bad | Passive | | | | | | Active |
| Sad | | | | | | Happy | Reliable | | | | | | Unreliable |
| Slow | | | | | | Fast | Nice | | | | | | Awful |
| Clean | | | | | | Dirty | Unpopular | | | | | | Popular |
| Strong | | | | | | Weak | Curious | | | | | | Indifferent |
| Cowardly | | | | | | Brave | Careless | | | | | | Careful |
| Honest | | | | | | Dishonest | Daring | | | | | | Afraid |
| Calm | | | | | | Nervous | Childish | | | | | | Mature |
| Unfair | | | | | | Fair | Attentive | | | | | | Inattentive |
| Graceful | | | | | | Awkward | Disorderly | | | | | | Orderly |
| Kind | | | | | | Cruel | Ungrateful | | | | | | Grateful |
| Unfriendly | | | | | | Friendly | Respectful | | | | | | Disrespectful |

### References to *Children's Perceptions*

1. G. Allport and H. Odbert, "Trait Names: A Psycho-lexical Study," *Psychological Monographs*, **47**, 1936.
2. D. P. Ausubel et al., "Perceived Parent Attitudes as Determinants of Children's Ego Structure," *Child Development*, **25**, 1954, 173–83.
3. A. S. Barr and R. E. Jones, "The Measurement and Prediction of Teacher Efficiency," *Review of Educational Research*, **28**, 1958, 256–64.
4. R. E. Bills et al., "An Index of Adjustment and Values," *Journal of Consulting Psychology*, **15**, 1951, 257–261.
5. W. W. Cook, "Significant Factors in Teachers' Classroom Attitudes," *Journal of Education*, **7**, 1956, 274–279.
6. A. Davis, *Social Class Influences Upon Learning*, Cambridge, Mass., Harvard University Press, 1952.
7. A. F. de Groat and G. G. Thompson, "A Study of the Distribution of Teacher Approval and Disapproval Among Sixth-Grade Pupils," *Journal of Experimental Education*, **18**, 1949, 57–75.
8. N. R. Dixon, "Social Class and Education," *Harvard Educational Review*, **23**, 1953, 330–338.

9. Rosalind F. Dymond, "A Scale for Measurement of Empathic Ability," *Journal of Consulting Psychology*, **13**, 1949, 127–133.
10. W. H. Friedhoff, "Relationships Among Various Measures of Socioeconomic Status, Social Class Identification, Intelligence, and School Achievement," *Dissertation Abstract*, **15**, 1955, 2098.
11. N. L. Gage et al., "Teachers' Understanding of Their Pupils and Pupils' Ratings of Their Teachers," *Psychological Monographs*, **69**, 1955.
12. H. G. Gough, *Reference Handbook for the Gough Adjective Check List*, Mimeographed (Berkeley, California: University of California, Institute of Personality Assessment and Research, 1955).
13. H. Hartshorne and H. A. May, *Studies in the Nature of Character, III: Studies in the Organization of Character*, New York, Macmillan Co., 1930.
14. R. A. Heimann and Q. F. Schenk, "Relations of Social Class and Sex Differences to High School Achievement," *School Review*, **62**, 1954, 213–21.
15. A. T. Jersild, *In Search of Self*, New York, Bureau of Publications, Teachers College, Columbia University, 1952.
16. S. M. Jourard and R. M. Remy, "Perceived Parental Attitudes, the Self, and Security," *Journal of Consulting Psychology*, **19**, 1955, 364–66.
17. J. G. Martire, "Relationship Between the Self Concept and Differences in the Strength and Generality of Achievement Motivation," *Journal of Personality*, **24**, 1956, 364–75.
18. R. M. Merrill and L. B. Heathers, "The Use of an Adjective Checklist as a Measure of Adjustment," *Journal of Consulting Psychology*, **1**, 1954, 137–43.
19. W. J. Meyer and G. G. Thompson, "Sex Differences in the Distribution of Teacher Approval and Disapproval Among Sixth-Grade Children," *Journal of Eaucational Psychology*, **47**, 1956, 285–396.
20. National Education Association, Research Division, "Teacher Opinion on Pupil Behavior," *Research Bulletin*, **34**, 1956, 51–107.
21. H. V. Perkins, "Factors Influencing Change in Children's Self Concepts," *Child Development*, **29**, 1958, 221–30.
22. ——— "Teachers' and Peers' Perceptions of Children's Self Concepts," *Child Development*, **29**, 1958, 203–220.
23. T. A. Reeder, "A Study of Some Relationships Between Level of Self Concept, Academic Achievement, and Classroom Adjustment," *Dissertation Abstract*, **15**, 1955, 2472.
24. C. R. Rogers, *Client-Centered Therapy*, Boston, Houghton-Mifflin, 1951.
25. B. C. Rosen, "The Achievement Syndrome: A Psychocultural Dimension of Social Stratification," *American Sociological Review*, **21**, 1956, 203–11.
26. T. R. Sarbin and B. C. Rosenberg, "Contributions to Role-Taking Theory: IV. A Method for Obtaining a Qualitative Estimate of the Self," *Journal of Social Psychology*, **42**, 1955, 71–81.
27. D. Snygg and A. W. Combs, *Individual Behavior*, New York, Harper and Brothers, 1949.
28. I. D. Steiner, "Self-Perception and Goal-Setting Behavior," *Journal of Personality*, **25**, 1957, 344–55.
29. P. H. Stevens, "An Investigation of the Relationship Between Certain Aspects of Self-Concept Behavior and Students' Academic Achievement," *Dissertation Abstract*, **16**, 1956, 2531–2532.
30. H. S. Sullivan, *Conceptions of Modern Psychiatry*, Washington, D. C., W. A. White Psychiatric Foundation, 1947.

31. P. M. Symonds, "Characteristics of the Effective Teacher Based on Pupil Evaluation," *Journal of Experimental Education*, **23**, 1955, 289–310.
32. L. M. Terman and L. E. Tyler, "Psychological Sex Differences," in L. Carmichael *Manual of Child Psychology*, Second edition, New York, Wiley and Sons, 1954.
33. E. L. Thorndike and I. Lorge, *The Teacher's Word Book of 30,000 Words*, New York, Bureau of Publications, Teachers College, Columbia University, 1944.

# EGO DEVELOPMENT AMONG SEGREGATED

# NEGRO CHILDREN

*David Ausubel and Pearl Ausubel*

In this paper we propose to do three things. First, we would like to consider the personality development of the segregated Negro child as a special variant of the more typical course of ego development in our culture. Here the approach is normative, from the standpoint of a personality theorist interested in subcultural differences. In what ways does the ego development of segregated Negro children differ from that of the text-book child growing up in the shadow of our dominant middle-class value system? Second, we would like to consider some kinds of and reasons for individual differences within this underprivileged group. Do all Negro children in the Harlem ghetto respond in the same way to the impact of their segregated lower-class environment? If not, why not? Are there social class, sex, and individual differences among Negro children? Questions of this type would be asked by a personality theorist concerned with idiosyncratic and group variability within a subcultural setting, or by a psychiatrist treating the behavior disorders of such children in a Harlem community clinic. Finally, we propose to consider the implications of this material for such practical issues as educational practice and desegregation.

## OVERVIEW OF EGO DEVELOPMENT IN WHITE MIDDLE-CLASS CHILDREN

Before turning to a description of ego development in segregated Negro communities, it may be helpful to examine briefly the typical middle-class

231

model with which it will be compared. In doing this we do not mean to imply that the developmental pattern in suburbia is necessarily typical of the American scene. Obviously only a minority of America's children live in the ecological equivalent of suburban culture. Nevertheless it is still a useful model for comparative purposes because it reflects the value system that dominates such official socializing institutions in our society as the school, the church, the youth organizations, the mass media, and the child-rearing manuals. Hence, it is the most widely diffused and influential model of socialization in our culture. It is the official model that most parents profess to believe in regardless of whether or not they practice it. It is the model that would most impress foreign anthropologists as typical of American culture.

The infant in suburbia, as in many other cultures, may be pardoned for entertaining mild feelings of omnipotence (7)*. Out of deference for his manifest helplessness, his altruistic parents are indulgent, satisfy most of his needs, and make few demands on him. In view of his cognitive immaturity, it is hardly surprising then that he interprets his enviable situation as proof of his volitional power than as reflective of parental altruism. As he becomes less helpless and more responsive to parental direction, however, this idyllic picture begins to change. His parents become more demanding, impose their will on him, and take steps to socialize him in the ways of the culture; and by this time the toddler has sufficient cognitive maturity to perceive his relative impotence and volitional dependence on them. All of these factors favor the occurrence of satellization. The child surrenders his volitional independence and by the fiat of parental acceptance and intrinsic valuation acquires a derived or attributed status. As a result, despite his marginal status in the culture and manifest inability to fend for himself, he acquires feelings of self-esteem that are independent of his performance ability. He also internalizes parental values and expectations regarding mature and acceptable behavior.

In suburbia, derived status constitutes the cornerstone of the child's self-esteem until adolescence. Beginning with middle childhood, however, forces are set in motion that bring about preliminary desatellization from parents. Both in school and in the peer group he is urged to compete for a primary status based on his academic proficiency, athletic prowess, and social skills. School and peer groups legislate their own values, impose their own standards, and also offer him a subsidiary source of derived status insofar as they accept him for himself in return for his loyalty and self-subordination. All of these factors tend to devalue the parents and to undermine their omniscience in the child's eyes. The home becomes only one of several socializing agents that foster the development of aspirations for academic and vocational success and of the pattern of deferred gratification necessary to achieve them. Nevertheless, until adolescence,

* Numbers in parentheses denote references at end of article.

parents remain the major socializing agents and source of values in the child's life. Compared to the derived status obtained from parents, the primary status available in school and peer group plays only a subsidiary role in the total economy of ego organization.

## EGO DEVELOPMENT IN YOUNG NEGRO CHILDREN

*Social Class Factors.* Many of the ecological features of the segregated Negro subculture that impinge on personality development in early childhood are not specific to Negroes as such, but are characteristic of most lower-class populations. This fact is not widely appreciated by white Americans and hence contributes to much anti-Negro sentiment: many characteristic facets of the Negro's value system and behavior pattern are falsely attributed to his racial membership, whereas they really reflect his predominant membership in the lower social class. Nevertheless, these characteristics are commonly offered as proof of the alleged moral and intellectual inferiority that is supposedly inherent in persons of Negro ancestry and are used to justify existing discriminatory practices.

Lower-class parents, for example, are generally more casual, inconsistent, and authoritarian than middle-class parents in controlling their children, and resort to harsh, corporal forms of punishment (30, 31, 70, 71, 74). Unlike middle-class fathers, whose wives expect them to be as supportive as themselves in relation to children, the lower-class father's chief role in child-rearing is to impose constraints and administer punishment (74). Even more important, lower-class parents extend less succorant care and relax closely monitored supervision much earlier than their middle-class counterparts (29, 30, 35, 54). Lower-class children are thus free to roam the neighborhood and join unsupervised play groups at an age when suburban children are still confined to nursery school or to their own backyards. Hence, during the preschool and early elementary-school years, the lower-class family yields to the peer group much of its role as socializing agent, and source of values and derived status. During this early period lower-class children undergo much of the desatellization from parents that ordinarily occurs during middle childhood and preadolescence in most middle-class families. They acquire earlier volitional and executive independence outside the home and in many cases assume adult responsibilities such as earning money and caring for younger siblings. Abbreviated parental succorance, which frustrates the dependency needs of middle-class children and commonly fosters over-dependence (100), has a different significance for and effect on these lower-class children. Since it reflects the prevailing subcultural norm, and since the opportunity for early anchorage to a free-ranging peer group is available, it tends to encourage the development of precocious independence.

This pattern of precocious independence from the family combined with the exaggerated socializing influence of the peer group, although characteristic of both white and Negro lower-class children, does not necessarily prevail among all lower-class minority groups in the United States. Both Puerto Rican (3) and Mexican (75) children enjoy a more closely knit family life marked by more intimate contact between parents and children. In Mexican families, maternal and paternal roles are also more distinctive, masculine and feminine roles are more clearly delineated in childhood, and the socializing influence of the peer group is less pronounced (75).

The working-class mother's desire for unquestioned domination of her offspring, her preference for harsh, punitive, and suppressive forms of control, and her tendency to maintain considerable social and emotional distance between herself and her children are probably responsible in part for the greater prevalence of the authoritarian personality syndrome in lower-class children than in middle-class children (36, 53, 69). Lower-class children tend to develop ambivalent attitudes toward authority figures and to cope with this ambivalence by making an exaggerated show of overt, implicit compliance, by maintaining formally appropriate social distance, and by interacting with these figures on the basis of formalized role attributes rather than as persons. Their underlying hostility and resentment toward this arbitrary and often unfair authority is later expressed in such displaced forms as scape-goating, prejudice, extremist political and religious behavior, ethnocentrism, and delinquency (36, 53, 69).

Much of the significant relationship between social class status and school achievement undoubtedly reflects pervasive social class differences in cognitive orientation and functioning that are operative from early childhood (15). Middle-class children are trained to respond to the abstract, categorical, and relational properties of objects, whereas lower-class children are trained to respond more to their concrete, tangible, immediate, and particularized properties. This difference in perceptual disposition is carried over into verbal expression, memory, concept formation, learning, and problem-solving. Hence, because schools place great emphasis on the learning of abstract relationships and on the abstract use of language, lower-class children, on the average, experience much greater difficulty than middle-class children in mastering the curriculum.

*Racial Factors.* All of the foregoing properties of the lower-class environment also apply to the segregated Negro community. Most authorities on Negro family life agree that well over 50 per cent of Negro families live at the very lowest level of the lower-class standard (56). In addition, however, Negro families are characterized by a disproportionate number of illegal and loosely connected unions (56). Illegitimacy is a very common phenomenon and is associated with relatively little social stigma in the Negro community (20); nevertheless, illegitimate Negro children, especially at the older age levels, are significantly inferior to their legitimate counterparts in I.Q., school achievement, and personal adjustment (59).

Negro families are much more unstable than comparable lower-class white families. Homes are more apt to be broken, fathers are more frequently absent, and a matriarchal and negative family atmosphere more commonly prevails (25, 28, 34, 56). Thus the lower-class Negro child is frequently denied the benefits of bi-parental affection and upbringing; he is often raised by his grandmother or older sister while his mother works to support the family deserted by the father (34). One consequence of the matriarchal family climate is an open preference for girls. Boys frequently attempt to adjust to this situation by adopting feminine traits and mannerisms (28).

Negro family life is even more authoritarian in nature than is that of the lower social class generally. "Children are expected to be obedient and submissive" (56), and insubordination is suppressed by harsh and often brutal physical punishment (28, 31, 56). "Southern Negro culture teaches obedience and respect for authority as a mainspring of survival" (51). Surveys of high-school and college students show that authoritarian attitudes are more prevalent among Negroes at all grade levels (50, 51, 108).

Being a Negro also has many other implications for the ego development of young children that are not inherent in lower-class membership. The Negro child inherits an inferior caste status and almost inevitably acquires the negative self-esteem that is a realistic ego reflection of such status. Through personal slights, blocked opportunities, and unpleasant contacts with white persons and with institutionalized symbols of caste inferiority (segregated schools, neighborhoods, amusement areas, etc.) —and more indirectly through mass media and the reactions of his own family—he gradually becomes aware of the social significance of racial membership (45).

As a consequence of prejudice, segregation, discrimination, inferior status, and not finding himself respected as a human being with dignity and worth,

... the Negro child becomes confused in regard to his feelings about himself and his group. He would like to think well of himself but often tends to evaluate himself according to standards used by the other group. These mixed feelings lead to self-hatred and rejection of his group, hostility toward other groups, and a generalized pattern of personality difficulties (58, p. 146).

### Segregation

... means that the personal worth, of either a white or Negro person, is measured solely by group membership regardless of individual merit. Such a measure is realistically false and of necessity distorts the developing self-image of Negro and white children as well as their view of each other. Under these psychological circumstances the Negro child, for example, is burdened with inescapable inferiority feelings, a fixed ceiling to his aspiration level which can constrict the development of his potentialities, and a sense of humiliation and resentment which can entail patterns of hatred against himself and his own group, as well as against the dominant white group (14, p. 151).

The Negro child perceives himself as an object of derision and disparagement (45), as socially rejected by the prestigeful elements of society, and as unworthy of succorance and affection (34); and having no compelling reasons for not accepting this officially sanctioned negative evaluation of himself, he develops a deeply ingrained negative self-image (14, 123).

It does not take long for Negro children to become aware of the unfavorable implications of their racial membership. In interracial nursery schools, most children show some type of racial awareness at the age of three (115), and this awareness increases rapidly between the ages of three and seven (116). Once aware of racial differences, they soon learn that "skin color is important, that white is to be desired, dark to be regretted" (68). Very significantly, racial self-recognition develops later in Negro than in white children (77, 116); in the light of doll play evidence indicating that they resist identifying with their own stigmatized racial group (23), this delay in racial self-recognition can only be interpreted as reluctance in acknowledging their racial membership.

All of the sociometric rejection and maltreatment experienced by Negro children in a mixed group cannot, of course, be attributed to their inferior caste status alone. Some of the victimization undoubtedly reflects the dynamics of a majority-minority group situation. Thus, when white children are in the minority, the values, judgments, and verbal expression of the Negro majority tend to prevail (96). Under these conditions, Negroes curse whites but the latter do not openly retaliate despite revealing anti-Negro prejudice to white investigators (96).

In addition to suffering ego deflation through awareness of his inferior status in society, the Negro child finds it more difficult to satellize and is denied much of the self-esteem advantages of satellization. The derived status that is the principal source of children's self-esteem in all cultures is largely discounted in his case since he can only satellize in relation to superordinate individuals or groups who themselves possess an inferior and degraded status. Satellization under such conditions not only confers a very limited amount of derived status but also has deflationary implications for self-esteem. We can understand, therefore, why young Negro children resist identifying with their own racial group, why they seek to shed their identities (34), why they more frequently choose white than Negro playmates (116), why they prefer the skin color of the culturally dominant caste (23, 47, 68), and why they tend to assign negative roles to children of their own race (116). These tendencies persist at least into late adolescence and early adult life, insofar as one can judge from the attitudes of Negro college students. These students tend to reject ethnocentric and anti-white ideologies and to accept authoritarian and anti-Negro propositions (114).

## EGO DEVELOPMENT IN OLDER NEGRO CHILDREN AND ADOLESCENTS

*Social Class Factors.* During middle childhood and preadolescence the ego development of the segregated Negro child also reflects the influence of both general social class factors and of more specific racial factors. As already pointed out, early experience in fending for himself both in the wider culture and in the unsupervised peer group, as well as in exercising adult-like responsibilities, accomplishes precociously much of the de-satellization from and devaluation of parents characterizing the ego development of middle-class children during this period.

In these developments, the school plays a much less significant role among lower-class than among middle-class children. The lower-class child of school age has fewer illusions about parental omniscience for the teacher to shatter, and is coerced by the norms of his peer group against accepting her authority, seeking her approval, or entering into a satellizing relationship with her (30). School can also offer him very little in the way of either current or ultimate primary status. His parents and associates place no great value on education and do not generally encourage high aspirations for academic and vocational success, financial independence, or social recognition (30, 54, 97). It is hardly surprising, therefore, that lower-class children are less interested in reading than are middle-class children, have lower educational aspirations, take their schoolwork less seriously, and are less willing to spend the years of their youth in school in order to gain higher prestige and more social rewards as adults (30, 54, 97).

Even if they equalled middle-class children in these latter respects, academic achievement would still be quite a valueless reward for a child who soon comes to realize that professional status is beyond his grasp (30). Hence, anxiety regarding the attainment of internalized needs for vocational prestige does not drive the lower-class child to excel in school (30). Also, because of low achievement and discriminatory treatment, he fails to obtain the current rewards of academic success available to middle-class school children (30). On what grounds could a child immersed in an intellectually impoverished environment be expected to actualize his genic potentials for verbal and abstract thinking, when he is unmotivated by parental pressures, by ambitions for vocational success, or by the anxiety associated with realizing these ambitions?

Lower- and middle-class adolescents differ markedly both in their social value systems and in their vocational interests. Middle-class youths and their parents are more concerned with community service, self-realization, altruistic values, and internalized standards of conduct (60, 112), and prefer demanding, responsible, and prestigeful occupational pursuits (88, 89, 103). They also make higher vocational interest scores in the literary, esthetic, persuasive, scientific and business areas than do lower-class adolescents. The latter adolescents and their parents, on the other hand, place greater stress on such values as money, security, respectability, obedience, and conformity to authority, and tend to prefer agricultural, mechanical, domestic service, and clerical pursuits (88, 89, 103).

The lower-class child's *expressed* levels of academic and vocational aspirations often appear unrealistically high (34), but unlike the analogous situation in middle-class children, these do not necessarily represent his *real* or functional levels of striving. They more probably reflect impairment of realistic judgment under the cumulative impact of chronic failure (99) and low social status (48), as well as a compensatory attempt to bolster self-esteem through the appearance rather than the substance of aiming high. Lacking the strong ego involvement which the middle-class child brings to schoolwork, and which preserves the attractiveness of academic tasks despite failure experience (98), he quickly loses interest in school if he is unsuccessful. Finally, since he does not perceive the eventual rewards of striving and self-denial as attainable for persons of his status, he fails to develop to the same degree as the middle-class child the supportive traits of ego maturity necessary for the achievement of academic and vocational success (30). These supportive traits include habits of initiative and responsibility and the "deferred gratification pattern" of hard work, renunciation of immediate pleasures, long-range planning, high frustration tolerance, impulse control, thrift, orderliness, punctuality, and willingness to undergo prolonged vocational preparation (30, 54, 86, 97).

Despite having less deep-seated anxiety with respect to internalized needs for academic achievement and vocational prestige, children of lower-class families exhibit more signs of personality maladjustment than do children of middle-class families (4, 6, 57, 101, 102, 111). This greater degree of maladjustment is largely a response to the greater vicissitudes and insecurities of daily living; to the greater possibility and actual occurrence of failure in an educational and vocational world dominated by middle-class standards in which they are greatly disadvantaged; to inner tensions engendered by conflict between the values of the family and those of the dominant middle-class culture; to feelings of shame about family background that are associated with impulses to reject family ties; to feelings of guilt and anxiety about these latter impulses (102); and to the personal demoralization and self-derogation that accompany social disorganization and the possession of inferior social status (5, 7, 111). In most instances, of course, the symptoms of maladjustment are uncomfortable rather than disabling; but the generally higher level of anxiety, and the more frequent occurrence of motivational immaturity in lower-class children and adolescents, also increase the incidence of such serious disorders as schizophrenia, drug addiction, and anxiety neurosis and its various complications (7, 57, 111). Proneness to delinquency is, of course, higher among lower-class adolescents because of greater family and social disorganization, the deep-seated resentments and aggressive impulses attributable to socioeconomic deprivation, the influence of organized, predatory gangs, and the tacit encouragement offered by the lower-class value system and the slum-urban teen-age cult of thrills, kicks, self-indulgence, violence, and non-conformity.

*Racial Factors.* All of the aforementioned factors inhibiting the development of high level ego aspirations and their supportive personality traits in lower-class children are intensified in the segregated Negro child. His over-all prospects for vertical social mobility, although more restricted, are not completely hopeless. But the stigma of his caste membership is inescapable and unsurmountable. It is inherent in his skin color, permanently ingrained in his body image, and enforced by the extra-legal power of a society whose moral, legal, and religious codes proclaim his equality (123).

It is proper to speak of a stigma as being "enforced" when the stigma in question is culturally derived rather than inherent in the physical existence of the mark per se (that is, a mark of inferiority in *any* culture such as lameness or blindness). Dark skin color is a stigma in our culture only because it identifies a culturally stigmatized caste. When we speak of the stigma being "inherent in his skin color," we mean that it is a stigma which the Negro inherits by virtue of being born with that skin color in a culture that places a negative valuation on it. Hence the stigma "inheres" in the skin color. But this does not imply that dark skin color is inherently (that is, apart from a particular set of cultural values) a mark of inferiority; the stigma is only inherent for the individual insofar as he acquires it by cultural definition rather than by anything he does.

Hence, since a culturally derived stigma refers to an identifying characteristic of a group which has been relegated to an inferiority status position in society, the stigma can only be perpetuated as long as the culture provides some mechanism for *enforcing* the low status position of the group in question. In the absence of cultural enforcement the stigma would vanish in as much as it is not inherent in the characteristic itself but is merely a symbol of membership in an inferior caste. In our society (unlike the Union of South Africa), there are no laws which explicitly create an inferior caste status for the Negro; even segregation statutes accord him a separate rather than an inferior status. Hence the "mark" is enforced extra-legally by preserving through informal social practices the social inferiority of which the mark is but a symbol.

If this situation exists despite the authority of God and the Constitution, what basis for hope does the Negro child have? It is not surprising, therefore, that, in comparison with lower-class white children, he aspires to jobs with more of the formal trappings than with the actual attributes of social prestige; that he feels impotent to strike back at his tormentors; that he feels more lonely and scared when he is by himself; and that he gives more self-deprecatory reactions when figuratively looking at himself in the mirror (34). He may have less anxiety about realizing high-flown ambitions than the middle-class child, but generalized feelings of inadequacy and unworthiness make him very prone to over-respond with anxiety to any threatening situation. In view of the general hopelessness of his position, lethargy, apathy, submission, and passive sabotage are more typical than aggressive striving of his predominant reaction to frustration (95, 105).

Rosen (95) compared the educational and vocational aspirations of Negro boys (age 8 through 14) and their mothers to those of white, Protestant Americans, French Canadians, American Jews, Greek-Americans, and Italian-Americans. The mean vocational aspiration score of his Negro group was significantly lower than the mean scores of all other groups except the French Canadian. Paradoxically, however, 83 per cent of the Negro mothers aspired to a college education for their sons.[1] Rosen concluded that although Negroes have been

. . . exposed to the liberal economic ethic longer than most of the other groups . . . their culture, it seems, is least likely to accent achievement values. The Negro's history as a slave and depressed farm worker, and the sharp discrepancy between his experience and the American Creed, would appear to work against the achievement values of the dominant white group. Typically, the Negro life-situation does not encourage the belief that one can manipulate his environment, or the conviction that one can improve his condition very much by planning and hard work (95, p. 55).

. . . Negroes who might be expected to share the prevalent American emphasis upon education, face the painfully apparent fact that positions open to educated Negroes are scarce. This fact means that most Negroes, in all likelihood, do not consider high educational aspirations realistic, and the heavy drop-out in high school suggests that the curtailment of educational aspirations begins very early (95, p. 58).

Ethnicity was found to be more highly related to vocational aspirations than was social class; sizable ethnic and racial differences prevailed even when the influence of social class was controlled. These results are consistent with the finding that white students tend to prefer "very interesting jobs," whereas Negro students are more concerned with job security (106).

[1] Another datum at variance with the general trend of the evidence is Grossack's finding that female Negro students in the South score significantly higher on need achievement measures than do comparable white females, and that the males of both groups are not significantly different (52).

The relatively low vocational aspirations of Negro children are apparently justified by the current facts of economic life. Negroes predominate in the unskilled occupations, receive less pay than whites for equivalent work, and exceed the percentage figured for whites in degree of unemployment (43, 105). In skilled occupations, Negroes are excluded at all educational levels (120): higher educational qualifications in Negroes are less frequently associated with higher-level vocational pursuits than they are in the case of whites (119). Thus,

... from long experience Negroes have learned that it is best to be prepared for the absence, rather than the presence of opportunity—or, at most, to prepare and strive only for those limited opportunities which have been open in the past. . . . Like most other people, Negroes tend to accept the views that prevail in the larger society about their appropriate role in that society, [and aspire and prepare] for only those positions where they are confident of acceptance (110, p. 461).

Negro children and lower-class white children who attend schools with a heterogeneous social class and racial population are in a more favorable developmental situation. Under these conditions, the unfavored group is stimulated to compete more aggressively, even to the point of unrealism (16, 109), with the more privileged group in every-day contracts and in aspirational behavior (16). In their self-judgments they compare themselves with *actual* models, who in fact are only slightly better off than they are, and hence do not feel particularly inferior (34). Negro children in segregated schools, on the other hand, are not only deprived of this stimulation, but in comparing themselves to other children paradoxically feel more depressed and less able to compete adequately (34), despite the fact that their actual contacts are confined to children in the incapsulated community who share their socioeconomic status. Apparently then, they must use idealized mass media models as the basis for comparison.

Negro children are placed in the same ambivalent, conflictful position with respect to the achievement values of western civilization as are the children of many native peoples experiencing acculturation and the socio-cultural impact of rapid industrialization. On the one hand, exposure to the new value system and its patent and alluring advantages makes them less able to accept the traditional values of their elders; on the other hand, both loyalty to their families and the excluding color bar established by the dominant group make it difficult for them to assimilate the new set of values (9, 11, 12, 35, 81). Resentment and hostility toward the rejecting whites, as well as disillusionment regarding white middle-class values and institutions, predispose them arbitrarily and indiscriminately to repudiate the aspirations and personality traits valued by the dominant culture. These negativistic tendencies are even manifested in speech patterns: minority group children tend to reject the accepted model of speech that is symbolic of superordinate status in a social order that accords them only second-class membership (2).

Further abetting these tendencies toward resistive acculturation are many organized and institutionalized forms of nationalism and counter-chauvinism. Among the Maori, "resistance took the form of unadaptive but adjustive messianic and magical cults, emphasis on moribund and ceremonial features of the ancient culture, and indiscriminate rejection of progressive aspects of European culture" (9, p. 221). Numerous parallels can be found among the American Negro—for example, the Father Divine and Black Muslim movements.

One of the most damaging effects of racial prejudice and discrimination on the victimized group is that it provides an all-embracing rationalization for personal shortcomings, lack of striving, and antisocial conduct.

Some Negroes use the objective injustice of [creating scapegoats] as an opportunity to relieve or ward off feelings of personal inadequacy, self-contempt, or self-reproach by projecting all the blame onto white prejudice and discrimination. For other Negroes, however, reaction-formation becomes a main defense against the negative racial image. . . . Thus they may develop extremes of moralistic, prudish, and compulsively meticulous attitudes [to disprove the stereotype] (14, p. 152).

The Negro child is offered an excuse for anti-social behavior and evasion of social responsibility through feeling deprived of the social rewards for self-denial which are part of a healthy socialization process. But since these reactions are at variance with the democratic ideal of many other teachings to which children of both races are exposed at home, at church, and at school, they arouse of necessity feelings of inner conflict, confusion, anxiety, and guilt. These constitute liabilities for optimal adjustment (14, p. 152).

A continuing set of small incidents, closed doors, and blocked opportunities contribute to feelings of insecurity and mistrust and lead to the building of faith only in immediate gratifications and personal possessions (14, p. 148).

### Withdrawal from Competition

An important factor helping to perpetuate the Negro's inferior social status and devalued ego structure is his tendency to withdraw from the competition of the wider American culture and to seek psychological shelter within the segregated walls of his own subculture. Such tendencies are particularly evident among middle-class Negroes who, instead of providing the necessary leadership in preparing their people to take advantage of new vocational opportunities in the emerging desegregated culture, often seek to protect their own vested interests in segregation. Negro businessmen, professionals, and teachers, for example, largely owe their clientele, jobs, and incomes to the existence of segregated institutions; furthermore, in the segregated community they do not have to meet the more stringent competitive standards prevailing in the wider culture (42, 93, 120). An additional complication is the fact that even though they "cannot escape altogether the discrimination and contempt to which

Negroes are generally subjected" (42, p. 299), they tend to identify with the values and ideology of the white middle-class and to dissociate themselves from other Negroes (42, 93, 107, 110, 114). Together with pride of race and grudging affirmation of their racial identity, members of intellectual Negro families "are led to assert their superiority over other Negroes and look down on those who are 'no account,' shiftless, and 'mean'" (93, p. 240).

The degree to which Negro potential can be developed in America depends, according to Smuts (110),

. . . not only on the willingness of the white community to grant greater opportunity to Negroes in the struggle for integrated schools and equal access to jobs; but it also depends at least as much on what the Negro community does to help its own members prepare themselves for new opportunities . . . In a democracy, how well the individual develops and utilizes his potential depends not only on the opportunities that come his way as a youth and a man, but equally on his own determination to seek and make the most of opportunity (p. 456).

In the past the real world that Negroes had to adjust to included segregation, discrimination, absence of opportunity. But the facts are changing and a new kind of adjustment is called for (p. 461) . . . The development of high ambition and firm self-confidence among Negro youth is one prerequisite for the fuller development of Negro potential (p. 462) . . . In a competitive society integration means competition, and successful competition requires at least equal preparation (p. 458) . . . Negroes will not be able to take full advantage of [new] opportunities unless they improve their preparation for work (p. 458) . . . Negro children cannot develop an image of themselves as free and equal members of American society unless they see their elders actually living that role (p. 463).

### Educational Aspirations and Achievement of Negro Children

Partly as a result of unequal educational opportunities, Negro children show serious academic retardation. They attend school for fewer years and, on the average, learn much less than white children do (5, 17, 21, 82, 110, 113). One of the chief reasons for this discrepancy is the inferior education and training of Negro teachers who themselves are usually products of segregated education. The inequality of educational facilities exists not only in the South (5, 17, 127), but in the urban North as well, where, for the most part, de facto segregation prevails (110, 113). Eighty-four per cent of the top 10 per cent of Negro graduates in one southern high school scored below the national mean on the Scholastic Aptitude Test (17). Thus the incentive of reaching the average level of proficiency in the group is not very stimulating for Negro children, since the mean and even the somewhat superior child in this group are still below grade level. Teachers in segregated schools also tend to be overly permissive and to emphasize play skills over academic achievement; they are perceived by their pupils as evaluating them negatively, and as more concerned with behavior than with schoolwork (34).

Even more important perhaps as a cause of Negro educational retardation is the situation prevailing in the Negro home. Many Negro parents have had little schooling themselves and hence are unable to appreciate its value. Thus they do not provide active, wholehearted support for high-level academic performance by demanding conscientious study and regular attendance from their children. Furthermore, because of their large families and their own meager schooling they are less able to provide help with lessons. Keeping a large family of children in secondary school constitutes a heavy economic burden on Negro parents in view of their low per capita income and the substantial hidden costs of "free" education. The greater frequency of broken homes, unemployment, and negative family atmosphere, as well as the high rate of pupil turnover (25, 104), are also not conducive to academic achievement.

Negro pupils are undoubtedly handicapped in academic attainment by a lower average level of intellectual functioning than is characteristic of comparable white pupils. In both northern and southern areas, particularly the latter, Negro pupils have significantly lower I.Q.s (19, 39, 80, 82), and are retarded in arithmetic, reading, language usage, and ability to handle abstract concepts (17, 82). The extreme intellectual impoverishment of the Negro home *over and above* its lower social-class status reflects the poor standard of English spoken in the home and the general lack of books, magazines, and stimulating conversation. In view of the educational and psychological inequality of segregated schools, the inferior intellectual status of Negro homes, and the negative motivational effects of membership in a socially stigmatized group, any inferences from the lower I.Q.s and educational retardation of Negro pupils regarding *innate* differences in intelligence are obviously unwarranted. Organic brain damage, however, is a more frequent occurrence in Negro children because of inadequate prenatal care and nutrition and because of the higher incidence of prematurity (85).

Similar kinds of family and community factors depress the vocational strivings and accomplishments of Negro youth. Practically all of the following description of the occupational aspirations of Maori adolescents in New Zealand applies to the Negro in America:

> Maori parents are less sophisticated than their [European] counterparts about vocational matters and are accordingly less capable of assisting their children with appropriate information, advice, and guidance. . . . In view of their smaller incomes and larger families, Maori parents are also more reluctant to commit themselves to supporting plans requiring long-term vocational preparation (9, p. 623).

> . . . Maori parents tend to adopt more permissive and laissez-faire attitudes than [European] parents toward their children's vocational careers. Despite occasional and inconsistent displays of authoritarianism in this regard, they are usually content to let them drift. They apply fewer coercive pressures and extend less support and encouragement in relation to the long-term occupational

ambitions of their children. Their own values concerning vocational achievement and the example they set their children also tend to encourage the adoption of a short-term view. In practice they make few demands for the deferment of immediate hedonistic satisfactions and for the internalization of supportive traits consistent with high academic and occupational attainment (p. 263).

. . . [Still] another factor limiting the vocational achievement of Maori youth is the relatively low occupational status and morale of Maori adults. Young people lack the encouragement [of visible emulatory models], of a tradition and a high current standard of vocational accomplishment in the ethnic group. They are also denied the practical benefits of guidance and financial backing that would follow from the existence of such a standard and tradition. On the other hand, they are discouraged by the marginal economic position of their elders [and] by social demoralization (p. 624).

Maori pupils also receive less encouragement from their peers than [European] pupils do to strive for vocational achievement. Not only is occupational success less highly valued in the Maori than in the European peer culture, but the greater availability of *derived status*—based solely on membership in and intrinsic acceptance by the group—also removes much of the incentive for seeking *primary status* based on individual competence and performance. In districts where community morale is low and juvenile delinquency flourishes, vocational achievement tends to be negatively sanctioned (p. 624).

Low vocational aspirations, of course, are in large part a reflection of the distressingly high rate of unemployment among Negro youth in the urban slums. Conant reports that in one large city 48 per cent of male Negro high school graduates and 63 per cent of non-graduates were unemployed (25).

The tone is not one to encourage education or stimulate ambition. One often finds a vicious circle of lack of jobs and lack of ambition; one leads to the other. It is my contention that the circle must be broken both by upgrading the educational and vocational aspirations of slum youth and, even more important, by finding employment opportunity for them, particularly for high school graduates. It does no good whatever to prepare boys and girls for nonexistent jobs (25, p. 36).

Finally, because of their precocious desatellization and emancipation from parents, Negro youths have greater needs for *immediate* financial independence. They therefore find psychologically more intolerable a prolonged period of psychological dependence on parents, such as would be required in preparing for a profession.

### Personality Adjustment

The destructive impact of prejudice, discrimination, segregation, an inferior caste status on self-esteem, in addition to the usual mental hygiene consequences of lower social class membership, result in a much higher incidence of behavior disorders in Negroes than in whites (51, 111, 128). Personality disturbance is also more highly correlated with intelligence test scores in Negroes than in whites (94). Quite understandably, both high anxiety level (83, 94) and suppressed feelings of aggression (61) are prominent symptoms of Negro maladjustment. Overt expression of these same aggressive impulses leads to a juvenile delinquency rate that is two to three times as high as among white teen-agers (37, 38). The occurrence of delinquent behavior is abetted by the high rate of unemployment (25) and by many characteristic features of lower-class Negro family life, such as illegitimate births, broken homes, desertion, neglect, employment of the mother, intra-familial violence, harsh punishment, and tolerance for minor dishonesties (20). Under these circumstances, aggressive antisocial behavior may be considered both a form of individual and social protest (38), as well as an effective means of obtaining and maintaining status in the peer group of the lower-class Negro subculture (22). Drug addiction, on the other hand, represents a particularly efficient type of "dead-end" adjustment for the hedonistic, motivationally immature adolescent who refuses to face up to the responsibilities of adult life (10, 41).

## SEX DIFFERENCES

One of the most striking features of ego development in the segregated Negro community is the relatively more favored position enjoyed by girls in comparison to the middle-class model. It is true that middle-class girls have certain advantages over boys in early ego development. Since girls perceive themselves as more highly accepted and intrinsically valued by parents (13) and have a more available emulatory model in the home (84), they tend to satellize more and longer. In addition to enjoying more derived status in the home, they can also acquire more primary status from household activities (84) and from school achievement. The opportunity for acquiring primary status in school is greater for girls than for boys because of their superior verbal fluency and greater conformity to adult authority, and because school success is less ambivalently prized by their peers. In general, girls are less negativistic (46), more amenable to social controls (66), and less alienated from adults.

Middle-class boys, however, are not excessively disadvantaged. Their mothers tend to prefer them to girls (100), and their fathers are responsible and respected status figures in the home and the principal source of economic security. Furthermore, although girls enjoy more current primary status during childhood, boys have higher ultimate aspirations for primary status; their aspirational level both for laboratory tasks (121) and for possessions and achievement (24) are higher. Unlike boys, girls do not *really* expect to prove their adequacy and maintain their self-esteem as adults by means of their vocational accomplishments. Their fathers are satisfied if they are "pretty, sweet, affectionate, and well-liked" (1).

Finally, the superordinate position of men in our society, and the accompanying male chauvinism, is reflected in childhood sex roles. From an early age boys learn to be contemptuous of girls and their activities; and although girls retaliate in kind by finding reasons for deprecating the male sex, they tend to accept in part the prevailing view of their inferiority (65). Whereas boys seldom if ever desire to change sex, girls not infrequently wish they were boys (124). The male counterpart of a "tom-boy" who relishes sewing and reads girls' books is indeed a rarity.

In contrast to this picture, we find girls in the *segregated* Negro community showing much greater relative superiority in academic, personal, and social adjustment (34). They not only outperform boys academically by a greater margin, but do so in all subjects rather than only in language skills (34). These girls have higher achievement needs (44, 52) and a greater span of attention; they are more popular with classmates; they show more mature and realistic aspirations; they assume more responsible roles; and they feel less depressed in comparing themselves with other children (3). Substantially more Negro girls than Negro boys complete every level of education in the United States (110). Adequate reasons for these differences are not difficult to find. Negro children in this subculture live in a matriarchal family atmosphere where girls are openly preferred by mothers and grandmothers, and where the male sex role is generally deprecated. The father frequently deserts the family and in any case tends to be an unreliable source of economic and emotional security (28, 34). Hence the mother, assisted perhaps by her mother or by a daughter, shoulders most of the burdens and responsibilities of child rearing and is the only dependable adult with whom the child can identify. In this environment male chauvinism can obtain little foothold. The preferential treatment accorded girls is even extended to opportunities for acquiring ultimate primary status. If the family pins all of its hopes on one child and makes desperate sacrifices for that child, it will often be a daughter in preference to a son.[2] Over and above his handicaps at home, the Negro boy also faces more obstacles in the wider culture in realizing his vocational ambitions, whatever they may be, than the Negro girl in fulfilling her adult role expectations of housewife, mother, nurse, teacher, or clerical worker (34).

It seems, therefore, that Negro girls in racially incapsulated areas are less traumatized than boys by the impact of racial discrimination. This is precisely the opposite of what is found in studies of Negro children from less economically depressed and less segregated environments (45, 117). The discrepancy can be attributed perhaps to two factors: (1) the preferential treatment accorded girls in the incapsulated community is more pervasive, unqualified, and continuous, and (2) the fact that, unlike

[2] In lower-class Puerto Rican and Mexican families, just the opposite situation is to be found; that is, male dominance and superiority prevail (40, 49, 75).

Negro girls in mixed neighborhoods, these girls are less exposed to slights and humiliation from white persons. However, because of less tendency to internalize their feelings and greater openness in their social organization, Negro boys are able to adjust more easily than girls to the initial impact of desegregation (18).

## INDIVIDUAL DIFFERENCES IN REACTIONS
## TO THE SEGREGATED NEGRO ENVIRONMENT

Only extreme culture determinists would argue that all children in the incapsulated Negro community necessarily respond in substantially identical ways to the impact of their social environment. Although common factors in cultural conditioning obviously make for many uniformities in personality development, genetically determined differences in temperamental and cognitive traits, as well as differential experience in the home and wider culture, account for much idiosyncratic variation. Would it be unreasonable, for example, to anticipate that an intellectually gifted Negro child in this environment might have a different fate than an intellectually dull or average youngster; that an active, assertive, outgoing, and tough-skinned child might react differently to discriminatory treatment than one who is phlegmatic, submissive, sensitive, and introverted?

Differences in early socializing experience with parents are probably even more important, especially since they tend to generalize to interpersonal behavior outside the home. At this point it is worth noting that, generally speaking, racial discrimination affects children indirectly through their parents before it affects them directly through their own contacts with the wider culture. This indirect influence is mediated in two ways. (1) General parental attitudes toward the child are undoubtedly determined in part by the parent's own experience as a victim of discrimination. Some racially victimized parents, seeking retribution through their children, may fail to value them intrinsically and may place exaggerated emphasis on ego aggrandizement. Others may be so preoccupied with their own frustrations as to reject their children. Still others may accept and intrinsically value their children, and through their own example and strength of character encourage the development of realistic aspirations and mature, self-disciplined behavior. (2) Parents transmit to their children some of their own ways of responding to discrimination, such as counter-aggression, passive sabotage, obsequious submission or strident counter-chauvinism. Individual differences such as these undoubtedly explain in part why some Negroes move into unsegregated neighborhoods and transfer to unsegregated schools when these opportunities arise, whereas other members of the race choose to remain in the segregated environment. The decision to transfer or not to transfer to an unsegregated school, for example, was found to be unrelated to both social class status and academic ability (27).

Much inter-individual variability therefore prevails in the reactions of children to minority group membership. Fortunately, sufficient time is available for establishing some stable feelings of intrinsic adequacy within the home before the impact of segregation on ego development becomes catastrophically destructive. It was found, for example, that Negro children who are most self-accepting also tend to exhibit more positive attitudes toward other Negro and white children (117), and that Negro college students who identify most with their own race tend to be least prejudiced against other minority groups (64). Hence, while appreciating the generally unfavorable effects of a segregated environment on all Negro children, we may conclude on the more hopeful note that the consequences of membership in a stigmatized racial group can be cushioned in part by a foundation of intrinsic self-esteem established in the home (7, 76).

## IMPLICATIONS FOR EDUCATION

Before Negroes can assume their rightful place in a desegregated American culture, important changes in the ego structure of Negro children must first take place. They must shed feelings of inferiority and self-derogation, acquire feelings of self-confidence and racial pride, develop realistic aspirations for occupations requiring greater education and training, and develop the personality traits necessary for implementing these aspirations. Such changes in ego structure can be accomplished in two different but complementary ways. First, all manifestations of the Negro's inferior and segregated caste status must be swept away—in education, housing, employment, religion, travel, and exercise of civil rights. This in itself will enhance the Negro's self-esteem and open new opportunities for self-fulfillment. Second, through various measures instituted in the family, school and community, character structure, levels of aspiration, and actual standards of achievement can be altered in ways that will further enhance his self-esteem and make it possible for him to take advantage of new opportunities.

*Desegregation.* Desegregation, of course, is no panacea for the Negro child's personality difficulties. In the first place, it tends to create new problems of adjustment, particularly when it follows in the wake of serious community conflict. Second, it cannot quickly overcome various long-standing handicaps which Negro children bring with them to school "such as their cultural impoverishment, their helplessness or apathy toward learning, and their distrust of the majority group and their middle-class teachers" (14, p. 158); nor can it compensate for "oversized classes, inappropriate curriculums, inadequate counseling services, or poorly trained or demoralized teachers" (14, p. 158). Yet it is an important and indispensable first step in the reconstitution of Negro personality, since the school is the most strategically placed social institution for effecting rapid change both in ego structure and in social status. A desegregated school offers the Negro child his first taste of social equality and his first experience of first-class citizenship. He can enjoy the stimulating effect of competition with white children and can use them as realistic yardsticks in measuring his own worth and chances for academic and vocational success. Under these circumstances, educational achievement no longer seems so pointless, and aspirations for higher occupational status in the wider culture acquire more substance.

It is also reasonable to anticipate that white children will be prejudiced and continue to discriminate against their Negro classmates long after desegregation accords them equal legal status in the educational system. Attitudes toward Negroes in the South, for example, are remarkably stable, even in periods of rapid social change involving desegregation (130), and are not highly correlated with anti-Semitic or other ethnocentric trends (50, 62, 90, 91). Prejudice against Negroes is deeply rooted in the American culture (92) and is continually reinforced both by the socioeconomic gain and by the vicarious ego enhancement it brings to those who manifest it (14, 55, 95). It is hardly surprising, therefore, that racial prejudice is most pronounced in lower social-class groups (125) and that these groups constitute the hard core of resistance to desegregation (63, 118); anti-white prejudice is similarly most pronounced among lower-class Negroes (26, 126). Increased physical contact per se between white and Negro children does little to reduce prejudice (78, 122), but more intimate personal interaction under favorable circumstances significantly reduces social distance between the two groups (62, 73, 129).

Artificial attempts to end de facto school segregation, caused by neighborhood segregation of Negroes in particular urban slums, are socially and psychologically unsound (25). It is not only impractical to transport white children to schools in distant, predominantly Negro neighborhoods just for the purpose of maintaining the principle of racially mixed classes, but it also victimizes individual white children and thereby increases racial tensions. Unless de facto segregation is accomplished by the gerrymandering of school districts, and unless schools in Negro districts are *actually* inferior, it seems more reasonable to work for the elimination of this type of school segregation by directly attacking its underlying cause, that is, neighborhood segregation (25).

*Community Action.* The support of parents and of the Negro community at large must be enlisted if we hope to make permanent progress in the education of Negro children.

One needs only to visit . . . a [slum] school to be convinced that the nature of the community largely determines what goes on in the school. Therefore to attempt to divorce the school from the community is to engage in unrealistic thinking, which might lead to policies that could wreak havoc with the school and the lives of children (25, p. 20).

Whatever can be done to strengthen family life and to give the fathers a more important role in it will make a significant contribution to the development of Negro potential (110, p. 462).

Working with mothers and getting them to adopt a more positive attitude toward school is an important first step in improving the educational achievement of urban Negro children (25). Typically only 10 per cent of Negro parents are high-school graduates and only 33 per cent complete elementary school (25). Thus enrollment of parents in adult-education programs would significantly raise the cultural level of the Negro home and "stimulate an interest in newspapers, magazines and possibly even books. One of the troubles . . . is that when the children leave the school they never see anyone read anything—not even newspapers" (25, p. 25). The "Higher Horizons" project in New York City is a good example of a recent attempt to discover academically talented children in slum areas and encourage them to aspire to college education. This program embodies cultural enrichment, improving counseling and instruction, and the sympathetic involvement of parents.

*Counseling.* Because of current grave inadequacies in the structure of the lower-class urban Negro family, the school must be prepared to compensate, at least in part, for the deficiencies of the home, that is, to act, so to speak, *in loco parentis.* Teachers in predominantly Negro schools actually perform much of this role at the present time. As one Negro teacher said to Conant:

We do quite well with these children in the lower grades. Each of us is, for the few hours of the school day, an acceptable substitute for the mother. But when they reach about 10, 11, or 12 years of age, we lose them. At that time the "street" takes over. In terms of schoolwork, progress ceases; indeed many pupils begin to go backward in their studies (25, p. 21).

It is apparent, therefore, that trained counselors must assume the role of parent substitute during preadolescence and adolescence. They are needed to offer appropriate educational and vocational guidance, to encourage worthwhile and realistic aspirations, and to stimulate the development of mature personality traits. In view of the serious unemployment situation among Negro youth, they should also assist in job placement and in cushioning the transition between school and work. This will naturally require much expansion of existing guidance services in the school.

Research has shown that Negro children's distrust of white counselors and authority figures in general makes it

. . . difficult for a white counselor to create an atmosphere wherein a Negro could gain insight . . . The fundamental principle of counseling—to view the social or personal field as the counselor does—is difficult to attain in such a situation. The white person can only imagine, but never know, how a Negro thinks and feels, or how he views a social or personal situation. The cultural lenses which are formulated from unique milieus are not as freely transferable as it is assumed, or as we are led to believe (87, p. 188).

*Educational Measures.* Specially trained teachers and smaller classes are obviously required to cope with the difficulties of educating culturally disadvantaged minority group children. Emphasis must be placed on acquiring such basic intellectual skills as reading, writing, and arithmetic before any attempt is made to teach algebra, literature, science, or foreign languages. In many urban high schools today, pupils who cannot read at a fifth-grade level, and who cannot speak or write grammatically or do simple arithmetical calculations, are subject to irregular French verbs, Shakespearean drama, and geometrical theorems. Nothing more educationally futile or better calculated to destroy educational morale could be imagined! Slow readers and pupils with other educational disabilities should be identified early and given intensive remedial work (25). Going even one step further, Professor Strodtbeck of the University of Chicago is attempting to teach underprivileged children to read at the age of 4, combining instruction with personal attention and affection, in order to forestall later reading difficulties (79).

If Negro youth is to be adequately prepared for the changing job market, more realistic prevocational courses, integrated in some instances with work experience programs, should be established in the "general" urban high schools (25). In connection with vocational education, Conant makes these four important points:

First and foremost, vocational courses should not replace courses which are essential parts of the required academic program for graduation. Second, vocational courses should be provided in grades 11 and 12 and not require more than half the student's time in those years; however, for slow learners and prospective dropouts these courses ought to begin earlier. Third, the significance of the vocational courses is that those enrolled are keenly interested in the work; they realize the relevance of what they are learning to their future careers, and this sense of purpose is carried over to the academic courses which they are studying at the same time. Fourth, the type of vocational training programs should be related to the employment opportunities in the general locality (25, p. 44).

Opportunities should also be made available for part-time high school study in conjunction with trade apprenticeships, as well as for more advanced vocational training in community colleges and technical institutes. For underprivileged urban students capable and desirous of pursuing a regular course of university studies, programs such as the previously described "Higher Horizons" project, supplemented by liberal scholarship aid, are necessary. Finally, a special public works and job training program is currently needed to alleviate the calamitous problem of unemployment among urban youth (25).

## SUMMARY AND CONCLUSIONS

The ego development of segregated Negro children in the United States manifests various distinctive properties, both because Negroes generally occupy the lowest stratum of the lower-class subculture, and because they possess an inferior caste status in American society. Their inferior caste position is marked by an unstable and matriarchal type of family structure, by restricted opportunities for acquiring educational, vocational, and social status, by varying degrees of segregation from the dominant white majority, and by a culturally fixed devaluation of their dignity as human beings. The consequences of this regrettable state of affairs for Negro children's self-esteem and self-confidence, for their educational and vocational aspirations, and for their character structure, interpersonal relations, and personality adjustment, constitute the characteristic features of their ego development.

Beginning in the preschool period, the Negro child gradually learns to appreciate the negative implications of dark skin color for social status and personal worth. Hence he resists identifying with his own racial group and shows definite preference for white dolls and playmates. This reluctance to acknowledge his racial membership not only results in ego deflation, but also makes it difficult for him to identify with his parents and to obtain from such identification the derived status that universally constitutes the principal basis of self-esteem during childhood. Much of the derived status that white children obtain from their parents is made available to the Negro child by virtue of his membership in an unsupervised peer group, which accordingly performs many of the socializing functions of the white middle-class home. This is especially true for the Negro boy who often has no adult male with whom to identify in the frequently father-less Negro family, and who finds maleness deprecated in his matriarchal and authoritarian home. Early experience in fending for himself results in precocious social maturity, independence, and emancipation from the home.

During preadolescence and adolescence, segregated Negro children characteristically develop low aspirations for academic and vocational achievement. These low aspirations reflect existing social class and ethnic values, the absence of suitable emulatory models, marked educational retardation, restricted vocational opportunities, lack of parental and peer group support, and the cultural impoverishment of the Negro home. Because of loyalty to parents and rejection by the dominant white group, Negro adolescents develop ambivalent feelings toward middle-class achievement values and the personality traits necessary for their implementation. In many instances they use the objective facts of racial prejudice and discrimination as a rationalization for personal inadequacies, apathy, lack of striving, and anti-social behavior. The seeming hopelessness of attaining adequate vocational and social status in the wider American culture induces many Negro youths to withdraw from contact and competition with whites, and to seek the psychological shelter of their own segregated subculture. Girls tend to develop a more mature ego structure than boys because of their favored position in the home, but face greater adjustment problems during desegregation. The detrimental effects of segregation and inferior caste status on Negro ego development naturally vary from one child to another depending on ability, temperament, and the degree of intrinsic self-esteem and ego maturity that can be acquired within the home environment.

The problem of raising aspirational and achievement levels among Negro youth is presently acute because Negroes can no longer adjust comfortably to their segregated caste status, and because automation has eliminated many of the unskilled jobs which formerly made some type of stable economic adjustment possible. Two different but complementary approaches are available in dealing with this problem. The more general approach, which primarily applies to educators in their role as citizens, involves the elimination of existing racial barriers in housing, education, employment, religion, and civil rights. The more specific educational approach is to attempt, through various family, school and community measures, an upgrading of the Negro child's aspirational level, standards of achievement, and character structure that will both enhance his self-esteem and enable him to take advantage of new opportunities.

In the educational sphere, school desegregation is an indispensable prerequisite for raising aspiration and achievement levels, but obviously cannot compensate, in and of itself, for the longstanding educational handicaps of the Negro child or for existing inadequacies in schools, teachers, curriculums, and counseling services. Before we can expect any permanent improvement in the educational performance of Negro children, we must strengthen Negro family life, combat the cultural impoverishment of the Negro home, and enlist the support and cooperation of Negro parents in accomplishing this objective. More intensive guidance services, utilizing Negro personnel, are required to provide the socializing and supportive functions that are currently lacking in many Negro homes. Other important needs are smaller classes, specially trained teachers, abundant remedial facilities, the provision of expanded and more realistic vocational education, and a public works program to alleviate the explosively dangerous problem of unemployment among urban Negro youth.

References to *Ego Development Among Segregated Negro Children*

1. Aberle, D. F., and K. D. Naegele, "Middle-Class Fathers' Occupational Roles and Attitudes Toward Children," *American Journal of Orthopsychiatry*, **22,** 1952, 366–378.

2. Anastasi, Anne, and F. A. Cordova, "Some Effects of Bilingualism upon the Intelligence Test Performance of Puerto Rican Children in New York City," *Journal of Educational Psychology*, **44**, 1953, 1–19.

3. Anastasi, Anne, and C. DeJesus, "Language Development and Non-verbal IQ of Puerto Rican Preschool Children in New York City." *Journal of Abnormal and Social Psychology*, **48**, 1953, 357–366.

4. Angelino, H., J. Dollins, and E. V. Mech, "Trends in the 'Fears and Worries' of School Children as Related to Socioeconomic Status and Age," *Journal of Genetic Psychology*, **89**, 1956, 263–276.

5. Ashmore, H. S., *The Negro and the Schools*, Chapel Hill, N.C., University of North Carolina Press, 1954.

6. Auld, B. F., "Influence of Social Class on Personality Test Response," *Psychological Bulletin*, **49**, 1952, 318–332.

7. Ausubel, D. P., *Ego Development and the Personality Disorders*, New York, Grune and Stratton, 1952.

8. ———, "Ego Development Among Segregated Negro Children," *Mental Hygiene*, **42**, 1958, 362–369.

9. ———, "Acculturative Stress in Modern Maori Adolescence," *Child Development*, **31**, 1960, 317–631.

10. ———, "Causes and Types of Drug Addiction: a Psychosocial View," *Psychiatric Quarterly*, **35**, 1961, 523–531.

11. ———, "The Maori: A Study in Resistive Acculturation," *Social Forces*, **39**, 1961, 218–227.

12. ———, *Maori Youth*, Wellington, New Zealand, Price, Milburn, 1961.

13. ———, et al., "Perceived Parent Attitudes as Determinants of Children's Ego Structure," *Child Development*, **25**, 1954, 173–183.

14. Bernard, Viola W., "School Desegregation: Some Psychiatric Implications," *Psychiatry*, **21**, 1958, 149–158.

15. Bernstein, B., "Some Sociological Determinants of Perception: an Enquiry into Sub-cultural Differences," *British Journal of Sociology*, **9**, 1958, 159–174.

16. Boyd, G. F., "The Levels of Aspiration of White and Negro Children in a Non-segregated Elementary School," *Journal of Social Psychology*, **36**, 1952, 191–196.

17. Bullock, H. A., "A Comparison of the Academic Achievements of White and Negro High School Graduates," *Journal of Educational Research*, **44**, 1950, 179–192.

18. Campbell, J. D., and Marian R. Yarrow, "Personal and Situational Variables in Adaptation to Change," *Journal of Social Issues*, **14**, 1958, 29–46.

19. Carson, A. S., and A. I. Rabin, "Verbal Comprehension and Communication in Negro and White Children," *Journal of Educational Psychology*, **51**, 1960, 47–51.

20. Cavan, Ruth S., "Negro Family Disorganization and Juvenile Delinquency," *Journal of Negro Education*, **28**, 1959, 230–239.

21. Clark, K. B., "The Most Valuable Hidden Resource," *College Board Review*, **29**, 1956, 23–26.

22. ———, "Color, Class Personality, and Juvenile Delinquency," *Journal of Negro Education*, **28**, 1959, 240–251.

23. ———, and M. P. Clark, "Racial Identification and Preference in Negro Children," in T. M. Newcomb and E. L. Hartley (eds.), *Readings in Social Psychology*, New York, Holt, 1947, pp. 169–178.

24. Cobb, H. V., "Role-Wishes and General Wishes of Children and Adolescents," *Child Development*, **25**, 1954, 161–171.
25. Conant, James B., *Slums and Suburbs: A Commentary on Schools in Metropolitan Areas*, New York, McGraw-Hill, 1961.
26. Cothran, T. C., "Negro Conceptions of White People," *American Journal of Sociology*, **56**, 1951, 458–467.
27. Crockett, Harry J., "A Study of Some Factors Affecting the Decision of Negro High School Students to Enroll in Previously All-White High Schools, St. Louis, 1955," *Social Forces*, **35**, 1957, 351–356.
28. Dai, B., "Some Problems of Personality Development in Negro Children," in C. Kluckhohn and H. A. Murray (eds.), *Personality in Nature, Society and Culture*, New York, Knopf, 1949, pp. 437–458.
29. Davis, A., *Deep South: a Social Anthropological Study of Caste and Class*, Chicago, University of Chicago Press, 1941.
30. ———, "Child Training and Social Class," in R. G. Barker, J. S. Kounin, and H. F. Wright (eds.), *Child Behavior and Development*, New York, McGraw-Hill, 1943, pp. 607–620.
31. ———, and J. Dollard, *Children of Bondage*, Washington, D.C., American Council on Education, 1940.
32. Davis, A., and R. J. Havighurst, "Social Class and Color Differences in Child Rearing," *American Sociological Review*, **11**, 1946, 698–710.
33. Deutsch, Martin P., "Minority Group and Class Status as Related to Social and Personality Factors in Scholastic Achievement," *Society for Applied Anthropology Monograph*, **2**, 1960.
34. ———, et al., "Some Considerations as to the Contributions of Social, Personality, and Racial Factors to School Retardation in Minority Group Children," paper read at American Psychology Association, Chicago, September 1956.
35. De Vos, G., and H. Miner, "Algerian Culture and Personality in Changes," *Sociometry*, **21**, 1958, 255–268.
36. Dickens, Sara L., and C. Hobart, "Parental Dominance and Offspring Ethnocentrism," *Journal of Social Psychology*, **49**, 1959, 297–303.
37. Dinitz, S., Barbara A. Kay, and W. C. Reckless, "Group Gradients in Delinquency Potential and Achievement Score of Sixth Graders," *American Journal of Orthopsychiatry*, **28**, 1958, 598–605.
38. Douglass, J. H., "The Extent and Characteristics of Juvenile Delinquency Among Negroes in the United States," *Journal of Negro Education*, **28**, 1959, 214–229.
39. Dreger, R. M., and K. S. Miller, "Comparative Psychological Studies of Negroes and Whites in the United States," *Psychological Bulletin*, **57**, 1960, 361–402.
40. Fernandez-Marina, R., E. D. Maldonado-Sierra, and R. D. Trent, "Three Basic Themes in Mexican and Puerto Rican Family Values," *Journal of Social Psychology*, **48**, 1958, 167–181.
41. Finestone, H., "Cats, Kicks, and Color," *Social Problems*, **5**, 1957, 3–13.
42. Frazier, E. F., "The Negro Middle Class and Desegregation," *Social Problems*, **4**, 1957, 291–301.
43. Frumkin, R. M., "Race, Occupation, and Social Class in New York," *Journal of Negro Education*, **27**, 1958, 62–65.
44. Gaier, E. L., and Helen S. Wambach, "Self-evaluation of Personality Assets and Liabilities of Southern White and Negro Students," *Journal of Social Psychology*, **51**, 1960, 135–143.

45. Goff, R. M., *Problems and Emotional Difficulties of Negro Children*, New York, Bureau of Publications, Teachers College, Columbia University, 1949.
46. Goodenough, F. L., "Anger in Young Children," *Inst. Child Welf. Monogr.*, 1931, No. 9.
47. Goodman, M. E., *Race Awareness in Young Children*, Cambridge, Mass., Addison-Wesley, 1952.
48. Gould, R., "Some Sociological Determinants of Goal Strivings," *Journal of Social Psychology*, **13**, 1941, 461–473.
49. Green, Helen B., "Comparison of Nurturance and Independence Training in Jamaica and Puerto Rico with Consideration of the Resulting Personality Structure and Transplanted Social Patterns," *Journal of Social Psychology*, **50**, 1960, 27–63.
50. Greenberg, H., A. L. Chase, and T. M. Cannon, "Attitudes of White and Negro High School Students in a West Texas Town Toward School Integration," *Journal of Applied Psychology*, **41**, 1957, 27–31.
51. Greenberg, H., and D. Fane, "An Investigation of Several Variables as Determinants of Authoritarianism," *Journal of Social Psychology*, **49**, 1959, 105–111.
52. Grossack, M. M., "Some Personality Characteristics of Southern Negro Students," *Journal of Social Psychology*, **46**, 1957, 125–131.
53. Hart, I., "Maternal Child-Rearing Practices and Authoritarian Ideology," *Journal of Abnormal and Social Psychology*, **55**, 1957, 232–237.
54. Havighurst, R. J., and H. Taba, *Adolescent Character and Personality*, New York, Wiley, 1949.
55. Herr, D. M., "The Sentiment of White Supremacy: an Ecological Study," *American Journal of Sociology*, **64**, 1959, 592–598.
56. Hill, M. C., "Research on the Negro Family," *Marriage and Family Living*, **19**, 1957, 25–31.
57. Hollingshead, A. B., and F. C. Redlich, *Social Class and Mental Illness*, New York, Wiley, 1958.
58. Jefferson, Ruth B., "Some Obstacles to Racial Integration," *Journal of Negro Education*, **26**, 1957, 145–154.
59. Jenkins, W. A., "An Experimental Study of the Relationship of Legitimate and Illegitimate Birth Status to School and Personal Adjustment of Negro Children," *American Journal of Sociology*, **64**, 1958, 169–173.
60. Kahn, M. L., "Social Class and Parental Values," *American Journal of Sociology*, **64**, 1959, 337–351.
61. Karon, B. P., *The Negro Personality*, New York, Springer, 1958.
62. Kelly, J. G., J. E. Ferson, and W. H. Holtzmann, "The Measurement of Attitudes Toward the Negro in the South." *Journal of Social Psychology*, **48**, 1958, 305–317.
63. Killian, L. M., and J. L. Haer, "Variables Related to Attitudes Regarding School Desegregation Among White Southerners," *Sociometry*, **21**, 1958, 159–164.
64. Kirkhart, R. O., "Psychological and Socio-psychological Correlates of Marginality in Negroes," *Dissertation Abstracts*, **20**, 1960, 4173.
65. Kitay, P. M., "A Comparison of the Sexes in Their Attitudes and Beliefs About Women: a Study of Prestige Groups," *Sociometry*, **3**, 1940, 399–407.
66. Koch, H. L., "Some Personality Correlates of Sex, Sibling Position, and Sex of Siblings Among Five- and Six-Year-Old Children," *Genetic Psychology Monographs*, **52**, 1955, 3–51.

67. Kvaraceus, W. C., "Culture and the Delinquent," *NEA Journal*, **48,** 1959, 14–16.
68. Landreth, C., and B. C. Johnson, "Young Children's Responses to a Picture and Inset Test Designed to Reveal Reactions to Persons of Different Skin Color," *Child Development*, **24,** 1953, 63–79.
69. Lipset, S. M., "Democracy and Working-Class Authoritarianism," *American Sociological Review*, **24,** 1959, 482–501.
70. Maas, H., "Some Social Class Differences in the Family Systems and Group Relations of Pre- and Early Adolescents," *Child Development*, **22,** 1951, 145–152.
71. Maccoby, Eleanor, P. K. Gibbs, et al., "Methods of Child Rearing in Two Social Classes," in W. E. Martin and C. B. Stendler (eds.), *Readings in Child Development*, New York, Harcourt, Brace, 1954, pp. 380–396.
72. McLure, W. P., "Challenge of Vocational and Technical Education," *Phi Delta Kappan*, **44,** 1962, 212–217.
73. Mann, J. H., "The Effect of Interracial Contact on Sociometric Choices and Perceptions,", *Journal of Social Psychology*, **50,** 1959, 143–152.
74. Markley, Elaine R., "Social Class Differences in Mothers' Attitudes Toward Child Rearing," *Dissertation Abstracts*, **19,** 1958, 355–356.
75. Maslow, A. H., and R. Diaz-Guerrero, "Delinquency as Value Disturbance," in J. G. Peatman and E. L. Hartley (eds.), *Festschrift for Gardner Murphy*, New York, Harper, 1960, pp. 228–240.
76. Milner, Esther, "Some Hypotheses Concerning the Influence of Segregation on Negro Personality Development," *Psychiatry*, **16,** 1953, 291–297.
77. Morland, J. K., "Racial Recognition by Nursery School Children in Lynchburg, Virginia," *Social Forces*, **37,** 1958, 132–137.
78. Neprash, J. A., "Minority Group Contacts and Social Distance," *Phylon*, **14,** 1953, 207–212.
79. *The New York Times*, Sunday, March 11, 1962.
80. North, R. D., *The Intelligence of American Negroes*, New York, Anti-Defamation League of B'nai B'rith, 1954.
81. Omari, T. P., "Changing Attitudes of Students in West African Society Toward Marriage and Family Relationships," *British Journal of Sociology*, **11,** 1960, 197–210.
82. Osborne, R. T., "Racial Differences in Mental Growth and School Achievement: a Longitudinal Study," *Psychological Reports*, **7,** 1960, 233–239.
83. Palermo, D. S., "Racial Comparisons and Additional Normative Data on the Children's Manifest Anxiety Scale," *Child Development*, **30,** 1959, 53–57.
84. Parsons, T., "Age and Sex in the Social Structure of the United States," *American Sociological Review*, **7,** 1942, 604–616.
85. Pasamanick, B., and Hilda Knobloch, "The Contribution of Some Organic Factors to School Retardation in Negro Children," *Journal of Negro Education*, **27,** 1958, 4–9.
86. Pawl, J. L. H., "Some Ego Skills and Their Relation to the Differences in Intelligence Between the Middle and Lower Classes," *Dissertation Abstracts*, **21,** 1960, 368.
87. Phillips, W. B., "Counseling Negro Students: an Educational Dilemma," *California Journal of Educational Research*, **10,** 1959, 185–188.
88. Pierce-Jones, J., "Socioeconomic Status and Adolescents' Interests," *Psychological Reports*, **5,** 1959, 683.

89. ——, "Vocational Interest Correlates of Socio-economic Status in Adolescence," *Educational and Psychological Measurement*, 1959, **19**, 65–71.

90. Pompilo, P. T., "The Relationship Between Projection and Prejudice with a Factor Analysis of Anti-Semitic and Anti-Negro Attitudes," unpublished doctoral dissertation, Catholic University, Washington, D.C., 1957.

91. Prothro, E. T., "Ethnocentrism and Anti-Negro Attitudes in the Deep South," *Journal of Abnormal and Social Psychology*, **47**, 1952, 105–108.

92. Raab, E., and S. M. Lipset, *Prejudice and Society*, New York, Anti-Defamation League of B'nai B'rith, 1959.

93. Record, W., "Social Stratification and Intellectual Roles in the Negro Community," *British Journal of Sociology*, **8**, 1957, 235–255.

94. Roen, S. R., "Personality and Negro-White Intelligence," *Journal of Abnormal and Social Psychology*, **61**, 1960, 148–150.

95. Rosen, B. C., "Race, Ethnicity, and the Achievement Syndrome," *American Sociological Review*, **24**, 1959, 47–60.

96. Rosner, J., "When White Children Are in the Minority," *Journal of Educational Sociology*, **28**, 1954, 69–72.

97. Schneider, L., and S. Lysgaard, "The Deferred Gratification Pattern: a Preliminary Study," *American Sociological Review*, **18**, 1953, 142–149.

98. Schpoont, S., "Some Relationships Between Task Attractiveness, Self-evaluated Motivation, and Success or Failure," unpublished doctoral dissertation, University of Illinois, Urbana, Ill., 1955.

99. Sears, P. S., "Levels of Aspiration in Academically Successful and Unsuccessful Children," *Journal of Abnormal and Social Psychology*, 1940, **35**, 498–536.

100. Sears, R. R., et al., "Some Child-Rearing Antecedents of Aggression and Dependency in Young Children," *Genetic Psychology Monographs*, **47**, 1953, 135–234.

101. Sewell, W., and A. O. Haller, "Social Status and the Personality Status of the Child," *Sociometry*, **19**, 1956, 113–125.

102. ——, "Factors in the Relationships Between Social Status and the Personality Adjustment of the Child," *American Sociological Review*, **24**, 1959, 511–520.

103. ——, and M. A. Strauss, "Social Status and Educational and Occupational Aspiration," *American Sociological Review*, **22**, 1957, 67–73.

104. Sexton, Patricia C., "Social Class and Pupil Turn-over Rates," *Journal of Educational Sociology*, **33**, 1959, 131–134.

105. Siegel, A. I., and P. Federman, *Employment Experiences of Negro Philadelphians: A Descriptive Study of the Employment Experiences, Perceptions, and Aspirations of Selected Philadelphia Whites and Non-Whites*. Wayne, Pa., Applied Psychological Services, 1959.

106. Singer, S. L., and B. Staffire, "A Note on Racial Differences in Job Values and Desires," *Journal of Social Psychology*, **43**, 1956, 333–337.

107. Smith, B. F., "Wishes of High School Seniors and Social Status," *Journal of Educational Sociology*, **25**, 1952, 466–475.

108. Smith, C. U., and J. W. Prothro, "Ethnic Differences in Authoritarian Personality," *Social Forces*, **35**, 1957, 334–338.

109. Smith, M. G., "Education and Occupational Choice in Rural Jamaica," *Social and Economic Studies*, **9**, 1960, 332–354.

110. Smuts, R. W., "The Negro Community and the Development of Negro Potential," *Journal of Negro Education*, **26**, 1957, 456–465.

111. Srole, L., T. S. Langner, S. T. Michael, M. K. Opler, and T. A. C. Rennie, *Mental Health in the Metropolis: the Midtown Manhattan Study*, New York, McGraw-Hill, 1962.
112. Staffire, B., "Concurrent Validity of the Vocational Values Inventory," *Journal of Educational Research*, **52**, 1959, 339–341.
113. *The Status of the Public School Education of Negro and Puerto Rican Children in New York City*, New York, Public Education Association, 1955.
114. Steckler, G. A., "Authoritarian Ideology in Negro College Students," *Journal of Abnormal and Social Psychology*, **54**, 1957, 396–399.
115. Stevenson, H. W., and N. G. Stevenson, "Social Interaction in an Interracial Nursery-School," *Genetic Psychology Monograph*, **61**, 1960, 37–75.
116. Stevenson, H. W., and E. C. Stewart, "A Developmental Study of Racial Awareness in Young Children," *Child Development*, **29**, 1958, 399–409.
117. Trent, R. D., "An Analysis of Expressed Self-Acceptance Among Negro Children," unpublished doctoral dissertation, Teachers College, Columbia University, New York, 1954.
118. Tumin, M. M., "Readiness and Resistance to Desegregation: a Social Portrait of the Hard Core," *Social Forces*, **36**, 1958, 256–263.
119. Turner, R. H., "Negro Job Status and Education," *Social Forces*, **32**, 1953, 45–52.
120. ———, "Occupational Patterns of Inequality," *American Journal of Sociology*, **59**, 1954, 437–447.
121. Walter, L. M., and S. S. Marzolf, "The Relation of Sex, Age, and School Achievement to Levels of Aspiration," *Journal of Educational Psychology*, **42**, 1951, 285–292.
122. Webster, S. W., "The Influence of Interracial Contact on Social Acceptance in a Newly Integrated School," *Journal of Educational Psychology*, **52**, 1961, 292–296.
123. Wertham, F., "Psychological Effects of School Segregation," *American Journal of Psychotherapy*, **6**, 1952, 94–103.
124. West, J., *Plainville, U.S.A.*, New York, Columbia University Press, 1945.
125. Westie, F. R., "Negro-White Status Differentials and Social Distance," *American Sociological Review*, **17**, 1952, 550–558.
126. ———, and D. Howard, "Social Status Differentials and the Race Attitudes of Negroes," *American Sociological Review*, **19**, 1954, 584–591.
127. Wilkerson, D. A., "Conscious and Impersonal Forces in Recent Trends Toward Negro-White School Equality in Virginia," *Journal of Educational Sociology*, **32**, 1959, 402–408.
128. Wilson, D. C., and E. M. Lantz, "The Effect of Culture Change on the Negro Race in Virginia as Indicated by a Study of State Hospital Admissions," *American Journal of Psychiatry*, **114**, 1957, 25–32.
129. Yarrows, Marian R., J. O. Campbell, and L. J. Yarrow, "Acquisition of New Norms: a Study of Racial Desegregation," *Journal of Social Issues*, **14**, 1958, 8–28.
130. Young, R. K., W. M. Benson, and W. H. Holtzman, "Change in Attitudes Toward the Negro in a Southern University," *Journal of Abnormal and Social Psychology*, 1960, **60**, 131–133.

# THE EFFECTS OF DESEGREGATION

# ON THE PERFORMANCE OF NEGROES[1]

*Irwin Katz*

This is a review of evidence regarding the effects of educational desegregation on the scholastic achievement of Negroes. It focuses on the problem of identifying the important situational determinants of Negro performance in the racially mixed classroom. Only a few studies have dealt directly with this problem, so that much of the evidence to be surveyed is only inferential. Included are the following: reports on the academic progress of Negro children attending integrated schools, evidence on aspects of the minority child's experience in desegregation that presumably affect his motivation to learn, relevant research on the behavioral effects of psychological stress, and, finally, a series of experiments on Negro productivity in biracial settings.

## Negro Americans

In this paper the term "Negro Americans" refers to a minority segment of the national population that is more or less distinguishable on the basis of skin color, hair texture, etc., and that occupies a subordinate position in American culture. The extent of subordination varies in different regions and localities, but usually includes some degree of restriction on educational and economic opportunities, as well as social exclusion by whites

[1] This paper was prepared at the request of the Society for the Psychological Study of Social Issues because of the social importance of the problem. The author wishes to express gratitude to John R. P. French for his warm encouragement and helpful suggestions during the preparation of this paper. Thanks are due also to my many colleagues who read and commented on an earlier draft.

From "Review of Evidence Relating to Effects of Desegregation on the Performance of Negroes," by Irwin Katz, *American Psychologist*, **19**, 6 (June 1964), 381–399. Reprinted by permission of the author and the American Psychological Association.

and an attribution by whites of intellectual inferiority. While the term "race" will be used for convenience, no meaning is intended other than that of distinctiveness of appearance and commonality of experience; the issue of whether there are consequential differences in the genetic endowment of Negroes and whites will not be considered. Thus the present discussion should be more or less applicable to any American minority group whose status is similar to that of Negroes.

### Desegregation

Educational desegregation is a politico-legal concept referring to the elimination of racial separation within school systems. As such it embraces a great variety of transitional situations having diverse effects upon the scholastic performance of Negro children. The meaning of desegregation has been broadened in recent years to include the reduction of racial clustering due to factors other than legal discrimination—i.e., de facto segregation. A number of recent court decisions in the North have ruled that "racial imbalance" in a school (a predominance of minority-group children) constitutes de facto segregation (United States Commission on Civil Rights, 1962a, 1962b). Also described as de facto segregation by various social scientists are the racially homogeneous classes often found in schools where children are grouped according to ability (Deutsch, 1963; Dodson, 1962; Tumin, 1963).

The present concern is mainly with instances of desegregation that are marked by a substantial increase in the proportion of white peers, or both white peers and adult authorities, in the immediate environment of the Negro student. (In the South integration with white classmates is usually also the occasion of initial contacts with white teachers, while in the North the proportion of white teachers may be high even in schools where Negro students predominate.) Almost invariably in this type of desegregation experience the minority group child is confronted with higher educational standards than prevail in segregated Negro schools (United States Commission on Civil Rights, 1962a, 1962b). Both aspects of the Negro's experience—change in the racial environment and exposure to relatively high academic standards—are likely to have important influences on his scholastic motivation.

# POSTULATED SITUATIONAL DETERMINANTS
# OF NEGRO PERFORMANCE IN DESEGREGATION

### Social Threat

Social threat refers to a class of social stimulus events that tend to elicit anxious expectations that others will inflict harm or pain. One may assume that novel types of contact with white strangers possess a social-threat component for members of a subordinated minority group. The degree of threat should be a direct function of (*a*) the amount of evidence of white hostility (or the extent to which evidence of white friendliness is lacking) and (*b*) the amount of power possessed by whites in the contact situation, as shown by their numerical predominance, control of authority positions, etc. It seems likely that Negro children would be under some degree of social threat in a newly integrated classroom. Mere indifference on the part of white peers may frustrate their needs for companionship and approval, resulting in lowered self-esteem and the arousal of impulses to escape or aggress. In more extreme instances, verbal harassment and even physical hazing may elicit strong fear responses. These external threats are likely to distract the minority child from the task at hand, to the detriment of performance.

In addition, psychological theory suggests that the Negro's own covert reactions to social threat would constitute an important source of intellectual impairment. In discussing the effect of psychological stress on the learning of skills, Deese (1962) mentions distraction by the internal stimuli of autonomic activation, as well as disruption of task responses by neuromuscular and other components of the stress reaction. Mandler and Sarason (1962) and others call attention to the disruptive role of task-irrelevant defensive responses against anxiety. Spence (1958) and Taylor (1963) propose that anxiety, conceptualized as drive, increases intratask response competition. And according to Easterbook (1959), emotion lowers efficiency on complex tasks by narrowing the range of cue utilization. Also relevant is Bovard's (1959) hypothesis of a specific physiological mechanism to account for the apparent lowering of the stress threshold under conditions of social isolation.

Another way in which social threat may impair performance is by causing Negro children to abandon efforts to excel in order not to arouse further resentment and hostility in white competitors. That is, the latter may possess what French and Raven (1960) refer to as "coercive power." When academic success is expected to instigate white reprisals, then any stimulus which arouses the motive to achieve should also generate anxiety, and defensive avoidance of such stimuli should be learned. This response pattern would not be wholly non-adaptive in a situation where a small number of Negro students stood relatively powerless against a prejudiced white majority—if one assumes that evidence of Negro intellectual competence might have an ego-deflating effect on these white students. The Group for the Advancement of Psychiatry (1957) has put the matter this way:

A feeling of superior worth may be gained merely from the existence of a down-graded group. This leads to an unrealistic and unadaptive kind of self-appraisal based on invidious comparison rather than on solid personal growth and achievement . . . [p. 10].

Finally with regard to possible social threat emanating from a white teacher—given the prestige of the adult authority, any expression by a white teacher of dislike or devaluation, whether through harsh, indifferent, or patronizing behavior, should tend to have unfavorable effects on Negro performance similar to those just described, and perhaps of even greater intensity.

### Social Facilitation

When the minority newcomer in a desegregated school is accepted socially by his white classmates, his scholastic motivation should be influenced favorably. It was noted earlier that achievement standards tend to be higher in previously all-white schools than in Negro schools. From studies based on white subjects, it is apparent that individuals are responsive to the standards of those with whom they desire to associate (reviewed by Bass, 1961; French & Raven, 1960; Thibaut & Kelly, 1959). That Negro children want friendship with white age mates was shown by Horowitz (1936), Radke, Sutherland, and Rosenberg (1950), and Yarrow (1958). Another study, by Criswell (1939), suggests that Negro children in racially mixed classrooms accept white prestige but increasingly withdraw into their own group as a response to white rejection. Thus, if their desire for acceptance is not inhibited or destroyed by sustained unfriendliness from white children, Negro pupils should tend to adopt the scholastic norms of the high-status majority group. Experimental support for this supposition comes from Dittes and Kelley (1956), who found with white college students that private as well as public adherence to the attitudinal standards of a group were highest among persons who had experienced a fairly high degree of acceptance from the group, with a possibility of gaining even fuller acceptance, while those who received a low degree of acceptance showed little genuine adherence to group norms.

Friendliness and approval on the part of white teachers should be beneficial to Negro motivation by increasing the incentive strength of scholastic success. Assuming that white teachers have more prestige for the minority child than do Negro teachers, the prospect of winning their approval should be more attractive. Hence, when such approval can be expected as a reward for good performance, motivation should be favorably influenced.

### Probability of Success

When the minority child is placed in a school that has substantially higher scholastic standards than he knew previously, he may become discouraged and not try to succeed. This common sense proposition is derived from Atkinson's (1958a) theory of the motivational determinants of risk taking and performance. For individuals in whom the tendency to approach success is stronger than the tendency to avoid failure, task motivation is assumed to be a joint function of the subjective probability of achieving success and the incentive value of success. From a postulated inverse relationship between the latter two variables (assuming external influences on incentive strength are held constant) he derives a hypothesis that the strength of motivation is at a maximum when the probability of success is .50, and diminishes as this probability approaches zero or unity. The hypothesis is supported by findings on arithmetic performance of white college students (Atkinson, 1958b), and white elementary-school children (Murstein & Collier, 1962), as well as on digit-symbol performance of white high-school students (Rosen, 1961). (In these studies, the effect occurred regardless of whether subjects had scored relatively high or low on a projective personality measure of the motive to approach success.) It follows that if the Negro newcomer perceives the standards of excellence in a desegregated school as being substantially higher than those he encountered previously, so that the likelihood of his attaining them seems low, his scholastic motivation will decline.

### Failure Threat

Failure threat is a class of stimulus events in an achievement situation which tend to elicit anxious expectations of harm or pain as a consequence of failure. High probability of failure does not by itself constitute failure threat—it is necessary also that the failure have a social meaning. Thus in Atkinson's formulation, the negative incentive strength of failure varies inversely with the subjective probability of failure, so that fear of failure is most strongly aroused when the probability of failure is at an intermediate level. This leads to the paradoxical prediction that as the probability of failure increases beyond .50, fear of failure declines. The paradox is resolved when one recognizes that Atkinson's model deals only with that component of incentive strength that is determined by the apparent difficulty of the task. Sarason, Davidson, Lighthall, Waite, and Ruebush (1960) call attention to the important influence of anticipated disapproval by parents and teachers on the negative valence of failure. (While their primary interest is in test anxiety as a personality variable, their discussion seems applicable to the present problem of identifying situational determinants of fear of failure.) Presumably, the child's belief that his failure to meet prevailing standards of achievement will bring adult disapproval is relatively unaffected by his own perception of the difficulty of a given task. Hence, fear of disapproval should increase as it becomes more probable— i.e., as the subjective probability of failure increases. Sarason and his associates suggest that a high expectancy of failure arouses strong unconscious hostility against the adults from whom negative evaluation is foreseen. The hostility is turned inward against the self in the form of self-derogatory attitudes, which strengthen the expectation of failure and the desire to escape the situation. Distraction by these and other components of emotional conflict may cause a decrement in the child's performance.

## REPORTS ON ACADEMIC ACHIEVEMENT OF NEGROES IN DESEGREGATED SCHOOLS

There is a dearth of unequivocal information about Negro performance in desegregated schools. A number of factors have contributed to this situation.

1. Many desegregated school systems have a policy of racial nonclassification, so that separate data for Negroes and whites are not available.

2. Where total elimination of legal segregation has occurred, it has usually been accompanied by vigorous efforts to raise educational standards in *all* schools; hence the effects of desegregation per se are confounded with the effects of improved teaching and facilities.

3. In several Southern states only small numbers of highly selected Negro pupils have been admitted to previously all-white schools, and since before-after comparisons of achievement are not usually presented, reports of "satisfactory" adjustment by these Negro children shed little light on the question of relative performance.

Taking the published information for what it is worth, most of it presents a favorable picture of Negro academic adjustment in racially mixed settings. Stallings (1959) has reported on the results of achievement testing in the Louisville school system in 1955–56, the year prior to total elimination of legal segregation, and again 2 years later. Gains were found in the median scores of all pupils for the grades tested, with Negroes showing greater improvement than whites. The report gave no indication of whether the gains for Negroes were related to amount of actual change in the racial composition of schools. Indeed, Stallings stated, "The gains were greater where Negro pupils remained by choice with Negro teachers." A later survey on Louisville by Knowles (1962) indicated that Negro teachers had not been assigned to classrooms having white students during the period covered by Stallings' research. This means that the best Negro gains observed by Stallings were made by children who *remained in segregated classrooms*, and can only be attributed to factors *other* than desegregation, such as a general improvement in educational standards.

In both Washington and Baltimore, where legal segregation was totally abolished in 1954, the United States Commission on Civil Rights found "some evidence that the scholastic achievement of Negroes in such schools has improved, and no evidence of a resultant reduction in the achievement of white students [*Southern School News*, 1960]." A detailed account of academic progress in the Washington schools since 1954 has been given by Hansen (1960). The results of a city-wide testing program begun in 1955 indicated year-to-year gains in achievement on every academic subject tested at every grade level where the tests were given. The data were not broken down by race. As in the case of Louisville, it seems reasonable to attribute these gains primarily to an ambitious program of educational improvement rather than to racial mixing. For several years the Washington schools have had a steady increasing predominance of Negro pupils (over 76 per cent in 1960); this, combined with a four-track system of homogeneous ability grouping which has the effect of concentrating Negroes in the lower tracks, has resulted in a minimal desegregation experience for the majority of Negro children.

Little relevant data have been published on other Southern states where desegregation has been initiated. In 1960, 12 administrators of desegregated school systems testified at a Federal hearing on whether integration had damaged academic standards (United States Commission on Civil Rights, 1960). They unanimously replied in the negative, but only one official (from Louisville) mentioned gains in the achievement of Negro pupils. Reports of widespread academic failure on the part of desegregated Negro children are rare. Among those that have appeared recently is one by Day (1962) on Chapel Hill, North Carolina. Referring to a total of about 45 Negroes in predominantly white schools, he stated that the experience of 2 years of desegregation has shown "a disturbing portion of Negro children attending desegregated schools have failed to keep pace with their white classmates. . . . The question remains as to how to raise the achievement of Negro pupils disadvantaged by their home background and lack of motivation [p. 78]." Wyatt (1962) quoted the Superintendent of Schools in Nashville, Tennessee, as stating there was substantially more difficulty with Negro students entering desegregated situations in the upper grades. The official ascribed most of the difficulties to problems of social adjustment, although the cumulative effect of the generally lower achievement in the Negro schools was credited with some responsibility for the situation.

The academic achievement of Negro graduates of segregated Southern high schools who attended integrated colleges has been reviewed by the National Scholarship Service and Fund for Negro Students (NSSFNS, 1963). In a period of 15 years, NSSFNS helped over 9,000 Negro students to enroll in interracial colleges, situated mostly in the North. The report stated:

Tabulations of the academic progress of former NSSFNS counselees and scholarship holders show that 5.6 per cent of these students had a scholastic average of A or A— ; 50.3 per cent B+, B, or B— ; 32.4 per cent C+, C, or C— ;

and .7 per cent D or below. Not listing grades were 11 per cent. Fewer than 5 per cent withdrew from college for any reason. This record of college success of an educationally and economically underprivileged group is far above the national average, which shows an over 40 per cent incidence of dropouts from all causes.

It should be noted that these students were carefully selected by NSSFNS for their academic qualifications. Nonetheless, the NSSFNS experience demonstrates that qualified Southern Negro youth can function effectively in predominantly white colleges of good quality. Later, there will be mention of additional material on these students which suggests that academic success was associated with social acceptance on the campus.

## EVIDENCE OF DESEGREGATION CONDITIONS THAT MAY BE DETRIMENTAL TO THE PERFORMANCE OF NEGROES

It was proposed that the achievement motivation of Negro children in desegregation may be strongly influenced by the social behavior of their white classmates and teachers (social threat and facilitation), by their level of expectancy with regard to academic success (probability of success), and by their perception of the social consequences of failure (failure threat). In this section, evidence about conditions of desegregation that are assumed to have unfavorable effects will be considered. The focusing on negative factors is not meant to suggest that conditions favorable to Negro performance are lacking in present-day situations of desegregation, but rather that the former have received more attention from social scientists —apparently because they are more salient.

### Social Rejection and Isolation

The rationale for assuming that social rejection is detrimental to the minority child's academic behavior has already been discussed. To what extent are Negroes rejected by white classmates? It is clear that this varies greatly from one community to another. The bulk of early studies on the racial attitudes of white school children in the North indicated that from an early age they expressed strong preference for their own racial group (e.g., Criswell, 1939; Horowitz, 1936; Radke et al., 1950; Radke, Trager, & Davis, 1949). Two examples of desegregation that were highly stressful for Negro children have been described by a psychiatrist, Coles (1963). He writes of the first Negroes to enter white schools in Atlanta and New Orleans:

When they are in school they may experience rejection, isolation, or insult. They live under what physicians would consider to be highly stressful circumstances. . .

During a school year one can see among these children all of the medical and psychiatric responses to fear and anxiety. One child may lose his appetite, another may become sarcastic and have nightmares. Lethargy may develop, or excessive studying may mark the apprehension common to both. At the same time one sees responses of earnest and effective work. . . . Each child's case history would describe a balance of defenses against emotional pain, and some exhaustion under it, as well as behavior which shows an attempt to challenge and surmount it.

Out of 13 original students who were studied during the first 2 years of integration, and 47 who became involved in integration 1 year later and were studied during the second year, "only one child has really succumbed to emotional illness." Coles does not present a systematic analysis of the various specific sources of fear and anxiety, but he suggests that worries about school work were of less importance than reactions to the prejudice of white children. Nor does he present adequate information about academic success, merely noting that very few learning difficulties "were insurmountable."

Severe stress due to social rejection has been experienced also by Negro students at various newly desegregated colleges and universities in the South. For example, several months after entering the University of Mississippi as its first Negro student, during which time he was often in considerable physical danger, James Meredith emphasized that rejection and social isolation were the most difficult features of his experience. He referred to himself as "the most segregated Negro in the world" despite his enrollment at the University. "Through it all," he said, "the most intolerable thing has been the campaign of ostracising me [*Southern School News*, 1963]."

Two Negro students who initiated integration at the University of Georgia experienced rejection and isolation during their entire 2-year enrollment (Trillin, 1964).

As Hamilton [Holmes] began his final ten-week quarter at Georgia, he had never eaten in a University dining hall, studied in the library, used the gymnasium, or entered the snack bar. He had no white friends outside the classroom. No white student had ever visited him and he had never visited one of them.

The other student, Charlayne Hunter, eventually entered into friendly relationships with several white classmates, and was generally in the company of other students when walking to and from classes or eating on campus. However, she remained totally ostracized in the dormitory where she occupied a room by herself. She suffered from stomach trouble off and on during her entire stay at the University. Both Negroes have since graduated, Holmes with a distinguished academic record. Charlayne Hunter is now married to a white Southerner who was a fellow student at the University.

Desegregation under more favorable conditions has been investigated by Yarrow (1958). Comparable groups of Negro and white children of both sexes were observed in segregated and desegregated summer camps during 2-week sessions. The campers were from low-income families in Southern and Border states. The biracial camps had integrated adult staffs that were highly motivated to "make desegregation work." It was found that the behavior of children in segregated and integrated groups was quite similar. An initial tendency for both white and Negro children to prefer white friends lessened during the 2-week period studied. Satisfaction with the camp experience, as indicated by the percentage of children who expressed a desire that the camp session be extended, was somewhat higher in the desegregated camps. However, there were also indications of social conflict and emotional tension associated with the integration process. In older groups (ages 12 and 13) white children directed almost twice as much aggression toward Negro cabin mates as toward white age peers. At the beginning of contact 29 per cent of all actions by white campers toward Negroes were hostile. On the other hand, Negro children of all ages aggressed more against one another than against whites. Overt manifestations of white prejudice tended to diminish during the 2-week period. Nonetheless, tension symptoms appeared in almost twice as many children in desegregated as in segregated groups (71 per cent compared with 38 per cent). Frequencies were the same for Negroes and whites. But Negro children in desegregation were more likely to manifest covert or internalized signs of distress (enuresis, fears, nightmares, withdrawal, physical symptoms) than those that were more overt (fighting, generally disruptive behavior, obscene language, complaining). Of the Negro campers showing tension, 85 per cent showed reactions of the covert type. For the white children showing tension, neither covert nor overt responses predominated. That Negroes were particularly fearful of white disapproval is suggested by their oversensitiveness in desegregation to aggressive and dominative behavior in other Negroes, and their denial of such impulses in themselves. Both reactions are further evidence of a tendency to conceal tensions in the presence of whites.

Regarding the relevance of this study to school integration, it should be noted that the total period of interracial contacts was brief, but peer interactions were probably more intimate and intense than the usual classroom contacts. A generally favorable picture of race relations in Southern integrated schools is presented in a recent article by a journalist, Tanner (1964):

On the social side, younger white and Negro children attending desegregated classes seem to accept each other better than the older ones. Negro and white youngsters can be seen playing together on the slides and swings of almost any desegregated Southern elementary school's playground. At Nashville's Buena Vista Elementary School, Negro boys have won two of the three positions of captain on the school's safety patrol. And in Birmingham, often called the most segregated U. S. city, a Negro boy was chosen vice president of a sixth-grade class that was desegregated last fall.

Even in desegregated high schools, some Negroes win quick social acceptance. When a lone Negro was admitted to the tenth grade of one high school in a small Texas town, he was elected vice president of the class his first day. A Negro also has become president of Oklahoma City's integrated Central High School student council.

One investigation has shown that experiences of social acceptance are associated with academic success. In the earlier-mentioned NSSFNS program of placing qualified Negro graduates of Southern high schools in Northern integrated colleges, it was found that those who participated in extracurricular activities, dated, and had a satisfactory number of friends got better marks than those who did not (NSSFNS, 1960). Though this finding is merely correlational, it is consistent with the proposition that acceptance by white peers is beneficial to the achievement motivation of Negro students.

### Fear of Competition with Whites

It was suggested that low expectation of success is an important detrimental factor in the performance of minority children attending integrated schools. The evidence is strong that Negro students have feelings of intellectual inferiority which arise from an awareness of actual differences in racial achievement, or from irrational acceptance of the white group's stereotype of Negroes.

### Inadequacy of Previous Training

The low quality of segregated Negro education is well documented. Plaut (1957) has summarized the overall situation:

Negroes, furthermore, have long been aware that most of their schools in the South, and often the *de facto* segregated schools in the North, are rundown, poorly staffed, and short-handed. Second- and third-rate schooling for Negroes leaves them without the ability to compete with white students and robs them of the initiative to compete. Even the 1955 Speaker of the Georgia House of Representatives admitted recently that "Negro education in Georgia is a disgrace. What the Negro child gets in the sixth grade, the white child gets in the third."

A few specific instances of educational disparity at the grade-school level will be cited. Findley (1956) found in testing for achievement in the Atlanta schools that from 40 per cent to 60 per cent of white pupils met the standards set by the top 50 per cent of a national sample on the different tests; but only 2 per cent to 10 per cent of Negro pupils met this standard on the various tests. In Tennessee, according to Wyatt (1962) Negro students averaged 1½ to 2 years behind grade level when transferred to biracial schools in the upper grades. In earlier grades, transfers performed satisfactorily. The same report described the status of Negro and white teachers in a Tennessee urban area. Only 49 per cent of 901 academically qualified Negro teachers passed the National Teachers Examination; among white teachers, more than 97 per cent of 783 qualified teachers passed the test. The Tennessee survey showed that the academic retardation of the segregated Negro elementary-school pupil is progressive.

The situation in northern Virginia was summarized by Mearns (1962) in a report written for the United States Commission on Civil Rights:

The Negroes themselves have recognized that the achievement gap exists, but the only obvious reaction among most Negroes is reluctance to transfer to white schools. The question is raised as to whether Negroes really obtain a better education in desegregated schools where they must compete with better prepared, highly motivated white students. Frustration and failure engulf the ill-prepared Negro pupils. . . .

Other data indicate that the racial gap in achievement continues to widen through high school and college. Roberts (1963) pointed out that less than 3 per cent of Negro graduates of segregated high schools would meet the standards of nonsegregated colleges. Roberts estimated that not more than 10 to 15 per cent of Negro American college youth were capable of exceeding the threshold-level score on the American Council on Education test that was recommended by the President's Commission (100 on the 1947 edition).

Even in the urban North, where schools are legally integrated, the education afforded Negroes tends to be inadequate. Deutsch (1960), for example, found that in time samples of classroom activity, from 50 per cent to 80 per cent of all classroom time in New York elementary schools with predominantly Negro, lower-class children was "devoted to disciplining and various essentially non-academic tasks." By comparison, only 30 per cent of classroom time was given over to such activities in elementary schools attended mainly by white children of roughly similar economic status.

The foregoing material indicates that when grade-a-year plans of desegregation are adopted, it is obviously desirable from an educational standpoint to begin integration at the lowest grade and work upward. However, many Southern school systems are on grade-a-year plans of reverse order, with integration starting in the twelfth grade and proceeding down.

### Unrealistic Inferiority Feelings

Apparently, the Negro child's feeling of intellectual inferiority is based not only on reality experience, but reflects an emotional accommodation to the demeaning role in American culture that had been imposed upon his racial group by the dominant white majority. The Group for the Advancement of Psychiatry (1957) has summarized the observations of numerous investigators of Negro personality:

Wherever segregation occurs, one group, in this instance the Negroes, always suffers from inferior social status. The damaging effects of this are reflected in unrealistic inferiority feelings, a sense of humiliation, and constriction of potentialities for self-development. This often results in a pattern of self-hatred and rejection of one's own group, sometimes expressed by antisocial behavior toward one's own group or the dominant group. These attitudes seriously affect the levels of aspiration, the capacity to learn, and the capacity to relate in interpersonal situations.

Two experiments with Negro male college students suggest the marked extent to which loss of confidence when competing with whites can override reality. Preston and Bayton (1941) found that when students at a Negro college were told that their own scores on intellectual tasks were the same as the average scores of white students, they tended to set their goal levels lower on the next few trials than they did when told that their scores equalled those of other Negro students. The results can be interpreted on the basis of Atkinson's (1958a) theory of goal-setting behavior. Assuming that the Negro subject's motive to succeed tended to be stronger than his motive to avoid failure, he should have set his goal where the probability of success was .50. When a given level of performance was said to represent the white norm its apparent difficulty became greater than when it was supposed to represent the Negro norm, hence the goal level at which the expectancy of success was .50 tended to be lower immediately following the announcement of these norms. In an investigation of small biracial work terms at a Northern university, Katz and Benjamin (1960) observed that Negro students who had actually scored as well as their white teammates on various intellectual tasks afterwards rated their own performance as inferior. Here knowledge of white performance levels apparently influenced the Negro subjects' cognitions of their own *actual* performance, rather than just their estimations of *future* performance.

In an experiment suggested by Whyte's (1943) observations of status influence in a white street-corner gang, Harvey (1953) had members of white high-school cliques take turns on a dart-throwing task. After several practice trials, the boys openly estimated their own and their companions' future performance. Guesses were directly related to social rank in the group. Only boys of lower rank showed a tendency to *under*estimate own performance. Moreover, they were expected by those of middle and high status to perform more poorly than they actually did. It should be noted that it is unclear from Harvey's results whether rank influenced perception of own ability or merely what one was willing to say in front of higher-ranking clique mates who had coercive power (French & Raven, 1960) to keep those of lesser rank "in their place."

## EXPERIMENTS ON STRESS AND PERFORMANCE

Earlier some situational factors were described that presumably are detrimental to Negro academic achievement: social threat, low expectancy of success, and failure threat. Also, evidence was presented (some of it inferential) of their occurrence in actual situations of racial integration. A good deal of experimentation having to do with the influence of these factors on verbal and motor performance has been stimulated by the concept of psychological stress. Applezweig and Moeller (1957) proposed a definition of stress which focuses on the condition of the individual: Stress occurs when a motive or need is strongly aroused and the organism is unable to respond in such a way as to reduce its motivation. Deese (1962) finds it more useful to define stress as a class of stimulus events that elicit a set of correlated responses, among which are feelings of discomfort. He points out that the effects of stress on performance are specific to particular components of the performance under consideration—i.e., responses to stress may be either compatible or incompatible with the responses required in a given task.

Early studies of stress and performance did not employ the type of analytic comparison of stress responses and dimensions of ability in specific skills that Deese suggests. The general trend of findings on verbal performance (reviewed by Lazarus, Deese, and Osler, 1952) has been that stress impairs efficiency on relatively complex and difficult tasks, while on simple tasks stress has sometimes been shown to improve performance. The types of stress that have been used in experiments include failure feedback or threat of failure, exposure to highly difficult tasks (often under time pressure), annoying or painful stimulation such as electric shock, distraction such as flashing lights or noises, disapproval or disparagement.

Many investigations have employed stress inductions that apparently aroused fear of failure. For example, using 9-year-old boys, Lantz (1945) observed an impairment of Stanford-Binet scores following a failure experience, but no such effect after a successful experience. An examination by Lantz of the differential effects of this failure experience upon the various subtests indicated that tasks requiring visual or rote memory were not affected, while those involving reasoning or thinking suffered a decrement. In other studies that were reviewed by Lazarus, Deese, and Osler failure stress produced decrements in scores on the following verbal-symbolic tasks: learning and recall of nonsense syllables, digit-symbol substitution, arithmetic, recognition of briefly exposed sentences, sentence formation, and digit span. Similar effects were obtained on various types of perceptual-motor performance (e.g., card sorting, reaction time).

Turning to some representative studies of stress not directly involving failure, Barker, Dembo, and Lewin (1941) observed regression in the mental age of nursery-school children, as measured by the constructiveness of their play, when the children were frustrated by being denied access to attractive toys. Stress associated with the blocking of hostile impulses against an instigating agent (a teacher who arbitrarily disregarded the expressed desire of students) was found by Goldman, Horwitz, and Lee (1954) to impair performance on three tasks: retention of learned material, digit span, and problem solving. Laird (1923) reported loss of body steadiness in college students who were "razzed" by future fraternity brothers while working on simple motor tasks. Klein (1957) found that a strong task-irrelevant drive (thirst) caused a reduction in the accuracy of visual size judgments; and Callaway and Thompson (1953) obtained a similar effect when their subjects were required to hold one foot in a bucket of ice water.

During the past decade much research has been done on the role of personality factors in reactions to stress, with particular focus on the role of individual differences in chronic anxiety as measured by Taylor's Manifest Anxiety scale and Mandler and Sarason's Test Anxiety Questionnaire. A lengthy review of this work would fall outside the scope of this paper, inasmuch as the primary concern here is with *situational* factors that affect Negro performance. Yet it is of interest to note the general pattern of experimental results. Greater decrements due to stress are found in the performance of high-anxious individuals than in the performance of subjects lower in the anxiety-score distribution. These studies have been reviewed by Sarason (1960) and Taylor (1963).

Speculating about underlying physiological processes in stress, Bovard (1959) places the organizing center of bodily-emotional responses to stress in the posterior and medial hypothalamus. Of particular interest are his hypotheses that (*a*) activity in the anterior hypothalamus tends to inhibit or dampen posterior activity, and (*b*) excitation in the anterior hypothalamus is produced by certain types of social stimuli. *Thus an organism's vulnerability to stress depends upon the nature of its social environment.* Bovard reviewed studies which suggest that the presence of companions or members of the same species has a supportive effect under stress. At the human level it has been observed that separation from the family and evacuation from London was more stressful for London children than enduring the bombings with their family (Titmuss, 1950). Mandlebaum (1952) and Marshall (1951) dealt with the importance of social contact among soldiers in resisting battle stress. Research at Boston Psychopathic Hospital (1955) has shown that lysergic acid diethylamide (LSD) taken in a group situation results in less anxiety and inappropriate behavior than when taken individually. Schachter (1959) reported that fear, as well as hunger, increased the affiliative tendency in college students; and Wrightsman (1960) found that being with others in a similar plight was anxiety reducing for students who were first-born or only children.

Similar phenomena have been observed at the animal level. Liddell (1950) found that the presence or absence of the mother goat determined whether young goats would develop an experimental neurosis in a conditioning situation. In experiments with rats, animals tested together under stressful conditions gave less fear response (Davitz and Mason, 1955) and had less resultant ulceration (Conger, Sawrey, and Turrell, 1957) than animals tested alone. Similarly, monkeys showed fewer fear responses in a strange situation when another monkey was present (Mason, 1960). Monkeys raised in total isolation from age peers were deficient in normal defensive responses to environmental threat (Harlow and Harlow, 1962).

If Bovard's theory is correct, the extreme social isolation that is often experienced by Negroes in predominantly white environments would weaken their resistance to other stress conditions, such as might arise from the inherent difficulty of academic work, time pressure, financial problems, etc.

Various theories have been invoked to account for the tendency of stress to reduce efficiency on complex tasks, but to facilitate performance, or have no effect, on simple tasks. Sarason and others (Child, 1954; Mandler and Sarason, 1952; Sarason et al., 1960) have dealt primarily with the effects of individual differences in vulnerability to failure stress. They emphasize the interference that occurs when expectation of failure generates anxiety which, in turn, acts as an internal stimulus for defensive, task-irrelevant responses. Similarly, Deese (1962) mentions task interference from responses to the internal stimuli of stress-induced autonomic activity.

Some writers have concerned themselves with the effect of drive on specific characteristics of task-relevant behavior. Thus Easterbrook (1959) postulates an inverse relationship between drive level and the range of cue utilization. Complex tasks require a relatively broad awareness of cues for optimal efficiency, whereas simple tasks by definition require apprehension of only a few cues for successful responding. Hence, when drive is very high (as in stress), relevant cues will be missed on hard tasks, but more closely attended to on easy tasks. Hullian theory, as developed with respect to anxiety drive and learning by Spence, Taylor, and others, deals with the energizing effect of drive on task responses. As strength of drive increases the number of habitual response tendencies that can be elicited in a given task increases also. When activation is strong (as in stress) intratask response competition is heightened. The theory is supported by the results of experiments in which high and low scorers on Taylor's Manifest Anxiety scale were required to learn competitional and noncompetitional paired-word lists (reviewed by Spence, 1958; Taylor, 1963). Thus Easterbrook and the Hullians have each dealt with a particular component of a great number of tasks, and have tried to predict either favorable or detrimental effects of stress from the presence or absence of this component.

Discussing the effects of stress on perceptual-motor skills, Deese (1963) points out the need for systematic analysis of (a) the characteristics of motor arousal under stress, in relation to (b) the dimensions of psychomotor abilities that are requisite for various task performances. Both Deese and Spence (1958) mention that a fundamental weakness of present thinking about the effects of stress on *verbal* learning is that not enough dimensions of verbal skills have yet been explored to know what kinds of effects to look for.

Summarizing this section, there is a considerable amount of experimental evidence that types of stress which may be present in desegregation (as varieties of social threat and failure threat) impair certain kinds of verbal and perceptual-motor learning. However, there does not exist at present any comprehensive system of variables for predicting the specific effects of different conditions of stress on the Negro child's performance of various academic tasks.

## EXPERIMENTS ON NEGRO PERFORMANCE IN BIRACIAL SITUATIONS[2]

In recent years this author and his associates have been engaged in a series of experiments on the intellectual productivity of Negro male college students in situations involving white peers and/or white authority figures. The general aim of the research is the identification of underlying psychological factors that have either favorable or detrimental effects on Negro efficiency. In connection with the interpretation of the results that are now to be presented there evolved the set of postulated situational determinants of performance that were discussed in an earlier section of this paper.

### Biracial Teams

In two exploratory studies, conducted at a Northern university (Katz and Benjamin, 1960; Katz, Goldston, and Benjamin, 1958), various cognitive and motor tasks were assigned to groups composed of two Negro students and two white students. Initially the men were total strangers. They worked together in several sessions for a total of twelve and a half hours. In general, it was found that Negroes displayed marked social inhibition and subordination to white partners. When teams were engaged in cooperative problem solving, Negro subjects made fewer proposals than did whites, and tended to accept the latter's contributions uncritically. On all tasks combined, Negroes made fewer remarks than did whites and

[2] All of the research by the author and his associates that is reviewed in this section was conducted under Contract Nonr 285 (24) between the Office of Naval Research and New York University.

spoke more to whites, proportionately, than to one another. White men, on the other hand, spoke more to one another, proportionately, than to the Negroes. These behaviors occurred even when group members could expect a monetary bonus for good teamwork, and were informed that their abilities were higher than those of subjects in other teams. Moreover, in the second experiment Negro and white partners were matched on intelligence, and were even made to display equal ability on certain group tasks (by means of secret manipulation of tasks). Yet on a terminal questionnaire Negroes ranked whites higher on intellectual performance, preferred one another as future work companions, and expressed less satisfaction with the group experience than did whites.

The findings on Negro behavior may have been a result of (*a*) social threat (i.e., Negroes were fearful of instigating white hostility through greater assertiveness), (*b*) low task motivation in confrontation with white achievement standards (as derived earlier from Atkinson's model), or (*c*) failure threat (high expectancy of failure combined with anxious anticipation of disapproval and rejection by white peers and the white experimenter). The experimental data provide no basis on which to reject any of these factors as irrelevant.

In the next experiment, Katz and Cohen (1962) attempted to modify Negro behavior toward white partners in the direction of greater assertiveness and autonomy. It was predicted that (*a*) when Negroes were compelled to achieve on a task that was performed cooperatively with a white peer, they would subsequently display an increased amount of achieving behavior on another shared task of different content, and (*b*) Negro subjects who were not compelled to achieve on the first task would show an opposite tendency. Negro-white student dyads at a Northern university engaged in cooperative solving of problems adapted from the Raven Progressive Matrices. Some of the problems were made easy, to insure that both participants would perceive the correct answer. On other problems the subjects unknowingly received different information, so that one person had an insoluble version. Each subject had the easy version half the time. On every problem partners had to agree on a single team answer, after which the experimenter announced the correct solution. Before and after the problem-solving experience a disguised measure of social influence between the two men was obtained on a task which required group estimates of certain quantitative characteristics of briefly exposed photographs (e.g., the number of paratroopers in the sky).

In a control condition, the rules of the problem-solving situation did not require that each person openly propose an answer to every problem. It was found that Negroes tended to accept passively the suggestions of their white companions *even when they held the easy version and the team-mate had to be in error.* Regarding intellectual efficiency, the private responses of Negroes, which they wrote down before each discussion began, showed *more errors than were made on the same problems at an earlier, individual testing session.* White subjects, on the other hand, made *fewer* private errors than they had made previously. As a consequence of the problem-solving experience in the control condition, Negroes showed increased social compliance on the picture estimations.

In an "assertion-training" condition the men were given their answer sheets from the previous session when they had worked alone. On every problem the two partners were required to read aloud their previous answers before negotiating a team reply. Thus, Negro subjects had the experience of openly announcing correct solutions in about half of all instances of disagreement (both men read off approximately the same number of correct answers). In the subsequent interactions over picture estimation there was an *increase* in the amount of influence Negroes had over the white partner. Further, Negro subjects were now inclined to accept the other person's influence only to the extent that he had displayed superior accuracy on previous pictures.

Thus, unless *forced* to express opinions at variance with those of a white peer, Negro students tended to suppress their own ideas in deference to the other person, and to show increased compliance on another task. But when they were *forced* to act independently on one task, they achieved greater autonomy in the second situation. The responses of white subjects on a postexperimental questionnaire indicate there may have been some hostility aroused against Negro partners who displayed intellectual competence. After working in the assertion-training condition whites tended to downgrade the Negro's performance and to accept him less as a future co-worker. However, since there were no all-white control groups, it is not known whether these reactions of white subjects were specifically interracial.

The results suggest that Negro submissiveness with the white companion was an effect primarily of social threat, and that probability of success was a relatively unimportant factor. As already mentioned, in both the assertion-training and control condition disagreement was experimentally arranged on almost all problems, with random alternation between partners in the assignment of easy and insoluble versions (on a few items *both* men had either easy or hard versions). Also, after each team decision the experimenter announced the correct answer (fictitious when both men had hard items) so that subjects could check the accuracy of their own private response and of the solution the partner had openly proposed. While there was a stable tendency in control teams for whites to make slightly fewer private errors than Negroes (all partners had been matched on pretest scores), it is doubtful that the average race difference of about two private errors on 49 items could have been discriminated by the average Negro subject. Hence the relative accuracy of own and partner's solutions was much the same for Negro subjects in the two experimental conditions, and the only difference between conditions was that in assertion training the Negro subject was forced to *disagree openly* with the partner. The disinhibiting effect of this experience on the Negro subject's behavior on another task seems attributable to a reduction in anxiety about instigating white hostility.

## The Effect of Induced Threat in Different Racial Environments

In the next experiment, Katz and Greenbaum (1963) examined more directly the influence of threat on Negro verbal performance by systematically varying the level of threat in different racial environments. Individual Negro students at a predominantly Negro college in the South were given a digit-symbol substitution task in the presence of two strangers who were both either white or Negro—an adult administrator and a confederate who pretended to be another student working on the same task. In order to minimize the amount of uncontrolled threat implicit in the white condition, there was no social interaction between the Negro subject and his white peer, and the task was described as a research instrument of no evaluative significance.

In addition to the variation of racial environment, the students were exposed to a condition of either high or low threat. Since the purpose of the threat variation was to determine whether individual Negroes were more vulnerable to debilitative effects of stress when they were alone with whites than when they were with other Negroes, it seemed desirable to use a threat stimulus that would not lead to intentional suppression of responses, by changing the social meaning of the task situation. The experimenters used an announcement that severe electric shock (high-threat condition) or mild electric shock (low-threat condition) would be administered to the subject and the co-worker at random times during the task. No shocks were actually delivered.

The results indicated that Negro students' scores on the digit-symbol task depended upon the particular combination of stress and racial-environment conditions under which they worked. When only mild shock was threatened they performed better in the presence of whites than of other Negroes. But when told to expect strong shock their efficiency in the Negro condition improved, while in the white condition it went down. Apparently, the prospect of successful competition against a white peer, and of approval from a white authority figure, had greater incentive strength than the corresponding prospect in the all-Negro situation. This is reasonable on the assumption that the whites (particularly the experimenter) had higher prestige for the subject than their Negro counterparts. Since in all experimental conditions the instructions for the task played down its intellectual significance, Negro subjects in the white-environment–low-shock threat condition would not have experienced strong failure threat. Hence, they could respond to the stronger incentive strength of success in the white condition.

There are a number of ways of looking at the effects of shock threat. First, if Negro subjects cared more about performing well in the white condition they would have been more fearful lest the strong shock disrupt their task responses (failure threat). The expected stimulus would thus become more salient and distracting. An upward spiral of debilitation could then be set in motion as distraction and fear made the task seem more difficult, and this in turn aroused further emotion. Subjects in the Negro environment, on the other hand, had a relatively relaxed attitude toward the task in the low-threat condition (*too* relaxed for good performance). Hence they would not have been fearful of possible decrements due to shock, but perhaps just enough concerned to work harder than before. Also relevant to these data is Bovard's earlier-mentioned notion that the ability to withstand stress is strengthened by the presence of familiar social stimuli that have nurturant associations (in this case other Negroes).

The Hullian conception of the energizing effect of drive is also applicable: Efficiency declined in the white condition because the subject's initial stimulation in this racial environment, in combination with the additional stimulation of the strong shock threat, produced a total drive strength that exceeded the optimum for the assigned task. In the Negro condition, initial stimulation was relatively low, so that the increment in arousal due to strong threat brought the total drive level closer to the optimum than it had been under mild threat.

### Effects of I.Q. versus Non-I.Q. Instructions

In a follow-up on the preceding experiment, Katz, Roberts, and Robinson (in press) investigated the effects of three factors on Negro students' efficiency; the race of the task administrator, the difficulty of the task, and the evaluative significance of the task. All subjects were students at a Southern Negro college. Half of them were tested individually by a Negro adult and the other half were tested by a white adult. In addition, one-third of the total sample worked on a relatively easy digit-symbol code, one-third were given a code of medium difficulty, and one-third had to do a relatively hard code. In order to attach a relatively nonthreatening significance to the situation, the task was described as a research instrument for studying eye-hand coordination, a nonintellectual characteristic. Unlike the Katz and Greenbaum experiment, there was no experimental confederate who posed as a second subject. The findings were consistent with results obtained in the low-threat condition of the earlier study— Negro subjects worked more efficiently when tested by a white adult than when tested by a Negro adult. However, the favorable influence of the white administrator was apparent only on the most difficult of the three tasks. On the two easier codes there were no statistically reliable differences in achievement associated with the skin color of the experimenters. Apparently the easier tasks were too simple to reflect the differences in motivation.

Then two additional groups of Negro students were tested by the same Negro and white administrators on the most difficult task only. But instead of being told that the task measured eye-hand coordination, it was presented to the subjects as a test of intelligence. Now the subjects did not attain higher scores in the presence of a white experimenter; rather, the effect of the I.Q. instructions was to slightly elevate performance with a Negro tester and to lower scores markedly in the white-tester group, so that the means for both testers were at about the same level. Thus in this experiment, making the most difficult task relevant to intellectual ability had effects not unlike those of strong threat in the previous study by Katz and Greenbaum. On the assumption that intellectual instructions were more highly motivating than the motor-test instructions, one can again apply the Hullian interpretation that motivation in the I.Q. test white-administrator treatment was excessive.

More directly relevant is Atkinson's (1958a) conception of motivation as a joint function of the subjective probability and incentive value of success, which was discussed earlier. Assuming again that a white experimenter has higher prestige for the Negro student than does a Negro experimenter, the prospect of eliciting the white person's approval would be more attractive. It follows that when the likelihood of winning approval by scoring well is equally high whether the tester is Negro or white, the subject will work harder for the white person. Thus in this experiment Negro students performed better with a white adult than with a Negro adult when the task was supposed to assess an ability which Negroes are not stereotyped as lacking (eye-hand coordination). Presenting the task as an intelligence test ought to have raised the incentive value of achievement in both racial conditions, with perhaps an even greater increment occurring when the experimenter was white (since *intellectual* approval by a white adult might be uniquely gratifying to the Negro students' self-esteem).

But suppose that on the intellectual task the Negro subject saw very little likelihood of meeting the white experimenter's standard of excellence. Unless the incentive strength of success increased enough to counterbalance the drop in subjective probability, Atkinson's model would predict a reduction in task motivation. As an additional source of impairment in this situation, low expectancy of success could have aroused fear of earning the white tester's *dis*approval (failure threat).

Turning now to the situation where the tester is Negro, there is no reason to assume that the subject's expectation of success would be markedly lower when the task was described as intellectual than when it was presented as a motor test. In both instances the racial identity of the tester would tend to suggest to the subject that he was to be compared with other Negroes. Accordingly, performance with the Negro tester ought to go up under I.Q. instructions. The fact that it rose only slightly in our experiment may be ascribed to the subject's unclarity about the tester's frame of reference for evaluating his score. That is, he was not actually informed whether he would be compared with norms for Negro students only, or with norms for *all* college students. The next study deals directly with this issue.

## Effects of Variations in Anticipated Comparison

Katz, Epps, and Axelson (1964) investigated the effects on Negro students' digit-symbol performance of being told that they would be compared intellectually with other Negro students, or with white students. Hard and easy versions of the digit-symbol task were administered to different groups of students at a Southern Negro college under three different instructions: no test, scholastic aptitude test with own college norms, and scholastic aptitude test with national (i.e., predominantly white) college norms. Scores in all three conditions were reliably different from one another, with highest achievement occurring in the Negro-norms condition, intermediate achievement in the white-norms condition, and lowest achievement when no comparison was expected. These differences tended to be larger on the hard task than on the easy one.

Again referring to Atkinson's model, Negro performance was lowest in the no-test condition because of low incentive, while the difference between the two test conditions was due to higher subjective probability of success (closer to .50) when Negro subjects believed they were competing with members of their own race than when they expected to be compared with whites.

White students from a nearby state university were tested under comparable instructions on the hard task only. It was found that scores of the two norms groups—i.e., own college and national—did not differ, and *both* groups were more efficient than subjects in the no-comparison condition.

Future research can determine the usefulness of this application of Atkinson's theory for understanding Negro behavior in integrated schools. For example, the present formulation predicts that if the subjective probability of success were held constant, Negro subjects would perform *better* on certain types of intellectual test when the administrator was white than when he was Negro, or when they were competing with white peers rather than with Negro peers.

## A Pilot Experiment on the Effect of Probability Feedback

In a recent pilot study (unpublished), done in preparation for a larger experiment, students at a Southern Negro college were individually given a digit-symbol task by a white administrator under two conditions of probability of success. All subjects performed an initial trial under instructions that the task measured intelligence. Upon completing the first trial, every subject was informed that his final score would be compared with racially integrated norms. Half of all the subjects were told, in addition, that on the basis of their first-trial scores there was a statistical probability of about 60 per cent that their final scores would exceed the mean for their age group. Then a second trial was administered to everyone. It was found that subjects who were given the probability information performed better on the second trial than those who were not. This preliminary investigation gives further weight to the suggestion that the perceived probability of success is an important determinant of Negro reactions to competition with whites.

### Emotional Reactions to Test Situations

Another line of investigation has to do with the appraisal of Negro subjects' emotional reactions to various test situations. In connection with the earlier discussion of failure threat, reference was made to the research of Sarason and his associates (Sarason, 1960; Sarason et al., 1960) on emotional factors in the test-taking behavior of white school children. In their view, the child who chronically experiences anxiety when tested is reacting with strong unconscious hostility to the adult tester, who he believes will in some way pass judgment on his adequacy. The hostility is not openly expressed, but instead is turned inward against the self in the form of self-derogatory attitudes, which strengthen the child's expectation of failure and his desire to escape the situation. Thus he is distracted from the task before him by his fear of failure and his impulse to escape.

Sarason has not as yet presented direct evidence that situations of adult evaluation arouse hostility in highly test-anxious children. However, in clinical studies by Lit (1956), Kimball (1952), and Harris (1961), difficulty in expressing aggression openly was found to be associated with scholastic underachievement. Rosenwald (1961) found that students who were relatively unwilling to give aggressive responses on a projective test showed greater impairment in solving anagrams after a hostility induction than did students who showed less inhibition of aggression on the projective test. Mention has been made of a study by Goldman, Horwitz, and Lee (1954), which demonstrated an association between the degree to which strong hostility against an instigator was denied expression and the amount of disruption of intellectual functioning.

These studies are pertinent to the problem of Negro children's learning efficiency in integrated classrooms, because these children often have to suppress strong hostility. It was seen that Yarrow (1958) found a much higher incidence of covert symptoms of emotional disturbance in Negro children than in white children at a desegregated summer camp. White children, it will be recalled, aggressed openly against their Negro cabin mates, but the latter did not respond in kind. Rather, they tended to deny aggressive impulses in themselves and to show heightened alertness to aggressive behavior in other Negro children. Another investigator who has reported stronger trends toward denial of hostile impulses in Negro children than in white children is Karon (1958), who examined individual personality by means of a projective technique, the Picture Arrangement Test.

It was suggested earlier that when the administrator of an intellectual test is white, or when comparison with white peers is anticipated, Negro subjects tend to become fearful of failure. Anticipation of failure would tend to generate feelings of victimization and covert hostility against the white tester. Since hostility against white authorities is dangerous, the hostile impulse would be strongly inhibited. Katz, Robinson, Epps, and Waly (in press) undertook to find out whether suppression of hostile responses occurs when a white adult makes Negro students take an intelligence test. Negro male students at a segregated high school in the South were given a test of aggression disguised as a concept-formation test. It consisted of 58 four-word items, with instructions to "circle the word that does not belong with the others." In half of the items one word had aggressive meaning, one word nonaggressive, and two words were ambiguous. Hence the subject could choose either a hostile or a neutral concept. Two equivalent forms of the test were administered on successive days. On the first day it was given informally to all subjects by a Negro teacher. The following day the entire sample was divided into four groups, each of which was tested by either a white or a Negro adult stranger, with instructions that described the task as either an intelligence test or a research instrument.

The results show that when neutral instructions were used on the second day, average scores in both the white-tester and Negro-tester groups were the same as on the pretest. But in the intelligence-test condition, hostility scores *increased* over the previous day when the experimenter was a Negro, and they *decreased* when the experimenter was white. The authors' interpretation is that both administrators instigated hostile impulses in the subjects when they announced that the task would be used to evaluate intelligence; when the adult authority was a Negro person, students revealed their annoyance by responding to the aggressive connotations of ambiguous words, but when the adult was a white person, the need to deny hostile feelings resulted in avoidance of aggressive word meanings. (The "denial" interpretation is of course inferential, since the results merely show that hostility scores in the white-adult–I.Q.-test condition went down; there was no *direct* evidence of increased emotional conflict in this condition.)

Assuming that these findings actually reflect variations in ability to express hostile impulses under different testing conditions, they furnish an interesting clue as to the nature of emotional processes attendant upon the disruption of Negro student's performance in the white-adult–I.Q.-test condition of an earlier experiment (Katz, Roberts, and Robinson).

## SUMMARY

This paper brings together evidence relating to the effect of school desegregation on the academic performance of young Negroes. Negro Americans are defined as a subordinated minority group, and the focus of attention is on their adjustment in schools where white age peers and teachers predominate. In situations of this type there appear to be a variety of favorable and detrimental influences on Negro performance.

*Low Probability of Success*—where there is marked discrepancy in the educational standards of Negro and white schools, or where feelings of inferiority are acquired by Negro children outside the school, minority-group newcomers in integrated classrooms are likely to have a low expectancy of academic success; consequently, their achievement motivation should be low. *Social threat*—given the prestige and power of the white majority group, rejection of Negro students by white class-mates or teachers should tend to elicit emotional responses (fear, anger, and humiliation) that are detrimental to intellectual functioning. *Failure threat*—when academic failure entails disapproval by significant others (parent, teachers, and perhaps also classmates), low expectancy of success should elicit emotional responses that are detrimental to performance.

On the other hand, *acceptance* of Negroes by white peers and adults should have a *social facilitation* effect upon their ability to learn, by motivating them to adhere to white standards of academic performance; anticipation that high performance will win white approval should endow scholastic success with *high-incentive value*.

Reports on the academic progress of Negro children in desegregated schools are on the whole inadequate for drawing any conclusions about the effects of biracial environments upon Negro performance. However, other types of evidence indicate that any or all of the situational factors mentioned above may be operative in specific instances. Research on psychological stress generally supports the assumption that social threat and failure threat are detrimental to complex learning.

Experiments on Negro male college students by the author and his associates have shown that in work teams composed of Negro and white students of similar intellectual ability, Negroes are passively compliant, rate their own performance as inferior even when it is not, and express less satisfaction with the team experience than do their white companions. These results are seen as due to social threat and/or failure threat. Later studies have sought to identify specific situational determinants of Negro behavior in biracial settings.

Forcing Negro subjects into attempts to influence nonhostile white partners in problem solving had the effect of increasing their ascendancy on another task with the same white partner, apparently mainly through reduction of their fear of instigating hostility.

Experimentally creating a verbal-task situation that was low in both social threat and failure threat resulted in better performance by Negroes in the presence of whites than in the presence of other Negroes, suggesting that the incentive value of success was greater in the white environment. But when threat of strong electric shock was introduced, the white setting became less favorable to performance than the Negro one. Thus, *vulnerability* to stress was greater in the white condition, even though it was not apparent until a strong explicit threat was introduced.

The evaluative significance of a verbal task (e.g., whether it was described as a perceptual-motor test or an intellectual test) interacted with race of the tester in determining Negro performance, in a manner consistent with the notions that (*a*) the incentive value of success was higher with a white tester than a Negro tester, and (*b*) the probability of success was lower with a white tester than with a Negro tester only when the task was defined intellectually.

Anticipated intellectual comparison with Negro peers was found to produce a higher level of verbal performance than anticipated comparison with white peers, in accordance with the assumption that the subjective probability of success was lower when the expected comparison was with whites. Also, performance was facilitated when a white tester raised the subject's expectancy of attaining a white standard of performance by giving him suitable "information" about his score on a previous trial.

Finally, suppression of hostile impulses appeared to occur in Negro students who were tested by a white adult, but not in those who were tested by a Negro adult.

Further research is needed to clarify the effects of the various situational factors mentioned above on the cognitive functioning of Negroes in biracial settings. However, it is possible even now to point out some implications for educational practice of the findings that have been reviewed.

## IMPLICATIONS FOR EDUCATIONAL PRACTICE

The foregoing is relevant to a number of recent suggestions by social scientists on ways to foster movement toward equal education for all children (e.g., Klopf and Laster, 1963):

1. Educational standards of Negro schools should be raised to the level of white schools, so that minority-group children who transfer to previously

all-white schools will have a reasonable chance of succeeding academically. This means, among other things, that the quality of training received by Negro teachers and the criteria used in selecting them for jobs must be raised to white levels, and racial integration of school faculties must be carried out.

2. Programs should be instituted for contacting parents and helping them to understand what they can do to prepare children for schooling, and to foster achievement once children are in school.

3. There should be in-service training of teachers and other personnel in newly integrated schools to develop awareness of the emotional needs of children in biracial situations. The training should include the imparting of techniques for helping children get acquainted with one another.

4. The widely accepted practice of assigning children to homogeneous ability groups (the "track" system) should either be abandoned entirely or modified to afford maximum opportunity for periodic re-evaluation of potentiality. Ability grouping tends inevitably to freeze teachers' expectations as well as children's own self-images, hence it is particularly dangerous to intellectual development in the early grades.

5. Where grade-a-year plans of desegregation are adopted, the process should begin at the lowest grades, where Negro children have the smallest educational handicap and where unfavorable racial attitudes are least strongly learned.

#### References to *The Effects of Desegregation on the Performance of Negroes*

Applezweig, M. H., and G. Moeller. "The role of Motivation in Psychological Stress," *Office of Naval Research Technical Report*, 1957, **3**.

Atkinson, J. W. "Motivational Determinants of Risk Taking Behavior," in J. W. Atkinson (ed.), *Motives in Fantasy, Action, and Society*, New York, Van Nostrand, 1958, pp. 322–340, (a).

—— "Towards Experimental Analysis of Human Motives in Terms of Motives, Expectancies, and Incentives," in J. W. Atkinson (ed.), *Motives in Fantasy, Action, and Society*, New York, Van Nostrand, 1958, pp. 288–305, (b).

Barker, R., Tamara Dembo, and K. Lewin. "Frustration and regression: An Experiment with Young Children," *University of Iowa Studies of Child Welfare*, 1941, **18**, 1.

Bass, B. M. "Conformity, Deviation and a General Theory of Interpersonal Behavior," in I. A. Berg and B. M. Bass (eds.), *Conformity and Deviation*, New York, Harper, 1961, pp. 38–100.

Boston Psychopathic Hospital. "Experimental psychoses," *Scientific American*, 1955, **192**(6), 34–39.

Bovard, E. W. "The Effects of Social Stimuli on the Response to Stress," *Psychological Review*, 1959, **66**, 267–277.

Callaway, E., and S. V. Thompson. "Sympathetic Activity and Perception," *Psychosomatic Medicine*, 1953, **15**, 443–455.

Child, I. L. "Personality," in C. P. Stone and Q. McNemar (eds.), *Annual Review of Psychology*, Stanford, Calif., Annual Reviews, 1954, pp. 149–170.

Coles, R. *The Desegregation of Southern Schools: A Psychiatric Study*, New York, Anti-Defamation League, 1963.

Conger, J. J., W. L. Sawrey, and E. S. Turrell. "An Experimental Investigation of the Role of Social Experience in the Production of Gastric Ulcers in Hooded Rats," *American Psychologist*, 1957, **12**, 410. (Abstract)

Criswell, Joan H. "A Sociometric Study of Race Cleavage in the Classroom," *Archives of Psychology, New York*, 1939, 235.

Davitz, J. R., and D. J. Mason. "Socially Facilitated Reduction of a Fear Response in Rats," *Journal of Comparative Physiological Psychology*, 1955, **48**, 149–151.

Day, R. E. Part 2, North Carolina. In United States Commission on Civil Rights, *Civil Rights U.S.A.—public schools, Southern states*. Washington, D. C.: United States Government Printing Office, 1962. Pp. 57–104.

Deese, J. "Skilled Performance and Conditions of Stress," in R. Glaser (ed.), *Training Research and Education*. Pittsburgh, Univer. Pittsburgh Press, 1962, pp. 199–222.

Deutsch, M. "Minority Group and Class Status as Related to Social and Personality Factors in Scholastic Achievement," *Society for Applied Anthropology Monograph*, 1960, No. 2.

——— "Dimensions of the School's Role in the Problems of Integration," in G. J. Klopf and I. A. Laster (eds.), *Integrating the Urban School*, New York, Teachers College, Columbia University, Bureau of Publications, 1963, pp. 29–44.

Dittes, J. E., and H. H. Kelley. "Effects of Different Conditions of Acceptance upon Conformity to Group Norms," *Journal of Abnormal and Social Psychology*, 1956, **53**, 100–107.

Dodson, D. Statement read at *Conference before the United States Commission on Civil Rights: Fourth annual education conference on problems of segregation and desegregation of public schools*. Washington, D. C.: United States Commission on Civil Rights, 1962. Pp. 137–141.

Easterbrook, J. A. "The Effect of Emotion on Cue Utilization and the Organization of Behavior," *Psychological Review*, 1959, **66**, 183–201.

Findley, W. G. *Learning and Teaching in Atlanta Public Schools*, Princeton, N. J., Educational Testing Service, 1956.

French, J. R. P., Jr., and B. Raven. "The Bases of Social Power," in D. Cartwright and A. Zander (eds.), *Group Dynamics*, (2nd ed.), Evanston, Ill., Row Peterson, 1960, pp. 607–623.

Goldman, M., M. Horwitz, and F. J. Lee. "Alternative Classroom Standards Concerning Management of Hostility and Effects on Student Learning," *Office of Naval Research Technical Report*, 1954.

Group for the Advancement of Psychiatry. *Psychiatric Aspects of School Desegregation*, New York, GAP, 1957.

Hansen, C. F. "The Scholastic Performances of Negro and White Pupils in the Integrated Public Schools of the District of Columbia," *Harvard Educational Review*, 1960, **30**, 216–236.

Harlow, H. F., and Margaret K. Harlow. "Social Deprivation in Monkeys," *Scientific American*, 1962, **207**(5), 136–146.

Harris, I. *Emotional Blocks to Learning*, Glencoe, Ill., Free Press, 1961.

Harvey, O. J. "An Experimental Approach to the Study of Status Relations in Informal Groups," *American Sociological Review*, 1953, **18**, 357–367.

Horowitz, E. "The Development of Attitudes Toward the Negro," *Archives of Psychology, New York*, 1936, No. 194.

Karon, B. P. *The Negro Personality: A Rigorous Investigation of the Effects of Culture*, New York, Springer, 1958.

Katz, I., and L. Benjamin. "Effects of White Authoritarianism in Biracial Work Groups," *Journal of Abnormal and Social Psychology*, 1960, **61**, 448–456.

———, and M. Cohen. "The Effects of Training Negroes upon Cooperative Problem Solving in Biracial Teams," *Journal of Abnormal and Social Psychology*, 1962, **64**, 319–235.

———, E. G. Epps, and L. J. Axelson. "Effect upon Negro Digit-Symbol Performance of Anticipated Comparison with Whites and with Other Negroes," *Journal of Abnormal and Social Psychology*, 1964, **69**, in press.

———, Judith Goldston, and L. Benjamin. "Behavior and Productivity in Biracial Work Groups," *Human Relations*, 1958, **11**, 123–141.

———, and C. Greenbaum. "Effects of Anxiety, Threat, and Racial Environment on Task Performance of Negro College Students," *Journal of Abnormal and Social Psychology*, 1963, **66**, 562–567.

———, S. O. Roberts, and J. M. Robinson. "Effects of Difficulty, Race of Administrator, and Instructions on Negro Digit-Symbol Performance, *Journal of Abnormal and Social Psychology*, 1965, **2**(1), 53–59.

———, J. M. Robinson, E. G. Epps, and Patricia Waly. "Effects of Race of Experimenter and Test vs. Neutral Instructions on Expression of Hostility in Negro Boys," *Journal of Social Issues*, 1964, **20**(2), 54–60.

Kimball, Barbara. "Sentence-Completion Technique in a Study of Scholastic Underachievement," *Journal of Consulting Psychology*, 1952, **16**, 353–358.

Klein, G. S. "Need and Regulation," in M. R. Jones (ed.), *Nebraska Symposium on Motivation: 1957*, Lincoln, Univer. Nebraska Press, 1957, pp. 224–274.

Klopf, G. J., and I. A. Laster (eds.). *Integrating the Urban School*, New York, Teachers College, Columbia University, Bureau of Publications, 1963.

Knowles, L. W. Part 1, Kentucky. In United States Commission on Civil Rights, *Civil Rights U.S.A.—public schools, Southern states*. Washington, D. C.: United States Government Printing Office, 1962. Pp. 19–56.

Laird, D. A. "Changes in Motor Control and Individual Variations under the Influence of 'Razzing,'" *Journal of Experimental Psychology*, 1923, **6**, 236–246.

Lantz, Beatrice. "Some Dynamic Aspects of Success and Failure," *Psychological Monographs*, 1945, **59**(1, Whole No. 271).

Lazarus, R. S., J. Deese, and Sonia F. Osler. "The Effects of Psychological-Stress upon Performance," *Psychological Bulletin*, 1952, **49**, 293–317.

Liddell, H. "Some Specific Factors that Modify Tolerance for Environmental Stress," in H. G. Wolff, S. G. Wolf, Jr., and C. C. Hare (eds.), *Life Stress and Bodily Disease*, Baltimore, Williams & Wilkins, 1950. Pp. 155–171.

Lit, J. "Formal and Content Factors of Projective Tests in Relation to Academic Achievement," *Dissertation Abstracts*, 1956, **16**, 1505–1506. (Order No. 16,311)

Mandlebaum, D. G. *Soldier Groups and Negro Soldiers*, Berkeley, Univer. California Press, 1952.

Mandler, G., and S. B. Sarason. "A Study of Anxiety and Learning," *Journal of Abnormal and Social Psychology*, 1952, **47**, 166–173.

Marshall, S. L. A. *Men Against Fire*, Washington, D. C.: Combat Forces Press, 1951.

Mason, W. A. "Socially Mediated Reduction in Emotional Responses of Young Rhesus Monkeys," *Journal of Abnormal and Social Psychology*, 1960, **60**, 100–104.

Mearns, E. A., Jr. Part 4, Virginia. In United States Commission on Civil Rights, *Civil Rights U.S.A.—public schools, Southern states.* Washington, D. C.: United States Government Printing Office, 1962. Pp. 155–217.

Murstein, B. I., and H. L. Collier. "The Role of the TAT in the Measurement of Achievement as a Function of Expectancy," *Journal of Projective Techniques* 1962, **26,** 96–101.

National Scholarship Service and Fund for Negro Students, *Annual Report 1959–1960,* New York, NSSFNS, 1960.

National Scholarship Service and Fund for Negro Students, *Annual Report 1962–1963,* New York, NSSFNS, 1963.

Plaut, R. L. *Blueprint for Talent Searching,* New York National Scholarship Service and Fund for Negro Students, 1957.

Preston, M. G., and J. A. Bayton. "Differential Effect of a Social Variable upon Three Levels of Aspiration." *Journal of Experimental Psychology,* 1941, **29,** 351–369.

Radke, Marian, Jean Sutherland, and Pearl Rosenberg. "Racial Attitudes of Children," *Sociometry,* 1950, **13,** 154–171.

————, Helen G. Trager, and Hadassah Davies. "Social Perceptions and Attitudes of Children," *Genetic Psychology Monograph,* 1949, **40,** 327–447.

Roberts, S. O. "Test Performance in Relation to Ethnic Group and Social Class," Report, 1963, Fisk University, Nashville. (Mimeo)

Rosen, M. "Valence, Expectancy, and Dissonance Reduction in the Prediction of Goal Striving," *Dissertation Abstracts,* 1961, **21,** 3846. (Order No. 61-2062)

Rosenwald, G. "The Assessment of Anxiety in Psychological Experiments," *Journal of Abnormal and Social Psychology,* 1961, **63,** 666–673.

Sarason, I. G. "Empirical Findings and Theoretical Problems in the Use of Anxiety Scales," *Psychological Bulletin,* 1960, **57,** 403–415.

Sarason, S. B., K. S. Davidson, F. F. Lighthall, R. R. Waite, and B. K. Ruebush. *Anxiety in Elementary School Children,* New York, Wiley, 1960.

Schachter, S. *The Psychology of Affiliation,* Stanford, Stanford Univer. Press, 1959.

Southern School News. Untitled. *Southern School News,* 1960 (Aug.), **7,** 6 (Cols. 1–2).

Southern School News. Untitled. *Southern School News,* 1963 (Apr.), **9,** 11 (Col. 2).

Spence, K. W. "A Theory of Emotionally Based Drive (D) and its Relation to Performance in Simple Learning Situations," *American Psychologist,* 1958, **13,** 131–141.

Stallings, F. H. "A Study of the Immediate Effects of Integration on Scholastic Achievement in the Louisville Public Schools," *Journal of Negro Education,* 1959, **28,** 439–444.

Tanner, J. C. "Integration in Action," *Wall Street Journal,* January 26, 1964, **64,** 1.

Taylor, Janet A. "Drive Theory and Manifest Anxiety, in Martha T. Mednick and S. A. Mednick (eds.), *Research in Personality,* New York, Holt, Rinehart & Winston, 1963, pp. 205–222.

Thibaut, J., and H. H. Kelley. *The Social Psychology of Groups,* New York, Wiley, 1959.

Titmuss, R. M. *Problems of Social Policy,* London, England, Her Majesty's Stationery Office and Longmans, Green, 1950.

Trillin, C. *An Education in Georgia,* New York, Viking Press, 1964.

Tumin, M. "The Process of Integration," in G. J. Klopf and I. A. Laster (eds.), *Integrating the Urban School*, New York, Teachers College, Columbia University, Bureau of Publications, 1936, pp. 13–28.

United States Commission on Civil Rights. *Second annual conference on education, Gatlinburg, Tenn.* Washington, D. C.: United States Government Printing Office, 1960.

United States Commission on Civil Rights. *Civil Rights U.S.A.—public schools, cities in the North and West.* Washington, D. C.: United States Government Printing Office, 1962. (a)

United States Commission on Civil Rights. *Civil Rights U.S.A.—public schools, Southern states.* Washington, D. C.: United States Government Printing Office, 1962. (b)

Whyte, W. F. *Street Corner Society; the Social Structure of an Indian Slum,* Chicago, Univer. Chicago Press, 1943.

Wrightsman, L. S., Jr. "Effects of Waiting with Others on Changes in Level of Felt Anxiety," *Journal of Abnormal and Social Psychology*, 1960, **61,** 216–222.

Wyatt, E. Part 1. Tennessee. In United States Commission on Civil Rights, *Civil Rights U.S.A.—public schools, Southern states.* Washington, D. C.: United States Government Printing Office, 1962. Pp. 105–130.

Yarrow, Marian R. (Issue Ed.) "Interpersonal Dynamics in a Desegregation Process, *Journal of Social Issues*, 1958, **14**(1, entire issue).

# B. *Motivational Characteristics*

# I WANT TO BE A LAWYER . . .

*Benjamin H. Bagdikian*

"I'm going to be a lawyer," said Harry, aged six. "Lawyers make good money. I'm going to keep my money."

"I'm going to be a doctor," said his seven-year-old brother firmly. "And I'm going to take care of my family."

Their eight-year-old sister announced serenely:

"I'm going to be a nurse in a big hospital and wear a real uniform and help people."

The sweet optimism of youth could have been heard in millions of homes, but this home was rather special.

It was midafternoon but the tenement was dark. Grey plastic sheeting was tacked to the insides of the living room windows except for one window where a stick was propped against the collapsed Venetian blind to keep it against the cracked glass. Plaster was off an expanse of ceiling and walls, and strands of hair on the laths trembled with the passing wind from outside. A double doorway gave onto the kitchen which was almost invisible. Its windows, too, were sealed with grey plastic, presumably to preserve heat. But the darkness was thickened by a crisscross of clothes-lines that filled the room with the hangings of what looked like shapeless cloth. In one corner of the kitchen was a small refrigerator, in another a table with three legs and one chair. There was a stained stove bearing a basin full of children's clothes soaked in cold soapy water. Next to the clothes basin was a pan of cold red beans and beside that an iron frying pan containing a single short rib congealed with fat. Through one kitchen door was a bathroom dominated by a toilet covered by boards; it had frozen and burst during the winter. Through another door was "the kids' room," a murky chamber with one window insulated by a roller shade tacked at the top and held down at the bottom sill with a stone. In this room slept seven children, in two beds. Neither bed had a mattress. The children slept on the springs.

"Look at this book I got from school," Harry said, calling from the living room. "Want to hear me read?"

Harry read about Dick and Jane and their dog, Spot. Dick and Jane were cleancut, well-dressed, blonde and red-headed Anglo-Saxon children who lived behind a white picket fence in a red-roofed cottage with geraniums in the window. Their mother was a smiling blonde with clear, square teeth. The father wore a snap brim hat, a conservative suit, and carried a briefcase. And they all lived happily in a schoolbook called *Friends and Neighbors*.

Little Harry might as well have read science fiction about Mars. He had never seen a cottage like that, never knew such parents of his own or anyone else, and so far as one could tell had never seen a geranium or a father in a business suit. His own family, for example, had never in his memory eaten a meal together. There weren't enough chairs, dishes, or forks. But Harry was still eager to please. He had not yet learned that other people expected him to be like Dick and his sister to be like Jane, and expected them to have parents like Dick's and Jane's, to live in a house like Dick's and Jane's, and that as a Negro slum kid all of this was as remote to him as the canals of Mars. And unless he was uncommonly lucky, this book and the school it came from would soon seem as remote.

Harry's mother, Mrs. Martin—to use a fictitious name that will not further burden young Harry—is a weary, round-faced, bewildered woman of indeterminate age in appearance but only twenty-seven. Conversation swirled without touching her most of the time, her brow perpetually creased, a half-smile in constant apology. She looked toward the tangle of clothes hanging from the kitchen ropes.

"The school, they said the kids' clothes had gotta be cleaner and better. Ah kep' theys clothes jess as clean as ah could but now ah washes 'em every night. Kids they get undressed about five-thirty an' then ah washes. Ah gets up at six in the mornin' and sometimes ah irons what ah washed an' hung the night before."

# ANOTHER LOOK AT THE CULTURALLY DEPRIVED AND THEIR LEVELS OF ASPIRATION

*Max Weiner and Walter Murray*

Several studies have suggested that middle-class parents place greater emphasis on the maintenance of high levels of school and vocational success than lower socioeconomic parents do. For example, Ausebel[1] supports the thesis that middle-class parents desire that their children achieve high academic success. Conversely, other studies[2] have suggested that lower socioeconomic parents are more concerned about their children's scholastic achievements than are middle-class parents.

In view of the conflicting evidence available, it is important that some factors other than the superficial ones are operative in a resolution of the issue. What are some of the superficial factors now operative? To the writers, it would seem that differences in social class position denote differences in attitudes about success. A second factor might be that the school and its teachers, oriented in terms of middle-class values, may fail to recognize that there is a common denominator among all social class groups, such as the need to succeed, to be recognized, to belong. What then are some of the "real" factors which are operative, but which need further analysis and interpretation? (1) The difference in the kinds of symbols and behavior that are requirements for membership in the several social class positions, (2) value systems, which require behavioral differences, as regard success and failure, (3) the types of models and the basis for their success. To be sure, there may be obstacles on either side. But

[1] Ausubel, David P., *Theory and Practice of Child Development*, New York, Grune and Stratton, 1958.
[2] Sears, Robert, *Patterns of Child Rearing*, Evanston, Row, Peterson and Co., 1952.

From *Journal of Educational Sociology*, **36** (March 1963), 319–321. Reprinted by permission of the authors and the *Journal of Educational Sociology*.

in attempting a resolution of the issue one must attempt to explore the several causes which account for differences in the willingness to preserve goals while encountering obstacles. It is the purpose of this paper to explore two of these "real" factors, namely, (1) the difference in the willingness to preserve goals while encountering obstacles, and (2) the difference between the *reality* and the *ideal* of these goals. Our contention is that lower socioeconomic parents also have high levels of aspiration for their children's education.

The differences lie not so much in desires, but rather in the attitudes that parents (and, it often follows, their children) have that the educational goals can be attained. When a middle-class child and his parents are asked whether the child plans to attend college, the answer is likely to be an emphatic "yes." The same response, it is submitted, would be elicited were a low socioeconomic level child given the same query. What then is the difference? When the middle-class parent answers in the affirmative, he has no doubts. His entire energy, if need be, will be given over to assure his child's entrance into a college. He sees college as the "natural" follower of a high school education. He "knows" his child will go to college. The lower socioeconomic level parent, on the other hand, answers "yes" as a wish, not as a fact. That is, he is not at all sure that his child will be able to go. College has a different meaning for him. Only certain children are able to attend. It requires an "unreachable" amount of money. It's something he'd *like* his child to do.

To cite an analogous illustration of the last point, the question can be stated thusly: "Would you like to be a millionaire?" It is assumed that all respondents would say "yes." It can be seen readily that "yes" has different meanings. There are some who would enjoy being a millionaire yet feel that their chances of being one are not only slight, but well nigh impossible. They live their lives not striving to reach "millionairehood." Others, however, feel it is possible to become a millionaire and therefore live, work, and are willing to face hazards in order to reach their goal. It is, then, the feeling of "reachableness" or "within my grasp" that differentiates the children who are in the lower socioeconomic status from these in higher social classes as far as educational aspirations are concerned. So important is this feeling, that the writers believe its lack is a major obstacle to lowering drop-out rates and inspiring the culturally deprived to continue their education.

Changes or improvements of schools are not enough. In a study conducted in a Westchester community,[3] which has one of the best school systems in the nation, it was found that lower socioeconomic level children and their parents are generally in agreement concerning vocational

---

[3] Weiner, Max, and Marion Graves. "A Study of Educational and Vocational Aspirations of Junior High School Pupils from Two Socioeconomic Levels." (Dittoed Paper) White Plains, N. Y. Board of Education, 1960.

aspirations. Most parents and children of both groups listed a professional occupation as the goal. When the lower socioeconomic level children were asked how far they expected to go in school, 52 per cent reported they would continue their education through college and 33 per cent through high school. When the curriculum in which those students were enrolled was checked, only 37 per cent were taking college preparatory courses. This compares to the middle class group, 95 per cent of whom said they intended to go on through college and 100 per cent of whom were enrolled in a college preparatory course of study.

What can be done? The writers have these suggestions as a start. First, parents and children in culturally deprived environments must learn to feel they can reach higher levels of aspiration. This can be accomplished, in part, by parent education classes and groups. These classes would be devoted to helping the parents become increasingly aware of the accessibility of a college or trade school education for their children. Economic status need not be an insurmountable obstacle because part-time employment, scholarships, or grants for educational purposes are available. In addition, savings plans might also be utilized. These parents and their children must see that many among their group do, in part, go on to higher levels of accomplishment. This does not mean the exceptional child, who is brought back to the home area as a "proof" of success. What might be attempted is an all out effort to encourage eligible children to apply to colleges or trade schools outside their immediate environment with the aid of guidance personnel. For it is submitted, there are many children who would be considered college material were they located in a less competitive community. As in the Westchester study cited earlier, many of the lower socioeconomic children could well be above average were they compared with pupils in a more urban environment.

# EDUCATIONAL AND OCCUPATIONAL
# ASPIRATIONS OF "COMMON MAN" BOYS

*Joseph A. Kahl*

## THE COMMON MAN CLASS

The cases were chosen from the minor white-collar, skilled, and semi-skilled occupational groups. Preliminary interviews indicated that most of these families thought of themselves as belonging to a status level which I shall call the "common man" class. A few families in the sample as it was first chosen fell outside the common man class and they were eliminated in picking the final 24 for analysis.[1]

Most parents spoke about a three-class system with themselves in the middle. But they did not call themselves middle class; they used such phrases as "common man," "average sort," "ordinary folks," "working people." They saw a "lower class" beneath them—people who lived in slums, had rough manners and morals, and had tough kids who were a bad influence on their own children. And they saw a group of "rich people," "business class" or "professionals" above them; I shall call this the "middle" class. A few respondents detected a fourth level, "the very rich," but their understanding of this group was hazy, for, as many studies

[1] The scores of the 24 families on the Warner Index of Status Characteristics ranged from 43 to 71, with 57.5 as the median—right in the center of his "upper-lower" class. Warner writes that the upper-lower is the "least differentiated from the adjacent levels and hardest to distinguish in the hierarchy," and so he often combines it with the lower-middle and calls the combination the level of the "Common Man." See W. Lloyd Warner et al., *Social Class in America* (Chicago: Science Research Associates, 1949), Chap. 1. My data indicate that in the urban scene the line between lower-middle and upper-lower cannot usefully be distinguished. The overlap between the lower levels of the white collar world and the upper levels of the blue collar world is pronounced and growing. For additional evidence see "Survey No. 244" (Chicago: National Opinion Research Center, March 1947).

From *Harvard Educational Review*, **23** (1953), 190–202. Reprinted by permission of the *Harvard Educational Review* and by permission of the author.

have indicated, people make subtle distinctions at levels close to themselves but merge people who are far from themselves into indistinct clusters.

The respondents used two main criteria for making status distinctions between people: prestige and consumption. The prestige ratings did not refer to personal reputation in the community, perhaps because these are big towns where people do not know many of their fellows by name. Instead, the ratings referred to the moral repute of people who lived a certain way. The respondents thought in terms of prestige categories which were based essentially on consumption behavior or general "style of life," and they recognized that consumption depends on income, which in turn depends on occupation. But the ranking of occupations was derivative—a halo effect from the consumption privileges they bought.

No symbol better represents the common man in these communities (and of course it is a local symbol) than the two-family wooden frame house in good condition. These houses stretch out mile after mile all over the metropolitan area. They are crowded rather closely together; there is little lawn space except, perhaps, for a small yard in the rear. The houses have a living room, dining room, kitchen, two or three bedrooms and a bathroom. They are furnished for comfort, not for conspicuous style: furniture is not remodeled just to "bring it up to date." The furnishings are in the Sears-Roebuck tradition, usually 10 to 20 years old, and not necessarily conforming to any matched pattern. The walls are usually covered with flowered paper, and often the dining room has a linoleum rug. There is a small TV set, and in front is parked a second-hand Ford or Chevrolet. Most of the upkeep of the house is taken care of by father, who is "handy with tools."

The subjects thought themselves well off because nowadays father had a steady job, and they remembered well when jobs were scarce. But they faced a constant struggle with inflation, and often mother or older children worked part time to help balance the weekly budget. Savings accounts with more than a couple of hundred dollars were rare.

There were rather wide variations in income among these families, coming from differences in father's paycheck and from the number of family members who worked. But these variations were often matched by variations in the size of the family. A policeman who earned $3600 a year and had two young children lived approximately the same way as a milkman who earned $5000 and had nine children, including an older daughter who contributed $5 a week from her secretarial earnings. The respondents recognized the variations in income, even to the extent of noting that some neighbors could afford a two week vacation in the country; yet they considered all people who lived about as they did, just getting by on a weekly paycheck, as similar to themselves. They readily distinguished themselves from people who could afford a large single family house with a yard, and from slumdwellers.

They did not make sharp distinctions between white and blue collar work. Often the fathers had had both types of jobs during their careers, and quite common was the family where one son worked in a factory while another was a clerk. Prestige was based on income and style of life, not on the color of one's work collar.

About half of the parents had gone at least part way through high school; only one had attended a liberal arts college; and a few fathers had gone to a business college or technical trade school for a year or less after high school. Most of the parents were native born; they came predominantly from Yankee, Irish, Italian and French-Canadian stock.

This sample of common man families had a style of life, a set of value-attitudes about it, and a class-consciousness which distinguished people like themselves from others who lived differently. (The class-consciousness concerned a definition of social space and not an idea of joint action.) They felt that they were ordinary people who were respectable but unimportant; who were decent but powerless; who lived comfortably but without the flamboyance, the freedom and the fun of conspicuous consumption; who, compared to the middle class, had inadequate income, inadequate education, inadequate understanding of the way things *really* worked, inadequate social and technical skills.[2]

The parents were articulate in varying degrees about these matters; a few seemed to live the daily routine without much awareness of their place in the social scheme of things, but most had at least some perceptions of social space and some way of placing themselves within it. Fifteen of the 24 families tended toward the view that the social scheme and their own place in it were morally proper and legitimate. They believed that people like themeslves who were not overly bright or ambitious had, as a matter of course, a certain style of life which might be questioned in detail but not in substance. Some said this way of life was not only to be accepted but to be preferred, that the competitive game to rise higher was not worth the candle. These 15 families could be said to espouse the core value of "getting by."

Eight families felt that the general social scheme was not bad, but that they had not risen quite as high as they should have. And one man raised serious questions about the moral justice of the scheme itself—he had flirted with radicalism in his youth, but lacked the courage to stick to it in the face of social ostracism. These 9 families could be said to believe in the core value of "getting ahead."

The distinctions just made were based on the fathers' attitudes toward their own success in life. In a few instances the fathers were considerably more satisfied with their achievements than were their wives, but usually both spouses told the same story.

[2] For a vivid description of the attitudes of similar industrial workers, see Ely Chinoy, "The Tradition of Opportunity and the Aspirations of Automobile Workers," *American Journal of Sociology*, **42**, March 1952, 453–459.

Let us first examine the attitudes of those who accepted the scheme of things and their own place within it—who believed in just "getting by."[3] They were concerned with balancing the budget each week, with living for the moment in a smooth manner. They looked neither to the past nor the future. Father wanted a job which offered congenial workmates, an easy boss, a regular paycheck. Mother would work occasionally if current bills demanded it or if she enjoyed it—she generally had no strong principles for or against women working. The children were encouraged to enjoy themselves while they were young and before the burdens of life bound them to regular work—sometimes the school-age children were encouraged to work part-time to bring in a little extra money to the family purse, but the pressure was weak. The children were told to stay in high school because a diploma was pretty important in getting jobs nowadays, but they were allowed to pick their own curriculum according to taste. The value "doing what you like to do" was applied to schoolwork, to part-time jobs, and to career aspirations. Rarely was the possibility of a college education seriously considered: "we can't afford such things," or "we aren't very bright in school." Indeed, their perception of college and the kind of jobs college-trained people held were exceedingly vague; they understood that such people were professionals and made a lot of money, but they did not know any such people socially and had no concrete images of what such a life might be. In sum, they felt that common people like themselves were lucky to have a regular job, that the sons would be as the fathers, that such was life and why think about it.

By contrast, the parents who believed in "getting ahead" were more sensitive to social hierarchies and thought more about the subject than those who were satisfied with their lot. They used the middle class as a reference group that was close enough to have meaning, though far enough away to be different. They kept thinking: "there, but for a few small difficulties, go I." The difficulty they usually referred to was lack of education. These people spoke with monotonous regularity about their handicap of poor education. Sometimes they blamed themselves for not taking advantage of their opportunities when young; they said that they did not realize when they still had time how important it was to get advanced training. Others merely shrugged their shoulders with the comment that they came from large families without much money; everyone had to go to work.

Often fathers pointed to the men immediately above themselves in the work hierarchy: machinists to mechanical engineers, carpenters to archi-

---

[3] For another way of phrasing the same observations, see Florence R. Kluckhohn, "Dominant and Substitute Profiles of Cultural Orientations: Their Significance for the Analysis of Social Stratification," *Social Forces*, **28**, May 1950, 376–393. See also Clyde Kluckhohn and Florence R. Kluckhohn, "American Culture: Generalized Orientations and Class Patterns," in *Conflicts of Power in Modern Culture*, ed. by Lyman Bryson et al., New York, Harper, 1948.

tects, clerks to office managers. Comparing themselves to those from whom they took orders, the fathers would say: "those fellows are better trained than I and can do things I can't do." Rarely did they complain that the people who got ahead were the sons of the bosses of people with good connections. Instead, they saw an occupational world stratified according to the basic principle of education, and education was something you got when you were young. These people felt vaguely guilty: they accepted the middle class value of getting ahead, they knew they had not gotten ahead, and thus they felt they were to some degree inadequate. They rationalized that it may not have been their fault that they had not received a good education, but nevertheless they felt themselves at least partial failures. Yet if they were blocked, their sons were not. Consequently, they encouraged their sons to take school seriously and to aim for college. By way of contrast, it is interesting to observe that two middle class fathers though admitting that education was important, denied it was crucial. They pointed to "self-made" men who got up because they were smart and worked hard, and they pointed to educated men who were loafers or stuffed with useless book-learning and were not successful in business. Thus it seems that a sense of failure seeks to excuse itself by an external factor like education, whereas a sense of success seeks to glorify itself by an internal factor like brains or "push."

Here are some witnesses to support the general statements made above about the values of these common men:

Case A: The father went to work as a machinist right after high school graduation. Two years later his parents talked him into going to Business College. After that training, he did very well as a sales manager but didn't like the work. He returned to the machine shop, and has been happy for 30 years. His wife points to the moral of his story: "I want my boy to do what he likes. Now take my husband. He was very smart in school. He graduated a year young; he skipped a grade. Then his mother wanted him to go to the Business College and he did and he took a job selling, but he wasn't happy with it and so he went back to the machinist work that he had done. You know, he has been told several times that with all of that schooling he should have a better job but he likes what he is doing and I think if that makes him happy that is all that is important. I don't think a person should be made to do something he doesn't like. I don't like housework, and I know I would just have hated it if I had had to do housework for somebody else; why, I would be the most unhappy woman in the world. . . . During the war my husband made a lot of money working overtime, but you had to work extra for it and I don't think it is good for them to have to work too hard. If you do you come home all tired out and it just doesn't seem worth it, so I'd just as soon have him work the regular day and get the regular day's pay."

Case B: The father is a bread salesman; he has five children. He is a high school graduate. "I was never a bright one myself, I must say. The one thing I've had in mind is making enough to live on from day to day; I've never had much hope of a lot of it piling up. However, I'd rather see my son make an improvement over what I'm doing and I'm peddling bread. . . . I think he's lazy. Maybe I am too, but I gotta get out and hustle. . . . I don't keep after him. I have five kiddos. When you have a flock like that it is quite a job to keep your finger on this and the other thing. . . . I really don't know what he would like to do. Of course, no matter what I would like him to do, it isn't my job to say so as he may not be qualified. I tried to tell him where he isn't going to be a doctor or lawyer or anything like that, I told him he should learn English and learn to meet people. Then he could go out and sell something worth while where a sale would amount to something for him. That is the only suggestion that I'd make to him. . . . I took typing, shorthand, bookkeeping and we had Latin, French, Geometry. We had everything. But anything I would know then I've forgotten now. . . . I suppose there are some kids who set their mind to some goal and plug at it, but the majority of kids I have talked to take what comes. Just get along. . . . I don't think a high school diploma is so important. I mean only in so far as you might apply for a job and if you can say, 'I have a diploma,' it might help get the job, but other than that I don't see that it ever did me any good."

Case C: The father is a baker; the mother works in a chainstore. Both parents have had some high school. They have eight children. She said: "I don't go to see the teachers. I figure the teachers know what they're doing. When I go up there I can't talk good enough. Some women go up there, and I don't know, they're so la-ti-ta. But I can't talk that way. Me, I'm just plain words of one syllable and that's all. And the teachers, they'd just as soon not have you get in their way, I figure. They know what they're doing. . . . I hate to push the kid. I figure he'll get his knocks later on, and he should do what he wants to now. . . . College would be out of the question. We figure we're lucky to be able to put them through high school. When they get out of school, I try to make them get a job as soon as they can. . . . I don't make them do homework or anything. I figure they're old enough to know what they want to do and they'll get their work done by and by. . . . If I didn't go to work, the boy would have had to leave school and go to work, and I didn't want that. It's better to have me working, so it all isn't on one kiddo. . . . They're not very friendly here. I don't really know the neighbors at all. It was different where we used to live. Of course, it wasn't as good a neighborhood as it is here, but I liked it better. Everybody was friendly. We'd all be in each other's house for tea all the time. And we were always having babies. There was about ten women always pregnant. And we'd always be sitting out on the steps talking to each other. . . . I'm not very deep-minded. We don't talk about things like that [the future]."

Case D: The father is a petty foreman in a factory with about 20 men under him. He had three years of high school, and is convinced he would have gotten further ahead if he had had more education. "Down at the shop we see a lot of men come in and try to make their way. The ones with the college education seem to succeed better. They seem better able to handle jobs of different sorts. They may not know any more than the other fellows but they know how to learn. Somehow they've learned how to learn more easily. Not only that, they know how to find out about things. If they don't know the answer to a question, they know how to find out about it. They know where to go to look it up. . . . If they get a job and see that they aren't going to get anywhere they know enough to get out of it or to switch. They know enough to quit. I don't blame them either. After they've sacrificed to go to college and had that training. So that's why I hope my boy will go to college. . . . The college men seem also better able to handle themselves socially. They seem smoother in getting along with people and more adaptable to new situations. I think that I would have gotten along a lot better myself if I had had that sort of an education."

## BOYS' ATTITUDES TOWARD SCHOOL AND WORK

School and the possibility of college were viewed by all the boys solely as steps to jobs. None was interested in learning for the subtle pleasures it can offer; none craved intellectual understanding for its own sake. The most common phrase in the entire body of interviews was "nowadays you need a high school diploma (or a college degree) to get a good job." Often a distinction was drawn between the diploma and the education it symbolized; the boys wanted the parchment, not the learning. In this pragmatic approach toward schooling, the boys reflected the views of their parents (and of most of their teachers).

All the boys who were convinced that a college degree was the basic essential for a job were seeking middle class jobs. Often they had a specific occupation in mind, such as engineering or accounting. Sometimes they just knew the level of job which they wanted, and talked more about the style of life that the income would buy than the details of the work itself. By contrast, the boys who were not aiming toward college occasionally had a specific common man job as their goal, but more often had no firm goal at all—they would "take anything that comes along."

It was not always clear which came first: the job ambition or the school performance. Sometimes the desire for the job did seem to be the base for the school motivation, yet sometimes a boy who did well in school became slowly convinced that he was good enough to think of a middle class job and sought for one that would be suitable without knowing in advance what it might be. Here are two contrasting examples: One boy had always wanted to be an architect. His hobby was drawing, and he proudly showed me the plans for many homes he had designed in his spare time. He wanted to go to the Massachusetts Institute of Technology, and was taking the technical college preparatory course. Another boy, who had always done very well in school, planned to be a high school teacher because everybody told him that a boy who did well with books would be a good teacher—but he had no special subject in mind and wasn't sure he would like teaching.

The attitudes of the boys toward schoolwork itself ranged from mild interest in a few courses that seemed to have the closest connection with future work, through tolerance for an activity that was simply a part of life to be taken for granted, through boredom, to active dislike of a dull and difficult task that distracted from more important activity. The mode was somewhere between taking it for granted and boredom. For example:

"I don't hate school, but I don't think there are many who are dying to go." (This boy gets the best marks in his class.)
"Yes, I think school is important. If you don't know anything you won't be anything is the way I look at it. If you are going to make a name for yourself in the world you have to know something."

"I'd much rather be working and earning money than going to school and spending it. I'll be glad when I get through. . . . I'll stay until I graduate. . . . I might be trying to get a job sometime and they'd want to know how good I was. Then I could show them my high school diploma, and I might want to set up a small business, too. And then I'd want to know bookkeeping and how to type and how to spell."

"You do well in things you like."

"I don't see why you have to take English if you want to be a mechanic. I suppose it broadens your mind."

"I like school but not schoolwork."

"I think English is a lot of bunk. I don't mean it that way but I mean that we spend a lot of time reading books and poetry. I just don't see it. Then there's stuff like Trig. I can't see taking that unless you are going after a high position— like a doctor or scientist. If you've high ideals, have set high standards, it's O.K., but otherwise I can't see it's any help."

The boys, like the parents, can be divided into two groups: those who believed in "getting by" and those who believed in "getting ahead." This basic split was reflected in their more specific attitudes towards the details of schoolwork, after school recreation, and jobs. The boys who believed in just "getting by" generally were bored with school, anticipated some sort of common man job, and found peer group activity to be the most important thing in life. They were gayer than those who felt a driving ambition to do things and be successful. By contrast, the strivers who believed in "getting ahead" seemed to take schoolwork more seriously than recreational affairs. Each group noticed the difference in the behavior of the other. The nonstrivers said the strivers "didn't know how to have any fun." The strivers said that the nonstrivers were "irresponsible; didn't know what was good for them."

It is interesting to speculate about the development of those attitudes in the future, using the fathers as indicators of how the boys might feel when they are further along in the life cycle. The fathers all had common man jobs, and with the exception of a few skilled workers they found work a dull routine, not a creative activity. Their sons did not know from direct experience the monotony of work; instead many boys looked forward to a job in romantic terms. It symbolized to them an escape from childhood, an end to the school routine, a freedom from dependency on father's pocket-book, a chance to get money for cars and girls. But the boys who went into common man jobs would, if they repeated their fathers' experiences, suffer at least some disillusionment. Not only would they learn that work can be duller and more empty than school, but many would feel some pangs of failure, for even though they did not all embrace the middle class norm of getting ahead, they were aware that it existed and was to some degree the dominant norm of their society. They would feel just a little on the outside of things. Many fathers and sons who perceived this value conflict comforted themselves with the philosophy of just getting by—enjoy what you can and don't bother to worry or plan because there's nothing you can do about it. The irony of the situation lay in the fact that the sons looked forward to adulthood as their greatest chance to live according to this philosophy, while the fathers looked back on adolescence as their period of greatest glory. It may well be that the boys' gang is the one institution of our culture which best transforms the values of getting by into organized interaction and satisfying ceremony, yet the boys did not know it.

Those boys who were aiming at middle class jobs were sacrificing some adolescent freedom and fun in order to channel more energy into schoolwork; for some, the sacrifice would lead to professional careers that would have creative meaning. At any rate, while in school they felt that their books were tied in with important aspects of their future lives, even though the books were not very exciting in themselves. Both of these ways of life contained satisfactions and dissatisfactions; the important thing to notice is that they were different.

Let us turn to a consideration of the development through time of the boys' attitudes toward school and work. In many ways, the grammar school years were crucial in "defining the situation." From his experiences in those years, each boy gradually formed a conception of himself as a pupil based on his estimate of his intelligence and his interest in books.

Each boy's performance defined the situation for his parents as well as for himself. The parents in this sample had not studied Gesell; they had no scientific standards for estimating the intelligence of their children. Yet, intelligence is a basic value in American culture; people who are "smart" are expected to act differently from those who are "dumb." Parents used early school performance as their main criterion for placing their children. If a boy did well, his parents expected him to continue doing well; if he did poorly, they usually decided that he was just one of those who was not smart and good at books and often emphasized his other qualities, such as skill with his hands or ability to get on well with people. The boy who was defined as smart and then later began to slip seriously in his schoolwork often got into trouble with his parents: they would assume he had gotten lazy or had started to run around with bad companions who were ruining him.

These common man parents seemed to have more tolerance for individual differences than do middle class parents. Often they themselves had done poorly in school and felt that they could not expect all their children to be brilliant. Consequently, they paid much attention to their sons' demonstration of ability in grammar school. There was a feedback situation: the better a boy did in school, the better he was expected to do. Said a father of nine:

"John and his sister are the only two that have talent—I think those are the only two that are college timber. One of the boys is going to work with his hands—he hasn't said anything about it, but I can watch him, I can see that he wants to do carpentry or mechanical work, machine work of some kind. Couple of the children have been held back in school—none of them are as good as John. You know, I try and keep him from being too much a model for them to follow. I think it's good, but I don't want them to feel that they have to do as well as he can because I know they can't—he's exceptional."

A boy from another family echoed the sentiments in the terse remark: "I suppose they figure: if ya got it, ya got it; if ya haven't, ya haven't."

The average marks for the first six years of school were significantly higher for the 12 boys who were college oriented than for the 12 who did not plan further education after high school. But the difference was not great; the first group averaged just above "B," the second group just below it. As has been remarked, the casual direction was not always the same; some boys had ambitions for college while in high school because they had done well in grammar school; some boys did well in grammar school in order to prepare themselves for college (probably more because their parents pushed them than because they understood the connection.)

By the time a boy entered junior high school in seventh grade he had a conception of himself as a scholar: he knew how he *ought* to behave. But his behavior did not always match his own norms, for the situation contained cross-pressures. When homework first appeared (around eighth grade), it became a question of homework versus baseball, homework versus daydreaming, homework versus after school job that brought in precious money and independence from father's pocketbook. Before this time, it was easy for a bright boy to do well: spontaneous intellectual curiosity was all the teacher asked. Homework was a different matter.

Other difficulties arose about the same time. The boys had to choose their curricula and it was known to all that the four programs increased in difficulty as follows: trade, general, commercial, and college preparatory. The unanimity on this rank order was complete, even to those boys who admitted they were more interested in mechanical than verbal activity but wouldn't go to trade school because the trade diploma was not as "good" as the regular one. As one boy put it, and his words were repeated almost verbatim by many others:

"I chose commercial because it was sort of in-between the general and the college course. I didn't want to take the general course, figuring, oh, you know, people would say, 'oh, he must be failing.' I didn't want to go to college; I don't have a brilliant mind."

There is another factor that became important about the same time: peer group pressures. If a boy wanted to aim higher than his friends, he had to accept derision or isolation from those who thought it was stupid and sissified to join the "fruits" in the college course who carried books home at night. An occasional boy of exceptional social skill was able to stick with the old gang even though he followed a higher curriculum than they did; others gave up their aspirations; still others became isolates or managed to switch into a college-oriented peer group. This problem was of course more acute for ambitious boys from the common man than the middle class, for in the lower status neighborhoods the majority of boys were not oriented toward college, whereas the reverse was true in the upper status areas.

The questionnaire study discussed at the beginning of this article indicated that I.Q. was the one factor that best accounted for marks received in early grammar school, though the correlation was not very high. It also indicated that social status of family became an important explanatory variable *after* grammar school. For common man boys, the interviews seem to have given some of the reasons why status became important only in the later years. It was in junior high that school became a problem to the boys: homework, the increased difficulties of the work in the college preparatory curriculum (and the much greater competition therein that followed from the selection procedures for entering it), and peer group pressures all combined to make it harder for a bright common man boy to continue doing well in school—natural intelligence was no longer enough. In addition, he then began to worry about the availability of money for college—and college was the reason for doing well in high school. Some boys surmounted these difficulties and continued to do well. But this occurred because they had specific motivation that was strong enough to carry them over the hurdles—motivation which was more rare in the common man than the middle class. The interviews suggested that such motivation came from four directions:

1) If a boy had done well in the early years, *and* had built up a self-conception in which good school performance was vital, he would work hard to keep up his record. But an idea that school was vital occurred only when that early performance was truly exceptional, or if the importance of his standing to him was reinforced by one or more of the other factors listed below.

2) A boy would sacrifice other pleasures for homework when they weren't important to him. If a boy was not good at sports, if he did not have close and satisfying peer contacts, or if he had no hobby that was strongly rewarding as well as distracting, then the cost of homework was less and the balance more in its favor. In extreme cases frustrations in these alternative spheres motivated a boy to good school performance as compensation.

3) If a boy's family rewarded good school performance and punished poor performance, and the boy was not in rebellion against the family for emotional reasons, he was more likely to give up some play for homework.

4) If a boy had a rational conviction about the importance of schoolwork for his future career, he would strive to keep up his performance. But that conviction never appeared unless the parents emphasized it.

There were no cases in which the boy found in schoolwork sufficient intellectual satisfactions to supply its own motivation. And there were no cases where a sympathetic and encouraging teacher had successfully stimulated a boy to high aspirations.

As a result of the four motivational factors in combination, each boy chose his curriculum and reacted to homework in his own way. Sometimes the balance of factors shifted after the first decision. About one-fifth of the boys moved down from one curriculum to a lower one; one boy moved up a step. These adjustments resulted from a difference between a boy's anticipation of what the college preparatory work would be like and his discovery of the facts.

The argument so far is that an intelligent common man boy was not college oriented in high school unless he had a very special reason for so being. Behind all the reasons stood one pre-eminent force: parental pressure.

Parents who believed in the value of "getting ahead" started to apply pressure from the beginning of the school career. They encouraged high marks, they paid attention to what was happening at school, they stressed that good performance was necessary for occupational success, they suggested various occupations that would be good for their sons. Their boys reached high school with a markedly different outlook from those who were not pushed. The strivers tended to have more specific occupational goals, they had educational aims to match, they worked harder in school, they thought more of the future, they were more sensitive to status distinctions, and they believed they could somehow manage to pay their way through college and reach the middle class.

*Table 1*—Relation between Parental Pressure and Son's Aspiration, 24 Boys*

| Son's aspiration | Parental pressure toward college | |
|---|---|---|
| | NO | YES |
| College | 4 | 8 |
| No College | 11 | 1 |

* Chi Square = 6.4; probability < .02.

The reader is referred back to Table 1, above. In all the cases therein, except two, families who applied pressure were families who believed in "getting ahead." That usually meant that the father was dissatisfied with his own occupational success. In the two exceptional cases where the father was satisfied, the pressure came from the mother, who was less content than her husband.

Two of the four boys who were aiming for college without pressure from home were instances of the "feed-back" phenomenon. They came from large families where the parents would support any aims of children without expecting them all to be alike. The boys had always done exceptionally well in school, and came to think of themselves as the kind of people who "ought" to go to college. The parents fully supported the high ambitions but did not initiate them. The other two boys who were aiming for college without pressure came from homes that were ambivalent:

the father was more satisfied with his job than was the mother. The mother did not desire to repudiate her husband, so offered only the softest of suggestions that her son should try to do better.

The connection between parental pressure and sons' response was not just in the mind of the outsider who rated the cases; the boys were aware of it. One boy expressed clearly the relation between his views and those of his parents in these words:

"I'd like to learn to specialize in college. My folks want me to go to college too. My father didn't get through high school, and he wishes he'd gone to college. He has a good job now but he says if he had just a little bit of college he could have gone much higher. He's got a good job but he's gone as high as he can without a college education. . . . My mother and father don't want me to be a hired man. They want me to be in the upper bracket. They want me to learn by going to school and college, to go ahead by getting a higher education."

A boy who was not being pushed by his parents took an entirely different approach:

"I'm not definite what I'd like to do. Any kind of job. Anything as long as I get a little cash. . . . My folks tell me to go out and get a job, anything, just as long as it's a job. They say I'm old enough to start turning in board. . . . I haven't got much brain for all that college stuff. . . . You know, nobody would believe me now, but I was an "A" student in grammar school. I dunno what happened; just started dropping gradually. . . . I guess the work just started getting harder. . . . I could do better work if I wanted to. As long as I pass I don't care. What the hell? I got nothin' to look forward to. . . . I was told to take the college course by the teachers. But I didn't want to. I wanted to take it easy."

The interviews indicated that the boys learned to an extraordinary degree to view the occupational system from their parents' perspective. They took over their parents' view of the opportunities available, the desirability and possibility of change of status, the techniques to be used if change was desired, and the appropriate goals for boys who performed as they did in school. The occasional boy who differed from his parents had gotten his ideas from a friend—never from an abstract medium of communication, such as books or movies.

# ACHIEVEMENT, CULTURE, AND PERSONALITY:

# THE CASE OF THE JAPANESE AMERICANS

*William Caudill and George de Vos*

Much of the literature on achievement has focused on the importance of hereditary or learned individual abilities, as in the relationship between I.Q. scores and educational or occupational success. In these studies, when discrepancies occur in expected predictions, the discrepancies are attributed to "other factors." For example, Terman and Oden use the added factor of individual personality traits to distinguish between otherwise matched groups—their high achievers being greater in "prudence and foresight," "self-confidence," "will-power and perseverence," and "desire to excel." Recent workers have gone on to emphasize that such traits should be seen not only within the framework of the individual personality structure, but that these traits are also related to cultural values receiving very different emphases in lower and middle-class levels of American society.

Some attention has also been given to the factor of ethnic background in accounting for differences in achievement. For example, Terman and Oden found that their Jewish subjects, while not differing significantly in mean I.Q. scores from the total group, had higher grades in college, received a higher income, and were concentrated more heavily in professional occupations. Thus, the indication is for something specific in Jewish culture to account for these differences, but beyond allusion to its probable importance, this factor has received little systematic elaboration.

Early psychological studies of Japanese American children compared with other social and racial groups in California public schools give indication of a cultural factor at work which was not fully recognized or

From *The American Anthropologist*, **58** (1956), pp. 1102–1126. Reprinted by permission of *The American Anthropologist*, and the authors.

explored at the time. Strong, in summarizing the achievement tests, grades obtained in school, and Binet I.Q. scores of Japanese American pupils in comparison with other groups in California schools, asks: "How shall we explain the fact that the Japanese pupils in Los Angeles have about the same I.Q. as the average pupil and score about the same on educational tests but obtain strikingly better grades? It may be that they possess to a greater degree than whites those qualities which endear pupils to a teacher; that is, they are more docile, occasion less disciplinary trouble, and give the appearance of being busy and striving to do their best . . . Another explanation would be that they come from poorer homes than the average and early realize that they must make their own way in the world; in consequence, they are better motivated to do their best." Strong does not develop the further question of why the Japanese Americans, out of the numerous low income ethnic groups in California at the time these studies were done, should show this remarkable striving and intensity of purpose.

The burden of this paper is that much further study of the cultural variable in achievement is needed in terms of understanding: (1) the achievement goals that are emphasized in the value system of the specific culture from which the subjects are drawn; (2) the processes by which these goals are implemented in the interpersonal behavior of individuals in the family, the peer group, the school, on the job, and in leisure time activities; and (3) the range and most frequent types of individual personality adjustment to these goals within the context of the specific culture, rather than a consideration of personality traits solely as an independent variable. The methods used in the research reported below were both quantitative analysis of data on the groups in question, and intensive clinical analysis of testing, interview, and psychotherapeutic data on specific individuals.

Between 1943 and 1946, approximately 20,000 Japanese Americans arrived in Chicago from relocation camps set up by the federal government when all persons of Japanese ancestry were evacuated from the Pacific Coast shortly after the United States entered World War II. Roughly a third were Issei—first generation immigrants who came to America during the early part of the century; the other two-thirds were Nisei—second generation, who are American citizen children of the Issei. The cultural and personality adjustment of this group to life in Chicago was studied for three years (1947–1950) by an interdisciplinary team from the University of Chicago. Although the problem of achievement was not a central focus of the research, the data serve to point up the success of the Japanese Americans in this regard, and to show the necessity of a thorough consideration of cultural factors in the further study of achievement.

In terms of the usual sociological or anthropological approach, there are many reasons why the 342 Japanese American families represented in the Chicago research, or the Japanese American group in general, should experience great difficulty in achievement in the United States. Traditionally, Japanese culture, social structure, values, and religion are thought of as alien to those of America. Moreover, the Issei had a background of rural, peasant, substance farming, and came to the United States with only temporary settlement in mind. Most important of all, the Japanese are a racially visible group to race-conscious Americans.

Yet the data show that by 1947 the Nisei, almost as a group, held white collar and skilled trade jobs within the general employment market of the city. White employers and fellow employers accepted the Nisei and were enthusiastic in their praise of them. The median level of education for the Nisei in Chicago was, as it had been on the Pacific Coast, beyond highschool graduation. Almost all who did not go on to college took vocational training in order to become secretaries, laboratory technicians, beauty operators, or skilled workers. It must be noted, however, that the Issei had a surprisingly high level of education for immigrants—a median of ten years. A summary of Japanese American educational data may be seen in Table 1.

*Table 1*—Education of Japanese Americans Compared with American Sample

| Education level | Issei (277 persons) Percent | Nisei (488 persons) Percent | Chicago Americans (60 persons) Percent |
|---|---|---|---|
| Elementary school | | | |
| Uncompleted | 7 | 0 | 0 |
| Graduated | 34 | 2 | 12 |
| Secondary school | | | |
| Uncompleted | 10 | 8 | 35 |
| Graduated | 32 | 56 | 40 |
| College | | | |
| Uncompleted | 11 | 21 | 10 |
| Graduated | 6 | 13 | 3 |
| Total | 100 | 100 | 100 |

*Note.*—Includes all persons who had completed their education as of January 1, 1947 from 342 Chicago families. Vocational and Trade School training not included. Right hand column is a normal control sample.

The Japanese Americans first found housing in some of the least desirable sections of Chicago. However, they disliked living in these sections and many families soon moved into predominantly white upperlower and lower-middle-class neighborhoods. The Japanese Americans were accepted in these areas. Neighbors and landlords liked them because they improved the property, paid their rent promptly, and were quite and courteous. In their clothing and general appearance the Nisei were almost stereotypes of the American middle class. This was particularly true for the women, who invariably appeared well-groomed, in conservative but chic dresses, blouses always snow white, nylons, and high heels. In their attitudes and aspirations the Nisei were oriented toward careers, white-collar work, or small businesses. They wanted little to do with factory jobs. They saw in unions a block to rapid advancement through individual achievement. In their social life the Nisei tended to stay within their own group. While they interacted freely with their white fellow workers on the job and in casual social intercourse at lunch, they had not yet achieved close intimate social contact with the white middle class they emulated. Yet they had achieved more in the space of four years in Chicago than other ethnic groups who had long been in the city, and who appear far less handicapped by racial and cultural differences.

Since occupation (as well as education) is a major avenue to achievement in America, it is worthwhile to look in a little more detail at the Japanese American data in this respect. The jobs the Japanese Americans were first able to obtain in the city were menial, unskilled, and poorly paid. Very shortly they left such jobs for semiskilled factory and service work at which the Issei stayed, while the Nisei, having higher aspirations, moved on rapidly to better employment. By 1947, the Japanese Americans showed the occupational distribution presented in Table 2, where it can be seen that 19 per cent of the Issei and 60 per cent of the Nisei fall in the categories of skilled workers, white-collar workers, small business owners, or managerial and professional jobs.

*Table 2*—Occupations of Japanese Americans

| Occupational category | Issei (197 persons) Percent | Nisei (383 persons) Percent |
|---|---|---|
| Unskilled workers and laborers | 1 | 1 |
| Domestic and service workers | 24 | 7 |
| Semi-skilled workers | 56 | 32 |
| Skilled workers | 2 | 10 |
| White collar workers | 2 | 35 |
| Small business ownership | 13 | 6 |
| Managerial and professional | 2 | 9 |
| *Total* | 100 | 100 |

*Note.*—Includes all members from 342 Chicago families who were employed as of January 1, 1947.

There were some interesting job differences between men and women. The Issei men were concentrated in semiskilled factory and service jobs. In the factories they worked on the assembly lines, as machine operators, or at such jobs as carpentry workers in trailer manufacture. Their jobs were as kitchen helpers, cooks, waiters, elevator operators, and janitors. There was also a considerable percentage of Issei men in building ownership and management, but the buildings were deteriorated and were operated as cheap hotels, or rooming and boarding houses. Even more than the Issei men, the Issei women were found in semiskilled factory and service jobs. Forty-three per cent of all Issei women in the sample worked in the garment trades.

The Nisei men tended to be spread throughout all occupational divisions. Their major concentration was in apprentice and skilled trade jobs, and also in the white collar field. In the skilled trades the Nisei men worked as printers, welders, electricians, mechanics, and jewelry and watch repairmen. Some of these Nisei men had achieved jobs as foremen and supervisors, where they had authority over white workers. In the white collar field the Nisei men worked as clerks, draftsmen, laboratory technicians, commercial artists, and studio photographers. The percentage of Nisei men in managerial and professional positions was of considerable significance. As managers they worked in personnel departments, as laboratory heads, and as editors. As professional men they were doctors, dentists, lawyers, pharmacists, research workers, and teachers.

Nisei women were concentrated in white collar work, with 49 per cent of the sample so employed. Here they were evenly distributed between secretarial-stenographic and clerical duties. Nisei women were also in the garment trades, but much less so than Issei women. Other important jobs for Nisei women were beauty operators, social workers, and registered nurses.

The aspirations of the Nisei indicated that small business would become increasingly important. In the sample, Nisei men owned grocery stores, garages, and cleaning shops, while the Nisei women owned such businesses as beauty parlors. All of these served the general public rather than merely the Japanese American community.

It must be remembered that the sample had been in the city for only a few years, and that the Nisei are young—clustering between twenty and thirty years of age—and have not yet reached their occupational peak.

Alan Jacobsen and Lee Rainwater investigated employers' evaluations of their Japanese American employees from 79 firms. These were owned by white businessmen, within the general economic and industrial structure of the city, and drew their employees from the general employment market. Firms owned by Japanese Americans were excluded, as were such organizations as social agencies, which might be expected to be somewhat more liberal in their employment policies. Better than two-thirds of the employers were very positive in their evaluations of Japanese Americans as workers; they considered them to be as good as the best employees they had ever had. The remaining one-third of the employers considered Japanese Americans to be no better and no worse than their average employees. An occasional negative evaluation usually took the form of criticizing the Nisei for being too ambitious and wanting to move on to a better job too quickly. In general, Japanese Americans were praised for their technical abilities such as speed and efficiency, and for their character traits of honesty, punctuality, willingness to work overtime, general moral standards, personal appearance, and so forth. They were also praised for the way they got along with other workers in informal relations. Japanese Americans had been up-graded in job and salary in 46 of the 79 firms, and in 5 others in salary alone. Seventeen Nisei were promoted to jobs which gave them authority over white workers.

Why was this so? How was it possible for the children of an immigrant group to succeed as well as the Nisei have in Chicago in approximating the American middle-class way of life, when the culture of their parents seems to diverge in so many respects from the American pattern?

Certainly relocation was a factor. No matter how well the Nisei were prepared in attitudes, behavior, and education for living a middle-class life, it seems unlikely that they would have been able to do so on the Pacific Coast because of anti-Oriental prejudice. Also, the Japanese Americans on the Coast had formed tight, self-contained communities controlled by parental authority and strong social sanctions, from which it was difficult for the Nisei to break free. Secondly, Chicago had had a Japanese population of only 390 persons, and had no social techniques for dealing with this group. Thirdly, with the scarcity of labor during the war, the highly trained Nisei were in a relatively favorable position in terms of the employment market.

These reasons may help to explain why the Nisei got their jobs, but will not satisfactorily explain why they were able to keep them and to please their employers and fellow workers.

A major hypothesis used as an orientation to our research was: there seems to be a significant compatibility (but by no means identity) between the value systems found in the culture of Japan and the value systems found in American middle-class culture. This compatibility of values gives rise to a similarity in the psychological adaptive mechanisms which are most commonly used by individuals in the two societies as they go about the business of living.

It is necessary to be aware that the hypothesis does not say that the social structure, customs, or religion of the two societies are similar. They are not, and Japan and the American middle class differ greatly in these respects. But the hypothesis does say that it is often overlooked that the Japanese and American middle-class cultures share the values of politeness, respect for authority and parental wishes, duty to community, diligence, cleanliness and neatness, emphasis on personal achievement of long-range goals, importance of keeping up appearances, and others. Equally, the hypothesis does not say that the basic personality or character structure of Japanese and middle-class American individuals is similar; but it does say that, for example, both Japanese and middle-class Americans characteristically utilize the adaptive mechanism of being highly sensitive to cues coming from the external world as to how they should act, and that they also adapt themselves to many situations by suppression of their real emotional feelings, particularly desires for physical aggressiveness.

Given this sort of relationship between the two cultures, when they meet under conditions favorable for acculturation (as in Chicago) Japanese Americans, acting in terms of their Japanese values and personality, will behave in ways that are favorably evaluated by middle-class Americans. Nevertheless, because the values and adaptive mechanisms are only compatible (and not identical), and because the social structures and personalities of the two groups are different, there are many points of conflict as well as agreement for the Nisei individual attempting to achieve in American middle class life. Certain points of conflict are made all the more poignant by the fact that the points of agreement are sufficiently strong to hold out much promise to the individual that he will succeed.

The direct relation of the general hypothesis to Japanese American achievement involves the problem of variant cultural orientations. Whenever cultural values are considered in current research studies on achievement, it is usually in terms of the dominant cultural values, whereas there may be many subgroups and individuals who do not subscribe to these values and who are, in this sense, variant. As Orville Brim says in an unpublished paper, "What is necessary is some systematic knowledge of differences between groups in the acceptance of the goals of the larger society, and it is of high importance that research operations be developed which will enable us to appraise the hierarchy of goals perceived as desirable by different *segments* of society, whether these be religious, ethnic, economic, or the like. Once accomplished, future studies could be directed toward relative individual achievement within discrete subcultures, with each of these sharing homogeneous goals."

Japanese Americans provide an excellent example for Brim's argument. The fact that they succeed in approximating middle-class American standards in education and occupation does not necessarily mean that they are motivated by middle-class values and goals, nor that their achievement orientation should be thought of in these terms. What is needed is an analysis of Japanese American values and psychological adaptive mechanisms underlying those goals that are of crucial importance to Japanese Americans in their conception of what constitutes achievement.

From the foregoing, it appears that much more than a surface evaluation of behavior is necessary for the understanding of achievement. Japanese American and white middle-class behavior looks very much the same in many areas of life, but the psychological motivations underlying such behavior may occur within quite different cultural matrices. The following sections of this paper will present material illustrating this problem, as well as the further problem of individual differences in achievement within the Japanese American group itself.

In order to further the understanding of the success of the Japanese Americans in Chicago, Thematic Apperception Tests, Rorschachs, and psychoanalytic and social agency case studies were used. This paper, however, limits itself to the projective material pertaining to those aspects of personality dynamics that seem most relevant to achievement among Japanese Americans.

TAT material will be discussed before the Rorschach analysis because it tends to provide data on the more conscious aspects of the personality structure—internalized values, goals, and preferred ways of relating to others and to oneself. The Rorschach provides data concerning more generalized, and perhaps deeper-lying and unconscious attributes of the content and structure of the personality. Thus, the TAT can be useful in indicating the manner in which an individual approaches problems of achievement, while the Rorschach can suggest related, but often hidden, motivations and conflicts in this area.

A random sample of TAT records was gathered from Japanese Americans and compared with samples of white Americans from several socioeconomic levels. In this paper only the material from TAT pictures 1 and 2 will be presented in detail. The manifest content of these pictures

*Table 3*—Positive Achievement Responses on TAT Pictures 1 and 2, by Cultural Group

| Group | Total cases | PERCENT POSITIVE ON: Picture 1 | Picture 2 |
|---|---|---|---|
| Issei | 30 | 67 | 83 |
| Nisei | 40 | 43 | 55 |
| White middle class | 40 | 38 | 48 |
| White lower class | 20 | 0 | 30 |

is such that they usually elicit stories concerning achievement. Picture 1 is of a young boy looking at a violin on a table in front of him. Picture 2 is a country scene: in the foreground is a young woman with books in her hand, while in the background a man is working in the fields and an older woman is looking on.

Table 3 shows that the rank order of positive achievement responses to both pictures goes from the Issei who have the highest proportion, through the Nisei and white middle class, who are roughly equivalent, to the white lower class who have the lowest percentage of positive responses.

In rating the stories told in picture 1, responses were considered to be positive achievement oriented when: (a) the boy wants to be a violinist (a long-range goal) and succeeds by working hard; (b) he is puzzled how to solve the task but keeps working at it; (c) his parents want him to become a violinist and he does so successfully, etc. Stories were considered to be negatively achievement oriented when: (a) the boy openly rebels against his parents' wishes for him to play the violin (against a long-range goal) and seeks immediate pleasure gratification in baseball or in breaking the violin; (b) he negativistically complies with his parents' demands and does poorly; (c) he engages in great fantasy about becoming a famous violinist, but gives no indication of how he will realistically reach this goal, etc.

Positive achievement-oriented responses on picture 2 were scored when: (a) the girl wants to leave the farm for a career, does so successfully (with or without help of her parents), and either returns later to help her parents, or is of benefit to society elsewhere; (b) the farmers in the picture are continually striving to do a better job, etc. Negative achievement-oriented stories were when: (a) the girl wants to leave, but feels she cannot and so she stays and suffers; (b) she is disgusted with farm life and wants to go see the bright lights of the city, etc.

Picture 1 reveals a second point: whether the boy is seen as self-motivated to work on a task, or whether he is assigned one by his parents or other adults. The distribution of the four cultural groups in this respect is shown in Table 4. The rank order here is the same as with reference to positive achievement responses.

Table 4—Self Motivation and Task Assignment Responses on TAT Picture 1, by Cultural Group

| Group | Total cases | Self-motivated Percent | Task assigned Percent |
|---|---|---|---|
| Issei | 30 | 93 | 7 |
| Nisei | 40 | 62 | 38 |
| White middle class | 40 | 75 | 25 |
| White lower class | 20 | 35 | 65 |

On picture 1, then, the Issei are high in positive achievement orientation and self-motivation. Taking these characteristics with a content analysis of the stories, a major value and psychological adaptive mechanism found in the Issei is to strive for success at all costs. Even if one is tired and puzzled, and the outer world presents many difficulties in living, one must keep on and never give up. Such a characterization is frequent in the literature on the Japanese, and is often referred to as "the Japanese spirit" or *yamato damashii*. The Issei attempt to live up to this value by hard realistic work with little use of fantasy or magical thinking, as can be seen in the following story:

What is this? A violin? He has a violin and he's thinking, "How shall I do it?" It looks very difficult and so he rests his face on his hand and worries. He thinks, "I can't play it yet, but if I study hard, someday maybe I'll be a good musician." In the end because he holds steady, he becomes a good player. He'll grow up to be a fine persevering young man.

Like the Issei, the Nisei see the boy as positively achieving and self-motivated, but they also often see him as assigned a task and in conflict with his parents. In the latter case, the adaptive mechanism is one of negativistic compliance and self-defeat. As will be seen later, this method of adapting is in considerable contrast to that used by the white lower class who tend to be openly hostile and rebellious. Typical Nisei stories are:

Probably gifted along musical lines. . . . Perhaps mature enough to realize it isn't a plaything but something that, well, takes both skill and practice to master.

. . . Perhaps he's been playing but still can't get the same tone or master it with such ease as an accomplished musician could. Doesn't seem to be thinking of baseball or anything like that, that would be keeping him away. . . . Well, if he had real talent, lived for music and is guided and counseled in the right manner by his parents and teacher, he might have the making of a musician in the real sense, toward classical rather than modern big name dance orchestras. . . . Probably strive more for immaterial things to make his life satisfactory in a spiritual sense rather than purely monetary, economic. Probably would be a musician in some large municipal symphony orchestra or through his love of music be a teacher in some university. He never would be very rich, but probably won't regret it and through his music he will be living a full rich life. That's about all.

Is he supposed to be sleeping? Probably practicing. I guess the mother must of . . . something the mother is forcing on him. He's a littled bored and disgusted, but he can't go against his mother's wishes. He's probably just sitting there day-dreaming about the things he'd like to do rather than practicing. Something that was forced upon him. He'll probably be just a mediocre player.

The white middle-class stories are very similar in their emphasis on self-motivation toward long-range goals, to those told by the Nisei. The situation is reversed in the lower-class stories where such goals are not valued, and where the boy is largely seen as assigned a task. When parental pressure is applied in the lower class stories, the reaction is either one of open rebellion and refusal, or doing only what one has to and then quitting.

An example of a white middle-class story is:

He is an intellectual looking young man. He probably has had an inspiration from some other violinist. He is intelligent. There seem to be two possibilities. Either he isn't too well prepared or he wonders why he isn't getting the same results from his violin that greater musicians get. He doesn't seem to register despair of any kind. Probably making an analysis of why he doesn't get the results although he seems rather young for much in the way of analytical work. He will probably go on with his studies of the violin and do quite well.

Whereas, in the white lower class:

Doesn't want to play his violin. Hates his music lessons. His mother wants him to be a musician but he's thinking about breaking the violin.

It strikes me as if he isn't thinking about the music there. He is thinking about a swimming hole, something like that. He has a violin there but he has his eyes closed and he's thinking about something else, probably what the other kids are doing out on the playground. He'll probably grow up to be a fiddler like Jack Benny. Probably grow up to drive a milk wagon [which is the subject's job]. When his mother quits pushing the violin on him, he will break away from it altogether.

In general, it may be said from an analysis of picture 1 that the Issei, Nisei and white middle class are self-motivated and achievement-oriented, while the white lower class are not. The determination to push ahead no matter what the obstacles, which is evident in the Issei stories, is a part of the Japanese value system and character structure, and it is this orientation that has been passed on to the Nisei in somewhat attenuated form. In addition, the Nisei give evidence of being in some conflict with the Issei parents, although they cannot openly express this. A further aspect of this conflict can be seen in the stories to picture 2, and is summarized in Table 5.

When the Issei tell stories of the girl leaving the farm to further her ambitions, it is usually in a positive manner. This is because it is a Japanese value that parents should help their children achieve long-range goals since it is (for the Issei) the unquestioned expectation that the children will then return to fulfill their obligations to their parents. For example:

This child is going to school. It's morning and her parents are farmers and they work and she's off to school. Her mother wants her to do well in school. In the end this girl goes to school to improve herself, and she wants to grow up so she can repay her obligation to her parents.

As on picture 1, the Issei are primarily concerned with working hard in a difficult environment in their stories to picture 2, and such stories make up the bulk of "other responses" for the Issei in Table 5. A typical story is:

Papa and Mama is working hard. One girl is about to go to school, I think. This picture mother work hard. She is working hard at something. This life is pretty hard. That's what these two are thinking—look like girl must see this situation and decide she must study diligently because Papa and Mama are concerned over her. Finally the girl becomes a nice girl, looks nice.

*Table 5*—Responses on TAT Picture 2 Indicating "Ability to Leave Farm," by Cultural Group

| Group | Total cases | Leave positively Percent | Leave negatively Percent | Other responses Percent |
|---|---|---|---|---|
| Issei | 30 | 37 | 7 | 56 |
| Nisei | 40 | 35 | 25 | 40 |
| White middle class | 40 | 35 | 28 | 37 |
| White lower class | 20 | 10 | 50 | 40 |

The Nisei, unlike the aging Issei, must find achievement and success within an American white middle-class world. The Japanese values and adaptive mechanisms learned from the Issei help the Nisei in such achievement, but they cannot both live up to the expectations of the American world and, at the same time, fulfill their Japanese obligations to their parents. Therefore the Nisei tell stories to picture 2 which are indicative of this conflict:

Well, let's see. This older woman over by the tree is watching her son till the soil. The young girl with the books is this woman's daughter and this boy's sister. She sort of has disdain for this life in a farm community, it's so limiting. So she goes to a nearby school in hopes of emancipating herself from this environment. But in her face you could see that she feels a very real sense of responsibility to her family and almost a guilty feeling for not sharing the life that her family had tried to create for her. And her feelings are always changing. She feels one day that she should stay and be contented with this life, and the next day that she should go on and seek a new life, but she is committed to school, so she guiltily looks back at her family and proceeds to school.

Like the Nisei, the white middle class see the girl in picture 2 as leaving the farm to achieve a career or higher education. Almost no lower class subjects see the picture in this manner. Unlike the Nisei, the white middle class do not see the girl so much in conflict with her parents as they see her neither being helped nor hindered by the parents, but simply leaving and becoming successful. Often this success is stated in too pat a fashion to be realistic. This reflects the American lower-middle-class overevaluation (particularly in the women's stories) of education as morally good in its own right; also, one "gets an education" as a status symbol in much the same sense as one buys a new car or a house. Education is likewise valued as a status symbol by Japanese Americans, but the emphasis is more on the knowledge and learned background it gives one, or as a down-to-earth means to further achievement. A representative middle-class woman's story to picture 2 is:

The daughter was brought up on a farm. She is striving for better things. She wants to read books, go to school, see the rest of the world. She is now in the process of going away from the farm, the early things you see on the farm. She will succeed in her book learning and will become a very successful author, authoress.

The lower-class responses to picture 1 are quite distinctive. When they see the girl leaving the farm, it is not to seek a long-range goal, but instead she leaves the farm because she is "disgusted with farm life" and wants to go to the city:

What kind of a field is that? It must be a wheat field. Girl is coming home from school. She's disgusted with the farm, doesn't like the farm. Like to get away from it all to the big city. Woman standing by the tree is her step-mother. She's very selfish. Father is a nice person. Looks to me like a very disgusted girl.

The TAT material just presented has shown some of the similarities and differences in Japanese and American achievement orientations in the area of life concerned with education, occupation, and other long-range goals. It would also be possible to make the same sort of analysis for parental, sexual, general interpersonal, and other aspects of life.

The Rorschach data offer a complementary analysis of Japanese American personality structure. The areas of mental striving and ambition drive as usually reflected in the Rorschach Test can be seen by comparing representative samples of 50 Issei and 60 Nisei with 60 American Normals ranging from lower to middle class socioeconomic status.

The perceptual organization of both the Issei and Nisei, when compared with the American sample, proves to be much more concerned with a straining to produce some over-all response to a Rorschach card (scored as W), with a neglect of both the easily perceived details (scored as D), and the smaller, usual detail responses (scored as Dd). . . . This sort of approach, along with an effort to organize the blot into complex concepts or configurations, indicated a great deal of striving in the intellectual sphere. The results also show a significantly large number of individuals among the Japanese Americans who exhibit an imbalance between an ability to be freely creative and spontaneous (as measured by movement responses on the Rorschach) and their intellectual strivings (as measured by whole responses). This finding suggests that the strong drive to accomplish outstrips, in some cases, the actual capacities available to the individual.

Although there is an over-all agreement as to striving among both Issei and Nisei, the personality context in which this striving is manifested is markedly different between the generations. The indications for a somewhat extreme intellectual constriction among the Issei are not as readily found in the Nisei. In both groups, where this constriction appears it sometimes leads to excessive associative blocking (refusal to continue responding to a particular Rorschach card) that suggests a lack of liberation of intellectual abilities, and in other cases to intense preoccupation with bodily functions, and a considerably narrowed range of interests or contacts with the outer environment. The associative blocking prevalent in the Issei was frequently accompanied by verbalization of a sense of defeat when the individual could not give an over-all response. When in a test of limits the examiner attempted to have the individuals respond to the details, in numerous instances they would not respond, feeling that they had already failed the task. They would, in many cases, only say, "*Ammari muzukashii* (it's too difficult)." This trend among the Issei is similar to their refusal to use fantasy or magical thinking even in the face of defeat as described in the TAT analysis. The American Normal group, on the other hand, shows more of a tendency to caution and momentary blocking in associative functioning. Rather than the severe blocking found in the Issei, those in the American Normal sample who show some sign of blocking recover and give responses, whereas in many cases the Issei totally reject the stimulus material.

The data suggest that oppositional trends (as measured by the frequency of white space responses) are most prevalent in the Nisei women, less common in the Nisei men, and notably lacking in the Issei group. Psychotherapy material in three of the extended treatment cases of Nisei women supports this conclusion. A strong theme running through many of the therapy cases was to oppose the mother to the extent of acting out rebellious behavior in various subtle ways. In none of the cases treated, however, was continuing difficulty with authority or supervisory figures expressed through direct opposition, probably because such direct opposition is not allowable in Japanese values. Instead, opposition was more indirectly manifested in the ways that assigned tasks would be done. The rebelliousness toward authority was prompted more toward women than men. In these cases, some break with the family always appeared, with the girl determined to make her own way, but with considerable turmoil and strong guilt feelings over neglecting the internalized obligation of obedience to family.

The kind of breakdown in ego controls observed in the Japanese American records often seems to be related to their sense of striving. The tendency to respond to the Rorschach cards in terms of confabulatory wholes found in both Issei and Nisei, the presence of vague abstract responses, the use of poorly conceived anatomy responses in which the parts were ill-defined at best, all serve to confirm the implication of an overstraining to accomplish. This strain to accomplish in spite of severe limitation is particularly present in the Issei. The observed selectivity of immigration from Japan does not allow one to infer that our results would hold true for all Japanese, and controlled studies in Japan should substantiate or modify these findings. The American normal group used here, in comparison with whom the Japanese tendency toward striving seems so marked, may on the other hand reflect a certain environmental selectivity related to their occupational framework. There is a tendency for this group to show a certain sluggishness of intellectual drive in comparison with the usual expectations of Rorschach workers. However, since the American normal group used as a sample in this study is composed of lower as well as middle class persons (unskilled and semiskilled, as well as skilled and executive groups), the results in terms of the greater striving shown in the Nisei adjustment would indicate that the orientation of the Nisei is more of a middle-class sort than is that of the Normal sample itself. The Japanese American Rorschach material has yet to be compared with Rorschach data gathered from a group of subjects with a strictly middle-class background.

In general, the over-all results of the research on Japanese Americans in Chicago seem to bear out the hypothesis that the values and adaptive mechanisms of the Japanese Americans and lower middle class are highly compatible, while the upper lower class diverges from both these groups and presents a different psychological adjustment. Where Japanese American values differ in emphasis by comparison with middle-class values, these differences are not of such a nature as to draw unfavorable comment from the middle class. Indeed, the differences would probably be considered praiseworthy by the middle class, if a little extreme, as in the extent of duty to one's parents, and the need to be of benefit to society.

The Issei place a high value on the attainment of such long-range goals as higher education, professional success, and the building of a spotless reputation in the community. These goals the Issei have passed on to their children, and the Issei willingly help the Nisei to achieve them because it is the unquestioned expectation of the Issei that their children will in turn fulfill their obligations to their parents. It is this "unquestioned expectation" that is the source of greatest conflict for the Nisei, who feel deeply their obligations to their parents but who also are striving for integration into American middle-class life.

What appears to have occurred in the case of the Japanese Americans is that the Nisei, while utilizing to a considerable extent a Japanese set of values and adaptive mechanisms, were able in their prewar life on the Pacific Coast to act in ways that drew favorable comment and recognition from their white middle-class peers and made them admirable pupils in the eyes of their middle-class teachers. This situation repeated itself in Chicago, and personnel managers and fellow workers also found the Nisei to be admirable employees. What has happened here is that the peers, teachers, employers, and fellow workers of the Nisei have projected their own values onto the neat, well dressed, and efficient Nisei in whom they saw mirrored many of their own ideals.

Because of this situation, the Nisei tend to be favorably evaluated by the American middle class, not only as individuals but as a group. Hence in Chicago, where they are removed from the high level of discrimination to be found on the Pacific Coast, the Nisei can be thought of as an entire group which is mobile toward, and attempting to achieve in, the American middle class. They are tremendously helped in this process by the praise both of their parents and of the white middle class; conversely, they are thrown into conflict over their inability to participate as fully as they would like in the middle class way of life, and at the same time fulfill their Japanese obligations to their parents.

A simile is useful in pointing up the similarities and differences between Japanese American and white middle-class achievement orientations: the ultimate destinations or goals of individuals in the two groups tend to be very similar; but Japanese Americans go toward these destinations along straight narrow streets lined with crowds of people who observe their every step, while middle-class persons go toward the same destinations along wider streets having more room for maneuvering, and lined only with small groups of people who, while watching them, do not observe their every movement. In psychoanalytic terminology, this means that the Japanese Americans have an ego structure that is very sensitive and vulnerable to stimuli coming from the outer world, and a superego structure that depends greatly upon external sanction. This tends to be true of middle-class Americans as well, but not nearly to such an extent. For example, individuals in both groups are interested in acquiring money in amounts sufficient to be translated in the achievement of social-class prestige; however, every move of a Japanese American toward amassing money is carefully watched, and the way he does it and the ultimate use he makes of it in benefiting the community are equal in importance to the financial success itself. This is less true of the American middle class, where an individual can make his money in a great variety of ways and, so long as these are not downright dishonest, the ways are sanctioned because of the end product—the financial success.

The Japanese Americans provide us, then, with the case of a group who, despite racial visibility and a culture traditionally thought of as alien, achieved a remarkable adjustment to middle-class American life because certain compatibilities in the value systems of the immigrant and host cultures operated strongly enough to override the more obvious difficulties.

The foregoing summary should by no means be taken to imply that all Japanese Americans will meet with success in the achievement of their goals. What is meant is that, because of the compatibility between Japanese and American middle-class cultures, individual Nisei probably have a better chance of succeeding than individuals from other ethnic groups where the underlying cultural patterns are less in harmony with those of the American middle class.

# RACE, ETHNICITY, AND THE

# ACHIEVEMENT SYNDROME

*Bernard C. Rosen*

*The disparity between the vertical mobility rates of some racial and ethnic groups can, in part, be explained as a function of their dissimilar psychological and cultural orientations towards achievement. Three components of this orientation—achievement motivation, achievement values, and educational-occupational aspirations—which have important consequences for social mobility in this country, are examined. Converging bodies of historical and ethnographic data indicate that differences between groups in motivation, values, and aspirations existed before their arrival in the Northeast, and had their origins in dissimilar socialization practices, traditions, and life-situations. Current attitudinal and personality data reveal that, for the most part, these differences still exist.*

The upward mobility rates of many racial and ethnic groups in America have been markedly dissimilar when compared with one another and with some white Protestant groups. For example, among the "new immigration" groups that settled primarily in the Northeast, the Greeks and Jews have attained middle class status more rapidly than most of their fellow immigrants. In general, ethnic groups with Roman Catholic affiliation have moved up less rapidly than non-Catholic groups. And the vertical mobility of Negroes, even in the less repressive environment of the industrial Northeast, has been relatively slow.[1]

The reasons offered to explain these differences vary with the group in question. Thus, differences in group mobility rates have sometimes been

[1] Cf. W. L. Warner and L. Srole, *The Social Systems of American Ethnic Groups*, New Haven, Yale University Press, 1945; F. L. Strodtbeck, "Jewish and Italian Immigration and Subsequent Status Mobility," in D. McClelland, A. Baldwin, U. Bronfenbrenner and F. Strodtbeck, *Talent and Society*, Princeton, Van Nostrand, 1958; M. Davie, *World Migration*, New York, Macmillan, 1936.

From *American Sociological Review*, **24** (1959), pp. 47–60. Reprinted by permission of the author and the *American Sociological Review*.

interpreted as a function of the immigrant's possession of certain skills which were valuable in a burgeoning industrial society. In this connection, there is some evidence that many Jews came to America with occupational skills better suited to urban living than did their fellow immigrants. Society mobility seems also to be related to the ability of ethnic and racial groups to organize effectively to protect and promote their interests. Both the Greeks and the Jews were quicker to develop effective community organizations than were other immigrants who had not previously faced the problem of adapting as minority groups. For the Jews, this situation grew out of their experiences with an often hostile gentile world; for the Greeks, out of their persecution by the Turks. The repressiveness of the social structure or the willingness of the dominant groups to permit others to share in the fruits of a rich, expanding economy has also been given as an explanation of differential group mobility. This argument has merit in the case of Negroes, but it is less valid in a comparison of the Jews with Southern Italians or French-Canadians. Finally, it has been suggested that groups with experiences in small town or urban environments were more likely to possess the cultural values appropriate to achievement in American society than were ethnic and racial groups whose cultures had been formed in rural, peasant surroundings. Here, again, it has been noted that many Jews and a small but influential number of Levantine Greeks had come from small towns or cities, while most of the Roman Catholic immigrants from Eastern and Southern Europe (and Southern Negroes before their migration to the North) came from rural communities.[2]

As valid as these explanations may be—and we believe they have merit —they overlook one important factor: *the individual's psychological and cultural orientation towards achievement*; by which we mean his psychological need to excel, his desire to enter the competitive race for social status, and his initial possession of or willingness to adopt the high valuation placed upon personal achievement and success which foreign observers from Tocqueville to Laski have considered an important factor in the remarkable mobility of individuals in American society.

Three components of this achievement orientation are particularly relevant for any study of social mobility. The first is a psychological factor, *achievement motivation*, which provides the internal impetus to excel in situations involving standards of excellence. The second and third components are cultural factors, one consisting of certain *value orientations*

[2] Cf. N. Glazer, "The American Jew and the Attainment of Middle-Class Rank: Some Trends and Explanations," in M. Sklare (ed.), *The Jews: Social Patterns of an American Group*, New York, Free Press, 1958; W. L. Warner and L. Srole, *op. cit.*; T. Burgess, *Greeks in America*, Boston, Sherman, French, 1913; T. Saloutos, "The Greeks in the U. S.," *The South Atlantic Quarterly*, 4, January, 1945, 69–82; T. Kalijarvi, "French-Canadians in the United States," *Annals, American Academy of Political and Social Science*, September, 1942; F. L. Strodtbeck, "Family Interactions, Values and Achievement," in D. McClelland, et al., *op. cit.*; G. Myrdal, *An American Dilemma*, New York, Harper, 1944.

which implement achievement-motivated behavior, the other of culturally influenced *educational-vocational aspiration levels*. All three factors may affect status achievement; one moving the individual to excel, the others organizing and directing his behavior towards high status goals. This motive-value-aspiration complex has been called the *Achievement Syndrome*.[3]

It is the basic hypothesis of this study that many racial and ethnic groups were not, and are not now, alike in their orientation toward achievement, particularly as it is expressed in the striving for status through social mobility, and that this difference in orientation has been an important factor contributing to the dissimilarities in their social mobility rates. Specifically, this paper examines the achievement motivation, values, and aspirations of members of six racial and ethnic groups. Four of these are "new immigration" ethnic groups with similar periods of residence in this country who faced approximately the same economic circumstances upon arrival: the French-Canadians, Southern Italians, Greeks, and East European Jews. The fifth is the Negro group in the Northeast, the section's largest "racial" division. The last, and in some ways the most heterogeneous, is the native-born white Protestant group. Contributing to the fact that these six groups have not been equally mobile, we suggest, are differences in the three components of the achievement syndrome: their incidence is highest among Jews, Greeks, and white Protestants, lower among Southern Italians and French-Canadians, and lowest among Negroes.

## RESEARCH PROCEDURE

The data were collected from a purposive sample of 954 subjects residing in 62 communities in four Northeastern states: 51 in Connecticut, seven in New York, three in New Jersey, and one in Massachusetts. The subjects are 427 pairs of mothers and their sons; 62 pairs are French-Canadians, 74 are Italians, 47 are Greeks, 57 are Jews, 65 are Negroes, and 122 are white Protestants. Most subjects were located through the aid of local religious, ethnic, or service organizations, or through their residence in neighborhoods believed to be occupied by certain groups. The subject's group membership was determined ultimately by asking the mothers in personal interviews to designate their religion and land of national origin. The interviewers, all of whom were upper-classmen enrolled in two sociology classes, were instructed to draw respondents from various social strata.[4] The respondent's social class position was determined by a

[3] B. C. Rosen, "The Achievement Syndrome: A Psychocultural Dimension of Social Stratification," *The American Sociological Review*, 21, April, 1956, pp. 203–211.
[4] The interviewers were trained by the writer; efforts were made to control for interviewer biases. It should be remembered that the sample is not random at any point in the selection process. Hence, the reader is cautioned to regard the data presented here as tentative and suggestive.

modified version of Hollingshead's Index of Social Position, which uses occupation and education of the main wage-earner, usually the father, as the principal criteria of status. Respondents were classified according to this index into one of five social classes, from the highest status group (Class I) to the lowest (Class V).[5] Most of the mothers and all of the sons are native-born, the sons ranging in age from eight to 14 years (the mean age is about 11 years). There are no significant age differences between the various groups.

Two research instruments were a projective test to measure achievement motivation and a personal interview to obtain information on achievement value orientations and related phenomena. Achievement motivation has been defined by McClelland and his associates as a redintegration of affect aroused by cues in situations involving standards of excellence. Such standards usually are imparted to the individual by his parents, who impart the understanding that they expect him to perform well in relation to these standards of excellence, rewarding him for successful endeavor and punishing him for failure. In time he comes to have similar expectations of himself when exposed to situations involving standards of excellence and re-experiences the affect associated with his earlier efforts to meet these standards. The behavior of people with high achievement motivation is characterized by persistent striving and general competitiveness.

Using a Thematic Apperception Test, McClelland and his associates have developed a method of measuring the achievement motive that involves identifying and counting the frequency with which imagery about evaluated performance in competition with a standard of excellence appears in the thoughts of a person when he tells a brief story under time pressure. This imagery now can be identified objectively and reliably. The test assumes that the more the individual shows indications of connections between evaluated performance and affect in his fantasy, the greater the degree to which achievement motivation is part of his personality.[6] This projective test, which involves showing the subject four ambiguous pictures and asking him to tell a story about each, was given privately and individually to the sons in their homes. Their imaginative responses to the pictures were scored by two judges; the Pearson product moment correlation between the two scorings was .86, an estimate of reliability similar to those reported in earlier studies using this measure.

Following the boys' testing, their mothers were interviewed privately. The interview guide included several standardized questions designed to indicate the mother's achievement value orientations, her educational and vocational aspirations for her son, and the degree to which she had trained him to be independent.

[5] A. B. Hollingshead and F. C. Redlich, "Social Stratification and Psychiatric Disorders," *American Sociological Review*, 18 April, 1953, 163–169.
[6] D. C. McClelland, J. Atkinson, R. Clark, and E. Lowell, *The Achievement Motive*, New York, Appleton-Century-Crofts, 1953.

# FINDINGS AND INTERPRETATION

*Achievement Motivation.* Empirical studies have shown that achievement motivation is generated by (at least) two kinds of socialization practices: (1) *achievement training*, in which the parents, by imposing standards of excellence upon tasks, by setting high goals for their children, and by indicating their high evaluation of his competence to do a task well, communicate to him that they expect evidences of high achievement; (2) *independence training*, in which the parents indicate to the child that they expect him to be self-reliant and, at the same time, grant him relative autonomy in decision-making situations where he is given both freedom of action and responsibility for success or failure. Essentially, achievement training is concerned with getting the child to *do things well*, while independence training seeks to teach him to do things *on his own*. Although both kinds often occur together and each contributes to the development of achievement, achievement training is the more important of the two.[7]

Two bodies of information—ethnographic studies of the "old world" or non-American culture and recent empirical investigations of the training practices used by Americans of various ethnic backgrounds—strongly indicate that the six groups examined here, in the past and to some extent today, differ with respect to the degree to which their members typically emphasize achievement and independence training. Ethnic differences in these matters were first studied by McClelland, who noted that the linkage between independence training and achievement motivation established by recent empirical studies suggests an interesting parallel with Weber's classic description of the characterological consequences of the Protestant Reformation. Weber reasoned, first, concerning salvation, that an important aspect of the Protestant theological position was the shift from reliance on an institution (the Church) to a greater reliance upon self; it seemed reasonable to assume that Protestant parents who prepared their children for increased self-reliance in religious matters would also tend to stress the necessity for the child to be self-reliant in other aspects of his life. Secondly, Weber's description of the personality types produced by the Reformation is strikingly similar to the picture of the person with high achievement motivation; for example, the hard-working, thrifty Protestant working girl, the Protestant entrepreneur who "gets nothing out of his wealth for himself except the irrational sense of having done his job well."[8]

[7] M. Winterbottom, "The Relation of Need for Achievement to Learning Experiences in Independence and Mastery," in J. Atkinson (ed.), *Motives in Fantasy, Action and Society*, Princeton, Van Nostrand, 1958; B. C. Rosen, "The Psychosocial Origins of Achievement Motivation," mimeographed progress report to the National Institute of Mental Health, 1957.

[8] D. C. McClelland, "Some Social Consequences of Achievement Motivation," in M. R. Jones (ed.), *Nebraska Symposium on Motivation, 1955*, Lincoln, University of Nebraska Press, 1955.

The hypothesis deduced from these observations was put to the test by McClelland, who questioned white Protestant, Irish-Catholic, Italian-Catholic, and Jewish mothers about their independence training practices. He found that Protestants and Jews favored earlier independence training than Irish and Italian Catholics.[9] These findings are supported and enlarged upon by data derived from questioning the 427 mothers in this study about their training practices. The mothers were asked, "At what age do you expect your son to do the following things?" and to note the appropriate items from the following list (taken from the Winterbottom index of training in independence and mastery):[10]

*1]* To be willing to try things on his own without depending on his mother for help.
*2]* To be active and energetic in climbing, jumping, and sports.
*3]* To try hard things for himself without asking for help.
*4]* To be able to lead other children and assert himself in children's groups.
*5]* To make his own friends among children of his own age.
*6]* To do well in school on his own.
*7]* To have interests and hobbies of his own. To be able to entertain himself.
*8]* To do well in competition with other children. To try hard to come out on top in games and sports.
*9]* To make decisions like choosing his own clothes or deciding to spend his money by himself.

An index of independence training was derived by summing the ages for each item and taking the mean figure. The data in Table 1 show that the Jews expect earliest evidence of self-reliance from their children (mean age 6.83 years), followed by the Protestants (6.87), Negroes (7.23), Greeks (7.67), French-Canadians (7.99), and Italians (8.03). Both primary sources of variation—ethnicity and social class—are significant at the .01 level.

Data on the relative emphasis which racial and ethnic groups place upon achievement *training* (that is, imposing standards of excellence upon tasks, setting high goals for the child to achieve, and communicating to him a feeling that his parents evaluate highly his task-competence) are much more difficult to obtain. Achievement training as such, in fact, is rarely treated in studies of ethnic socialization practices. Hence, inferences

[9] D. C. McClelland, A. Rindlisbacher, and R. C. deCharms, "Religious and Other Sources of Parental Attitudes Towards Independence Training," in D. C. McClelland (ed.), *Studies in Motivation*, New York: Appleton-Century-Crofts, 1955.
[10] Winterbottom, *op. cit.* Though primarily a measure of independence training, two items in this index—items 6 and 8—are considered measures of mastery training, a concept akin to our notion of achievement training. The failure to disentangle independence training from mastery (achievement) training has been responsible for some confusion in earlier studies of the origins of achievement motivation. (For an analysis of this confusion, see Rosen, "The Psychosocial Origins of Achievement Motivation," *op. cit.*) The two components were kept in the index in order to maintain comparability between this study and the earlier work on ethnic groups by McClelland reported above.

about achievement training were drawn primarily from ethnographic and historical materials, which are usually more informative about achievement as such than about relevant socialization practices.

The groups about which the most is known concerning achievement training, perhaps, are the Protestants, the Jews, and, to a lesser extent, the Greeks. These groups traditionally have stressed excellence and achievement. In the case of the Protestants, this tradition can be located in the Puritan Ethic with its concept of work as a "calling" and the exhortation that a job be done well. Of course, not all Protestants would be equally comfortable with this tradition; it is much more applicable, for example, to Presbyterians and Quakers than to Methodists and Baptists. Nonetheless, the generally longer residence of Protestants in this country makes it

*Table 1*—Mean Age of Independence Training by Ethnicity and Social Class

| Ethnicity | I-II-III | SOCIAL CLASS* IV | V | $\bar{x}$ | N |
|---|---|---|---|---|---|
| French-Canadian | 8.00 | 7.69 | 8.08 | 7.99 | 62 |
| Italian | 6.79 | 7.89 | 8.47 | 8.03 | 74 |
| Greek | 6.33 | 8.14 | 7.52 | 7.67 | 47 |
| Jew | 6.37 | 7.29 | 6.90 | 6.83 | 57 |
| Negro | 6.64 | 6.98 | 7.39 | 7.23 | 65 |
| Protestant | 5.82 | 7.44 | 7.03 | 6.87 | 122 |
| $\bar{x}$ | 6.31 | 7.64 | 7.59 | | |

Ethnicity: $F = 8.55$   $P < .01$
Social Class: $F = 21.48$   $P < .001$
Ethnicity × Class: $F = 6.25$   $P < .01$

* The three-class breakdown was used in an earlier phase of the analysis. An examination of the means of cells using a four-class breakdown revealed no change in pattern and did not warrant new computations.

probable that they would tend to share the American belief that children should be encouraged to develop their talents and to set high goals, possibly a bit beyond their reach. The observation that Jews stress achievement training is commonplace. Zyborowski and Herzog note the strong tendency among *shtetyl* Jews to expect and to reward evidences of achievement even among very young children. The image of the Jewish mother as eager for her son to excel in competition and to set ever higher goals for himself is a familiar one in the literature of Jewish family life.[11] Careful attention to standards of excellence in the Greek home is stressed by the parents: children know that a task which is shabbily performed will have to be re-done. In this country, the Greek is exhorted to be "a credit to his group." Failure to meet group norms is quickly perceived and where possible punished; while achievement receives the approbation of the entire Greek community.

Among the Southern Italians (the overwhelming majority of American-

[11] M. Zyborowski and E. Herzog, *Life Is With People*, New York, International University Press, 1952.

Italians are of Southern Italian extraction), French-Canadians, and Negroes the tradition seems to be quite different. More often than not they came from agrarian societies or regions in which opportunities for achievement were strictly curtailed by the social structure and where habits of resignation and fatalism in the face of social and environmental frustrations were psychologically functional. Under such conditions children were not typically exhorted to be achievers or urged to set their sights very high. Of course, children were expected to perform tasks, as they are in most societies, but such tasks were usually farm or self-caretaking chores, from which the notion of competition with standards of excellence is not excluded, but is not ordinarily stressed. As for communicating to the child a sense of confidence in his competence to do a task well, there is some evidence that in the father-dominant Italian and French-Canadian families, pronounced concern with the child's ability might be perceived as a threat to the father.[12]

On the whole, the data indicate that Protestants, Jews, and Greeks place a greater emphasis on independence and achievement training than Southern Italians and French-Canadians. The data on the Negroes are conflicting: they often train children relatively early in self-reliance, but there is little evidence of much stress upon achievement training. No doubt the socialization practices of these groups have been modified somewhat by the acculturating influences of American society since their arrival in the Northeast.[13] But ethnic cultures tend to survive even in the face of strong obliterating forces, and we believe that earlier differences between groups persist—a position supported by the present data on self-reliance training. Hence, the hypothesis that the racial and ethnic groups considered here differ with respect to achievement motivation. We predicted that, on the average, achievement motivation scores would be highest among the Jews, Greeks, and white Protestants, lower among the Italians and French-Canadians, and lowest among the Negroes. Table 2 shows that the data support these predictions, indicated by the following mean scores: Greeks 10.80, Jews 10.53, Protestants 10.11, Italians 9.65, French-Canadians 8.82, and Negroes 8.40.

A series of $t$-tests of significance between means (a one-tail test was used in cases where the direction of the difference had been predicted) was computed. The differences between Greeks, Jews, and Protestants are not statistically significant. The Italian score is significantly lower (P < .05) than

[12] P. H. Williams, *South Italian Folkways in Europe and America*, New Haven, Yale University Press, 1938; H. Miner, *St. Dennis: A French-Canadian Parish*, Chicago, University of Chicago Press, 1939.
[13] It does not necessarily follow that the impact of American culture has reduced the differences between groups. An argument can be made that for some groups life in America has accentuated differences by allowing certain characteristics of the groups to develop. We have in mind particularly the Greeks and Jews whose need to excel could find little avenue for expression through status striving in Europe.

the score for the Greeks, but not for the Jews and Protestants. The largest differences are between the French-Canadians and Negroes on the one hand and the remaining groups on the other: the French-Canadian mean score is significantly lower (P <.01) than those of all other groups except Italians and Negroes; the mean score for all Negroes is significantly lower (P <.01) than the scores for all other groups except French-Canadians. A "Roman Catholic" score was obtained by combining Italian and French-Canadian scores, and scores for all non-Negro groups were combined to form a "White" score. The differences between group means were tested for significance (by a one-tail $t$-test) and it was found that the "Catholic" score is significantly lower than the scores for Protestants, Greek Orthodox, and Jews (P <.01). The Negro mean score is significantly lower than the combined score of all white groups (P <.002).

*Table 2*—Mean Achievement Motivation Scores by Ethnicity and Social Class

| Ethnicity | I-II | III | IV | V | $\bar{x}$ | N |
|---|---|---|---|---|---|---|
| | | | SOCIAL CLASS | | | |
| French-Canadian | 10.00 | 10.64 | 8.78 | 7.75 | 8.82 | 62 |
| Italian | 8.86 | 12.81 | 7.54 | 10.20 | 9.65 | 74 |
| Greek | 9.17 | 12.13 | 10.40 | 8.75 | 10.80 | 47 |
| Jew | 10.05 | 10.41 | 10.94 | 11.20 | 10.53 | 57 |
| Negro | 11.36 | 9.00 | 8.23 | 6.72 | 8.40 | 65 |
| Protestant | 11.71 | 10.94 | 9.39 | 7.31 | 10.11 | 122 |
| $\bar{x}$ | 10.55 | 11.26 | 9.01 | 8.32 | | |

Ethnicity: F = 1.23  P >.05
Social Class: F = 5.30  P <.005
Ethnicity × Class: F = 1.32  P >.05

A comparison of ethnic-racial differences does not tell the whole story. There are also significant differences between the social classes. In fact, analysis of Table 2 indicates that social class accounts for more of the variance than ethnicity: the F ratio for ethnicity is 1.23 (P> .05), for class 5.30 (P <.005). The small number of cases in Classes I and II greatly increases the within-group variance; when these two classes are combined with Class III the variance is decreased and the F ratio for ethnicity increases sharply to 2.13 (P <.06). Social class, however, remains more significantly related to achievement motivation than ethnicity. This finding is especially important in this study since the proportion of subjects in each class varies for the ethnic groups. There are relatively more middle class than lower class subjects among the Jews, Greeks, and Protestants than among Italians, French-Canadians, and Negroes. To control for social class it was necessary to examine the differences between cells as well as between columns and rows. A series of $t$-tests of differences between the means of cells revealed that for the most part the earlier pattern established for total ethnic means persists, although in some instances the differences between groups are decreased, in others increased, and in a few cases the direction of the differences is reversed. Neither ethnicity not social class alone is sufficient to predict an individual's score; both appear to contribute something to the variance between groups, but on the whole social class is a better predictor than ethnicity. Generally, a high status person from an ethnic group with a low mean achievement motivation score is more likely to have a high score than a low status person from a group with a high mean score. Thus, the mean score for Class I-II Negroes is higher than the score for Class IV-V white Protestants: the score for the former is 11.36, for the latter, 7.31; a *t*-test revealed that the difference between these two means is significant at the .05 level, using a two-tail test. This relatively high score for Class I-II Negroes, the third highest for any cell in the table, indicates, perhaps, the strong motivation necessary for a Negro to achieve middle class status in a hostile environment. Generally, the scores for each group decrease as the class level declines, except for the Jews whose scores are inversely related to social status—a finding for which we can offer no explanation.

*Achievement Value Orientations.* Achievement motivation is one part of the achievement syndrome; an equally important component is the achievement value orientation. Value orientations are defined as meaningful and affectively charged modes of organizing behavior—principles that guide human conduct. They establish criteria which influence the individual's preferences and goals. Achievement values and achievement motivation, while related, represent genuinely different components of the achievement syndrome, not only conceptually but also in their origins and, as we have shown elsewhere, in their social correlates.[14] Value orientations, because of their conceptual content, are probably acquired in that stage of the child's cultural training when verbal communication of a fairly complex nature is possible. Achievement motivation or the need to excel, on the other hand, has its origins in parent-child interaction beginning early in the child's life when many of these relations are likely to be emotional and unverbalized. Analytically, then, the learning of achievement oriented values can be independent of the acquisition of the achievement motive, although empirically they often occur together.

Achievement values affect social mobility in that they focus the individual's attention on status improvement and help to shape his behavior so that achievement motivation can be translated into successful action. The achievement motive by itself is not a sufficient condition of social mobility: it provides internal impetus to excel, but it does not impel the individual to take the steps necessary for status achievement. Such steps in our society involve, among other things, a preparedness to plan, work hard, make sacrifices, and be physically mobile. Whether or not the individual will understand their importance and accept them will depend in part upon his values.

[14] Rosen, "The Achievement Syndrome," *op. cit.*, pp. 208–210.

Three sets of values (a modification of Kluckhohn's scheme[15]) were identified as elements of the achievement syndrome,[16] as follows:

1. *Activistic-Passivistic Orientation* concerns the extent to which the culture of a group encourages the individual to believe in the possibility of his manipulating the physical and social environment to his advantage. An activistic culture encourages the individual to believe that it is both possible and necessary for him to improve his status, whereas a passivistic culture promotes the acceptance of the notion that individual efforts to achieve mobility are relatively futile.

2. *Individualistic-Collectivistic Orientation* refers to the extent to which the individual is expected to subordinate his needs to the group. This study is specifically concerned with the degree to which the society expects the individual to maintain close physical proximity to his family of orientation, even at the risk of limiting vocational opportunities; and the degree to which the society emphasizes group incentives rather than personal rewards. The collectivistic society places a greater stress than the individualistic on group ties and group incentives.

3. *Present-Future Orientation* concerns the society's attitude toward time and its impact upon behavior. A present oriented society stresses the merit of living in the present, emphasizing immediate gratifications; a future oriented society encourages the belief that planning and present sacrifices are worthwhile, or morally obligatory, in order to insure future gains.

Examination of enthnographic and historical materials on the cultures of the six ethnic groups revealed important differences in value orientation —differences antedating their arrival in the Northeast. The cultures of white Protestants, Jews, and Greeks stand out as considerably more individualistic, activistic, and future-oriented than those of the Southern Italians, French-Canadians, and Negroes. Several forces—religious, economic, and national—seem to have long influenced the Protestants in this direction, including, first, the Puritan Ethic with its stress upon individualism and work; then the impact of the liberal economic ethic (Weber's "Spirit of Capitalism") emphasizing competitive activity and achievement; and finally, the challenge of the frontier, with its consequent growth of a national feeling of optimism and manifest destiny. All of these factors tended very early to create a highly activistic, individualistic, future-oriented culture—the picture of American culture held by foreign observers since Tocqueville.[17]

The Jews, who for centuries had lived in more or less hostile environments, have learned that it is not only possible to manipulate their environment to insure survival but even to prosper in it. Jewish tradition stresses

[15] F. Kluckhohn, "Dominant and Substitute Profiles of Cultural Orientations," *Social Forces,* **28,** May, 1950, 376–393.
[16] For the most part, the value orientations examined in this study, their description, and the items used to index them, are identical with those which appear in Rosen, "The Achievement Syndrome," *op. cit.*
[17] For a history of the development of the liberal economic ethic and its manifestation on the American scene, see J. H. Randall, *The Making of the Modern Mind,* Boston, Houghton Mifflin, 1926; J. K. Galbraith, *The Affluent Society,* Boston, Houghton Mifflin, 1958.

the possibility of the individual rationally mastering his world. Man is not helpless against the forces of nature or of his fellow man; God will provide, but only if man does his share. Like Protestantism, Judaism is an intensely individualistic religion and the Jews an intensely individualistic people. While the family was close knit, it was the entire *shtetyl* which was regarded as the inclusive social unit; and in neither case was loyalty to the group considered threatened by physical mobility. The Jews typically have urged their children to leave home if in so doing they faced better opportunities. *Shtetyl* society, from which the vast majority of American Jewry is descended, vigorously stressed the importance of planning and working for the future. A *shtetyl* cultural tradition was that parents save for many years, often at great sacrifice to themselves, in order to improve their son's vocational opportunities or to provide a daughter with a dowry.[18]

In some respects, Greek and Jewish cultures were strikingly similar at the turn of the century. The ethos of the town and city permeated the Greek more than most other Mediterranean cultures, although only a small proportion of the population was engaged in trade—with the important exception of the Levantine Greeks, who were largely merchants. The image of the Greek in the Eastern Mediterranean area was that of an individualistic, foresighted, competitive trader. Early observers of the Greek in America were impressed by his activistic, future-oriented behavior. E. A. Ross, a rather unfriendly observer, wrote as early as 1914 that "the saving, commercial Greek climbs. From curb to stand, from stand to store, from little store to big store, and from there to branch stores in other cities—such are the stages in his upward path."[19]

Though separated by thousands of miles, French-Canadian and Southern Italian cultures were similar in many respects. Both were primarily peasant cultures, strongly influenced by the Roman Catholic Church. Neither could be described as activistic, individualistic, or future-oriented. In Southern Italian society, the closed-class system and grinding poverty fostered a tradition of resignation—a belief that the individual had little control over his life situation and a stress upon the role of fate (*Destino*) in determining success. The living conditions of French-Canadians, although less harsh, were sufficiently severe to sharply limit the individual's sense of mastery over his situation. In neither group was there a strong feeling that the individual could drastically improve his lot; for both groups the future was essentially unpredictable, even capricious. Extended family ties were very strong in both groups: there is the Southern Italian saying, "the family against all others;" the French-Canadian farmer in need of

[18] Zyborowski and Herzog, *op. cit.*; B. C. Rosen, "Cultural Factors in Achievement," mimeographed, 1952; Strodtbeck, "Family Interactions, Values and Achievement," *op. cit.*
[19] Quoted in Saloutos, *op. cit.*, p. 71. The writer is indebted to J. Gregoropoulos, a native of Athens, for many helpful comments on European and American Greek communities.

help will travel many miles to hire a kinsman rather than an otherwise convenient neighbor.[20]

Ironically, although Negroes are usually Protestant (however, not ordinarily of the Calvinistic type) and have been exposed to the liberal economic ethic longer than most of the other groups considered here, their culture, it seems, is least likely to accent achievement values. The Negro's history as a slave and depressed farm worker, and the sharp discrepancy between his experiences and the American Creed, would appear to work against the internalization of the achievement values of the dominant white group. Typically, the Negro life-situation does not encourage the belief that one can manipulate his environment or the conviction that one can improve his condition very much by planning and hard work.[21] Generally, family ties have not been strong among Negroes, although traditionally the mother was an especially important figure and ties between her and her children, particularly sons, may still be very strong.[22]

Another and more direct way of studying ethnic values is to talk with group members themselves; thus our personal interviews with the mothers. (Their sons in many cases were too young to give meaningful answers.) They were asked whether they agreed or disagreed with the following statements, listed here under the appropriate value orientation categories.

(1) *Activistic-Passivistic Orientation*

Item 1. "All a man should want out of life in the way of a career is a secure, not too difficult job, with enough pay to afford a nice car and eventually a home of his own."

Item 2. "When a man is born the success he is going to have is already in the cards, so he might just as well accept it and not fight against it."

Item 3. "The secret of happiness is not expecting too much out of life and being content with what comes your way."   .

(2) *Individualistic-Collectivistic Orientation*

Item 4. "Nothing is worth the sacrifice of moving away from one's parents."

Item 5. "The best kind of job to have is one where you are part of an organization all working together even if you don't get individual credit."[23]

[20] Miner, *op. cit.* See also Williams, *op. cit.*; Strodtbeck, "Family Interactions, Values and Achievement," *op. cit.*

[21] We recognize that to infer a group's values from its life-situation and then to use these values to explain an aspect of that situation is to reason circularly. However, the temporal sequence between values and mobility has a chicken-egg quality which is difficult to avoid because values and life-situation interact. To some extent, knowledge of ethnic cultures prior to their arrival in the United States helps to establish the priority of values to mobility. In the case of the Negroes, however, relatively little is known about their several cultures before their transportation to this country.

[22] E. F. Frazier, *The Negro Family in the United States*, Chicago, University of Chicago Press, 1939; see also Frazier's *The Negro in the United States*, New York, Macmillan, 1957, especially Chapters 13 and 24.

[23] Of course, if Whyte is correct about the growth of the organization man and the importance of the "social ethic," agreement with this statement may indicate an asset rather than a handicap to social mobility. See W. H. Whyte, Jr., *The Organization Man*, New York, Simon and Schuster, 1957.

(3) *Present-Future Orientation*

Item 6. "Planning only makes a person unhappy since your plans hardly ever work out anyway."

Item 7. "Nowadays with world conditions the way they are the wise person lives for today and lets tomorrow take care of itself."

Responses indicating an activistic, future-oriented, individualistic point of view (the answer "disagree" to these items) reflect values, we believe, most likely to facilitate achievement and social mobility. These items were used to form a value index, and a score was derived for each subject by giving a point for each achievement-oriented response. In examining the mothers' scores two assumptions were made: (1) that they tend to transmit their values to their sons, and (2) that the present differences between groups are indicative of at least equal, and perhaps even greater, differences in the past.

*Table 3*—Mean Value Scores by Ethnicity and Social Class

| Ethnicity | I-II | III | IV | V | $\bar{x}$ | N |
|---|---|---|---|---|---|---|
| | | | SOCIAL CLASS | | | |
| French-Canadian | 4.00 | 4.21 | 4.60 | 2.46 | 3.68 | 62 |
| Italian | 5.86 | 4.00 | 3.96 | 3.40 | 4.17 | 74 |
| Greek | 6.33 | 5.52 | 4.80 | 3.25 | 5.08 | 47 |
| Jew | 5.94 | 5.47 | 5.41 | 4.80 | 5.54 | 57 |
| Negro | 6.00 | 5.00 | 4.90 | 4.67 | 5.03 | 65 |
| Protestant | 5.86 | 5.50 | 4.97 | 3.54 | 5.16 | 122 |
| $\bar{x}$ | 5.91 | 5.08 | 4.78 | 3.49 | | |

Ethnicity: $F = 11.62$  $P < .001$
Social Class: $F = 33.80$  $P < .001$
Ethnicity × Class: $F = 2.43$  $P < .01$

The ethnographic and historical materials led us to expect higher value scores for Jews, white Protestants, and Greeks than for Italians, French-Canadians, and Negroes. In large measure, these expectations were confirmed. Table 3 shows that Jews have the highest mean score (5.54), followed closely by Protestants (5.16), Greeks (5.08), and Negroes (surprisingly) (5.03). The Italians' score (4.17) is almost a point lower, and the French-Canadian score (3.68) is the lowest for any group. The scores for Jews, Protestants, and Greeks do not significantly differ when the two-tail test is used (we were not able to predict the direction of the differences), but they are all significantly higher than the scores for Italians and French-Canadians. When Italian and French-Canadian scores are combined to form a "Roman Catholic" score, the latter is significantly lower ($P < .001$) than the scores for Jews, Protestants, or Greeks.

The prediction for the Negroes proved to be entirely wrong. Their mean score (5.03) is significantly higher ($P < .001$) than the scores for Italians and French-Canadians. Nor is the Negro score significantly different from those for Protestants and Greeks, although it is significantly lower than the Jewish score ($P < .05$) when the one-tail test is used. The skeptic may regard the relatively high Negro value score as merely lip-service to the liberal economic ethic, but it may in fact reflect, and to some extent be responsible for, the economic gains of Negroes in recent years.[24]

Social class also is significantly related to achievement values and accounts for more of the variance than ethnicity: the F ratio for class is 33.80 (P < .001) for ethnicity 11.62 (P < .001). Almost without exception, the mean score for each ethnic group is reduced with each decline in status. *Social class, however, does not wash out the differences between ethnic groups.* A series of *t*-tests between cells across each social class reveals that Greek, Jewish, and Protestant scores remain significantly higher than Italian and French-Canadian scores. Negro scores also remain among the highest across each social class. Ethnicity and social class interact and each contributes something to the differences between groups: the individual with high social status who also belongs to an ethnic group which stresses achievement values is far more likely to have a high value score than an individual with low status and membership in a group in which achievement is not emphasized. For example, the Class I-II Greek score is 6.33 as compared with the Class V French-Canadian score of 2.46—the difference between them is significant at the .001 level. On the other hand, the score for Class I-II Italians, an ethnic group in which achievement values are not stressed, is 5.86 as compared with 3.25 for Class V Greeks—the difference between them is significant at the .001 level. Neither variable, then, is sufficient to predict an individual's score; and for some groups social class seems to be the more significant factor, for others ethnicity appears to play the greater role. Thus, for Jews and Negroes the mean scores remain relatively high for each social class; in fact, Class V Jews and Negroes have larger mean scores than many French-Canadians and Italians of higher social status.

*Aspiration Levels.* Achievement motivation and values influence social mobility by affecting the individual's need to excel and his willingness to plan and work hard. But they do not determine the areas in which such excellence and effort take place. Achievement motivation and values can be expressed, as they often are, through many kinds of behavior that are not conducive to social mobility in our society, for example, deviant, recreational, or religious behavior. Unless the individual aims for high vocational goals and prepares himself appropriately, his achievement motivation and values will not pull him up the social ladder. Increasingly, lengthy formal education, often including college and post-graduate

[24] The relatively high value score for Negroes supports our contention that achievement motivation and achievement values are genuinely different components of the achievement syndrome. It will be remembered that the Negroes had the lowest mean motivation score. If achievement motivation and values are conceptually and empirically identical, there should be no difference between the two sets of scores.

study, is needed for movement into prestigeful and lucrative jobs. An educational aspiration level which precludes college training may seriously affect the individual's chances for social mobility.

Their cultures, even before the arrival of the ethnic groups in the Northeast, were markedly different in orientation towards education.[25] The Protestants' stress upon formal education, if only as a means of furthering one's career, is well known. Traditionally, Jews have placed a very high value on educational and intellectual attainment; learning in the *shtetyl* society gave the individual prestige, authority, a chance for a better marriage. Contrariwise, for Southern Italians, school was an upper class institution, not an avenue for social advancement for their children, booklearning was remote from everyday experience, and intellectualism often regarded with distrust. French-Canadians, although not hostile to education and learning, were disinclined to educate their sons beyond the elementary level. Daughters needed more education as preparation for jobs in the event they did not marry, but sons were destined to be farmers or factory workers, in the parents' view, with the exception at times of one son who would be encouraged to become a priest. Greeks—generally no better educated than Italians or French-Canadians—on the whole were much more favorably disposed towards learning, in large part because of their intense nationalistic identification with the cultural glories of ancient Greece.[26] This identification was strengthened by the relatively hostile reception Greeks met on their arrival in this country, and is in part responsible for the rapid development of private schools supported by the Greek community and devoted to the teaching of Greek culture—an interesting parallel to the Hebrew School among American Jews. Finally, Negroes, who might be expected to share the prevalent American emphasis upon education, face the painfully apparent fact that positions open to educated Negroes are scarce. This fact means that most Negroes, in all likelihood, do not consider high educational aspirations realistic. And the heavy drop-out in high school suggests that the curtailment of educational aspirations begins very early.

To test whether and to what degree these differences between groups persist, the mothers were asked: "How far do you *intend* for your son to go to school?" It was hoped that the term *intend* would structure the question so that the reply would indicate, not merely a mother's pious wish, but also an expression of will to do something about her son's schooling. The

[25] For a comparison of ethnic group education and vocational aspirations, see R. M. Williams, Jr., *American Society*, New York, Knopf, 1951, Chapter 8; F. J. Woods, *Cultural Values of American Ethnic Groups*, New York, Harper, 1956, Chapters 5 and 7.
[26] Attempts by Mussolini to create a similar bond between his people and ancient Rome, or even the more recent Renaissance, were unsuccessful. French-Canadians for the most part have long refused to be impressed by the "secular" achievement of European anti-clerical French society.

data show that 96 per cent of the Jewish, 88 per cent of the Protestant, 85 per cent of the Greek, 83 per cent of the Negro (much higher than was anticipated), 64 per cent of the Italian, and 56 per cent of the French-Canadian mothers said that they expected their sons to go to college. The aspirations of Jews, Protestants, Greeks, and Negroes are not significantly different from one another, but they are significantly higher than the aspirations of Italians and French-Canadians (P < .05).

Social class, once more, is significantly related to educational aspiration. When class is controlled the differences between ethnic groups are diminished—particularly at the Class I-II-III levels—but they are not erased: Jews, Protestants, Greeks, and Negroes tend to have aspirations similar to one another and higher than those of Italians and French-Canadians for each social class. The differences are greatest at the lower class levels: at Class V, 85 per cent of the Protestants, 80 per cent of the Jews, and 78 per cent of the Negroes intend for their sons to go to college as compared with 63 per cent of the Greeks, 50 per cent of the Italians, and 29 per cent of the French-Canadians.

The individual, to be socially mobile, must aspire to the occupations which society esteems and rewards highly. An individual, strongly motivated to excel and willing to plan and work hard, who sets his heart on being the best barber will probably be less vertically mobile than an equally endowed person who aspires to become the best surgeon. Moreover, the individual who aspires to a high status occupation is likely to expend more energy in competitive striving—and in so doing improve his chances for social mobility—than someone whose occupational choice demands relatively little from him.

Since many of the boys in this study were too young to appraise occupations realistically, we sought to obtain a measure of ethnic group vocational aspiration by questioning the mothers about their aspirations for their sons, once again assuming that they would tend to communicate their views of status levels and their expectations for their sons. Ten occupations were chosen which can be ranked by social status; seven of our ten occupations (marked below by asterisks) were selected from the N.O.R.C. ranking.[27] The occupations, originally presented in alphabetical order, are given here in the order of status: Lawyer*, Druggist, Jewelry Store Owner, Machinist*, Bank Teller, Insurance Agent*, Bookkeeper*, Mail Carrier*, Department Store Salesman*, and Bus Driver*. The mothers were asked: "If things worked out so that your son were in the following occupations, would you be satisfied or dissatisfied?" To obtain

[27] National Opinion Research Center, "Jobs and Occupations: A Popular Evaluation," *Opinion News*, **9**, September 1, 1947. We substituted store salesman for store clerk and bus driver for streetcar motorman. The position of the three occupations which did not appear in the N.O.R.C. survey are ranked according to their similarity to occupations in the survey.

aspiration scores for each mother, her responses were treated in three ways:

1. The number of times the mother answered "satisfied" to the ten occupations was summed to give a single score. In effect this meant giving each occupation a weight of one. Since the subject must inevitably select lower status occupations as she increases her number of choices, the higher the summed score, the lower the aspiration level. The basic limitation of this method is that it is impossible to know from the summed score whether the occupations chosen are of low or high status.

2. To correct for this, a second index was derived by assigning weights to the seven occupations taken from the N.O.R.C. study according to their position in the rank order. Thus the highest status position, lawyer, was given a rank weight of 1.0 and the lowest a weight of 6.5 (store salesman and bus driver were tied for last place). Here again, the higher the score, the lower the aspiration level.

3. A third method of weighting the occupations was devised by taking the percentage of the entire sample of mothers who said that they would be satisfied with a particular occupation, and using the reciprocal of each percentage as the weight for that occupation. (The reciprocal was first multiplied by one thousand to eliminate decimals.) The mothers ranked the occupations somewhat differently than the N.O.R.C. ranking (assigning a higher status to bookkeeper and insurance agent and lower status to machinist and mail carrier). The assumption here is that the higher the percentage who answered "satisfied," the higher the status of the occupation. A score for each mother was obtained by summing the reciprocal weights for each occupation chosen. With this method, the highest status occupation is lawyer (score of 11.0), the lowest bus driver (48.0). All ten occupations were used in this index. The higher the subject's score, the lower her aspiration level.

Although these indexes differ somewhat, they provide very similar data on ethnic group vocational aspirations. Table 4 shows the same rank ordering of groups for all three indexes, in descending order as follows: Jews, Greeks, Protestants, Italians, French-Canadians, and Negroes. A series of $t$-tests of differences between group mean scores revealed differences and similarities much like those found for achievement motivation. Thus the Jews, Greeks, and Protestants show significantly higher mean scores (that is, they tend to be satisfied with fewer occupations and indicate satisfaction with only the higher status positions) than the Roman Catholic Italians and French-Canadians.[28] The mean score for Jews is significantly

[28] Similar Jewish-Italian differences are reported in F. L. Strodtbeck, M. McDonald, and B. C. Rosen, "Evaluation of Occupations: A Reflection of Jewish and Italian Mobility Differences," *American Sociological Review*, 22, October, 1957, 546–553.

higher than the scores for Protestants and Greeks, but there are no significant differences between Greeks and Protestants, or between Italians and French-Canadians. The mean score for Negroes is significantly lower than the scores for all other groups except French-Canadians. In examining the aspirations of Negroes it should be remembered that most of these occupations are considered highly desirable by many Negroes, given their severely limited occupational opportunities, so that their aspiration level may appear low only by "white" standards. There are, however, these problems: are the Negro mothers (83 per cent) in earnest in saying that they intend for their sons to go to college? And, if so, how is this to be reconciled with their low vocational aspirations?

*Table 4*—Mean Scores and Rank Position of Six Ethnic Groups Using Three Indexes of Vocational Aspiration*

| | INDEX OF VOCATIONAL ASPIRATION | | | |
| Ethnicity | Number satisfied | Rank weight | Reciprocal weight | N |
|---|---|---|---|---|
| French-Canadian | 6.60 (5) | 14.43 (5) | 119.90 (5) | 62 |
| Italian | 5.96 (4) | 12.66 (4) | 104.55 (4) | 74 |
| Greek | 4.70 (2) | 7.78 (2) | 73.51 (2) | 47 |
| Jew | 3.51 (1) | 6.02 (1) | 59.48 (1) | 57 |
| Negro | 6.95 (6) | 16.18 (6) | 138.74 (6) | 65 |
| Protestant | 5.28 (3) | 10.12 (3) | 88.19 (3) | 122 |

* Rank positions are shown by figures in parentheses.

Social class, too, is significantly and directly related to vocational aspiration—a familiar finding—*but it is not as significant as ethnicity*. Analysis of variance of data for each of the three indexes reveals that ethnicity accounts for more of the variance than social class. For example, when the number of occupations with which the mother would be satisfied for her son is used as an index of vocational aspiration, the F ratio for ethnicity is 12.41 ($P < .001$) as compared with a ratio of 9.92 for social class ($P < .001$). The same pattern holds for data derived from the other two indexes. Although ethnicity and class interact, each contributing to the differences between groups, the effects of class are more apparent at the middle class (Classes I-II-III) than at the working and lower class (Classes IV-V) levels.

As the question was worded in this study, in one sense it is misleading to speak of the "height" of vocational aspirations. For all groups have "high" aspirations in that most mothers are content to have their sons achieve a high status. The basic difference between groups is in the "floor," so to speak, which they place on their aspirations. For example, at least 80 per cent of the mothers of each ethnic group said that they would be satisfied to have their sons be lawyers, but only two per cent of the Greeks and seven per cent of the Jews were content to have their sons become bus drivers, as compared with 26 per cent of the French-Canadians and 43 per cent of the Negroes. Again, 12 per cent of the Jewish, 22 per cent of the

Protestant, and 29 per cent of the Greek mothers said that they would be satisfied to have their sons become department store salesmen, as compared with 48 per cent of the Italians, 51 per cent of the Negro, and 52 per cent of the French-Canadian mothers.

## SUMMARY

This paper examines differences in motivation, values, and aspirations of six racial and ethnic groups which may explain in part their dissimilar social mobility rates. Analysis of ethnographic and attitudinal and personality data suggests that these groups differed, and to some extent still differ, in their orientation toward achievement. The data show that the groups place different emphases upon independence and achievement training in the rearing of children. As a consequence, achievement motivation is more characteristic of Greeks, Jews, and white Protestants than of Italians, French-Canadians, and Negroes. The data also indicate that Jews, Greeks, and Protestants are more likely to possess achievement values and higher educational and vocational aspirations than Italians and French-Canadians. The values and educational aspirations of the Negroes are higher than expected, being comparable to those of Jews, Greeks, and white Protestants, and higher than those of the Italians and French-Canadians. Vocational aspirations of Negroes, however, are the lowest of any group in the sample. Social class and ethnicity interact in influencing motivation, values, and aspirations; neither can predict an individual's score. Ethnic differences persist when social class is controlled, but some of the differences between ethnic groups in motivations, values, and aspirations are probably also a function of their class composition.

# NEGRO AND WHITE CHILDREN'S

# PLANS FOR THEIR FUTURES

*Albert J. Lott and Bernice E. Lott*

## OUTLOOK

The Background and Outlook Questionnaire includes a number of items that attempt to assess the students' plans for the future, their perceived position within society, and their general degree of reality orientation. From answers to questions relevant to these points, information was obtained regarding what we have called "outlook" for the future. Discussion of the over-all findings will follow presentation of all the specific results.

### Plans for the Future: Residence

The students were asked to specify the state in which they *wanted* to live, and also to predict the place in which they actually *expected* to be living, in 10 years. Answers were categorized in terms of: Kentucky; Southern states (other than Kentucky); and other states. Table 1 indicates the number and proportion of responses in each category made by the total Negro and white groups in answer to both the "desire" and "expectation" questions. A "no-response" category, which can be interpreted as indicating uncertainty, was included in the data analysis.

Chi-square analyses of the data in Table 1 revealed a significant relationship between the Negro–white variable and both desired location. ($\chi^2 = 52.64$, $p < .001$) and expected location ($\chi^2 = 66.40$, $p < .001$). The great majority of the Negro students (59 per cent) wanted to leave Kentucky in favor of a non-Southern state; only 24 per cent wanted to remain in Kentucky, and 4 per cent desired to live in another Southern state.

Among the white students, 53 per cent desired to stay in Kentucky and an additional 18 per cent wished to move to another Southern state. The figures for expected location reveal the same basic difference between the Negro and white students, with 50 per cent of the former expecting to be in a non-Southern state in 10 years compared with only 9 per cent of the latter.

A comparison between the matched groups, with responses dichotomized into two categories, Southern states (including Kentucky) and other states, yielded similar results. A significantly smaller proportion of

*Table 1*—Desired and Expected Geographic Locations in Ten Years

| Subjects | Kentucky | DESIRED LOCATION<br>Southern<br>state | Other state* | No<br>response | N |
|---|---|---|---|---|---|
| Negro | | | | | |
| Frequencies | 28 | 5 | 68 | 15 | 116 |
| Proportions | .24 | .04 | .59 | .13 | |
| White | | | | | |
| Frequencies | 92 | 32 | 45 | 6 | 175 |
| Proportions | .53 | .18 | .26 | .03 | |
| Total | | | | | 291 |
| | | EXPECTED LOCATION | | | |
| Negro | | | | | |
| Frequencies | 42 | 3 | 58 | 13 | 116 |
| Proportions | .36 | .03 | .50 | .11 | |
| White | | | | | |
| Frequencies | 139 | 7 | 16 | 13 | 175 |
| Proportions | .79 | .04 | .09 | .07 | |
| Total | | | | | 291 |

\* Included in this category are choices of a foreign country. Three white students made such desired location responses.

the Negro than the white matched group both wanted to live in a Southern state ($\chi^2 = 13.53$, $p < .001$) and expected to ($\chi^2 = 17.28$, $p < .001$). The Negro college-bound group differed from the white college-bound group in precisely the same way (desired location, $\chi^2 = 27.04$, $p < .001$; expected location, $\chi^2 = 38.94$, $p < .001$). That more of the Negro students are eager to leave their home state for states outside the Southern region is, thus, clear.

## PLANS FOR THE FUTURE: OCCUPATION

Respondents were asked to name the occupation they both *desired* and *expected* to be employed at in 10 years. The data obtained for the boys are presented in Table 2, and for the girls in Table 3. Separate analyses were performed since vocational choice is expected to differ according to sex. The occupational categories utilized in ordering responses are as follows:

*1*] Professional I and business—for example, medicine, law, business ownership or management

*2*] Professional II—for example, social work, nursing, teaching, or the ministry

*3*] CSS—clerical, sales, or skilled trade jobs

*Table 2*—Occupations Desired and Expected in Ten Years by Males

| Subjects | Professional I and business | Professional II | CSS | Glamorous | No response | N |
|---|---|---|---|---|---|---|
| **DESIRED OCCUPATION** | | | | | | |
| Negro | | | | | | |
| Frequencies | 10 | 16 | 25 | 8 | 5 | 64 |
| Proportions | .16 | .25 | .39 | .12 | .08 | |
| White | | | | | | |
| Frequencies | 14 | 20 | 13 | 20 | 6 | 73 |
| Proportions | .19 | .27 | .18 | .27 | .09 | |
| Total | | | | | | 137 |
| **EXPECTED OCCUPATION** | | | | | | |
| Negro | | | | | | |
| Frequencies | 5 | 14 | 26 | 10 | 9 | 64 |
| Proportions | .08 | .22 | .40 | .16 | .14 | |
| White | | | | | | |
| Frequencies | 12 | 18 | 11 | 17 | 15 | 73 |
| Proportions | .16 | .25 | .15 | .23 | .21 | |
| Total | | | | | | 137 |

*Table 3*—Occupations Desired and Expected in Ten Years by Females

| Subjects | Professional I and business | Professional II | CSS | Glamorous | Housewife | No response | N |
|---|---|---|---|---|---|---|---|
| **DESIRED OCCUPATION** | | | | | | | |
| Negro | | | | | | | |
| Frequencies | 5 | 28 | 14 | 4 | 0 | 1 | 52 |
| Proportions | .10 | .54 | .27 | .07 | .00 | .02 | |
| White | | | | | | | |
| Frequencies | 5 | 32 | 22 | 17 | 25 | 1 | 102 |
| Proportions | .05 | .31 | .22 | .17 | .24 | .01 | |
| Total | | | | | | | 154 |
| **EXPECTED OCCUPATION** | | | | | | | |
| Negro | | | | | | | |
| Frequencies | 5 | 26 | 14 | 2 | 1 | 4 | 52 |
| Proportions | .10 | .50 | .27 | .04 | .02 | .07 | |
| White | | | | | | | |
| Frequencies | 3 | 24 | 17 | 10 | 40 | 8 | 102 |
| Proportions | .03 | .23 | .17 | .10 | .39 | .08 | |
| Total | | | | | | | 154 |

*4*] Glamorous—a job in the arts or other out-of-the-ordinary fields such as advertising, diplomacy, politics, and flying

*5*] Housewife.

No category for unskilled jobs was necessary since not a single one of the respondents made such a choice, either for desired or expected occupation.

The chi-squares obtained on the four sets of data are all significant (male desires, $\chi^2 = 9.70$, $p < .05$; male expectations, $\chi^2 = 12.26$, $p < .02$; female desires, $\chi^2 = 17.79$, $p < .01$; female expectations, $\chi^2 = 27.30$, $p < .001$).[1] Examination of Tables 2 and 3 reveals the direction of differences between the Negro and white seniors.

Negro males are more heavily concentrated in the CSS, and less heavily in the glamorous category, than the white males with respect to both desired and anticipated occupations. With respect to anticipated jobs, the professional I-business category has a proportionately greater white than Negro representation. As might be expected, when we move from desired to expected occupations there is a decline, within both the Negro and white male groups, in the number of high status occupations chosen and an increase in the number of no-responses (or uncertainties).

A comparison of white and Negro girls indicates that proportionately more of the latter desire top status occupations (professional I-business and professional II), but that fewer desire glamour jobs or the role of housewife. It is noteworthy that not one of the 52 Negro girls stated a desire to be a housewife in 10 years. The findings are similar with respect to expectations: proportionately more Negro than white girls expect to have top status jobs, and proportionately fewer expect to be housewives or be in a glamour job. Inspection of Table 3 indicates that the differences between desire and expectation responses by the females are small and due, mainly, to shifts in response on the part of the white girls rather than on the part of the Negroes.

Since the number of students in the two matched groups is small, male and female responses were not separated, and occupational choices were dichotomized into the categories of CSS and other. The differences between Negro and white responses to both the questions on desire and expectation were found to be nonsignificant. The Negro–white variable, in other words, in the case of these groups, matched on I.Q. and parent's occupation, and similar on other background indices, is not a discriminating one with respect to vocational choice.

This same lack of significance for the Negro–white variable was found when the desire and expectation responses of the college-bound males were analyzed. Only one of the 23 Negro boys and none of the 46 white boys wanted a CSS job, and only 3 Negro and 2 white males expected to be in one in 10 years; consequently the CSS category was excluded from consideration in analyzing the data. These students were, therefore, compared on choice of professional I, professional II, and glamorous jobs. The professional II category received the heaviest concentration of choices for both of the groups.

In analyzing job choices made by the college-bound girls the categories

---

[1] A no-response category was included in the expectation analyses but not in the analyses of desires because of the small number of such responses in the latter data.

of professional I-business and professional II were combined, since only a small number chose the former. The Negro–white variable proved not to be a reliable one with respect to the choices made by the girls, as was also the case for the college-bound boys. For the female data, however, the obtained chi-squares fell just short of the 5 per cent level of confidence. Proportionately more of the college-bound Negro than white girls chose the higher status occupations, while none of the Negro girls either expected to be or desired to be a housewife or to pursue a glamour occupation. In addition, a greater proportion of the Negro than white girls chose CSS occupations.

### Identity of Desire and Education

It was possible for the students to respond differently or identically to the questions regarding their expectations and their desires. To see whether or not the Negro and white groups differed in the proportion who anticipated doing what they wanted to do, a frequency count was made of those seniors whose expectations for both residence and occupation were identical with their desires and of those whose expectations and desires were disparate. These data are shown in Table 4.

*Table 4*—Number of Individuals whose Occupational and Residence Expectations are Identical with Their Desires

| Subjects | Identical | Not identical | N |
|---|---|---|---|
| Males | | | |
| Negro | | | |
| Frequencies | 29 | 35 | 64 |
| Proportions | .45 | .55 | |
| White | | | |
| Frequencies | 37 | 36 | 73 |
| Proportions | .51 | .49 | |
| Total | | | 137 |
| Females | | | |
| Negro | | | |
| Frequencies | 31 | 21 | 52 |
| Proportions | .60 | .40 | |
| White | | | |
| Frequencies | 40 | 62 | 102 |
| Proportions | .39 | .61 | |
| Total | | | 154 |

The obtained chi-square for males is not significant. For the females, a reliable relationship with the Negro–white variable was found ($\chi^2 = 5.78$, $p < .02$). A greater proportion of the Negro than white girls expected to do what they desired to do whereas there was no substantial difference in this respect between the Negro and white boys.

No significant difference was found between the matched groups. The

Negro–white variable also proved to be not reliable for both the college-bound males and the college-bound females.

### Immediate Postgraduation Plans

In addition to being asked to think of themselves 10 years in the future, the seniors were questioned about their plans immediately following graduation. The answers, placed within the categories of college, vocational training, job, and armed forces, are shown in Table 5.

*Table 5*—Immediate Postgraduation Plans

| Subjects | College | CATEGORIES Vocational training | Job | Armed forces | N |
|---|---|---|---|---|---|
| **Males** | | | | | |
| Negro | | | | | |
| Frequencies | 23 | 17 | 10 | 14 | 64 |
| Proportions | .36 | .26 | .16 | .22 | |
| White | | | | | |
| Frequencies | 47 | 0 | 17 | 8 | 72 |
| Proportions | .65 | .00 | .24 | .11 | |
| Total | | | | | 136 |
| **Females** | | | | | |
| Negro | | | | | |
| Frequencies | 18 | 22 | 10 | | 50* |
| Proportions | .36 | .44 | .20 | | |
| White | | | | | |
| Frequencies | 48 | 19 | 30 | | 97† |
| Proportions | .49 | .20 | .31 | | |
| Total | | | | | 147 |

\* Omitted is one subject who said she planned to stay at home.
† Three girls planned to stay at home and one planned to get married.

The Negro–white variable is significantly related to the immediate plans of both the boys ($\chi^2 = 27.80$, $p < .10$) and the girls ($\chi^2 = 9.84$, $p < .01$). A larger proportion of the white than Negro males were planning either to attend college or to get a job right after graduation. These two categories together include 89 per cent of the white males in contrast to only 52 per cent of the Negro males. The other Negro males were, instead, planning either direct vocational training or entrance into one of the armed services. It is assumed that the services are viewed by the students as means for training rather than as permanent career areas, an assumption supported by our interview data. Eleven per cent of the white boys said they were going to join the armed forces, but it is particularly noteworthy that not one of the 73 white males indicated plans for direct vocational training.

The findings for the females are similar to those for the males. A smaller proportion of the Negro than white girls were planning to enter college or to get a job. Instead, vocational training was indicated by 44 per cent of the Negro girls in contrast to only 20 per cent of the white girls.

The same direction of results was obtained for the small matched groups, although the Negro–white difference in choice distribution did not prove to be statistically significant. Of the Negroes, 45 per cent, versus 59 per cent of the whites, were planning to attend college. Since the frequencies in the other categories were small, they were combined, and the Negro and white matched subjects were, therefore, compared only with respect to plans for college versus other plans.

All of the individuals in the college-bound groups were, of course, planning to enter college right after high school, this having been the criterion for their placement within the college subgroups.

Since the students had been asked to indicate both their long-range vocational plans and their immediate plans, it was possible for the investigators to put these two responses side by side and to make a judgment about their relationship. A judgment of positive relationship was made if the student's plans seemed to be in line with, or could lead to, his desired vocation, as for example, in a case where college is the immediate plan and teaching is the desired occupational goal. A senior who wants to be a dancer but is planning nurse's training illustrates a negative relationship. An indeterminate category was used for those cases in which a confident judgment could not be made.

*Table 6*—Judged Relationship between Desired Vocation and Immediate Post-graduation Plans

| Subjects | Positive | Negative | Indeterminate | N |
|---|---|---|---|---|
| Negro | | | | |
| Frequencies | 85 | 26 | 5 | 116 |
| Proportions | .73 | .23 | .04 | |
| White | | | | |
| Frequencies | 135 | 31 | 9 | 175 |
| Proportions | .77 | .18 | .05 | |
| Total | | | | 291 |

The relevant data are presented in Table 6. No significant relationship was found with the Negro–white variable, and it can be seen that a similar proportion of individuals within both groups was judged to have made plans that were congruent with long-range occupational aspiration. This similarity was also found between the Negro and white matched groups.

### Class Placement

One further outlook comparison was made. Students were asked to place themselves in one of three socioeconomic classes, working, middle, or upper, with no description of these classes given beyond the simple labels. The responses to this question are tabulated in Table 7. A reliable relationship between class placement and the Negro–white variable was found ($\chi^2 = 53.77$, $p < .001$), a greater proportion of the Negro than white subjects having placed themselves in the working class and a greater proportion of the white than Negro subjects in the middle class. Only a very small proportion of both groups see themselves as part of the upper class.

Because of the small number of students in the matched groups, responses to the class placement item were dichotomized into working class versus a combined middle and upper class category. This latter is primarily a middle class category since few upper class responses were given. Again, the Negro–white variable proved to be significant ($\chi^2 = 3.98$, $p < .05$).

*Table 7*—Social Class in which Subjects Placed Themselves

| Subjects | Upper | CLASS Middle | Working | N |
|---|---|---|---|---|
| Negro | | | | |
| Frequencies | 8 | 40 | 63 | 111 |
| Proportions | .07 | .36 | .57 | |
| White | | | | |
| Frequencies | 8 | 137 | 30 | 175 |
| Proportions | .05 | .78 | .17 | |
| Total | | | | 286 |

The majority of the Negroes and a greater proportion than the whites indicated working class identification (61 per cent versus 29 per cent). For the college-bound students this general difference in class placement between Negroes and whites is again maintained, although the proportion of Negroes who identified themselves with the working class is less than the proportions found within either the total or the matched Negro groups. In the college-bound group 38 per cent of the Negroes and 11 per cent of the white students placed themselves in the working class. Middle and upper class responses were combined and account for the remainder of each of the two groups. A chi-square analysis of these data revealed a statistically reliable Negro–white difference ($\chi^2 = 13.94$, $p < .001$).

### Summary and Discussion

The comparisons between the Negro and white students on outlook suggest that the Negro youth are looking toward the future with a generally realistic view of themselves and of their opportunities in contemporary society.

One important indication of this is that a vast majority of the Negro students intended to leave their home state and the South in favor of some other state. This was found for the total Negro group as well as for both the matched and college-bound subgroups. Among these other areas, New York, California, and the District of Columbia rank highest. That these are places in the United States in which Negroes have better than average occupational opportunities is well known. It appears, then, that the Negro students are very much aware of the limited opportunities available to them in Kentucky and in the South, and that they also know where their chances are better for a higher standard of living.

The tendency in recent years for Negroes to leave Kentucky, suggested by our findings, is confirmed by an analysis of 1950 census data by Coleman, Pryor, and Christiansen (1956). These investigators have reported that, as is true of most other Southern states,[2] the Negro population of Kentucky has been decreasing. In 1950 there were fewer Negroes in the state than there had been at any time during the past 50 years, and those Negroes who continued to live in Kentucky represented, by and large, an older population. Compared with the general distribution of U.S. Negroes, the Kentucky Negro distribution had, in other words, proportionately more persons over 39 and fewer persons under 35 years of age. This is attributed to both a low birth rate and a heavy out-migration of young adults. Indicative of this out-migration is the fact that almost 40 per cent of the living Negroes born in Kentucky were living outside the state in 1950 as compared with about 30 per cent of the white persons born in the state. These facts serve to increase confidence in the reliability of our results.

Our findings with respect to occupational aspirations and expectations highlight, again, the reality orientation of the Negro seniors. Negroes and whites differ significantly in the distribution of both their occupational desires and their occupational expectations. Whereas 27 per cent of the white boys, for example, desired a glamour job, such as pilot, politician, and so on, this was true of only 12 per cent of the Negro boys. On the other hand, 39 per cent of the Negro boys, in contrast to 18 per cent of the whites, desired a job in the CSS category. The proportions of Negro and white males choosing business or professional careers were relatively similar (41 per cent of the Negroes and 46 per cent of the whites). It is of interest to note, however, that only 30 per cent of the former actually expected to be in such a position in contrast to 41 per cent of the latter.

The choices of the Negro males are clearly for those fields where their opportunities are, at the moment, greatest: electronics rather than politics, auto repair rather than advertising, and so on. The emphasis by the Negro males on middle status occupations is clear from the fact that 40 per cent of them expected, in 10 years, to be working at a CSS job in contrast to 15 per cent of the white males. This is interpreted as representing a realistic appraisal of the Amercan scene in combination with a high,

---

[2] It has been estimated that "by the end of the present decade, if the movement continues, half the total Negro population of this country will be living outside the 13 traditionally southern states" (Jones, 1957).

rather than low, level of aspiration. Within the higher status occupations, for example, choices for the more attainable professions, such as teaching or the ministry, exceeded those for the less attainable, such as law or medicine. This was true for the white males as well as the Negro. Furthermore, not one of the seniors, Negro or white, either desired or expected to be doing lowest status, unskilled work.

A comparison of the white and Negro girls indicates that proportionately more of the Negro females are interested in all the occupational categories with the striking exceptions of the glamorous category (desired by only 7 per cent of the Negro, in contrast to 17 per cent of the white, girls and expected by 4 per cent of the Negro, versus 10 per cent of the white, girls) and the housewife category (desired by none of the 52 Negro females and expected by only 1). The majority of the Negro girls (54 per cent) chose a profession such as social work, teaching, and nursing, while only 27 per cent chose a clerical-sales-trade vocation. This is again interpreted as indicating knowledge of real opportunities, since job possibilities for Negro women in the latter fields are not nearly so good as they are in the former.

The striking lack of interest shown by the Negro girls in home-making as a primary goal may, at first consideration, be surprising. This, again, however, can be viewed as an accurate reflection of reality. Since the majority of the Negro mothers were reported to be employed outside the home, it is not difficult to understand how a young Negro girl might come to see herself as a source of income, first, and take for granted the secondary role of housewife. In other words, we do not interpret the lack of choice for the housewife role as indicating no desire to marry, although this is certainly a possibility that should be explored in subsequent research.

That our data on occupational aspirations and expectations are primarily a reflection of differences in present background conditions between the Negro and white groups rather than a reflection of the Negro–white variable, per se, is a conclusion which is supported by the results obtained when the matched groups are compared and when the male college-bound groups are compared. Both comparisons yielded no significant differences between the Negroes and the whites in either job desired or expected. Thus, in our small matched subgroups the proportions choosing CSS jobs versus other jobs are roughly the same, for Negroes and whites. Between Negro and white males who were planning to attend college there is also no reliable difference in distribution of occupational choices. The majority of choices for both of these latter groups falls, understandably, in the highest status categories. With respect to occupational choices of the college-bound females, the Negro–white variable again failed to be significant although, as was mentioned earlier, in the case of both expected and desired occupations the obtained chi-squares fell just short of the 5 per cent level of confidence. The college-bound Negro girls, like the total Negro female group, tended not to choose either a glamorous occupation or to see themselves as housewives. Thus, of the general differences found between our Negro and white students on occupational desires and anticipations, those which may truly be a reflection of the complex Negro–white variable rather than socioeconomic factors are the differences between the females, namely, the total neglect of housewife as a goal by the Negro girls and their decidedly lesser interest in careers in the arts and other off-beat fields.

Our results on occupational choice are, by and large, contrary to reports found elsewhere. Ginzberg, for example, in his book, *The Negro Potential*, has written (1956, p. 108):

For decades the Negro had little basis for rational planning of his preparation for work. He set himself either no goals or badly skewed goals. As a result of his background, the ambitious young Negro is even more likely than the white youth to scorn skilled work and to overestimate the importance of achieving status through white collar or professional employment.

We did not find this to be the case. Perhaps Ginzberg has accurately described a past situation that is now somewhat different, as a function, we suspect, of improved Negro education and of changing conditions, in general, which make realistic goals for the Negro youth not so distasteful that they cannot be faced. Another possibility is that our results cannot be generalized beyond border state communities because in such communities the probability of developing realistic aspirations is, for some reason, increased. This has been suggested by Frazier. In his report of Negro youth in the thirties, in Washington, D.C., and Louisville, Kentucky, two "middle state" communities, Frazier noted (1940, p. 266) that "in the border states, where the separate schools approximate more or less the white schools in equipment and personnel, education stimulates in Negro pupils about the same aims and ambitions as in the white." On the basis of our data, we would add that this seems to be most true where the Negroes and whites also share some important background characteristic.

Many of the investigations that have reported "skewed" aspirations for Negro youth were carried on prior to the Second World War or were studies of youth in deeper Southern states or both. For example, 129 high school and college students in Greensboro, North Carolina, were reported, in 1941 (Atwood et al.), to have "aimed high, showing a preference for the professional positions that seem to guarantee both high income and social prestige." An even more dramatic example of unrealistic aspirations was reported by Johnson (1941) in his study of more than 2000 Negro youth in the rural South. Over 65 per cent of the girls and almost 39 per cent of the boys questioned about their occupational preferences, chose one of the professions. Johnson concluded that, "the gap between occupational expectation and reality is at present so great as to suggest that the expectation itself borders on fantasy" (p. 223). Another early study, by Hyte (cf. Antonovsky and Lerner, 1957) of Negro high school boys in Indiana and Kentucky in 1936 obtained similar results. In their study 70 per cent of the boys, for example, were reported as expecting to attend college; 75 per cent were reported as aspiring to professional jobs.

A 1941 report by Witty et al. (cf. Antonovsky and Lerner, 1957) represents an exception to the general direction of findings in these early studies. This investigation compared a large group of Negro and white high school students in Chicago and the occupational preferences of the Negro youth were found to be no higher than those of the white. This is what we found to be true when comparing Negro and white groups matched for I.Q. and parent's occupation, as well as when comparing Negro and white groups matched on the basis of plans for college. Other studies, however, in which matched groups have been utilized and which have been conducted in recent years, have presented evidence of higher aspirations among Negro than white youth. One such investigation, by Boyd (1952), found higher occupational ambitions within a group of Negro than white elementary school children in Oregon. In another, the Elmira, New York, study (Antonovsky and Lerner, 1957), which investigated youth from a low socioeconomic background, one of the major findings was that the Negro youth had a higher level of occupational aspiration than the white.

It is difficult to reconcile our findings with many of those reviewed above. With the possible exception of the Negro girls, we found no evidence that the occupational goals of the Negro students were any higher than those of the white students. Instead, we found that professional and business occupations were chosen by roughly the same proportion of Negro as white boys but that a far greater proportion of the Negro males chose CSS jobs and a lesser proportion chose glamour jobs. When our Negro and white college-bound groups and when our Negro and white matched groups were compared, these differences in distribution of occupational choices disappeared.

What is responsible for the apparent reality orientation within the Negro group investigated in the present study, as compared with groups studied earlier? The answer to this question probably requires consideration of the special characteristics of border state communities, changing patterns of job discrimination, changes in the degree of contact with, and awareness of, the general community on the part of Negro youth, and so on. That our results are reliable is strongly suggested by the totality of findings on outlook which, together, point to a relatively realistic self-appraisal on the part of the Negro youth studied, contrary to what previous investigations have led us to expect.

Another recent investigation provides data relevant to the present discussion. Rosen (1959) studied vocational aspirations within six ethnic groups living in northeastern communities (French-Canadians, Southern Italians, Greeks, East European Jews, Negroes, and native-born white Protestants) by questioning the mothers of eight-to-fourteen-year-old boys.

Each mother was asked if she would be satisfied if her son was a lawyer, druggist, jewelry-store owner, machinist, bank teller, insurance agent, bookkeeper, mail carrier, department-store salesman, or bus driver. Mothers who restricted their satisfaction responses to the first few vocations (top status) were said to have higher aspirations for their sons than mothers who indicated satisfaction with a greater range. On this basis the Negro sample was found to be lower in aspiration level than any of the other ethnic groups, except the French-Canadian. However, because all of the vocations presented are obviously high in status when compared with jobs that Negroes generally hold, interpretation of these findings is equivocal.

There is some indication in our data that the Negro girls may be less realistic about the future than the white girls. They tended, as was noted previously, not to see themselves as housewives. In addition, a significantly greater proportion of the Negro than white girls expected to achieve their desires with respect to residence and job (60 per cent of the former versus 39 per cent of the latter). Such a difference was not found between the white and Negro boys. An alternative explanation of this difference between the girls is that it indicates, perhaps, a greater degree of determination on the part of the Negro girls to attain their personal objectives. It will be recalled that the Negro females scored generally lower on esthetic value, and higher on the theoretical and political values than the white females. The Negro girls thus seem to be relatively more masculine or "hard-headed" in their interests and orientations, and relatively more concerned with attainment outside the home. This is congruent with the proposition that they are more determined than the white girls to do what they want to do, although it is probably also true that they are less realistic in estimating their chances for success.

Proportionately more Negro than white males were planning vocational training or entrance into the armed forces (48 per cent vs. 11 per cent) right after graduation, while proportionately less were planning to go to college (36 per cent vs. 65 per cent) or to get a job (16 per cent vs. 24 per cent). These results, again, clearly suggest a sophisticated and knowledge-able view on the part of the Negro youth regarding his present opportunities. A job for him right after high school graduation without additional training would mean low pay and low status work. Thus vocational training rather than college was the answer for many. This is a more possible and realistic plan. The attraction of the armed forces for the Negro male senior can also be safely attributed to its recent role of providing free vocational education as well as equal opportunity and status.

The immediate plans of the Negro and white girls were also found to differ, in similar directions to those found for the boys. Proportionately fewer Negro than white females planned to attend college (36 per cent vs. 49 per cent) or to get a job (20 per cent vs. 39 per cent) while proportionately more intended to get some kind of vocational training (49 per cent vs. 20

per cent). The differences between the Negro and white girls in the proportions planning an immediate job must be assumed to have some relationship to the fact that, whereas a white high school graduate can expect to get a fairly respectable job in the community as a typist or clerk or a salesgirl, a Negro girl of similar educational attainment cannot.

Judgments were made by the investigators of the relationship between the students' desired vocational goals and their immediate plans. On this comparison the Negro youth emerged no less sober, nor less aware of realities, than the white youth. The Negro group does not differ significantly from the white group in the proportion of individuals whose immediate plans were judged to be positively related to their stated aspirations.

One final indication in our data of the Negro youth's reality orientation is his tendency to see himself as belonging to the working class. This is in sharp contrast to the predominant middle-class self-placement of the white students. Fifty-seven per cent of the Negroes identified themselves as members of the working class whereas only 17 per cent of the whites did so. Seventy-eight per cent of the latter group placed themselves in the middle class in contrast to 36 per cent of the Negroes. When one considers the differences which exist between the Negro and white groups with respect to occupation of major breadwinner, for example, this difference in class placement appears reasonable and accurate. That this reliable Negro–white difference in class placement was maintained between the matched groups and also the college-bound groups is of especial interest.

What does it mean to think of oneself as belonging to the working class or to the middle class? From the work by Centers (1949) on class identification we find that, according to people in general,[3] the chief qualifications for membership in the middle class are a "fair amount of money, a comfortable standard of living, a good education and proprietorship of some sort. Minor criteria such as security in one's job and decent family connections play some part also." On the other hand, having a low income and being an employee or wage earner, having a lack of education and training, and a lack of security, are listed as differentiating members of the working class from others. Although surely not aware of these explicit criteria, both the Negro and the white seniors made intuitive choices which indicate that they perceive their relative positions in the contemporary social scene with remarkable clarity.

Certain of the differences in outlook which exist between the total Negro and white groups disappear when the college-bound groups and when the matched groups are compared. The differences which do not hold between the matched groups are those with respect to occupational goals and immediate postgraduation plans. Similarly, occupational goals do not reliably differentiate between Negro and white college-bound males

[3] Approximately 1100 men, representing a cross-section of the white male population in the United States, were interviewed.

or females, although, in the latter case, inspection of the data suggests that the greater avoidance by the Negro females of housewife and glamorous job choices may be a real rather than chance phenomenon. The outlook differences which are maintained between the Negro and white matched and college-bound groups are those regarding social class identification and choice of geographic residence. These findings would seem to justify the conclusion that these latter two components of outlook are truly a function of the complex Negro–white variable, whereas occupational goals (especially for males), and immediate plans, are more probably related to background factors of a generally socioeconomic nature.

References to *Negro and White Children's Plans for Their Futures*

Antonovsky, A., and M. Lerner. *Negro and White Youth in Elmira*, New York, State Commission against Discrimination, Nov. 1957.

Atwood, J. H., D. W. Wyatt, V. J. Davis, and I. D. Walker. *Thus be Their Destiny*, Washington, D.C., American Council on Education, 1941.

Boyd, G. F. The Levels of Aspiration of White and Negro Children in a Non-segregated Elementary School. *Journal of Social Psychology*, **36,** 1952, 191–196.

Centers, R. *The Psychology of Social Classes*, Princeton, N.J., Princeton University Press, 1949.

Frazier, E. F. *Negro Youth at the Crossways*, Washington, D.C., American Council on Education, 1940.

Ginzberg, E. *The Negro-Potential*, New York, Columbia University Press, 1956.

Johnson, C. S. *Growing Up in the Black Belt*, Washington, D.C., American Council on Education, 1941.

Rosen, B. C. Race, Ethnicity, and the Achievement Syndrome. *American Sociological Review*, **24,** 1959, 46–60.

# iv

---

# *Familial Factors*
# *and Environment*

## FAMILY ORGANIZATION

"I think it is very important to talk to parents as much as possible, but I don't seem to do it very well. I always have mixed feelings about it. It is pathetic to see how grateful a parent is to hear the least good thing about his child." Thus speaks one teacher in the first selection, "Parent Conferences are Always Rough."

It is commonplace among educators to say that part of the job of any teacher is knowing and working with families of children taught. However, this idea is sometimes more frequently proposed than practiced. To you, the teacher in the inner city of the metropolis, knowledge of and relations with the parents of your children is crucial because the environment of each child may differ so much from your own. The single group that is dominant in every child's situation is his family. It is, therefore, imperative that you as a teacher of children in the metropolis know what their family backgrounds are.

In the private world of the family each child you teach is trained to

363

enter the public world of the school, the neighborhood, and eventually the community. The kinds of families children are born into influence the ways in which they are readied for their roles outside. Arensberg and Kimball compare two contrasting communities in "West End and Crestwood Heights" in terms of family organization, transmission of culture through child-rearing, the relations with the outside world of work and school. In West End, a working-class Italian section of Boston, a form of social organization called the peer-group society is found.(22) This is a subculture in which "during adulthood, the family is its most important component." Adult West Enders spend almost as much time with siblings, in-laws, and cousins—that is, with relatives of the same sex and age—as with their spouses, and more time than with parents, aunts, and uncles. Limited participation beyond the family circle results in viewing the outside world as hostile or at best simply incompatible with the peer-group type of family.

In Crestwood Heights, (53) an upper middle-class suburb populated by Jews and Gentiles, one finds a "family of parents and children, isolated from its kin (often socially as well as geographically), temporarily anchored in its own separate dwelling and dependent upon the success of the father's career for its status and its future." Unlike the West Enders, the family maintains a direct relationship between itself and the outside world. Work in the outside world is valued as an activity that proves the value of the family and the status to which it belongs.

The effects of these two forms of family organization on you and the school are directly opposite. To the child from Crestwood Heights, the school is simply an extension of the family. To the child from West End, the school is a part of the public world that may be potentially destructive to his way of life. The authors suggest that the continued inability of middle-class institutions to penetrate or take root in the environment of West End is due to the fact that were they successful, the peer-group family system would be disrupted.

Ethnic and social class factors influence, in addition, the internal routines of life developed in different families. Bossard, in "Rituals in Family Living," describes the styles of life evolved in varied classes and explains these by saying "One aspect of these three ways of life may, at the outset, explain a good deal about certain variations in the rituals to be described. In these middle-class families, school and business hours coincide very closely. For the most part all the family must be up together at the same time, and leave home at nearly the same time. In a home not cramped, but not spacious either, this leads to one specific type of situation. In upper- and lower-class homes, on the contrary, the member's schedules do not coincide so closely. The business hours of father and working children are often at very different times, and school hours at yet another. In the lower-class home, cramped for space, this has one meaning; in the upper, with separate rooms and with servants quite another."

You can see that families can be and are organized differently according to the ethnic and status groups to which they belong. It should be apparent that children from these varied family experiences come to school with different understandings of the world. The lack of privacy and absence of schedules may make the public world of the school, with its emphasis on subordination to group standards and demands for punctuality, particularly difficult for the child from a poor home. In addition, the "Dick-and-Jane" type of family common in the curriculum of some schools may be totally removed from the experiences with families some of your children have had.(33)

Too often teachers assume that the middle-class family they knew as children or copied as successful aspirants to the middle class is the universal and, for some, the best pattern of family organization. But, as indicated in a previous section, even our monogamous form of marriage is in the minority in a world in which most societies practice polygamy.(19) We are also prone to believe that the partrilineal family as we know it is the natural form of tracing descent. However, there are many cultures in the world which are matrilineal, tracing descent and property through the mother's line. We sometimes feel that the nuclear family, composed of parents and their children, is the best kind of family. But many societies in the world find an extended family organization more acceptable. In such families, the child may live with many kin including grandparents, cousins, and other relatives.(38)

Anthropologists have done much to reduce ethnocentricism—or belief that one's way of life is best. Their study of kinship indicates that a child can be successfully raised with a number of mothers and fathers as defined by a particular culture. A child can be raised in a world that values clan above family. In Israel, for example, the child of the *Kibbutz* is raised in an environment in which central nursery schools largely replace family units.(59) However, we do not have to leave America to find different family patterns. The various ethnic groups which have contributed to our culture have brought with them or have evolved since arrival different ways of living in the family as can be seen in the West End of Boston or in any metropolis in our nation.

For example, Negro American families are often centered on the female. Historically, through the institution of slavery, the woman came to represent continuity in the family.(20) Lewis, in "The Changing Negro Family," quotes statistics indicating that female heads of families are still more prevalent today. He proposes, however, that the meaning of this fact for child-rearing and other family processes is insufficiently understood at this time. Nevertheless, it is more likely that the Negro child in your classroom comes from a family in which the father may be missing or secondary in central importance. This is more probable if the child is from a lower socioeconomic level because the role of the father becomes more dominant in middle-class Negro families.

The Puerto Rican child in your classroom is, on the other hand, more likely to come from a family in which the father is the center. Padilla, in *Up From Puerto Rico*, states, "The lines of authority in a family are supposed to radiate from the father, as center, to the mother and thence from the older to the younger children." The male in this cultural pattern is dominant, with wife and children subordinated to his authority, which is clearly defined for all. The father, for example, is not expected to tell the wife and children where he is going when he leaves the home. The mother, on the other hand, is expected to be explicit both to the father and in his absence to the children about her destination outside the home.

With time, these ethnic family constellations change. With urbanization in New York, Puerto Ricans have come to distinguish between "ancient" and "modern" families. The family that is rigidly controlled by the parent is considered ancient and different from the more flexible "modern" families. The effect of social change on the family in terms of migration, urbanization, and acculturation creates stresses on family members and on the unit as a whole. Rose Hum Lee, in "Chinese Culture, Social Organization and Personality," describes the traditional extended family system with its emphasis on clan. She indicates the disruption of this form of family: "For some time, the younger Chinese have learned to prize bravery and patriotism before clan and family associations, individualism, frankness, and self-assertion. The tendency of the older Chinese to conceive of China as she once was has caused many elders and leaders to impart norms and values that are unrealistic. This flight from reality stems from the inability of persons reared in a clan-oriented society to separate national, family, or district issues from personal issues."

The effects of acculturation and urbanization on the family are far-reaching. Lewis states that "Increases in illegitimacy rates among Negroes and in the proportion participating in the Aid to Dependent Children program are associated with recent increases in urbanization . . . There has been a tendency for the non-white rate to be higher in Northern urban centers than the estimated non-white percentage for the entire country including the Southern states." The process of change influences the ways in which families are organized and the methods they use in socializing children for roles in society. When change is, in addition, associated with low income, the urban family is particularly vulnerable to difficulties.

## SOCIALIZATION OF CHILDREN

However, some educators are too prone to blame families with problems for all the school difficulties children in the metropolis encounter. It is sometimes easier for the teacher to explain a child's learning problems as a result of his family than as a product of the teacher's or school's inability to help him. Perhaps the first article in this section, "I Want to Get Out," will help you see family problems from the perspective of three women who raise their children in slum neighborhoods. For example, the first mother interviewed says, "And the kids, you know, they don't understand. You don't just tell them there ain't no money for this and that. It's not like when they were little."

Your work as a teacher can be greatly enhanced if you increase your understanding of the feelings and problems of parents and the ways in which their own ethnic and societal backgrounds interact with the pressures of change and the heartaches of poverty. And most important of all, in order to help your children you must understand how their families raise them in relation to these environmental factors.

Bronfenbrenner in "Socialization and Social Class Through Time and Space," reviews research studies conducted to determine class differences in the training of children. In general, the author concludes that the bulk of evidence collected suggests that lower-class parents are less permissive toward the child's expressed needs and wishes in such diverse areas as oral behavior, toilet accidents, dependency, sex, aggressiveness, and freedom of movement outside the home. The middle-class parent has higher expectations for the child and trains him to accept more responsibilities about the home and to progress further in school. Parents from this class are more likely to rely on discipline involving the threat of loss of love, as isolation, reasoning, and appeals to guilt while lower-class parents are more likely to resort to physical punishment.

Not all research findings reviewed, however, are congruent. For example, the earlier study of Davis and Havighurst found middle-class parents to be more restrictive in child-training than lower-class parents.(16) Then several years later, Sears and his colleagues found the reverse, that lower-class parents were more restrictive in training.(52) This contradiction is resolved by Bronfenbrenner who concludes, "Class differences in feeding, weaning, and toilet training show a clear and consistent trend. From about 1930 till the end of World War II, working class mothers were uniformly more permissive than those of the middle class. . . . After World War II, however, there has been a definite reversal in direction; now it is the middle-class mother who is more permissive . . . Shifts in the pattern of infant care—especially on the part of middle-class mothers— show a striking correspondence to the changes in practice advocated in successive editions of U. S. Children's Bureau publications and similar sources of expert opinion . . . socialization practices are most likely to be altered in those segments of society which have most ready access to agencies or agents of change . . ."

We now know that change over time affects parents of different classes differentially. However, we are still left with many unresolved issues in the determination of how families from different positions in society raise their children. There is further need for clarification of terms used and activities subsumed under words like "permissive." As Langner points out in his article in the third section of this volume, permissive attitudes toward aggression from children, for example, must be understood in terms of the target of the aggression. His data indicate that aggression against parents is more often permitted at higher social levels, whereas aggression against non-family members is condoned or even encouraged at lower levels.

Wortis, in "Child-Rearing Practices in a Low Socioeconomic Group," presents evidence from a recent longitudinal study conducted over a five-year period that also indicates a complex relationship between factors rated as restrictive or permissive in child training. The author states, ". . . mothers who used a great deal of corporal punishment to enforce obedience were also permissive about matters that did not concern them. A relative indifference to manners and cleanliness at age 5 years went along with our previous finding that these were not areas of great concern to the mother at age $2\frac{1}{2}$ years. However, in areas where she was concerned, as in permission for aggression against the parent she was in fact very restrictive." It is clear that the parent-child relationship is a complex interaction of many factors that are influenced by environment differently. As a teacher, it is necessary to understand the complexity of these factors and to avoid over-simplification with generalized labels if you wish to help the children you teach.

One of the most important single variables to consider is the effect of family experiences on children of different sexes. McKinley in "Status and the Socialized Son," presents research indicating that the son of a lower-class family is less likely to identify with his father as the person he admires or resembles most. The author believes that this lack of identification with the lower-class father is a "consequence of his poverty in resources and power in society and the resulting emotional distance, lack of authority in the family, and severity in dealing with the son." The mother appears to be the more important figure of identification for the boy from lower socioeconomic levels.

This may be particularly the case in the large number of homes in which the father is absent, leaving the son with no adult male image to emulate. As Lewis indicates in the reading considered earlier in this introduction, the statistics for Negro broken homes is disproportionately high, but we are still not sure of the effect on children. McCord in "Some effects of Paternal Absence on Male Children," presents evidence which suggests, however, that behavior problems of white boys from poor homes in which fathers are missing are not necessarily a direct result of such absence. The investigator concludes, ". . . many of the effects often presumed to result from paternal absence can, largely, be attributed to certain parental characteristics—intense conflict, rejection, and deviance—which occur more commonly in broken families." A generally unstable environment, a mother who is rejecting or deviant, the boy's age when the father leaves, the replacement with a substitute are all factors found to influence boys from homes with no fathers. Again, we face the complexity of understanding the effects of family organization and training on children. You, as a teacher, must have a wide range of facts about a family before any child's problems can be attributed to paternal absence or to any other single factor *per se*.

Among children in our huge urban centers, there are also a large number who experience maternal deprivation from either the complete absence of a mother-person or from a relationship with a mother-person that is discontinued or insecure. Under the auspices of the World Health Organization, the conclusion reached from a careful assessment of all research conducted on the effects of maternal deprivation is simply that adverse results on children's development occur for a longer or shorter time depending on the point at which deprivation is relieved. There is little doubt that family disorganization in which maternal absence or inadequacy is paramount will have some negative effects on children. Although some critics maintain that it is stimulus deprivation as such that is experienced, there is considerable evidence to show that the interaction between child and mother is crucial to the child.(62)

It is important to note, however, that every culture or subculture develops a particular system of maternal care. If this includes a number of kin who are defined as acceptable mother-persons, the child who is cared for by more than one mother does not suffer ill effects. The Wortis article in this section indicates that only one-third of the Negro children in the study had been cared for exclusively by their own mothers. The other children had been cared for by an average of two mother-persons with 25 per cent of the total group cared for by three persons or more, excluding baby-sitters. This fact by itself does not necessarily mean a discontinuity or inadequacy in maternal care since the subculture involved has historically tended toward a wider kinship network in which many kin are involved in maternal care. There are, therefore, many ways of viewing the problem of maternal deprivation or inadequacy and again it is not possible to assume that any child in your classroom who has experienced a different pattern of maternal care is having problems due to this fact alone.

A related question about maternal care has been debated over the past few decades since women began to work outside the home. In general, research findings indicate no ill effects on children, although there are some conflicting results. Douvan, in "Impact of Employment of Mothers by Social Class," attempts to resolve some of the contradictory evidence by considering the mediating influence of family position in different strata in our society. She finds, "A part-time work commitment has a relatively stable meaning and implication in both the middle and working classes, but full-time maternal employment apparently depends upon different motivational sources in the two groups and has distinct meaning for family integration."

Girls more than boys, and girls from lower-class homes rather than middle-class homes, suffer most from the necessity of full-time employment. The author states that these girls ". . . carry very heavy responsibilities, lack normal leisure commitments, and apparently find in extra-family relationships (i.e., the steady dating relationship) the secure and stable companionship that they do not find at home." On the other hand, "girls whose middle-class mothers are working full-time are active in both organized and unorganized leisure activity, spend a good deal of time with their families, and are relatively autonomous in issues of judgment and authority."

Again we face the interrelated complexity of family influences on children. Whether or not a mother works is not the issue. Whether she *wants* to work, has a job she *wants*, and other similar factors are crucial in knowing whether any child's problems in your classroom are a result of maternal care. This selection, as well as all other readings in this section, points to one inescapable conclusion: You as a teacher must have a thorough knowledge of the complicated interrelations between environmental factors and personal successes and failures of children before you can adequately assess the source and effect of family influences on learning and behavior of your pupils. It is not enough to say that this fact or that event in the child's family caused the behavior of any one child. Rather, you must be able to say that the interrelationship of certain family attributes as they are affected by ethnic and socioeconomic level interact in specific ways to affect the learning of the child in your classroom.

This requires an awareness of different ethnic and socioeconomic patterns of family organization and child-rearing. It necessitates a knowledge of the effects of migration, acculturation, and urbanization on family structure and children's socialization to become part of the public world. And finally, it assumes a sophisticated understanding of the relative importance of the roles of mother and father in both organized and disorganized family units in terms of the cultural and social backdrop against which these are played. With large classes still common in urban schools, it is obviously a difficult task for you as a teacher. But only with thorough and complete understanding can you avoid the unsatisfactory and, at times, banal explanations given for a child's behavior or the excuses for his lack of learning because of a "bad family environment."

*A. Family Organization*

# PARENT CONFERENCES ARE

# ALWAYS TOUGH . . .

*Dorothy M. McGeoch, et al.*

I think it is very important to talk to parents as much as possible, but I don't seem to do it very well. I always have mixed feelings about it. It is pathetic to see how grateful a parent is to hear the least good thing about his child. Pamela's mother was almost crying when she walked out of her conference, because she was so proud that Pamela is doing well. And Pamela *is* doing very well. I was not pouring on any oil. I was telling her exactly what I meant—that I was proud to have Pamela in my class and that she was an asset to the class. I told this to Oscar's mother, too, and the look on her face was as if I had handed her a million dollars. It made me wince, because I thought maybe I did not sound sincere.

One interesting thing about the conference days was that I often saw sisters—not parents, but sisters—who were really the most responsible people I have met. They were intelligent, inquisitive young people, and I felt as if I were talking to adults, not high school kids. It was amazing. I couldn't get over it.

But none of the mothers of my problem children ever came to see me except Eddy's mother and that was under the most tremendous pressure. Maybe that has something to do with their being problems.

I had one mother whose English was very limited, and I'm as ashamed of my Spanish as she is of her English. Her daughter, who is in my class, came with her. I was very careful of my verbs and I said things slowly, and I pointed out things on papers. This mother has really been a help to me. Since we sat and talked that evening, I have had no trouble with the girl at all. The mother came a second time, too. Apparently, she values education highly.

I feel very inadequate in parent conferences because I don't know how to conduct them and my principal and all the books in the world can't help me until I have done it a lot of times. The things you have to say sound so insignificant compared with the problems they have. I read in some books at college that you should try to get background in these first conferences. But it's very hard. It sounds so funny to say, "Does he like to come to school in the morning?" "Is he enjoying school this year?" I don't know how to question a parent delicately and tactfully in order to find out how he feels about his child, so I really don't know how to approach the situation.

I also have trouble with report-card marks. If the parent were able to analyze the report cards, he would find practically nothing there. Anyhow, when I'm making out report cards, I don't know what to put down. I don't have marks for some subjects. I just have not given the children written tests. I have tested them in conversation which is not a formal yardstick of achievement. I can't test them if they can't read the questions; if they don't know what I'm asking, I can't find out anything. There are some children who never volunteer. Either they don't understand what I'm asking, or they just don't know the answer. Either way it amounts to the same thing.

The parent conferences are always tough. I get butterflies in my stomach every time I know that some parent is coming up to see me. There's one mother who has eleven children and has worked herself to death to at least let them breathe. She's so tired and withdrawn and so wrapped up in her own problems. She looks at me, standing there in my nylon stockings and my nice new dress and fresh lipstick on, and, you know, everything in place. I think to myself, "I really don't know anything," I can't get over the feeling of aloneness. I'm an outsider. Maybe it would be better if I came in a slouchy pair of shoes. It's like walking into a candy store; everyone knows right away that you can't be anything but a social worker or a teacher. You can't be a "member of the family" because of the way you dress and the way you look. I feel, then, the way I do when I put on my coat to go home and the kids rub their faces against it and talk about it being so nice and soft. It doesn't matter that it only cost $24.95. That's not it. It's just the feeling when they look at me. I'm their ideal, and it makes me so uncomfortable. I feel that I have so much and they have so little.

On the other hand, I have to be like that and look like that in order to give them something to look up to because I represent what an educated person is. That is what the parents want for their youngsters so they want me to look different.

I have never gotten used to being looked at with admiration. I feel very uncomfortable and embarrassed when it happens. When a little girl comes in with long leather gloves because I have long leather gloves, it makes me very self-conscious.

I am very aware of how little experience I have. I can't imagine what it would be like to bring up eleven children. My parents found it hard enough to bring up two. I think about all the heartaches of trying to put a child from these families through business school or nursing school. Sometimes, when an older sister comes for a parent conference, I ask, "Are you going to school?" and she says, "Oh, yes, I am going to business school." She's so proud, and she has a right to be.

I think to myself how wonderful it is that with this impoverished background and with the tremendous needs of the family, some of them can keep so close together and be so loving to each other. There are people like Gregory with twelve children in the family—twelve of the nicest, neatest, cleanest, most polite, most aspiring children. You wonder, what do you look like to people like that? You're middle-class, urban, and very civilized, and intelligent, but you feel that you really don't know anything about life in the slums. I always feel that I may seem to be "talking down" to the parents when I want so much to help.

When Edgardo's father came to the school because Edgardo's coat was ripped, I felt like a shirker, because I couldn't do anything about it. He is a very young father who never went to school and he is terribly concerned for his son. He came to New York from Puerto Rico so his son could get an education and be with people who aspired to higher things. He doesn't want his son to be what *he* is. He wants his son to have a better life. It shows in the way he dresses his children that he doesn't want them to be considered slum children or lower class. He just wants them to be very Americanized —to be "real" Americans.

When you see this—when you see parents who almost get tears in their eyes when you say good things about their children, you almost haven't got the heart to sit there and say, "Well, now that I've told you all the good, let me tell you the bad." It may be that with some of the parents, I would get further by not mentioning the bad—by giving them something to be proud about. Maybe, when the parent goes home and says, "I got good news from the teacher," the child will feel that the teacher must really like him or she wouldn't have said good things to the parent. It could be.

# WEST END AND CRESTWOOD HEIGHTS

*Conrad M. Arensberg and Solon T. Kimball*

## THE WEST END

It is not surprising that the family system congenial to the American-born Italians of Boston's West End resembles that of their immigrant parents. It is a society of intense relationships and deep loyalties to those of the same blood and to the friends with whom one has grown to adulthood. This restrictive grouping of conjoined age mates has led Gans to refer to this form of organization as a "peer-group society," in which "during adulthood, the family is its most important component. Adult West Enders spend almost as much time with siblings, in-laws, and cousins—that is, with relatives of the same sex and age—as with their spouses, and more time than with parents, aunts, and uncles."[1]

Within this tightly knit group of adults—kin and peers—each child learns the behavior and values which he carries with him as he joins with those whose similar backgrounds provide a familiar environment of personal relationships. Here he builds the ties that persist beyond the time when the young man takes a bride and establishes his own family.

In this adult-centered family system, the child encounters "a continuous barrage of prohibitions and threats, intertwined with words and deeds of reward and affection."[2] He is viewed as a little adult, for whom it is necessary to prescribe the behavior that is expected of him, but with little evidence of parental concern "about how he receives their messages."[3] "Impulsive child-rearing is possible because West Enders are not concerned with *developing* their children, that is, with raising them in accord-

[1] Gans, Herbert J., *The Urban Villagers*, New York, Free Press, 1962, p. 37.
[2] *Ibid.*, p. 59.　　　　　　　　[3] *Ibid.*, p. 59.

ance with a predetermined goal or target which they are expected to achieve. Unlike adult-directed or even child-centered families found in the middle class, West Enders have no clear image of the future social status, occupational level, or life-style that they want their children to reach. And even when they do, they do not know how to build it into the child-rearing process."[4]

As Gans describes it, the "West Enders want for their children what they want for themselves."[5] But there is no pressure to push them toward this goal, although there is concern that the child may not equal his peers, and real fear that he may become a "bum."

The social environment that the family circle and peer group builds for its children is also the one to which the adolescent-become-adult turns in his search for a spouse. It should come as no surprise that intermarriage with non-Italians is rare in the second generation and not favored for the third, although if the choice is also a Catholic the disapproval is slight. In those rare instances where out-marriage occurs, there is the usual effort to bring the stranger into the orbit of established peers and the family circle.

The peer group shapes its members' perspectives and organizes their relations with those who differ from themselves and who are found in what is to them the "outside world." The institutions, values, and behavior of the outside are judged by the same rules that govern the peer group. Outside rejection of their norms leads them to expect exploitation (which is often justified) and, in turn, to a calculated exploitation of others. They view those who hold positions in government as uniformly corrupt and guilty of denying the citizen what should be naturally his. The services that reach the peer group from the world beyond are "to be used if they are desirable and to be ignored or fought if they seek to change or injure the individual or the peer group."[6]

It is in the setting of a potentially hostile, corrupt, and exploitative outside world that most members of the peer group must seek their means of livelihood. It is not surprising to discover that work as an end in itself, as an opportunity for self-development and improvement, or as a contribution to the welfare of the larger society, has little or no meaning. One works in order to make a living and to enjoy and extend the pleasures of life which are found beyond the job. Since work must be endured, the goal is to find employment where one is treated as an equal, or in some small firm that permits expression of relationships comparable to those within the peer group. This is rarely achieved. "What does matter is that identification with work, work success, and job advancement—while not absolutely rejected—are of secondary priority to the life that goes on within the family circle."[7]

The rejection of the outside contributes to the intense involvement

[4] *Ibid.*, pp. 59–60.     [5] *Ibid.*, p. 60.     [6] *Ibid.*, p. 121.     [7] *Ibid.*, p. 245.

in family and peer group and produces related effects that further preserve and accentuate separation from the remainder of the society. West Enders reject middle-class status and values. In particular, they do not understand nor wish to use the educational ladder as the device for upward social mobility. In fact the "worry about downward mobility is stronger than any desire for upward mobility. Consequently, the major hope is that in education, occupation, and general status, the child will not fall below that of his peers."[8] Exemplification of this rejection may also be found in the indifference, even hostility, to those cultural missionaries of the middle class found in settlement houses, libraries, and similar transplants from middle-class society.

## CRESTWOOD HEIGHTS

No yardstick extant can convey any true measure of the cultural gulf that separates the Italian, working-class West Enders from the upper-middle-class residents of Crestwood Heights (Seeley et al. 1956). Our recourse is to let the weight of comparative, empirical description carry the burden of establishing the differences.

The physical contrast alone is impressive enough. In the West End one found the massed tenements of an older American city in association with the small shops and street-corner bars catering to the local population, a setting in which street corner society flourished. In contrast, Crestwood Heights is a community of single family homes, each separated by lawn and shrubbery from those adjoining it, and a community in which "the massive centrality of the schools . . . assert the community as a physically organized entity, as a psychological reality, and as a social fact."[9]

In the Crestwood Heights family one encounters a pattern that is nearly identical to that found in the upper-middle-class suburbs which stretch across America. It is the family of parents and children, isolated from its kin (often socially as well as geographically), temporarily anchored in its own separate dwelling, and dependent upon the success of the father's career for its status and its future. In the limitation of emotional life to relatively few persons, disharmony in the relations among its members can be shattering to the psychic stability of the individual.

It is a family in which the finely balanced tensions between independence and dependence of its members impose upon children and parents alike a responsibility for its maintenance as a smoothly functioning unit. Within its confines and the adjunct activities of school, church, and com-

[8] *Ibid.*, p. 60.
[9] Seeley, John R. R., Alexander Sim, and Elizabeth W. Loosley, *Crestwood Heights*, New York, John Wiley, 1963, p. 224.

munity, the woman finds her validation as wife and mother. The man must also validate his roles as father and husband in his relationships with wife and children, but his success in these roles, and that of the others in theirs, is inexorably linked to his success in another realm of life, that of his career. It is "from this base of home and male career, which are almost inseparable, [that] the family can articulate with the community."[10]

It is a family formed from and held together by "love," in the union of man and woman through marriage and in the care for and attention to its children. This love unites but does not bind, since freedom and individuality are highly prized. Each family member values his independence in relations with the institutions of the community.

It is a family which in its orientation to the future is perpetually poised for mobility. Unattached to the past, which "tends to be obliterated from the collective thinking of the family,"[11] it presents a flexibility that permits change of residence, of job, and of friends, if the new promises to enhance status ranking and economic well being. When one joins the values of independence, hope in the future, and mobility, it is easy to understand why the successful separation of the child from his family of orientation and his own willful launching upon a career are both possible and necessary. But the potential and recognized consequences extend to the very nature of relations within the family itself. "Consciously, the future is optimistically viewed; and the task of the family is to equip the child as effectively as possible in the present with all available means for his later solitary climb to better and more prosperous worlds lying far ahead of him. . . . But the future nevertheless beckons with sufficient force that the parental generation, if it seriously hinders the child's upward progress, must be virtually abandoned; this is well understood by both parents and children. Only the promise of continuous upward social mobility (or, at the very least, continually validated status at the present level) can nerve the Crestwood Heights family to its obligations; and for its members to feel the full poignancy of the separation to which it, as a family, is dedicated, might well wreck the whole precarious structure."[12]

As the children move into their teens their participation with their parents lessens as that with their peers increases. Finally, there is an almost complete separation of social life from that of the parents. One consequence of this wide range of activity permitted the teen-ager outside the family is that the older children provide a model of behavior for the younger ones and in fact can open opportunities of participation for them and teach them ways of behavior "which may be new or strange to parents."[13]

The club or association is the focus of organized social life for the parents; the school serves the same purpose for their children. Here, in extracurricular activities, in planned social affairs, and in the exclusive system of fraternities and sororities, the young join with their peers in

[10] *Ibid.*, p. 163.    [11] *Ibid.*, p. 164.    [12] *Ibid.*, p. 164.    [13] *Ibid.*, p. 203.

reproducing a system of status differentials based upon competitive achievement, family background, and the religious separation of Jews and Gentiles which resembles that of their parents. It is here also that those friendships are formed that may prove so crucial later on in the careers of the males, and that courtships blossom which prepare young people for the social roles of male and female as husband and wife in the adult life of Crestwood Heights or in its suburban counterpart elsewhere.

Only one ideal, that of "love," is accepted as the proper basis for marriage. This concept is surrounded, however, by a series of beliefs that ostensibly supply the greatest possible latitude in the search for a mate but in reality restrict that choice to a narrow band of persons who closely resemble each other. The belief in equality, in the right of the individual to free choice, and in permissiveness in behavior and the selection of friends, might conceivably lead to an openness of groupings that would extend across class and religious lines (assuming that other groups were equally disposed). In fact, no such thing happens. The children early come to learn of the great disparity between the preachments of their parents and reality. They come to understand that the beliefs can be effected only if one is with those who resemble oneself.

The wall of exclusion that the parents throw around their children is maintained in the selection of a residence, in the summer camps to which their children go, in the arranged participation in adult social activities, and in the social affairs arranged by church or synagogue. If need be, the child may be sent to private school, further to assure his isolation from unacceptable associates and his inclusion with his own kind, or with those whom his parents hope he will emulate.

Prior to adolescence the necessity to maintain an exclusiveness of participation is not felt as strongly as it is after the child reaches that age. In practice, romantic love does not cross ethnic or class lines. With adolescence begins the subtly enforced guidance that directs the child toward those with whom courtship and marriage is approved. There can be no open rejection of the belief that romantic love recognizes no boundaries, but it is tacitly understood that Gentile boys do not date Jewish girls, and that Jewish boys do not date Gentile girls. There is set at this stage the barrier to intermarriage and, in turn, the definition of that group from which one seeks his marriage partner. But the system is much more precise and complicated than that based upon obvious designations of religion alone.

The ideology of the middle class in its romantic, liberal version stipulates that only those who also hold the same beliefs as it does are worthy of compatibility and intimacy. It matters not that the disjunction between belief and action is so great, because those who do not hold such beliefs (the other social classes) automatically repel the Crestwooder and hence "tend to render their possessors repugnant or less attractive as possible partners for intimacy or marriage. The very belief, therefore, that 'class is of no consequence' (which is on one side a middle-class view exclusively) becomes a token of compatibility and a basis for intimacy, and in so far as it determines friendship, membership in a clique, and marriage, a potent factor in the maintenance of the class boundaries which 'do not exist!' 'do not matter,' or 'ought not to be considered'."[14]

Thus the guides to marriage are far more pervasive than the simple prescription of romantic love. If the indoctrination of middle-class values is successful, then there is no necessity to enforce overtly the selection of a suitable marriage partner. The child, turned adult, has already deeply internalized exactly the kind of person with whom he or she is expected to, and will, fall in love with and marry. This, then, is the cultural situation within which mate selection occurs and which led the authors to state that beliefs "in the dignity of the individual and the sacredness of personality, in the valuation of people 'for what they are instead of what they have' . . . come to their ultimate expression and test in the 'romantic' view of how marriages of their children ought to be founded: on 'love,' sympathy, compatibility, and personality characteristics, 'without regard to race, creed or color' or, above all—ugly word—money. Despite these deeply held and pervasive views, the marriages that do occur are not notably different from those that might have been arranged in a caste system based on race, creed color, and—above all—money. Marriages between Jew and Gentile, Protestant and Catholic, rich and poor, are almost as rare as 'marriages out' in any group that punishes them by formal expulsion (for example, the Quakers until recently)."[15]

## WORK AND THE OUTSIDE

Unlike the West Enders, the upper-middle-class people of Crestwood Heights maintain a direct relationship between their way of life and the outside. It is this arena for which the young, especially the males, have been oriented since their childhood and which they enter upon completion of their schooling. It is here that, sometimes in cooperation with and sometimes in competition with others, they work and strive for success in the careers they have chosen. In its economic and status aspects the measure of that success is reflected in the recognition accorded to one's family. But wife and children are no passive recipients of career success. "Besides 'friends,' no partner is more important to the career than the wife; none can help more—and perhaps none can hinder more than she, though this is more difficult to establish."[16] And in the education and other advantages that he can provide for his children, a man demonstrates his own merits.

The career pattern follows a predictable course. Following the period

14 *Ibid.*, p. 400.          15 *Ibid.*, pp. 396–97.          16 *Ibid.*, p. 135.

of preparation, which is also a time of dependency, there begins the long climb. This is the period of renunciation, of "hard work," which is followed "by a relatively brief period of full realization, and a gradual decline shading into retirement."[17] Within career activity there are two often complementary but possibly antagonistic directions in which ambition may be channeled. Output may bring either monetary reward, or recognition for achievement, or both.

In Crestwood Heights work is highly valued, not as an end in itself, but as the activity through which one proves the validity of the other values of the culture, particularly status achievement and family welfare. In contrast to the West Enders, the parents do know how to build a view of the future, somewhat different from their own, into their child-rearing practices. "The Crestwood child who is reared in an environment of prosperity and success, comes to feel that life's opportunities are limitless, that he can become anything he wishes to become."[18] But the inability of the father to transmit his own status to his children is largely concealed. The father can help to open the way to his son, but when the chips are down, it is the latter on whom the full burden falls. It is the son who must struggle and strive and he who will reap the rewards. But in a most peculiar way success cannot be a solitary thing. It is closely tied to his wife and intimate friends, and its validation is also linked to the approving judgment of the others. In this sense there are two worlds in which each man orbits: "the exacting work schedules of life downtown" and "the world of leisure and affection uptown."[19]

## CONCLUSION

We are now ready to return to a consideration of the propositions and questions that were raised in the earlier sections of this chapter and to examine them in the comparative light of the empirical data drawn from the studies of the Italians in the West End of Boston and of the upper-middle-class residents of Crestwood Heights. There is a small problem in deciding which facet of the whole should be treated first, but since the various segments seem to reveal systemic interconnections it may be desirable to begin with the most comprehensive subject, the social structure of the metropolis.

It was suggested earlier that institutional arrangements could be divided into those associated with the private world of family and friends and the counterpoised but parallel public world of social superstructures. These latter contain the corporate and professional activities through which the essential goods and services are produced and distributed. It was also suggested that associated with the cultural and social dichotomy of public

[17] *Ibid.*, p. 133.                [18] *Ibid.*, p. 124.                [19] *Ibid.*, p. 155.

and private were two social class systems. The immediate problem, then, is to see to what extent the empirical data support this view.

For the West Enders the separation between the private world of family and peer group and the public world of outside is dramatically sharp. The outside includes all those institutions over which the West Enders exert a minimum of control, and which threaten the continued cohesion of the group. The threat is a double one: It arises from attempts to win allegiance from the group's members (and thus to alienate them) and from the fear of exploitation. In consequence, members of the peer group are thrown even closer together as they unite to reject the values of and participation in activities of the outside, but they are ready to exploit such activities when they appear advantageous. Among the values rejected are those of work and self-improvement as ends in themselves or for purposes of social mobility. The rejection even extends to education as a device for social mobility. In fact, aspiration for higher status is recognized as disruptive of the peer group and opposed to the core of values that give it meaning. The West Enders, by adherence to their own values and rejection of those of the middle class and its institutions, clearly demonstrate the separation between private and public worlds and the potential conflict between the two.

The evidence from Crestwood Heights is equally striking in its substantiation of the distinction between the private world of family and friends and the public world of profession and corporate structure. But here the two are related in a vastly different and almost opposite fashion from the West End. Although the activities of either private or public world are distinct in kind and separate in space, their interdependence is of such magnitude that success or failure in one has its repercussions on the other. The male Crestwooder learns early that the goal of his pre-adult training is to prepare him to do battle for the honors that can be won in the arena of profession or business. Only thus does he validate and perhaps improve upon the status to which he was born. The girl learns equally soon the significance of the complementary role that she must play as wife and mother. For both parents and children aspiration in self-development is the psychological counterpart of the achievement of higher social status. For the upper middle class of Crestwood the public world is no threatening "outside"; it is the familiar environment in which its members contest and attempt to control. They call their activities in it "work," and it is for this work that a part of their formal education prepares them. For some, work may become an end in itself, but this is not the social purpose that it serves.

We can extend and deepen our understanding of the dual structure of the metropolis and its relation to social class if at this time we turn to the first of three propositions offered earlier. There we postulated that social class is a manifestation of the social system rather than the system itself.

At first glance this statement might appear to be a truism that was hardly worthy of much attention. We could accept this view readily enough if it were not for the fact that all delineations of social class rely almost exclusively upon the determination of cultural configurations. Now the basis for such analyses has been derived from the grouping of attributes or qualities associated with things, activities, and individuals. This approach has yielded some good results, but we would argue that their validation rests upon the relationships of these attributes to interaction between specific individuals in specific events. We contend that such an examination would show that patterns of interaction contain the key to understanding social class systems. Evidence from two different sources may be adduced to illustrate the point. Since we have already discussed the system of status associated with the hierarchical organization of corporate superstructures, we will not elaborate further on demonstrating the relation between corporate organization and social class. Instead, we shall turn to a comparison of forms of family organization associated with the residents of the West End and of Crestwood Heights, respectively. The significant differences in relations with the "outside" have already been commented on. What is needed now is to look at the relations of family members with the non-work aspects of the community and the process of mate selection. For each of these it will be our purpose to show how the facts may be interpreted within the context of family structure.

Within the relations of parents and children in the peer-based family circle of the West Enders, certain implicit values find expression. Since it is within the family circle that those activities which are most highly valued are found, it seems logical, and is in fact true, that parental concern for children is that they might also experience a comparable style of life. The generational reconstruction of the peer-group type of family can be realized, however, only if there is relatively great stability. Hence it is easy to understand why middle-class values are meaningless and possibly threatening. The intense and frequent activity among peers ensures a commitment to the present rather than to the future, and ensures the avoidance of time-consuming and involving activities with other types of groups. In fact, limited participation beyond the borders of the family circle should not be viewed as a consequence of conscious avoidance but of the incompatibility between a family system of the peer-group type and other forms of institutional activity, including deep religious involvement. This formulation helps us to understand the continued inability of middle-class civic and cultural enterprises to penetrate or take root in this environment. If successful they would destroy the presently constituted family system.

The relations between the parents of Crestwood Heights and their children are almost entirely different. Parental orientation of children for the future must include a sense of autonomy and desire for achievement that leads to mobility. It is the obligation of the male-child-turned-adult to validate the aspirations of his parents through his success in the world of work, and of the female, in partnership with her husband, to shape the environment within which her children come to maturity. Hence the immediate community is of utmost significance. The activities associated with social clubs and the time devoted to civic and school betterment should not be viewed as ends in themselves but as part of the necesssary effort to create and preserve an environment compatible with the relations between members of the family and its adjunct values. Thus, as was argued earlier, the interconnections and inderdependencies between the relationships of a family system, its values, and the participation pattern in the non-work extra-familial activities can be made explicit. Further substantiation of this and other points appear when we turn to the processes of courtship and marriage.

Mating, reproduction, and care of the young are biological processes culturally organized among humans. Thus, variations in the processes may be examined as variations in culture. For this part of the analysis the crucial aspect is to examine the relation between the definition of a suitable mate and forms of human grouping. It is obvious from the empirical evidence that mates are chosen from those who are similar in cultural behavior and outlook. Among the West Enders marriage with other than an Italian is disapproved, and only rarely does it occur. In Crestwood Heights the separation of Jews from Gentiles appears in adolescence in dating behavior, a type of activity preliminary to later final mate choice. Both groups resemble each other, however, in the care with which the definition of a proper and improper marriage partner is inculcated in the young. What weight may be given to the several factors that contribute to the success of this effort is not entirely clear and possibly may not be completely determinable. Admonition and precept undoubtedly have an effect, but the relative power of verbal command to direct behavior must still be determined. This problem really belongs in the category of the dynamics of learning. Our own inclination is to give greater priority to patterns of relationships as explanatory.

The marriage partnership is fully intermingled with peer group and family circle in the West End. Between the period of adolescence and marriage the males separate themselves from the family setting to regroup as an all male peer group, congregating on street corners and in other locales. Marriage pulls them once again into the family circle, but in a gathering of their own age mates, and not that of their parents. For their wives they choose girls of similar backgrounds. Thus, through the joining of biological and cultural processes there is ensured a continuity of cultural tradition.

The process of mate selection and family formation for Crestwood Heights varies only in its details. So also is the consequence of cultural perpetuation the same. But the cultural stability, almost inertia, which this analysis suggests must also be examined in the context of the environment of the other institutional arrangements in the society. When these are taken into account we then inject a new dimension, one whose changes bring repercussions elsewhere. For this reason the rise of great social superstructures are relevant to the system of social class and to changes in its definition. For this reason social class, defined as the configuration of cultural elements, should be considered as a manifestation of the social system and not as the system itself. This leads to a further conclusion that each form of civilization has its own kind of social ranking.

Little additional comment seems necessary for the other two propositions presented earlier. The empirical data and their analysis support the proposition that social class should be examined from two perspectives— from the vantage point of those who are participants and from criteria that are external to the system. Finally, the insistence that comparative analysis requires concepts and procedures which are free of substantive particularism was exemplified in the comparisons between the West End and Crestwood Heights. It will be remembered that we utilized the categories of work and non-work, family organization, transmission of culture, and mate selection.

A final problem to which some brief attention should be given is the relation between social class and urban theory. Although no attempt was made to examine the multiple dimensions that inevitably must be considered by those who work with urban theory, much of the content of this chapter is relevant.

The formulation which we utilized was that modern urban society, in its metropolitan form, contains two major systems of social class, each one of which is related to separate organizational systems—that of family and its extensions, and those of the work system. Once these systems have been delineated and their relationships and processes understood, we will possess a working model of urban society. From this base of knowledge we can then proceed with some confidence to seek out principles that explain the processes of change.

# RITUALS IN FAMILY LIVING

*James H. S. Bossard and Eleanor S. Boll*

Even within a general rhythm, different ways of life lead to varied procedures of living. When the families in our study are divided into three classes, similarity of rites within classes and differences between them are marked. One aspect of these three ways of life may, at the outset, explain a good deal about certain variations in the rituals to be described. In the middle-class families, school and business hours coincide very closely. For the most part all the family must be up together at the same time, and leave home at nearly the same time. In a home not cramped but not spacious either, this leads to one specific type of situation. In upper- and lower-class homes, on the contrary, the members' schedules do not coincide so closely. The business hours of father and working children are often at very different times, and school hours at yet another. In the lower-class home, cramped for space, this has one meaning: in the upper, with separate rooms and with servants, quite another. Under such different circumstances, the degree of comfort to be attained by remaining at home as long as possible, or by getting away from it at the first practicable moment, also enters into the ritual picture. The following differences in rituals are in part results of these varied situations in the three classes.

## Awakening

From this study it would seem that the alarm clock is the modern American equivalent to "the first crowing of the cock," by which it was decreed that the ancient Chinese family must arise. Some one person in most of these homes is awakened by the alarm, and it then becomes his duty to set off the daily morning procedures.

In the lower-class home, this person is most frequently the father, who has to leave home even before the young babies are clamoring for attention. Upon his departure the baton is passed to the mother, who clock-watches for each other member of the family with a schedule to meet.[1]

In the middle-class family, a parent usually supervises the alarm clock, and it is a signal for a rapid succession of awakenings, well routinized according to time limits beyond which each member may not be permitted to remain in bed. It is in the middle-class family that there is found the practice of wakening with a kiss, a song, or some sort of familiar family game or by-play.

The upper-class family is more individualistic in its awakening. Sometimes a servant rises by the alarm, and notifies each family member at the appointed time. A call on the house phone, a tap at the door, a closing of the bedroom windows are all predetermined signs of the proper moment for getting up. The mother often takes this responsibility just as she does in the middle- and lower-class homes. But also, children who are past high school age have their own alarm clocks, and dependably rise by them.

### Bathroom Procedures

The fact that the middle-class family rises almost together, and has few bathrooms, has resulted in a problem for it, which has been resolved by a very narrowly prescribed ritual for many of them—a bathroom ritual. They have developed set rules and regulations that define who goes first (according to who must leave the house first), how long one may stay in, what are the penalties for overtime, and under what conditions there may be a certain overlapping of personnel. It is usually required that actual tub-bathing be done the evening before. But a good wash and a toothbrushing, as well as a daily shave for the men, must be fitted into this precedence- and time-defined rite.

Upper-class girls, most of whom had their own individual bathrooms, reacted with interest when told of middle-class procedures in this respect. The lower-class girls were amazed that such a thing was necessary. Probably privacy, which they had never had, and over-fastidiousness were not family values that made such arrangements important.

### Breakfast Rituals

In the material gathered from autobiographies published by adults, every family of each class considered breakfast a family meal. In the case

---

[1] This study did not happen to include families in which the father worked late afternoon shifts or night shifts. This would obviously lead to a different situation.

records the parent generation too, for the most part, observed this as a family rite. But from the present generation records, the American family breakfast seems to be fast dying out. Breakfast here is a peripatetic meal, eaten individually or in relays, in a rush, and with little service. There are several reasons why this may be so. (*a*) People stay up later at night than they did a generation or two ago. There is more to do at night. This being so, even a few minutes of extra sleep in the morning is precious. And, time schedules of members differing, family breakfast becomes a lesser value than sleep, a meal to be postponed till the last minute and not to be lingered over. (*b*) Breakfast can be prepared more easily, even by youngsters, nowadays, what with canned fruit juices, prepared cereals, chocolate milk, packaged melba toast, and instant coffee. (*c*) The day of having a "hired girl" live in, even in lower-class homes, is gone. Few even of the middle class have a servant actually living in the home. And when servants come in for the day, they are considered a nuisance at breakfast time, because it is easier not to be dependent upon them, and not to have to cater to their time requirements.

By the time a lower-class youngster in these families is old enough for school, he is quite well equipped to get his own breakfast and get himself off to school. From that time on he does so, standing in the kitchen and dodging around any other members of the family who may happen to be attending to their own breakfasts simultaneously. It is only the young babies, with their mother, who have any sort of table-breakfast. Even the father, for the most part, gets what he wants on his way to early work.

Since the middle-class family usually rises in rapid succession, there is a very well-worked-out procedure. Mother goes into the kitchen first, and starts breakfast. She serves the family in relays, working between stove and table: first the father, then the school children, and then often sits down herself and has her own breakfast with the remaining preschool children. This meal, usually in the kitchen, is short, brisk, and highly mobile. But the different relays do eat at table, have a regular table-setting, and often a semblance of family conversation.

Breakfast is a highly individual affair with the upper class as with the lower, but with these differences. The food is usually prepared by a servant, and is taken by each member from the refrigerator, the buffet, or is served individually when desired. It is almost always eaten in the dining room. For small children, the meal is more leisurely and settled. Mother, nurse, or maids take care of them, and if it is the sort of home that affords a mademoiselle and a nursery, the preschool children eat there. In such homes, the children often eat all their meals in the nursery until they are old enough to cope with the formalized intricacies of the evening meal that exist in this kind of home.

Upper- and middle-class families frequently make up for this sort of weekday breakfast with a late, large spread on Sunday morning. All the family sits at table, and the Sunday newspapers are conspicuous. Often this occasion includes the weekly entertaining of married siblings and their families. Sometimes it is the weekly occasion for entertaining guests.

### Leaving Notes

The period immediately after breakfast gives rise to a ritual common to both upper- and middle-class families: the reporting to the family as to one's whereabouts and one's activities during the day.

In the upper-class home it is considered polite and proper to give the family such information daily, and it is done in many homes by the leaving of notes in especially designated places, because personal communication in the early morning is not usual. Note exchange is also a custom of the middle-class home. But more often these exchanges are verbal, since the family members do see each other in passing. With both classes, this is definitely the time of the day for checking up between parents and children. No lower-class child interviewed had any such custom.

### Dinner

Dinner, in the American families represented here, is definitely at night, as it was not so consistently in the families of the autobiographers of an earlier era. It is often, indeed, the first time that the entire family meets together during the day.

In the lower-class family, however, dinner is almost the same kind of meal as is breakfast. The mother, or an older sister, does prepare the food, but the rest of the family comes and takes it when and where they want to. Some of these families never have a meal sitting down with the whole family together except for Sunday dinner, which is considered a very special occasion. Even at this meal some families have to eat in relays, or in different rooms, because there is not room enough for all of them at a table. In the smaller families, where the family does eat together every night, they do so in the kitchen, with the "everyday" tableware, the dining room tending to be reserved for holiday, Sunday, and entertaining, when the best china is brought out for use.

Middle-class dinner involves very formal procedures. It is at a certain time, usually six or six-thirty. It is a meal at which the whole family sits around the table, for the most part in the dining room, and at which each member has a special place to sit. Features of it, generally, are two: there are assigned tasks for different members of the family, such as serving, carving, clearing the table and doing the dishes; and second, though the dinnertime equipment is too varied to describe specifically, it is usually more formal and impressive than for other meals.

Dinner for the upper class is later, at about seven or seven-thirty, and is much more formal as to appointments and service. In all but three homes, servants took over the complete preparation and serving of the meal. White damask, well-polished silver, flowers, candlelight, dinner china and glassware, and a completely leisure atmosphere describe the situation of this meal. No one moves away from the table during the meal, except father, if he carves from the sideboard. Cocktails before dinner and after-dinner coffee in the living room are, in many cases, regular parts of the dinner ritual.

## WORK AND RECREATION

Work and recreation rituals, in the middle- and lower-class homes, are intimately related to each other, and in this respect: the time and opportunities for regular family recreation depend to a large extent upon the smooth functioning of necessary household routine. There is a definite maneuvering between household chores and the time left over to devote to leisure-time activities.

It is the middle-class family that has many organized work rituals that, once regularized, free it for regular periods of family entertainment. Housecleaning, marketing, dishwashing, preserving, even hair-washing, automobile- and dog-washing, and garden care are got through by having a certain day and time, certain jobs for each member, and ways considered most "correct," because most efficient, for doing them. . . . These families then can regularize, and do, one night as "family night"; Sunday afternoons as the time for a ride together, or a visit to relatives or friends; an evening for games or music, or entertaining. The family at the television in the living room for certain programs is a very popular rite, not only on Sunday evenings, but often several other times during the week. Certain news commentators are "musts" for the whole family every day. Saturday is definitely a day for recreation. When children are small, this means some kind of family frolic. But even with children of college age, some part of Saturday figures largely as the time when the whole family engages in some activity that is different from the spirit of the rest of the week. Going down town to lunch and the movies, or having friends in to dinner to a more than usually elaborate meal are the two most popular ways of celebrating Saturday in the present-generation middle-class homes.

Cooperative rites of a menial nature are practically non-existent in the upper-class homes. Even the few families that have no servant living in the house have day help to perform these duties. Sharing dishwashing is the only frequent rite of this sort mentioned. For a few it is every night, and for others on the servants' nights out. The upper class does have rigidly set times for family recreation of a specific kind, but it is more often outside the home than is the case with the middle class, which tends to outside recreation together only during weekends. Usual types of regular family participation in the upper class are these: the orchestra during the season; golf or tennis on Sunday in spring, summer, and autumn; a weekly or monthly visit to grandmother's; the theatre once a month; opera during the season; always the horse shows; the Orpheus Club; the Stagecrafters; charity bazaars: the Penn-Cornell Game. Season tickets for orchestra, theatre, and opera are fairly common to middle-class college students, but these affairs are attended individually or with friends, not within the family, as with the upper class. At home, for the upper class, there is: bridge once a week; television at night; playing the piano and singing each week. Saturday is very definitely a day for frolic, but not so often in family, as with the middle class. Many social obligations center around this day, but they are separated into children's obligations and parents' obligations.

Saturday has a sharply different meaning to the girls of the lower class. Saturday is housecleaning day. It meant the same thing to all the girls interviewed, though they came from different communities. Except in the smallest families, all the children old enough, and preferably girls, spend most of the day helping to clean up the house. If, and when, they are finished, they are free to amuse themselves separately. There are no times for family recreation together. Work and recreation interlock in this way: older children have certain nights when they stay at home each week to take care of the younger ones in order that their parents, or their mother and a married sister or friend, may go out. Aside from this time, the children seek out their own fun, and away from home. There are no family games and entertainments at home. Even the television is not a family affair. Teen-agers said that they had given up trying to compete with father's news programs, and the youngest's adventure serials. There are just too many people of too many ages to use one television together. There are too many people in a small space to gather together comfortably for any kind of games.

## RELIGIOUS RITUALS

There are two kinds of religious rituals observed in the families studied. First, there are rituals in the home, such as grace at meals, family prayers, Bible readings, Sunday procedures, celebration of sacred days. Second, there is regular family participation in religious services outside of the home.

Important in the interpretation of religious rituals on a class basis is the analysis of the religious and denominational make-up of the cases under discussion. Families belonging to the upper class in this study are all Episcopal or Presbyterian, with the former predominating. There are no Catholic families in this group. The middle class is composed of every major denomination and Catholics, with no preponderance of any one. The lower class represents the Catholic faith overwhelmingly, though there are Methodists and Baptists represented. The religious affiliation of the three classes as represented here may be characteristic of the general class population. But until this is ascertained, it must be admitted that religious affiliation may here have an influence on the rituals which unduly differentiates them, since the Catholic church is more dominantly the guardian of religion than is the case with Protestantism. Even in middle-class families in this study, religious rituals in the home are less usual in Catholic families than in Protestant ones. With this suggestion that the sample may be uncharacteristic in religious make-up, the rituals are described as they were discovered.

### At Home

It is the middle-class families here described that carry the torch of religion in the home, though they also represent all but one of the admitted agnostic families. Grace is frequently said at meals, and in many different forms. It is not something done on special occasions, but a form that children remembered as having always been in effect, and that was still occurring without question. Bedtime prayers are as common. Children were taught them by a parent as soon as they were old enough to talk, and they were "heard" each night, often kneeling, for many years, after which time a good proportion of the children continued them individually even on to college age. The most popular childhood prayer was "Now I Lay Me Down to Sleep;" and mothers who had learned this prayer are now still teaching it to their youngsters, without revision. It is only the middle-class family that has regular family prayers apart from bedtime prayers and grace. In this class only is there celebrated the old-fashioned type of Sunday, in which no toys, work, sewing, games, or cooking are permitted.

While the family was small, and the children young, the pattern for the lower class was similar to that of the middle class. But as it grew, these forms died out. The children interviewed "thought" that the babies still said their prayers, but were not certain. Grace is said often, on the occasions when dinner is formalized enough to permit of such a period. Some Catholic families have a form of simple altar tacked to a wall, with no specific procedures for its use. But this is all that could be construed as religious rites in these homes.

Upper-class children were also taught bedtime prayers by a parent or a nurse. At the time of the interview, however, only three of the girls still said their prayers independently at night. One interviewee explained this in these terms. "Nurse, or Mademoiselle, taught us our prayers, with the approval of our parents, and heard us as long as she put us to bed. After that, we were on our own." This quick giving up of the form may be related to a conspicuous absence of all other religious forms in the family. There is in these homes ample opportunity for grace at meals, but only four families observe it. There are no family prayers or Bible readings. The general attitude, whether a rationalization or not, is that anything deeply religious in nature is personal and intimate, and would be very embarrassing if indulged in openly in family life. It seems highly probable, from the comparison of these cases in the three classes, that though all the parents feel the responsibility for teaching religious rites to small children, the rites do not endure where there is no adult pattern to nourish them.

### Sunday Church Services

Only the small families in the lower class go to church together regularly on Sundays. With the larger ones it is an individual affair, and there is much more pressure between the priest and the child than between the parent and the child. Members can, in these cases, attend mass at the most convenient hours, and many of them do so in relays, so that someone is always at home to preside over the babies and to take care of the important occasion of the week—Sunday dinner.

More than half of the middle-class families always go to church together on Sunday morning. Some always attend midweek services. Children go to Sunday school, and to young people's services on up through their teens. The Sunday services are times for special dressing up, and certain Sundays mean corsages for the ladies, or new hats. Sunday dinner in these families is prepared for and set at a time that will not interfere with anyone's going to church.

In the upper class, nearly half the families go to church together regularly on Sunday mornings, and this also involves special dressing for the occasion. But there are two marked differences between the upper and middle classes. Even the upper-class families who always go on Sundays are conspicuous by their absence at other services, that day or during the week. The children who go to Sunday school and young people's organizations drop out at early teen-age. In the group there was one "younger sister" who was still going to Sunday school, and one teen-ager who teaches a class. At a fairly early age, in this group, other social activities come to crowd out church activities. Most of these children are, at this time, preparing for a very intricate sort of adult social life. The other difference is this: all the families, even those who never go to church regularly, usually go together on Thanksgiving, Christmas, Easter, and during Lent. These services are compulsory to the upper-class families in this study as they are not to non-church goers of the middle class. It seemed clear that these are occasions of high social, rather than of just religious, importance. Everybody who is anybody will be there. In respect to regarding certain ceremonies at church as social duties, one girl interviewed said, interestingly enough, that though her family never goes to church in the wintertime, if she is visiting and her host goes to church, she, of course, goes along too. . . .

## SUMMER VACATIONS

The summer vacation is becoming more individualized with the advent of easier and cheaper transportation and more freedom for young people. In published autobiographies, most families who could afford a vacation described a regular vacation ritual. A far lesser proportion of the present-day families did so. But with some it is still well established, and varies among the classes.

With the upper class, summer is the time when there is a transplanting of the family to a more favorable location. Usually this is a removal to a second home where, though it may be on a simpler scale, the same kinds of social relationships and activities are carried on as in the wintertime, and often with many of the same people, since people from the same winter communities cluster at the same resorts. Members may take trips abroad, or go on visits across the continent; but they do it from this summer center, where they all automatically go for the season. Newport was, of course, the grand model for this kind of resort,[2] and there are many of them, in descending scale of affluence and formality, which maintain rather tight little circles of social life. In one New Jersey resort, to which some of the families under study move each summer, there is one beach labeled as the "swank set beach." There are no ordinances to prevent anyone from using it, yet no one but the "set" bathes therefrom. Sightseers walk through, but return to the other beaches for their swimming. The "set" have a quite separate social life, and do not mingle with others at the resort. Many of them own homes there, and appear at this beach year after year, beginning as small babies and ultimately appearing with their own offspring.

The middle-class vacation is not so predetermined, for they do not so often own a home just for summer use. There is a time in the year, however, when father brings home a few road maps to plan the trip, or mother goes to the shore or mountains to hire a cottage for the season or for a few weeks. If it is for the season, father usually commutes over weekends, except during his own short vacation. The middle-class vacation is less often a transplanting of a community of friends, and more often a meeting of new and different people, or of the "regular summer friends." Life is lived on

[2] For a description of the model of such resorts, see *Cleveland Amory*, "Newport: There She Sits," *Harper's Magazine*, February, 1948.

a much less formal scale, and is usually definitely planned to be very different from the winter regimen.

A week at the shore or at grandmother's is the best that the lower-class family can expect regularly. And this is only for the smaller families. Furthermore, it is definitely not a continuation of regular family life, but an escape from it. In the large families, the oldest children are required, in some cases, to take care of the household each year while the parents go off for a few days of change. Many of the children have short yearly vacations at free camps, and this is a time of exhilaration and preparation for the family. Its climax comes when trains or buses loaded with the children of the neighborhood are "seen off" by parents, siblings, and other neighbors.

## FAMILY BUDGETING AND ALLOWANCES

Wherever there was a family council on budgeting and expenditures, it occurred in the middle-class family. In some cases the children are even given a vote on the purchasing of home improvements and new cars when something else has to be sacrificed for them. These children are pretty well aware of their fathers' salaries and what sort of arrangements are made between father and mother for household and personal expenses. Usually there is a set sum, given to the mother at whatever interval the father receives his pay. Children get allowances by the week, often supplementing them, in their teens, with money they earn, which is considered strictly their own.

The lower- and upper-class children know next to nothing about their parents' incomes or about budgeting. They are not called in to council on such subjects.

Most of the lower-class children do not get allowances, but simply ask for money, and are never sure whether or not they will get it. It came to light that the young married brother, or brother-in-law, is an especially good source to tap in this respect for these girls—in fact, older working siblings in the lower class showed considerable generosity toward all younger children. When these children are small and do odd jobs, the money they earn is their own. But when they grow older and have steadier work with better pay, they are supposed to contribute to the family in board.

All the upper-class children have their own allowances. When they were younger, this was the same sort of weekly sum that is still being meted out to the middle class at college age. By early teen-age, however, the upper-class child's allowance is almost in every case in the form of a bank account, into which the father or mother deposits a check every month, ranging from $100 up. This is specified to be for certain purposes and varies from "incidentals" to "all personal expenses and clothing, except fur coats." Some of the girls have private incomes, plus allowances, and some have full-time paying positions. But in all cases their incomes are considered their own, and there is no contribution to the family expected, except through personal gifts.

## PRESENT-GIVING

The middle class seems to enjoy gift-giving rituals and goes out of its way to provoke such occasions quite apart from celebrations such as birthdays and Christmas. These rituals . . . are characteristic of this class. There are certain regulations concerning their gift-giving . . . Gifts for non-holiday times may be food and necessities, but for birthdays and Christmas they are almost always extra luxuries. An exception is that of a needed dress for a special party; one that would not be forthcoming otherwise. Another exception is the gift given to the middle-class father. From this report, he corresponds to the cartoonists' conception of him, in that he receives only presents that he would have to buy for himself anyway: ties, shirts, socks, etc. An examination of upper-class gift-giving to father leads to the possible explanation that the middle-class father is discriminated against chiefly because he indulges in so few hobbies, except smoking, that his wife and children are hard pressed to find interesting gifts for him.

The upper-class males do have hobbies which enable their families to give them wider varieties of presents. Golf, gunning, fishing, photography, stamp collecting, and so on, result in very different habits in family presentations. In this class, gift-giving is more restricted to appropriate occasions—birthdays, Christmas, and anniversaries predominating—and is on a more spectacular scale at these times. To give a downright necessity is something not to be tolerated. Even if such an article as a smoking jacket, underwear, or housecoat is given, it must be of the extraordinary sort that precludes its ever being bought by the recipient.

In the lower class, gift-giving is pretty well restricted to birthdays and Christmas. Even birthday celebrations belong chiefly to the smaller children. One girl interviewed responded matter-of-factly, "Oh, I didn't have any birthday this year. I was fifteen." A special dinner with ice cream and cakes is generally the only birthday festivity for parents and older children, except in the smallest families. Christmas is a more liberal time, but the gifts are predominantly in the form of foods of some kind. Another girl described Christmas at her house: a wooden bowl on the center of the dining-room table, containing presents for all the members of the family from the rest of the family. Every gift in the bowl is something to eat.

A very common ritual of the middle-class parent generation was the practice for family and close relatives to present a girl baby at birth, and on subsequent birthdays, with the kind of gift which was a symbol of what it was hoped her adult status would one day be. The most usual gift was a piece of sterling silver flatware, which gradually, through the years, was built up into a whole set. Jewelers aided in this conspiracy, keeping in their files the names of the recipient, the pattern of the silverware, and the pieces already accumulated. The gift second in popularity was the necklace to which a pearl was added annually. The initial gift was the largest, center pearl. Jewelers are still advertising their willingness to aid in this family ritual. In this way many a middle-class girl whose parents and friends might not have been able to present them all at once with these gifts at the proper time, were, upon marriage, equipped with two of the valued symbols of "gracious living."

# THE CHANGING NEGRO FAMILY

*Hylan Lewis*

The recent rapid urbanization has affected Negro families unevenly and in a variety of ways. One reason is that all of the movement is not that of poorly educated, unsophisticated rural persons and families. It is likely, despite their generally poor background, that recent migrants are on the whole better equipped than their predecessors of a generation or more ago. Yet, they are relatively at a greater disadvantage because of changes in the quality of the demand for workers in industry, service, and commerce. On the other hand, particularly, in the urban communities of the North and West, their public rights and interests are better protected—if for no other reason than the political strength of Negroes already settled in those communities.

Today, two out of every three Negroes live in urban areas; and more than one-third of all Negroes now live in urban areas outside of the South. If present trends continue, it is estimated that by the end of the next fifteen years one-fourth to one-third of the population of a number of the larger cities, and as much as one-fifth of the population of some of the larger metropolitan areas will be Negro. An extreme example, and special case in many ways, is Washington, D.C., where Negroes now represent about 45 per cent of the population. About nine out of every ten Negroes in the nation's capital live in the central city. Washington is likely to be a predominantly Negro community in 1970. It is important to note that among Southern cities there is a tendency for the proportion of Negroes to decline.

From *The Nation's Children: I. The Family and Social Change*, editor Eli Ginzberg (New York: Columbia University Press, Copyright © 1960 Golden Anniversary White House Conference on Children and Youth, Inc.), pp. 115–129. Reprinted by permission of Columbia University Press.

397

The gross statistics reveal that Negro families in urban areas significantly exceed the total population with respect to rates of residence in older parts of the central city, female heads of families, working wives, sub-families, doubling-up in households, separations, widowhood, illegitimacy, and participation in the Aid to Dependent Children program.

In standard metropolitan areas, approximately four out of five Negroes live in the central cities in contrast to about three out of five of the white population. Concentrated in the central parts of metropolitan areas, the Negro family has less housing available. And much of the new housing available is that vacated by whites moving to suburban areas and new developments, from which Negroes are excluded by policy or high costs.

The Negro population increased slightly more than one-sixth between 1940 and 1950, but there was an increase of only one-seventh in the number of their dwelling units. On the other hand, the white population increased about one-seventh and there was an increase of nearly one-fourth in the number of dwelling units.

Between 1940 and 1954, the doubling rate among non-white couples was close to twice that for white couples.[1] The significantly higher doubling rate in Negro households is not only a function of lower income, although it is an important factor. It reflects also the small supply of housing for all Negroes and the significant role of kinship, particularly among low-income families. As Frazier points out, this does not mean that the urban Negro family has retained the character of an extended family. This is a pragmatic urban cultural form. The rate of doubling for Negroes in 1954 was about the same as the rate for whites in 1940.

Despite the fact that fertility rates are higher for Negro couples than white couples, proportionately fewer Negro sons and daughters under eighteen years old still live with their parents. Larger proportions of Negro youths in their teens live apart from relatives or live in families of relatives other than their parents. This is also true of younger Negro children but to a lesser extent. In urban areas both in and out of the South, the proportion of middle-age Negro families with young sons and daughters in their homes is significantly lower than that for white families. For farm areas, the reverse is true.

The likelihood that a Negro family is a "project dweller" in a public housing unit is much greater than the likelihood that a white family is—and the Negro ratio appears to be increasing. In 1954, Negro families occupied more than a third (37.7 per cent) of all such units available; in 1957, the proportion exceeded two-fifths (43.7 per cent.) This represents an upgrading of housing for some Negro families. An increasing proportion of low-income urban Negro families are either aspirants to or graduates of public housing projects. There are many relative gains for Negro families

[1] Many of the family statistics cited here and following are taken or adapted from Paul C. Glick, *American Families*, New York, Wiley, 1957.

that live in public housing projects, but complaints and invidiousness with respect to these units and their residents are increasing within the Negro community, as well as the larger community.

Public housing continues to be both the first and last best hope of low-income, marginal families, and those involved with social and welfare agencies. The fact that such housing is under attack for a variety of reasons threatens, and increases the invidiousness with respect to, an important setting for a large slice of Negro family life. The gap between the housing-project dweller and the rest of the Negro community is likely to widen as general upgrading of living and status standards occurs.

More than 25,000 Negro families are "living under conditions of open-occupancy," according to Public Housing officials. Housing experts point out, however, that experience has shown that where racial barriers in public housing have been broken by public policy or law, there is a tendency for the units to become all-minority.

Negro families are disproportionately involved in the displacement and relocation problems related to slum clearance, urban redevelopment, and urban renewal programs. Over-all approximately two out of every three persons displaced are Negroes. In seventeen communities in the Southeastern Region, for example, 95 per cent of the families displaced were Negro; and less than two out of three of these families were relocated in "decent, safe, and sanitary" houses. One of every five families went into substandard housing.

Improved job opportunities and increased incomes since the 1940s have contributed to the marked increase in home ownership among Negroes and significant upgrading in housing among the middle- and upper-income families in urban areas, as a result of both individual efforts and new, privately sponsored but government-insured housing projects for Negroes. Despite this improvement, with the increased population and concentration in the central city, the housing market for the Negro family continues severely restricted. The chances are overwhelming that the Negro family will live in a segregated area or a new transition area that will soon become segregated—a slum or a housing project for low-income groups; and an upgraded all-Negro development, or fringe area for middle- and upper-income groups. And the chances are overwhelming that the Negro family will be paying premium prices for the housing it has.

The Negro family has become increasingly self-conscious and anxious about housing. This development is related not only to scarcity, lack of free choice, and neighborhood and community tensions, but also to changes in comfort, success, and status models. Added to the heightened family and personal value of decent housing and good neighborhoods as proper settings for child-rearing and family living, is the increased importance of housing as a status symbol and measure of mobility. This is, of course, a value that the Negro family shares with all American families. For the Negro family there is additional emphasis—and therefore added possibilities of frustration—because of what housing means now as an overt demonstration of achievement and worth to both the Negro and white communities.

The problem of public school education is directly related to, and aggravated by, the housing situation for Negroes, particularly in urban communities; and it is marked by similar values, needs, and anxieties among the Negro families. Because of the residential concentration of Negro families in the central and older parts of the city, a high proportion of Negro public school pupils are in older, overcrowded school buildings that tend to be segregated in fact, if not in law. The effects on the family are direct not only in terms of the quality of the education of the child but also in terms of the anxieties and resentments this situation arouses in Negro parents of the stable working class and middle class. The effects are more acute because of the high values placed on education as a means of advancement in all levels of the Negro community; of the effect of the Supreme Court decision and desegregation in the South, which spotlight and make more onerous segregated schooling in the North; and because of the great current public concern over the quality of public education.

Negro families, and organizations representing them, are showing increased sensitivity over what are perceived as any competitive disadvantages their children have, for whatever reasons. Negro family heads are likely to be concerned not just about the availability of schooling as such, but about the quality of education available to their children and the characteristics of particular schools. For the second successive year a group of Negro parents in New York City are refusing to send their children to what they describe as an inferior, over-crowded school.

The added value placed on education of children as a means of escaping low and achieving higher status is a myth-like cultural theme. It induces anxiety on all levels. The "compensatory projection of parental ambition" onto children in middle-class, white-collar Negro families is expected and understood; however, Merton points out that "in a recent research on the social organization of public housing developments, we have found among both Negroes and whites in lower occupational levels, a substantial proportion having aspirations for a professional career for their children." Reiss and Rhodes, in a Nashville study, found that "Negroes require a somewhat higher level of educational attainment than the general population and place a substantially greater value on schooling than do whites."

If, as Merton suggests, the "syndrome of lofty aspirations and limited realistic opportunities . . . is precisely the pattern which invites deviant behavior,"[2] the conclusions of Reiss and Rhodes provide an important clue to reasons why, and ways in which, Negro mothers might prime both achievement and deviant behavior in children:

[2] Robert K. Merton, *Social Theory and Social Structure*, Revised and Enlarged Edition, New York: Free Press, 1957, p. 159.

White mothers in the lower stratum of American society are less likely than Negro mothers to project high aspirations on to their children if they are low rather than high I.Q. children. . . . [We] suggest that the importance of schooling to the Negro family makes their members more likely than those of the white family to project unrealistic educational goals in the low I.Q. child. There is only a small race difference in subjects' educational aspirations such that Negroes are somewhat more likely to aspire toward a college education.[3]

The absolute chances of Negro youths for higher education are increasing: In 1950 more Negroes graduated from college than had graduated from high school in 1920. The rate of increase of Negro college enrollment during that period was six times that of whites. The fact that slightly better than one in ten Negro families include an adult with some college education in contrast to slightly more than one in four white families, shows a sizable gap still. Further, as suggested earlier, general anxiety about education is likely to make Negro families more concerned and anxious about the educational future and prospects of children. And all the more so when the increased costs of education are juxtaposed to the generally low income of the Negro family.

One of the most persistent and popular stereotypes is that lower-class parents have little or no interest in the education of their children. Refutation and an indication of the need to examine other factors are furnished in a study made in a New York school with a pupil population predominantly Puerto Rican and Negro. A field worker was assigned to work with the parents. The results:

A year and a half later there were forty-five Negro and Puerto Rican mothers working on the Executive and seven other committees that formed the leadership core of the PTA; the Executive Committee of fifteen Negro and Puerto Rican mothers had felt confident enough to visit the superintendent of all the elementary schools and make a request in non-hostile terms; a parent chorus was giving concerts in schools; the PTA had compiled and mimeographed a directory of available health services and had set up a polio clinic for the neighborhood; and one of the mothers, a Negro, had become president of the Community Health Committee. These parents, who had seemed to take no interest in their children's education, proved that, although oppressed with problems of living conditions, health, and economic security, they were deeply concerned with their school and had the capacity for positive action and leadership.[4]

The foregoing suggests the heavy impact now of housing and schooling values and anxieties as factors affecting one aspect of child rearing and the roles of adults. However, the ways in which, and the relative success with which, Negro families carry out these functions, are primarily related to family size and structure and class position.

[3] Albert J. Reiss, Jr. and Albert L. Rhodes, "Are Educational Norms and Goals of Conforming, Truant, and Delinquent Adolescents Influenced by Group Position in American Society?" *Journal of Negro Education*, **28**, Summer, 1959, 258, 261.
[4] John H. Niemeyer, "Splitting the Social Atom," *Saturday Review*, September 12, 1959, p. 18.

During the past generation, the decline in the average size of Negro households has been much less than that of white households, due to differences in the birth rate and in the practice and necessity of doubling. Negro households are significantly larger, containing on the average more children and more adults. Since 1950, the number of Negro households has been increasing at a rate more than twice that for white households. And Negroes have a relatively larger proportion of both small and large households. This is related to the large proportion of childless women, the high proportion of women with large numbers of children, and the high proportion of lodgers.

The chances continue disproportionately high that much of the socialization of the Negro child will take place in a household headed by a woman, not headed by both or either of his own parents, with relatives other than his own parents and brothers and sisters, or with nonrelatives, and with direct support or subsidy from public funds.

Since the conventional and stable type of family or household is not the instrument of socialization for many children, or of community-orientation and status-giving for many adults, it is probable that persons, institutions, and experiences outside of the family or household are relatively more important, and make their influence felt earlier, in the Negro family. And the relatively larger role played by nonfamily factors in socialization in the Negro community probably applies on all levels and for all family types. Evidence supporting this is found in one of the few recent examples of a follow-up study of Negro family functions. In 1953–56 John H. Rohrer and his associates in New Orleans did a follow-up investigation of the adolescent subjects used in Allison Davis' and John Dollard's 1937–38 study published as *Children of Bondage*. They studied "group patterning of primary social identification" in child training in a class-stratified sample of Negro women householders as well as among the original subjects of the Davis-Dollard study. Their study "failed to reveal that there was any universal systematic training given in caste etiquette, at least before school age."[5]

All that this finding suggests, however, is that the Negro child probably gets most of his racial training by absorbing informally and unsystematically clues and cues from members of the household and from outside the family. Merton points out: "Nor is the socialization confined to direct training and disciplining. The process is, at least in part, inadvertent . . . Not infrequently, *children detect and incorporate cultural uniformities even when these remain implicit and have not been reduced to rules*."[6]

Edward K. Weaver asked children at an elementary school in the

---

[5] John H. Rohrer, "Sociocultural Factors in Personality Development," National Conference on Social Welfare, *The Social Welfare Forum, Official Proceedings*, *Philadelphia*, 1957, New York, Columbia University Press, 1957, p. 195.
[6] Merton, *Social Theory*, p. 158.

South to write answers to the question "When did you first discover that you were a Negro?" In only three of the thirty replies cited as "typical" did a child report the first explicit revelation as having come from direct family instruction or from inside the home. And in these instances it was the grandparent who gave the instruction or warning.[7]

Statistics continue to confirm the classic pictures of disorganization, dependency, and inadequacy, and larger proportions of broken families and female heads. However, we have little or no recent data to tell us what these facts and forms mean and represent in the present context. It may be that the classic explanations are still valid, but we cannot be sure, and there is a risk in assuming or guessing, without the facts that go beyond the statistics and older studies.

The proportion of Negroes married but living apart from spouses is three to four times higher than that of whites. Approximately one in nine Negro married women and one in twelve Negro married men are living apart from their spouses. Negroes constitute about one in eleven of all families in the United States, one in fourteen of all husband-wife families, and one in five of all families with female heads.

Much of the incidence of these and the related characteristics is, of course, explained, as Frazier has done so effectively, by the persistence of rural-folk traditions and ways in interaction with urban, secular imperatives. However, not enough is known about the dynamics of present family forms and functions and about the behavior patterns which are distinctly urban products with a dynamic and history of their own. The forms, as in the case of the family headed by the female, may be the same but the context in which they fit and function has probably changed in important details. Knowledge of background and of a tradition, which itself is changing, are necessary but probably not sufficient to explain and understand the Negro family, particularly in the changing cities of today.

In this connection, it is probable that even the time-honored reference to desertion as "the poor man's divorce" needs closer examination and discrimination, although it is abundantly clear that the racial difference in desertion remains very significant. In a study made in Philadelphia, Kephart found that "when the bottom three occupational classes are combined . . . for the whites these classes are slightly overrepresented in desertions, while among Negroes, surprisingly, these classes are slightly underrepresented. . . . [Among] the Negroes the greatest overrepresentation is found in the semiskilled category." He suggests as explanatory factors possible underreporting because of ignorance of the law and the "lingering tradition" among Negro lower classes—the wives may not want husbands back. Balancing these, however, he adds, is the fact that lower-class wives

[7] Edward K. Weaver, "Racial Sensitivity Among Negro Children," *Phylon*, **17**, First Quarter, 1956, 52–60.

must have family support and cannot get public assistance unless the husband is reported.[8]

The census data indicate that "color is a differential in marriage impermanence only in separation and widowhood." Divorce rates for Negro women tend to rise as education rises up to, but not including, college graduation.

Increases in illegitimacy rates among Negroes and in the proportion participating in the Aid to Dependent Children program are associated with recent increases in urbanization. For the general population, the number of births to unmarried mothers has been rising at a faster rate than births to married mothers. The illegitimacy rate in 1956 was 46.5 per 1,000 live births as compared with 37.9 per 1,000 live births in 1940. Teenagers contributed nearly half the number of illegitimacies in 1940, and 40 per cent in 1956. The predominant part of the increase between 1940 and 1955 is to be accounted for by nonwhite illegitimate births, which increased at a rate more than twice that for whites. There has been a tendency for the nonwhite rate to be higher in Northern urban centers than the estimated nonwhite percentage for the entire country including the Southern states. It is undoubtedly true now as Frazier points out that "illegitimacy, like other forms of family disorganization, tends to become segregated in the poorer sections of the Negro community located in the slum areas of our cities." The fact that illegitimacy rates are increasing in urban areas at the same time that the general economic and educational level of the Negro population is improving may reflect a short-run rise attributable in the main to the disorganization related to the rapid influx and piling up of low-income groups. There are certainly other factors operating currently about which we know little, which are independent of race.

Another measure of family inadequacy or disorganization closely associated with increasing urbanization of the Negro is the rate of participation in the Aid to Dependent Children program. This is not surprising inasmuch as the family crises leading to need for ADC (absence or incapacity of father) occur relatively more frequently among low-income groups. Urbanization of ADC recipients is increasing, particularly among Negroes who make up an increasing portion of the ADC load—31 per cent in 1948; 40 per cent in 1956. More than one-half of the nonwhite family recipients live in cities of over 50,000 population; nearly two-thirds of the Negro recipients are in metropolitan counties. The overrepresentation of Negro families on ADC rolls is a political and administrative issue in both many Southern states and Northern communities with large concentrations of Negroes. This is another example of the acutely "political" character of the needs and rights of disadvantaged Negroes.

The increase, and the differential, in the labor force participation of

[8] William M. Kephart, "Occupational Level and Marital Disruption," *American Sociological Review*, **20**, August, 1955.

Negro wives reflect different values and pressure among them: the greater need to work to maintain or supplement a basically low family income, particularly among lower occupational and educational levels; increased incentive or wish to work, in order to improve or maintain a desired level of living, particularly among mobile, better-educated, middle-class families; and possibly, more favorable conditions for leaving children with relatives or others. The significance of this last is questionable, particularly among low-income newcomers to the large cities. Social workers report an increase in "door-key children" and an acute current shortage of low-cost nursery care in impoverished urban areas.

Negro wives in just over two-fifths of all Negro husband-wife families work; about half of those with no children under six work; and nearly one in four of those with children under six is in the labor force. The mothers of children under six are less than half as likely to be working as other mothers, regardless of race and other variables. And the differences in labor force participation of mothers, Negro and white, who share family responsibilities with a husband and those who are themselves the head of the family, as in the case of a disproportionate number of Negroes, are growing less. That this does not imply the same values and pressures is indicated by the fact that the income level of nearly one-half the broken families with female heads is below $2,000. There is some convergence in the employment of Negro and white wives, but the differences remain large.

# UP FROM PUERTO RICO

*Elena Padilla*

## HOME LIFE

The home life of Eastville Hispanos is conditioned by their living in New York. Though recent migrants' home life contrasts at many points with that of Hispanos who have grown up in New York, the home life of both is different from that of Puerto Ricans on the island. Hispanos who have grown up here regard "American" home life as being different and as suiting them better than that of Puerto Ricans. They overtly try to be different from Puerto Ricans and to come closer to American ideals of family living.

For recent migrants on the other hand, keeping the family functioning properly in New York is a new enterprise in living, requiring many adaptations. Young or old, the individual is oriented toward placing his family's interests before his own, and toward subordinating his own individual needs to the demands of family life. Recent migrants find that rules for family living are changing right before their eyes, and that new rules and codes for living are developing, regardless of whether they approve of them or live by them. These appear as part of the cultural adaptations taking place among Hispanos. Rules of behavior, authority patterns, decision-making channels, and the expectations of family members reflect the changes in the routine of everyday family life. This is an unavoidable aspect of the process of adaptation that migrants must undergo in order to live with minimal conflicts. The end-product may, however, prove to be maladaptive and hence destructive of the adequate functioning of the individual. Yet whatever happens to the Hispano family in New York is pivotal to what will happen to the personal and social development of the individual Hispano.

The Puerto Rican family in Eastville lives within the setting of a slum subculture, and is subject to the stresses and difficulties, as well as to the social, cultural, and psychological potentials of positive adaptation that that style of life offers the underprivileged in this society. The family is also affected by the rules and standards set up by the larger society and its institutions. In addition, the cultural influences stemming from the adaptations of the Hispano subculture in New York present the Puerto Rican family with changed rules and norms to live by. What will happen to the family in New York is contingent, too, upon the degree of cohesiveness and adequate functioning it had in Puerto Rico. It is likely that a migrant family which did not function adequately in the island will disintegrate in New York in the light of the additional conflicts in norms that its members will meet here. The family that functioned adequately in Puerto Rico, providing basic emotional and social supports to its members, on the other hand, has greater resources to cope with the changing sociocultural environment, though it too here faces severe conflicts and stresses that may bring about its destruction. The process of adaptation of the family involves an emphasis on cultural traditionalism. As a means of counteracting social and cultural changes that seem incompatible with the adequate functioning of the family and its members, the uprooted family tends to reinforce the values of the past and to channel these socially by stressing the importance of parental authority as a source of control. That authority acts as a guide in the selection and acceptance of new influences, and the parent in whom it is vested is expected to use his power to halt undesirable changes. Should the authority fail, the migrant family is likely to be shattered. In the framework of the historical and environmental contexts of the Hispano migrant family, then, it is unrealistic to expect its smooth transition in the direction of middle-class core American values.

To insure its own survival, and to insure some kind of social and emotional balance for its growing children, the Hispano family will tend to seek adaptations that are compatible with its cultural ideology as well as with its subcultural settings in New York. In Eastville these adaptations are made in the direction of learning to cope with American life from the starting point of the slum subculture. There, while the father is the boss of the family, the mother holds the responsibility for managing family matters. This responsibility has been delegated to her by her husband, to whom she, in turn, is responsible. She can make rules for the children and other members of the household (except her husband) to follow, and while she can be overruled by her husband, there are areas in which, to please her, he will go along with her. This is particularly so in matters pertaining to disciplining the children and teaching them to behave properly.

A family in which "order" is maintained is considered necessary to the development of "good" children. Good parents must inculcate respect in their children, as respect is essential to the maintenance of order in the family and to the smooth conduct of family affairs. The lines of authority in a family are supposed to radiate from the father, as center, to the mother, and thence from the older to the younger children. When authority channels operate thus, a family is said to be one in which respect has been instilled and order is maintained. A good father expresses his love for his children by his control over their conduct and by presenting them with an example of a good man. In practice this means he is to support, guide, and discipline them.

Juan Ramon is considered by his wife a good man, except for three faults. The first is that he is weak with his children; they do not respect him and he does not do anything about it. Second, he is a jealous man. And third, he is "a man of color." However, he is a good father otherwise, because he supports his children, not only those of his present wife, but also those he had by his first wife.

Eastville Puerto Ricans also distinguish between "ancient" (*a la antigua*) and "modern" families. The family that is rigidly ruled by the father, or the mother, is called "ancient," and is different from the "families of today." The ideal of greater leeway and tolerance for the children is more distinct among young adults, whether they came from Puerto Rico recently or grew up in New York. As a rule, the younger parents are better educated than their own parents, have broader outlooks, and uphold the idea that there should be fewer restrictions placed on children by their parents. Especially among adults whose fathers were of the "ancient" kind and who made their mothers suffer either by infidelity, mistreatment, physical punishment, or desertion of the family, is there outspoken criticism of this type of family. It is said that these are different times, that one should bring up the children in a different manner, giving them more freedom and allowing them to play. Yet even among these individuals decisions about family affairs reside in a central authority, usually the father. The difference is that the authority is more flexible, less restrictive, and less formidable.

Good parents are always right, for what they do is for the good of their child, so new rules may be invoked and all rules changed at will by the parents in order to resolve problems between them and their child. The child has no voice in decisions made by his parents about himself or anything else. One day when twelve-year-old Joe, and his ten-year-old brother, Jim, were playing in an alley behind their home, Joe found a knife. His father who watched their play from a window, noticed the object in Joe's hand and called both boys upstairs. In an angry tone the father asked Joe, "Where did you get it?" to which the reply was, "In the yard." "What were you doing there?" Jim: "Playing with a boy." The father took the knife out of Joe's hand and told both Jim and Joe that children should not play with knives. He warned them that "if the police see children playing with knives, they put them in jail." The father then said he was going to throw the knife out of the window. The mother, who had until then remained silent while watching the father scold the boys, noted that the knife belonged to some American Negroes who had lost it in the alley. The oldest son, a young man, said that the knife should not be thrown away but kept for stirring up the earth around the plants. The mother asked in astonishment, "What plants?" (there are no plants in the household), and continued, "I am going to use it in the kitchen; it is a good chopping knife." The father then went on with this scolding of Jim and Joe in the same angry tone: "If you find another knife, it must be brought immediately to your mother to see if she can use it in the kitchen." Then, looking at the fieldworker who had witnessed the scene, he added: "You see, they don't know how to play with knives, and did not know what to do with it." By this time the two boys were standing quietly beside the window in tears.

Thus the father switched his command arbitrarily in midstream, and whatever he might say or do could not be questioned by his children and at least not directly by his wife, for he holds the responsibility and authority. In most ways, the father is a "free agent." He can come and go as he pleases, but his wife is supposed to tell him or the children where she is going when leaving the household, or where she has been on returning.

At least once a week the father is likely to go out by himself, and seldom is he seen in the company of his wife. If they do go out together, he will probably walk in front while she lags behind with some of the children, as rarely does a woman go out at all without her children. Her husband, in fact, may be seen in the street more often with the children than with "the missus" (*la doña*). If he is invited to a party or some other recreational gathering, it may be specified that he "bring some of the children," which he will do. And even for other social occasions, unless he goes by himself, he will be much more inclined to take his older children than his wife. Hardly would both father and mother go out together socially leaving the children at home alone, for babysitters are not used. It is understood that the father is to spend part of his income on his own personal recreation and amusement, which includes buying beer for his friends, playing the numbers, and going to night clubs. Both at home and in the street he is likely to be better dressed than other members of his family. In a word his own economic needs are recognized to be of greater importance than those of any other individual member of his family, although as a father he is supposed to acknowledge his obligation to support his wife and children.

To carry out his obligation of support, the father assigns his wife an allowance (*un diario*). She decides the family menus on a day-to-day basis, and on Saturday prepares a list of items for her husband to bring from a supermarket or the city market which is located within walking distance of Eastville. Although the heavy shopping (*la compra*) is done only once a week, not all that is needed for the week ahead is purchased then, nor is it planned in accordance with a weekly menu. Rather, the weekly shopping consists primarily of approximate quantities of the bulky staple items, such as rice, potatoes, beans, and other grains, which form the foundation of the family's diet, plus the particular food that is to be consumed over the weekend. In addition, it includes a number of special items not considered essential to the family's diet, but which have status value, or are indexes that the family is well off. These are beer, both with and without alcohol (black malt), soda pop—especially cream soda—cakes, and canned pear, apricot, or orange juice. The father also makes arrangements with a near-by bodega for the family to buy on credit some of the daily incidentals, such as meat, milk, and eggs. Not only does the father take care of the family's food shopping, but also he does most of the shopping for their clothes, medicines, and articles of personal use. If he is too busy or if his wife complains too much about the quality of his shopping, he may tell her to go and do it herself, but the children are likely to have little to say about what either parent selects for their personal use.

The family depends on both cash income and credit to supply its needs, which are to be met as soon as they are recognized. As a rule, no one plans a budget for expenses. Wages earned by the father are already consumed or owed by the time he gets paid. His pay probably will not exceed forty dollars a week, and his job will probably be unskilled and seasonal, with layoffs. He may have to hock his watch or borrow from professional money lenders, a finance company, or friends at high interest rates in order to meet such emergencies as illness or requests made by the schools for the children, or to make a partial payment on an old debt. A wife may exaggerate to her husband the nature of family needs and debts and in this way acquire some money herself. Other ways she manages to obtain money are by shopping for bargains and by telling her husband she has had to borrow cash for an emergency. Either she will save this money for a real emergency, hiding it some place in the house—in an old purse, a shoe, or underclothes—or else she will use it to meet immediate needs of the children, the house, or herself. Most wives who earn money at home, like those who take care of working women's children, administer their earnings themselves. The husband of such a woman may, however, cut down on her allowance because now she has her own money.

The housewife who conforms to the expectations for a good wife is a "busy" woman. She is not idle, she does not gossip or wonder what the neighbors are doing. She stays home and works almost constantly, because "the work of a woman never ends."

In the morning the wife gets up before her husband and children, usually between six and seven, depending on the time her husband must be at work and the children in school. If she has a baby, it is to be fed soon after it wakes up, but one of her first chores is to prepare breakfast for her husband. She boils fresh milk and makes coffee, preferably a brand said to be of "Latin flavor" (*al gusto latino*), such as Cafe Bustelo or Cafe Crema. The coffee considered best is the strong and flavorful one, and this is at its best when served with a lot of milk—"quite white" (*bien blanco*)— and flavored with sugar. The husband may have a piece of white bread spread with margarine or butter with his coffee. While he eats his breakfast, his wife prepares his lunch, which usually consists of a sandwich of white bread, filled with a slice of processed meat or cheese, and a thermos of coffee. The wife may take a cup of coffee while she stands to fix her husband's lunch or does other early morning chores around the house, but she does not sit down to eat with him. If she has school-age children, she will call them, and it is her job to see that they clean themselves up properly. Breakfast for the children is not standardized except that all are expected to drink coffee with milk and sugar. This is the basic breakfast for both young and old. A child may refuse to consume more than this, but if circumstances permit, the children may be offered a choice of corn flakes, fritters, or a piece of cake. If they are skinny (*flacos*) or have no appetite (*desganados*), they may have to take "medicine"—cod liver oil or a liquid or semiliquid patent tonic "with vitamins." After breakfast, on leaving for school, the children are expected to ask a blessing from their mother and also one from their father, if he is still home.

Breakfast over, if she does not have to walk the children to school, the mother may start to reorganize the household by making beds and folding up cots, love seats, sofas, and other furniture used as beds. After she does this and her apartment looks tidy, she may go back to bed herself for a nap until around ten, when she is to start her mopping and the daily washing of shirts, bedding, diapers, dresses, pants, and so on. By afternoon one sees lines of clothing extending from one end of the kitchen to the other, or out of the window on a clothesline through the yard. While performing these duties the mother may have a second cup of coffee, and afterward she may have to go down to the bodega to buy milk or sugar or some other foodstuff, to use during the day, before she undertakes her other daily chores of ironing and mending. Several such trips may be necessary, and even when the children come home from school, they may be asked to bring up still other items that she "forgot" she did not have in the house and that will be needed for dinner or snacks. When the mother is not going far, she may leave the small children sleeping in the apartment by themselves, asking a next-door neighbor to look in on them occasionally while she is gone. While shopping she is likely to meet her friends and neighbors and exchange information with them, making it something of a social expedition.

For business that will require more time or take her out of the neighborhood, the mother will ask one of her school-age children to stay home to look after the younger ones, while another of her older children may have to go along with her. This child acts both as a translator and as a protector of her virtue, because a good woman is not to be seen alone in the street: a woman alone in the street must of necessity be doing something bad or looking forward to doing something bad.

The children attending school in or near Eastville may come home after having had their lunch at school for a second lunch at home—usually bread and butter or a slice of processed meat and a cup of coffee with milk and sugar. Children who claim they do not like the school lunch do not eat at school at all. They come home for their meals, which may consist of canned food, such as spaghetti or soup, with or without a slice of bread, coffee with milk and sugar, or just soda pop. The mother may have a cup of coffee and a slice of white bread for lunch unless there are guests in the house. When guests are present, she may either forego eating lunch altogether, or she may prepare sandwiches or canned food. After the children come home from school at around three, they are expected to have coffee with milk, and even a baby may be fed a bottle of coffee with milk in it at this time.

In the morning the mother will put beans in water to soak, and around two in the afternoon she will probably start to boil them and to prepare the dinner that will not be ready until sometime after six. Rice and beans, or rice and some other grain, are essential to a real dinner. The rice may be "white" or "stewed" (*guisado*). White rice is cooked in boiling water, and after it is soft, one or two large spoonfuls of lard are added. A basic method of making stewed rice is to fry chopped pieces of salt pork and add to this small chunks of tomatoes, garlic, onion, and greens, which are pounded on a wooden mortar with a pestle. The rice, which is first fried and then boiled in additional water until the grains are soft but loose, is added to this mixture, and on top is placed either *achiote* (a tropical fruit pulp, *annatto*) or tomato sauce, "to add color to it." To cook beans or other grains a similar procedure is followed, namely, small chunks of pounded ham, salt pork, tomatoes, and so on are fried and added to the beans or grains after they have boiled, and then the whole is simmered together.

Rice and beans do not constitute a balanced meal, however, though a complete dinner that includes them is considered necessary to good health, for "it is fattening and makes a person strong." To be complete a meal must include a "mixture" (*mixtura*). This can be fried eggs, fried potatoes, slices of fried plantains, or fritters of meal flour and dried codfish, meat, or chicken. After dinner, coffee is served again. Salads, green vegetables, fresh fish, and fresh fruits are seldom, if ever, part of the daily diet. Sunday meals, particularly the dinner in the middle of the day, usually consist of rice with chicken and beans; or rice and beans and pork chops; or filet of beef; or fried chicken as *mixtura*. Meats and poultry are cooked until well done.

As a rule, meals are not eaten by all the family together. Usually the father is served alone so that he will not be disturbed, unless a "person of importance" (*persona de cumplido*) or a close male friend of his has dropped in at dinnertime. For a person of importance a special meal must be prepared, or else he may be asked politely and without insistence, "Would you join us?" and he, according to convention, is to reply, "No, thanks. I already ate." A close friend, on the other hand, will be urged to stay for dinner, and such extras as canned soup, canned spaghetti, or more fritters prepared. That is, the wife improves on the *mixtura*, insisting that "there is enough for all."

On Sundays and holidays, it is expected that friends and relatives will drop in unexpectedly to "spend the day." They are invited to eat and are to be impressed with the good living the family is enjoying, as can be estimated by the quantity and quality of the food they are served. Such visiting at home, by one whole family with another whole family, or going to the parks or beaches in the summer represents almost the only recreation indulged in by the members of a family as a group. Otherwise, leisure-hour activities are contingent upon the age, sex, and position in the household of individual family members.

Children are not to eat with adults. The mother calls and serves them separately, and she may have to prepare something special for those who say they do not like rice and beans and for those who say they will eat later. Mothers often claim that their children do not like Puerto Rican food: "They eat only American [food]." And this kind of food may be prepared for them. When asked what American foods the children like, mashed potatoes, spaghetti, fried chicken, and canned foods are mentioned. Mothers also often claim that they have to cook rice and beans daily on account of their husbands, because they themselves will "eat anything." Mothers may also say, "I hate milk," or, "I hate eggs," or, "I don't like meat." These remarks reflect, on a latent level, an aspect of "good" motherhood conditioned by circumstances of scarcity, namely, that a mother is to keep secret from her husband and children her liking for "expensive foods." She justifies her rejection of them by saying she does not like them. When she buys these products, it is understood that she is not to consume them herself but to leave them for her husband and children.

A mother will also cook special food for those children who are considered to be underweight or to have a delicate taste that does not permit them to eat "regular food," because they might get sick. These children are termed *delicado* or *mañoso*. In Spanish the auxiliary verb *ser* is used with *delicado* to connote "delicate." *Estar delicado*, on the other hand, means to have pulmonary tuberculosis. A *delicado* child in the former sense is actually a spoiled child, and psychologically he can be characterized as a child with strong dependency needs for his parents, particularly his mother, which he satisfies through special food demands. This is also a culturally acceptable way of dealing with sibling rivalry. The father or mother may punish a child who does not eat, though not if he is *delicado*, but rather if he was eating candy or bread before the meal (eating *vicios*), which spoiled his appetite.

The mother will probably have her own dinner after everybody else has been served. No doubt she will be so tired by that time that she will have a few spoonfuls of food from the kettles and pans rather than serve herself on a dish. As she takes her few bites standing by the stove, she may remark, if visitors are present, that she never has enough time to sit down and eat. Afterward, perhaps she will ask one of her daughters to help her with the dishes and with cleaning up the kitchen, but she is not likely to ask her husband or sons to help her with these tasks because they are considered "womanly."

While the mother cleans up, the father and the children may move into the living room where several activities will probably take place simultaneously. One child may study, another watch "The Lone Ranger" on TV, the father listen to the "Spanish Hour" on the radio, and visitors come in to chat. Watching TV, listening to the radio, and engaging in conversation are the chief pleasure-time pursuits in the home, and talking is usually reserved to adults, especially men, as children are not allowed, or at least not supposed, to move around too much, to play, or to make noise at home. While the father and the after-dinner visitors are talking, he may offer the guests coffee, hot chocolate, soda pop, canned juices, or nonalcoholic beer, which he will call upon his wife to serve. Then, after she has finished the kitchen work, she may come and sit in the living room for a time, until around ten when the children are to take their baths. At this point she will bathe those "who do not know how to." In the meanwhile, the father may have gone out "to the corner." On his return he will probably retire. There are many nights when the mother is not likely to go to bed until after midnight, however, or whenever it is that she finishes her household chores.

A good woman is expected to attend to her household duties regardless of whether she must seek employment outside of her home. She may call on her mother in Puerto Rico to come to New York and help her or else send for her niece or godchild to help her maintain the order and cleanliness that bespeaks a good family. Should she fail on this score, she is considered dirty and can only be socially justified on account of illness. Seldom are the condition of the buildings, the dirt and garbage in the surroundings of her home considered justifiable explanations for not having a spic-and-span household, for in terms of standards of recent migrants, the condition of the household is solely a woman's responsibility. By the same token, the condition of neglect of the neighborhood buildings, streets, and alleys is seen as being solely the responsibility of the government.

Among women brought up in this country the ideal of a good woman as one who is responsible only to her home, husband, and children is considered old-fashioned. Rather, among them prevails the concept of womanhood as associated with equivalent responsibilities between husband and wife, the availability of time for recreation and enjoyment away from household chores, both for the family as a group and for the couple as husband and wife. These ideals of behavior call for a different kind of organization of daily activities for women reared in this country than that of recent migrant women. Caught between these sets of standards, many Eastville Hispano women fail to achieve their goals, even if they pay lip service to the cultural ideals of good womanhood.

# CHINESE CULTURE, SOCIAL ORGANIZATION,
# AND PERSONALITY

*Rose Hum Lee*

For the past several decades, there has been an undiminished interest in the impact of culture on social organization and personality.[1] The thesis underlying the interrelationship between these concepts is that a given culture, e.g. the Chinese one, contains broad patterns of behavior, known as cultural uniformities, which are transmitted through its institutions. These behavior patterns, reflected in the personalities of the general population, are used to distinguish the members of one society from another. Hence, Chinese differ from Koreans and Indonesians through being brought up in a cultural milieu that molds them into socially acceptable personalities suitable for their particular society. The foremost social organization transmitting and implanting such patterns is the family, but it is supplemented by educational, religious, political and other organizations.

This approach does not obviate the existence of individual differences resulting from family expectations, parent-child relationships, social class membership, education, occupation, religion, and other influences. Rather, broad cultural uniformities enable members of a society to utilize common denominators around which to interact in matters ranging from etiquette to interpersonal relations or from voting habits to abstract notions about war and peace. An understanding of the cultural uniformities enables a stranger coming into the society to establish and develop *rapport*

[1] Merrill, Francis E. and Eldredge, H. Wentworth. *Society and Culture*, Englewood Cliffs, New Jersey: Prentice-Hall, 1957, Ch. 10.

From *The Chinese in the United States of America* by Rose Hum Lee (Hong Kong: Hong Kong University Press, Copyright 1960), pp. 132–141. Reprinted by permission of Hong Kong University Press.

with the resident population, because they form the bases for mutual exchange of social amenities as well as of serious topics.

These broad cultural uniformities are centered around the institutional roles the members of a society assume and act out as they engage in reciprocal relations with others. These can be gleaned from the child-rearing practices used by the members of the family in socializing their young. In the Chinese society parents and elders are expected to transmit and implant the broad behavior patterns to succeeding generations through example, conditioning, punishment and rewards. They teach the young (1) the content of culture (actual behavior patterns), (2) the meaning of culture (what these patterns mean), (3) the organization of culture (internalizing the meanings and actions into a functional whole).

It becomes pertinent to determine which of the cultural uniformities are introduced by the immigrant Chinese who recreate as far as possible the kind of social organization they knew in China. By and large they created associations more frequently than institutions and these served to reaffirm and strengthen the behavior patterns carried from China through the clan, district, and benevolent associations. For the sake of brevity, attention will be centered around the behavior patterns which are found more frequently among the foreign-born and other China-oriented Chinese. The retention of these patterns caused persons of Chinese ancestry to be different from others in this society.

Although it may be argued that American-Chinese have these behavior patterns too, since they are partially the products of Chinese culture and institutions, the patterns grow weaker with each succeeding generation. Through interacting with another set of institutions, the native-born substitute cultural uniformities found in the American society. The latter are learned from the existing American institutions, while the Chinese family seeks to impart the old-world heritage. If old-world patterns are retained by the China-oriented native-born, they fulfill special personal needs, such as vested interests, social acceptance by foreign-born rather than by native-born, or the means for attaining status, power, and influence. Some may also retain these behavior patterns and participate in old-world organizations out of inertia or parental pressures.

In the transmitted old-world heritage most important are the associations that reflect the social organization of society in China, i.e., the clan and family associations, district associations, and the like. When these did not suffice, tongs or merchants associations and benevolent associations sprang up. Later, associations organized around common interest, professionalism, civic enterprise, etc., came into existence to satisfy the needs of the better-educated Chinese as well as the native-born. Although the old-world organizations are increasingly ineffective, they have not been abandoned, because some of the Chinese in America resist changes in their way of life. Indeed, there is overwhelming evidence that the associations and institutions the Chinese believe adequate for their needs in America are outmoded in China today, whether Taiwan or the Mainland. The cultural uniformities which the Chinese in America cling to are being rooted out and superseded by new ones.

However, there are several behavior patterns found among the foreign-born, and to a lesser degree among some native-born, which are contributing to the disorganizing of Chinese life and social organization. These behaviors are also hindering the acculturation, assimilation, and integration of the Chinese into American society. Foremost is the tendency of the Chinese to utilize indirect, rather than direct, methods of interaction. Second is the inclination to involve others, especially members of *tongs* and other associations, in personal or group problems, rather than rely on solutions offered by the larger society or act on an individual basis. Third is the creation and perpetuation of covert measures of social control which are enforced through associational backing of individuals whom the associations favor, as a device for presenting a united front to the American society and to hide the activities of the China-oriented Chinese whose behavior is counter to the prevailing norms and values. Fourth is the reliance on face-saving to reinforce social control and to justify the existence of China-oriented norms and behaviors. Fifth is the flight from reality, or the immigrants' habit of believing the world they left to be as it was, rather than as it has become.

It should be noted that very many Chinese in America and elsewhere have laudable traits which are widely acclaimed and admired: patience, tolerance, faith (or fatalism), honesty, industriousness, integrity and humility, to name a few. Ironically, the persons exhibiting these traits are also apt to transmit and retain those that are no longer effective in maintaining the best form of social organization or in helping the young to develop the best personality.

A summary of the important aspects of social organization and child-rearing practices in China as they are related to the transmission of the afore-mentioned cultural uniformities will help in understanding Chinese life and thought in the U.S.A., and will provide appropriate frames of reference.

## THE CLAN AND EXTENDED FAMILY

For over twenty centuries Chinese society revolved around clans, groups of individuals stemming from a common ancestor and bearing the same surname. Consequently, innumerable Chinese are related by consanguinity and these clan relationships form the basis for preferred social interaction, the extension of mutual aid and protection, and power interrelations. Clans are more important in southern than northern China; the immigrants from Kwangtung Province recreated clan or family associations here. Particular Chinatowns have been organized around a given clan. In time, other clans arrived and formed their own associations to counteract the power and influence of the entrenched clan or clans.

Since clan members are scattered throughout China, as they are in the U.S.A., a second basis for organization was used, namely the district of origin. District associations tied those of a given clan or several clans together for mutual aid and protection against the vicissitudes of life in a new land. Hence, the clan and district associations superseded the individual in importance; until several decades ago a Chinese individualist had difficulty in being accepted by other Chinese.

The superordinate position of the clan is evidenced by the surname, which precedes the personal name, e.g., in 'Dr. Sun Yat-sen', Sun is the surname and is placed uppermost because strangers can, through the exchange of surnames, quickly establish identification and kinship, or the opposite. Westernized Chinese native-born reverse the order, showing greater individualism as well as Americanization, through relegating the clan surname to a place behind their personal names. In fact, one of the greatest points of contention between foreign-born and native-born is the practice of changing surnames through romanizing them to the point where they negate clan membership. Few of the native-born who have never visited China have any interest in the home village or district of their original ancestors.

Since the Chinese are surrounded by many persons to whom they owe obligations and duties because of kinship relations, the preferred type of family arrangement in China was the extended-kinship family. This was a miniature clan, so to speak, important for persons needing food, shelter, employment, protection, and influence. Extended families are composed of several generations as well as collateral kinsmen living together under one roof, or in a big compound. Ideally the oldest members head the units, and their descendants and close kinsmen prefer to have their elders represent them as social heads.

An illustration is the Chew family in Hong Kong, living in a three-story brick house, filled with relatives. The family includes: the head of the household, his wife, his concubine, married and unmarried sons, wives and children of the married sons, unmarried female children, the first wife's distant female cousin, sometimes the brother of the latter, the unmarried sons and daughters of the household head's first cousin, a widowed fourth aunt, relatives visiting the village, and kinsmen in need of food and shelter during periods of unemployment or adversity. Frequently, others come and stay for companionship or personal reasons. In addition, there are servants for each of the family units (head of household, concubine, married sons) as well as two more servants to take care of the rest of the family. Then there are cooks, maidservants, and a handyman. At meal times, thirty places must be set.

In the United States, such units are rare because families were few until recently. In their place were the Chinese shops whose owners were likely to have their families and many kinsmen boarding with them, thus duplicating to some degree the extended family ties. It is well known that many persons are "related" while living in America who would not be so regarded in China; that is, they have the same surnames but are not related in the strict use of the term, as cousins, uncles, nephews, etc.

These consanguineous units are symbolic of comfortable middle-class status in China and came to be so regarded in the U.S.A., for they bolstered the status of the Chinese merchant and his family. In practice, the social head and his subordinates (younger male kin) signify that they are capable of (1) supporting a large number of dependents, (2) maintaining harmony among a large number of people, and (3) demonstrating the ability to extend power, influence, and status over a wide geographical area. Such units often own and control farm lands, businesses, or investments where they live and where other relatives live in the next city, in rural China, and elsewhere. People become equated with wealth and power, therefore, and their importance to the larger organization is based on their willingness to subordinate their personal desires in the interest of the group's well-being.

Individuals belonging to this form of organization must accept their position. The youngest members must respect those above them. For example, in the Chew family mentioned, the daughters of the first wife take precedence over those of the concubine. The latter are known as "nine" and "ten," meaning they are below eight and nine sisters or brothers to whom they must accord respect and obedience. Then they have to acknowledge the ascendancy of two mothers, a father, a fourth aunt, older cousins, and other elders. These hierarchical arrangements have an impact on personality. Persons thus reared in China, whether in villages or cities, behave accordingly after settling in the United States. This has contributed to reliance upon the older sojourners and foreign-born, who came as younger men but are now middle-aged, as leaders.


## IMPACT ON PERSONALITY

To maintain harmony, individuals in the Chinese family are taught to keep to their assigned status and rank. Ideally, group aims are achieved by respect and obedience to authoritarian elders. The young in Chinese society are taught to repress their own desires, to inhibit aggressions. Otherwise their parents are criticized for improper child-rearing. This has given rise to the seeming stoicism of the Chinese. True emotional reactions are seldom displayed by the properly reared child; and this is equated with "good breeding."

In contrast, the lower classes and the less educated are not bound by these restrictions and niceties. Their emotional reactions take shape in loud denunciations, assaults, conspiracies, and fights. Low-class females, particularly, wail aloud in public and weep copiously over any alleged mistreatment by family members. They are commonly heard to threaten suicide even in America.

The members of the large extended units learn to be secretive about their desires, in order to circumvent others who are envious, jealous, greedy, and conniving. In theory, the in-group members should be working in close harmony, but in practice such a state of affairs is seldom approximated. Children learn at an early age to be secretive, in order to safeguard their desires from the everwatchful adults around them. Indeed, parents teach children how to evade censure and punishment at the same time that they teach them how to connive against those who appear to be thwarting them. Obviously, the mothers more than the fathers impart the behavior patterns centering around indirection, secretiveness, slyness, intimidation, gossip, innuendoes, evasiveness, and intrigue. Moreover, children connive to act together against the dominance of collateral peers.

A strong measure of social control taught to the young is "face saving": not to embarrass others and not to be caught in embarrassing situations. In a large family, where many persons know one another and many interests must be reconciled, offenders are judged by many elders and peers, not only by their parents and siblings. There are many who know about petty quarrels, jealousies, competitiveness, distorted motives, or greed.

In its undiluted form, "face-saving" is a delicate concept and is intended to protect the innocent from the malicious. Those who have offended others want to be seen in the best possible light and do not wish to have to regain favor with all who are above them in status. The time may come, moreover, when the victims become the offenders and need to have their "faces" saved. Face-saving is a shield for both.

The desire to save face has resulted in many unfair situations remaining unsatisfactorily resolved. The persons aggrieved feel abused; while the abusers fear no retaliation, especially if they have status and prestige. In practice, face-saving has become perverted and is used to shield persons whose misdeeds should be exposed. They are exempted because of their status and institutional or associational roles so that face-saving then becomes equated with sanctioning dishonesty, oppression, and unfairness. . . . Then it is not a question of whether the one abused or the abuser is right or wrong, but upon whose rights and privileges someone has dared to tread. In America as elsewhere the strong override the weak through belonging to a powerful family, clan, or *tong* association.

The above traits are more pronounced in insecure personalities and they are found when relations between parents are distorted through tensions, anxieties, and hostilities. In old Chinese families, marriages are undertaken for the benefit of the clan and family line, rather than for the attainment of individual happiness. Compatibility between the spouses is not always present; through the displacement of affections, mothers and sons develop close emotional bonds. These sons are reared in the "women's chamber," in the Chinese expression, and acquire many cultural uniformities which properly belong to females—such as submissiveness, fearfulness, suspiciousness, indirection, gossip, undermining, etc.

Many sons are over-protected in Chinese families because of their roles in perpetuating the family line and ensuring their mothers' support. The care add rearing of sons bring Chinese mothers of the old-style families considerable status and recognition, a concept which has fast been ebbing in the last generation. Daughters, in contrast, do not give their mothers the same status and protection, nor can they be counted upon to exact the same rights and privileges for their mothers from their fathers or family elders. Hence, sons are reared more like females and females as sons. Patent evidence of the latter practice is seen in the games the Chinese boys are allowed to play in China, games minimizing aggressive competition and designed to avoid physical injury.

The permitted games are shuttlecock (using the heel), chess, tag (if not too vigorously), jacks, marbles, finger, and guessing games. Sons of families who can afford it have female servants accompanying them to and from school. Sisters too, if they are fortunate enough to be given an education, protect their brothers on the way.

The active, vigorous sports preferred for males in western society are shunned. It was not until the advent of modern education and the subsequent emphasis upon health education and physical development that active western sports such as basketball, volleyball, tennis, and soccer were adopted. These were accepted by the youth, rather than by their parents. In China, a more robust type of Chinese youth has emerged, and this applies equally to the girls. This has likewise been found to be true in the United States. The native-born are not only more active in sports but they are much larger in physique than their immigrant parents. The older Chinese are of slight build. Until recently, a robust physique was equated with a peasant background; and the foreign-born, especially in the upper classes, believed that a more frail physique implied higher status.

The absence of competitiveness between groups and individuals on an impersonal basis, rather than kinship ties, has resulted in the lack of emphasis on fair play, sportsmanship, man-to-man or team-to-team contests. China has never had a national sport, unless it be mahjong, a sedentary game preferred by men and women alike. The lack of a national sport has caused persons desiring to demonstrate gentility to reject masculine roles for which they were not prepared. For example, the students and intellectuals persist in denying that the militarists in China are included in the social structure. Yet, important events in China during the past century have revolved around military successes or reverses, wherein the leading militarists have undeniably shaped a new social order.

The tendency to transmit and acquire the more genteel cultural uniformities has resulted in the older Chinese persons exhibiting lack of candor, boldness, and bravery—attributes associated with masculinity. Although it can be argued that the sojourners were very brave and migrated to settle in a strange and hostile land, which is in itself evidence, nevertheless the behavior pattern of the settlers was largely unsuitable for a highly competitive, masculine-oriented culture. For example, the Chinese withdrew from overt and active competition with organized labor, instead of organizing among themselves to mitigate the strength of labor unions. They retreated from one industry after another. Instead of directing their aggressions against members of the dominant group, they turned their hostilities inward toward members of the Chinese society in America. Even today conspiracies are condoned, instead of fist fights, and examples are countless of Chinese relying on their *tongs* and other associational influence to exact undue rights and privileges rather than relying upon fair play.

Far too much attention has been paid to perpetuating and maintaining, within Chinatowns, a social organization which no longer suits the changing composition of the Chinese population in the United States. For some time, the younger Chinese have learned to prize bravery and patriotism before clan and family associations, individualism, frankness, and self-assertion. Unhappily, many China-oriented Chinese in the United States are unaware of these new attitudes current in China and they do not wish to change their behavior to fit changing times. The tendency of the older Chinese to conceive of China as she once was has caused many elders and leaders to impart norms and values that are unrealistic. This flight from reality stems from the inability of persons reared in a clan-oriented society to separate national, family, or district issues from personal issues. Since few of the older Chinese have ever participated in organizations that did not have clan, district, or dialect ties, their scope of operation as well as their ideational mobility are proscribed. They reject new abstract concepts. Instead they emphasize particularism, sectionalism, separatism.

When some of the old habits were transplanted to America by the early Chinese immigrants, the larger society's treatment of them reinforced these cultural uniformities. They had to be secretive, sly, and circuitous to counteract harsh laws, maltreatment, and abuse. Each later group of immigrants was taught by the older settlers to embrace these behavior patterns and forms of social organization. However, these preferences had their roots in China and were perpetuated in America because they found fertile ground.

At one time it became necessary also to exert strong social control on in-group behavior to attain the immigrants' objectives and to transmit the gains to succeeding generations. To prevent the larger society from learning of illegal activities, for example, subtle rather than overt measures of control were preferred. These are harder for the larger society's members to detect because intimidation, blackmail, extortion, and conspiracy are difficult to prove. Hence the Chinese have been unusually successful in being able to maintain two sets of norms and behavior patterns; but their refusal to change them has hindered their integration into American society.

## B. Socialization of Children

# I WANT TO GET OUT . . .

*Elaine Paul*

### FIRST MOTHER

"I want to get out. I wants to move. But what can you get? No sense in moving somewhere where I can't pay the rent. And the kids don't leave me no time to look for a place. But it's no good for the kids here. You see there by those cars," she said, pointing out the window toward a gas station on the corner. "One day I seen Edgar with some boys there between the cars, sniffing glue. And I told Edgar if I ever seen those boys there doing that again—I don't care if he's with them or not—I'm callin' the cops. I told him.

"One day, they fool me. They call me to school to talk about Mark and Ty, but I get there and there's some detectives asking me 'bout Edgar. They say they know there's some smoking and sniffing—pot and glue—goin' on 'round here and they know Edgar's in the middle of it and they think maybe more. I asked them if they find out he's shooting they let me know, and if I find out he's shooting I let them know. But I looks at his arms when he's at sleep and I know he ain't shooting. I still checks them—when he's asleep.

"Oh, but it's hard to keep up with them and do right by them. I got a job a little while back, but they told me I had to quit or they go to court 'cause the kids don't go to school. You see, I hadda leave the house by 7:30, and with nobody there, they just stayed home. So I hadda quit that job. And the kids, you know, they don't understand. You can't just tell them there ain't no money for this and that. It's not like when they little. Now they won't eat this and they don't eat that. And they only wear C——— (a brand of sneakers costing $8.50) or P——— (a moderately expensive

Unpublished manuscript. Printed by permission of the author.

425

brand of shoes). And they want this and that and go places like their friends. They just don't hear about no money. And they ain't no man 'round here to tell them what for. Their father—well, it's better he's gone. But sometimes they need someone bigger'n me to tell them what for. Edgar, he's bigger'n me now. I lay down the law to him. He got to be in the house by 10:00 except if he's right in front of the house where I can see him. Sometime he don't come in till 1 or 2 o'clock, but he's right in front of the house where I can see him.

". . . Now Edgar, he got a job beginning of this year when he stop goin' to school. He work in a store. His boss say he's a good boy. But I told him he's goin' back to school. I took him to court and they fix it so he can go back to school. And he's goin'—or he's goin' to the training school."

## SECOND MOTHER

[Mrs. Ortiz beamed as she brought out an imitation leather portfolio to show Luis' graduation awards. He had graduated from junior high school with honors in music and art and had won the Mayor's Salute to Youth Award for service to the community.] "My Luis is a good boy, a smart boy. He will go to college. All my children will go to college. Maria will be a teacher and Josefina will be a secretary. But I do not understand the school. Always I go to the school and help. I am president of the PTA, but no more. I go no more. I don't understand how they talk to me. I read in the paper that the schools here are no good. They do not teach the children so they can go to college. I go to the school but they do not listen. They do not talk to me.

"Last week I went to school about my Maria because they take her out of the academic class. They put her in merchandising. They don't talk to her or to me. They just told her to go to different classes one day. She went to summer school to stay in academic classes. She's a good girl, a smart girl, but they don't talk to her so she can learn. Look, she went to summer school and got 95 in English, but at that school she get 50 and they say she can't go to college. Last week, I went to the counsellor, but they don't talk to me. They just yell. They say Maria don't study. She study! All my children study. I make sure. But they don't listen.

"You know, once I saw in the paper where a teacher say bad things about the Spanish children. A teacher right over here. And, you know, she is still there, in that school. That's not right. She should not be allowed to say such things. She should not be allowed to teach there. . . .

"Everybody likes my children. They are good children. You see this watch. The lady in the country where Luis go, she gave it to him. She call me and say she hate to send him home. And Josefina, she shops for the old lady downstairs. And my girls are good girls. All the boys chase them.

You should see the Christmas presents. But they are still good girls. They don't have any boyfriends. And they are good at home. They help me. Look, they just washed all these walls. Soon, they will be grown and I will not have to worry any more. It does not matter what happens then. I just worry about them."

## THIRD MOTHER

"I just got back from the hospital with Billy. [Billy has a deformed hip and must spend most of his hours in a steel brace.] You know it takes most of a day to go to clinic, and they still don't say nothing about operating. They just say, 'At the right time. At the right time.' They want me to bring him in an extra day next week so they can start a new series of X-rays. They're good doctors and I trust them, but sometimes I wish't they'd let me in on what's going on. They say the operations is very . . . whatcha say, touchy, and maybe won't come out okay anyway, but everything has to be just right for it. It's funny, I don't like to take any of the other kids there 'cause we just gets kinda pushed around and nobody pays any attention to us, but they always done right by Billy. Sometimes it's hard to remember he's not well. He gets around and into everything. You can't leave anything out anywhere that's to eat. Even if it's high up, he gets it.

"Evelyn'll be coming home in a minute and she'll watch him while I go off to the cub scouts. Richy wanted to join but they said they wouldn't take no more boys unless their mothers join too to help. So I got to go to Den Mother classes, but Richy likes it and it's interesting talking to the other mothers. Last week we learned how to make wallets, and stuff like that. I never thought I'd be doin' stuff like that. Richy's all worked up now about going to camp.

"Evelyn? Oh, yes. She always come home after school, 'cept when she doin' something at school. She comes home and locks herself in her room to study all afternoon and evening. And she don't want nobody bothering her. She wants to be a doctor. She just found out she's in the top fifth of her class, which help to make up some for not getting into that school upstate. They didn't give her no reason or anything. They just said they weren't taking anybody from her school. She's got her heart set on going out of town to school, even though it would be easier money-wise to stay in town. She just say she'll get the money. I'm doing all I can to try and help her. I'm even trying to get a job at night. I figure if she want it so bad, I gotta try that hard to help her.

"Henry and Cyril and Sheila stay at school for the afterschool center, and then they come right home. I don't like none of them playing around here. This may be a project, but that's 'junky row' across the street there and I don't want my kids around none of that stuff. And I know what goes on in this building, too. Sheila told me about that Marylou upstairs in school. One day she went up to this other girl in school and taunted her about the girl's father being over at her house the night before. They always having parties up there and all sorts of goings on. The boy hit a teacher and got thrown out of school. No, I don't want my kids playing with anyone around here. They's enough of them to play amongst themselves.

"They good kids, mostly. The other day I went to see Henry's teacher. She call him the class clown. He always got something funny to say. But the teacher likes him. She say he's smart and he don't really act up. If he do, he knows he'll get it. All my kids know they won't get away with nothing. Even then, if they'd rather have a punishment, they get a whopping, and, if they'd rather have a whopping, they get a punishment. But I don't have to do too much of that. We have a good time together. We like to read out loud together, and sometimes play word games. The bigger kids give Cyril the easy words and let him win sometimes.

"Right now, Evelyn's all excited 'cause she's going to be in a fashion show at school. The girls picked her even though the teacher made some remark about her being too dark. I laughed to myself cause Evelyn don't know I gets most of her clothes at the Volunteers of America. I stop by often so I get all the good things that come in and then I just puts it into the self-service cleaners and she never knows the difference. I couldn't ever buy her such nice stuff new, but we get by pretty good that way."

# SOCIALIZATION AND SOCIAL CLASS

# THROUGH TIME AND SPACE

*Urie Bronfenbrenner*

## BACKGROUND AND RESOURCES

During the past dozen years, a class struggle has been taking place in American social psychology—a struggle, fortunately, not *between* but *about* social classes. In the best social revolutionary tradition the issue was joined with a manifesto challenging the assumed superiority of the upper and middle classes and extolling the neglected virtues of the working class. There followed a successful revolution with an overthrow of the established order in favor of the victorious proletariat, which then reigned supreme— at least for a time. These dramatic changes had, as always, their prophets and precursors, but they reached a climax in 1946 with the publication of Davis and Havighurst's influential paper on "Social Class and Color Differences in Child Rearing."[1] The paper cited impressive statistical evidence in support of the thesis that middle-class parents "place their children under a stricter regimen, with more frustration of their impulses than do lower-class parents." For the next eight years, the Davis-Havighurst conclusion was taken as the definitive statement of class differences in socialization. Then, in 1954, came the counterrevolution; Maccoby and Gibbs published the first report[2] of a study of child-rearing practices in the Boston area which, by and large, contradicted the Chicago findings:

[1] A. Davis and R. J. Havighurst, "Social Class and Color Differences in Child Rearing," *American Sociological Review*, 1948, **11**, 698–710.
[2] E. E. Maccoby, P. K. Gibbs, and the staff of the Laboratory of Human Development at Harvard University, "Methods of Child Rearing in Two Social Classes," in W. E. Martin and C. B. Standler (eds.), *Readings in Child Development*, New York, Harcourt, Brace and Co., 1954.

From *Readings in Social Psychology* third edition, edited by Eleanor Maccoby, Theodore Newcombe and E. Hartley, Copyright 1947, 1952, © 1958 by Holt, Rinehart and Winston, Inc. used by permission.

in general, middle-class parents were found to be "more permissive" than those in the lower class.

In response, one year later, Havighurst and Davis[3] presented a re-analysis of their data for a subsample more comparable in age to the subjects of the Boston study. On the basis of a careful comparison of the two sets of results, they concluded that "the disagreements between the findings of the two studies are substantial and large" and speculated that these differences might be attributable either to genuine changes in child-rearing practices over time or to technical difficulties of sampling and item equivalence.

A somewhat different view, however, was taken by Sears, Maccoby, and Levin[4] in their final report of the Boston study. They argued that Davis and Havighurst's interpretation of the Chicago data as reflecting greater permissiveness for the working-class parent was unwarranted on two counts. First, they cited the somewhat contrasting results of still another research: that of Klatskin[5] in support of the view that class differences in feeding, weaning, scheduling, and toilet training "are not very stable or customary." Second, they contended that the Chicago findings of greater freedom of movement for the lower-class child were more properly interpreted not as "permissiveness" but as "a reflection of rejection, a pushing of the child out of the way." Such considerations led the Boston investigators to conclude:

> This re-examination of the Chicago findings suggests quite clearly the same conclusion that must be reached from Klatskin's study and from our own: the middle-class mothers were generally more permissive and less punitive toward their young children than were working-class mothers. Unfortunately, the opposite interpretation, as presented by Davis and Havighurst, has been widely accepted in education circles during the past decade. This notion of working-class permissiveness has been attractive for various reasons. It has provided an easy explanation of why working-class children have lower academic achievement motivation than do middle-class children—their mothers place less restrictive pressure on them. It has also provided a kind of compensatory comfort for those educators who have been working hard toward the goal of improving educational experiences for the noncollege-oriented part of the school population. In effect, one could say, lower-class children may lack the so highly desirable academic motivation, but the lack stems from a "good" reason—the children were permissively reared.[6]

It would appear that there are a number of unresolved issues between

[3] Havighurst and Davis, "A comparison of the Chicago and Harvard Studies of Social Class Differences in Child Rearing," *American Sociological Review*, 1955, **20**, 438–442.

[4] R. R. Sears, E. Maccoby, and H. Levin, *Patterns of Child Rearing*, Evanston, Ill.: Row, Peterson and Co., 1957.

[5] E. H. Klatskin, "Shifts in Child Care Practices in Three Social Classes under an Infant Care Program of Flexible Methodology," *American Journal of Orthopsychiatry*, 1952, **22**, 52–61.

[6] Sears, Maccoby, and Levin, *op. cit.*, pp. 446–447.

the protagonists of the principal points of view—issues both as to the facts and their interpretation. At such times it is not unusual for some third party to attempt a reappraisal of events in a broader perspective with the aid of documents and information previously not available. It is this which the present writer hopes to do. He is fortunate in having at his disposal materials not only from the past and present, but also seven manuscripts unpublished at the time of this writing, which report class differences in child-rearing practices at four different places and five points in time. To begin with, Bayley and Schaefer[7] have reanalyzed data from the Berkeley Growth Study to provide information on class differences in maternal-behavior ratings made from 1928 to 1932, when the children in the study were under three years old, and again from 1939 to 1942, when most of them were about ten years old. Information on maternal behavior in this same locale as of 1953 comes from a recent report by Martha Sturm White[8] of class differences in child-rearing practices for a sample of preschoolers in Palo Alto and environs. Miller and Swanson have made available relevant data from their two comprehensive studies of families in Detroit, one based on a stratified sample of families with children up to 19 years of age,[9] the other a specially selected sample of boys, ages 12 to 14 years.[10] Limited information on another sample of adolescent boys comes from Strodtbeck's investigation of "Family Interaction, Values, and Achievement".[11] Also, Littman, Moore, and Pierce-Jones[12] have recently completed a survey of child-rearing practices in Eugene, Oregon for a random sample of parents with children from two weeks to 14 years of age. Finally, Kohn[13] reports a comparison of child-training values among working and middle-class mothers in Washington, D.C.

In addition to these unpublished sources, the writer has made use of nine published researches.[14] In some instances—notably for the monu-

[7] N. Bayley and E. S. Schaefer, "Relationships between Socioeconomic Variables and the Behavior of Mothers toward Young Children," unpublished manuscript, 1957.

[8] M. S. White, "Social Class, Child Rearing Practices, and Child Behavior," *American Sociological Review*, 1957, **22**, 704–712.

[9] D. R. Miller and G. E. Swanson, *The Changing American Parent*, New York, John Wiley and Sons, Inc., in press.

[10] Miller and Swanson, *Inner Conflict and Defense*, New York, Henry Holt and Co., Inc., 1959.

[11] F. L. Strodtbeck, "Family Interaction, Values, and Achievement," in A. L. Baldwin, Bronfenbrenner, D. C. McClelland, and F. L. Strodtbeck, *Talent and Society*, Princeton, N.J., D. Van Nostrand Co., 1958.

[12] R. A. Littman, R. A. Moore, and J. Pierce-Jones, "Social Class Differences in Child Rearing: A Third Community for Comparison with Chicago and Newton, Massachusetts," *American Sociological Review*, 1957, **22**, 694–704.

[13] M. L. Kohn, "Social Class and Parental Values," paper read at the Annual Meeting of the American Sociological Society, Washington, D.C., August, 27–29, 1957.

[14] H. E. Anderson (Chrmn.), *The Young Child in the Home*, report of the Committee on the Infant and Preschool Child, White House Conference on Child Health and Protection, New York, D. Appleton-Century, 1936; A. L. Baldwin, J. Kalhorn,

Table 1—Description of Samples

| Sample | Principal investigator source | Date of field work | Age | NO. OF CASES Total | Middle class | Working class | Description of sample |
|---|---|---|---|---|---|---|---|
| National Cross Section,* I II III IV | Anderson | 1932 | 0-1 1-5 6-12 1-12 | 494 2420 865 3285 | 217 1131 391 1522 | 277 1289 474 1763 | National sample of white families "having child between 1 and 5 years of age" and "representing each major geographic area, each size of community and socioeconomic class in the United States." About equal number of males and females. SES (seven classes) based on Minnesota Scale for Occupational Classification. |
| Berkeley, Cal., I-II | Bayley and Schaefer | 1928-32 1939-42 | 1-3 9-11 | 31 31 | Information not available | Information not available | Subjects of both sexes from Berkeley Growth Study, "primarily middle class but range from unskilled laborer, relief, and three-years education to professional, $10,000 income and doctoral degrees." SES measures include education, occupation (Taussig Scale), income, home and neighborhood rating, and composite scale. |
| Yellow Springs, Ohio | Baldwin | 1940 | 3-12 | 124 | Information not available | | Families enrolled in Fels Research Institute Home Visiting Program. "Above average" in socioeconomic status but include "a number of uneducated parents and from the lower economic levels." No SES index computed but graphs show relationships by education and income. |
| Chicago, Ill., I* | Davis and Havighurst | 1943 | 5 (approx.) | 100 | 48 | 52 | Middle-class sample "mainly" from mothers of nursery-school children; lower class from "areas of poor housing." All mothers native born. Two-level classification SES following Warner based on occupation, education, residential area, type of home, etc. |
| Chicago, Ill., II | Duvall | 1943-44 | 5 (approx.) | 433 | 230 | 203 | Negro and white (Jewish and non-Jewish) mothers. Data collected at "regular meetings of mothers' groups." SES classification (four levels) following Warner. |
| New Haven, Conn., I* | Klatskin | 1949-50 | 1 (approx.) | 222 | 114 | 108 | Mothers in Yale Rooming-in Project returning for evaluation of baby at one year of age. SES classification (three levels) by Hollingshead, following Warner. |

| Location | Authors | Year | Age | | | | Description |
|---|---|---|---|---|---|---|---|
| Boston, Mass.* | Sears, *et al.* | 1951–52 | 4–6 | 372 | 198 | 174 | Kindergarten children in two suburbs. Parents American born, living together. Twins, adoptions, handicapped children, and other special cases eliminated. Two-level SES classification follows Warner. |
| New Haven, Conn., II | Strodtbeck | 1951–53 | 14–17 | 48 | 24 | 24 | Third-generation Jewish and Italian boys representing extremes of under- and over-achievement in school. Classified into three SES levels on basis of occupation. |
| Detroit, Mich., I* | Miller and Swanson | 1953 | 12–14 | 112 | 59 | 53 | Boys in grades 7–8 above borderline intelligence within one year of age for grade, all at least third-generation Americans, Christian, from unbroken, nonmobile families of Northwest European stock. SES (four levels) assigned on basis of education and occupation. |
| Detroit, Mich., II* | Miller and Swanson | 1953 | 0–18 | 479 | Information not available | Information not available | Random sample of white mothers with child under 19 and living with husband. Step-children and adoptions eliminated. SES (four levels) based primarily on U.S. census occupation categories. |
| Palo Alto, Cal.,* | White | 1953 | 2½–5½ | 74 | 36 | 38 | Native-born mothers of only one child, the majority expecting another. Unbroken homes in suburban area SES (two levels) rated on Warner scale. |
| Urban Connecticut | McClelland *et al.* | 1953–54 | 6–18 | 152 | Information not available | Information not available | Parents between 30–60 having at least one child between six and eighteen and representing four religious groups. "Rough check on class status" obtained from educational level achieved by parent. |
| Upstate New York | Boek, *et al.* | 1955–56 | 3–7 months | 1432 | 595 | 837 | Representative sample of N.Y. state mothers of newborn children, exclusive of unmarried mothers. SES classification (five levels) as given on Warner scale. |
| Eugene, Oregon* | Littman, *et al.* | 1955–56 | 0–14 | 206 | 86 | 120 | Random sample of children from preschool classes and school rolls. Two SES levels assigned on same basis as in Boston study. |
| Washington, D.C. | Kohn and Clausen | 1956–57 | 10–11 | 339 | 174 | 165 | Representative samples of working- and middle-class mothers classified by Hollingshead's index of social position. |

* Denotes studies used as principal bases for the analysis.

434 FAMILIAL FACTORS AND ENVIRONMENT

mental and regrettably neglected Anderson report—data were reanalyzed and significance tests computed in order to permit closer comparison with the results of other investigations. A full list and summary description of all the studies utilized in the present review appear in Table 1. Starred items designate the researches which, because they contain reasonably comparable data, are used as the principal bases for analysis.

## ESTABLISHING COMPARABLE SOCIAL-CLASS GROUPINGS

Although in most of the studies under consideration the investigators have based their classification of socioeconomic status (SES) explicitly or implicitly on the criteria proposed by Warner,[15] there was considerable variation in the number of social class categories employed. Thus, in the Anderson report data were analyzed in terms of seven SES levels, the New York survey distinguished five, the second Chicago and the two Detroit studies each had four, and Klatskin used three. The majority, however, following the precedent of Havighurst and Davis, differentiated two levels only—middle vs. lower or working class. Moreover, all of these last studies have been reanalyzed or deliberately designed to facilitate comparison with each other. We have already mentioned Havighurst and Davis' efforts in this regard, to which the Boston group contributed by recalculating their data in terms of medians rather than means.[16] Both White and Littman et al. were interested in clarifying the contradictions posed by the Chicago and Boston studies and hence have employed many of the same indices. As a result, both necessity and wisdom call for dropping to the lowest common denominator and reanalyzing the results of the remaining researches in terms of a two-level classification of socioeconomic status.

In most instances, the delicate question of where to establish the cutting point was readily resolved. The crux of the distinction between middle and working class in all four of the studies employing this dichotomous break lies in the separation between white- and blue-collar workers. Fortunately,

[15] W. L. Warner, M. Meeker, and others, *Social Class in America*, Chicago, Science Research Associates, 1949.
[16] Sears, Maccoby, and Levin, *op. cit.*, p. 427.

---

and F. H. Breese, *Patterns of Parent Behavior*, Psychological Monographs, 1945, **58**, No. 3 (Whole No. 268): W. E. Boek, E. D. Lawson, A. Yankhauer, and M. B. Sussman, *Social Class, Maternal Health, and Child Care*, Albany, New York State Department of Health, 1957; Davis and Havighurst, *op. cit.*; E. M. Duvall, "Conceptions of Parenthood," *American Journal of Sociology*, 1946–1947, **52**, 190–192; Klatskin, *op. cit.*; E. E. Maccoby and P. K. Gibbs, *op. cit.*; D. C. McClelland, A. Rindlisbacher, and R. DeCharms, "Religious and Other Sources of Parental Attitudes toward Independence Training," in McClelland (ed.), *Studies in Motivation*, New York, Appleton-Century-Crofts, Inc., 1955; Sears, Maccoby, and Levin, *op. cit.*

this same differentiation was made at some point along the scale in each of the other researches included in the basic analysis. Thus, for the several studies[17] using four levels of classification (upper and lower middle, upper and lower lower), the split occurred, as might be expected, between the two middle categories. For the New York State sample an examination of the occupations occurring at each of the five class levels used pointed to a cutting point between Classes III and IV. Klatskin, in comparing the social-class groupings of the New Haven study with the middle and lower classes of the original Chicago research, proposed a division between the first and second of her three SES levels, and we have followed her recommendation. Finally, for the seven-step scale of the Anderson report, the break was made between Classes III and IV, placing major clerical workers, skilled mechanics and retail business men in the middle class, and farmers, minor clerical positions, and semiskilled occupations in the working class.

In all of the above instances it was, of course, necessary to compute anew percentages and average scores for the two class levels and to calculate tests of significance (almost invariably $\chi^2$, two-tailed test, with Fisher-Yates correction for continuity). These computations, the results of which appear in the tables to follow, were performed for the following samples: National I–IV, New Haven I, Detroit I and II, and Upstate New York. All other figures and significance tests cited are taken from the original reports.

The effort to make the division between middle and working class at similar points for the basic samples, however successful it may have been, does not eliminate many other important sources of difference among the several researches. We now turn briefly to a consideration of these.

## PROBLEMS OF COMPARABILITY

The difficulties involved in comparing the results of more than a dozen studies conducted at different times and places for somewhat different purposes are at once formidable, delicate, and perilous. First of all, even when similar areas are explored in the interview, there is the problem of variation in the wording of questions. Indeed, however marked the changes may be in child-rearing practices over time, they are not likely to be any more dramatic than the contrasts in the content and, above all, connotation of the queries put to mothers by social scientists from one decade to the next. Thus, the comprehensive report from the first White House Conference which covered the gamut from the number of children having rattles and changing their underwear to the number of toothbrushes by age, and the times the child was frightened by storms (analyzed by seven SES

[17] Duvall, *op. cit.*, Miller and Swanson, *Inner Conflict and Defense* and *The Changing American Parent, op. cit.*

levels), says not a murmur about masturbation or sex play. Ten years later, in Chicago, six questions were devoted to this topic, including such items as: "How did you frighten them out of the habit?" and "What physical methods did you use (such as tight diaper, whipping them, tying their hands, and so forth)?" In the next decade the interviewer in the Boston study (perhaps only a proper Bostonian) was more restrained, or simply less interested. He asked only two questions: first, whether the mother noticed the child playing with himself; then, "How important do you feel it is to prevent this in a child?" Nor is the difficulty completely eliminated in those all-too-few instances when a similar wording is employed in two or more studies, for there is the very real possibility that in different contexts the same words have different meanings.

Serious problems arise from the lack of comparability not only in the questions asked but also in the character of the samples employed. Havighurst and Davis, for example, point out that the Chicago and Boston samples had different proportions of cases in the two bottom categories of the Warner scale of occupations. According to the investigators' reports, the Palo Alto and Eugene studies deviated even further in both directions with the former containing few families from the lowest occupational categories, and the Oregon group exceeding previous studies in representation from these same bottom levels. The authors of several studies also call attention to the potential importance of existing differences in ethnicity, religious background, suburban vs. urban residence, and strength of mobility strivings.

A source of variation perhaps not sufficiently emphasized in these and other reports is the manner in which cases were selected. As Davis and Havighurst properly pointed out in their original publication, their sample was subject to possible bias "in the direction of getting a middle-class group which had been subjected to the kind of teaching about child rearing which is prevalent among the middle-class people who send their children to nursery schools." Equally important may be the relatively high proportion in the Chicago lower-class sample of mothers coming from East European and Irish backgrounds, or the four-year discrepancy in the average ages of the mothers at the two-class levels. The first New Haven sample consisted entirely of mothers enrolled in the Yale Rooming-in Project who were sufficiently interested to bring the baby back for a checkup a year after mother and child had left the hospital. As Klatskin recognized, this selectivity probably resulted in a "sample composed of the families most sympathetic to rooming-in ideology," a fact which, as she noted, was reflected in her research results. White's Palo Alto group consisted solely of mothers of only one child, most of whom were expecting a second offspring; cases were recruited from a variety of sources including friends, neighbors, personnel managers, nursery school teachers, Public Health nurses, and maternal prenatal exercises classes. In short, virtually every sample had its special eccentricities. For some of these, one could guess at the extent and direction of bias; in others, the importance or effect of the selective features remains a mystery. Our difficulties, then, derive as much from ignorance as from knowledge—a fact which is underscored by the absence, for many of the samples, of such basic demographic information as the distribution of subjects by age and sex.

It is clear that many factors, some known and many more unknown, may operate to produce differences in results from one sample to the next. It is hardly likely, however, that these manifold influences will operate in a consistent direction over time or space. The possibility of obtaining interpretable findings, therefore, rests on the long chance that major trends, if they exist, will be sufficiently marked to override the effects of bias arising from variations in sampling and method. This is a rash and optimistic hope, but—somewhat to our own surprise—it seems to have been realized, at least in part, in the analyses that follow.

## SOCIAL CLASS DIFFERENCES IN INFANT CARE, 1930–1955

In interpreting reports of child-rearing practices it is essential to distinguish between the date at which the information was obtained and the actual period to which the information refers. This caution is particularly relevant in dealing with descriptions of infant care for children who (as in the Eugene or Detroit studies) may be as old as 12, 14, or 18 at the time of the interview. In such instances it is possible only to guess at the probable time at which the practice occurred by making due allowances for the age of the child. The problem is further complicated by the fact that none of the studies reports SES differences by age. The best one can do, therefore, is to estimate the median age of the group and from this approximate the period at which the practice may have taken place. For example, the second Detroit sample, which ranged in age from birth to 18 years, would have a median age of about nine. Since the field work was done in 1953, we estimate the date of feeding and weaning practices as about 1944.[18] It should be recognized, however, that the practices reported range over a considerable period extending from as far back as 1935 to the time of the interview in 1953. Any marked variation in child-rearing practices over this period could produce an average figure which would in point of fact be atypical for the middle year 1944. We shall have occasion to point to the possible operation of this effect in some of the data to follow.

[18] It is true that because of the rising birth rate after World War II the sample probably included more younger than older children, but without knowledge of the actual distribution by age we have hesitated to make further speculative adjustments.

If dates of practices are estimated by the method outlined above, we find that the available data describe social-class differences in feeding, weaning, and toilet training for a period from about 1930 to 1955. The relevant information appears in Tables 2 through 4.

It is reasonable to suppose that a mother's report of whether or not she employed a particular practice would be somewhat more reliable than her estimate of when she began or discontinued that practice. This expectation is borne out by the larger number of statistically significant differences in tables presenting data on prevalence (Tables 2 and 3) rather than on the

### Table 2—Frequency of Breast Feeding

| | | NO. OF CASES REPORTING | | | PERCENTAGE BREAST FED | | | |
| 1. Sample | 2. Approx. date of practice | 3. Total sample | 4. Middle class | 5. Working class | 6. Total sample | 7. Middle class | 8. Working class | 9. Differ- ence* |
|---|---|---|---|---|---|---|---|---|
| National I | 1930 | 1856 | 842 | 1014 | 80 | 78 | 82 | −4† |
| National II | 1932 | 445 | 201 | 244 | 40 | 29 | 49 | −20† |
| Chicago I | 1939 | 100 | 48 | 52 | 83 | 83 | 83 | 0 |
| Detroit I | 1941 | 112 | 59 | 53 | 62 | 54 | 70 | −16 |
| Detroit II | 1944 | 200 | 70 | 130 | Percentages not given | | | + |
| Eugene | 1946–47 | 206 | 84 | 122 | 46 | 40 | 50 | −10 |
| Boston | 1947–48 | 372 | 198 | 174 | 40 | 43 | 37 | +6 |
| New Haven I | 1949–50 | 222 | 114 | 108 | 80 | 85 | 74 | +11† |
| Palo Alto | 1950 | 74 | 36 | 38 | 66 | 70 | 63 | +7 |
| Upstate New York | 1955 | 1432 | 594 | 838 | 24 | 27 | 21 | +6† |

\* Minus sign denotes lower incidence for middle class than for working class.
† Denotes difference significant at 5-percent level of confidence or better.

### Table 3—Scheduled versus Self-demand Feeding

| | | NO. OF CASES REPORTING | | | PERCENTAGE FED ON DEMAND | | | |
| 1. Sample | 2. Approx. date of practice | 3. Total sample | 4. Middle class | 5. Working class | 6. Total sample | 7. Middle class | 8. Working class | 9. Differ- ence* |
|---|---|---|---|---|---|---|---|---|
| National I | 1932 | 470 | 208 | 262 | 16 | 7 | 23 | −16† |
| Chicago I | 1939 | 100 | 48 | 52 | 25 | 4 | 44 | −40† |
| Detroit I | 1941 | 297 | 52 | 45 | 21 | 12 | 53 | −41† |
| Detroit II | 1944 | 205 | 73 | 132 | 55 | 51 | 58 | −7 |
| Boston | 1947–48 | 372 | 198 | 174 | Percentages not given | | | — |
| New Haven I | 1949–50 | 191 | 117 | 74 | 65 | 71 | 54 | +17 |
| Palo Alto | 1950 | 74 | 36 | 38 | 59 | 64 | 55 | +9 |

\* Minus sign denotes lower incidence of self-demand feeding in middle class.
† Denotes difference significant at 5-percent level of confidence or better.

timing of a particular practice (Tables 4–6). On the plausible assumption that the former data are more reliable, we shall begin our discussion by considering the results on frequency of breast feeding and scheduled feeding, which appear in Tables 2 and 3.

*General Trends.* We may begin by looking at general trends over time irrespective of social-class level. These appear in column 6 or Tables 2 and 3. The data for breast feeding are highly irregular, but there is some suggestion of decrease in this practice over the years.[19] In contrast, self-demand feeding is becoming more common. In both instances the trend is more marked (column 8) in the middle class; in other words, it is they especially who are doing the changing. This fact is reflected even more sharply in column 9 which highlights a noteworthy shift. Here we see

### Table 4—Duration of Breast Feeding
(for those breast fed)

| Sample | Approx. date of practice | NO. OF CASES†† | | | MEDIAN DURATION IN MONTHS | | | |
|---|---|---|---|---|---|---|---|---|
| | | Total sample | Middle class | Working class | Total sample | Middle class | Working class | Differ- ence** |
| National II* | 1930 | 1488 | 654 | 834 | 6.6 | 6.2 | 7.5 | −1.3† |
| Chicago I | 1939 | 83 | 40 | 43 | 3.5 | 3.4 | 3.5 | −.1 |
| Detroit I* | 1941 | 69 | 32 | 37 | 3.3 | 2.8 | 5.3 | −2.5 |
| Eugene | 1946–47 | 95 | 34 | 61 | 3.4 | 3.2 | 3.5 | −.3 |
| Boston | 1947–48 | 149 | 85 | 64 | 2.3 | 2.4 | 2.1 | +.3 |
| New Haven I* | 1949–50 | 177 | 97 | 80 | 3.6 | 4.3 | 3.0 | +1.3 |
| Upstate New York | 1955 | 299 | 145 | 154 | 1.2 | 1.3 | 1.2 | +.1 |

\* Medians not given in original report but estimated from data cited.
† Denotes difference significant at 5-percent level if confidence or better.
\*\* Minus sign denotes shorter duration for middle class than for working class.
†† Number of cases for Chicago, Eugene, Boston, and Upstate New York estimated from percentages cited.

### Table 5—Age at Completion of Weaning
(either breast or bottle)

| Sample | Approx. date of practice | NO. OF CASES | | | MEDIAN AGE IN MONTHS | | | |
|---|---|---|---|---|---|---|---|---|
| | | Total sample | Middle class | Working class | Total group | Middle class | Working class | Differ- ence* |
| Chicago I | 1940 | 100 | 48 | 52 | 11.3 | 10.3 | 12.3 | −2.0† |
| Detroit I | 1942 | 69 | 32 | 37 | 11.2 | 10.6 | 12.0 | −1.4† |
| Detroit II | 1945 | 190 | 62 | 128 | —Under 12 months— | | | — |
| Eugene | 1947–48 | 206 | 85 | 121 | 13.6 | 13.2 | 14.1 | − 9 |
| Boston | 1948–49 | 372 | 198 | 174 | 12.3 | 12.0 | 12.6 | −.6 |
| New Haven I | 1949–50 | 222 | 114 | 108 | —Over 12 months— | | | — |
| Palo Alto | 1951 | 68 | 32 | 36 | 13.1 | 14.4 | 12.6 | +1.8 |

\*Minus sign denotes earlier weaning for middle than for working class.
† Denotes difference significant at 5-percent level of confidence or better.

that in the earlier period—roughly before the end of World War II—both breast feeding and demand feeding were less common among the middle class than among the working class. In the later period, however, the direction is reversed; it is now the middle-class mother who more often gives her child the breast and feeds him on demand.

The data on duration of breast feeding (Table 4) and on the timing of weaning and bowel training (Tables 5 and 6) simply confirm, somewhat less reliably, all of the above trends. There is a general tendency in both social classes to wean the child earlier from the breast but, apparently, to

[19] As indicated below, we believe that these irregularities are largely attributable to the highly selective character of a number of the samples (notably, New Haven I and Palo Alto) and that the downward trend in frequency and duration of breast feeding is probably more reliable than is reflected in the data of Tables 2 and 4.

allow him to suck from a bottle till a somewhat later age. Since no uniform reference points were used for securing information on toilet training in the several studies (i.e., some investigators report percentage training at six months, others at ten months, still others at 12 or 18 months), Table 6 shows only the direction of the difference between the two social classes. All these figures on timing point to the same generalization. In the earlier period, middle-class mothers were exerting more pressure; they weaned their children from the breast and bottle and carried out bowel and bladder training before their working-class counterparts. But in the last ten years the trend has been reversed—it is now the middle-class mother who trains later.

### Table 6—Toilet Training

| Sample | Approximate date practice begun | NO. OF CASES Bowel training | Bladder training | DIRECTION OF RELATIONSHIP Beginning bowel training | End bowel training | Beginning bladder training | End bladder training |
|---|---|---|---|---|---|---|---|
| National II | 1931 | 2375 | 2375 | | −† | | −* |
| National I | 1932 | 494 | 494 | | − | | − |
| Chicago I | 1940 | 100 | 220† | −† | − | −†** | +† |
| Detroit I | 1942 | 110 | 102 | − | − | + | − |
| Detroit II | 1945 | 216 | 200 | +† | | − | |
| Eugene | 1947–48 | 206 | 206 | + | − | + | + |
| Boston | 1948–49 | 372 | | − | +† | | |
| New Haven I | 1950–51 | 214 | | +† | | | |
| Palo Alto | 1951 | 73 | | +† | | | |

\* Minus sign indicates that middle class began or completed training earlier than lower class.
† Denotes difference significant at 5-percent level of confidence or better.
\*\* Based on data from 1946 report.

These consistent trends take on richer significance in the light of Wolfenstein's impressive analysis[20] of the content of successive editions of the United States Children's Bureau bulletin on *Infant Care*. She describes the period 1929–38 (which corresponds to the earlier time span covered by our data) as characterized by:

... a pervasive emphasis on regularity, doing everything by the clock. Weaning and introduction of solid foods are to be accomplished with great firmness, never yielding for a moment to the baby's resistance ... bowel training ... must be carried out with great determination as early as possible. ... The main danger which the baby presented at this time was that of dominating the parents. Successful child training meant winning out against the child in the struggle for domination.

In the succeeding period, however,

... all this was changed. The child became remarkably harmless. ... His main active aim was to explore his world. ... When not engaged in exploratory under-

[20] M. Wolfenstein, "Trends in Infant Care," *American Journal of Orthopsychiatry*, 1953, **23**, 120–130. Similar conclusions were drawn in an earlier report by Stendler surveying 60 years of child-training practices as advocated in three popular women's magazines. *Cf.* C. B. Stendler, "Sixty Years of Child Training Practices," *Journal of Pediatrics*, 1950, **36**, 122–134.

takings, the baby needs care and attention; and giving these when he demands them, far from making him a tyrant, will make him less demanding later on. At this time mildness is advocated in all areas: thumbsucking and masturbation are not to be interfered with; weaning and toilet training are to be accomplished later and more gently.[21]

The parallelism between preachment and practice is apparent also in the case of breast feeding. Up until 1945, "breast feeding was emphatically recommended," with "warnings against early weaning." By 1951, "the long-term intransigence about breast feeding is relaxed." States the bulletin edition of that year: "Mothers who find bottle feeding easier should feel comfortable about doing it that way."

One more link in the chain of information completes the story. There is ample evidence that, both in the early and the later period, middle-class mothers were much more likely than working-class mothers to be exposed to current information on child care. Thus Anderson cites table after table showing that parents from higher SES levels read more books, pamphlets, and magazines, and listen to more radio talks on child care and related subjects. This in 1932. Similarily, in the last five years, White, in California, and Boek, in New York, report that middle-class mothers are much more likely than those in the working class to read Spock's best-seller, *Baby and Child Care*[22] and similar publications.

Our analysis suggests that the mothers not only read these books but take them seriously, and that their treatment of the child is affected accordingly. Moreover, middle-class mothers not only read more but are also more responsive; they alter their behavior earlier and faster than their working-class counterparts.

In view of the remarkably close parallelism in changes over time revealed by Wolfenstein's analysis and our own, we should perhaps not overlook a more recent trend clearly indicated in Wolfenstein's report and vaguely discernible as well in the data we have assembled. Wolfenstein asserts that, since 1950, a conservative note has crept into the child-training literature; "there is an attempt to continue . . . mildness, but not without some conflicts and misgivings . . . May not continued gratification lead to addiction and increasingly intensified demands?"[23] In this connection it is perhaps no mere coincidence that the differences in the last column of Tables 2 to 4 show a slight drop after about 1950; the middle class is still more "relaxed" than the working class, but the differences are not so large as earlier. Once again, practice may be following preachment—now in the direction of introducing more limits and demands—still within a permissive framework. We shall return to a consideration of this possibility in our discussion of class differences in the training of children beyond two years of age.

[21] Wolfenstein, *op. cit.*, p. 121.
[22] Benjamin Spock, *Baby and Child Care*, New York, Pocket Books, Inc., 1957.
[23] Wolfenstein, *op. cit.*, p. 121.

Taken as a whole, the correspondence between Wolfenstein's data and our own suggests a general hypothesis extending beyond the confines of social class as such: *child-rearing practices are likely to change most quickly in those segments of society which have closest access and are most receptive to the agencies or agents of change (e.g., public media, clinics, physicians, and counselors).* From this point of view, one additional trend suggested by the available data is worthy of note: rural families appear to "lag behind the times" somewhat in their practices of infant care. For example, in Anderson's beautifully detailed report, there is evidence that in 1932 farm families (Class IV in his sample) were still breast feeding their children more frequently but being less flexible in scheduling and toilet training than nonfarm families of roughly comparable socioeconomic status. Similarly, there are indications from Miller and Swanson's second Detroit study that, with SES held constant, mothers with parents of rural background adhere to more rigid techniques of socialization than their urban counterparts. Finally, the two samples in our data most likely to contain a relatively high proportion of rural families—Eugene, Oregon and Upstate New York—are also the ones which are slightly out of line in showing smaller differences in favor of middle-class permissiveness.

The above observations call attention to the fact that the major time trends discerned in our data, while impressive, are by no means uniform. There are several marked exceptions to the rule. True, some of these can be "explained" in terms of special features of the samples employed. A case in point is the New Haven study, which—in keeping with the rooming-in ideology and all that this implies—shows the highest frequency and duration of breast feeding for the postwar period, as well as the greatest prevalence of feeding on demand reported in all the surveys examined. Other discrepancies may be accounted for, at least in part, by variations in time span encompassed by the data (National 1930 *vs.* 1932), the demonstrated differential rate in breast feeding for first *vs.* later children (Palo Alto *vs.* National 1930 or Boston), ethnic differences (Boston *vs.* Chicago), contrasting ages of mothers in middle- *vs.* working-class samples (Chicago), etc. All of these explanations, however, are "after the fact" and must therefore be viewed with suspicion.

*Summary.* Despite our inability to account with any confidence for all departures from the general trend, we feel reasonably secure in our inferences about the nature of this trend. To recapitulate, over the last 25 years, even though breast feeding appears to have become less popular, American mothers—especially in the middle class—are becoming increasingly permissive in their feeding and toilet-training practices during the first two years of the child's life. The question remains whether this tendency is equally apparent in the training of the child as he becomes older. We turn next to a consideration of this issue.

# CLASS DIFFERENCES IN THE TRAINING
# OF CHILDREN BEYOND THE AGE OF TWO

Once we leave the stage of infancy, data from different studies of child training become even more difficult to compare. There are still greater variations in the questions asked from one research to the next, and results are reported in different types of units (e.g., relating scales with varying numbers of steps diversely defined). In some instances (as in the Chicago, Detroit II, and, apparently, Eugene surveys) the questions referred not to past or current practices but to the mother's judgment about what she would do at some later period when her child would be older. Also, when the samples include children of widely varying ages, it is often difficult to determine at what period the behavior described by the mother actually took place. Sometimes a particular age was specified in the interviewer's question and when this occurred, we have made use of that fact in estimating the approximate date of the practice. More often, however, such information was lacking. Accordingly, our time estimates must be regarded as subject to considerable error. Finally, even though we deal with substantially the same researches considered in the analysis of infant care, the total period encompassed by the data is appreciably shorter. This is so because the mothers are no longer being asked to recall how they handled their child in infancy; instead they are reporting behavior which is contemporary, or at least not far removed, from the time of the interview.

All of these considerations combine to restrict severely our ability to identify changes in practices over time. Accordingly, the absence of evidence for such changes in some of the data is perhaps more properly attributed to the limitations of our measures than to the actual course of events.

*Permissiveness and Restriction on Freedom of Movement.* The areas of impulse expression documented in Table 7 reflect a continuity in treatment from babyhood into early childhood. With only one minor, statistically insignificant exception, the results depict the middle-class parent as more permissive in all four spheres of activity: oral behavior, toilet accidents, sex, and aggression. There is no suggestion of a shift over the somewhat truncated time span. The now-familiar trend reappears, however, in the data on restriction of freedom of movement shown in Table 8.

In Table 8 we see a gradual shift over time with the middle class being more restrictive in the 1930's and early 1940's but becoming more permissive during the last decade.

*Training for Independence and Achievement.* Thus far, the trends that have appeared point predominantly in one direction—increasing leniency on the part of middle-class parents. At the same time, careful consideration of the nature of these data reveals that they are, in a sense, one-sided: they

Table 7—Permissiveness toward Impulse Expression

| Sample | Approx. date of practice | No. of cases reported | Oral behavior | Toilet accidents | Sex | Aggression |
|---|---|---|---|---|---|---|
| | | | | DIRECTION OF TREND FOR MIDDLE CLASS | | |
| National I | 1932 | 470 | | | More infants allowed to play on bed unclothed.* | More children allowed to "fight so long as they don't hurt each other badly."* |
| Chicago | 1943 | 100 | | Treated by ignoring,* reasoning or talking,* rather than slapping,* scolding, or showing disgust.* | | |
| Detroit II | 1946 | 70–88 | Less often disciplined for thumb sucking. | | Less often disciplined for touching sex organs. | |
| New Haven | 1949–50 | 216 | Less often disapproved for thumb sucking, eating habits, mannerisms, etc.* | | | |
| Eugene | 1950 | 206 | | Less often treated by spanking or scolding. | More permissive toward child's sexual behavior.* | |
| Boston | 1951–52 | 372 | Less restriction on use of fingers for eating.* | Less severe toilet training.* | Higher sex permissiveness (general index).* | More permissive of aggression toward parents,* children† and siblings. Less punishment of aggression toward parents.* |
| Palo Alto | 1953 | 73 | | Less severe toilet training.* | | More permissive of aggression toward parents.* Less severe punishment of aggression toward parents. |

* Indicates difference between classes significant at the 5-percent level or better.
† The difference between percentages is not significant but the difference between ratings is significant at the 5-percent level or better.

have been concerned almost entirely with the parents' responses to the expressed needs and wishes of the child. What about the child's response to the needs and wishes of the parent, and the nature of these parental demands? The results presented in Table 9 are of especial interest since they shed light on all three aspects of the problem. What is more, they signal a dramatic departure from the hitherto unchallenged trend toward permissiveness.

### Table 8—Restriction on Freedom of Movement

| Sample | Approx. date of practice | No. of cases reported | Age | Item | Direction of relationship* |
|--------|--------|--------|-----|------|-------------|
| National II | 1932 | 2289 | 1–5 | Play restricted to home yard | — |
| | | | | Play restricted to block | + |
| | | | | Play restricted to neighborhood | + † |
| | | | | No restriction on place of play | + † |
| National III | 1932 | 669 | 6–12 | Child goes to movie with parents | + |
| | | | | Child goes to movie with other children | + |
| National IV | 1932 | 2414 | 1–12 | Child goes to bed earlier | + |
| Chicago | 1943 | 100 | 5 | Age at which child is allowed to go to movie alone or with other children | + † |
| | | | | Age at which child is allowed to go downtown | — † |
| | | | | Time at which children are expected in at night | + † |
| New Haven I | 1949–50 | 211 | 1 | Definite bed time | — † |
| Boston | 1951–52 | 372 | 5 | Restriction on how far child may go from home | — |
| | | | | Frequency of checking on child's whereabouts | — ** |
| | | | | Strictness about bed time | — † |
| | | | | Amount of care taken by persons other than parents | — † |
| Detroit II | 1953 | 136 | 0–18 | Child supervised closely after 12 years of age | — † |
| Palo Alto | 1953 | 74 | 2½–5½ | Extent of keeping track of child | 0 |

\* Plus sign denotes greater restriction for middle class.
† Denotes difference significant at 5-percent level or better.
\*\* The difference between percentages is not significant but the difference between mean ratings is significant at the 5-percent level or better.

Three types of questions have been asked with respect to independence training. The first is of the kind we have been dealing with thus far; for example, the Boston investigators inquired about the mother's reaction to the child's expression of dependence (hanging on to the mother's skirt, demanding attention, etc.). The results for this sort of query, shown in column 6 of Table 9, are consistent with previous findings for the postwar period; middle-class mothers are more tolerant of the child's expressed needs than are working-class mothers. The second type of question deals with the child's progress in taking care of himself and assuming responsibility (column 7). Here no clear trend is apparent, although there is some

*Table 9*—Training for Independence and Academic Achievement

| 1. Sample | 2. Approx. date of practice | 3. No. of cases reported | 4. Age | 5. Item | DIRECTION OF RELATIONSHIP | | | |
|---|---|---|---|---|---|---|---|---|
| | | | | | 6. Parents' response to child's dependency | 7. Child's behavior* | 8. Parental demands and expectations | 9. Academic aspirations for child* |
| National II | 1932 | 2380 | 1–5 | Dress self not at all | | ++ | | |
| | | | | Dress self partially | | − | | |
| | | 2391 | | Dress self completely | | − | | |
| | | | | Feed self not at all | | − | | |
| | | | | Feed self partially | | + | | |
| | | 2301 | | Feed self completely | | − | | |
| | | | | Children read to by parents | | | | + |
| National III | 1932 | 865 | 6–12 | Runs errands | | 0 | | +† |
| | | | | Earns money | | − | | +† |
| | | | | Receive outside lessons in music, art, etc. | | | | |
| National IV | 1932 | 2695 | 1–12 | Books in the home | | | | +† |
| Chicago I | 1943 | 100 | 5 | Age child expected to dress self | | | 0 | |
| | | | | Expected to help at home by age 5 | | | +† | |
| | | | | Expected to help with younger children | | | +† + | |
| | | | | Girls expected to begin to cook | | | | |
| | | | | Girls expected to help with dishes | | | | |
| | | | | Child expected to finish high school only | | | | +† |
| | | | | Child expected to finish college | | | | +† |
| | | | | Father teaches and reads to children | | | | + |

| Location | Year | N | Age | Item | Class difference |
|---|---|---|---|---|---|
| Detroit II | 1946 | 128 | | All right to leave three-year-old with sitter | 0 |
| | 1947 | 127 | | Expected to pick up own toys | + |
| | 1948 | 126 | | Expected to dress self by age 5 | ++† |
| | 1948 | | 0–18 | Expected to put away clothes by age 5 | +0 |
| | | | | Children requested to run errands at age 7 | + |
| | | | | Agree child should be on his own as early as possible | |
| Urban Connecticut | 1950 | 152 | 6–18 | Age of expected mastery (Winterbottom scale) | ++† |
| Eugene | 1950 | 206 | 0–18 | Household rules and chores expected of children | + |
| Boston | 1951–52 | 372 | 5 | Parent permissive of child dependency | −† |
| | | | | Punishment, irritation for dependency | −† |
| | | | | Parents give child regular job around house | |
| | | | | Importance of child's doing well at school | |
| | | | | Expected to go to college | 0 |
| New Haven II | 1951–53 | 48 | 14–17 | Father subscribes to values of independence and mastery | +† |
| | | 1151** | 14–17 | Expected to go to college | −† / ++ |
| | | | | Family checks over homework | ++ / ++ |
| Palo Alto | 1953 | 74 | 2½–5½ | M's report of child's dependency | − |
| | | | | Amount of attention child wants | + |
| | | | | Child objects to separation | − |
| | | | | Judge's rating of dependency | + |
| Upstate New York | 1955 | 1433 | 0–1 | Mother's educational aspirations for child | +† |

* Plus sign denotes greater independence or achievement required for middle-class child.
† Difference between classes significant at the 5-percent level or better.
** This is the entire high-school sample which Strodtbeck surveyed in order to select his experimental and control group.

suggestion of greater solicitousness on the part of the middle-class mother. For example, in the 1932 material the middle-class child excelled in dressing and feeding himself only "partially," not "completely." In the 1935 Palo Alto study, the middle-class mother viewed her child as more dependent even though he was rated less so by the outsider observer. It would appear that middle-class mothers may be on the alert for signs of dependency and anxious lest they push too fast.

Yet, as the data of column 8 clearly indicate, they push nevertheless. By and large, the middle-class mother expects more of her child than her working-class counterpart. All five of the statistically significant differences support this tendency and most of the remaining results point in the same direction. The conclusion is further underscored by the findings on class differences in parental aspirations for the child's academic progress, shown in column 9. The only exception to the highly reliable trend is in itself noteworthy. In the Boston study, more middle-class mothers expected their children to go to college, but they were less likely to say that it was important for their child to do well in school. Are these mothers merely giving what they consider to be the socially acceptable response, or do they really, as Sears and his colleagues suggest, have less cause for concern because their children are living up to expectations?

The preceding question raises an even broader and more significant issue. Our data indicate that middle-class parents are becoming increasingly permissive in response to the child's expressed needs and desires. Yet, these same parents have not relaxed their high levels of expectations for ultimate performance. Do we have here a typical instance of Benedict's "discontinuity in cultural conditioning,"[24] with the child first being encouraged in one pattern of response and then expected to perform in a very different fashion? If so, there are days of disappointment ahead for middle-class fathers and mothers. Or, are there other elements in the parent-child relationship of the middle-class family which impel the child to effort despite, or, perhaps, even because of, his early experiences of relatively uninhibited gratification? The data on class differences in techniques of discipline shed some light on this question.

*Techniques of Discipline.* The most consistent finding documented in Table 10 is the more frequent use of physical punishment by working-class parents. The middle class, in contrast, resort to reasoning, isolation, and what Sears and his colleagues have referred to as "love-oriented" discipline techniques.[25] These are methods which rely for their effect on the child's fear of loss of love. Miller and Swanson referred to substantially the same class of phenomena by the term "psychological discipline," which for

[24] R. Benedict, "Continuities and Discontinuities in Cultural Conditioning," *Psychiatry*, 1938, **1**, 161–167.
[25] These investigators also classify "isolation" as a love-oriented technique, but since this specific method is reported on in several other studies as well, we have tabulated the results separately to facilitate comparison.

Table 10—Techniques of Discipline

| Sample | Approx. date of practice | No. of cases reporting | Age | DIRECTION OF RELATIONSHIP* | | | | Nature of love-oriented technique | Other significant trends for middle class |
|---|---|---|---|---|---|---|---|---|---|
| | | | | Physical punishment | Reasoning | Isolation | Love-oriented technique | | |
| National II | 1932 | 1947 | 1–5 | −† | | | | | |
| National III | 1932 | 839 | 6–12 | | | +† | | | |
| National IV | 1932 | 3130 | 1–12 | | +† | | | | Infractions more often ignored†; More children deprived of pleasure as punishment |
| Chicago I | 1943 | 100 | 5 | + | | − | +† | Praise for good behavior | Soiling child more often ignored† rather than spanked† or shown disgust |
| Detroit I | 1950 | 115 | 12–14 | −† | | | +† | Mother expresses disappointment or appeals to guilt | |
| Detroit II | 1950 | 222 | 0–19 | − | | | + | Mother uses symbolic rather than direct rewards and punishments | |
| Eugene | 1950 | 206 | 0–18 | − | | +† | 0 | No difference in overall use of praise or withdrawal of love | |
| Boston | 1951–52 | 372 | 5 | −† | + | + | | | Less use of ridicule,† deprivation of privileges** or praise for no trouble at the table† |

* Plus sign indicates practice was more common in middle class than in working class.
† Denotes difference between classes significant at 5-percent level or better.
** The difference between percentages is not significant but the difference between mean ratings is significant at the 5-percent level or better.

them covers such parental behaviors as appeals to guilt, expressions of disappointment, and the use of symbolic rather than direct rewards and punishments. Table 10 shows all available data on class differences in the use of corporal punishment, reasoning, isolation, and "love-oriented" techniques. Also, in order to avoid the risks, however small, involved in wearing theoretical blinders, we have listed in the last column of the table all other significant class differences in techniques of discipline reported in the studies we have examined.

From one point of view, these results highlight once again the more lenient policies and practices of middle-class families. Such parents are, in the first place, more likely to overlook offenses, and when they do punish, they are less likely to ridicule or inflict physical pain. Instead, they reason with the youngster, isolate him, appeal to guilt, show disappointment,— in short, convey in a variety of ways, on the one hand, the kind of behavior that is expected of the child; on the other, the realization that transgression means the interruption of a mutually valued relationship.

These consistent class differences take on added significance in the light of the finding, arrived at independently both by the Boston and Detroit investigators, that "loved-oriented" or "psychological" techniques are more effective than other methods for bringing about desired behavior. Indeed, both groups of researchers concluded on the basis of their data that physical punishment for aggression tends to increase rather than decrease aggressive behavior. From the point of view of our interest, these findings mean that middle-class parents, though in one sense more lenient in their discipline techniques, are using methods that are actually more compelling. Moreover, the compelling power of these practices, rather than being reduced, is probably enhanced by the more permissive treatment accorded to middle-class children in the early years of life. The successful use of withdrawal of love as a discipline technique implies the prior existence of a gratifying relationship; the more love present in the first instance, the greater the threat implied in its withdrawal.

In sum, to return to the issue posed in the preceding section, our analysis suggests that middle-class parents are in fact using techniques of discipline which are likely to be effective in evoking the behavior desired in the child. Whether the high levels of expectation held by such parents are actually achieved is another matter. At least, there would seem to be some measure of functional continuity in the way in which middle-class parents currently treat their children from infancy through childhood.

Before we leave consideration of the data of Table 10, one additional feature of the results deserves comment. In the most recent study reported, the Boston research, there were three departures from the earlier general trend. First, no class difference was found in the over-all use of praise. Second, working-class parents actually exceeded those of the middle class in praising good behavior at the table. Third, in contrast to earlier findings, the working-class mother more frequently punished by withdrawing privileges. Although Sears *et al.* did not classify "withdrawal of privileges" as a love-oriented technique, the shift does represent a change in the direction of what was previously a method characteristic of the middle-class parent. Finally, there is no clear trend in the differential use of love-oriented techniques by the two social classes. If we view the Boston study as reflecting the most recent trends in methods of discipline, then either middle-class mothers are beginning to make less use of techniques they previously relied upon, or the working class is starting to adopt them. We are inclined toward the latter hypothesis in the belief that the working class, as a function of increasing income and education, is gradually reducing its "cultural lag." Evidence from subsequent studies, of course, would be necessary to confirm this speculative interpretation, since the results cited may merely be a function of features peculiar to the Boston study and not typical of the general trend.

*Over-all Character of the Parent-child Relationship.* The material considered so far has focused on specific practices employed by the parent. A number of researches document class differences as well in variables of a more molar sort—for example, the emotional quality of the parent-child relationship as a whole. These investigations have the additional advantage of reaching somewhat further back in time, but they also have their shortcomings. First of all, the results are not usually reported in the conventional form of percentages or means for specific social-class levels. In some studies the findings are given in terms of correlation coefficients. In others, social status can only be estimated from educational level. In others still, the data are presented in the form of graphs from which no significance tests can be computed. Partly to compensate for this lack of precision and comparability, partly to complete the picture of available data on class differences in child rearing, we cite in Table 11 not only the results from these additional studies of molar variables but also all other statistically significant findings from researches considered previously which might have bearing on the problem at hand. In this way, we hope as well to avoid the bias which occasionally arises from looking only at those variables in which one has a direct theoretical interest.

The data of Table 11 are noteworthy in a number of respects. First, we have clear confirmation that, over the entire 25-year period, middle-class parents have had a more acceptant, equalitarian relationship with their children. In many ways, the contrast is epitomized in Duvall's distinction between the "developmental" and "traditional" conceptions of mother and child. Durall asked the mothers in her sample to list the "five things that a good mother does" and the "five things that a good child does." Middle-class mothers tended to emphasize such themes as "guiding and understanding," "relating herself lovingly to the child," and making sure that he "is happy and contented," "shares and cooperates with others," and "is

### Table 11—Overall Character of Parent-child Relationship

| Sample | Approx. date of practice | No. of cases reported | Age | Middle-class trend | Working-class trend |
|---|---|---|---|---|---|
| Berkeley I | 1928–32 | 31 | 1–3 | Grants autonomy Cooperative Equalitarian | Expresses affection Excessive contact Intrusive Irritable Punitive Ignores child |
| National I | 1932 | 494 | 0–1 | | Baby picked up when cries† |
| National IV | 1932 | 3239 | 1–12 | Higher percentage of children punished† | Nothing done to allay child's fears† |
| Yellow Springs, Ohio | 1940 | 124 | 3–12 | Acceptant-democratic | Indulgent Active-rejectant |
| Berkeley II | 1939–42 | 31 | 9–11 | Grants autonomy Cooperative Equalitarian Expresses affection | Excessive contact Intrusive Irritable Punitive Ignores child |
| Chicago I | 1943 | 100 | 5 | | Father plays with child more† |
| Chicago II | 1943–44 | 433 | 1–5 | "Developmental" conception of "good mother" and "good child"† | "Traditional" conception of "good mother" and "good child"† |
| New Haven I | 1949–50 | 219 | 1 | More necessary discipline to prevent injury or danger† | More prohibitive discipline beyond risk of danger or injury |
| Boston | 1951–52 | 372 | 5 | Mother warmer toward child† Father warmer toward child* Father exercises more authority* Mother has higher esteem for father† Mother delighted about pregnancy† Both parents more often share authority* | Father demands instant obedience† Child ridiculed† Greater rejection of child† Emphasis on neatness, cleanliness, and order† Parents disagree more on child-rearing policy* |
| New Haven II | 1951–53 | 48 | 14–17 | Fathers have more power in family decisions† Parents agree in value orientations† | |
| Palo Alto | 1953 | 73 | 2½–5½ | Baby picked up when cries† | Mother carries through demands rather than dropping the subject† |
| Eugene | 1955–56 | 206 | 0–18 | Better relationship between father and child† | |
| Washington, D.C. | 1956–57 | 400 | 10–11 | Desirable qualities are happiness,* considerateness,* curiosity,* self-control* | Desirable qualities are neatness-cleanliness,* obedience* |

* Trend significant at 5-percent level or better.
† The difference between percentages is not significant but the difference between mean ratings is significant at the 5-percent level or better.

eager to learn." In contrast, working-class mothers stressed the importance of keeping house and child "neat and clean," "training the child to regularity," and getting the child "to obey and respect adults."

What is more, this polarity in the value orientation of the two social classes appears to have endured. In data secured as recently as 1957, Kohn[26] reports that working-class mothers differ from those of the middle class in their choice of characteristics most desired in a child; the former emphasize "neatness, cleanliness, and obedience," while the latter stress "happiness, considerateness, and self-control."

Yet, once again, it would be a mistake to conclude that the middle-class parent is exerting less pressure on his children. As the data of Table 11 also show, a higher percentage of middle-class children are punished in some manner, and there is more "necessary" discipline to prevent injury or danger. In addition, though the middle-class father typically has a warmer relationship with the child, he is also likely to have more authority and status in family affairs.

Although shifts over time are difficult to appraise when the data are so variable in specific content, one trend is sufficiently salient to deserve comment. In the early Berkeley data the working-class parent is more expressive of affection than his middle-class counterpart. But in the follow-up study of the same children eight years later the trend is reversed. Perhaps the same mothers behave differently toward younger and older children. Still, the item "Baby picked up when cries" yields a significant difference in favor of the working-class mother in 1932 and a reliable shift in the opposite direction in 1953. *Sic transit gloria Watsoniensis!*

Especially with terms as heavily value laden as those which appear in Table 11, one must be concerned with the possibility that the data in the studies examined document primarily not actual behavior but the middle-class mother's superior knowledge of the socially acceptable response. Undoubtedly, this factor operates to inflate the reported relationships. But there are several reassuring considerations. First, although the items investigated vary widely in the intensity of their value connotations, all show substantially the same trends. Second, four of the studies reported in Table 11 (Berkeley I and II, Yellow Springs, and New Haven II) are based not on the mother's responses to an interview but on observation of actual interaction among family members. It seems highly unlikely, therefore, that the conclusions we have reached apply only to professed opinions and not to real behavior as well.

## RETROSPECT AND PROSPECT

It is interesting to compare the results of our analysis with the traditional

[26] Kohn, *op. cit.*

view of the differences between the middle- and lower-class styles of life, as documented in the classic descriptions of Warner,[27] Davis,[28] Dollard,[29] and the more recent accounts of Spinley,[30] Clausen,[31] and Miller and Swanson.[32] In all these sources the working class is typically characterized as impulsive and uninhibited, the middle class as more rational, controlled, and guided by a broader perspective in time. Thus Clausen writes:

> The lower class pattern of life . . . puts a high premium on physical gratification, on free expression of aggression, on spending and sharing. Cleanliness, respect for property, sexual control, educational achievement—all are highly valued by middle class Americans—are of less importance to the lower class family or are phrased differently.[33]

To the extent that our data even approach this picture, it is for the period before World War II rather than for the present day. The modern middle class has, if anything, extended its time perspective so that the tasks of child training are now accomplished on a more leisurely schedule. As for the lower class the fit is far better for the actual behavior of parents rather than for the values they seek to instill in their children. As reflected in the data of Tables 10 and 11, the lower-class parent—though he demands compliance and control in his child—is himself more aggressive, expressive, and impulsive than his middle-class counterpart. Even so, the picture is a far cry from the traditional image of the casual and carefree lower class. Perhaps the classic portrait is yet to be seen along the skid rows and Tobacco Roads of the nation, but these do not lie along the well-trodden paths of the survey researcher. He is busy ringing doorbells, no less, in the main section of the lower-class district, where most of the husbands have steady jobs and, what is more important, the wife is willing to answer the door and the interviewer's questions. In this modern working-class world there may be greater freedom of emotional expression, but there is no laxity or vagueness with respect to goals of child training. Consistently over the past 25 years, the parent in this group has emphasized what are usually regarded as the traditional middle-class virtues of cleanliness, conformity, and control, and although his methods are not so effective as those of his middle-class neighbors, they are perhaps more desperate.

Perhaps this very desperation, enhanced by early exposure to impulse

[27] W. L. Warner and P. S. Lunt, *The Social Life of a Modern Community*, New Haven, Yale University Press, 1942; Warner, Meeker, and Others, *op. cit.*

[28] A. Davis, B. Gardner, and M. R. Gardner, *Deep South*, Chicago, University of Chicago Press, 1941.

[29] J. Dollard, *Caste and Class in a Southern Town*, New Haven, Yale University Press, 1937.

[30] B. M. Spinley, *The Deprived and the Privileged: Personality Development in English Society*, London, Routledge & Kegan Paul, Ltd., 1953.

[31] J. A. Clausen, "Social and Psychological Factors in Narcotics Addiction," *Law and Contemporary Problems*, 1957, **22**, 34–51.

[32] Miller and Swanson, *The Changing American Parent*, *op. cit.*

[33] Clausen, *op. cit.*, p. 42.

and aggression, leads working-class parents to pursue new goals with old techniques of discipline. While accepting middle-class levels of aspiration he has not yet internalized sufficiently the modes of response which make these standards readily achievable for himself or his children. He has still to learn to wait, to explain, and to give and withhold his affection as the reward and price of performance.

As of 1957, there are suggestions that the cultural gap may be narrowing. Spock has joined the Bible on the working-class shelf. If we wish to see the shape of the future, we can perhaps do no better than to look at the pages of the newly revised edition of this ubiquitous guidebook. Here is a typical example of the new look—a passage not found in the earlier version.

If the parent can determine in which respects she may be too permissive and can firm up her discipline, she may, if she is on the right track, be delighted to find that her child becomes not only better behaved but much happier. Then she can really love him better, and he in turn responds to this.[34]

Apparently "love" and "limits" are both watchwords for the coming generation of parents. As Mrs. Johnson, down in the flats, puts away the hairbrush and decides to have a talk with her unruly youngster "like the book says," Mrs. Thomas, on the hill, is dutifully striving to overcome her guilt at the thought of giving John the punishment she now admits he deserves. If both ladies are successful, the social scientist may eventually have to look elsewhere in his search for everlarger $F$'s and $t$'s.

Such speculations carry us beyond the territory yet surveyed by the social scientist. Perhaps the most important implication for the future from our present analysis lies in the sphere of method rather than substance. Our attempt to compare the work of a score of investigators over a score of years will have been worth the labor if it but convinces future researchers of the wastefulness of such uncoordinated efforts. Our best hope for an understanding of the differences in child rearing in various segments of our society and the effects of these differences on personality formation lies in the development of a systematic long-range plan for gathering comparable data at regular intervals on large samples of families at different positions in the social structure. We now have survey organizations with the scientific competence and adequate technical facilities to perform the task. With such hopes in mind, the author looks ahead to the day when the present analysis becomes obsolete, in method as well as substance.

## RECAPITULATION AND CODA

A comparative analysis of the results of studies of social-class differences in child rearing over a 25-year period points to the following conclusions.

[34] Spock, *op. cit.*, p. 326.

### Trends in Infant Care

1. Over the past quarter of a century, American mothers at all social-class levels have become more flexible with respect to infant feeding and weaning. Although fewer infants may be breast fed, especially over long periods of time, mothers are increasingly more likely to feed their children on demand and to wean them later from the bottle.

2. Class differences in feeding, weaning, and toilet training show a clear and consistent trend. From about 1930 till the end of World War II, working-class mothers were uniformly more permissive than those of the middle class. They were more likely to breast feed, to follow a self-demand schedule, to wean the child later both from breast and bottle, and to begin and complete both bowel and bladder training at a later age. After World War II, however, there has been a definite reversal in direction; now it is the middle-class mother who is the more permissive in each of the above areas.

3. Shifts in the pattern of infant care—especially on the part of middle-class mothers—show a striking correspondence to the changes in practices advocated in successive editions of U.S. Children's Bureau bulletins and similar sources of expert opinion.

4. In addition to varying with social-class level, methods of infant care appear to differ as a function of cultural background, urban vs. rural up-bringing, and exposure to particular ideologies of child rearing.

5. Taken together, the findings on changes in infant care lead to the generalization that socialization practices are most likely to be altered in those segments of society which have most ready access to the agencies or agents of change (e.g., books, pamphlets, physicians, and counselors).

### Trends in Child Training

6. The data on the training of the young child shows middle-class mothers, especially in the postwar period, to be consistently more permissive toward the child's expressed needs and wishes. The generalization applies in such diverse areas as oral behavior, toilet accidents, dependency, sex, aggressiveness, and freedom of movement outside the home.

7. Though more tolerant of expressed impulses and desires, the middle-class parent, throughout the period covered by this survey, has higher expectations for the child. The middle-class youngster is expected to learn to take care of himself earlier, to accept more responsibilities about the home, and—above all—to progress further in school.

8. In matters of discipline, working-class parents are consistently more likely to employ physical punishment, while middle-class families rely more on reasoning, isolation, appeals to guilt, and other methods involving the threat of loss of love. At least two independent lines of evidence suggest

that the techniques preferred by middle-class parents are more likely to bring about the development of internalized values and controls. Moreover, the effectiveness of such methods, should, at least on theoretical grounds, be enhanced by the more acceptant atmosphere experienced by middle-class children in their early years.

9. Over the entire 25-year period studied, parent-child relationships in the middle class are consistently reported as more acceptant and equalitarian, while those in the working class are oriented toward maintaining order and obedience. Within this context, the middle class has shown a shift away from emotional control toward freer expression of affection and greater tolerance of the child's impulses and desires.

In the past few years, there have been indications that the gap between the social classes may be narrowing. Whatever trend the future holds in store, let us hope that the social scientist will no longer be content to look at them piecemeal but will utilize all the technical resources now at his command to obtain a systematic picture of the changes, through still more extended space and time, in the way in which humanity brings up its children.

# CHILD-REARING PRACTICES IN A LOW

# SOCIOECONOMIC GROUP

## The Mothers of Premature Infants

*H. Wortis, J. L. Bardach, R. Cutler, R. Rue, and A. Freedman*

In 1949, Warner(1)* combined occupation, source of income, dwelling area, and type of house lived in as a scale which he used to measure differences in American social status. Using this scale, he found a close relationship between class placement and certain characteristics of behavior. Warner believed that class position was determined not only by socioeconomic factors, but also by social relations, a person being a member of that class in which most of his social participation occurs. This viewpoint, that of social anthropology, postulates that the social system consists of acts and beliefs which are passed from the old generation to all members of the new. Children are born into the same class as their parents, since they live together and participate in their social activity; the parents, through example and precept, train the child to act appropriately within their own group. "As participants in the society in which they are growing up, they (the new generation) internalize the prevailing way of life in the community and make it part of themselves to the extent that, by the time they reach adolescence, much of the basic beliefs and clues of the total group become part of the emotional structure of each individual."(2).

This concept of the American social structure was later expanded to include a second form of social stratification existing side by side with the class system. This is the caste system which separates people by their skin color and differentiates between an "upper" white caste and a "lower" black caste. While the lines between classes are fairly flexible and allow for upward and downward movement, the lines between the castes are

* Numerals in parentheses denote references at end of chapter.

From *Pediatrics*, **32**(2), August 1963, 298–307. Reprinted by permission of the American Academy of Pediatrics and the authors.

458

inflexible and do not permit change. Within each caste, a separate class system exists, and ethical and social values are much alike in the parallel class levels. The caste system, however, does not permit merging of the parallel and co-existing classes.

It is thus anticipated that women of the same class will have similar standards and expectations for their children, whatever their caste. The study of child-rearing practices in a particular group becomes a study of how children are prepared to function as members of their parents' social class.

This concept of the stratification of American society has been used in studies by Dollard, Hollingshead, and others to differentiate groups in our apparently homogeneous culture.

Studies of child-rearing practices in relation to class have, however, not resulted in uniform findings. In an early and often quoted study conducted in Chicago, Davis(3) interviewed Negro and white mothers of 5-year-old children. He found working-class mothers more permissive toward their children in weaning and toilet training, and more likely to punish and less concerned with educational goals than middle-class mothers. In a more recent study at Harvard, Sears and his co-workers(4) interviewed white mothers of 5-year-old kindergarten children. He found working-class mothers less permissive, more punitive, and with the same concern about education as his middle-class mothers. Sears also found a number of other attributes where there were significant differences between middle-class and working-class mothers of 5-year-old children. Various reasons have been given to explain the differences between the Harvard findings and Chicago findings. Havighurst(5) has suggested that although both studies were of working-class mothers, the Chicago group contained more lower-class mothers.

The present study pertains to a group of Negro working-class women who all belong to the lowest social class. Our interest in them derived from the fact that each had delivered a premature infant in a municipal hospital in Brooklyn. Because we were engaged in an anterospective study, we were able to observe the mothers and children over a 5-year period. We have reported elsewhere on several aspects of our study(6, 7). Here we shall discuss only certain aspects of child-rearing practices at $2\frac{1}{2}$ and at 5 years.

Our sample consisted of the mothers of 250 Negro premature children of low social class. Most of the mothers lived in the same congested, segregated, urban area. Few of them had completed high school, and almost all of them had worked as domestics or as unskilled factory workers. On Warner's Occupational Scale(1), almost all the mothers rated in classes 6 and 7. All of the children had been followed since birth in a study of the relation of certain neonatal experiences to development. The children were seen at regular intervals and the study group established good rapport with the mothers. Our present report on child-rearing practices is based on two interviews, the first given when the child was 2½ years old, the second when the child was 5 years old.

Our information when the child was 2½ was derived during the period 1959 to 1962 from the responses of 212 natural mothers, 14 substitute mothers, 6 fathers, and 18 other persons. Two social workers performed all the interviews, using a prepared schedule which included questions regarding child-rearing practices and measures of the child's behavior selected from the Vineland Social Maturity Scale(8). The answers were

*Table 1*—Social Characteristics of Families of 250 Premature Negro Children of Low Social Class, Studied at Age 2½ Years

| Characteristics | Per cent |
| --- | --- |
| Number of persons per room more than 1.5 | 34 |
| Where employed, father a manual or unskilled worker | 89 |
| Where employed, mother a domestic or unskilled factory worker | 88 |
| Mother has not completed high school | 71 |
| Family supported wholly by earnings | 69 |
| Annual household income $3,900 or less | 67 |
| Family supported wholly or in part by public assistance | 29 |
| Number of minor children in the home (mean) | 3.2 |

*Table 2*—Living Arrangements with Natural Parents of 250 Premature Negro Children of Low Social Class, Studied at Age 2½ Years

| Living arrangements | No. | % |
| --- | --- | --- |
| Living with both natural parents | 134 | 53.6 |
| Living with natural mother only | 95 | 38.0 |
| Living with natural father only | 2 | 0.8 |
| Living with neither natural parent | 19 | 7.6 |
| Total | 250 | 100.0 |

recorded at the time of the interview and subsequently rated. In order to obtain reliability in rating, the two interviewers had previously independently rated a number of interviews and then compared results until they reached a high level of agreement. All ratings were then made by one of the interviewers (R.R.).

When the child was 2½, the characteristics of the family in which he lived were those of very low social class (Table 1). The family structure in which the 2½-year-old lived was further characterized by a large number of broken homes. Only 53.6 per cent of the children lived in homes with both parents (Table 2).

Thirty-eight per cent of the children lived in homes where the natural mother, but not the father, was present (Table 2). Seven and six-tenths per cent of the children lived in homes where neither parent was living. In a third of the households, the head of the family was a woman, usually the mother herself (Table 3). The conventional family pattern of both natural parents living together with their offspring did not exist for almost half of these children; for a third, an unattached woman was the only paternal figure. The child's relation to the parent was further attenuated by the fact that only a third of the children had been exclusively cared for by their own mothers. Almost half of the mothers had worked for considerable periods since this child's birth, and provision had been made for the child's care, often out of the home, and not infrequently in another state. A few of the mothers had abandoned the child, and two mothers had died. When we estimated the number of mother-persons who had exclusive responsibility for the child since his birth (excluding baby sitters), the average number of mother-persons was two. Twenty-five per cent of the children had three or more mother-persons.

*Table 3*—Family Structure in Household of 250 Premature Negro Children of Low Social Class, Studied at Age 2½ Years

| Family structure | No. | % |
|---|---|---|
| Husband-wife family | 151 | 60.4 |
| Other male head | 12 | 4.8 |
| Female head: mother | 73 | 29.2 |
| Female head: other | 12 | 4.8 |
| Institution and unknown | 2 | .8 |
| Total | 250 | 100.0 |

*Table 4*—Household Characteristics in Families of 250 Negro Children of Low Social Class, Studied at Age 2½ Years

| Characteristics | Per cent |
|---|---|
| Ownership of television set | 94.4 |
| Child has own bed | 52.9 |
| Ownership of children's toys | 80.4 |
| Someone reads or tells the child a story | 48.0 |
| Ownership of children's books | 70.7 |
| Ownership of automobile | 12.0 |

Other characteristics of the household in which he lived gave further clues to the social experiences of the 2½-year-old (Table 4). Possessions in these homes were meager. Almost half of these children shared a bed with siblings or adults. There were few toys, and 19.6 per cent of the households reported no toys of any description. The small number of families that owned an automobile was not an unexpected finding, but one which was related to the child's limited social experience. Few of these children had visited a park or a zoo or had gone on an excursion. In 48 per cent of the households, there was no story-telling to the 2½-year-old. However, 94.4 per cent of the homes owned a television set, and two-thirds of these young children were reported to watch television programs for at least an hour a day, while a few watched at intervals throughout the day.

Encouragement to work was also a characteristic of the way the 2½-year-old was brought up. While few of the children had set tasks, most were expected to perform small duties, fetching diapers, mopping up, or helping mother by using the dust pan or dusting.

In the Chicago and Harvard studies, retrospective information had been collected on the methods of toilet-training and weaning from the breast. In the Chicago study, the working-class mothers were reported to be more permissive than middle-class mothers in regard to training the children for feeding and cleanliness. In the Harvard study, the working-class mothers were found more restrictive in toilet-training, weaning and cleanliness habits.

Since our first interview was with mothers of 2½-year-old children, we were able to ascertain the mother's attitude toward the child's present level of toilet-training and dependence on the bottle at a time when the child was still often incompletely trained.

At 2½, two-thirds of the children whose mothers were interviewed had not completed their toilet-training, and half of them still drank milk from a bottle (Table 5). However, most of our mothers showed little affect in

*Table 5*—Level of Social Development among 250 Premature Negro Children of Low Social Class, Studied at Age 2½ Years

| Development | % |
|---|---|
| Eats table food only | 90 |
| Usually feeds self | 86 |
| Never uses a bottle | 49 |
| Able to use spoon, fork, and cup | 46 |
| Can completely undress and unbutton | 32 |
| Never wets or soils | 32 |

discussing either toilet-training or weaning from the bottle; these were not subjects which evoked much emotional response from the mother. She expected the 2½-year-old to have "accidents," and his bottle drinking had absolutely no negative connotation for her. On the other hand, the mother usually permitted the 2½-year-old child to feed himself and to eat table food. She seldom, however, permitted him to assist with dressing, even though some children were quite able to do so. "It's quicker to do it myself" was her reason.

In general, indeed, it seemed largely a consideration of her own convenience that was the basis for the mother's child-rearing practices, and not a theory of good child care. The 2½-year-old was permitted, or even expected, to act like a baby. But he was also permitted to achieve independence at his own rate of speed, provided that in doing so it made things easier for the mother. The mother did not set up high achievement goals for the 2½-year-old, and her handling of the child was usually based on her own immediate needs. Middle-class mothers are very responsive to questions about toilet-training or bottle drinking, and our selection of questions in this area was an indication of our own middle-class bias. It might be that the lack of response to these questions was a reflection of a completely different set of values in these working-class mothers, and that we might have tapped different responses with different kind of questions.

Davis and Sears both agreed that the working-class mother was more punitive toward the child than the middle-class mother. We found that corporal punishment, often with a strap, was the form of punishment most often used to control the 2½-year-old. Children were most often punished for disobeying the mother or fighting with siblings. We regarded the use of corporal punishment to enforce obedience in the 2½-year-old as restrictive maternal behavior. However, the mother did not regard herself as strict. There were evidently important semantic differences between the mother and the interviewer.

Our interview included the following question: "Some mothers are strict, some are easy-going, and some worry a lot. How would you describe yourself? Only 17 per cent of the mothers used the word "strict" to describe themselves, and 29 per cent used "worrisome"; 49 per cent used the word "easy-going" (Table 6). Even though most mothers used corporal punishment to enforce obedience, the absence of strong strictures in relation to time of getting up, meal-times, bottle drinking, and use of eating implements, made us agree that most mothers were "easy-going" in these areas.

*Table 6*—Mother's Evaluation of Her Own Strictness among 248 Premature Negro Children of Low Social Class

| Evaluation | No. | % |
| --- | --- | --- |
| Mother used "strict" to identify self | 46 | 17 |
| Mother used "worrisome" to identify self | 81 | 29 |
| Mother used "easy-going" to identify self | 136 | 49 |
| "Can't say," or other | 13 | 4 |
| Total | 276* | 99 |

* Number of responses are greater than number of subjects, since some mothers used combinations of words to identify themselves.

We regarded the more frequent use of the word "worrisome" as significant, since many of the mothers appeared to us to be subdued, apathetic, and unhappy. Indeed, we rated 8 of every 100 mothers as seriously depressed. This was perhaps not surprising in view of the social situations we have described.

In general, the mother's attitude toward the 2½-year-old child could be characterized as being vaguely positive. When asked to describe him in her own words, two-thirds of the mothers described the child in positive terms, but usually in words that were general and impersonal, and did not suggest an individualization of the child. One-third of the mothers whom we interviewed used negative terms in describing the child, and 4 per cent expressed extreme dislike or antagonism toward him. An example of a response rated "very positive" was, "He's very lovable, easy going, sweet, mischievous, an imp." The following responses were rated as "vaguely positive," the category into which most fell: "She's all right"; "A nice kid, not too bad to take care of, obeys me nice"; "He's pretty well behaved"; "He's easy to manage, not real bad, not bad tempered; he does as he's told." A vaguely negative reply was: "She doesn't like to be petted too much. If you tell her she can't have something, she'll fight." A very negative reply was: "He's just a problem child to me. He does things he's not supposed to, like pushing his sister and hitting. He wants everything his own way—more than the rest—I just can't figure him" (Table 7).

*Table 7*—Informant's Description of 248 Premature Negro Children of Low Social Class

|  | No. | % |
|---|---|---|
| Strongly positive | 47 | 19 |
| Vaguely positive | 119 | 48 |
| Balance of positive and negative | 46 | 19 |
| Vaguely negative | 24 | 9 |
| Strongly negative | 9 | 4 |
| "Can't say" | 3 | 1 |
| Total | 248 | 100 |

The presence of severe social disorganization and the poverty of the homes did not prevent good maternal care. A "growth fostering" score was rated on a scale which included the mother's encouragement of self-care, her approval of the child's behavior, her enjoyment of the child, and her use of moderate and consistent discipline. We also scored each family separately on a scale of social disorganization which indicated the degree of social pathology in the home. There was a significant correlation[1] between the degree of social disorganization and the quality of maternal care, the better organized homes tending to have better maternal care. However, the distributions were not identical, and some homes with a high degree of social disorganization had high scores of growth fostering care. The following scales were used in evaluating the situations.

### Estimate of Family Organization at 2½ Years

(The score is the sum of the subscores)

| | |
|---|---|
| Both natural parents not in home | 1 |
| Social pathology or psychiatric history (score 1 when 1 instance of social pathology; score 2 for 2 or more): | 2 |

Psychiatric illness
Alcoholism
Drug addiction
Marital discord
Prostitution
Child abandonment
Unmarried parents
Out of wedlock children by different fathers
Others

| | |
|---|---|
| Child has had three or more caretakers | 1 |
| Mother is rejecting | 1 |
| Mother shows some or marked emotional disturbance | 1 |

[1] Pearson product-moment coefficient of correlation = 0.414 (p <0.01).

*Growth Fostering Scale at 2½ Years*
(The score is the sum of the subscores)

| | |
|---|---|
| Mother encourages child in self-care | 1 |
| Mother generally approves of child's behavior | 1 |
| Mother enjoys child | 1 |
| Mother affectionate and warm towards child | 1 |
| Child receives moderate and consistent discipline | 1 |

The mean score in the Estimate of Family Organization was 2.2; the mean score in the Growth Fostering Scale was 3.

If we attempt to sum up the 2½-year-old child's social experience and maternal care in this very low social class, we can say that he lived in a very disorganized family and often lacked an exclusive relationship to one maternal or paternal figure. He was more likely to have a relationship to a female than to a male parental figure. His personal characteristics were not of great concern to his parent. He was one of a large family group, and possibly for this reason he was encouraged to be independent in self-feeding and eating table food, but not in dressing himself. His mother generally approved of his behavior. If he were still drinking from a bottle or wetting, his mother showed little concern. He received a good deal of corporal punishment, although his mother thought of herself as easy-going and was in fact, quite permissive in many respects. He had few toys or books, but had ample opportunity to watch television. The quality of maternal care he received was sometimes better than the social organization of the family in which he lived.

We turn now to an interview with a sample of the same population when the children were aged 5 years. When the children reached their fifth birthdays, we called them back for an examination and for an interview with the mothers. In a 9-month period, we interviewed the mothers or mother-substitutes of all those who had become 5 years of age within this period and who were available, 72 children in all. At age 5, the social conditions under which the children were living did not differ from those we described at 2½ years, except that more children were living with the mother only.

In the 5-year interview, we utilized parts of the interview, the rating scale and the definitions which were developed by Sears and the Harvard group.[2] Sears' interview was concerned with maternal attitudes and child-rearing practices. He had administered it to working-class and middle-class mothers and had found certain significant differences between them.

Our interviews were performed by two social workers who recorded the responses at the time of the interview and subsequently rated them, using Sears' definitions and rating scales. The inter-reliability of the rating was previously established by each social worker independently rating the

[2] We wish to express our thanks to Dr. Robert Sears who made available to us the Harvard study interview, the rating scale and instructions on rating. We used all the child-rearing scales which Sears reported to have a user-rater reliability of 0.485 or better and which in his factor analysis correlated ±0.30 with the factors A-G (Sears, 1957).

same two interviews and subsequently comparing the ratings. All ratings were found to be identical or very similar.

In order to make our populations comparable with Sears, we will report only on information derived from interviews with the natural mother. There were 47 such interviews.

Table 8 describes the Harvard study and the Brooklyn working-class mothers. The two groups were composed of native born, natural mothers of 5-year-old children. They differed in that Brooklyn mothers were all Negro, of lower social class, and did not all live in intact families.[3]

*Table 8*—Comparison of Harvard and Brooklyn Studies of Working-Class Mothers of 5-year-old Children

| Comparative item | Harvard (174 children) | Brooklyn (47 children) |
|---|---|---|
| Ethnic origin | Native born whites | Native born American Negro |
| Occupation | Warner's Occupational Scale, Class 4-7; primarily blue collar workers, the largest number being relatively skilled workers | Primarily unskilled, Warner's Occupational Scale, 6, 7 |
| Religion | Protestant; Catholic; Jewish | Almost all Protestants; a few Catholics |
| Marital status | All married and living with child's father* | A large number of separated unmarried women |
| Relation to 5-year-old child | Living with child | Living with child |

* Sears had excluded separated and unmarried mothers from his study.

We were able to compare ratings for 24 of the dimensions in which Sears had found statistically significant differences between his middle-class and working-class mothers (Table 9). We were not able to compare them in all dimensions because of the nature of the sample. For instance, we could not inquire about weaning from breast feeding since the enforced hospital stay of these premature infants had precluded breast feeding.

In 15 of the 24 dimensions, the Brooklyn working-class mothers rated in the same direction as the Boston working-class mothers. Low permissiveness for dependency; low sex permissiveness; low permissiveness for aggression toward parents; high severity of punishment for aggression toward parents; high strictness about bedtime; high use of physical punishment; low maternal warmth to child; high percentage of mothers showing some rejection of the child; low percentage of mothers delighted over pregnancy; low mother's esteem for father; high parental disagreement on child-rearing practices; on the scales which measured family authority, high on the authority exercised primarily by the mother.

[3] Sears had excluded separated and unmarried mothers from his study.

Although the Brooklyn and Harvard mothers were similar in these dimensions, a larger portion of the Brooklyn mothers had those attributes which Sears had found characteristic of his working-class sample. In three dimensions (Table 9) there was a highly statistically significant difference between the Harvard and Brooklyn working-class mothers, although they both rated in the same direction.[4] The Brooklyn mothers were much less permissive in aggression against parents, much lower in maternal warmth and far lower in delight when they first learned of their pregnancy. The greater proportion of "working-class responses" in the Brooklyn mothers we attributed to the fact that they were lower in the working-class scale than the Harvard mothers.

*Table 9*—Comparison of Child-Training Practices among Harvard Study and Brooklyn Mothers

| *Items rating high\** *(percentage rated)* | HARVARD *Middle class* *(%)* | *Working class* *(%)* | BROOKLYN *Lowest working class* *(%)* |
|---|---|---|---|
| Permissiveness for dependency | 42 | 29 | 25 |
| Sex permissiveness | 53 | 22 | 6 |
| Permissiveness for aggression toward parents | 19 | 7 | 4† |
| Severity of punishment for aggression toward parents | 36 | 51 | 61 |
| Strictness about bed-time | 28 | 38 | 39 |
| Importance of child's doing well at school | 35 | 50 | 52 |
| Use of physical punishment | 17 | 33 | 43 |
| Mother's warmth toward child | 51 | 37 | 16.3‡ |
| Percentage of mothers showing some rejection of child | 24 | 40 | 43 |
| Percentage of mothers delighted over pregnancy | 73 | 65 | 10† |
| Mother's esteem for father high | 54 | 37 | 34§ |
| Parents' disagreement on child-rearing practices | 15 | 19 | 20§ |
| Family authority exercised primarily by: | | | |
| Father | 29 | 25 | 28 |
| Both equally | 62 | 59 | 42 |
| Mother | 9 | 16 | 30 |

\* In all the scales, the Harvard Study and Brooklyn working class mothers rated in the same direction.
† Differences between Brooklyn and Harvard working-class significant at 0.001 level.
‡ Difference between Brooklyn and Harvard working-class significant at 0.01 level.
§ Scored only in intact families.

Since it seemed very possible that the large number of unmarried mothers had influenced their report on "delight" in pregnancy, we compared the responses of the married and unmarried mothers and found no difference in their responses. Both groups were equally displeased when they learned of their pregnancy. The number of negative responses in regard to "delight in pregnancy" is so large that it suggests further study.

In nine dimensions, we found a reversal of Sears' findings (Table 10). We found the Brooklyn working-class mothers more permissive of aggression towards neighborhood children, less restrictive in use of fingers for

[4] Differences 0.01 level or less.

eating, less restrictive in care of house and furniture, exerting less pressure for orderliness and cleanliness, using less praise of the child if he gave no trouble at table, and less depriving of privileges. This is in apparent support of Davis' findings that working-class mothers are permissive, but this support is more apparent than real. As we saw earlier, mothers who used a great deal of corporal punishment to enforce obedience were also permissive about matters which did not concern them. A relative indifference to manners and cleanliness at age 5 years went along with our previous finding that these were not areas of great concern to the mother at age $2\frac{1}{2}$ years. However, in areas where she was concerned, as in permission for aggression against the parent, she was in fact very restrictive. The fact that she did not use deprivation of privileges to punish the child went along with her greater use of corporal punishment as a means of control. The low use of praise went along with the relative coldness of these mothers.

*Table 10*—Comparison of Child-Training Practices among Harvard Study and Brooklyn Mothers

| | HARVARD | | BROOKLYN |
|---|---|---|---|
| Items rating high* (percentage rated) | Middle class (%) | Working class (%) | Lowest working class (%) |
| Permission for aggression toward neighborhood children | 38 | 31 | 60† |
| Amount of restriction for use of fingers in eating | 66 | 81 | 61‡ |
| Restrictions for conformity in table standards | 23 | 39 | 16 |
| Restrictions on care of house and furniture | 65 | 78 | 57* |
| Pressure for orderliness and cleanliness | 43 | 57 | 39 |
| Use of praise if child gives no trouble at table | 49 | 63 | 29† |
| Deprivation of privileges | 34 | 42 | 26 |
| Percentage who want child to go to college | 70 | 24 | 39 |
| Father's warmth to child | 60 | 56 | 74 |

* In these scales, there is a reversal of direction when ratings of the Harvard study and the Brooklyn working-class mothers are compared.
† Differences between Brooklyn and Harvard working-class significant at 0.001 level.
‡ Differences between Brooklyn and Harvard working-class significant at 0.01 level.

The higher rate, in Brooklyn mothers, of "desire that the child go to college" was comparable to Davis' earlier finding that the lowest class Negro mother was more likely to say that she wanted her child to go to college. There was, indeed, a great interest among the Brooklyn mothers in good education for their children, but they actually did not have specific educational goals. Rather, the expression of a desire for college was part of the mother's generalized feeling that she wished the child's situation to be better than her own, and it was symptomatic of her rejection of her own class and caste status.

An unexpectedly high percentage of the fathers were rated as showing a high degree of warmth to the child. We had rated paternal warmth only in those homes where a father was present. This could very well be a selective finding since in our families, the father who was fond of his child was more likely to be present in the home. Our finding suggests a high degree of paternal warmth in those homes where a father was present, but we have already demonstrated that many of these homes had no father.

We would call attention to the very high number of Brooklyn mothers who encouraged their children in aggression toward neighborhood children. Again, our own interpretation of this was that in encouraging her child to fight back, the mother showed a realistic understanding of the social problems in her neighborhood. It might also be her own hostility to, and rejection of, the miserable circumstances of her own economic and segregated status.

## CONCLUSIONS

Our findings support the view that there are characteristics in child-rearing practices which are related to class status, and that these differences become more pronounced with the extremes of class.

In this sample of low-class mothers interviewed when the child was $2\frac{1}{2}$ years of age, we found some maternal rejection of the child, coldness, and physical punishment. There was lack of restrictiveness in regard to toilet training and training for manners. At 5 years there was much restrictiveness in regard to aggression against parents, and against sex play. There was great concern for education for the child, and a strong feeling that the child should fight back if molested. Some of these attitudes, we believe, came out of the mother's rejection of her own social situation and segregation into a lower caste.

The maternal attitudes and child-rearing practices which we have described and which were related to class, undoubtedly helped mold the developing child. If we can speculate, we would say that certain things in his environment were helpful to the child. He was permitted to grow at his own speed. If he was unable to perform, he did not meet with criticism and pressure to do better. He learned how to work. He was encouraged to fight for his rights. On the other hand, there was confusion as to who had authority over him and what behavior was acceptable, since many persons with different expectations had a parental role. He was accustomed to extremes of adult authority, being very controlled at times, and not at all controlled in others. He early became used to corporal punishment. He was treated with relative coldness and he was not praised for achievement. The stimuli which are supplied by books, toys, and cultural experiences were often missing. There was little opportunity for a boy to identify with a male figure. There was lack of interest in the personality characteristics which differentiate one individual from the other and which contribute to a strong feeling of self-identification.

Other elements in the environment were preparing the child to take over a lower class role. The inadequate incomes, crowded homes, lack of consistent familial ties, the mother's depression and helplessness in her own situation, were as important as her child-rearing practices in influencing the child's development and preparing him for an adult role. It was for us a sobering experience to watch a large group of newborn infants, plastic human beings of unknown potential, and to observe over a 5-year period their social preparation to enter the class of the least-skilled, least-educated, and most-rejected in our society.

### References to *Child-rearing Practices in a Low Socioeconomic Group*

1. Warner, W. L., M. Meeker, and K. Eells, *Social Class in America; A Manual of Procedure for the Measurement of Social Status*, Chicago, Science Research Associates; 1949.
2. Warner, W. L., "A Methodological Note," in *Black Metropolis*, by St. Clair Drake and Horace R. Cayton, New York, Harcourt, Brace and Company, 1945.
3. Davis A., and R. J. Havighurst, "Social Class and Color Differences in Child-rearing." *American Sociological Review*, **11**, 698, 1946.
4. Sears, R. E., E. E. Maccoby, H. Levin, *Patterns of Child-Rearing*, New York, Row, Peterson, 1957.
5. Havighurst, R. J., and A. Davis, "A Comparison of the Chicago and Harvard Studies of Social Class Differences in Child-Rearing," *American Sociological Review*, **20**, 438, 1955.
6. Freedman, A. M., et al., "The Influence of Hyperbilirubinemia on the Early Development of the Premature," *Psychiatric Research*, Report 13, December, 1960.
7. Wortis, H., et al., "Children Who Eat Noxious Substances," *Journal of American Academy of Child Psychiatry*, **1**, 536, 1962.
8. Doll, E. A., "Vineland Social Maturity Scale: Manual of Directions," Educational Test Bureau, 1947.

# STATUS AND THE SOCIALIZED SON

*Donald G. McKinley*

We have evidence that parents at the lower levels of society are more severe, more likely to use physical modes of discipline, and less warm. We also have evidence that the relative severity of mothers and fathers varies from class to class. It appears that mothers are almost as severe or are even more severe than fathers at the higher levels of society, but that fathers become increasingly severe and cool to the child, relative to mothers, in the lower strata of society. It also appears that, at least in relation to sons, mothers are very central figures in lower-level families but become decreasingly significant in the higher levels. The complement to this is that fathers become less significant as one moves down the classes—they have less authority, play less significant parts in the emotional life of the family, and seem to be generally less involved in the family. What would be some expected consequences of these patterns and what data can we offer to support our expectations and hypotheses?

From our research on sociological conditions leading to external expression of aggression, we found that parents in those statuses with few positive sanctions for socialization resort to negative sanctions to train and control the child. Though negative sanctions are effective to some degree, they are less effective (in bringing about socialization and identification with the parental image) than the emotional closeness possible with positive sanctions. In Freudian perspective, if the parental image and ideals are not sufficiently internalized, the superego suffers atrophy. This suggests that impulses are subject to fewer controls and that individual initiative and personal responsibility operate at a lower level.

471

By contrast, the parent who receives esteem, security, and love from society can use these resources as positive sanctions for the more effective moulding of the child in the parental image. A more "adult" personality is the product: the superego is more highly developed and life is lived by the "reality principle" rather than by the "pleasure principle." This means that certain impulses (love and aggression) are held within and perhaps expressed in other areas or at other times in a more "realistic" fashion.

This view seems to provide a social structural or social status explanation of several forms of behavior which characteristically vary at different class levels. The reduced control of hostile impulses (as a consequence of status-determined patterns of socialization) at the lower levels of society is reflected in the higher rates of homicide, general crimes against persons, and wife-beating, and in the norm of being tough.

This reduced control of impulses may also have some objective advantages. Thus, positive affect is expressed more freely and without the self-conscious and inhibiting mechanisms of the superego. Perhaps the greater amount of sexual behavior, the patterns of jovial horseplay and joking, and the nearly constant tide of emotionally charged social involvement of many lower-class individuals are manifestations of this condition. The picture may be accurate even though some researchers find the number of highly isolated individuals (often defined by the middle-class criterion of frequency of "visits") to be larger at the lower levels.

Just as lack of control of impulses may have certain advantages as well as disadvantages, so also control and introjection of emotions may have certain disadvantages as well as the recognized advantages. For example, we observe that suicide rates seem to complement homicide rates as we move up and down the class ladder. The higher rate of suicide at the upper levels of society may be a consequence of the check on the external expression of aggression and a turning it in on the self: one commits the final act of self-aggression in suicide. And other, less extreme psychological phenomena seem to support this interpretation. We find guilt and depressive psychosis, relative to other psychoses, more common at the upper levels of society; and assaultive psychoses, e.g., paranoid schizophrenia, more frequent at the lower levels of the social system.

This picture is in agreement with an earlier statement about social interaction at different class levels in our society. The individualism of the upper levels of society is revealed in a person who seems to be more self-contained—he characteristically hates himself, condemns himself, feels guilt (commits suicide), or loves himself (is proud and self-appreciative). By contrast, the lower-class individual seems more other-involved, directing both positive and negative affect more freely. His personality is less *self*-conscious and more permeable. It is a relatively open system of affective exchange with other affective systems (personalities or groups).

*A Brief Review of Theories of Identification*

Let us talk about the process of socialization in a somewhat more limited but detailed way. In the process of socialization the child is taught by the parent, through explicit and implicit rewards and punishment, to behave in certain ways. Other processes are operating, however, besides this action by the parent. The child is trying to relate his own behavior to the parent's. As viewed by Winch (1962), he may try to fashion his behavior after that of the parent (similar identification) or he may try to model his behavior not to copy but to complement the parent's behavior (reciprocal identification). Finally, for various reasons he may strive to be quite the opposite of the parent (negative identification). However the processes take place, behaviorally, psychologically, or even unconsciously, Winch assumes that the parental model is of central significance.

Several theorists have taken social learning and identification as a basic focus in the analysis of human behavior. For example, George Mead's discussion (1934) of the importance of words or symbols in role-taking and role-playing gives added meaning to the process of identification with family roles, either as played by the child's particular parents or as defined in his community.

Freud saw perhaps three basic stages in identification. The first stage is fused or primary identification in which the infant fails to distinguish between himself and the significant social objects in his environment, particularly the mother. The second stage comes about when differentiation is made between self and significant others but when a strong emotional tie or dependency exists between the child and certain social objects. Freud saw two basic processes operating in the third stage, and he seems to have given varying degrees of importance to each in different writings. In the third stage one process is perhaps an exaggeration of the second stage, for there is a loss of the loved object in growing up and identification of the ego with the abandoned but *desired* object. Part of the individual's personality becomes like the lost object, perhaps to fill the felt void. The other process in this third stage is an identification with the stern and perhaps aggressive authority figure, the powerful but *feared* father. This whole latter stage is involved in the resolution of the Oedipal problem and the development of an adult and "socially mature" superego.

Another interesting theory and set of stages is proposed by Sears (1957a). The process begins with the infant's biological dependence on the mother and its psychological corollary of gratification or dissatisfaction. The condition of dissatisfaction is particularly important if it occurs when the mother is absent, as any mother occasionally will be. When this situation exists the infant attempts to reduce the tension and frustration by recreating stimuli similar to those produced by the mother. This attempt will sometimes produce actual satisfaction; probably the mere presence of familiar stimuli (or stimuli associated with gratification) will itself produce gratification on another level. This gratification will reinforce the imitating (modeling and identifying) behavior and the child will begin to become like the mother.

Sears points out that this reduces the problems of socializing the child because the process is intrapsychic to an important degree, even though the original stimuli were social in nature. He hypothesizes that socialization will take place most easily when (1) the mother (or socializing figure) provides great affection and nurturing, (2) the mother is occasionally absent, so that the child is required to create his own substitute satisfaction through imitation, (3) the socializing figure uses withdrawal of love as a means of disciplining the child (withdrawal of love being a psychological absence which requires imitating behavior just as the physical absence does).

## Class and Patterns of Identification

Our data do not allow us to study these various kinds of identification (e.g., reciprocal versus similar), nor are we able to analyze the process of identification in terms of the special ideas of the theories just discussed. They require more detailed data on processes of an earlier period than our research provides.

Here we will look at the pattern and degree of positive identification as a consequence of variation in the emotional significance, power, and severity (hostility) of the two parents. . . . Parents in lower status (reward) levels have less resources available for the process of socialization. We reasoned that this fact, plus special frustrations felt by the father which result in greater expression of hostility, make the process of identification with the paternal image less complete.

Two telling questions developed by Daniel J. Funkenstein and asked the subjects give evidence on this. The son was asked what relative he admired most (could take as a model) and which parent he was said to resemble more in personality. One might conjecture that the answer to the first question reveals the somewhat conscious attempt to identify with the parent and that the second question probes the consequences of this process. The responses at different class levels, given in Table 1, show a much stronger "identification" with the father than with the mother at the upper class levels. This decreases rather strikingly at the lower levels.

The difficulty of finding adequate masculine models among other relatives was also found in the lower levels. In the top class (Hollingshead's Class I) all boys who did not admire their father most chose another male relative as the most admired. In Classes IV and V only about 58 per cent of the sons admired their fathers or other male relatives most. The others chose female relatives. In order to simplify Table 1 this data is not presented.

Status and the Socialized Son

Another way of looking at the data indicates that the two parents are less "admired" in the lower levels than in the upper levels. Instead, other relatives are chosen. Sixty-nine per cent of our upper class (Hollingshead's I and II) sons chose their fathers or mothers as most admired among their various relatives. This falls to 56 per cent in our middle class (III) and to 54 per cent in our lower class (IV and V). This perhaps creates problems of inculcating values and channeling the child according to parental ideals.

Table 1 provides evidence in support of the views . . . that certain components of masculine identification, commitment to "mature" work and to the husband-father role, become problems through the lack of an

*Table 1*—Percentage of Sons Who Admire and Resemble Father More than Mother at Five Social Class Levels

| Class level (Hollingshead's) | Per cent who admire father more[a] | Per cent who resemble father more[b] |
|---|---|---|
| I (Upper) | 100 (10)[c] | 72 (18) |
| II (Upper middle) | 77 (30) | 63 (46) |
| III (Lower middle) | 69 (39) | 67 (67) |
| IV (Working) | 46 (28) | 58 (52) |
| V (Lower) | 44 (9) | 45 (11) |

[a] The question asked, "Whom do you admire most in your family or among your relatives?"
[b] The question asked, "Which parent are you said to resemble more in personality?"
[c] Numbers in parentheses are total numbers of cases choosing father or mother, and exclude those choosing other relatives.

*Table 2*—The Mother's Work Role and the Son's Identification (Son's Report of What Others Say)

| Class level | Work role | Number resembling mother | Number resembling father | Percentage resembling mother |
|---|---|---|---|---|
| Upper | Works | 6 | 6 | 50.0 |
| | Doesn't work | 16 | 35 | 31.4 |
| Middle | Works | 10 | 17 | 37.0 |
| | Doesn't work | 12 | 28 | 30.0 |
| Lower | Works | 14 | 18 | 43.7 |
| | Doesn't work | 14 | 15 | 48.2 |

"adequate" father figure and the presence of a powerful and adequate mother. One can imagine the conflicts and problems of a familial, sexual, and general social nature that this creates. It also creates problems that are sustained and exaggerated in the father-son relationship of the next generation.

The son's commitment to work (as an adult) may not be as impeded as one would think, for the mother (with whom he may be identifying) is more likely to be working in the lower classes. This leads us to expect that the working mother is more likely to be an identification figure for the son for two reasons: by working she becomes a more important figure in the family, and as a worker she may have a personality more consistent with the needs of a maturing son in an achievement-oriented society. Table 2 shows this to be true in the upper and middle classes but not true in the lower class. It is in this latter class where we had expected it to be most strikingly true. Evidently the controlling, expressive, and home-oriented mother who does not work is such an emotionally important figure at this level that the son "identifies" with her despite her probable inappropriateness for the son. This factor might increase rather than ameliorate the problem of identification with and commitment to the adult work role.

*    *    *

## IDENTIFICATION AND FAMILY STRUCTURE

The position has been that the lack of identification with the lower-class father is a consequence of his poverty in resources and power in society and the resulting emotional distance, lack of authority in the family, and severity in dealing with the son. Tables 3, 4, and 5 give evidence on these matters. These conditions and these consequences for the son are not limited to the lower class. Only because of social experiences and the distribution of social rewards is it more likely that certain father-son relationships impeding identification will occur in the lower classes than in the higher strata of society.

### Severity of Socialization and Identification

Table 3 shows that if the father's methods of socialization are severe the son is less likely to resemble the father (75 and 66 per cent versus 56 and 59 per cent). This suggests that identification with the "aggressor" is not operating, or at least not to the degree that identification with mild disciplinarians is occurring.

The figures of Table 3 bring to mind but hardly support other interesting ideas concerning the mother's role and the son's identification. If the mother is severe the son may be insufficiently confident to take the Oedipal step from identification with the mother to identification with the father. Or in the terms of George Mead, the mother's harshness produces anxiety in the son. This anxiety inhibits flexible symbolic behavior and impedes the kind of imaginative role-taking necessary if identification with the husband-father role is to occur. The son is anxiously frozen in a kind of femininity or "immaturity." It may be that nonhostile socialization by the mother is in this primary stage more important for the son in transferring identification from the mother to the father. In later years the tone of the father's socialization gains in importance and becomes more influential.

### Emotional Support and Identification

Table 4 shows that though social class is an important condition in explaining whether identification with the father will or will not occur, the emotional relationship that exists between father and son is even more predictive of "identification." If the father operates effectively in the area of emotional support then the son has high identification with him ("admires" and resembles him) rather than with the mother at all three levels. In a general way this evidence is parallel to the findings of Sears, Maccoby, and Levin (1957) . . . which showed that the development of a conscience (a measure of identification for them) occurs more frequently for the child when the parent is warm and accepting.

*Table 3*—General Level of Severity of Socialization Techniques and "Identification"

| Father's level | Mother's level | Son resembles mother (number) | Son resembles father (number) | Son resembles father (per cent) |
|---|---|---|---|---|
| Mild | Mild | 11 | 33 | 75.0 |
| | Severe | 10 | 19 | 65.5 |
| Severe | Mild | 18 | 23 | 56.1 |
| | Severe | 32 | 46 | 59.0 |

*Table 4*—Relationship Between Emotional Support from Father and Tendency for Son to Admire and Resemble Father More Than Mother

| Class level | Emotional support from father | Per cent admire father | Per cent resemble father [a] |
|---|---|---|---|
| Upper | High | 100 (11) | 92.9 (14) [b] |
| | Low | 74.7 (27) | 53.4 (45) |
| Middle | High | 100 (10) | 78.9 (19) |
| | Low | 61.5 (26) | 62.5 (48) |
| Lower | High | 66.7 (6) | 70.0 (10) |
| | Low | 41.9 (31) | 54.9 (51) |

[a] Son's report of what others say.
[b] Numbers in parentheses equal total cases.

Results similar to these for adolescent boys were obtained by Pauline Sears (1953) in a study of 379 kindergarten children. She found that boys who chose to play the father in projective doll play (and were thus adjudged appropriately sex typed and identified with their fathers) came from families where the fathers were reported to be warmer than the fathers of other subjects. Boys who chose the mother role in doll play tended to come from families where the mothers (but not the fathers) were high in warmth, where the mothers were quite permissive generally but tended to restrict the boys to the home area. This restriction increased the mothers' authority over their sons. These mothers also tended to be critical of the fathers in interviews.

Though the emotional relationship between father and son is more predictive of identification than social class, this does not mean that social status is an unimportant factor in identification. The whole framework of the research should be recalled. We have reasoned that the amount of positive affect the father has to direct toward the son is a consequence of the amount of positive sanctions (power, possessions, and prestige) that his status in society provides him. It is thus partially the amount of emotional support received from the father *as structured by the father's status* that brings about the son's resemblance to the father as a model. Again, we see that a warm and relatively intimate relationship between father and son brings about identification with the father rather than the mother. Warm support and rather mild discipline create the "emotional bridge" between father and son which facilitates an acceptance of the parental model.

## The Structure of Authority and Identification

It would seem that if the father plays the significant role in the area of authority, this would be another factor bringing about the son's identification with him. If the father is making decisions about behavior and the distribution of sanctions within the family, then identification might come about for two reasons. If the father is powerful he becomes admired as a

*Table 5*—Relationship Between Parental Authority Over Son and Tendency for Son to Admire and Resemble Father More Than Mother

| Class level | Authority over son | Per cent admire father | Per cent resemble father[a] |
|-------------|-------------------|------------------------|-----------------------------|
| Upper | Father | 88.5 (26) | 70.0 (30)[b] |
| | Mother | 64.3 (13) | 61.3 (31) |
| Middle | Father | 78.6 (28) | 78.6 (28) |
| | Mother | 45.5 (11) | 52.9 (34) |
| Lower | Father | 41.7 (24) | 51.7 (29) |
| | Mother | 53.8 (13) | 59.4 (32) |

[a] Son's report of what others say.
[b] Numbers in parentheses equal total cases.

respected and adequate person to be copied. Secondly, if he is controlling and sanctioning behavior then it would become advantageous for the son to accept the father's ideals and modes of behavior as his own. This would bring about harmonious and rewarded social interaction in his presence, and following Sears, security and gratification in his absence. Table 5 shows that this expectation is strongly confirmed in the middle and upper classes.

The opposite is found to be the case in the lower class. The reversal also holds when the authority structure is measured in a somewhat different manner (using additional questions) and when the source of authority is trichotomized into these categories: father, parents equal, and mother.

Though we should again avoid explaining away every exception, we do feel that we may get these results at the lower level because the father's authority and control are here particularly hostile and rigid in nature. Again, this may be indirect evidence in opposition to theories of identification with the aggressor.

## STATUS, IDENTIFICATION, AND SEXUAL BEHAVIOR

Sexual behavior, like other physiological functions, is not met without social and psychological experiences and norms controlling its expression and molding its meaning. The child's training in areas of body function, the parental attitude expressed toward his body and toward pleasure at this level, his early feelings toward adult individuals of the same and opposite sex in society and in the family, and his relationships to sibs and peers of both sexes interact to channel sexual behavior and to create varying sexual interests and attitudes.

The child begins life in a situation of intimate body care, and with a focus on care in certain more sensitive areas. This intimate attention and its derivative emotional attitudes of encompassing approval and security must be given up, to a certain extent, in the process of maturing. Body care becomes less and less intimate, the child is expected to become *independent*, to express and be satisfied with verbal and symbolic expressions of love and interest in him, to accept criticisms, and to respond to increasing expectations for achievement. As the child matures, some of the intimacy lost in the family is regained in the latency peer group. Individuals are able to move from the natal family as their intimate reference group to the peer group with varying success. Similarly, individuals are with varying success able to move from the natal family or the peer group to the behavior system of adult sexuality (dating, courtship, heterosexual love and activity, and marriage).

For those who achieve adult behavior there remain certain rather overlaid needs to recapture the intimate emotional nature of the parent-child or family relationships and the peer-group relationships. This motivation, when combined with the operation of the incest taboo, interests in validating one's adult sex status, and development of genital sexuality on a physiological level, provide the impetus for sexual behavior, dating, marriage, and having children of one's own.

These needs for physical and emotional intimacy and regression must be met, it would seem, if the level of adult performance is to be maintained. The absence of an approved social situation in which the single individual can express these needs may account for part of the higher mental disorder rate of this group.

## Achieved Status and the Emergence of Subcultural Sexual Norms

This sociopsychological interpretation of the development of erotic interests allows us to view sexual behavior as not merely a release of physical tension and needs but as the expression of attitudes and social desires learned in a particular subculture, and of needs resulting from a particular social situation. Patterns of sexual behavior, and here we use data from one of the Kinsey reports (Kinsey et al., 1948) as a test of our predictive interpretation, should be related to an achieved social status, education.

In the strictest sense this is not an interpretation but a group of hypotheses. . . . Here are some basic findings relevant to our interest in this section and our approach:

1. The percentage of heterosexual acts expressed extramaritally is greater in the lower social-class levels than in the upper-class levels, but with age this pattern reverses. That is, by the age of 40 or 45 the lower-class male is relatively more faithful than the upper-class male (Table 6).

Table 6—Percentage of Total Sexual Outlet Obtained by Marital Intercourse Among Married Males by Age and Educational Level

| Years of education | 16–20 | 21–25 | 26–30 | AGE 31–35 | 36–40 | 41–45 | 46–50 |
|---|---|---|---|---|---|---|---|
| 13+ | 85.4 (3.47)[a] | 83.9 (3.07) | 82.8 (2.61) | 78.3 (2.05) | 74.4 (1.89) | 76.4 (1.48) | — |
| 9–12 | 82.2 (4.10) | 81.6 (3.35) | 81.7 (2.88) | 85.2 (2.83) | 88.2 (2.29) | — | — |
| 0–8 | 79.9 (3.74) | 81.0 (3.28) | 86.2 (3.00) | 88.1 (2.26) | 88.1 (1.95) | 90.0 (1.72) | — |

[a] Numbers in parentheses equal mean frequency per week.
Source: Selected columns from Alfred Kinsey, Wardell Pomeroy, and Clyde Martin, Sexual Behavior in the Human Male (Philadelphia: W. B. Saunders Company, 1948), p. 356.

Table 7—Percentage of Total Sexual Outlet Obtained Homosexually by Age and Educational Level

| Years of education | Marital status | Adol.–15 | 16–20 | 21–25 | AGE 26–30 | 31–35 | 36–40 | 41–45 | 46–50 |
|---|---|---|---|---|---|---|---|---|---|
| 13+ | Married | — | .16 | .53 | .96 | .75 | .89 | 1.64 | 3.0 |
| | Single | 3.14 | 2.43 | 3.72 | 8.82 | 17.90 | — | — | — |
| 9–12 | Married | — | 2.11 | 1.05 | .96 | 1.38 | .73 | — | — |
| | Single | 8.73 | 10.81 | 16.31 | 25.95 | 18.83 | — | — | — |
| 0–8 | Married | — | 3.08 | 1.33 | .46 | .14 | .30 | .08 | — |
| | Single | 8.03 | 6.85 | 8.06 | 14.04 | 27.43 | 18.60 | — | — |

Source: Selected columns from Alfred Kinsey, Wardell Pomeroy, and Clyde Martin, Sexual Behavior in the Human Male (Philadelphia: W. B. Saunders Company, 1948), pp. 378, 382.

2. The percentage of total outlets homosexual in nature among married men is greater in the lower classes than in the upper classes at the early ages, but again this relationship has been reversed by 35 or 40 years of age (Table 7).

3. The percentage of homosexual outlets among single men is greatest among those with some high school education (and nearly as great among those with only elementary schooling), but least in the upper-status level (Table 7).

Why did we look for these kinds of trends and how do we interpret them from our general position? Let us look at sexual behavior as it interacts with social status and identification in the family.

### Identification and Extrafamilial Sexual Expression

Though findings (1), (2), and (3) deal with both homosexual and heterosexual behavior of married and single individuals, they are all related to the degree of erotic expression occurring *extrafamilially*. This common quality of the several kinds of sexual behavior, which are quite different in other ways, requires some common explanatory device.

During his younger years the lower-class man engages in more extrafamilial sexual activity, but this relationship becomes reversed after 20 or 25 years of married life. We were led to expect this for reasons already spelled out to some degree. The situation of the lower-class father makes it particularly difficult for him to direct the kind of warmth necessary for appropriate intimacy and the son's identification with the father-husband role. Thus, the high extramarital heterosexual and homosexual behavior is a manifestation of absence of identification with the father-as-husband role, alienation from the family group, and a relatively strong involvement in the same sex peer group. This latter group takes over much of the socialization function and it is here that many needs are satisfied and sexual interests first molded.

The peer group has its own incest taboo also, the homosexual taboo. If we generalize many of the proposed reasons for the functional relationship between the family as a socializing group and the incest taboo to the socializing processes and emotional needs in the peer group, we would be led to make certain predictions. We would predict that many of the erotic impulses do not find expression in the intimate peer group as a personality-maintaining and socializing "family" where much of the motivation originates, but with females and occasionally males outside this group.

Within the peer group the individual in the lower levels of society learns certain conceptions of sexuality (of both heterosexual and homosexual nature) independent of the family situation. This forceful, emotional, and extrafamilial socialization leads to an extrafamilial expression of eros on the adult level.

By contrast, the problem for the upper-level male is freeing himself libidinally from a more secure and emotionally consistent family. He is sexually more restrained (both heterosexually and homosexually), but the sex that is expressed shows a great integration of his family role (married status) and his sexual role (lower rate of extramarital intercourse and homosexual behavior).

It is true that solitary sexual activity among the higher-status (college-educated) groups carries over into marriage at a higher rate for both males (Kinsey et al., 1948, p. 382) and females (Kinsey et al., 1953, p. 181). Perhaps they are at some psychosexual level still much more involved with their natal families, indicating the strong sense of satisfaction and obligation there. Perhaps they are also still involved psychosexually with themselves, a behavioral consequence of a cultural philosophy of individualism.

We would explain the reversing trends in fidelity at the different status levels in this way: with increasing age the lower-level married male, despite certain problems, is placed in a situation which socializes him increasingly for fusion of the family role and sex role activity. Thus the decrease in extramarital and homosexual activity. With increasing age the higher-level married male is increasingly freed from the emotional control and definition of behavior learned in his natal family. This freeing attitude is carried over into his attitude toward his marital family and he begins to express himself emotionally and sexually in other ways. Thus, the increased extramarital heterosexual and homosexual behavior with increasing age in the higher level male. This, we feel, indicates a learning to separate the father-husband sex role, which he learned by strong identification with his father, from an extrafamilial erotic role which had been relatively inhibited in development. The evidence is indirect and not beyond dispute.

It is difficult to make a similar interpretation of the association between status and the sexual behavior of women. This seems to result primarily from the fact that the sexual behavior of women seems to vary less by educational level and is associated less with such achieved statuses (Kinsey et al., 1953, p. 685). These conditions may be an additional example of a general condition—the female and mother roles vary less from class to class. Intimate natal family experiences are more likely to be influential for the woman.

*Summary*

The various tables presented thus far in this chapter support our general orientation in several ways. First, they show that the expected consequences at various class levels do occur. The mother becomes a more important figure of identification at the lower levels of society and the father a more important figure at the upper levels. Secondly, within each class we see that identification takes place for the reasons we have hypothesized to be operating to varying degrees in the different classes. We see that variation in the amounts of hostility expressed in socialization, of emotional intimacy, and of authority exercised influence identification.

And finally, we find that adult erotic behavior, which is closely linked to the process of psychosexual identification in the family, can be interpreted as a consequence of certain patterns of family roles at different status levels.

To continue our chain of reasoning and analysis, we should expect that certain patterns of emotional relationship between father and son or mother and son, and certain patterns of identification, should result in the choice of particular levels and types of occupations by the socialized son.

References to *Status and the Socialized Son*

Kinsey, Alfred, Wardell Pomeroy, and Clyde Martin. *Sexual Behavior in the Human Male*, Philadelphia, W. B. Saunders Co., 1948.

Kinsey, Alfred, et al. *Sexual Behavior in the Human Female*, Philadelphia, W. B. Saunders Co., 1953.

Mead, George H. *Mind, Self and Society*, Charles Marris (ed.), Chicago, University of Chicago Press, 1934.

Sears, Pauline S. "Child-Rearing Factors Related to Playing of Sexed-Type Roles," *American Psychologist*, Vol. **8,** 1953, p. 431 (abstract).

Sears, Robert R. "Identification as a Form of Behavioral Development," in D. B. Harris (ed.), *The Concept of Development*, Minneapolis: University of Minneapolis Press, 1957, pp. 149–161.

Sears, Robert R., E. Maccoby and H. Levin. *Patterns of Child Rearing*. New York: Harper Row, 1957.

Winch, Robert F. *The Modern Family*, New York, Holt, Rinehart & Winston, Inc., 1952.

# SOME EFFECTS OF PATERNAL ABSENCE

# ON MALE CHILDREN

*Joan McCord, William McCord, and Emily Thurber*

"That children are best reared in a home with two loving and understanding parents is so obvious as to need no statement" Dorothy Barclay (1959) has commented, typifying current opinion. This viewpoint is so prevalent that it comes close to heresy to question it. Although William Goode (1956), in his comprehensive study of divorce, points to the almost total lack of research on the effects of divorce on children, he concludes:

> At every developmental phase of childhood, the child needs the father (who is usually the absent parent) as an object of love, security, or identification, or even as a figure against whom to rebel safely. . . . It would be surprising if the absence of the father had no effect on the child.

The same view prevails throughout social science. Few empirical studies of child development fail to include the words "intact homes" as a criterion of sample selection. It has long been the tradition to view anxiety as a primary outcome of father absence (Fenichel, 1945; Freud, 1953; Gardner, 1959). Such disorders as alcoholism, homosexuality, and totalitarian tendencies have been attributed to paternal absence (Meerloo, 1956). The high incidence of broken homes among the delinquent population has led to theories which might account for the apparent causative relationship (Burton and Whiting, 1960; Whiting, Kluckhon, and Anthony, 1958).

In research comparing united homes with those in which the father is permanently or temporarily absent, and in psychological and psycho-analytic theory concerning paternal absence, attention has been particularly centered on three areas of personality development: the extent to which the child develops a feminine as opposed to a masculine self-image, the

From *Journal of Abnormal and Social Psychology* (1962), **64**(5), 361–369. Reprinted by permission of the authors and the American Psychological Association.

intensity and type of anxiety which he experiences, and the probability of his engaging in antisocial behavior. In the following pages, we will examine various hypotheses in these areas as they relate to a (primarily) lower-class sample of boys. In the analyses, comparisons are made between boys raised in permanently broken homes and those in united homes. By varying the subgroups compared, the dynamic relationship between family disorder and abnormal behavior is assessed.

## METHOD

### Design of the Research

During the 1930s, Richard Clark Cobot initiated the project, from which the subjects for this study of broken homes were taken, as an adjunct of an experimental program aimed at the prevention of delinquency in Cambridge and Somerville, Massachusetts (Powers and Witmer, 1951).

For an average period of 5 years, between the ages of 10 and 15, 255 boys[1] were observed at home, at school, and at play. Trained social workers, who visited the families approximately every other week, noted the behavior of the parents as well as the child. The counselors would appear unannounced, with a frequency which made it possible to observe the families at meals, during their leisure, in the midst of crises, and during their ordinary daily routines. They recorded their observations after each visit. Thus, running records were kept for 255 subjects between 1939 and 1945.[2]

In 1956 and 1957, trained researchers read each case record and rated the boy and his parents on a number of variables ranging from occupation and religion to affectional interaction. Interrater agreement, tested on a random sample, was high[3] and several factors point to the

[1] Originally 325 boys had been included. Because of heavy case load, 65 boys were retired from the project in 1941, 5 additional boys were dropped because of their death or moving out of Massachusetts. The original sample was selected as follows: Teachers, police, and other officials recommended boys whom they believed showed signs of incipient delinquency. The Cambridge-Somerville Youth Study staff gathered information about them for the matching procedure (one boy to receive treatment and the other to be placed in a control group) so that the criteria of selection consisted in a willingness to participate and ability to find two boys with similar backgrounds in family structure, age, and "general personality." To avoid stigmatizing the boys in the project, an approximately equal number were added who were considered "normal" by the same authorities (again, equally divided between the treatment and the control groups).

[2] Between 1955 and 1957, these subjects and a matched control group who had received no direct attention from the project were traced through the Massachusetts Board of Probation, mental hospitals, and various agencies dealing with alcoholism. It was found that the treatment program had no discernible effect upon criminality or alcoholism (McCord and McCord, 1959, 1960).

[3] The reliability of each of the ratings is fully discussed in *Origins of Alcoholism* (McCord and McCord, 1960).

validity of the information obtained in this manner. Expected relationships which might have indicated a middle-class bias or operation of a halo effect were not found (e.g., the lower-class boys were not pictured as more aggressive and the brighter boys were not pictured as leaders). Most importantly, the categorized ratings of the case records yielded strong relationships to completely independent measures of social deviance among the subjects when they had become adults (McCord and McCord, 1960).

### Sample Characteristics

Among the 255 boys[4] in the study, 105 had lost one or both parents. Because we wished to focus on the effects of paternal absence, we dropped boys who were not living with their natural mothers (12 had lost both parents and 20 had lost their mothers) and the 18 who had step- or foster fathers. The remaining 55 boys from broken homes were living with their natural mothers; these were children whose fathers had died (24), deserted (8), been placed in mental hospitals (4), were serving long prison terms (3), or whose parents had been divorced or legally separated (16). The 150 boys whose natural parents were living together were used for the control group.

A number of studies have indicated that broken homes are associated with low socioeconomic status (Burgess, 1950; Hollingshead, 1950; Weeks, 1943). To the extent that social class affects personality development, this relationship between social class and family stability may lead to false conclusions regarding the effects of broken homes. Since the Cambridge-Somerville Youth Study centered upon the congested areas of these two cities, the entire sample had a strong lower-class representation. A comparison of fathers' occupations between broken and united homes within the sample showed slight (not statistically significant)[5] differences between the groups.

Various studies have indicated that Catholic families may be slightly more stable, although they seem to contribute more than their share of desertion cases (Bell, 1938; Monahan and Kephart, 1954). In our sample, records of the mother's religion showed that 65 per cent of the boys raised in united homes and 64 per cent of the boys in broken homes had been raised by Catholic mothers.

Theorists have also suggested that the wife may alter her behavior to compensate for her husband's absence. P. O. Tiller (1958) reports that Norwegian sailors' wives whose husbands were absent for extended periods

[4] From 237 families.
[5] Throughout the research, the chi square test, two-tailed, was used when $N > 30$ and the Fisher test, two-tailed, was used when $N < 30$. Differences were considered significant if $p < .05$.

of time exceeded matched mothers whose husbands were not absent in being overprotective and stressing obedience and politeness (in contrast to happiness and self-realization). In our sample, we did not find a significantly greater incidence of either maternal overprotection (31 per cent/29 per cent) or punitiveness (49 per cent/44 per cent) in the broken homes than in the united homes. Nor did we find significant differences between the mothers' attitudes toward their sons[6] in united homes and broken homes.

Two potentially important variables, however, strongly differentiated broken home boys from boys in united homes. William Goode (1956) reported that about a third of his sample of divorced women cited sexual or alcoholic deviance of their husbands as the primary cause of divorce. We found a significantly higher proportion of deviant (i.e., alcoholic, criminal, or promiscuous) fathers ($p < .001$) and deviant mothers ($p < .025$) among the boys from broken homes than among the boys whose parents were living together (see Table 1).

### Table 1—Parental Deviance

| Condition | Broken homes (N = 55) | United homes (N = 150) |
|---|---|---|
| Father deviant | 30% | 31% |
| Mother deviant | 1 | 4 |
| Both deviant | 24 | 5 |
| Neither deviant | 45 | 60 |

In addition, a significantly lower proportion of the boys in broken homes had immigrant fathers ($p < .001$). Fifty-eight per cent of the fathers in united homes, compared to 29 per cent in broken homes, were immigrants.

To insure that the effects of these differences were not attributed to paternal absence, we matched each boy from a broken home to a boy similar in background whose parents were living together. Besides parental deviance and father's birthplace, the mother's attitude toward the boy, her disciplinary technique, her degree of control over her son, and the consistency of her discipline were used as criteria for matching.

We anticipated that paternal absence might have different effects under various conditions. Therefore, we divided the broken home boys on three dimensions:

1. The reason for the father's absence. The father's death might be presumed to have a different effect on the child than would his disappearance from the home after preliminary quarrels.

2. The age of the boy at the time when his father left. The child's age at the time of the break was divided roughly into preschool, preadolescent (or middle childhood), and adolescent.

[6] "Warm" mothers openly expressed their affection; "cold" mothers showed passive concern, but seldom demonstrated affection; "ambivalent' mothers displayed extreme variation between overt affection and overt rejection; and "rejecting' mothers cared little for their children or their welfare.

3. The affectional relationship and stability (non-deviance) of the mother. Warm, nondeviant mothers were considered "normal." The distribution of the boys in broken homes on these three dimensions is shown in Table 2.

Table 2—Distribution of Broken Homes

| Father | Mother | AGE OF BOY AT TIME OF BREAK | | |
|--------|--------|------|------|---------|
| | | 0–5 | 6–12 | Over 12 |
| Dead | Normal[a] | 4 | 6 | 4 |
| Living | Normal[a] | 4 | 6 | 1 |
| Dead | Abnormal[b] | 3 | 3 | 4 |
| Living | Abnormal[b] | 7 | 11 | 2 |

[a] Warm, nondeviant.
[b] Deviant, cold, ambivalent, or rejecting.

Since overt conflict probably precedes divorce and separation, and may have preceded desertion or death, the putative effects of broken homes may actually be the result of parental conflict. Ratings from direct observation of parental interaction were used to divide the boys whose parents were living together into two groups: the 30 whose parents quarreled constantly and were in overt conflict, and the 120 whose homes were relatively tranquil.

## RESULTS

### Feminine Identification

One of the most widely held beliefs about the effects of paternal absence is that male children will develop unusually strong feminine components in their personalities. Three sets of ratings on the 205 boys in our study were used to test feminization in the father-absent group: homosexual tendencies, dependency, and lack of aggressiveness.[7] Although the trend of past evidence would suggest that father-absent boys would be relatively more feminine (Burton and Whiting, 1960; Leichty, 1960; Lynn and Sawrey, 1959; Winch, 1949), more dependent (Stolz, 1954), and less aggressive (Bach, 1946; Sears, Pintler, and Sears, 1946), we found that neither homosexuality nor dependency differentiated significantly between the boys whose fathers were absent and those whose fathers were present and that the aggression scale was significantly related—but in the opposite direction from that predicted. (Eighty-seven per cent of the broken home

[7] Boys were considered to have strong homosexual tendencies if they played with dolls, sometimes wore dresses, frequently expressed the wish to be a girl, or were overtly homosexual. They were considered to be dependent if they showed an unusually strong desire for adult approval. Femininity and dependency were not significantly related to each other. A three-point scale of behavioral aggression, ranging from little to unrestrained, was used.

boys, as opposed to 67 per cent of those from tranquil homes, were moderately or strongly aggressive.)

Since aggressive behavior may be considered as an exhibition of "masculinity," it seemed probable that those who were both aggressive and showed signs of feminine identification[8] were expressing an instability in sex role identification or defending against feminine identification. This combination of feminine-aggressive behavior (as compared to feminine-non-aggressive behavior) was found significantly more frequently among boys in broken homes than among boys in tranquil homes ($p < .001$).

Since both parental conflict and paternal absence were related to feminine-aggressive behavior, it seemed likely that either parental conflict or parental deviance (found in almost equal proportions among broken and conflictful homes)[9] might fully account for the difference. Neither of these explanations, however, fit the data. We reasoned that parental conflict would have been less among homes severed by death of the father; yet a higher proportion (58 per cent) of the sons in these homes showed feminine-aggressive behavior (see Table 3).

### Table 3—Sex Role Behaviour

| Sex role | Broken home (N = 55) | Conflictful home (N = 30) | Tranquil home (N = 120) |
|---|---|---|---|
| Masculine[a] | 49% | 43% | 58% |
| Feminine-nonaggressive | 4 | 14 | 20 |
| Feminine-aggressive | 47 | 43 | 22 |

[a] Nine per cent of the broken home boys, none of those in conflictful homes, and 13 per cent of those in tranquil homes showed masculine role behavior but were not aggressive.

To check whether the home milieu rather than paternal absence itself was responsible for the high rate of feminine-aggressive behavior, we used the group of boys with similar backgrounds in united homes.

Because the comparison with matched controls (see Table 4) showed higher feminine-aggressive behavior among broken home boys ($p < .005$), the difference in sex role behavior could not be attributed simply to conditions which might have precipitated the family break.

Analysis of the father-absent boys provided a clue to their reasons for sex role conflict. We contrasted sons whose mothers were normal (affectionate and nondeviant) with those having mothers rated abnormal. In these two groups of boys, the age at which paternal absence began and the reason

[8] Boys who evidenced high dependency or strong homosexual tendencies were classified as showing feminine identification. We hypothesized that feminine identification (with or without aggression) would arise from the "teasing' effect of an ambivalent nondeviant mother or from the combination of rejection from a stable father and affection from a stable mother; among the 22 boys whose parents were of these types, 77 per cent evidenced feminine identification.

[9] Immigrant families, too, were found in almost equal proportions among broken and conflictful homes, i.e., they were less likely to be either conflictful or severed.

for such absence had different relationships to sex role behavior. These differences suggest that feminine-aggressive behavior has different origins in broken homes in which a normal, as opposed to an abnormal, mother had remained.

Whereas the child's age when his father left was of great importance among boys whose mothers were warm and nondeviant, it had slight relationship to feminine-aggressive behavior for boys raised by abnormal mothers (see Table 5).

*Table 4*—Sex Role Behaviour

| Sex role | Father absent | Matched controls |
|---|---|---|
| Masculine | 49% | 45% |
| Feminine-nonaggressive | 4 | 24 |
| Feminine-aggressive | 47 | 31 |

*Table 5*—Percentage Who Exhibited Feminine-Aggressive Behavior

| | BOY'S AGE WHEN FATHER LEFT | | |
|---|---|---|---|
| | 0–5 | 6–12 | Over 12 |
| Normal mother | (N = 8)  0 | (N = 12) 75[a] | (N = 5)  0*** |
| Abnormal mother | (N = 10) 70 | (N = 14) 50 | (N = 6) 50 |

[a] Twenty-five percent of matched group exhibited feminine-aggressive behavior ($p < .05$).
*** $p < .01$.

Boys reared by normal mothers showed feminine-aggressive behavior only if their fathers left when the boys were between the ages of 6 and 12 ($p < .01$). Since only 25 per cent of their matched controls indicated sex role conflict of this type, the home milieu of these boys were apparently not responsible for their high rate. Studies of children's sex differentiated behavior give reason to believe that the years of middle childhood may be critical ones in the development of sex identification. In an early study, P. H. Furfey (1927) noted little sex differentiation in the play of 6–8-year-olds, with increasing separation and differentiation after that age. Observations of recreational clubs at the Merrill-Palmer School in Detroit indicated that 5- and 6-year-olds seem to ignore sex as a basis for choosing play groups, but that sex segregation is almost complete for 10- and 11-year-olds (Campbell, 1939). Studies of friendship choices point to the same phenomenon (Moreno, 1934).

Previous research with father-separated samples whose mothers were probably "normal" by our criteria tend to point also to the importance of age at the time of separation. A study by Sears et al. (1946) found that early differences in sex role behavior between father-absent and father-present boys had begun to disappear by age 5. Bach (1946), however, reported evidence of feminization among 6–10-year-olds whose fathers had been absent 1–3 years.

Early separation, as Sears et al. (1946) suggested, may result in sex typing delay—but both their and our evidence indicates that this effect is of relatively short duration: probably because the boy is able to find substitute role models during the period of sex identification. During the critical years of sex identification, perhaps because memory of the father interferes with adoption of a substitute model, loss of the father seems to have a more permanent affect on sex role identification. By age 12, the process of sex role identification is probably fairly complete, thus explaining the absence of feminine-aggressive behavior among the other boys raised by normal mothers.

Among boys raised by abnormal mothers, age at the time of separation was of relatively minor importance in relation to feminine-aggressive behavior; death of the father (see Table 6), however, seemed to be highly productive of this type of confused sex role behavior ($p < .05$).

*Table 6*—Percentage Who Exhibited Feminine-Aggressive Behavior

| | REASON FOR FATHER'S ABSENCE | |
| | Death | Other |
|---|---|---|
| Normal mother | (N = 14) 36 | (N = 11) 36 |
| Abnormal mother | (N = 10) 90[a] | (N = 20) 40* |

[a] Ten per cent of matched group exhibited feminine-aggressive behavior ($p < .01$).
* $p < .05$.

One can argue that death of the father raises a conflict in the male child between his desire to replace the father and his denial of this desire; yet this theory does not explain the *lower* proportion among those whose mothers were affectionate ($p < .05$) who showed feminine-aggressive behavior.

It seems reasonable to explain this type of sex role instability among boys exposed to cold or rejecting mothers in terms of dependency needs and their satisfactions: When resources for satisfaction of dependency needs are limited (as they would be in broken homes of this type), the child becomes more dependent on this limited source and also more resentful of his dependency because it fails to bring satisfaction.[10] Thus, such children respond to the conflict by being relatively dependent and feminine, and simultaneously behaving aggressively, in a compensatory masculine fashion.

[10] It seems likely that a relationship between maternal rejection and parental separation or divorce (see Newell, 1936) leads to disproportionate representation of this type of home in some studies of the effects of broken homes on sex role identification. Whiting (1961) suggested that cultures in which there are exclusive mother-child sleeping arrangements also tend to define the maternal role in terms which would be considered abnormal in our society (i.e., maternal rejection and promiscuity are common among them). It seems possible that the cross-cultural relationship found between father separation in infancy and evidence of sex role conflict is dependent upon the limited resources for satisfaction of dependency needs in these cultures.

### Anxiety

Although it has received less research attention, the belief that paternal absence results in anxiety is widespread. Specific research relating anxiety to paternal absence has yielded conflicting results. A number of studies have linked such various manifestations of anxiety as feelings of inferiority, poor school performance, immaturity, and tensions to paternal absence (Hardy, 1937; Lynn and Sawrey, 1959; Rouman, 1956; Stolz, 1954). Other studies have found no evidence of increased anxiety (Leichty, 1960; Rowntree, 1955; Russell, 1957). In an attempt to clarify this confusion in the literature, we tested three hypotheses derived from clinical theories.

*Hypothesis 1.* Father-separated boys should manifest many or intense fears because their heightened Oedipal desires cannot be brought to gratification (Freud, 1953), or because the child fears that his mother will desert him (Gardner, 1959). We found no confirmation of this hypothesis that loss of the father results in abnormal fears. Forty per cent of the

*Table 7*—Percentage Who Exhibited Sex Anxiety

| Condition | Percentage |
|---|---|
| Broken home (*N* = 55) | 47[a] |
| Conflictful home (*N* = 30) | 57 |
| Tranquil home (*N* = 120) | 27 |

[a] Forty-nine per cent of the matched group exhibited sex anxiety.

broken home boys and 40 per cent of those raised in tranquil homes gave evidence of abnormal fears (e.g., fear of the dark or excessive fear of bodily injury). Among boys reared in conflictful homes, 50 per cent had abnormal fears. These negative results relating paternal absence to abnormal fears tend to confirm the findings of Rowntree (1955) for matched pairs of pre-school children in Britain and Russell (1957) for matched pairs of school age children in America.

*Hypothesis 2.* Father-separated boys should have anxiety about sex; this should be particularly strong for those whose fathers have died (Fenichel, 1945). A number of boys expressed to their counselors their concern over achieving normal sexual relations or about their sexual adequacy; others publicly masturbated during periods of tension.[11] These boys were considered to be sexually anxious. Although a significantly higher proportion of those whose fathers were absent than of those whose homes were tranquil evidenced sex anxiety ($p < .02$), roughly the same proportion of those whose parents were in open conflict were sexually anxious (see Table 7).

There was little variation within the father-absent group in the proportions who showed sex anxiety: 45 per cent of those whose fathers were living, compared to 50 per cent of those whose fathers had died:

[11] The two measures were significantly related in the sample ($p < .01$).

54 per cent of those whose mothers were rejecting and 41 per cent of those whose mothers were affectionate evidenced sex anxiety. None of the four boys with affectionate deviant mothers evidenced sex anxiety. Although sex anxiety was prominent among boys raised without their fathers, the fact that 49 per cent of the matched controls (compared to 47 per cent) exhibited sex anxiety suggests that high sex anxiety may not be specifically related to paternal absence.

*Hypothesis 3.* Father-separated boys should show signs of regression (Fenichel, 1945). Thumb sucking, nail biting, excessive smoking, and constant playing with the mouth were used as behavioral signs of oral tendencies. Since these forms of behavior may also indicate general anxiety, only those who did not exhibit abnormal fears were classified as showing oral regression. Oral regression, though not oral anxiety, was found most frequently among the father-absent group. The relationship was not, however, strong enough to reject the possibility that it had occurred by chance (see Table 8).

#### Table 8—Oral Tendencies

|  | Broken home (N = 55) | Conflictful home (N = 30) | Tranquil home (N = 120) |
|---|---|---|---|
| Oral regression | 22%[a] | 13% | 10% |
| Oral and anxious | 15 | 23 | 16 |
| Neither | 63 | 64 | 74 |

[a] Thirteen per cent of the matched group exhibited oral regression.

#### Table 9—Percentage Who Showed Signs of Oral Regression

|  | Father absent | Matched controls |
|---|---|---|
| Normal mother | (N = 25)  8% | (N = 25) 20% |
| Abnormal mother | (N = 30) 33 | (N = 30)  7** |

** $p < .025$.

As a further check, we examined oral regression in relation to normal and abnormal mothers among the father-absent boys. Although the proportion showing oral regression was not higher among the normal mother group than among those raised in tranquil homes (8 per cent/10 per cent), the comparison revealed a significantly higher proportion (see Table 9) showing signs of oral regression (33 per cent) among those whose mothers were rejecting or deviant ($p < .005$).

Rejection or deviance, with or without paternal absence, might have explained oral regression. Comparison with the matched group led to rejection of this hypothesis.

Reasoning that death of the father would most fully realize the Oedipal wish, we hypothesized greater regression among boys whose fathers had died. This hypothesis, too, was not supported. These comparisons indicate that paternal absence, probably following conflict, *in combination with* maternal deviance or rejection result in oral regression.

### Antisocial Behavior

The lay public as well as professional criminologists have linked broken homes to antisocial behavior. There seems to be general agreement that the proportion of broken homes among criminals is greater than that of the general population (Schulman, 1959). It was possible to use two measures of antisocial behavior for our sample. The counselors' reports of direct observations permitted ratings of primary reference groups during adolescence. Boys whose primary reference groups were delinquent gangs participated in behavior disapproved by the majority in their community. In 1955, court records for each of the subjects were obtained as an additional independent record of criminality; these traced the boys into adulthood. Those who had been convicted for a felony (or for a crime which would be a felony if the boy were an adult) were considered criminals.

*Table 10*—Percentage Who Had Delinquent Reference Groups

| Condition | Percentage |
|---|---|
| Broken home ($N = 55$) | 20 |
| Conflictful home ($N = 30$) | 43 |
| Tranquil home ($N = 120$) | 18 |

There was little support for the theory that paternal absence led to delinquent gang activities. A significantly higher proportion of those boys whose parents continued to live together despite considerable overt conflict than *either* those whose parents were in little conflict ($p < .01$) or those whose fathers were absent ($p < .05$) were gang delinquents (see Table 10).

That parental conflict rather than paternal absence tends to result in gang delinquency is given further support by the fact that the older the boy at the time of the break, the more likely he was to become a gang delinquent. It should further be noted that a significantly higher proportion of those who had parent substitutes (34 per cent) than of those who lived in tranquil homes had become gang delinquents. This latter group, it appears, is responsible for the apparently high rate of juvenile delinquency among the broken home population of the lower class—a correlation which has been erroneously attributed to the absence of a paternal model.[12]

[12] With this theory in mind, we recomputed the Glueck (Glueck and Glueck, 1950) figures reported in *Unraveling Juvenile Delinquency*, breaking down the broken home boys into those who did and those who did not have parent substitutes. Recomputed, the Glueck figures no longer support the theory that broken homes as such are causally related to delinquency: Among their 500 delinquents, 72 were from broken homes without parent substitutes; among their 500 nondelinquents, 111 were from broken homes without parent substitutes. In contrast, 230 of the delinquents, compared to 60 of the nondelinquents, had substitute parents.

Using convictions for felonies as a measure of antisocial behavior, the expected relatively high rate of criminality was found among the father-absent group (see Table 11). Tranquil homes produced a significantly lower proportion of criminals than did the father-absent homes and the conflictful homes ($p < .025$).

Several findings point to the fact that the absence of a generally stable home environment, rather than the specific absence of the father, is related to criminality: (a) boys reared by parents who were in overt conflict were

*Table 11*—Percentage Who Became Criminals

| Condition | Percentage |
|---|---|
| Broken home ($N = 55$) | 36 |
| Conflictful home ($N = 30$) | 40 |
| Tranquil home ($N = 120$) | 22 |

as likely to become criminals as boys from father-absent families; (b) the criminal rate among boys who had parent substitutes was identical (i.e., 36 per cent became criminals) to that of the father-absent boys; (c) the criminal rate increased with an increase in the age of the boys at the time of the family break; and (d) none of the 13 father-absent boys cared for by warm nondeviant mothers whose fathers had not been deviant became criminals.[13]

## SUMMARY

Repeated direct observations of 205 boys and their families during a period of approximately 5 years of their early adolescence and court records for convictions for felonies were used to assess the effects of paternal absence upon boys. The sample, drawn from former members of the Cambridge-Somerville experiment, came from a lower-class, relatively deprived environment. The results of this study suggest the following conclusions:

1. Although feminine-nonaggressive behavior was negatively related to paternal absence, feminine-aggressive behavior appeared to be produced by paternal absence if the boy was between 6 and 12 when his father left, or the mother was deviant or rejecting (especially if the father had died).

2. No support was found for the theory that paternal absence leads to abnormal fears.

3. Intense sexual anxiety was found among almost half of the boys who had lost their fathers. Yet this anxiety seemed to be a response to a generally unstable environment rather than to paternal absence per se.

[13] Nine of the 10 father-absent boys whose mothers were both rejecting and deviant had been convicted for felonies.

4. Oral regression was related to father-absence only among those whose mothers were deviant or rejecting.

5. Gang delinquency was found to be unrelated to paternal absence, although it did occur more frequently in broken homes in which the father or mother had been replaced by substitutes. In fact, the proportion of gang delinquents among boys whose parents quarreled but remained together was significantly higher than among those whose fathers were absent.

6. The relationship between criminality and paternal absence appears to be largely a result of the general instability of broken homes rather than of paternal absence in itself.

The evidence drawn from this sample indicates that many of the effects often presumed to result from paternal absence can, largely, be attributed to certain parental characteristics—intense conflict, rejection, and deviance—which occur more commonly in broken families.

### References to *Some Effects of Paternal Absence on Male Children*

Bach, G. R. "Father-Fantasies and Father Typing in Father-Separated Children," *Child Development*, 1946, **17**, 63–79.

Barclay, Dorothy. "When One Parent Plays the Double Role," *N. Y. Times Magazine*, **69**, April 5, 1959.

Bell, H. *Youth Tell Their Story*, Washington, D. C., American Council on Education, 1938.

Burgess, E. W. "Predictive Methods and Family Stability," *Annual of the American Academy of Political and Social Sciences*, 1950, **272**, 47–52.

Burton, R. V., and J. W. M. Whiting. "The Absent Father: Effects on the Developing Child," (Rev.) Paper read at American Psychological Association Convention, Chicago, 1960.

Campbell, E. H. "The Social-Sex Development of Children," *Genetic Psychology Monograph*, 1939, **21**, 461–552.

Fenichel, O. *The Psychoanalytic Theory of Neurosis*, New York, Norton, 1945.

Freud, S. "Three Essays on Sexuality," in *Standard Edition*, Vol. VII (Originally published 1905) London, Hogarth, 1953.

Furfey, P. H. "Some Factors Influencing the Selection of Boys' Chums," *Journal of Applied Psychology*, 1927, **11**, 47–51.

Gardner, G. E. "Separation of the Parents and the Emotional Life of the Child," in S. Glueck (ed.), *The Problems of Delinquency*, Boston, Houghton Mifflin, 1959, pp. 138–143.

Glueck, S., and Eleanor T. Glueck. *Unraveling Juvenile Delinquency*, Cambridge, Mass., Harvard Univer. Press, 1950.

Goode, W. J. *After Divorce*, New York, Free Press, 1956.

Hardy, M. C. "Aspects of Home Environment in Relation to Behavior at the Elementary School Age," *Journal of Juvenile Research*, 1937, **21**, 206–225.

Hollingshead, A. B. "Class Differences in Family Stability," *Annual of the American Academy of Politicial and Social Sciences*, 1950, **272**, 39–46.

Leichty, Mary. "The Absence of the Father During Early Childhood and Its Effect Upon the Oedipal Situation as Reflected in Young Adults," *Merrill-Palmer Quarterly*, 1960, **6**, 212–217.

Lynn, D. B., and W. L. Sawrey. "The Effects of Father-Absence on Norwegian Boys and Girls," *Journal of Abnormal and Social Psychology*, 1959, **59**, 258–262.

McCord, W., and Joan McCord. *Origins of Crime*, New York, Columbia Univer. Press, 1959.

———, and Joan McCord. *Origins of Alcoholism*, Stanford, Calif., Stanford Univer. Press, 1960.

Meerloo, J. A. M. "The Father Cuts the Cord: The Role of the Father as Initial Transference Figure," *American Journal of Psychotherapy*, 1956, **10**, 471–480.

Monahan, T. P., and W. M. Kephart. "Divorce and Desertion by Religious and Mixed-Religious Groups," *American Journal of Sociology*, 1954, **59**, 454–465.

Moreno, J. L. *Who Shall Survive?* Washington, D. C., Nervous and Mental Disease Publishing Co., 1934.

Newell, H. W. "The Psycho-dynamics of Maternal Rejection," *American Journal of Orthopsychiatry*, 1936, **6**, 576–588.

Powers, E., and Helen Witmer. *An Experiment in the Prevention of Delinquency*, New York, Columbia Univer. Press, 1951.

Rouman, J. "School Children's Problems as Related to Parental Factors," *Journal of Educational Research*, 1956, **50**, 105–112.

Rowntree, Griselda. "Early Childhood in Broken Families," *Population Studies*, 1955, **8**, 247–263.

Russell, I. L. "Behavior Problems of Children from Broken and Intact Homes," *Journal of Educational Sociology*, 1957, **31**, 124–129.

Sears, R. R., M. H. Pintler, and Pauline S. Sears. "Effects of Father-Separation on Preschool Children's Doll Play Aggression," *Child Development*, 1946, **17**, 219–243.

Shulman, H. M. "The Family and Juvenile Delinquency," in S. Glueck (ed.), *The Problems of Delinquency*, Boston, Houghton Mifflin, 1959, pp. 128–136.

Stolz, Lois M., et al. *Father Relations of War-Born Children*, Stanford, Calif., Stanford Univer. Press, 1954.

Tiller, P. O. "Father-Absence and Personality Development of Children in Sailor Families: A Preliminary Research Report," *Nord. Psykol.*, 1958, Monogr. No. 9.

Weeks, A. H. "Differential Divorce Rates by Occupations," *Social Forces*, 1943, **22**, 334–337.

Whiting, J. W. M. Paper read to Graduate Colloquium in Psychology, Stanford University, January 19, 1961.

———, R. Kluckhon, and A. Anthony. "The Function of Male Initiation Ceremonies," in Eleanor E. Maccoby, T. M. Newcomb, and E. L. Hartley (eds.), *Readings in Social Psychology*, (3rd ed.) New York, Holt, 1958, pp. 359–370.

Winch, R. F. "The Relation Between the Loss of a Parent and Progress in Courtship," *Journal of Social Psychology*, 1949, **29**, 51–56.

# IMPACT OF EMPLOYMENT OF MOTHERS

# BY SOCIAL CLASS

*Elizabeth Douvan*

. . . It seemed highly probable to us that the meaning of maternal employment would be different in the two [major] social classes, and, in the case of the full-time working mother, this is borne out in the analysis. A part-time work commitment has a relatively stable meaning and implication in both the middle and working classes, but full-time maternal employment apparently depends upon different motivational sources in the two groups, and has distinct meanings for family interaction. The findings we have reported for this group represent a combination of two quite different patterns.

## Middle Class

In the middle class the girls of full-time working women look more like those whose mothers work part-time: they are relatively active, autonomous girls who admire their mothers but are not unusually closely tied to the family. They have a high rate of participation in leisure activities and in organized groups—higher than either working-class girls whose mothers work full-time or middle-class girls whose mothers do not work. They do not have as active leisure lives as girls in the middle-class part-time group, but the differences between the two patterns are not large on our measures of leisure activity.

The serious and adult-like activities decrease in this group when we factor out class: middle-class girls in the full-time pattern do not have as

From "Employment and the Adolescent," in Francis Nye, ed., *The Employed Mother in America* (Chicago: Rand McNally, Copyright 1963), pp. 155–164. Reprinted by permission of Rand McNally & Company.

much responsibility at home, and they do not hold part-time jobs as often as girls in the working class whose mothers work full-time. They date just as actively, but again look more like other girls of their class level whose mothers work part-time: they do not go steady as often as their counterparts in the working class. They spend more time with their families than the daughters of full-time working women in the lower class, and their relationships within the family look like those we have described for the part-time working mother pattern. Their parents expect them to be self-reliant, give them a share in rule-making, and apparently permit discussion and open disagreement. In all these respects, girls in the middle-class full-time group are more like those in the part-time patterns and different from girls in the working class whose mothers work full-time. They choose their mothers as ideals more than daughters of non-working women—this holds for all the working mother groups at both class levels—but they do *not* choose in-family models as exclusively as do their working-class counterparts. They think of the mother as confidante, but they also think that a friend can be as close to one as a family member. They do not characteristically think that a girl should yield personal work interests to return home to a lonely mother.

### Working Class

·The dependency which distinguished the total group of girls whose mothers hold full-time jobs is primarily a feature of working-class girls in the pattern. Here we find both a strong positive affection for the mother and a strong dependency component. The working-class girls in families where the mother works full-time show the primary characteristics of premature seriousness, deprivation in social and leisure activities, and emotional dependency. Compared to other working-class girls or to middle-class daughters of full-time working women, they have fewer group memberships and leisure activities, and they are more often responsible for major housekeeping tasks and part-time jobs. They are not striving toward emotional independence, nor are they encouraged by their parents to be self-reliant. In this regard they look most like girls whose mothers do not work and differ from all of the other working mother groups.

Compared to any other group in this analysis, the working-class girls whose mothers work full-time have strong emotional ties to the family: they admire and feel close to their mothers, and seem psychologically highly dependent on the family. In choosing an adult ideal, girls in this group name their mothers as often as girls in other working mother categories, and when we consider all in-family choices, they are far and away the group most family-oriented (76 per cent of this group name an ideal from the family group, compared to 60 per cent of the working-class non-working mother group, the second highest of all categories in this regard). They have

*Table 1*—Full-Time Maternal Employment in Relation to Girls' Activities and Attitudes in the Middle- and Working-Class Groups*

| Item: Adolescent girls' behavior, attitudes | FULL-TIME MATERNAL EMPLOYMENT | |
|---|---|---|
| | Middle class (N = 104) | Working class (N = 131) |
| | Per cent | |
| **Leisure activities** | | |
| Low | 18 | 34 |
| Medium | 42 | 51 |
| High | 40 | 15 |
| **Group membership** | | |
| None | 21 | 34 |
| Belongs to 1 or 2 groups | 54 | 49 |
| Belongs to 3 or more groups | 25 | 17 |
| **Household responsibilities** | | |
| Major | 15 | 27 |
| Moderate | 32 | 28 |
| Light or none | 47 | 39 |
| **Work** | | |
| Holds job | 74 | 86 |
| **Dating†** | | |
| Goes steady | 5 | 16 |
| Dates | 49 | 33 |
| Doesn't date | 45 | 51 |
| **Spends leisure time** | | |
| Alone | 5 | 17 |
| With friend(s) | 43 | 48 |
| With family | 47 | 32 |
| **Parents' expectations** | | |
| Self-reliance | 19 | 5 |
| Good manners | 54 | 43 |
| Obedience | 21 | 28 |
| **Part in rule-making** | | |
| R shares in rule-making | 71 | 57 |
| **Disagreement with parents** | | |
| Reports no disagreement | 15 | 36 |
| **Index of disagreement (specific issues)** | | |
| Disagrees with parents on 3 issues or more | 43 | 28 |
| **Adult ideal** | | |
| Mother | 40 | 43 |
| Father | 1 | 1 |
| All in-family choices | 55 | 76 |
| **Intimacy of friendship** | | |
| Can be as close as family tie | 46 | 25 |
| **Choice of confidante** | | |
| Mother | 60 | 44 |
| Friend | 28 | 18 |
| No one | 7 | 16 |
| **Response to lonely mother** | | |
| Return home | 37 | 56 |

* Middle-class status was assigned whenever the father's job was a professional, managerial, or white-collar one. The working class category includes all girls whose fathers hold manual jobs.
† Analysis of dating patterns with age and class both controlled reduced numbers severely. In the interest of reliability, we have run the analysis for all age groups. The class groups did not differ significantly in age, in any case.

fewer disagreements with their parents than any other group of girls, and they more often reject the notion that friendship can be as close as kinship. On the question about the lonely mother who wants her daughter to come to live with her, girls in this group give the traditional response of loyalty to the mother more than girls from any other constellation. The contrast is again a striking one—56 per cent of this group think the girl should return, compared to 42 per cent of the next highest group.

On the other hand, these girls do not spend a great deal of time with their families; they are more likely than other girls to say they spend most of their free time alone or with a friend. In many cases, this friend may be a steady boyfriend, since a large proportion of these girls go steady. If we take steady dating to indicate a transfer of emotionality from the family, then we are faced with the paradoxical fact that girls in this pattern are both very tied to their families and at the same time more likely to have shifted the focus of their emotional lives. One other indication that at least in some spheres they do not in fact rely on their mothers as much as one might think from their attitudes toward family relationships: they do not think of the mother as confidante as often as girls in the other working mother groups.

### Patterns of Effects

The analysis of maternal employment within social classes has distinguished two patterns of effects that may accompany a mother's full-time work commitment. The patterns break on class lines in the following manner: in the middle class the effect of the mother's working full-time appears to be similar to the effects of a partial work commitment in either class group—family interaction is high and is geared to training children toward autonomy and self-reliance. Girls in such families are active in both organized and non-organized leisure activity, spend a good deal of time with their families, and are relatively autonomous in issues of judgment and authority. They admire their mothers, but do not seem particularly dependent on them.

The lower-class girl whose mother works full-time is not like other daughters of working women. The girls in this pattern come closest to our original conception of the girl who is neglected and suffers a serious loss in family life because her mother is overextended in her commitments, harassed, perhaps resentful. Here we find girls who carry very heavy responsibilities, lack normal leisure commitments, and apparently find in extra-family relationships (i.e., the steady dating relationship) the secure and stable companionship which they do not find at home. Though in fact they share very little time with their families, the girls in this group have a strong and sentimental conception of the importance of family ties, and continue to be emotionally dependent on the family at an age when other girls have begun to break their ties of dependency. This last set of findings does not, we think, contradict our original notion that full-time maternal employment might imply neglect: one reason girls from such families might be sentimental about the family and more dependent on it is that their needs for family-based security have never been adequately met. At the same time that girls with such backgrounds take unusual responsibility for daily realities, they may continue to yearn for the closeness and security of more normal family interaction.

### Explanation

Why should full-time maternal employment have such different effects in the two status groups? The simplest hypothesis relies on economic factors: the middle-class mother who works either part- or full-time very likely has some degree of choice in the matter. In the working class the two commitments may reflect quite different degrees of personal choice and financial press—the lower-class woman who works full-time may be responding to a much simpler and more imposing condition of economic need. Two minor findings from our study support this suggestion. When we asked girls to think of ways in which a girl might like her parents to be different, the girls in our working-class full-time group differed clearly from the other three working mother groups in one respect: while the other three groups all stand out for their reference to the parents' life style ("she'd like them to have a nicer home, go out, entertain more"), the working-class full-time group rarely gives such answers. On the other hand, the working-class full-time group gives economic *problems* as a source of worry for girls much more than any of the other working mother groups.

If in fact this is the case—that the working-class full-time pattern is the only one of our four working mother groups that represents serious economic deprivation—then we can make some ordered interpretations of our findings. The mother who works because of serious economic need is not necessarily one whose psychological make-up prepares her for the dual roles of homemaker and worker. She may feel herself taxed by the demands of a life complication which she did not choose and does not feel up to. Sheer economic deprivation adds a further burden of concern, and in many cases we might expect to find such women both harried and resentful or passively resigned to an unsatisfying and burdensome life situation. The pattern is similar to the one Lois Hoffman has characterized as guilt-free (4).* Pressed themselves, such women feel no special obligation to their families. They expect to get their children to take a good deal of responsibility at home; they spend very little time and energy in managing or sharing their children's leisure affairs; and they engender in their children a strong sympathy and sentimental loyalty.

* Numerals parenthesized denote references at end of article.

One is reminded of the mothers who so regularly appear in the short stories of Frank O'Connor and other Irish authors: the strong and stable support in a family whose father deals primarily in alcoholic charm and irresponsibility. The key for such a woman is to convert the children to her side, as emotional suppliers and supporters in the real problems of life. She inspires her children with both the strength to cope with reality and also the dependency that assures her some emotional gratification in an otherwise bleak life. To be sure this fictional Irish mother is an exaggerated form, but we suspect that such pattern is the paradigm for understanding the emotional nexus that dominates many lower-status families in which the mother's employment is a condition for family survival.

We have already described the motivational pattern that we think underpins part-time maternal employment. The distinctive features here are that the woman herself chooses to work and that she maintains a vivid sense of obligation and responsibility toward her family. She chooses a complex rather than a simple life pattern, but the conditions of the pattern are set by her primary commitment to her family role. We see this as a pattern requiring unusual energy and one which results in a high degree of family interaction. Derivative effects of the pattern we note in the degree of parent participation in the leisure lives of their adolescent children and in the energy, autonomy, and responsibility that characterize girls from this family setting. These psychological features of the girls develop, we suggest, from a modeling process in which the girls identify with and draw their ideals from their own active and autonomous mothers.

The only pattern remaining to be accounted for is the middle-class mother who works full-time. We found this group of girls to be indistinguishable in most critical respects from the daughters of women who work part-time. We must now ask how a full-time work commitment might for a middle-class woman be the same—have the same meaning—as part-time employment. One suspects that economic need alone does not distinguish the two kinds of employment for middle-class women, and the woman of higher social status who works full-time does so, at least in part, because of personal choice.

## MATERNAL EMPLOYMENT AND ADOLESCENT BOYS

One would expect—from the findings in the girls' study—that maternal employment might be a less important factor in the life of the adolescent boy. If we are right in our view that much of the influence of maternal employment comes about through a modeling process in which the girl fashions her ego-ideals and activities in keeping with the pattern set by her mother, then we can expect that this pattern will be less effective in predicting the boy's developing integration. For the boy, the model provided by his father will be the key to ego development, and the mother's activity or employment should be a comparatively minor factor.

Our interpretations of the meaning of work to mothers in the part-time and full-time patterns gain some general support from our data on boys. Here again we find that the lower-class family in which the mother works full-time has more pressing financial troubles—or, at least, that financial problems come through to the children more clearly. Boys in this group think of financial problems as a source of worry and also as something they would like to change about their own lives more often than do boys in any of the other working mother patterns, and often more than those whose mothers do not work at all. The other three types of working mother (i.e., higher-status women who work full-time and women of either high or low status who hold part-time jobs) again seem to be women who are unusually conscientious, active mothers. Their sons, like their daughters, report sharing leisure activities with their parents more than other boys do, and they have a larger number of leisure activities of the kind that imply parental involvement (i.e., membership in organized groups and active sports and hobbies).

Beyond these few findings, the working mother variable shows relatively little power to predict the boy's activities and psychological characteristics. When the mother's work stems from personal choice—or so we infer, at least—the boy has a relatively high leisure activity index, but he differs in no other area from boys whose mothers do not work. He is no more likely to work or date; he shows no signs of unusual achievement striving,[1] of special forms of ego development, or of precocious loosening of dependency ties.

The boys from families in which the mother's work is the product of economic necessity (i.e., lower-status women who work full-time) do differ from other boys in some respects, and this seems to us interesting in light of the fact that this is the one case in which maternal employment implies something about the father as a model. The fact that a mother "must" work —irrespective of her personal wishes—does not speak well for the father's capacity as a provider. Considering the importance of economic prowess in the American definition and evaluation of the male, a father who cannot or does not support his family adequately can hardly serve as an effective ideal for his son. And it is in the area of modeling that the boys differ most clearly

[1] When we consider only urban boys from lower-middle and upper-middle working-class homes, we do find a relationship between the boys' mobility aspirations and maternal employment. Boys who aspire to upward mobility more often report that their mothers work part-time than do boys whose orientation is non-mobile or downwardly mobile. While maternal employment is generally a less imposing force in the life of the boy, this finding suggests that in certain cultural settings, the fact that a boy has an ambitious mother may crucially affect the direction of his development. Kahl's work (5) supports this suggestion.

from their age mates. They choose their own fathers significantly less often than other boys do, and they more frequently say that they have no adult ideals. Beyond this we find that boys in this group are somewhat rebellious in response to adult authority, and that they show signs of a poor ego integration. They have a relatively short time perspective and a low level of general activity. Only in dating are they especially active. They do not have part-time jobs as often as other boys; they have very few organizational ties and active leisure engagements. Our information on their family attitudes is limited: we did not ask boys as many questions in this area as we did girls.

*Table 2*—Working-Class Boys with Full-Time Working Mothers Compared to Other Boys on Selected Measures of Activity, Ego Development

| Item: Boys' attitudes, behavior | MATERNAL EMPLOYMENT | |
|---|---|---|
| | Full-time working-class (N = 71) | All other patterns (N = 631) |
| | Per cent | |
| *Adult ideals* | | |
| Father | 12 | 27 |
| No ideal | 15 | 6 |
| In-family models (including father) | 45 | 41 |
| *Time perspective* | | |
| Extended | 32 | 45 |
| Restricted | 12 | 5 |
| *Dating* | | |
| Date | 68 | 53 |
| Doesn't date | 32 | 47 |
| *Group membership* | | |
| None | 43 | 26 |
| Belongs to 1 or 2 groups | 48 | 53 |
| Belongs to 3 or more groups | 9 | 21 |
| *Leisure activities* | | |
| Low | 33 | 18 |
| Medium | 38 | 45 |
| High | 29 | 37 |
| *Work* | | |
| Holds a job | 51 | 47 |
| *Intimacy of friendship* | | |
| Can be as close as family relationship | 46 | 41 |
| Cannot be as close | 52 | 56 |
| *Reliance on parents: advice on issues* | | |
| Relies heavily on parents | 40 | 44 |
| Relies somewhat on parents | 47 | 45 |
| Does not rely on parents | 13 | 10 |

But boys in the lower-class full-time group do not seem to be emotionally dependent on the family in any way that compares with our findings for girls from similar family backgrounds. They do not think that family ties are always closer than friendships, and they do not rely heavily on parental advice or on in-family models more than other boys do. We would very much like to have information on the boy's relationship to his mother distinguished from his attitude toward his father, but in this our data on boys are specifically lacking.

We can say, by way of a general conclusion, that the effect of maternal employment in the boy's development is significant only when it serves to inform us about general features of family integration and, specifically, about the relationship between the boy and his father. When the mother's work rests to any significant degree on factors of personal choice—when, that is, it reflects qualities and motives of the mother but does not yield specific information about the father—it fails to predict a unique pattern of adjustment in the boy, although it appears to be an important force in the girl's integration. This difference in the findings for boys and girls supports our earlier view that the kind of woman who assumes an occupational role through a desire for some self-realization exerts an influence on her daughter's development through a modeling process in which the girl identifies with and incorporates many of her mother's ego characteristics.

References to *Impact of Employment of Mothers by Social Class*

1. Bergsten, Jane W. "A Nationwide Sample of Girls from School Lists," *Journal of Experimental Education*, **26,** March, 1958, 197–208.
2. Douvan, Elizabeth, and Joseph Adelson. *Themes in American Adolescence*, Unpublished manuscript in preparation.
3. ————, and Carol Kaye. *Adolescent Girls*, Ann Arbor, Mich., Survey Research Center, University of Michigan, 1956.
4. ————, and S. B. Withey. *A Study of Adolescent Boys*, Ann Arbor, Mich., Survey Research Center, University of Michigan, 1955.
5. Kahl, J. A. "Educational and Occupational Aspirations of 'Common Man' Boys," *Harvard Education Review*, **23,** Spring, 1953, 186–203. See this book, pp. 298–310.

---

# Educational Factors
# and Environment

## INTRODUCTION

"Maria's Composition," the first reading in this part, is written by a 13-year-old Puerto Rican girl who has witnessed the death of a neighbor from wounds inflicted in a knife fight in Maria's own building. She puts into five paragraphs her shock and terror. Her teacher puts in one sentence her reaction, "Too long."

In this final section, you, the teacher, are asked to look at the place at which and the people with whom the child spends approximately thirteen years of his early life. In previous sections of this book, you have read about the intellectual and personal attributes of children from various ethnic groups and social strata. You have considered the families from which urban children come and the training they receive in their homes. With this background, it is now appropriate to assess the effects of teachers and school systems on children from poor families in the metropolis.

The little five-year-old from an urban slum enters an educational bureaucracy, a huge organizational complex of which his own school is only a small unit. This organization is different, however, from the bureaucracies of business or industry in that the child has no choice but to go to school. Employees may choose to quit and go elsewhere. But the child is prohibited from doing the same. He remains in an institution that differs in another way from those of the non-academic world: His teacher is part of a profession and, at the same time, part of a bureaucracy. She is caught between the demands of giving full devotion and unlimited time to her career as a professional should and punching the timeclock or signing in every morning as a bureaucratic employee must.

It is within this very familiar bureaucratic structure with its unique educational peculiarities, that the young child is trained to take his place in society and in the public world of work for which he is destined. How well does the school achieve this goal for the child from lower socioeconomic levels? To what extent does the school enable the child to use his full academic and social potential?

Cuber, in "Who Shall Be Educated?" presents evidence that the social status of children influences the nature of curriculum and coursework as well as physical condition and academic calibre of the school. The result of these educational inequalities is glaringly apparent in a study of children who were all "college material" with I.Q.'s of 110 and over. "Slightly over one fourth of the 'superior' children of below-average socioeconomic status did not even finish high school; approximately 60 per cent more finished high school but did not attend college. Not quite 13 per cent of these intellectually potential college students eventually attended college. About 57 per cent of the superior children of above-average socioeconomic status, by contrast, attended college. Only a handful did not at least graduate from high school."

Why don't the schools enable these and other children of lower socioeconomic status to realize their full potential? Sexton, in "Education and Income," provides some answers in her 1960 study of an urban school system in one of our fourteen largest cities. Her data indicate that *all* schools in income areas above $7,000 are achieving *above* grade level and *all* schools below $7,000 average family income are achieving *below* grade level. The differences between the two groups of students from different income levels do *not* improve as a result of exposure to the Big City schools. Instead, there is a progressive increase in the difference so that by the eighth grade, the children from the lowest income groups are almost two years behind their more privileged peers in achievement test scores.

Though many environmental factors pointed out in earlier sections of this book impinge on school achievement, it is not unreasonable to expect that with prolonged exposure to the school, the handicaps of poverty would lessen in importance with a concomitant increase in achievement levels. This does not happen.

What help did the school system in the city studied by Sexton give to the children from lower income areas to help them overcome their learning problems? A remedial reading program was developed that, unfortunately, allowed only those children who scored at least C on reading tests to enroll. The obvious consequence was that children in the upper-income groups participated in larger numbers because they scored higher on the tests to begin with. At the same time, a special program for gifted children showed an enrollment of 3.7 students per 10,000 children in lower-income areas under $7,000 compared with 34.4 per 10,000 pupils from areas in which average family income was over $7,000. Again, lower-income children even if bright were not helped since they did not qualify for the status of "gifted." Regardless of which end of the intellectual continuum the lower-income child was located, he lost the benefits of additional assistance from the schools, either because he was thought too retarded or not quite bright enough.

What happens to children in these schools of our metropolitan masses? They leave. Those who leave acquire a label in the process—the dropouts. Havighurst, in "A Study of High School Dropouts," says that 35 per cent of the students in River City quit school. This is *not* atypical of other cities (12). Of those leaving, the majority come from lower-income groups. Of those leaving in River City, 47 per cent gave negative experiences in and negative attitudes toward school as their reasons for leaving. After dropping from the system, 56 per cent wished they had remained, but their dislike of school had closed that chapter of the book for them. The author of this study concludes, "As early as the sixth grade it is possible to discover those who will go farthest in school. If these subgroups are recognized and treated wisely, it should be possible to make the school system into a more effective institution for helping the various types of children to grow up successfully."

But children are not the only people in schools in lower-income areas of our cities who are dissatisfied. What happens to teachers in these schools? They leave. Those who leave acquire a label, too, the transfers. Havighurst turns his attention to this problem in the next research presented, "Teachers in Chicago Schools." In this our second largest city, teachers from schools in lower-class or slum areas request transfers about twice as frequently as their colleagues in upper-income school areas. What about those who stay on? How do they feel? Among elementary school teachers, 65 per cent have very favorable attitudes toward their present position *if* they are located in upper-income area schools. Of those in lower class or slum schools, 17 per cent feel very favorably about their positions. And to top it off, 22 per cent have unfavorable or very unfavorable attitudes toward their positions in these areas. Obviously, something is wrong. Teachers transfer; children drop out. Fortunately, however, the administrators and public at large are beginning to scrutinize the system of education in our urban centers. Hopefully, changes will be made which will aid teachers and students who are both disadvantaged under the present conditions(30).

Whatever changes are needed in urban school systems, our concern is with you, the teacher. So we return to the analysis of teaching difficulties set forth in the introduction to this volume. If you will recall, the conflict generated by environmental differences experienced by the teacher in contrast to her students was considered basic to many misunderstandings and much difficulty in the classroom.

Charters, in "Consequences of Educators' Social Position on the Teaching-Learning Process," reviews the limited research done on this problem. The basic question he seeks to answer is, "How is the teaching-learning process influenced by the positions teachers occupy in the American social structure?" Of the many theoretical approaches, the anthropological approach is perhaps the most promising. The basic premise is that ". . . the social environment is seen to shape the generalized value orientations by which a person lives and works. The significant aspect of the teaching-learning process in the classroom is the transmission of value orientations from teacher to pupil. It proceeds not so much through didactic teachings as through the reward and punishment system and subtleties of the flow of interaction. Which values will be transmitted depends upon the teacher's own value orientation, which, in turn, is determined by his position in the groups and subcultures of the social structure. Problems arise in those cases where pupils are located at different points in the larger social structure and enter the classroom with conflicting value orientations."

Social class is seen as a part of the social environment which influences the classroom interaction. Those who emphasize social status see the school as serving "the upward mobile child of the lower class as a secondary acculturating agency, a place where he can assimilate the values, customs, morals and manners essential to acceptance in the higher strata." Charters points out, however, that the school, on the other hand, "preserves the stability of the stratification system by limiting upward mobility to those youth who are willing and able to play within the rules of the game or, more specifically, to acquire the value orientations and motivations appropriate to middle-class membership."

The teacher may, even unknowingly, enforce this state of affairs by the intrusion of her own value orientations in two ways: "by governing the distribution of reward and punishment and by determining what kinds of pupil behavior will be rewarding to the teacher." We do have evidence indicating that "Teachers' ratings of the personal or social adjustment of particular pupils have been found to correlate with the social class position of the pupils in a number of studies." Furthermore, one study found that the kind of contact teachers had with their students from lower classes tended to be characterized by teacher domination with conflict. The kind of contact the teacher had with students from upper classes tended to show greater teacher integration with evidence of working together.

However, as Charters points out, the evidence is sparse and subject to a number of questions of interpretation. That this should be the case is not surprising. There is little research available on most of the problems of the poor in either their contact with each other or in their contact with representative people from other positions in society. This neglect leads to many questions for which there are either no specific answers or at best contradictory evidence; consequently, concrete assistance in eliminating difficulties in your schools is somewhat limited. However, your acquaintance with the present thinking in the field should enable you to assume a more knowledgeable approach to yourself and to your children.

This knowledge is increasingly necessary as the schools become more and more the central concern of most Americans. Education is the crucial question of our century, because people everywhere now know that progress and peace are dependent on your present efforts or your future efforts if you are training to be a teacher as well as on those of teachers throughout the world today. Increasingly, the education of children in the schools of our inner cities has come under fire from various critics(14). Some of these criticisms are or can be valuable aids in your own efforts to improve the teaching-learning process in your classroom.

Typical of the more thoughtful and hopefully helpful appraisals of teaching is the research presented by Clark in "Defeatism in the Ghetto Schools." He says, "The schools in the ghetto have lost faith in the ability of their students to learn and the ghetto has lost faith in the ability of the schools to lead. There are two conflicting points of view—one, that the pupils do not learn because they cannot; the other, that they do not learn because they are not taught. The fact is they are not learning. The problem is to see that they do, and only when the attempt is made with enthusiasm and competence will the answer be clear."

Clark believes that the expectations of teachers are negative. They do not really believe that children from slum areas can learn under the present conditions. He says, "As HARYOU gathered data on the schools, it became increasingly clear that the attitude of the teachers toward their students was emerging as a most important factor in attempting to understand the massive retardation of these children." The author goes on to give evidence that children of lower income levels do achieve under certain conditions: "The pilot experiments in St. Louis, New York, and elsewhere are encouraging evidence that children can learn when they are expected to learn."

Though this is a valid and necessary viewpoint, there is little doubt that more than a change in teachers' expectations is required to achieve the goal of maximum learning and optimal personal and social functioning of children in the metropolis. Teachers' expectations are, in part, based on their membership in a human organization, the school with its policies and practices. This institution is one major source of influence in the child's total environment. As such, institutional personnel must gage their impact on the child from the slum just as they must evaluate the influence of other human groups and organizations on the child. This section is, therefore, presented to you so you may examine the effects of the school as an institution with policies and procedures, of teachers as organizational personnel with their own values and expectations, and of children who interact or react to this part of their environment with their own values and expectations.

# MARIA'S COMPOSITION

[Maria is a thirteen-year-old Puerto Rican girl in an East Harlem Junior High School. Her composition is copied with all its errors and innocence.]

"Stop don't do it" "Please stop them" "Help" She screamed.

That was the words she prenounce when I was coming from the store. When I was coming up the stairs I saw blood down the stair and I look up I saw three policeman and two detective and I said what's wrong, were does blood come from? The detective said in a deep voice this blood come from the second floor two neighbors had a fight, and we are waiting for the ambulance. My heart stop for one second, and then I ran up the stairs and I said. "That is where I live." When I came up and saw Mr. Lopez with blood all over his shirt and I kneel down and said "Mr. Lopez what happen" and he said "That no good Luis he" he stop and then I said go on, but the policeman interb and said please goung girl don't try to make him talk, then a policeman and a fat lady the lady was the nurse and she said take this man immediately! to the ambulance he is bleeding to much. The policeman took him to the ambulance. The other she put some bandage around his shoulders and then she said go to your home and report tomorrow at the hospital. Then the nurse call me over and said do you know the man that I sent in the ambulance? Yes nurse. "Then will you answer some questions." Yes. Will you please companion me to the hospital. Yes nurse.

Mr. Lopez die in the ambulance, I call Mrs. Lopez and gave her the bad news. She started to scream and cry. I came back from the hospital after I answer the question. The first thing that came in my mine was "why" "why" two neighbors fight. "Why" because they maybe don't understand each other or maybe one ask for a advice and the other said why come to me why don't you go to your family.

From *Bridges to Slum-Ghetto Children*, Leonard Kornberg, ed. (Queens, New York: BRIDGE Project, Department of Education, Queens College, Copyright 1962). Reprinted by permission.

To be a neighbor is not necessary to be in the neighborhood, it can be country or city or and town anything. For example if you go to a country that you never gone before. All during your travels you would see people staring at your odd clothing, people who would not understand the language you spoke.

Then you would land in a strange country. Everything would be different. You would have to learn a strange language, learn a new trade. Then you try to be kindful and helpful with people. The people will adore you truly. "Why" because you been not only a good neighbor but helpful and friendly with them. This is one of the simple ways to be kind with people, by helping them in anything they need your help today and to-morrow they help you. This composition is for the adolescent to give them an ideal to understand other persons. When a boy or girl comes into a classroom for the first time you try to make a conversation with him or her. Show the boy or girl around the school introduct the boy or girl to your friends so she don't feel lonely. In a way you are helping the boy or girl getting around.

[At the end of this composition, the teacher had written: "too long!"]

# WHO SHALL BE EDUCATED?

*John F. Cuber and William F. Kenkel*

## EQUALITY OF EDUCATIONAL OPPORTUNITY

If all children were able to continue their formal education as long as they were able to profit from it, and wished to pursue it, then we could say that educational opportunities are available to all. There is considerable evidence, however, that this ideal is seldom attained; a person's opportunity to remain in school seems to be closely linked simply with the socioeconomic status of his parents.

Warner reports on a study of 910 Pennsylvania grade-school children, all with I.Q.'s of 110 or above, and thus all "college material." The group was separated into those of "above average" and "below average" economic levels. It was evident that children of similar intellectual ability were not receiving a similar amount of education. Slightly over one fourth of the "superior" children of below-average socioeconomic status did not even finish high school; approximately 60 per cent more finished high school but did not attend college. Not quite 13 per cent of these intellectually potential college students eventually attended college. About 57 per cent of the superior children of above average socioeconomic status, by contrast, attended college. Only a handful did not at least graduate from high school.

A study was made of a similar group of students in Milwaukee. From the standpoint of ability, the students were much the same; all had I.Q.'s of 117 or above. The yearly income of their parents, however, ranged from under $500 to over $8000. Table 1 clearly indicates that the higher the yearly income of the parents, the more likely it was that the child attended college.

From *Social Stratification in the United States* by John F. Cuber and William F. Kenkel (New York: Appleton-Century-Crofts, Inc., Copyright 1954), pp. 263–276. Reprinted by permission of Appleton-Century-Crofts. Charts and text from *Who Shall be Educated?* by W. Lloyd Warner, et al. Copyright 1944 by Harper and Brothers. Reprinted by permission of Harper and Row, Publishers.

Other studies have also discovered this direct relationship between economic status and school attendance. If, however, the children of lower economic origins do not *want* to remain in school to the same extent as do their wealthier intellectual peers, the statistics do not necessarily indicate a status-bias in our school system. Warner presents three types of evidence which would seem to indicate that economic factors bear heavily on the decision to remain in school. One study discovered that many students give "lack of money" as their reason for leaving school.[1] There was a large response to the National Youth Administration school program which offered financial aid to school students. It is difficult to estimate how many of the students would have dropped out of school were it not for this financial assistance. To be eligible for this aid, however, a child had to

*Table 1*—Relation of Parental Income to Full-time College Attendance of Superior Milwaukee High School Graduates*

| Parental income | Per cent in college full-time |
|---|---|
| $8000– | 100.0 |
| 5000–7999 | 92.0 |
| 3000–4999 | 72.9 |
| 2000–2999 | 44.4 |
| 1500–1999 | 28.9 |
| 1000–1499 | 25.5 |
| 500– 999 | 26.8 |
| Under 500 | 20.4 |

* Adapted from W. Lloyd Warner, Robert J. Havighurst, and Martin B. Loeb, *Who Shall Be Educated?* (New York, Harper and Bros., 1944), p. 53. Used by permission.

demonstrate he "needed" the funds to remain in school. There is the fact that it *does* cost money to go school, even to the so-called "free" schools in the United States. One study, for example, discovered that even ten years ago, the "incidental" expenses connected with attending a public high school amounted to $125 a year.[2]

This type of evidence, though certainly significant, does not give us the full story. Many a lower-status child will probably say that he dropped out of grade or high school or failed to go to college because this is what he "wanted" to do. But let us investigate how the school system "works" in selecting students for higher education. Perhaps then we will better realize why it is that many lower-status children "want" to leave school.

[1] Howard M. Bell, *Youth Tell Their Story* (Washington, D.C., American Council on Education, 1938), pp. 64 ff.
[2] A Committee of North Central Association of Colleges and Secondary Schools, *General Education in the American High School* (Chicago, Scott, Foresman and Co., 1942), pp. 17–20.

## SEPARATE SCHOOL CURRICULA AND
## DIFFERENTIAL SOCIAL STATUS

### Elementary Schools

It may seem that social status would not affect the course of training in our elementary schools, since all students in the public schools usually receive the same formal training. We must remember, however, that the "best" families sometimes do not send their children to the public elementary schools. They register their sons, instead, at an "exclusive" military school and send their daughters to a "nice" girls' school where "music is emphasized" and where the "young ladies" can learn to ride and swim and cultivate the "right" friendships. Thus, children in our public elementary schools do not often even get to know their age-mates from socially prominent families. During Christmas vacation, perhaps, they may hear exciting tales of life in the different "cottages" or of strict but easily outwitted "headmasters," but all in all they learn little about how the highest 1 per cent live. In this manner, then, social status enters into elementary school education; at a very early age children are somewhat segregated according to the possessions and prestige of their parents.

But social status operates at this time of life in still other ways. A child in the higher grades in elementary school is well aware that in high school he can "elect" some courses or can choose from several different curricula. His parents, perhaps, have already instructed him concerning which courses he should choose and his teachers may have talked to him to assure that he will make a "wise" decision. Most children of lower status are not encouraged to talk about college-preparatory courses but are told of the "fine vocational courses" that they can take. Even while still in grade school, children of higher status begin to realize that high school, for them, is but a means of preparing themselves for college. Let us see, then, what happens when children of various statuses get to high school.

### High Schools

In Yankee City, a typical small New England town, the high school has four curricula. Two, the science and the Latin courses, prepare the students for college; the general and the commercial curricula are usually considered terminal.

The college-preparation curricula are said to be "better" than the terminal ones for these reasons:

1. Scholastic standards are higher in the Latin and scientific courses. A "D" is not considered a passing grade in these courses, whereas it is in the general and commercial ones.

2. The college-preparatory courses are taught better. The principal of

Yankee City High School stated that the standard of teaching lowers as one goes from the college-preparatory curricula to the general and commercial ones. "It is like having two schools within one building."[3]

3. The college-preparatory courses are more difficult and comprehensive. The principal cited, as one example, the difference between the General Science Course III and the Chemistry course in the scientific curriculum. "The latter," he stated, "is more difficult and includes more material. . . ."[4]

4. The goals of the college-preparatory curricula are "higher." They prepare students for the occupations which directly or indirectly can place them in a higher social position.

In view of these differences, one might suppose that the more able and ambitious students would choose the Latin and scientific courses. Social status, however, seems to affect the students' choice of curricula in the Yankee City and Hometown high schools. In general, the higher an adolescent's social status, the more likely he is to choose the Latin and scientific courses.

Thus, the status system is, in part, perpetuated. Children from families of higher status generally prepare themselves for higher statuses; many children of lower-status origin prepare themselves for a social position similar to that of their parents.

Table 2 indicates, however, that a sizable minority of lower-class children do enroll in the college-preparatory curricula. Some of these children will eventually graduate from college and will accomplish a substantial rise in status. But why do not more lower-status children prepare themselves for college? Several "reasons" are offered to explain this phenomenon.

1. *Lower-status Children Lack Ability*. No objective studies support this theory. Intelligence differences between children of different status are not sufficient to account for their differential preparation for college.[5]

2. *Lower-status Children Lack "Ambition."* It is sometimes suggested that lower-status children lack the "will to get ahead" and that anyone with ability who "really wanted to" could manage a college education. Many high school students, however, have stated that they would like to go to college, but simply cannot afford it. Among those who state that they do not want a college education there are many, undoubtedly, who have accepted what they believe is the inevitable. Their knowledge of the cost of a college education and the experiences of their friends support this belief.

3. *Lower-status Children Lack Encouragement*. It cannot be denied that

---

[3] Warner, *op. cit.*, p. 61.                                    [4] *Ibid.*
[5] For conclusions regarding the relationship between ability and status and appropriate references see Stephen Abrahamson, "Our Status System and Scholastic Rewards," *Journal of Educational Sociology*, 25 (April, 1952), pp. 441–450.

some lower-status families encourage their children to pursue a course of study that will enable them to "get a job" after completion of high school. In many cases this is probably a quite "realistic" approach to the situation, because of the inability of the parents to pay for a college education. It is probably not as well known that teachers, too, dissuade students from preparing for college. Sometimes they "have a talk" with the student; other times they give failing grades to those who they think should not pursue the college-preparatory curricula. Warner implies that in Yankee City, status factors, and not necessarily achievement, enter into teachers' judgments of who "belongs" in the college-preparatory courses.

*Table 2*—College Expectations and Social Position*
Proportion of High-School Students Expecting to Go to College

| Class | Hometown per cent | Yankee City per cent |
|---|---|---|
| Upper upper | | |
| Lower upper | 100 | 100 |
| Upper middle | 80 | 88 |
| Lower middle | 22 | 45 |
| Upper lower | 9 | 28 |
| Lower lower | 0 | 26 |

* W. Lloyd Warner, Robert J. Havighurst, and Martin B. Loeb, *Who Shall Be Educated?* (New York, Harper and Bros., 1944), p. 66.

We have some evidence, then, that students' choice of curricula is in part dependent upon their social status rather than upon their ability to learn. There are some who do not like to admit that factors other than ability seem to determine who goes to college and especially that these "other factors" are closely tied up with our stratification system. Such people emphasize the fact that *some* lower-status children do, in fact, go to college. They point out, furthermore, that each year college scholarships are offered to able students and that a certain proportion of the scholarships always go unused. Later we will investigate factors in our schools, other than curricula differences, that are related to social status. Perhaps this will help answer these objections. Let us turn first to those schools that have but one curriculum for all students.

## SCHOOLS WITHOUT DIFFERENT CURRICULA

In some public high schools there is no differentiation of curricula; the same courses are available to all students. In general, there are three types of undifferentiated high schools: (1) the school whose enrollment is too small to permit different curricula; (2) the school whose population is similar in its status make-up; and (3) the school that is large enough to permit differentiation but chooses instead not to have hard divisions based on collegiate intentions.

*The Small High School.* In Hometown, as in most small cities, the high school enrollment is too small to have a separate curriculum for the college-bound students. There are, of course, a certain number of "elective" courses, but students of all statuses are in the same "required" courses. It should be added, however, that in many such schools the curriculum is built around college-entrance requirements.

*The High School that Serves a Relatively Homogeneous Population.*[6] In homogeneous suburbs such as Lake Forest (Ill.), Grosse Pointe (Mich.), and Shaker Heights (Ohio) it is usually unnecessary to have different curricula. Most of the students are college-bound and the remainder seem to accept the curriculum that is built around the needs of the majority.

*The Large, Undifferentiated High School.* In some large cities the high schools contain no separate curricula despite the fact that their enrollments are large enough to make differentiation possible.[7] The distinguishing characteristic of the undifferentiated high school is the lack of the split between the college-preparatory group and the "others" and the differential prestige that is attached to the two groups. In such a situation children should have a greater chance to compete with one another and to demonstrate their ability.

Perhaps if we examine how social status affects still other aspects of the school situation we will understand why even in the undifferentiated high schools students who go to college do not come from the various status levels proportionately.

## STATUS AND THE "SECTION SYSTEM"

Some elementary schools have a section system by which the students in the same grade are separated into two, three, or more groups. In Old City, for example, each grade has three sections: A, B, and C. The sections meet in different classrooms and are taught by different teachers. In Old City the children are said to be divided into the sections on the basis of their ability. The junior-high-school principal explains that the "ability" of the students is estimated simply by teachers' judgments.[8, 9]

Accordingly, if ability is distributed more or less evenly among children of various statuses, we should expect to find the same proportion of children

---

[6] Warner, *op. cit.*, p. 70.      [7] *Ibid.*, pp. 69–70.      [8] *Ibid.*, p. 73.
[9] A recent study discovered that teachers in small schools can estimate a student's I.Q. with a fairly high degree of accuracy. Errors in estimates were made, to be sure, but the coefficient of correlation between teachers' rating of their students and their subsequent scores on an I.Q. test was discovered to be +0.72. (Robert E. Hubbard and William R. Flesher, "Intelligent Teachers and Intelligence Tests—Do They Agree?" *Educational Research Bulletin,* **32** (May 13, 1953), pp. 113–122.) If we can generalize on the basis of this study, it would seem that teachers *can* estimate the ability of their students. The question in relation to this study concerns whether they estimate ability *alone* when assigning students to various sections.

from each social level in each of the three sections. But this is not the case. The higher-status levels are represented in Section A up to twice as frequently as they are in the total sample, whereas there are over three times as many lower-status students in the sample as there are in the highest section. These facts lend themselves to two interpretations: (1) higher-status students in general have more ability than do those of lower status; or (2) students are placed in the section on the basis of factors other than ability alone. Perhaps the statement of two school officials will help us decide which is the more likely interpretation. When the junior-high-school principal was asked whether there were any status distinctions between the sections he responded:[10]

There is to some extent. You generally find that children from the best families do the best work. That is not always true but usually it is so. The children from the lower class seem to be not as capable as the others. I think it is to some extent inheritance. The others come from people who are capable and educated, and also the environment probably has a great effect. They come to school with a lot of knowledge already that the others lack.

The principal's theory seems to support the first interpretation. A teacher in the junior high school had a somewhat different story when asked if there was "much class feeling in the school." She replied:[11]

Oh, yes, there is a lot of that. We try not to have it as much as we can but of course we can't help it. Now, for instance, even in the sections we have, it is evident. Sections are supposed to be made up just on the basis of records in school but it isn't and everybody knows it isn't. I know right in my own A section I have children who ought to be in B section, but they are little socialites and so they stay in A. I don't say there are children in B who should be in A but in the A section there are some who shouldn't be there. We have discussed it in faculty meetings but nothing is ever done. . . .

Of course, we do some shifting around. There are some borderliners who were shifted up to make the sections more nearly even. But the socialites who aren't keeping up their standard in the A section were never taken into B or C section and they never will. They don't belong there socially. Of course, there are some girls in A section who don't belong there socially, but almost everyone of the socialites is in A.

Studies dealing with the relationship between ability and social status would support this teacher's viewpoint that it is not always ability that places a student in the highest section.[12] Whatever the interpretation, however, the fact remains that higher-status students are overrepresented in the A section. By and large, students from a given status level are placed with one another, and thus learn to exclude those of quite different status.

[10] Warner, *op. cit.*, p. 74.
[11] *Ibid.*
[12] For the relationship between academic achievement and social status see Stephen Abrahamson, *op. cit.*, p. 443. See also pp. 172–173.

## YANKEE CITY SCHOOLS

There are two kinds of groupings in the Yankee City elementary school system: (1) there are different schools for children from different sections of the city; and (2) the schools employ the section system for grouping the students in each grade.

Dorland School is situated in the south end of Yankee City. Over 80 per cent of the children in this school are either upper-lower or lower-lower class. Most higher-status children go to Ashton School, situated in one of the "better" neighborhoods. "In the case of those who live near the border-line of the school districts the assignment of the students by the school authorities is based more on class status than ability."[13]

Social status is reflected in the physical facilities of the Yankee City schools as well as the make-up of the school populations. The Dorland School has the dubious distinction of being the only school in town without lighting in all of its classrooms. Its heating system has been called inadequate and even hazardous. In general, the school is dirty and run-down. The school authorities spend less money for this and other schools in the poorer areas than for other schools. With respect to this situation Warner concludes, "There can be no doubt that the powerful middle-class, by their influence on the schools, tend to contribute to the subordination of the lower classes by refusing equipment to schools which are predominately lower class."[14]

The Dorland School operates with a section system similar to that previously described. The children purportedly are placed in the sections according to their ability but the superintendent of schools commented that, "A section is for Hill Streeters, B for the middle group, and C for the Riverbrookers."[15] The school principal does not seem to like the implications of this remark and emphasizes that students are allowed more individual attention because of the section system.

But status differences among students in the three sections *are* evident. All of the upper-middle class (the highest class in the school) students are in A section, while 91 per cent of the students in C section are lower-lower class. Regardless of how we account for this, it is manifest that children tend to be segregated along lines of social status in some of our grade and high schools.

## COLLEGES AND THE STATUS SYSTEM

Most students are probably well aware that there are status differences among the many colleges and universities in this country. The "Ivy League" institutions and a few others largely attract the higher-status

[13] Warner, *op. cit.*, p. 75.          [14] *Ibid.*, p. 76.          [15] *Ibid.*

students. State universities and liberal-arts colleges draw mainly from the middle-status levels. College students of lower status are found disproportionately in our teachers' colleges and municipal junior colleges.

Equally as significant as the status differences among institutions of higher learning is the relationship between the curricula choices of college students and the economic status of their families. In a study cited by Warner, an interesting pattern is discovered when the college courses are ranked according to the median income of the families of students pursuing each. (The study was first published in 1940, so it is to be expected that the average incomes are lower than those that would be found today.) It seems safe to generalize from Table 3 that status differences are often related to curriculum choices at the collegiate level.

*Table 3*—Parental Income and College Courses*

| Curriculum | Median parental income |
|---|---|
| Law | $2118 |
| Medicine and dentistry | 2112 |
| Liberal arts | 2068 |
| Journalism | 1907 |
| Engineering | 1884 |
| Teaching | 1570 |
| Commercial | 1543 |
| Nursing | 1368 |
| Industrial trades | 1104 |

* W. Lloyd Warner, Robert J. Havighurst, and Martin B. Loeb, *Who Shall Be Educated?* (New York, Harper and Bros., 1944), p. 72. Used by permission.

Concerning social status and the school system Warner concludes: "The evidence from the Yankee City schools demonstrates that the school reinforces the class standards in the general community, from an early period in the child's life through high school and into college."[16]

## SOCIAL MOBILITY THROUGH EDUCATION

So far we have shown only one side of the picture, how the school system operates to fit students into social positions similar to their parents'. But there are always a number of "exceptional" cases. Some boys and girls of lower status are placed in the higher sections of elementary school, choose the college-preparatory course in high school, and eventually graduate from college.[17]

Education as a means of social mobility operates differently for different children, however. It depends, in part, on how far the mobile person rises and from where he starts. Warner cites some case histories of successful social mobility which illustrate how education fits into the picture. One is

[16] *Ibid.*, p. 80.   [17] *Ibid.*, pp. 81–82.

the story of Martha, a lower-status girl from one of the poorest residential areas of Hometown. "When Martha first appeared at school," we are told, "she was a shy, thin blonde child, looking like a fresh version of her pale, prematurely old mother."[18] She soon attracted the attention of her teachers, however, by her seriousness, her willingness and ability to learn, and her persistence in doing simple tasks for them during recess. Her teachers generally reciprocated with extra help in school work, and some-times they gave her a book or two. As a result of her presumably pleasant experiences in grammar school, Martha had no misgivings about enrolling in high school.

Apparently Martha readily adjusted to high school and was very happy there. Despite the fact that her mother died and she was forced to keep the family going, she managed to remain in high school with the help of a scholarship arranged for by her teachers. Her school history was in marked contrast to her half-brothers and half-sisters who disliked school, were "kept back" at one time or another, and generally "grew to be unrecogniz-able among the other Boxtown children."[19] Finally, Martha graduated from high school and took a job as a domestic in a "respectable" home.

From the Browns, Martha learned "refined ways" and "some of the niceties of living room conduct." For quite a time she was happy with them, then she announced one day that she was going to visit her mother's people in Indiana. The real story was this. She had become enamoured of a magazine salesman who professed both his love for her and his intentions of marriage. Martha's letter informing him she was going to bear his child had been returned with the conclusive stamp, "not known at this address." She bore the child in a maternity home in a nearby city and six months later returned to Hometown where she obtained a job through the assist-ance of her former employer, Mrs. Brown.

Another chapter in Martha's life began the night she met Dick Johnson, a run-of-the-mill lawyer, at a dance sponsored by a women's organization.[20] A few months later they were married.

And so the shy little girl from the tarpaper shack in Boxtown settled down in a neat white house in a "nice" neighborhood. Throughout her story many factors stand out as having contributed to her successful mobility. Martha had ambition; she was determined and calculating as well. She knew what she wanted and soon learned how to satisfy her wants. But we are concerned here with how education fits into the story of our socially mobile heroine.

From the time that Martha started school it was apparent that she was not like the rest of "those Boxtowners." Her clean clothes and person belied her lower status. Nor did she *act* like the typical "slum kids." She took an interest in school, helped her teachers, and so on. Her teachers, in turn, were willing to put forth some extra effort when they discovered that

[18] *Ibid.*, pp. 88–89.          [19] *Ibid.*, p. 90.          [20] *Ibid.*, pp. 94–95.

she was interested in "getting ahead." It was through their help that she managed to graduate from high school, a somewhat rare accomplishment for the "typical Boxtowner." Her first job was found by one of her teachers. Certainly education alone was not responsible for Martha's rise in status but it is almost equally as certain that it played an important part.

Most cases in which education contributes to a rise in status are not so spectactular as that cited. The more frequent cases are those of children who are able to raise their status only a little above that of their parents.

# EDUCATION AND INCOME

*Patricia Cayo Sexton*

## ELEMENTARY SCHOOLS

These were the methods used in setting up the study:

First we found out the average family income levels in each school area. For this purpose, revised census data were used (the revisions having been made by a local newspaper). It was necessary to use average income figures, since median income data were not available. Although average figures are higher than median, they proved to be just as suitable for our purposes.

Schools with the same or very similar income levels were then grouped together. These school groups were ranked, from the lowest to the highest income group. As it turned out, there were twenty-six groups of schools with separate and distinct income levels.

Table 1 lists these income groups and also shows the number of schools included in each group.

In addition, this table shows the "major income groups." These major groups are simply divisions which have been made of the minor groups after every $2000 of income. Thus major group I includes all schools where family income is between $3000 and $5000. (Exception: major group IV includes all schools over $9000, the exception having been made in order to keep this group up to a workable size.)

The table is rather complicated, but it will be necessary to understand it completely in order to move on to other things.

### Success or Failure

*Achievement Scores.* Achievement tests show—perhaps better than any other measure, and certainly better than report-card marks—how much students are learning in school. It may be, of course, that students are learning many important things that do not show up on these achievement tests. And it may also be that these tests include some, perhaps many, detailed bits of information that students do not really need to know. Still, the tests give us a fairly good idea of how well students are coming up to the academic standards which the schools themselves have set.

*Table 1*—Income Groups

| Major income group | Minor income group | Average family income, 1957 | Number of elementary schools in each group |
|---|---|---|---|
| Group I | 1 | $3500 | 3 |
| | 2 | 3800 | 10 |
| | 3 | 4520 | 5 |
| | 4 | 4700 | 6 |
| | 5 | 4857 | 7 |
| Group II | 6 | 5300 | 9 |
| | 7 | 5500 | 6 |
| | 8 | 5689 | 9 |
| | 9 | 5800 | 13 |
| | 10 | 5900 | 11 |
| | 11 | 6000 | 18 |
| | 12 | 6200 | 2 |
| | 13 | 6312 | 11 |
| | 14 | 6500 | 21 |
| | 15 | 6695 | 7 |
| Group III | 16 | 7100 | 17 |
| | 17 | 7404 | 8 |
| | 18 | 7600 | 17 |
| | 19 | 7700 | 4 |
| | 20 | 7900 | 16 |
| | 21 | 8000 | 5 |
| | 22 | 8207 | 7 |
| | 23 | 8500 | 11 |
| Group IV | 24 | 9112 | 16 |
| | 25 | 9933 | 1 |
| | 26 | 11,055 | 3 |

The test used in Big City is the Iowa Achievement Test, a nationally standardized test which has been given to large numbers of students all over the country. It is claimed to be essentially a test of "skills" rather than simply of facts and information.

The test includes five divisions: language skills, work skills, arithmetic skills, reading and vocabulary. It will be noticed that three of these five divisions (more than half of the test) have directly to do with verbal skills: reading, vocabulary, and language skills. The other two sections (work skills and arithmetic skills) also depend on the ability to use language well, since the Iowa tests are written tests and students must be able to read them quickly and accurately in order to do well on them. This is the way it is with most written tests, if not all of them. They lean their whole weight on the student's ability to read and his skill at taking written tests.

In Big City the Iowa test was recently given to all students at three grade levels: fourth, sixth, and eighth; Table 2 shows the relationship between test scores and family income levels.

Table 2—Iowa Achievement Test Composite Scores

| Income | Income group | Fourth grade | Sixth grade | Eighth grade |
|---|---|---|---|---|
| $3000— | 1 | 3.10 | 5.30 | — |
| | 2 | 3.45 | 5.06 | 6.50 |
| | 3 | 3.63 | 5.32 | — |
| | 4 | 3.55 | 5.35 | 7.30 |
| | 5 | 3.46 | 5.28 | — |
| $5000— | 6 | 3.69 | 5.50 | 7.13 |
| | 7 | 3.55 | 5.40 | — |
| | 8 | 3.58 | 5.45 | — |
| | 9 | 3.70 | 5.57 | — |
| | 10 | 3.72 | 5.61 | 7.10 |
| | 11 | 3.62 | 5.54 | 7.50 |
| | 12 | 3.40 | 5.50 | — |
| | 13 | 3.80 | 5.59 | — |
| | 14 | 3.94 | 5.85 | 7.70 |
| | 15 | 3.88 | 5.75 | 7.44 |
| $7000— | 16 | 4.21 | 6.16 | 7.91 |
| | 17 | 4.28 | 6.38 | 8.00 |
| | 18 | 4.46 | 6.45 | 8.19 |
| | 19 | 4.53 | 6.60 | 8.27 |
| | 20 | 4.43 | 6.49 | 8.22 |
| | 21 | 4.48 | 6.68 | 8.37 |
| | 22 | 4.56 | 6.62 | 8.29 |
| | 23 | 4.60 | 6.80 | 8.44 |
| $9000— | 24 | 4.78 | 6.95 | 8.56 |
| | 25 | 4.90 | 7.30 | 9.10 |
| | 26 | 5.10 | 7.50 | 9.30 |

Key

4.00 = fourth grade
6.00 = sixth grade
8.00 = eighth grade

Note: Blank spaces indicate that there are no students in the elementary schools at the eighth-grade level in these income groups; instead these students are attending junior high schools.

Three things are immediately striking in this table:

One: All schools *above* $7000 income are achieving *above* grade level (with only one exception in the eighth grade). All schools *below* $7000 income are achieving *below* grade level.

Two: In general, achievement scores tend to go up as income levels go up.

Three: In the fourth grade, group 1 is achieving almost one whole year below grade level. At the same time, group 26 is achieving more than a year above grade level. Thus the highest income group is achieving at a level *two whole years* above the lowest-income group.

The scores in the table are "composite" scores; that is, they are the sum of the scores in the five separate areas: language skills, work skills, arithmetic skills, reading, and vocabulary.

The composite scores for the major income groups show that without exception achievement scores rise with family income levels (Table 3).

As we see, the difference between groups I and IV becomes greater with each passing grade. In the eighth grade the lowest-income students are almost two years behind the highest-income students. Some observations and explanations that have been made about this situation follow.

Jackson Toby: "School subjects are cumulative. Within a few years, the child from a deprived background is retarded in basic skills, such as reading, absolutely necessary for successful performance in the higher grades. This makes school still more uninteresting, if not unpleasant, and he neglects his work further. Eventually he realizes he can never catch up."(1)*

*Table 3*—Iowa Composite Scores, Major Income Groups

| Major income group | Fourth grade | Sixth grade | Eighth grade |
|---|---|---|---|
| I ($3000—) | 3.48 | 5.23 | 6.77 |
| II ($5000—) | 3.73 | 5.61 | 7.38 |
| III ($7000—) | 4.42 | 6.47 | 8.22 |
| IV ($9000—) | 4.84 | 7.05 | 8.67 |
| Difference between groups I and IV | 1.36 | 1.82 | 1.90 |

Joseph Kahl: "Social status was not an important factor in the earliest grades; it began to take effect around the fourth grade and had an increasing effect as each year passed."(2)

Howard Becker: "One resultant of this situation—in which less is expected of those teachers whose students are more difficult to teach—is that the problem becomes more aggravated in each grade, as the gap between what the children should know and what they actually do know becomes wider and wider."(3)

Only the composite scores of the Iowa test have been included in these tables. The scores in the five separate areas (language skills, work skills, arithmetic skills, reading, and vocabulary) give us valuable clues about the learning problems of lower-income students. They also tell us something about why upper-income students are so successful in school.

Relatively speaking (relative to their *composite* scores, that is), lower-income groups did well in arithmetic and work skills. Upper-income groups did poorly in these two "non-verbal" areas, relative to their composite scores. Upper-income groups, however, did very well on the reading section of the test, while lower-income groups did worse in reading than in the other areas.

The figures in Table 4 represent the difference between the scores in work skills, arithmetic, and reading in the fourth grade, and the total (or composite) scores. A minus sign before the number indicates that the score was below the composite score, a plus sign that it was above.

* Numerals in parentheses denote references at end of chapter.

The greatest difference in these scores is in reading; lower-income groups are unusually weak and upper-income groups are unusually strong in reading. Perhaps this explains why the over-all performance levels of lower-income groups on these tests is below that of upper-income groups.

Approaching these important Iowa scores from still another angle, we see them in perhaps an even more startling perspective.

Table 5 shows the percentage of schools that are above or below grade level in each income group. This table seems to speak for itself—clearly, perhaps eloquently.

### Table 4—Fourth-Grade Iowa Achievement Scores

| Major income group | Total work skills* | Total arithmetic* | Reading* |
|---|---|---|---|
| I ($3000—) | 0 | +.09 | −.14 |
| II ($5000—) | −.03 | +.07 | −.06 |
| III ($7000—) | −.09 | −.01 | +.07 |
| IV ($9000—) | −.19 | −.15 | +.20 |

* Relative to total *composite* score.

### Table 5—Schools Above and Below Grade Level, Fourth-Grade Composite Iowa Achievement Scores (Percentage of schools in each income group)

| | MAJOR INCOME GROUPS | | | |
| | Group I $3000— | Group II $5000— | Group III $7000— | Group IV $9000— |
|---|---|---|---|---|
| Schools below grade level | 96% | 82% | 5% | 0 |
| Schools a *half*-grade or more below grade level | 72 | 24 | 0 | 0 |
| Schools a *full* grade or more below grade level | 4 | 1 | 0 | 0 |
| Schools above grade level | 4 | 18 | 95 | 100 |
| Schools a *half*-grade or more above grade level | 0 | 1 | 49 | 89 |
| Schools a *full* grade or more above grade level | 0 | 0 | 1 | 22 |

*     *     *

### The "Gifted"-Child Program

Shortly after Sputnik and the sudden alarm about Soviet scientific development, Big City set up a special city-wide program for "gifted" children. Since Soviet schools do not segregate the "gifted" (except the artistically "gifted"), it is strange that concern about Soviet education should have finally put such a program into operation.

The fact is that a heated and protracted debate in the Soviet during the last few years ended in complete defeat for the scientists who proposed the segregation of the scientifically "gifted."

But perhaps Sputnik was simply an excuse for doing what some influential people in the schools wanted to do anyway.

The program was set up for the first year of high school (ninth grade) and 436 students were selected from among all eighth-grade students in the city. The selected students were then sent to special schools to take part in an intensified program of study, with the best possible facilities and teachers available for their instruction. One of the schools offering this program was a technical school; the other two were among the highest-income high schools in the city.

Selections were made on the basis of I.Q. and Iowa Achievement Test scores. All students had to have at least an A I.Q. rating, and all had to be achieving at least at grade level.

Table 6 shows the income groups from which these "gifted" children came. The pattern of selection is quite astonishing. Not one of the 436 students selected came from an income group below $5000! At the same time, 148 students came from the highest-income group, even though there were almost 10,000 fewer students in this group than in the below-$5000 group.

*Table 6*—Program for "Gifted" Children

| Income group | Number of "gifted" chosen | Rate per 10,000 students |
|---|---|---|
| I (below $5000) | 0 | 0 |
| II ($5000—) | 4 | 1.1 |
| III ($6000—) | 41 | 6.1 |
| IV ($7000—) | 120 | 20.1 |
| V ($8000—) | 123 | 36.0 |
| VI (over $9000) | 148 | 78.8 |

In this table, in order to provide a more complete picture of selections, major income group divisions have been made after every one thousand dollars of income rather than after every two thousand.

By income halves, the rate per 10,000 students was:

A (under $7000)    3.7
B (over $7000)    34.4

It appears that this "gifted"-child program is servicing upper-income groups almost exclusively. Perhaps this explains why so many spokesmen for upper-income groups have fastened upon "gifted"-child programs as a major solution to our educational problems. "Educate the elite," they say, "and forget about the others." The "elite," of course, often includes themselves and their own children.

\*    \*    \*

### Delinquency

Now that we are acquainted with the children who do well in school—the "gifted"—let us turn to the others, the failures, the problem children, the delinquents.

These are the children, as University of Chicago Professor Robert J. Havighurst has put it, whose "fathers are seldom or never at home and pay little attention to them when they are." These are the children who "come to school in the morning unwashed and in dirty clothes, sometimes without breakfast, often needing a doctor's care. They have trouble learning to read, the first thing in a long series of school difficulties. Their second disadvantage is verbal intelligence below average—a serious handicap in a society that places more and more reliance on verbal agility. Finally, the school fails this group. When they are very young the teacher too often passes over their problems. She is so busy with those who get along passably well that she may allow these three or four children in her class to drift. Eventually, at thirteen or fourteen, they are reading at the level of third or fourth graders but are in the seventh or eighth grade. At about this point they become troublesome problems to the school and grow more so in the ninth grade or the freshman year of high school."(4)

When such students become troublesome in Big City schools they may be put in an "Ungraded Class" or they may be sent to a special school for problem children. If they commit a crime they may end up in the Detention School, which is operated by Big City's board of education. Information was available only on enrollments in Ungraded Classes and the Detention School; the social class origins of students in the several special schools for problem children (sometimes euphemistically called trade or vocational schools) were not known.

The Ungraded Class: This special class is called "Ungraded" because it is made up of students from different grade levels, much like a one-room school. These classes are held in regular schools and children are put into them when they are too troublesome for regular classes.

The "Ungraded Class" is not for the retarded student but rather for the child who is considered a behavior problem. The retarded, the handicapped, and the sickly are often put in other special classes, which are also ungraded. The rate per 10,000 students in each income group in these "Ungraded Classes" was as follows.

| Income group | Students in ungraded classes |
|---|---|
| I ($3000—) | 37.7 |
| II ($5000—) | 14.8 |
| III ($7000—) | 4.2 |
| IV ($9000—) | 0 |

Detention School: The same pattern of distribution holds for admissions to the city's Detention School. This school is operated by the board of education and is attached physically to the juvenile court. Its function is to educate school-age youths who are serving brief sentences in the Detention Home, or who are being held pending trial or transfer to another institution.

Some of the students in this school (one out of eleven) are simply homeless youths who have committed no crime but are being held in the Detention Home (often with serious juvenile offenders) because there is *no other place in the city for them to live*—a brutal indication of the neglect of children who are in trouble and without means.

In analyzing admissions to the Detention School two types of divisions have been used: admissions from regular elementary schools, and admissions from regular schools *plus* admissions from the city's special schools for problem children.

The distribution of youths in the Detention School who were previously enrolled in a *regular* Big City school was (per 10,000 students in the schools of origin) as follows.

| Income group | Detention school students from regular schools |
|---|---|
| I ($3000—) | 31.3 |
| II ($5000—) | 21.7 |
| III ($7000—) | 6.9 |
| IV ($9000—) | 2.7 |

The enrollment in Detention School is topheavy with students from lower-income groups. But, when those students are included who were admitted to the school from the special schools for problem children, the distribution is even more unbalanced, as the following figures indicate.

| Income group | Detention school students |
|---|---|
| I ($3000—) | 85.7 |
| II ($5000—) | 40.2 |
| III ($7000—) | 6.9 |
| IV ($9000—) | 2.7 |

The rate of admissions in group I is *thirty-two times greater* than the rate in group IV. Quite the reverse of admission rates to the "gifted"-child program! While the "gifted" come almost exclusively from upper-income groups, the delinquents apparently come almost exclusively from lower-income groups.

Why is delinquency so much more common among lower-income youths? In our present state of at least semicivilized awareness, few people would claim that delinquents are "born that way." Delinquents are made, not born; that much is known.

But if the youths themselves and their "perverse natures" are not to blame, who or what *is*? Parents, neighborhood environment, schools, society? Perhaps all share in the blame, some more than others. But this study is concerned mainly with the schools and with the role they play in the training of youth, so we shall restrict ourselves to a brief consideration of school policies which may contribute to delinquency.

Item: The schools give better services and more of them to upper-income groups. Lower-income groups and their problems are generally neglected.

Item: The school "culture," being predominantly middle class, tends to alienate the lower-income child. Since he cannot share the values of the school, he is inclined to rebel against them in order to assert his own values.

Item: Because schools are often dominated by "female" attitudes, interests, and standards of behavior, lower-income boys (who seem to place a much higher value on masculinity than do upper-income boys) have difficulty finding a place in school life. Lower-income boys, judging by Detention School admissions, are heavily overrepresented in the delinquency statistics.

Item: The schools do not spend any real money on treatment for emotionally disturbed delinquents. Nor do they spend more than token sums on counseling services for lower-income, delinquency-prone youths. Nor do they make much effort to reach the parents of lower-income youths to help them or to consult with them about the behavior and welfare of their children. Upper-income parents, when their children are in trouble, can afford to pay for private care.

Item: Too many people in the schools are convinced (though usually only in private) that lower-income "troublesome" children are not worth very much and that the "gifted" students are the only ones that really matter. Too few people are concerned in any significant way about lower-income, delinquency-disposed youths, and too little time, attention, and money is being spent on the solution of their problems.


*          *          *


### Rewards and Punishments

Perhaps all human behavior is controlled by systems of rewards and punishments. We work because we know that if we do we will win favor in our family and in society, and, perhaps more important, that we will get a paycheck at the end of the week. We know, in other words, that we will be rewarded for our work.

Some of us, perhaps, refrain from injuring other people or stealing their property only because we know that, unless we do, we will probably be punished for our behavior.

While rewards and punishments both affect behavior, rewards are almost always preferable to punishments as a means of control. Rewards are positive and punishment negative. Rewards stimulate desire and voluntary participation, while punishment stimulates fear and often hatred, rebelliousness, and delinquency.

Moreover, prolonged punishment tends to discourage children and to undermine their confidence in themselves and in the world. In brief these excessive and continuous punishments tend either to destroy a child's self-esteem or to create in him a desire to destroy others. In either case the results are tragic for the individual and for society.

The schools therefore should aim at controlling, or disciplining, students by rewards rather than by punishment. Very often they do. The trouble is, however, that, though the schools offer many rewards, these rewards are not open to all students. In most cases the schools deliberately restrict the number of students who can win important rewards, limiting, for example, the percentage of students who can get A's or who can be admitted to special programs. Because of these restrictions a great many children are not able to win rewards. Moreover, many don't know what the rewards are worth and so do not *seek* to win them. The end result is that, in general, upper-income groups win most of the rewards and lower-income groups get most of the punishment.

School rewards are put too far out of the reach of lower-income students. They are not equipped to win rewards in competition with more privileged groups, and since there are not enough rewards to go around, they usually give up. In many cases their reaction is "I didn't want them anyhow, I'm not interested and I'm not even going to try." Often the reaction is anger, loss of confidence and self-esteem, and withdrawal from school life.

While a great many lower-income students pretend they do not want school rewards (knowing they can't get them anyway), many genuinely do not seek these rewards. They have little natural interest in them, and they have no knowledge of what the rewards are worth (what can you do with a gold star that's worth the effort of getting it?)

Perhaps the biggest prize and the most coveted reward offered by the schools is the possibility of a college education. Going to college usually means getting a better job than average, with higher pay, better working conditions, greater security and prestige, and a generally richer, fuller life.

Most lower-income children do not understand this. They cannot appraise the value of a college education nor do they understand that students must begin to prepare for college even in the elementary school grades. Perhaps even more to the point, they do not realize that a college education could ever be *possible* for them.

This is a reward, then, which they do not seek or respond to. Under present conditions they would be more likely to respond to an offer of candy or a trip to a ball game. They know that candy is good—but what good is a college education?

The truth is that lower-income children have never been "sold" on the value of a college education. Education beyond high school, in fact, is rarely put to them as a possibility. Until students come right up to the finishing line (at high-school graduation time) the importance or possibility of a continuing education is seldom even mentioned in lower-income schools. Upper-income students usually know about college through their family or friends, and they are driven to perform well in school in order to win this coveted prize, a college education (preferably at a prestige school). Lower-income students don't compete because they usually do not know what the prize is, what it is worth, or how one goes about getting it.

## SENIOR HIGH SCHOOLS

### The Selecting and Sorting Process

*Subjects Studied.* In elementary schools all students study essentially the same subjects; in high schools, because of the variety of curriculums and elective subjects, they tend to pursue different studies. This "open range" of subjects is the basis of the selecting and sorting process in the high school, a process which prepares some students for professional and managerial careers, some for white-collar and "vocational" jobs, and others for nothing much at all.

Subjects studied in high school tend to vary with social class position, as indicated in Table 7.

*Table 7*—Big City Enrollments in Various Subjects (percentage of total number of students in each income group)

| Income group | Health education | Home economics | Industrial education | Math | Music | Retailing |
|---|---|---|---|---|---|---|
| I | 61.0% | 19.4% | 29.1% | 43.7% | 23.5% | 2.3% |
| II | 62.2 | 17.0 | 39.0 | 32.8 | 17.3 | 3.1 |
| III | 57.2 | 11.7 | 34.5 | 56.7 | 14.6 | 1.8 |
| IV | 44.3 | 12.7 | 24.5 | 62.8 | 22.8 | 3.6 |
| V | 46.2 | 4.6 | 15.7 | 66.5 | 9.8 | 3.7 |
| A | 62.3 | 18.5 | 32.1 | 40.2 | 20.9 | 2.2 |
| B | 49.5 | 11.2 | 26.5 | 61.4 | 18.0 | 2.3 |

| Income group | Art | Business education | Family living | Foreign language | Science | ROTC |
|---|---|---|---|---|---|---|
| I | 11.2% | 73.2% | 4.3% | 12.5% | 45.5% | 7.1% |
| II | 8.4 | 88.4 | 2.8 | 16.7 | 50.7 | 7.7 |
| III | 10.3 | 67.4 | 2.9 | 24.1 | 44.1 | 4.6 |
| IV | 10.7 | 54.5 | 4.5 | 29.4 | 44.1 | 3.5 |
| V | 7.9 | 37.1 | 3.0 | 52.5 | 56.5 | 3.1 |
| A | 9.8 | 79.9 | 3.7 | 14.2 | 46.7 | 7.6 |
| B | 10.5 | 57.8 | 3.2 | 30.8 | 45.0 | 3.1 |

Among the significant items in this table are these: Enrollment in health education is 14.8 per cent heavier in group A (below $7000) than in group B.

The home economics enrollment varies in almost strict accordance with income, a big drop-off occurring in group V, where families are likely to hire domestic help to do home chores.

Industrial education enrollments also vary in accordance with income, except that enrollments in group I are unusually low. This lowest income group tends to be excluded from the skilled trades and also to have poor industrial education facilities in its schools.

Enrollment in business education (shorthand, typing, etc.) is unusually high in group II. Apparently many students in this group plan to work in secretarial and white-collar jobs.

Group V enrollments in foreign language are extremely high.

Enrollments in math are 21.2 per cent higher in group B than in group A.

Enrollments in science are higher in the lower-income groups than would be expected, but the highest enrollment percentage is found in group V.

Comparing the lowest and the highest income groups, we find that group I is heavily enrolled in health education, home economics, music, art, business education, family living, and ROTC. Group V, on the other hand, is heavily enrolled in "academic" subjects—foreign language, math, and science. The other income groups seem to be enrolled in subjects in accordance with their own special occupational destinations.

One of the liveliest and longest-standing disputes in education concerns high-school electives. Some argue that all students should study essentially the same subjects, much as they do in elementary school; others argue that students should have more electives and a broader range of choices. The pros and cons of the argument run about as follows.

*More Choice:* Students are all different; they have different interests, aptitudes, and occupational plans. Therefore they should all study different subjects. In Big City high schools, English, social studies and some math and science are now required of all students; this is enough "standardization," perhaps more than enough.

*Less Choice:* Students are more nearly equal in their aptitudes and potential than most people assume and should share more common experiences. Many have no "occupational plans" other than what counselors or teachers have suggested. Variety in curriculum offerings results in students' being "guided" into paths which perpetuate social class origins. Moreover, students find a wide range of electives more confusing than rewarding.

The argument is carried on in different ways and at various levels, usually does not involve an extremist either-or position. It is more a matter of the direction in which we should proceed from our present position— whether toward more electives or toward more "standardization."

Both sides argue persuasively but, at the present time in Big City, it appears that there are too many elective offerings and too much premature type-casting of students. Obviously culturally deprived students have different academic needs from those of culturally privileged students. But what they need, mainly, is more attention, not an inferior or "vocational" curriculum. Little evidence exists to support the assumption that these students cannot master "academic" subjects or that they are "fit only for manual labor and unskilled jobs." In so far as their high-school training is different from that of upper-income groups, it should be mainly training which repairs deficiencies in their backgrounds so that they can compete on more nearly equal terms with upper-income groups. It should go without saying, however, that the "academic" offerings, to upper- and lower-income groups alike, should be sensible, meaningful, and interesting. In Big City most students in low-income groups are being prepared for low-income jobs, as the following material on curriculum enrollments makes clear.

### Curriculum Enrollment

Not all school systems separate students into different curriculums in high school. A school system adjacent to Big City, which has a reputation for being one of the best in the country does not make curriculum separations at all, but simply guides students into various subjects according to their interests. This system is typical of many throughout the country.

Big City, however, makes these curriculum separations. All high schools in the city offer three distinct courses of study, or curriculums: college preparatory, general, and business-and-vocational. The business-and-vocational curriculum is designed for those students who plan to work in offices or in the trades, skilled or semi-skilled. The general curriculum is designed for those who do not seem to fit anywhere else. Most of the students who enroll in this curriculum will eventually become unskilled workers.

Since students are usually only fourteen when they enter high school (fifteen if they enter from junior high school), the decision to enter a fixed curriculum, with its occupational limitations, seems very premature. What is more, the decision seems unnecessary. A student who wants to prepare for college can take suitable courses without being put in a special curriculum and segregated from students in other curriculums. In fact, all students could be processed through high school on the assumption that they might some day want to go to college. At fourteen most students know little about college or about the occupational possibilities open to them. They are too young to make an informed and free choice of curriculums; as a consequence the choice is very heavily influenced, if not actually made in most cases, by teachers and counselors and, in upper-income groups especially, by parents.

Considering the accelerated tempo of technological change and the resulting changes in the nature of work assignments, it may be doubted that schools can successfully train students for particular work assignments. Certainly employers would prefer potential employees who are literate rather than partially trained in an already outmoded "vocational" skill. Consequently, it would seem wiser to concentrate on "general" education at all levels.

By the school's own standards, curriculum choices are very often misguided. Professor Samuel A. Stouffer says: "A nation-wide survey shows that among seniors in the top 30 per cent of ability, a third of the boys and nearly half of the girls were not, at the time of the survey, in college preparatory courses."(6) Curriculum assignments are often made on the basis of social class factors; again, Stouffer says: "It is known, for example, that even very able boys from working-class homes who fail to make really good grades in the seventh and eighth grades are seldom advised to take a college preparatory course. This is not equally true of boys from white-collar homes."

Indications of the influence of social class on curriculum assignments are shown in Table 8.

*Table 8*—Curriculum Enrollments (Percentage of students in each school)

| Income group | College preparatory | Business and vocational | General |
|---|---|---|---|
| 1 $5000— | 15% | 30% | 55% |
| 2 | 19 | 41 | 40 |
| 3 | 16 | 27 | 57 |
| 4 | 18 | 27 | 55 |
| 5 | 25 | 40 | 34 |
| 6 $6000— | 25 | 40 | 35 |
| 7 | 15 | 60 | 25 |
| 8 | 34 | 39 | 27 |
| 9 $7000— | 33 | 35 | 32 |
| 10 | 54 | 23 | 24 |
| 11 | 37 | 33 | 30 |
| 12 | 35 | 34 | 31 |
| 13 $8000— | 50 | 25 | 25 |
| 14 | 59 | 17 | 24 |
| 15 | 53 | 22 | 25 |
| 16 | 64 | 19 | 17 |
| 17 $9000— | 79 | 11 | 10 |
| I ($5000—) | 19 | 33 | 48 |
| II ($6000—) | 25 | 46 | 29 |
| III ($7000—) | 40 | 31 | 29 |
| IV ($8000—) | 57 | 21 | 23 |
| V ($9000—) | 79 | 11 | 10 |

Almost half the students in group I are enrolled in the free-floating general curriculum. This is five times the enrollment in group V.

Only 19 per cent of students in group I are enrolled in college preparatory; in group V, 79 per cent are enrolled.

Enrollments in all three curriculums follow a regular income pattern in the major income groups. The only exception is the unusually heavy enrollment of group II in the business and vocational curriculum.

In interpreting college-preparatory enrollments it should be kept in mind that many of the group V students enrolled in non-college curriculums are probably lower-income students who "happen" to attend this highest-income high school, and that well over half the students in lower-income groups drop out of school before graduation. Thus it cannot be said that 19 per cent of *all* group I students take college-preparatory courses. Counting drop-outs, and considering the curriculums the drop-outs would have been enrolled in, the percentage would be much lower than this.

What effect does enrollment in one or another of these curriculums have on a student's chances for social and academic success? One senior high-school girl quoted in Hollingshead's Elmtown study claimed that enrollment in the college-preparatory curriculum was the key to success in high school.

If you take a college preparatory course, you're better than those who take a general course. Those who take a general course are neither here nor there. If you take a commercial course, you don't rate. It's a funny thing, those who take college preparatory set themselves up as better than the other kids. Those that take the college preparatory course run the place.

I remember when I was a freshman mother wanted me to take home economics, but I didn't want to. I knew I couldn't rate. You could take typing and shorthand and still rate, but if you took a straight commercial course, you couldn't rate. You see, you're rated by the teachers according to the course you take. They rate you in the first six weeks. The teachers type you in a small school and you're made in classes before you get there. College prep. kids get good grades and the others take what's left. The teachers get together and talk, and if you are not in college prep. you haven't got a chance.(7)

From long experience with the situation, we suspect that approximately the same prestige attaches to the college-preparatory curriculum in Big City; those who are "in" are usually enrolled in college prep, and those who are "out" are usually in general or vocational curriculums.

Through the use of separate curriculums and other devices, including segregated groupings of various sorts, the schools establish a class system which is more rigid in its way than the class system in the outside world, since all students have curriculum and "ability" labels which segregate them from other students in a clearly defined rank order. In this school social system, the college preparatory curriculum is the upper class, the vocational curriculum the middle, and the general curriculum the lowest class. Within this class structure there is apparently little movement either up or down. Once assigned to a curriculum and status level in the high school, students seldom change to other curriculums and class categories.

\*     \*     \*

### Who Goes to College?

It seems safe to assume that all, or nearly all, students who were in the college-prep curriculum will at least *try* to go to college. Many who try will not succeed. And many who succeed will not last out the first semester.

College drop-outs among lower-income students are reported to be very high, though exact figures are not available. In the state university located inside Big City (attended at least in the freshman year by numbers of lower-income students) about *one-third* of all registered students drop out in their first year.(8) An undetermined number return and finish school.

No doubt large numbers of these drop-outs are lower-income students. A study conducted at the university shows "financial difficulties" to be the most common cause of drop-out, with "lack of interest in studies" coming in second.

Though drop-out, even when students later return, would seem to indicate serious problems of an economic, emotional, or academic nature, colleges seem as unconcerned about the problems involved as the public schools seem to be.

For those who can hang on, college attendance means a great deal—good jobs, higher pay, an enriched life, and higher status. In a sense, college attendance is the most important element in class structure. Indeed, Vance Packard advances the theory in *The Status Seekers* that college attendance is now the most decisive factor in separating the "Haves" from the "Have Nots" in modern society.(9)

The only relevant information available in Big City about college attendance had to do with the number of students in Big City "requesting transcripts for college," and the educational and occupational plans of high-school graduates.

The percentage of students requesting transcripts of their high-school credits in order to apply for college admission was as follows.

| | |
|---|---|
| I ($5000—) | 22.8% |
| II ($6000—) | 34.0 |
| III ($7000—) | 46.3 |
| IV ($8000—) | 60.6 |
| V ($9000—) | 81.0 |
| A (below $7000) | 27.0 |
| B (above $7000) | 57.4 |

According to these figures there is a difference of 58.2 per cent between groups I and V in the percentage of students applying for college. The percentage figure in group B (the upper-income half) is more than twice as great as in group A.

Responses to a survey of Big City high-school graduates about their future plans revealed the information shown in Table 9. (Some students had no plans and checked only the "Further Counseling Wanted" category; some checked "Job Promised" as well as other categories.)

It may be seen in this table that the percentage of students planning to go to college "immediately" increases as income increases, with a great forward leap in group V. The percentage in group V is more than three times greater than in group I.

In group I, 60 per cent of the graduates feel they need further counseling from the schools—almost twice the percentage found in group V.

*Table 9*—After Graduation

| Income group | College immediately | Work—college later | Work permanently | Job promised | Further counseling wanted |
|---|---|---|---|---|---|
| I ($5000—) | 27% | 36% | 26% | 5% | 60% |
| II ($6000—) | 32 | 18 | 41 | 13 | 57 |
| III ($7000—) | 43 | 14 | 33 | 11 | 47 |
| IV ($8000—) | 57 | 12 | 26 | 18 | 53 |
| V ($9000—) | 87 | 5 | 6 | 23 | 35 |
| A (below $7000) | 28 | 29 | 32 | 8 | 59 |
| B (above $7000) | 55 | 14 | 26 | 16 | 48 |

Almost one out of every four graduates in group V already has a job promised, though they have not yet started college. In this group, 92 per cent of the graduates plan to enter college either now or later. The percentage in the other major income groups with plans for college *now or later* is:

| Income group | Percentage planning for college |
|---|---|
| I ($5000—) | 63% |
| II ($6000—) | 50 |
| III ($7000—) | 57 |
| IV ($8000—) | 69 |
| V ($9000—) | 92 |

It is most interesting that 63 per cent of all graduates in group I *want* to go to college at some time or another. Possible explanations for this might be:

One: High-school graduates in group I are much more highly selected than those at other income levels. Drop-outs in this lowest-income group are so heavy that only unusually serious and determined students remain in school long enough to graduate, the social and economic pressures to leave school being what they are in the lower-income environment. We could expect, then, that many of those who graduate from high school would have enough interest in education at least to *want* to go to college.

Of course most of those in the "Work—College Later" category will probably never get to college. Their desire to go may in fact represent quite unrealistic job and educational aspirations, which may lead to final disappointment.

Two: It is so difficult for students in this lowest-income group to find jobs, much less desirable jobs, that going to college is often the only way out for them. Some evidence of the job scarcity for lower-income youths is found in the "Job Promised" column of Table 9. While a total of 62 per cent of group I students plan to work after high-school graduation, only 5 per cent have jobs promised; at the same time 11 per cent of students in the highest-income groups plan to work immediately, yet 23 per cent of them have jobs promised.

Three: Related to point two, very low-income groups are often denied job opportunities because of racial and class factors. For example, either because of prejudice or lack of "know how," individuals from these groups rarely enter business or the skilled trades. Often the best way for them to get "better jobs" is through education for the professions or white-collar and government service.

Again an illustration can be taken from the "Job Promised" column. Jobs are usually promised in the business or trade of the father or other relatives. The fact that few jobs have been promised to group I students indicates that they probably do not have relatives in business or trade and that these avenues of escape tend, therefore, to be closed to them.

Why does college attendance (or the likely prospect) vary in almost strict accord with family income? All the social class factors discussed in this study provide possible answers to this question. Those which may be especially pertinent are:(10)

One: College is expensive, even for many upper-income families. For lower-income families the costs are usually prohibitive. The average annual expense of college students (unmarried undergraduates, 1959–60) is $1550. Of this amount, most is paid out of the parents' pockets— $950, or about 61 per cent of the total. Students themselves contribute an average of only $360 toward college expenses. Scholarships provide only $130, on the average—or about 8 per cent of the total costs. Perhaps because college is largely a parental expense, and a costly one, college students are recruited mainly from upper-income families, those who can afford to pay. Among families above the $10,000 income bracket, 95 per cent with children under ten expect them to attend college. This bracket now sends 70 per cent of its eighteen-to-nineteen-year-olds to college. Among families earning $5000 to $7500, 80 per cent aspire to college, and only 40 per cent get there. In the lowest-income bracket, among families earning less than $3000 a year, 40 per cent would like to attend, and only 20 per cent manage to do so. Undoubtedly college drop-outs among this 20 per cent are numerous, judging by the heavy drop-outs in state colleges attended by lower-income students.

Often lower-income students will be admitted to college, yet fail to appear at registration time. In Big City, over *one-fourth* of all students admitted to the state university in the city failed to enroll in classes, either there or elsewhere. Study revealed that, on an average, this vanished group had somewhat better admission qualifications than those finally admitted. "Thus they had good potentiality for college work. *Inability to finance collegiate work* proved to be a significant factor for a large majority of them."

\*    \*    \*

Of course scholarships are available—some half-million of them—but they tend to go to higher-income students. Those from lower-income families either do not meet the standards, do not apply, or cannot afford to go to college, even with scholarship money.

At no college subscribing to the College Scholarship Service (mostly high-prestige colleges) do as many as half the scholarship winners come from the neediest half of our nation's population.

It is estimated that the median income of the scholarship holder's family is between $6000 and $7000 a year, as compared with a national median of $5000 per family. The figures, interestingly, are largely estimates, since very few colleges keep family income records.

A recent study of two hundred selected colleges puts the figures for applicants even higher. According to this report, the median family income of scholarship *applicants* was almost $7500. Nearly one-third had incomes over $8000, and one out of ten had incomes over $12,000. At the same time, only one out of ten applicants had incomes below $4000. Thus lower-income students are unlikely even to make application for scholarship money.

The *New York Times* comments about these figures: "Admissions officers are much concerned over what they regard as the serious implications of these figures, for the colleges, for the nation's youth, and for the national welfare. These figures, some of them say, reflect forces inducing a kind of collegiate segregation, which will be accentuated as college fees rise, as they are continuing to do."(11)

According to the director of the College Scholarship Service, Rexford G. Moon, Jr., the nation is now losing the talents of 150,000 able youths a year from the lower-income levels, or three quarters of all the able students who for one reason or another do not continue their education beyond high school.(12)

Dean Munro of Harvard wants colleges to "stop making scholarship awards for embellishment purposes to well-off students." He also thinks that college representatives should explore the whole field. "Why should three hundred college representatives visit New Trier High School each year and hardly any, except coaches, visit the big downtown Chicago high school only twenty miles away?" At the present time, of the nation's 26,500 high schools, a mere 5000 produce 82 per cent of all college students.

The big need, Munro says, is for coordination of the college talent hunters. Plaut of the National Scholarship Service and Fund for Negro Students has recently urged a national program, costing up to $100 million, for developing the neglected talents of Negro and other underprivileged children.

Of course, college admission is easier now than it used to be for lower-income students, and class distinctions are not as exaggerated as they once were. Today, including all part-time students, 20.6 per cent[2] of all youths

---

[2] This figure represents a careful recalculation by Bernard Berelson (*The Graduate School in the United States*) of previous estimates which have generally overstated college enrollment, some putting it as high as 40 per cent of those of college age. Comparable figures from other countries are not available. Indications are, however, that enrollment in the USSR is roughly comparable, and that the rate of increase there is more rapid.

eighteen to twenty-one are in colleges and universities in this country. The doors of higher education have opened somewhat and permitted a relatively small inflow of the underprivileged.

In John Adams' day at Harvard matters were worse. Students were graded according to family social standing, and if the student's father was a man of power and position, the son was ranked first and given the head seat at the table, the best room, the first place in academic processions, the privilege of helping himself first in the commons.

Harvard today is not that bad, but in all honesty it's not very much better. The class distinctions are simply less obvious and objectionable. Though Harvard, rich and lavish with its scholarships, is perhaps the most "democratic" of the Ivy Leaguers, only 18 per cent of its *scholarship* students come from families with less than $4000 income (not much below the national median).

Two: Lower-income students usually lack even the crudest information about such simple matters as how to prepare for college, which college to choose, how to get in, how to get along, once in, how to fill out acceptable applications. They don't have the "know how" of the upper-income student. Their parents and friends, typically, have not been to college or even inside a college classroom. Thus they cannot give directions or show them the way. The upper-income student, on the other hand, learns the way from his parents, who have usually been there before. He is headed in the right direction early in his life, equipped with a rather complete blueprint of the route to school success.

The lack of "know how" among lower-income groups was recently illustrated in the author's own experience. A semi-skilled factory worker consulted the author about the possibility of his son's going to college. He wanted to know how his son should go about applying, whether he should write or call, to whom he should talk, what schools there were in the area, etc.

The questions were posed in such a simple and puzzled sort of way that it seemed almost as though he were inquiring about how to get to the moon, the distances and the difficulties of the trip appearing to be equally great. The upper-income parent would probably know the answers to these questions, and a great deal more, out of his own experience. And not only would he be able to guide his son into college admittance, he would also be able to counsel him about the hundreds of problems that trouble students during the course of their college careers. The lower-income student who manages somehow to get into college often hangs on there by a thin thread; perhaps more often than not the thread breaks and the student drops out in his first semester. The pace of college life is fast, and human relations are very impersonal; if a student does not know the way and has no one to show him, the thread will often break at the first sign of strain. As we have mentioned, the drop-out rate among lower-income

college students is reported to reach disaster proportions during the first
semester of attendance. These students don't know how to go to college;
their failure to get along is so tragic for them and so wasteful of human
resources (not to mention school resources) as to demand intensive study
and attention.

### References to *Education and Income*

1. Toby, Jackson, "Orientation to Education as a Factor in the School Maladjustment of Lower-Class Children," *Social Forces*, **35**(3), March, 1957.
2. Kahl, Joseph A., "Educational and Occupational Aspirations of Common-
   Man Boys." *The Harvard Educational Review*, **23**(3), Summer, 1953.
3. Becker, Howard S. "Social Class Variations in the Teacher-Pupil Relationship." *Journal of Educational Sociology*, **26**(8), April, 1952.
4. Havighurst, Robert J., "Knowledge of Class Status Can Make a Difference."
   *Progressive Education*, **27**(4), February, 1950.
5. Bond, Horace Mann, "The Productivity of National Merit Scholars by
   Occupational Class," *School and Society*, **85,** September 28, 1957.
6. Stouffer, Samuel A., "The Student—Problems Related to the Use of
   Academic Ability." *The Identification and Education of the Academically
   Talented Student in the American Secondary School*, The Conference
   Report, NEA, February 1958.
7. Hollingshead, August B., *Elmtown's Youth*, New York, John Wiley, 1949.
8. Smith, Margaret Ruth, "A Study of First Year Drop Outs" (entered
   September 1953).
9. Packard, Vance, *The Status Seekers*, New York, McKay, 1959.
10. "How People Pay for College," Ann Arbor, Michigan, Survey Research
    Center, 1940.
11. *The New York Times*, April 5, 1959.
12. Moon, Rexford G., Jr., *The New York Times*, April 5, 1959.

# A STUDY OF HIGH SCHOOL DROPOUTS

*Robert J. Havighurst, Paul H. Bowman, Gordon P. Liddle,*
*Charles V. Matthews, and James V. Pierce*

It is clear that progress through school is related to social status, ability, personal and social adjustment, and personal motivation for education. These factors are all interrelated, and therefore it is not possible to say what factors are most truly causes and what ones are results or consequences of these causes.

It is important, though, to recognize the fact that dropping out of school before high-school graduation under present conditions in River City is a sign of general maladjustment to society and is an unfavorable prognosis for the future. Whereas dropping out of school to go to work was a normal thing in 1900, and even as late as 1930 a young person who quit school for a job might be taking a solid step forward toward adulthood, this is seldom the case in 1960.

A special study of dropouts in River City has made this conclusion abundantly clear. This study was planned to include every dropout except the few who completed the twelfth grade but did not get enough credits to win a high-school diploma.

## Numbers and Ages of Dropouts

Of 432 students for whom educational career records are complete, 35 per cent (152) did not graduate from high school. There were 138 who dropped out before completing the twelfth grade, and 14 others who finished the grade but did not earn a high-school diploma.

Thirty per cent of the dropouts left school in the first six months after their sixteenth birthday. Forty-six per cent left school after 16½ years of age. This leaves 24 per cent who quit school before the legal school-leaving age of 16. One student dropped out when in the seventh grade, several in the eighth grade, and the largest number when in the ninth grade. About equal numbers dropped out of the tenth, eleventh, and twelfth grades.

Because 24 per cent dropped out before reaching the legal school-leaving age of 16, some explanation is needed. This number did not include any who quit school in June but reached their sixteenth birthday before the following September. They were all counted as age 16 on the dropout roll. About two-thirds of the "illegal" dropouts were girls. One of them was 14 when she dropped out due to pregnancy. Several were married before they were 16, and dropped out at the time of marriage, frequently because they were pregnant at the time. The school authorities generally regarded obvious pregnancy as a good reason for dropping out of school, regardless of the age of the girl. One girl moved out of town and did not enter school in the town to which she moved. Another had illness in the family and dropped out in order to help at home. A few said they didn't like school and managed to stay out of sight of the truant officer until they were 16. This was the usual history of the boys who dropped out before age 16. These boys were generally in so much trouble at school that the school authorities tacitly accepted the fact that the boys were not in school. None of the early dropout boys was married during the first year out of school, and only 6 of 13 boys found a steady job. Nine of them had been arrested for various degrees of delinquency.

. . . Forty per cent of the dropouts came from the lowest quartile of intelligence, as against 13 per cent of the stayins. However, there were 6 per cent of dropouts from the top quartile of intelligence.

Social class differences are evident. . . . Forty-six per cent of the dropouts came from the lowest social class, compared with 13 per cent of the stayins.

It is clear that low intelligence and low socioeconomic status are important factors in dropping out of school, but it is also clear that these factors alone are not adequate explanations. For instance, although some 70 students of the lower social class dropped out of school, yet about 40 did stay in school until high-school graduation. Most of the Class A and B students finished high school, but one in seven dropped out. Consequently additional factors that influence dropping out of school were sought by comparing the dropouts with a control group matched as far as possible for intelligence and social class.

Since it was known that dropping out of school was associated with below average intelligence and social status, it would not be useful to compare dropouts with those who stayed in school unless these particular factors could be kept constant. That is, a comparison group of boys and girls who stayed in school was needed, and it was important that this comparison group have the same socioeconomic status and intelligence as the dropout group. However, it is not easy to find as many boys and girls of lower socioeconomic status and lower mental ability who stay in school as the number who drop out.

There were 138 dropouts; that is, boys and girls who quit school before completing the twelfth grade. The ideal comparison group would have been a group of equal size in which for every dropout there was a boy or girl of the same sex, quartile in I.Q., and social class. Thus the two groups, dropouts and control stayins, would consist of matched pairs. A total of 85 boys and girls were found who could match 85 dropouts on these factors. Beyond that some more were added who matched the remaining dropouts on sex and *either* intelligence or social class, but not both. Eventually the control group consisted of 127 people of whom 111 were matched with dropouts for I.Q., 101 for social class, with 85 appearing in both the I.Q. control and the social-class control groups. Comparisons could then be made between dropouts and the total control group of 127, or one or the other of the two partial control groups.

### Comparisons of Dropouts with Their Control Group

The dropouts have been compared with their control group in five areas of experience: personal-social adjustment, attitudes and values, finances, school experiences, and area of residence. These comparisons were based on data in the files of the study and on information determined from an interview made four to six months after the dropout had left school, and parallel interviews with the members of the control group.

*Personal-social Adjustment.* It will be remembered that the California Test of Personality, given in the sixth grade, showed that those who stayed longer in school had higher scores. But when the dropouts are compared with the control group of the same social class and intelligence, this difference largely disappears. At the sixth grade, there is not a reliable difference between the two groups. However, at the tenth grade the stayins were reliably higher than the dropouts on the California Psychological Inventory, which is designed to measure personal-social adjustment in an indirect manner. This difference was present in spite of the fact that the earliest and more maladjusted half of the dropouts were not in school and did not take this test.

*Attitudes and Values with Respect to Education and Work.* In the interviews the boys and girls were asked why they dropped out or stayed in school, as the case might be. The dropouts give the following major reasons:

Negative experiences and negative attitudes in school—47 per cent
Poor social adjustment—18 per cent
Preference or need for work—16 per cent
Marriage with or without pregnancy—9 per cent

In contrast, the control group gave the following reasons for wanting to stay in school:

Education is needed for getting a job or getting into college—50 per cent
Education is valued for itself—30 per cent
Parental guidance or pressure—13 per cent

Apparently the control group of stayins was more concerned about holding a job and making a vocational success, and they saw education as a means to this end. The control group also showed more positive attitudes to work through their work records. Eighty per cent of controls and 40 per cent of dropouts held part-time jobs while they were in school. Of the controls, 40 per cent had held their jobs for more than a year, whereas only 2 per cent of dropouts had held jobs that long while still in school. The dropouts apparently had ill-defined goals for themselves, or wanted to achieve these goals without effort. But their experience after dropping out of school was generally disappointing. Despite speaking to an interviewer who was markedly permissive, and to whom they frequently expressed great hostility toward school, 56 per cent said they wished they had stayed in school.

Parental attitudes were also involved in the distinction between dropouts and control-group members. The boy or girl was asked how his parents felt about his dropping out or staying in school. The interview generally took place in the home, and the interviewer could often obtain this information directly from a parent. Of the control group, 68 per cent of the parents strongly insisted that their children remain in school. Among the dropouts only 13 per cent of the parents opposed their dropping out. Thirty-four per cent of the dropouts reported their parents to be indifferent about school; only 7 per cent of the controls indicated parental indifference. Six per cent of the dropouts actually were urged to drop out of school by their parents.

*Financial Factors.* When the dropouts were interviewed six months or more after they had dropped out of school, only 5 per cent gave clear evidence of having to leave school for financial reasons. Seventy-five per cent of them stated quite clearly that there was no financial necessity for leaving school. Furthermore, it was possible to compare the dropouts with their socioeconomic controls who were still in school on the extent to which they contributed to their own support through jobs, payment for board and room, clothing purchases, and the like. When the two groups were compared on these items, it was found that 70 per cent of the controls were mainly self-supporting, whereas 55 per cent of the dropouts were mainly self-supporting.

The two groups could also be compared on ownership of an automobile. At the time of the interview 26 per cent of dropouts and 11 per cent of controls owned cars. It seems that the dropouts were less thrifty and industrious than the controls, although they had much more time free for earning money.

*School Experiences.* By any criterion that is used the dropouts had less successful, more frustrating experiences in their school lives. Their difficulties at school began in the first and second grade and continued throughout their school careers. In either the academic or the extra curricular fields the story is the same.

For example, there were four times more dropouts than controls retarded at least one year in school. None of the controls failed of promotion after the fifth grade, while some dropouts have failed each year. In elementary school 4 per cent of the dropouts were in the upper third of their classes in school marks against 19 per cent of the controls; this was just reversed in the lowest third of the class marks. In high school the dropouts again made much poorer grades. None of the dropouts was in the upper quartile of the class in grade-point average; 18 per cent of the controls scored in the top quarter. Of the dropouts, 70 per cent were in the lowest quarter against 8 per cent of the controls. Half of all the grades made

*Table 1*—Comparison of Dropouts and Controls on Reading Achievement

| Per cent of pupils | 1ST GRADE | | | 4TH GRADE | | | 7TH GRADE | | |
| | Drop out | Intell. control | Soc. class control | Drop out | Intell. control | Soc. class control | Drop out | Intell. control | Soc. class control |
|---|---|---|---|---|---|---|---|---|---|
| Reading scores at or above grade level | 40 | 50 | 53 | 56 | 67 | 73 | 20 | 36 | 53 |
| Reading scores below grade level | 60 | 50 | 47 | 44 | 33 | 27 | 80 | 64 | 47 |

by the dropouts in high school were D's and F's (failing grades), and only one per cent were A's; the A's were almost all in music and physical education. In reading-achievement scores the controls were consistently higher at every grade level. Table 1 shows that both dropouts and controls improved somewhat in their reading scores through the fourth grade, but then both dropped sharply at the seventh grade. This apparent change may be an artifact of the tests that were used.

Attendance at school is an indicator of general adjustment to school. From kindergarten through seventh grade the dropouts were absent about 20 per cent more than their controls. Then, in the eighth and ninth grades the absences of the future dropouts increased rapidly while the absences of controls decreased sharply. The future dropouts were absent an average of 22 days during the eighth and ninth grades; their controls were absent an average of 8.5 days. It seems clear that the future dropouts were already dropping out "in their own minds" a couple of years before they dropped out physically.

Dropouts were equally unsuccessful in extracurricular activities. Only one dropout held any school government office, and controls were about twice as active as dropouts in all activities. The major participation of dropouts was in attending athletic events and dances. These experiences led 67 per cent of the dropouts to express strong dislike for school as did 12 per cent of the controls. The majority of the dropouts were thus finding school to be a very frustrating place which they would like to avoid as much as possible.

Some attitudes toward extracurricular activities are shown in the following excerpts from interviews with dropouts.

"Were you interested in the Girls Athletic Association or the Y Teen group?"
"No, I wasn't."
Sister: "She went down to the Y.M. for swimming."
"What did you think of the social life at junior high school, did you care at all for the dances?"
"I didn't know that they had them."
"Did you go to any of the games?"
"No."
"Do you feel that you were generally a part of the junior high school as far as the activities were concerned?"
"No, I don't. I went to one dance and stayed for ten minutes. I never went to another one."
"Do you feel like you were happy in junior high school?"
She laughed. "Just before school started and after school was out."

In spite of their frustrations in school, the experience of a few months out of school made many of the dropouts doubt the wisdom of their "decision." They were asked, "Is it better out of school or in school?" "If you had it to do over, would you go on or drop out?" The quotations that follow give something of the doubt and uncertainty of these young people.

No. I wasn't expecting to quit when I was sixteen. I was just not getting along well out there and then they wrote that note home. I think that if I had been getting along better, I would have kept on going to school. I don't know though. I like the job a lot better. I have had this same job since I left school. . . . I don't know. It would have been all right to go on in school if things were going all right. But if things weren't going all right I suppose I would quit again. If I'd been successful in school I would have stayed on."

"It just seemed to me that all the other kids were out playing while I was in school. They said to me, 'Stay in.' I said, 'You found out the hard way, let me find out the hard way. Let me find out for myself.' It's the same way about getting married. I always say, 'Let me get married and find out the hard way if it's no good . . .' "

"I couldn't get along with teachers. That was the main reason. I really didn't like any of them. . . . In a way it seems better (being out of school) and in a way it don't. When you are in school, at least, you have some place to go and pass the time."

"If I had it to do over again, I am sure I would go on."
"Why do you say that?"

"Well, really, I was thinking about the vacation I would have here but I find it really is not a vacation. It is a lot of work keeping a house." Here she shook her head and continued. "And when the baby comes, it will be a lot more. One baby is all I want."

*Residential Area.* A family of low social status generally lives in an area of similar families, but occasionally such a family lives in a neighborhood where the families are generally of higher status, and the children therefore attend a school with children of generally higher status. In this situation, the children may tend to follow the educational values of the neighborhood and to stay in school.

. . . There is a tendency for dropouts to live in the lower social class areas, whereas their socioeconomic controls live in areas with more middle-class neighbors.

## CONCLUSIONS

School provides the only pathway to adolescence in River City, and high school is the only easily travelled route through adolescence to adulthood. For the third of River City youth who do not finish high school the way to adulthood is not an easy one. . . . The dropouts have the greatest difficulty in growing up successfully. They are the most vulnerable to delinquency. They get the poorest jobs, if they get jobs at all. They have the most trouble with marriage. The churches see very little of them.

These boys and girls are somehow alien to the society in which they are trying to live. The evidence is clear that they start school with cultural handicaps, they have inadequate help and encouragement from their parents, and they accumulate a record of failure and frustration in school which drives them out of school at the earliest possible date. Early failure in school starts a process of alienation from society that leads them into delinquency and other forms of adolescent maladjustment.

With its present type of program, the school serves these children poorly. As late as a generation ago this group had the alternative of juvenile work leading to adult competence. Now this alternate pathway has narrowed and seems to be disappearing. The school is challenged to create a new and more satisfactory way to adulthood for a third of our youth.

In contrast to the dropouts we find another third of River City youth moving through high school and on to college and other post-high-school institutions with relative success. For them the educational system is working well.

As early as the sixth grade it is possible to discover the probable dropouts with considerable accuracy, and also to discover those who will go farthest in school. If these subgroups are recognized and treated wisely it should be possible to make the school system into a more effective institution for helping the various types of children to grow up successfully.

# TEACHERS IN CHICAGO SCHOOLS

*Robert J. Havighurst*

This chapter will report some of the results of a study of classroom teachers made with a questionnaire. . . . This chapter will concentrate on the attitudes of teachers toward the job of teaching in Chicago schools, and the sources of satisfaction and dissatisfaction in their work.

The questionnaire was given to all teachers below the rank of principal. Thus a number of people who are not now teaching a regular classroom were included, such as counselors, adjustment teachers, assistant principals, nurses, psychologists, librarians, physical education teachers, and teachers of special education classes. However, most of the analyses and tables in this chapter are limited to regular classroom teachers. This category included 75 per cent of the teachers working in elementary schools, and 64 per cent of those working in high schools. In the case of the high schools, the teachers of vocational and shop subjects were placed in a separate category, which includes 16 per cent of all high school teachers. Their responses to the questionnaire are not included in most of the tables, but their responses were similar, for the most part, to those of teachers of the academic subjects. The limitation of the analyses to regular classroom teachers has the advantage of concentrating on the main body of teachers and bringing out some things about their attitudes that would tend to be obscured if all the teachers were lumped together.

The most general facts about the teachers are given in Table 1. The majority are women, comprising 86 per cent of elementary school teachers and 53 per cent of high school teachers. The teachers with the most

From *The Public Schools of Chicago: A Survey for the Board of Education of the City of Chicago* by Robert J. Havighurst (Chicago: The Board of Education of the City of Chicago, 1964), pp. 338–347. Reprinted by permission of the author.

554

experience are mainly women. Even in the high schools, where the total group is almost evenly divided between men and women, 70 per cent of the teachers with 16 years of experience or more are women. Men are most strongly represented in the group with three to 15 years of teaching experience. Furthermore, it is clear that the proportions of men have been increasing since World War II, especially in the elementary schools. About 21 per cent of the teachers are "substitutes" who are teaching fulltime. That is, they have state teachers' certificates but have not yet passed the examination for a certificate in the Chicago system. Most of these people do pass the Chicago examination after a few months or a few years, if they stay in Chicago. The questionnaire was not given to day-to-day substitutes.

It is on the whole an experienced group, 68 per cent of the elementary school teachers and 67 per cent of high school teachers having six years or more of teaching experience. With respect to their training, about half of

*Table 1*—Years of teaching experience and sex of teachers

(Percentages, unless otherwise stated)

| Years of experience | ELEMENTARY SCHOOLS | | | HIGH SCHOOLS | | |
|---|---|---|---|---|---|---|
| | Male | Female | Number | Male | Female | Number |
| 1–2 | 16 | 84 | 801 | 41 | 59 | 428 |
| 3–15 | 18 | 82 | 2,738 | 59 | 41 | 1,243 |
| 16+ | 5 | 95 | 1,581 | 30 | 70 | 689 |
| Total | 14 | 86 | 5,120 | 47 | 53 | 2,360 |

the elementary school teachers were trained in Chicago Teachers College and about half in liberal arts colleges and universities. Among high school teachers, 75 per cent were educated in a liberal arts college or university, while most of the rest went to Chicago Teachers College.

## RELATIONS OF AGE, SEX, AND TEACHING EXPERIENCE TO SOCIOECONOMIC AREA OF THE SCHOOL

One of the most difficult problems of a big city school system is to equalize the quality of teaching among the many different types of schools. Teachers have preferences, and they have a right to consideration for their preferences. Teachers with the most service experience generally have some rights and priorities due to seniority.

Wherever there are some schools that teachers think are preferable to other schools in a school system, there will be a tendency to gravitate toward the preferred schools. Reasons for a school being preferred are generally the following: it is near a teacher's home; it has a principal whom the teacher likes, its neighborhood and its pupils are attractive. There are also other motives that influence a teacher to choose one or another type of school. A teacher may want a different kind of school than he has had in the past, for the sake of greater professional experience; or he may want a school where he thinks he can be of most service to people.

The net effect of these motives of teachers, together with the rules set up by the school administration regarding assignment and transfer, and

*Table 2*—Characteristics of teachers related to socioeconomic area of school
(Percentages, unless otherwise stated)

| | *Upper- or middle-class* | *Mixed middle- and working-class* | *Stable working-class* | *Lower-class or slum* | *Total* |
|---|---|---|---|---|---|
| | | A. *Elementary schools* | | | |
| *Sex* | | | | | |
| Male | 10 | 9 | 12 | 19 | 14 |
| Female | 90 | 91 | 88 | 81 | 86 |
| *Age* | | | | | |
| 20–25 | 3 | 9 | 13 | 19 | 14 |
| 26–30 | 7 | 11 | 15 | 21 | 16 |
| 31–40 | 19 | 23 | 22 | 32 | 27 |
| 41–50 | 26 | 21 | 18 | 15 | 18 |
| 51–65 | 45 | 34 | 30 | 13 | 24 |
| 66+ | 1 | 1 | 2 | 1 | 1 |
| *Experience* | | | | | |
| 1 year | 2 | 5 | 7 | 11 | 8 |
| 2 | 3 | 4 | 7 | 12 | 8 |
| 3–5 | 6 | 12 | 16 | 26 | 19 |
| 6–15 | 31 | 36 | 32 | 36 | 35 |
| 16+ | 58 | 44 | 38 | 16 | 31 |
| *Number* | 264 | 1,537 | 912 | 2,409 | 5,122 |
| Per cent of total | 5 | 30 | 18 | 47 | 100 |
| | | B. *High schools* | | | |
| *Sex* | | | | | |
| Male | 47 | 44 | 54 | 52 | 47 |
| Female | 53 | 56 | 46 | 48 | 53 |
| *Age* | | | | | |
| 20–25 | 14 | 16 | 17 | 23 | 18 |
| 26–30 | 18 | 15 | 22 | 21 | 18 |
| 31–40 | 23 | 22 | 23 | 28 | 24 |
| 41–50 | 12 | 17 | 14 | 12 | 15 |
| 51–65 | 31 | 26 | 21 | 15 | 23 |
| 66+ | 2 | 3 | 3 | 2 | 3 |
| *Experience* | | | | | |
| 1 year | 5 | 7 | 11 | 11 | 9 |
| 2 | 5 | 8 | 11 | 14 | 10 |
| 3–5 | 19 | 20 | 23 | 29 | 22 |
| 6–15 | 35 | 31 | 28 | 31 | 31 |
| 16+ | 36 | 34 | 27 | 16 | 29 |
| *Number* | 242 | 1,187 | 391 | 504 | 2,328 |
| Per cent of total | 10 | 51 | 17 | 22 | 100 |

the actual situation in the schools, is to produce a pattern in which the youngest and least experienced teachers tend to get the least desirable teaching assignments. This pattern is illustrated in Tables 2A and 2B. . . .

Teachers were asked, "In what kind of socioeconomic area is your school located?" They were asked to check one of the following: upper- or middle-class area; mixed middle- and working-class area; stable working-class area; lower-class or slum area. There was a difference between elementary school and high school reporting on this question, with 65 per cent of elementary school teachers seeing their schools in stable working-class areas or in slum areas, while 39 per cent of high school teachers reported their schools to be in these two categories. There is a real difference of this sort, because elementary schools are more likely to be located in slum neighborhoods than high schools are.

In Table 2 are presented the data on age, sex, and teaching experience in relation to socioeconomic area of the school. It will be seen that the younger teachers and those with least experience tend to be assigned to schools in the lower socioeconomic areas. On the other hand, the teachers over 50 years of age and with 16 or more years of experience are heavily clustered in the higher status areas and in the mixed middle- and working-class areas.[1] It will also be seen that there is a tendency for men to be assigned to working-class and slum area schools more than women. This tendency is stronger in the elementary schools, where most of the men are younger and less experienced than the women teachers. Probably it is the factor of age and experience rather than sex that accounts for the difference.

## ATTITUDE TOWARD PRESENT POSITION RELATED TO TEACHING EXPERIENCE, SEX, AND SOCIOECONOMIC AREA OF SCHOOL

The attitude a teacher has toward his present position is a matter of importance in his teaching. To secure some information on the matter, the teachers were asked, "What is your attitude, in general, about your present position?" They could indicate their attitudes by checking on a five-point scale as follows: very favorable, favorable, neutral, unfavorable, very unfavorable. Their answers were heavily "favorable" and "very favorable" with 72 per cent of elementary school teachers and 71 per cent of high school teachers giving these two responses.

However, there are some reliable differences between subgroups of teachers, as can be seen in Table 3. The older and more experienced teachers are more favorable than the younger and less experienced. Also, women are more favorable than men in their answers to this question.

The type of school area has the closest relation to attitude toward present position. Elementary school teachers in upper- and middle-class areas are 65 per cent very favorable toward their present position, while

---

[1] The reliability of trends which are pointed out here has been tested by the usual statistical methods, but the statistics will not be given, since this is not a technical report. Whenever a difference or a trend is pointed out, it is statistically reliable unless a statement is made to the contrary.

*Table 3—Attitude toward present position related to experience, sex, and type of school area*
(Percentages, unless otherwise stated)

| | ELEMENTARY SCHOOLS | | | | | | HIGH SCHOOLS | | | | | |
| --- | --- | --- | --- | --- | --- | --- | --- | --- | --- | --- | --- | --- |
| | VF | F | N | U | VU | Number | VF | F | N | U | VU | Number |
| *Years of teaching experience* | | | | | | | | | | | | |
| 1–2 | 20 | 42 | 19 | 14 | 5 | 806 | 19 | 50 | 16 | 12 | 3 | 428 |
| 3–15 | 25 | 43 | 16 | 12 | 4 | 2,768 | 21 | 48 | 16 | 12 | 3 | 1,254 |
| 16+ | 46 | 36 | 9 | 6 | 2 | 1,592 | 36 | 41 | 14 | 7 | 2 | 693 |
| Total group | 31 | 41 | 14 | 11 | 4 | 5,166 | 25 | 46 | 16 | 11 | 3 | 2,375 |
| *Type of school area* | | | | | | | | | | | | |
| Upper- and middle-class | 65 | 25 | 6 | 4 | 0 | 264 | 35 | 46 | 11 | 5 | 3 | 242 |
| Mixed middle- and working-class | 41 | 41 | 11 | 5 | 2 | 1,537 | 29 | 47 | 13 | 8 | 3 | 1,187 |
| Stable working-class | 38 | 39 | 13 | 7 | 3 | 912 | 19 | 47 | 18 | 13 | 2 | 391 |
| Lower-class and slum | 17 | 43 | 18 | 16 | 6 | 2,409 | 14 | 45 | 21 | 16 | 4 | 505 |
| Total group | 31 | 41 | 14 | 11 | 4 | 5,122 | 25 | 46 | 16 | 11 | 3 | 2,343 |
| *Sex* | | | | | | | | | | | | |
| Male | 9 | 14 | 19 | 20 | 21 | 720 | 41 | 47 | 53 | 49 | 65 | 1,123 |
| Female | 91 | 86 | 81 | 80 | 79 | 4,430 | 60 | 53 | 47 | 51 | 35 | 1,250 |
| *Number* | 1,576 | 2,083 | 731 | 541 | 185 | 5,150 | 581 | 1,087 | 363 | 246 | 66 | 2,373 |

Note: VF = very favorable; F = favorable; N = neutral; U = unfavorable; VU = very unfavorable.

those in lower-class or slum area schools are only 17 per cent very favorable, with 22 per cent unfavorable or very unfavorable. There is a similar difference, though not so striking, among high school teachers.

## WHY TEACHERS REQUEST TRANSFERS

Among those who answered the questionnaire, 12 per cent of elementary school teachers and 8 per cent of high school teachers said their names are on the transfer list. That is, they wished to change to another school. They wrote out their reasons freely, and these were then put into the categories that seemed most appropriate. The results are shown in Table 4. The most

*Table 4*—Why teachers have requested transfers

(Per cent of regular classroom teachers)

|  | Elementary | H.S. |
| --- | --- | --- |
| *Per cent with name on transfer list* | 12 | 8 |
| *Socioeconomic area of school* |  |  |
| Upper- or middle-class | 6 | 6 |
| Mixed middle- and working-class | 9 | 6 |
| Stable working-class | 12 | 9 |
| Lower-class or slum | 15 | 11 |
| Number | 616 | 164 |
| *Reasons given for requesting transfers* |  |  |
| Personal convenience | 34 | 27 |
| Professional advancement | 15 | 17 |
| Dissatisfaction with principal | 15 | 20 |
| Other professional dissatisfaction | 16 | 21 |
| Dissatisfaction with pupils and/or community | 16 | 12 |
| Operation of system | 4 | 2 |

frequent reason was one of personal convenience, which consisted mainly of such reasons as distance of the school from home. Next in frequency was a desire for professional advancement and growth through experience in another type of school. The category of professional dissatisfaction was equal in frequency to the category of professional advancement. This included such reasons as unsatisfactory working conditions, and relations with colleagues. The specific reason of dissatisfaction with the principal was given by 15 per cent of elementary and 20 per cent of high school teachers whose names were on transfer lists. Dissatisfaction with pupils and/or the local community was given by 16 per cent of elementary and 12 per cent of high school teachers as the main reason for wishing to transfer. Finally, there was the category of mechanical operation of the system which caused a person to transfer, usually because he was taking the place of someone returning from leave of absence, and therefore must move to another place.

The percentages of teachers on the transfer list from different socioeconomic types of school are also shown in Table 4. Lower-class or slum schools have about twice as many transfer requests as the middle- and upper-class area schools.

## THE MAJOR INFLUENCE OF THE SOCIO-ECONOMIC TYPE OF SCHOOL

There is a deep ambivalence about teaching in a "difficult" school, which is a school in a high transiency and low-income area. Of the 82 per cent of elementary school teachers and the 66 per cent of high school teachers who have had experience in such a school, they divide almost evenly when asked whether they like working in such a school.

Some experienced teachers choose to work in such a school. Sometimes they do this out of loyalty and satisfaction with a principal who is competent and who gives them recognition and security. Sometimes they teach in such a school because they feel that they can be of most service there. Still, the median years of teaching experience of regularly assigned teachers in these schools is only four, compared with 19 for teachers in the most favored areas.

It is clear that the present situation works against a retention of experienced teachers in the schools in low socioeconomic areas. This means that young and inexperienced teachers must work their apprenticeship in such schools—the most difficult schools in the city.

While the energy and the spirit of youth are desirable traits to bring to a difficult job, the job cannot be done well without more maturity on the staff as well as more help to the young and inexperienced. It is urgently necessary to make the work in the difficult schools more satisfactory to young teachers and to mature ones.

# CONSEQUENCES OF EDUCATORS' SOCIAL POSITION ON THE TEACHING-LEARNING PROCESS

*W. W. Charters, Jr.*

How is the teaching-learning process influenced by the positions teachers occupy in the American social structure? When we turn to this question, we meet far more conjecture than research. Nevertheless, it may be of some value to summarize the major assumptions, bringing to bear, where possible, the research studies relating to them.

With a few exceptions, the modes of reasoning have been of two major kinds, one representing an educational tradition and the other an anthropological approach. In both, a person's position in the social structure is viewed as having a formative influence, as producing certain enduring attributes which he carries into the classroom and which affect his teaching behavior.

In the tradition of educational studies of social composition, assumptions are made as to what social statuses are likely to produce the *best* teachers. These assumptions entail two sets of subsidiary assumptions concerning, first, the particular personal attributes necessary for effective performance as a teacher and, second, those segments of society which produce persons with the "proper" attributes.

The emphasis of the anthropological approach is different. Position in the social structure is regarded as shaping the general value orientations which affect a teacher's behavior in the classroom rather than as a determiner of the specific cognitive abilities, pedagogical skills, or attributes of personal and moral character deemed necessary for effective teaching. Thus, the anthropological approach goes beyond the issue of teaching effectiveness to the more general question of the impact of teacher values on the teaching-learning process.

From *Handbook of Research on Teaching*, N. L. Gage, Ed. (Chicago: Rand McNally and Co., 1963), pp. 722–740. Reprinted by permission of AERA.

## Teaching Effectiveness and Societal Position

In the educational studies of social composition, assumptions regarding the connection between societal position and effective teaching have been little more than the embodiment of popular conceptions or stereotypes. The personal attributes deemed necessary for teaching effectiveness and presumed to be formed by societal statuses are varied but may be roughly ordered as (1) cognitive competencies, skills, and abilities exercised in teaching, (2) character traits and personality attributes expressed in teaching, and (3) "appropriate" motivations for performing in the teaching role.

Coffman's early survey of teacher characteristics (1911) offers a convenient way to illustrate the rationale in these various realms. He based his study on over 5,200 questionnaires returned by teachers in 17 states, chiefly in the East. From them he sought information on such things as age, sex, salary, education, teaching experience, nativity of subjects and parents, parental occupation and income, and number of siblings. The following paragraphs contain, in germinal form at least, most of the assumptions on which 50 years of subsequent research on the social composition of teaching has been based:

> The kind of people we have in teaching necessarily affects the kind of teaching we get. Differences in race must make a vast difference in customs, traditions, moral and religious ideals, language habits, and originality. Differences due to social class, to economic station, to intellectaul maturity, to academic and professional training, and the like, must likewise be important factors affecting public opinion of the merits of the teacher and his work. . . .
>
> If we knew the class of people which is contributing the teachers, its fecundity, its ambitions and its outlook, its possibilities for refinement, for culture, and for personal improvement, we could, with the aid of modern science, tell something of the intellectual grade of people we are getting. If we knew the motive that impels teachers to choose it as a vocation, the preparation they make for it, and their recognition of its opportunities for social service, we would have some measure of how far there is a craft-spirit of professional ethics dominating the body of workers.[1]

*Assumptions Regarding Cognitive Competencies.* In the realm of cognitive competencies, skills, and abilities, Coffman spoke of "originality," of "intellectual grade," or of "intellectual maturity." How do these attributes tie up with societal positions? In part, Coffman exhibited a strong genetic bias, common in his day, implying an inherent superiority among the "favored" classes in the virtues necessary for teaching. Thus, he expected the higher social classes "naturally" to contain more intellectually capable persons than the lower social classes. This genetic bias, however, has been left by the wayside since Coffman's time; the alleged superiority of the higher classes is now more likely to be attributed to the influences of the social environment. Coffman included this in his rationale too: "The

[1] Coffman, L. D., "The Social Composition of the Teaching Population," *Teachers' College Contr. Education*, 1911, No. 41, pp. 14–15.

formative influence of any body of workers must always be in terms of their social class. Their strengths and limitations are determined not merely by their immediate ancestry but also by their social position."[2]

Thus, cognitive attributes are shaped by social position, but, in keeping with contemporary sociological doctrine, Coffman saw the impact of the environing social structure as a restricting one as well. Thus, after showing that teachers come from very large families (4 to 5 siblings) with very low incomes, Coffman wrote: "This condition means that the population that teaching selects is restricted as to its opportunities for personal improvement and for liberal culture, that in the main it must enter the field of teaching with little or no professional preparation."[3] Position in the social structure, then, is regarded as limiting or enhancing the life chances of the person. Low "economic station," especially, limits the opportunity for academic and professional training, which in turn affects the development of cognitive attributes.

The presumption that educational attainment, or more specifically, academic and pedagogical training, produces the cognitive competencies and skills requisite for teaching has become firmly embedded in the rationale underlying surveys of teacher characteristics in the ensuing years. Indeed, the presumption has been firmly institutionalized in the American educational system in teacher certification requirements, in criteria for accrediting schools, in salary promotion schedules, and in teacher-training programs. The presumption no longer is a matter of debate, except in regard to what kind of education is needed.

Societal statuses other than educational attainment and social class origins have also been seen as associated with the knowledge, skills, and abilities appropriate to teaching. Arguments concerning the suitability for teaching of males and females (their comparative ability to control, and ability to understand, children), the young and the older (fresh ideas versus tried methods), and the married and unmarried (maturity of judgment and experience in handling children) have waxed and waned with the decades. Such arguments often seem directed toward issues other than classroom performance, such as increasing the prestige of the occupational group, or enhancing the likelihood of professional commitment to the occupation, or increasing the stability of school staffs.

*Assumptions Regarding Character Traits and Motivations.* In the realm of character traits and personality attributes, Coffman spoke of "customs," "moral and religious ideals," "language habits," and the like. A review of subsequent writings would extend the list of attributes almost indefinitely to include the whole range of traits commonly associated with leadership capacity, congenial personal relations, devotion to study, and refinement of manners and taste. Such social statuses as religious affiliation (that is, activeness of membership, not particular affiliation), community of origin,

[2] *Ibid.*, p. 54.                                    [3] *Ibid.*, p. 79.

and social class background typically are seen as playing a part in fostering these attributes.

The rural and small town origins of teachers are said to forge a "parochial outlook" among them, especially when their normal occupational mobility fails to carry them into the broader world (L. A. Cook and Cook, 1950). In the early studies, lowly social class origin was in itself a mark of defective character. Or it was conceived to limit the opportunity for personal mobility in society, which in turn supports one's parochial outlook and values; it reduces the possibilities for "refinement" through contact with "cultural" or "broadening" experiences; it restricts opportunity for academic and professional training. Lieberman (1956) expressed this mode of reasoning in the more recent vein:

The majority of teachers are coming from homes which are culturally unpromising if not impoverished. They are coming from homes in which light popular books and magazines or none at all are the rule. If the future teacher's family subscribes to any magazines, it is likely to be *Colliers, Saturday Evening Post*, or the *Reader's Digest*. It is not likely to be *Harper's, Atlantic Monthly, Freeman, Saturday Review of Literature, American Mercury, Reporter*, or any other periodical devoted to serious writing on political, social, or cultural topics. The families from which teachers come are generally inactive both politically and in community affairs. Their social activities are likely to be confined to fraternal orders and lodges such as the Masons, Shriners, Order of Eastern Star, Elks, Moose, International Order of Odd Fellows, or Knights of Columbus. Families in the upper lower and lower middle classes usually have rather limited experience in the fine arts such as music or painting. Attending movies, playing cards, listening to radio and watching television, and visiting the neighbors are the most popular recreational outlets for these classes.[4]

(He tempers the extremity of his assertion in the subsequent paragraph by pointing out that the "impoverishment" is characteristic of the classes from which teachers are drawn, not necessarily of the teachers themselves.)

Moffett's (1929) survey of the social and "cultural" worlds of teachers college students in the 1920's epitomizes the line of reasoning which connects social class and community background with character attributes requisite for good teaching. From student reports in 15 training institutions, she describes the typical students in terms such as these: father is owner or manager of small business or farm, and family is unbroken by death or divorce; reared in a rural community or small town; recreation restricted to the resources of a small community; little participation in formal organizations and even less leadership experience; small group from which to select associates, and contact with people has been limited; no creative activities; "cultural standards" those of her community associates rather than those "generally held best" in her high school or college.

Finally, in the realm of motivations appropriate to the teaching status,

---

[4] Lieberman, M., *Education as a Profession*, Englewood Cliffs, N.J.: Prentice-Hall, 1956, p. 466.

the implicit assumptions are not strikingly different from the foregoing. Incentive for "personal improvement," embodiment of the "craft-spirit," and commitment to "social service" are some of the appropriate motives which Coffman mentioned. These are commonly seen to inhere in the "better" social classes or among males.

*Empirical Tests.* Research support for the various sets of implicit assumptions is virtually nonexistent. Some investigators, in the context of research on teacher effectiveness, have sought to establish relationships between social structure variables and teacher performance in the classroom. Since the findings, like those on teacher effectiveness generally, are either inconclusive or contradictory, only a few illustrations will be presented here. Herda (1935) found no differences between males and females in effectiveness as measured by a teachers' examination and by pupil ratings. Age showed a slight positive correlation with effectiveness when measured by supervisors' ratings (Odenweller, 1936), a slight negative correlation when the criterion was the Professional Test for Elementary Teachers (Bathurst, 1929), and a curvilinear relationship when the criterion was pupil gains on a history examination (Brookover, 1945). Peters' (1934) exhaustively controlled study of married and single females showed a slight advantage for married teachers on criteria of pupil achievement and mental growth, but, in accord with a previous study (Waits, 1932), no advantage on a criterion of supervisors' ratings. The teacher's socioeconomic status was found to be unrelated to teaching effectiveness as measured by supervisors' ratings (W. S. Phillips, 1935), by tests of teaching ability (Greene and Staton, 1939), or pupil gains (Brookover, 1945).

The Teacher Characteristics Study (Ryans, 1960) exemplifies a more direct approach to measures of performance and describes their relationships to various teacher statuses. In this study, teachers were scored on a number of dimensions of classroom behavior from ratings provided by trained observers and data furnished by responses of teachers to questionnaire items. Two of the bipolar dimensions, for example, were "warm, understanding, friendly teacher behavior" versus "aloof, egocentric, restricted teacher behavior" and "responsible, businesslike, systematic teacher behavior" versus "evading, unplanned, slipshod teacher behavior.", But simple relationships between the performance dimensions and age, sex, marital status, and extent of religious participation were not discernible. These statuses interacted in complex ways with teaching level and teaching field to produce different patterns of performance scores for teachers.

It is too much to expect, perhaps, that empirical relationships would support the unsophisticated assumptions of studies in the social composition tradition. The logical chain connecting the teacher's position in the social structure and performance in the classroom is long and tenuous, especially when performance is restricted to preconceptions of attributes necessary for effective teaching. Furthermore, decades of empirical research have failed to identify unequivocally the *behaviors* which *define* "effective teaching," much less to establish an association between such behaviors and enduring personal attributes of teachers. If the problem cannot be anchored on the "proximal" end, it can hardly be pursued fruitfully at the "distal" end.

### Value Orientations of Teachers

The second major mode of reasoning regarding the consequences of the teacher's position in the social structure is associated with the work of social anthropologists and sociologists. In this approach, the social environment is seen to shape the generalized value orientations by which a person lives and works. Simple societies with relatively homogeneous, internally consistent, unchanging patterns of culture present no complex "educational" problems. The educational issue in simple societies, if it is an issue at all, is one of providing the means of "teaching" most suitable for inducting the youth into the values dominant in the society.[5] But contemporary industrial societies consist of differentiated groups, or subcultures, each with a propensity to develop a different set of values in its members. Moreover, the groups may be hierarchically ordered with respect to prestige or power, which introduces further complexities into relationships among persons with different values. Nor are the value systems unchanging. The changes occurring in the dominant value system of the society proceed at different rates in the several groups and subcultures, producing, in another way, dislocations of value orientations among the society's members.

From this point of view then, the significant aspect of the teaching-learning process in the classroom is the transmission of value orientations from teacher to pupil. It proceeds not so much through didactic teachings as through the reward and punishment system and other subtleties of the flow of interaction, a point illustrated vividly in Henry's (1955b, 1957) accounts of interaction in elementary school classes. Which values will be transmitted depends upon the teacher's own value orientation, which, in turn, is determined by his position in the groups and subcultures of the social structure. Problems arise in those cases where classroom participants (teachers and pupils) are located at different points in the larger social structure and enter the classroom with conflicting value orientations.

Margaret Mead, in her analyses of American education (1946, 1951), postulates three distinct value orientations which teachers stress in the teaching situation. These she derives from her cross-cultural observations of the role of different age groups in inducting the young into society. One

[5] Henry's (1955a) provocative essay, distinguishing a number of characteristics of the instruction process in terms of communication theory, specifies in detail how instruction is suited to particular societies.

is a stress on conservatism and preservation of tradition, where the function of education is to transmit the accumulated wisdom of the society. This function, appropriate to highly stable preliterate societies, is performed by the elders, in what Mead calls the "grandparent role."

The second value orientation emphasizes the immediacy of the here and now, unfettered by concerns for the future or constraints of the past. In some societies it is the child's world of fantasy, of direct bodily expression, or communication by gesture and touch which is valued. Here the function of education is to preserve for society these resources of childhood; it is accomplished by relegating the socialization process to the older siblings who, themselves, have not emerged from the child's world. This is Mead's "child nurse role."

The third value orientation, appropriate to a society in the throes of rapid change, stresses the preparation of youth for the future, but for a future which cannot be comprehended in terms of the past, or, indeed, in terms of the present generation of parents. Parents can only raise their children to succeed them, to become the next possessors of a world still unknown and uncharted, and they find an ally in the school teacher who assumes the "parent role."

In contemporary American society, teachers assume these differing roles, depending upon the requirements of the school, according to Mead. Thus, the "grandparent role" is epitomized by the teacher in schools of small, provincial communities where he merely saves the time and energy of parents in teaching what the parents themselves could just as well teach. It is also epitomized by teachers in the academies (private high schools) and by high school teachers of mathematics, science, literature, and other classics who convey to pupils a sense of the relatedness of life.

The "child nurse role" is manifested in the nursery school and kindergarten where the upper middle-class girl, concerned less with verbal facility than material objects, allies herself with the world of the child and encourages the child's self-expression and self-indulgence.

Finally, the "parent role" is epitomized by teachers of middle-class suburbia, by teachers of modern history, current events, and scientific methods of exploration, and by teachers of the city schools charged with acculturating the flood of immigrants reaching our shores (e.g., the Puerto Ricans of the 1950's in New York City). These teachers convey to youth what their parents cannot. They represent the future as different from the past and induce youth to move beyond their parents. In order to do so, the youth are taught the virtues of sacrifice, of impulse restraint, of industry, and the wisdom of ignoring those traditions which block success.

Mead suggests that the teachers conveying these value orientations are drawn from, and have their values formed in, different sectors of the American society. Teachers in the city schools and in suburbia, for example, are selected from among urbanites raised in the midst of cultural diversity and change, from among middle and lower middle-class persons who, themselves, are seeking to transcend their past. Teachers in traditional communities are recruited from similar communities and are able to convey the provincial values with ease. Academy teachers and teachers of the academic subjects in public high schools tend to be drawn from the downward mobile sectors of the population, from persons who are clinging to the past. Thus, the value orientations transmitted in the classroom are reflections of the teachers' own societal circumstances, and an occupational selection process sorts them into school situations to which their value perspectives are congenial.[6] Mead's substantive propositions, however, have not been subjected to direct empirical check, either in terms of the societal positions of teachers in the various school situations or in terms of their characteristic value perspectives as manifested in teaching.

Spindler's (1955) conceptualization, in much the same vein as Mead's, provides a more fruitful base for empirical research in that his hypotheses are more explicitly formulated and his key variables are more readily operationalized. Spindler conceived of a major change occurring in the core values of American society, a change associated with our recent, unsettling history—our engagement in global wars, our experience with a "boom or bust" economy—and with the insecurities generated by an atomic age and its portent of cataclysm. In the present ethos, the *traditional values* which founded our society no longer serve, and they have tended to give way to a new value system, which Spindler calls the *emergent values*. Specifically, the traditional values of puritan morality, work-success ethic, individualism, achievement orientation, and future-time orientation are being supplanted by such emergent values as sociability, a relativistic moral attitude, consideration of others, conformity to the group, and a hedonistic present-time orientation.[7]

Three principal societal statuses help to determine a person's value orientation. One of these is social class. Spindler regarded the middle and the lower middle class as a stronghold of moral respectability, the work-success ethic, and, generally, the traditional value system. Another is position in the community power structure. Persons so located, Spindler

[6] There is a parallel between Mead's three teacher roles and the time dimension of societal value orientations proposed by Florence Kluckhohn (1953): value systems may emphasize the past ("grandparent role"), the present ("child nurse role"), or the future ("parent role"). Kluckhohn's analysis similarly tied differences in time orientation directly to social class position: the upper class adheres more to a past than a future orientation, the middle class more to a future orientation, and the lower class more to a present orientation. This observation has produced a number of empirical investigations which, however, are outside the field of education and beyond the scope of the present review.

[7] Spindler is by no means alone in noting a major shift in the dominant values of American society or the implications it holds for education or socialization patterns generally. While the details and emphases differ, his observations are closely similar to those of such writers as Getzels (1957), Riesman (1950), Swanson and Miller (1958), and Whyte (1956).

suggested, have a vested interest in the status quo and, hence, support traditional values. The third societal status is age. Assuming that value orientations are acquired early in life, we can say that the older generations, acculturated during a period when traditional values prevailed, are more likely to exhibit the traditional values today than are the younger generations. One further subculture enters Spindler's analysis as a determinant of values—the education profession itself, especially as represented in teacher-training institutions. The cultural force in schools of education, Spindler observed, is clearly in the direction of emergent values.

On the basis of these determinants, then, Spindler hypothesized that the various participants in the school and community will array themselves in the following order, from the traditional to the emergent pole on a value orientation continuum:

School board members
General public and parents
Some students
School administrators
Older teachers
Younger teachers
Other students

School board members are most traditional by virtue of their advanced age and the fact that they represent community power groups. Spindler's "general public and parents" refers particularly to the vocal critics of the school; others may well range over the entire continuum. Students are located in two places on the range, depending upon the location of their families. School administrators are in the middle, literally and figuratively, inasmuch as they must face the demands of persons with conflicting values. Older teachers differ from the younger teachers principally by virtue of the fact that they grew up and acquired their values at a time when the system was more traditional.

Spindler used this continuum to imply that the severity of value conflict increases as the difference in status of participants increases. For purposes of this review, it is especially noteworthy that the teacher, young or old, may well be faced with value conflicts within the classroom. Even the young teacher who finds close kinship in outlook with some students can still be confronted by other students from families whose basic value orientations diverge greatly from the teacher's.

Spindler's immediate interest in presenting his analysis was to uncover the roots of the conflict between the school and its public. The present-day ethos of anxiety leads to societal demoralization, disorganization, and conflict, he argued; the hostile feelings which result are vented in attacks of one group upon another, in attacks by persons with traditional values on other persons and institutions representing the emergent system of values, and vice versa. But Spindler's analysis goes beyond the school-community conflict. He suggested that conflicts may arise between participants in the school institution holding dissimilar values and, more important, within individual participants exposed to divergent cultural pressures during formative periods of their lives.

Spindler reserved special attention for teachers in his discussion of internal value conflict. He proposed that teachers typically are drawn from the middle and lower middle classes and, further, that within these classes the teaching occupation is selective of the more puritanical element, of those who emphasize self-denial, altruism, and a moralistic self concept— all adding up to a strong commitment to traditional values. But in their training, teachers encounter a new culture with a strong press toward emergent values, and they experience a discontinuity in their acculturation process.

The value conflict which ensues in teachers has one of three consequences: ambivalence, compensation, and adaptation. The ambivalent teacher is one prone to vacillation in matters of classroom discipline and authority, vacillation between laissez-faire and authoritarian relations with pupils. The compensating teacher goes to either the emergent or the traditional extreme in his classroom performance. At the emergent extreme are those thoroughly committed to the social adjustment movement and the "groupthink" cult; at the traditional extreme are those teachers who are downright authoritarian in their dominance over pupils and enter into formal, rigid relations with them. The adaptive teacher is one who manifests either of the preceding mechanisms of conflict resolution but in far less severe form.

Several empirical studies have given a modicum of support to Spindler's hypotheses regarding differential value orientations of participants in the school institution. Prince (1957) developed a 64-item forced-choice questionnaire designed to distinguish persons in their positions on the traditional-emergent continuum and administered it to principals, teachers, and students in 22 high schools. He reported that older teachers were significantly more traditional in their value orientations than young teachers, and that older principals were more traditional than younger principals.

Using the same questionnaire, McPhee (1959) studied 600 respondents in eight Mid-western communities, mainly citizen-members of a variety of civic organizations but also some school personnel. He, too, found greater traditionalism among the older respondents but no significant difference between teachers and laymen. Nor could he report differences in value orientations associated with occupation, income, educational attainment, home ownership, the school attended by the respondents' children, or participation in school elections.

Abbott's (1960) study of school board members and superintendents in 40 Mid-western school districts showed board members to be significantly more traditional than superintendents. But, in contrast to the other studies, he found among the superintendents a negative relationship between traditional value orientation and age. The older superintendents were more emergent in their values than the younger superintendents. Abbott found no relationships among board members between value orientations and occupation or type of community in which they were reared. From the brief published reports of these studies, it would appear that McPhee and Abbott examined only the first-order relationships between value scores and respondents' social characteristics. In Spindler's reasoning, the agent responsible for a person's value orientation is the cultural group in which he was raised and trained; social characteristics are but rough indicators of this prime variable. A faithful test of Spindler's hypotheses requires more sensitive analyses than Prince, McPhee, or Abbott provided. It should be noted, however, that none of them designed his study as a direct test of Spindler.

### Value Orientations: The Case of Social Class

Sociologists and anthropologists associated with Warner's theory of social stratification regard the social class strata as the most important set of subcultures in American society. In this view, the social class structure consists of a series of loosely formed groups larger than the friendship circle but smaller than the entire community and ordered on a scalar dimension of prestige.[8] Personal interaction tends to be limited between members of the different classes but relatively intense within class strata, a circumstance which favors the emergence of unique culture patterns and value systems within each class. A child born to a family within a particular stratum is acculturated by means of unique patterns of child training and then comes to internalize the appropriate value orientations. Nevertheless, personal movement from one stratum to the next is not uncommon in American society. Indeed, exponents of this theory of social class consider the aspiration to enhance one's social standing (or to maintain a favorable standing) as an extremely important human motivation. Movement from one stratum to another is never easy, and in some cases, for example, when the host stratum excludes those without a proper family lineage or those without white skin color, it is impossible. To be mobile, a person must acquire the value orientations, attitude, language habits, manners, and other cultural trappings appropriate to the host stratum, and this frequently requires him to renounce the values and way of life of the stratum from

[8] The Warner theory of social stratification departs in a number of important respects from classical Marxian theory and other sociological theories. Since educators are inclined to regard it as *the* theory of social class, the author recommends to them the excellent, authoritative review of contemporary social class theories by Mayer (1953) which places the Warner theory in perspective.

which he moves, running the risk, consequently, of alienating himself from his family and earlier friends.

In the view of the theorists, the school assumes a highly significant function in the stratification system of twentieth-century America (Warner, Havighurst, and Loeb, 1944). On the one hand, the school is one of the few remaining avenues of upward mobility from the lower to the middle classes or, within the middle class, from its lower to its higher reaches. Formal educational training is a *sine qua non* of membership in higher social strata. Not only is educational attainment itself a criterion for membership but it is a prerequisite for more "respectable" occupational or professional opportunities and higher or more secure incomes. Moreover, the theorists propose that the public school is a middle-class institution in the sense that it embodies the middle-class culture and thereby serves the upward mobile child of the lower class as a secondary acculturating agency, a place where he can assimilate the values, customs, morals, and manners essential to acceptance in the higher strata.

On the other hand, the school preserves the stability of the stratification system by limiting upward mobility to those youth who are willing and able to play within the rules of the game or, more specifically, to acquire the value orientations and motivations appropriate to middle-class membership. The public school serves as a sifting and sorting mechanism which differentiates between those who go to college and those who do not. Among those who do not go on to college, the school makes differential allocations to the various levels of occupational opportunity in the community; among the college-bound, to the various types of advanced training. As one analyst recently suggested (Parsons, 1959), the sorting process begins as early as the elementary school.

Our purpose is not to assess the adequacy of the social class theory nor to review the research which serves as its underpinning. Our discussion is offered as background for the task of examining the research pertinent to the impact of the teacher's social class position upon the teaching-learning process in the classroom. In undertaking such an examination, we will identify and elaborate on the main links in the chain of reasoning which connects the teacher's social class origins to his classroom performance. Given the fact that teachers derive principally from the middle class, one can draw certain conclusions concerning how the degree of success pupils will experience in the classroom and school will depend on the pupils' own social class position. But these conclusions can be drawn from the given fact only if three basic assumptions, or tenets, also hold. These tenets relate to (1) social class differences in values, (2) teachers' internalization of middle-class values, and (3) the manifestation of middle-class values in the classroom interaction process.

*Social Class Differences in Values.* The first basic tenet is that persons raised in middle-class families (or upper-class families) will hold values in their adulthood differing in certain critical respects from those held by persons raised in lower-class families. Two implications of this statement demand elaboration and some qualification. The statement reflects the strong emphasis social class theorists place on childhood as the formative period of adult character. While theorists of the Warner school do not disregard the influence on the adult's behavior of his contemporary social class position or of his social class aspirations and mobility, they are inclined to stress the enduring attributes of personality acquired during the early acculturation period. Hence the significance of their research on class differences in child training practices. The statement also posits major differences in value orientations and cultural patterns among the social strata of American society. This assumption has been abundantly supported by empirical research over the years, especially regarding differences between the middle and lower classes. Such demonstrated differences, however, do not preclude the existence of a dominant or core value system in American society, more or less internally consistent, more or less integrative of the variant values and ideologies in the several social strata and other subcultures.

At the risk of oversimplifying the research findings, we will outline some of the more important differences in ideology and value orientation between the middle class (representing most closely what Warner and others call the "common man" or lower middle class) and the lower (or working) class.[9] Orientation of the middle class is toward sacrifice of immediate gratifications to attain future rewards, together with long-term planning to tie future goals to instrumental acts of the present; orientation of the lower class is toward immediate impulse gratification and "getting by" in the present rather than "getting ahead." This difference in orientation is related to several other divergences, including the valuation of expressions of "raw" emotions. In the middle class, strong taboos are associated with the direct expression of aggressive or sexual impulses; such impulses are neither controlled nor denied in the lower class but, rather, are rewarded when prowess is displayed. In the middle class, money, property, and material goods are things to be accumulated and cared for; in the lower class, they are regarded as things to be used. Personal "ownership" is a concept less applicable to goods in the lower class; in the middle class, the distinction between "your" possessions and "mine" is taught early and reinforced by sanctions.

Schooling, study, and academic achievement, in the middle class, are

---

[9] It is impossible in the space available here to cite the supporting evidence regarding social class differences in culture patterns, and the literature *summarizing* the evidence is, perhaps, more voluminous than the research itself. In the following sketch we have drawn heavily upon the systematic schematization of value orientations presented by C. Kluckhohn and Kluckhohn (1947). The reader wishing to pursue the evidence should consult a standard textbook on sociology or social stratification.

viewed as instrumental to the attainment of occupational aspirations and "success"; in the lower class, they are either irrelevant or only vaguely instrumental, representing primarily a delay in entering the labor market and in establishing one's status as a nondependent adult. The person who is "too educated" is a misfit in the lower-class community. In the middle class, respect for a person depends on the extent of his conformity to standards of propriety, including proper forms for eating, address, greetings, exchange of gifts, expression of sympathy, offering of apology, language usage, and standards associated with tidiness of person, apparel, and possessions. In the lower class, respect is accorded on the basis of attributes of the person, such as being a "good fellow" or a "good-hearted woman," unmediated by conformity to many formal conventions. In the middle class, value is associated with the nuclear, but not the extended, family, with participation in formal organizations, and with allegiance to and respect for institutionalized authority. In the lower class, the extended family is the proper base of one's associations, and institutionalized authority of the law and courts, of the school, and of formal community organizations is feared or treated opportunistically, not respected.

The preceding sketch, as well as the evidence on which it is based, describes modal value orientations of the middle and lower classes in the aggregate. Even when the social strata are broken down into five or six divisions, or when classification is made on the basis of self-identification rather than objective placement, characterizations of the various classes represent modal tendencies distilled, in effect, from comparisons of statistical averages. Inspection of the original data reveals sizable departures from the modal tendencies within each stratum, due in part to the crudity of measurement. Such intrastratum variability is probably due in larger part, however, to differences among stratum members in their exposure to a wide gamut of value-forming experiences other than social class. This point becomes relevant as we examine the second tenet of the social class reasoning.

*Social Class Values of Teachers.* The second basic tenet is that teachers are drawn from the middle stratum of the American social class structure and, therefore, hold middle-class value orientations. Evidence for the first part of this tenet has been reviewed earlier. It is almost certainly true that a majority of the families of persons currently teaching are from the middle class. The second part of the tenet, however, does not necessarily follow from the first part. Does teaching select those middle-class members who hold the value orientations of the middle class? Is the teacher a member of the middle class who is fully imbued with the notions of sacrifice of present desires and denial of emotional expression, fraught with taboos regarding sex and aggression, conventional and proper, convinced of the instrumental worth of education? According to the popular stereotype, the answer would be yes, but the answer must be sought in facts. Other possibilities are open.

In any event, empirical investigation relating to the latter half of the second tenet is meager.

Few studies of class-related attitudes or values have been conducted so as to permit either (1) comparison of teachers with the general population from which they are drawn or (2) comparison among teachers of different social class memberships. The most relevant is Sims's (1951) study of several hundred public school teachers attending a summer session at the University of Alabama. Sims asked these teachers the six questions Centers (1949) had asked a nationwide sample five years earlier to assess positions on a "conservatism-radicalism" dimension of politico-economic attitudes. The questions were of the following kind: Do you agree or disagree that America is truly a land of opportunity and that people get pretty much what's coming to them in this country? In strikes and disputes between working people and employers, do you usually side with the workers, or with the employers?[10]

Centers had found a substantial positive relationship between degree of conservatism, as derived from responses to these questions, and social class membership, when measured either by self-placement or by objective placement. The distribution of attitude scores for the Alabama teachers showed them to be more conservative, on the average, than any of Centers' occupational categories except businessmen; they were more conservative in scores than the white-collar workers whom they would most closely approximate in social-class position.

Sims's study is far from definitive in regard to the issue of social class selectivity. One would anticipate higher conservatism scores from a Deep South sample, whether or not composed of teachers, than from a cross-sectional sample of the nation. Moreover, the Alabama summer session teachers almost certainly were largely composed of nonurban persons, a factor which Centers showed was associated with conservatism. Nevertheless, to the author's knowledge, Sims's study remains the most direct attempt to test the second tenet of the social class theory.

A test of the proposition that middle-class teachers internalize the value orientations of their social class might be sought in research, such as Wickman's (1928), on the kinds of pupil behavior teachers regard as serious problems. If teachers' standards of conduct were found to correspond to the values associated uniquely with the middle class, the hypothesis would be supported, assuming, of course, that the teachers studied were principally of middle-class origin. Among the 12 problems most frequently cited as serious by 511 elementary school teachers in Wickman's (1928) study, three related to sex taboos (heterosexual activity, masturbation, obscene notes and pictures), two related to disrespect for property (stealing, destroying school materials), two related to disrespect for authority (impertinence

[10] Sims, V. M., "The Social-Class Affiliations of a Group of Public School Teachers," *School Review*, 1951, 59, p. 332.

and defiance, disobedience), and one related to unbridled aggression (cruelty and bullying). Two of the remaining might also be regarded as class-typed standards—truancy, unreliability, and irresponsibility—but the last two might better be considered as related to core values of American society—untruthfulness and cheating.

As evidence for the second tenet, however, Wickman's data are highly equivocal. There is no assurance that social class differences would be shown *on these particular items.* Furthermore, certain variations appear in Wickman's data where no variations in social class of teachers would be expected, and no variations appear where differences in social class might be expected. In Wickman's study[11] 35 teachers in three villages in Minnesota and New York State (probably not varying substantially from the urban teachers in social class position) regarded selfishness, smoking and profanity as among the most serious behavioral problems, matters of considerably less concern to the teachers of New York City, Cleveland, and Newark. These differences may be more closely associated with the puritanical code of the rural areas than with social class mores. In his data from experienced teachers enrolled in college classes, Wickman observed that the departure of their ratings from the public school sample in some instances could be attributed to the course instruction and its emphases.[12] This would suggest that teachers' norms with respect to pupils are affected by professional training. Finally, Wickman obtained ratings from 10 male teachers in a private academy near Cleveland; these teachers, conceivably of a higher social class than the remainder of the public school sample, nevertheless rated pretty much the same problems as the most serious.[13]

Several replications of the Wickman study in the 1940's and 1950's supported the contention that influences other than social class membership affect standards of judgment regarding undesirable pupil behavior (Mitchell, 1943; Schrupp and Gjerde, 1953; Stouffer, 1952). While the same kinds of behavior problems that appeared in 1926 (when Wickman's data were collected) still appeared in the top ranks of seriousness—such as heterosexual activity, stealing, cruelty, obscenity, and lying—certain subtle shifts in ranking were observed. Mitchell (1943), for example, reported that such nonaggressive behaviors as sullenness, unhappiness, and resentfulness increased in rank between 1926 and 1940. Where the correlation between teacher rankings and the rankings by mental hygiene experts had been — .08 in the Wickman study, Mitchell's teachers and mental hygienists in 1940 agreed to the extent of a .70 correlation. Mitchell, however, gave his mental hygiene experts different instructions from those Wickman had given, and the two studies were hence not strictly comparable.

Schrupp and Gjerde (1953) exactly replicated the Wickman study and

---

[11] Wickman, E. K., *Children's Behavior and Teachers' Attitudes,* New York: Commonwealth Fund, 1928, pp. 246–247.
[12] *Ibid.,* pp. 105; 108–109.          [13] *Ibid.,* pp. 106–107.

found a correlation of .56 between the rankings of teachers and of mental hygienists in 1951. These authors showed that it was the teachers and not the experts who had changed their rankings in the intervening 25 years. Stouffer's (1952) study provided very similar evidence.

It is reasonable to attribute the shifts in teachers' judgments of behavior problems to changes which occurred in professional education in this period and even to the Wickman study itself. The Wickman research appeared just at the time the mental hygiene point of view was gaining a foothold in teacher-training curricula and the conclusion widely drawn from Wickman's data rightly or wrongly, that teachers do not appreciate the significance of withdrawal and autism as symptoms of personality disturbance in children, became a point of departure for mental hygiene courses and textbooks. There is no doubt that the generations of teachers trained after 1930 have been sensitized during their training to problems of personal and social adjustment far more than were earlier generations of teachers.

The simple fact is that no definitive conclusion can be drawn from existing data regarding the extent to which teachers internalize the value orientations unique to their social class position. One might anticipate considerable variation among teachers here, but the empirical tests have not been made.

*Manifestation of Values in Teaching.* The third basic tenet, completing the connection between the teacher's social class position and the teaching-learning process, is embedded in the following statement: "Since the teachers' judgments of the children and of standards of performance are inevitably based on their own personal standards, buttressed by those set up by the school as an institution, the lower-class child is at a disadvantage when competing with children from the middle classes."[14]

The key phrase here is that teachers' judgments of pupils are "inevitably based on their own personal standards," meaning, in the context of the paragraph, on their own *social class* standards. Thus, the tenet states that teachers guide their classroom behavior according to the general cultural values of the social stratum in which they were raised. This is a critical assumption, for it could very well be that, even though a teacher had thoroughly internalized the value orientations of his social class, his performance in the role of teacher is governed by frames of reference and value orientations other than those of his social class, such as those provided by his specialized occupational training, by the core values of society, or by requirements of the social organization of the learning process. Dahlke (1958) poses the latter alternative forcefully:

A current interpretation of the public school is that it merely reflects and upholds middle-class values. The norms apparently support this idea, but

[14] Warner, W. L., *American Life: Dream and Reality*, Chicago: University of Chicago Press, 1953, p. 177.

continuity of school and middle-class norms is incidental. Many of the norms and even value emphases occur not because of middle-class influence but because the school is a group. Emphasis on work, punctuality, getting the job done, control of aggression, avoidance of conflict, and being relatively quiet are necessary conditions if any group is to persist.[15]

Nevertheless, the assumption that the performance of teachers in the classroom is governed by their middle-class values is central to the line of argument. Davis and Dollard[16] used this reasoning in the most thoroughly detailed analysis of the operation of social class standards in the teaching-learning process available to us. In accord with the learning theory developing in the Yale Institute of Human Relations at the time (Miller and Dollard, 1941), Davis and Dollard proposed that behavioral responses of human beings are reinforced when accompanied by reward, especially the social rewards of privilege and approval, or when they reduce anxiety produced by the threat of punishment or of social disapproval. To understand the classroom situation, it is necessary to consider the teacher's distribution of social rewards and punishments and to examine the behavioral responses of pupils with which they are associated. Davis and Dollard argued that, initially at least, the teacher distributes rewards on the basis of the child's social class membership, not on the basis of his classroom performance.

[Children of middle- or upper-class membership] begin to receive favors and status privileges ... as soon as they enter school. They must work, as their parents and teachers demand, but they are also immediately rewarded. Their anxiety is thus reduced, and they are reinforced in repeating those actions which have pleased the teacher. Before long, the person of the teacher, her smile or praise, become sub-goal responses in themselves. The average lower-class child, however, who on status grounds is systematically punished by his teacher, becomes a sullen, hostile child. Anger, overt or repressed, is a barrier to effective learning. . . .

He sees the upper-class and upper-middle-class children being accorded preference, not only in classroom recitations but also in school entertainments and in intimate friendship relations with the teacher. He finds that he is not granted these privileges; instead, he is stigmatized by teachers and their favored students on grounds of the "ignorance" of his parents, the dialect which he speaks, the appearance of his clothes, and, very likely, the darkness of his skin. It does not take him long to discover that something is wrong and that the teacher's "pets" of high status are the only ones who can make the prestige goal responses. If there is no reward for learning, in terms of privilege and anxiety-reduction, there is no motive for work.[17]

The lower-class child is "systematically punished" for what he *is* and not for what he *does*. It is thereby impossible for him to learn which

---

[15] Dahlke, H. O., *Values in Culture and Classroom*, New York: Harper & Row, 1958, p. 253.
[16] Davis, A., and Dollard, J., *Children of Bondage*, Washington, D.C.: American Council on Education, 1940, chapter 13.     [17] *Ibid.*, pp. 281–285.

behavioral responses are instrumental in obtaining reward or in avoiding punishment. The case of the child of higher social class position is different. Initially, he is favored for what he is, but he is also "reinforced in repeating those *actions* which have pleased the teacher." This means that the teacher differentially rewards the behavioral responses of the middle-class child but not those of the lower-class child. This phase of the Davis and Dollard argument is rather awkward, for it leaves unexplained why in the one case reward and punishment remain attached to the class membership of the child and in the other case they are transferred to the behavioral responses of the child. But whether it is the child's social position as such or whether it is the propriety (by middle-class standards) of his behavior which inclines the teacher's actions, the fact remains, Davis and Dollard would argue, that lower-class children monopolize the punishments, higher-class children the rewards.

Reward and punishment, according to the underlying learning theory (Miller and Dollard, 1941), have very different consequences for the pupil. In brief, the middle- and upper-class child learns how to succeed in school while the lower-class child learns how to escape punishment in school. There are, of course, many ways of escaping punishment besides becoming a success. And, as the quoted passage intimates, punishment induces anger and aggressive impulses which not only interfere with cognitive learning but also, when overtly expressed, are likely to bring further punishment. A "circular reinforcement" process is instituted in the interaction between teacher and pupil which over time stabilizes the teacher's inclinations to favor the higher-class child and to discriminate against the lower-class child. The social reinforcement which a favored child receives from his teacher has consequences for the child and also for the teacher. In the first place, the acts of the teacher in praising the pupil and granting him dominant relationships to his fellow students diminishes the pupil's anxiety and thus reinforces him in learning his lessons and in maintaining good "deportment." At the same time, the student's successful learning reinforces the teacher in continuing her acts of preference toward him. The teacher is herself a member of the class system. She is rewarded by the behavior of the good student, first, because his habits are evidence that she is a proficient teacher, and, second, because through the child she is able to gain the approval of his upper middle-class or upper-class parents.[18] The upshot of the analysis by Davis and Dollard is that the social class value orientations of the teacher enter the teaching-learning process in two ways: by governing the teacher's distribution of reward and punishment, and by determining what kinds of pupil behavior will be rewarding to the teacher.

A markedly different form of analysis was offered by Brookover (1953) in which he centered his concern less on how the teacher's values govern

[18] *Ibid.*, pp. 281–282.

his classroom behavior than on what the teacher's values and social class position represent to the pupil.[19] In so doing, he proposed four ideal types of teacher which he called "upper-class," "established middle-class," "striving middle-class," and "unranked" teachers. These teacher types vary not only in the behavior patterns and beliefs they manifest but in such attributes as their sense of security in the stratification system, their capacity to appreciate, understand, and communicate with pupils of various social class levels, and their ability to provide the skills and incentive for upward mobility. Depending upon the social class position of the pupils involved, each type of teacher differs both in the kind of behavioral model he provides the pupil and in the likelihood that he will serve as a model at all. The pupil's identification with a given type of teacher is a major determiner of the pupil's own orientation to the social class structure. While Brookover advanced a number of specific hypotheses on these themes, none of them have been tested to date.

*Classroom Studies of Manifest Social Class Values.* What of the research evidence for the assumption that teachers govern their classroom behavior in accordance with the cultural orientations of their social class? Direct evidence on the issue is scanty, entailing, as it must, classroom observations of teacher-pupil interaction; we will shortly review the one study which bears precisely on the issue. Some circumstantial evidence is available in teachers' reports about their pupils and, as in studies of the Wickman type cited above, about the behavior of pupils which distresses them. We will first look at a few studies of teacher reports on pupils and pupil behavior, beginning with Becker's sociologically oriented investigation.

During interviews with 60 teachers in the Chicago public schools about the problems of teaching, Becker (1952b) found them spontaneously making evaluations in terms of the social class of the pupils they taught. (Becker presented no evidence regarding the incidence of these evaluations.) Problems with pupils centered in three areas, each varying in severity and kind with the pupils' social class. The first area was the problem of performing the task of teaching successfully. As Becker said, "The teacher considers that she has done her job adequately when she has brought about an observable change in the children's skills and knowledge which she can attribute to her own efforts. . . ."[20] In this respect, pupils in the "better neighborhoods"—i.e., of the upper middle class—furnished the teacher with the greatest reward, and those of the "slum" schools—i.e., the lower lower class—offered the least reward. "Ambivalent feelings are aroused by children of the middle group. While motivated to work hard in school they lack the proper out-of-school training. . . ."[21] The second area related to

[19] Getzels (1957) has approached the matter of value learning in much the same way as Brookover, emphasizing the process of the pupil's *identification* with the teacher.
[20] Becker, H. S., "Social-Class Variations in the Teacher-Pupil Relationship," *Journal of Educational Sociology*, 1953, p. 453.          [21] *Ibid.*, p. 455.

problems of discipline. "Slum" children were considered the most difficult to control, but those of the "better" neighborhoods were also hard to handle in some respects by virtue of their disinclination to submit to the authority of the teacher. The middle group was regarded as the least difficult to discipline.

Neither of the preceding two problem areas, however, directly implicates teachers' middle-class values. Indeed, they suggest that the occupational role of teacher induces standards of evaluation quite apart from the general cultural standards of the social stratum. The third area, on the other hand, directly involves social class standards—the problem of the moral acceptability of the students. Becker offers a variety of instances in which teachers were concerned with pupil transgressions against deeply felt moral standards, especially those of "health and cleanliness, sex and aggression, ambition and work, and the relations of age groups."[22] The most severe instances involved children of the "slum" schools, but again children of the "better" neighborhoods often violated teachers' standards regarding smoking, drinking, and respect for their elders. "Children of the middle group present no problem at this level, being universally described as clean, well dressed, moderate in their behavior, and hard working."[23]

Kaplan (1952) summarized annoying forms of pupil behavior as those which either violated the teachers' personal standards or challenged the teachers' authority in the classroom. He had asked elementary school teachers to write freely on "What problems or situations disturb or annoy you in your work and life as a teacher?" About one-half of the responses of teachers related to pupil behavior; others related to problems of school organization, professional status, and out-of-school obligations and pressures. From these free responses he prepared a 100-item check list and administered it to 250 experienced elementary school teachers in an Oregon summer school. Those pupil behaviors which two-thirds or more of the teachers agreed were "very disturbing" or "greatly annoying" referred to such matters contravening the teachers' sense of morality as stealing, lying, cheating, aggression, and destruction of property—items reminiscent of the Wickman list. Teachers also agreed on the annoying character of such matters as inattentiveness, indifference to school work, reluctance to work except under compulsion, nonconformity, and refusal to follow regulations, which Kaplan regarded as challenges to the teachers' roles as "leaders, disciplinarians, and instructors." A similar theme is found in Clark's (1951) report, but his conclusion—that teachers are more annoyed by behavior disruptive of classroom decorum than by behavior personally threatening to them—is not warranted by his data.

Teachers' ratings of the personal or social adjustment of particular pupils have been found to correlate with the social class position of the

[22] *Ibid.*, p. 461.                    [23] *Ibid.*, p. 461.

pupils in a number of studies. Objective measures of adjustment, however, often indicate that lower-class pupils are indeed less well adjusted. Hence, it is more parsimonious to attribute the correlation to veridical estimations by the teacher rather than to a "social class bias" on their part. A recent study (Glidewell, Gildea, Domke, and Kantor, 1959) demonstrated that teachers tend to see a lower incidence of adjustment problems among middle-class pupils than among either upper- or lower-class pupils, but the data they obtained simultaneously from parents led them to reject the "social class bias" explanation.

Thus, the ratings and reports of teachers about pupil behavior are not substantial evidence regarding the operation of social class values within the teaching-learning situation. More convincing would be investigations of the flow of classroom interaction, especially in terms of the privileges, favors, and attention accorded by the teacher to his pupils.

The study by Hoehn (1954) is the only systematic test made along this line to determine the extent of teachers' "unconscious discrimination against lower-class children."[24] Using a modification of the Anderson-Brewer schedule of dominative-integrative teacher behavior, he recorded the frequency and kinds of teacher contact with children high and low in social class position in 19 third-grade classrooms in central Illinois. The teachers were all middle class, Hoehn reports, but were heterogeneous with respect to age, experience, and marital status. He found no relationship between the frequency of teacher contacts, regardless of kind and social class position of the child; children of low social class position were just as likely to receive the teacher's "attention" as those of high social class position. With respect to the *kind* of contact involved, however, some differentiations were noted. The proportion of "domination with conflict" contacts was greater for low social class children than for high social class children. The proportion of "integration with evidence of working together" contacts was greater for high than for low social class children, and the ratio of integrative to dominative contacts favored the higher class children.

Hoehn introduced a note of caution in interpreting these results: He had studied the relationship between teacher contact and the achievement level of the pupils, measured by the Progressive Achievement Test. He reported that the low achievers received a greater share of the teacher contacts but also a greater proportion of the "less favorable" kinds of contact (dominative and conflictful) than the high achievers. The question

[24] Hoehn cited a dissertation by Clifton (1944) in which observations of the dominative-integrative behavior of teachers in second-grade classrooms were reported. The classrooms were located in three different socioeconomic areas. According to Hoehn, Clifton found little difference between the classrooms in the nature of teacher contacts with pupils, but there were somewhat fewer conflict contacts and somewhat more integrative contacts in the schools of the highest socioeconomic area.

was raised by Hoehn as to whether the teachers' discrimination against the lower-class children is not simply a reflection of their discrimination against low achievers, since the two are highly correlated. If we take the Davis and Dollard analysis seriously, though, we would expect to find a relationship between teacher discrimination by social class and discrimination by pupil achievement. Discrimination by social class leads to differential learning success which, in turn, stabilizes the teacher's social class discriminations (Davis and Dollard, 1940).

A more important qualification is found in Hoehn's remark that the absolute magnitude of the differences in teacher behavior toward low- and high-class pupils was small. (His presentation of data does not show the amount of difference; it only shows the number of the 19 classrooms in which differentiation occurred in *some* degree and the direction of such discrimination.) Hoehn was considerably more impressed by the variation *among teachers* in the extent of their discriminatory behavior. On the basis of his inspection of the data, he noted that some teachers did not discriminate consistently between either group of pupils, other teachers consistently favored the high social class children, and in one of the classrooms the teacher consistently favored the low social class pupils with the greater proportion of integrative and the smaller proportion of conflict contacts. Recall that all of these teachers, nominally at least, were members of the middle class.

Hoehn's study ties in with a long line of research on the implications of teacher-pupil interaction for promoting a healthy learning environment for pupils. Some of these studies, like Hoehn's, find teachers directing their promotive acts principally at high achieving pupils and their disruptive acts at the low achievers. Recording interaction in four New York State classrooms by means of a Teacher Approval-Disapproval Scale, DeGroat and Thompson (1949) found that children who received many approval responses but few disapproval responses from the teacher were significantly higher in intelligence test scores and in achievement than were those who received few approval but many disapproval teacher responses.

Subsequently, Meyer and Thompson (1956) recorded a sex discrimination in teachers' interactions with pupils in three sixth-grade classrooms: boys received a substantially greater proportion of the (female) teachers' disapproval responses than girls. No strong sex difference appeared in the approval responses. The authors interpreted the sex discrimination in terms of an interplay between the middle-class values of teachers and the societal definition of the male and female roles, especially as it regards assertive behavior. Boys are expected to be more aggressive, they argue, and in fact they are more aggressive in the classroom than girls. But this aggressive behavior of boys is unacceptable to teachers on the grounds of their middle-class standards, and the teachers consequently direct more disapproval toward the boys. The authors fail to explain, however, why teachers do not share in the societal expectations of differences in the male and female roles.

The key assumption of Warner and his followers—that teachers' middle-class standards inevitably determine their classroom responses—stands virtually untested at the present time. Persuasive as the illustrative anecdotes of writers may be, provocative as the indirect evidence may be, one central question remains unanswered: Do teachers with value orientations of the lower or the upper class behave differently in the classroom than those professing middle-class values? Affirmative evidence respecting relationships between teachers' social class and their distributions of reward and punishment, or respecting the value premises underlying their classroom actions and communication, would be compelling. To generalize, we submit that the greatest fruit will be borne by research which pits the assumption that middle-class values determine teacher behavior against one or more competing assumptions concerning the source of teachers' classroom standards. Such research would require specification of distinct points of discontinuity or conflict between middle-class values and professional values, or between middle-class orientations and orientations of the "core culture" of American society, or between middle-class standards and standards imposed by the requirements of social order in the classroom. Where conflict or discontinuity can be specified, observation in the classroom can be directed toward assessing the relative potency of the opposing forces acting on the teacher. Research can be set the task of delineating the conditions which predict which force will ultimately govern the teacher's performance in the teaching-learning situation. If, on the other hand, it is found impossible to specify points of discontinuity, serious doubt would be cast upon the conceptual stature of the social class argument.

*Social Class Differences in Pupil "Success."* The final link in the chain of reasoning concerning the teacher's position in the social class structure remains to be stated explicitly, although we have alluded to it throughout our discussion. Recall our three basic assumptions: (1) that persons raised in middle-class families hold values in their adulthood differing from those held by persons raised in lower-class familes, (2) that teachers are drawn from the middle stratum of the American social class system and thereby hold those values characterizing the middle class, and (3) that teachers guide their classroom behavior according to the values of their social stratum. Given these three basic tenets, it is proper to conclude that pupils of the lower classes will experience frustration and failure and pupils of the higher classes will experience gratification and success in their educational experiences. The evidence supporting this conclusion is overwhelming.

To categorize youth according to the social class position of their parents is to order them on the extent of their participation and degree of "success" in the American educational system. This has been so consistently confirmed by research that it now can be regarded as an empirical law.[25] It appears to hold, regardless of whether the social class categorization is based upon the exhaustive procedures used in Elmtown (Hollingshead, 1949) or upon more casual indicators of socioeconomic status such as occupation or income level. It seems to hold in any educational institution, public or private, where there is some diversity in social class, including universities, colleges, and teacher-training institutions as well as element- ary and secondary schools. Social class position predicts grades, achieve- ment and intelligence test scores, retentions at grade level, course failures, truancy, suspensions from school, high school drop-outs, plans for college attendance, and total amount of formal schooling. It predicts academic honors and awards in the public school, elective school offices, extent of participation in extracurricular activities and in social affairs sponsored by the school, to say nothing of a variety of indicators of "success" in the informal structure of the student society. Where differences in prestige value exist in high school clubs and activities, in high school curricula, or in types of advanced training institutions, the social class composition of the membership will vary accordingly.

The predictions noted above are far from perfect. Inasmuch as social class position rarely accounts for more than half the variance of school "success," the law holds only for differences in group *averages*, not for differences in individual success. The relationship in some instances may be curvilinear rather than linear, but the data rarely have been assembled to test this possibility. Finally, there are a few cases in the literature in which the expected relationships have failed to emerge. Nevertheless, positive findings appear with striking regularity.

The weight of evidence supporting the conclusion of the chain of argument does not, however, necessarily justify the assumptions from which the conclusion is drawn. To infer that it does is to commit the logical fallacy of affirming the consequent. Conditions other than the teacher's position in the social class structure may account equally well for the rela- tionship between the pupil's social class position and his degree of success in the educational system. The complexity of the situation was well recognized by Warner and his associates. In discussing the correspondence between social class and high school drop-outs, Warner drew this conclusion:

We believe this is a two-way relationship. On the one hand, the class culture of the child provides him with certain beliefs and values about the high school and what it has to offer. On the other [hand], the institutional values of the school,

---

[25] We cannot undertake to document each of the following statements separately. The reader is referred to the bibliographies of Dixon (1953) and Gordon (1957b), to the various community studies in the social class tradition, especially Hollings- head on Elmtown (1949), and Warner, Havighurst, and Loeb's (1944) monograph on education, to the comprehensive selection of readings in Stanley, Smith, Benne, and Anderson (1956, Part 2), and to the competent summaries of Brookover (1955b, Ch. 5) and Havighurst and Neugarten (1957, Chs. 10, 11).

represented by the Board of Education, the professional administrators and teachers, as well as the students, develop differential attitudes toward persons in different positions in the social structure which act as attractive or repellent agents to keep the adolescent in, or to force him out of, school.[26]

During the 1950's, research efforts moved strongly in the direction of explaining school success in terms of the motivational structure and cultural experiences provided by the pupil's family rather than in terms of the "bias" of the educational institution. Representative studies include those of Davie (1953), Douvan and Adelson (1958), Drews and Teahan (1957), Girard and Bastide (1955), Hieronymus (1951), Hyman (1953), Kahl (1953), and Toby (1957).

## CONCLUSION: THE CONSEQUENCES OF OCCUPATIONAL SELECTIVITY

It is obvious that teachers are drawn selectively from various statuses in the American social structure. At the same time, assumptions have been made regarding what this selectivity means for the teaching-learning process; some of these assumptions have been naïve and some sophisticated. In either case, research which tests the veridicality of the assumptions is meager, and what findings there are suggest that the assumptions are gross oversimplifications of the processes involved. We submit that the absence of positive findings regarding the relationship between societal statuses and performance in the teaching-learning situation is attributable in large part to the fact that programs of research and theoretical development have not concentrated on this problem as such. The research we have had to draw upon has more often emerged as a by-product of other research movements, such as those aimed at specifying the qualities of the "good teacher," the conditions under which more and better teachers may be induced to enter the teaching occupation, the mental hygiene implications of the classroom behavior of teachers, or the relation of social stratification to societal stability and change. Conceptualizations developed for these other purposes may be highly provocative for the problem of the relationship between occupational selectivity and the teaching-learning process, yet they are not necessarily adequate for the task. Indeed, they are almost bound to be partial accounts of the relationship. If and when the relationship in question is itself taken as a problem for investigation, theoretical models will almost certainly arise which will be capable of accounting for the complexities of the interdependence between the teacher's statuses in society and his conduct in the classroom. Such theoretical models, however, will also have to come to terms with other environmental forces acting on the teacher.

[26] Warner, E. L., et al., *Social Class in America*, Chicago: Science Research Associates, 1949, p. 206.

References to *Consequences of Educators' Social Position*

Abbott, M. G. Values and value-perceptions in superintendent-school board relationships. *Admin. Notebook*, 1960, **9**(4), 1–4.

Adorno, T. W., Frenkel-Brunswik, Else, Levinson, D. J., & Sanford, R. N. *The authoritarian personality*, New York: Harper, 1950.

Anderson, L. W. Teacher morale and student achievement. *J. educ. Res.*, 1953, **46,** 693–698.

Anderson, W. F. Attitudes of parents of differing socio-economic status toward the teaching profession. *J. educ. Psychol.*, 1954, **45,** 345–352.

Archer, C. P. In-service education. In C. W. Harris (Ed.), *Encyclopedia of educational research*. (3rd ed.) New York: Macmillan, 1960. Pp. 702–710.

Asch, S. E. *Social psychology*, New York: Prentice-Hall, 1952.

Atwood, M. S. An anthropological approach to administrative change. Unpublished doctoral dissertation, Columbia Univer., 1960.

Barkley, Margaret K. The concept of the home economics teacher held by high school students. Unpublished doctoral dissertation, Univer. of Illinois, 1956.

Barr, A. S. Supervision. In W. S. Monroe (Ed.), *Encyclopedia of educational research*. (Rev. ed.) New York: Macmillan, 1950. Pp. 1371–1373.

Bathurst, J. E. Relation of efficiency to experience and age among elementary teachers. *J. educ. Res.* 1929, **19,** 314–316.

Batten, T. R. The status and function of teachers in tribal communities. In R. K. Hall, N. Hans, & J. A. Lauwerys (Eds.), *The yearbook of education 1953*, Yonkers, N.Y., World Book Co., 1953, Pp. 76–94.

Baudler, Lucille, & Paterson, D. G. Social status of women's occupations. *Occupations*, 1948, **26,** 421–424.

Beale, H. K. *Are American teachers free?* New York: Scribner's, 1936.

Becker, H. S. The career of the Chicago public schoolteacher. *Amer. J. Sociol.*, 1952, **57,** 470–477. (a)

⸻ Social-class variations in the teacher-pupil relationship. *J. educ. Sociol.*, 1952, **25,** 451–465. (b)

⸻ The teacher in the authority system of the public school. *J. educ. Sociol.*, 1953, **27,** 128–141.

⸻ & Carper, J. The development of identification with an occupation. *Amer. J. Sociol.*, 1956, **61,** 289–298.

⸻ & Geer, Blanche. The fate of idealism in medical school. *Amer. sociol. Rev.*, 1958, **23,** 50–56.

Benedict, Ruth. Continuities and discontinuities in cultural conditioning. *Psychiatry*, 1938, **1,** 161–167.

Benne, K. D., & Muntyan, B. (Eds.) *Human relations in curriculum change*. New York: Dryden, 1951.

Berner, M. K. Development of procedures and techniques for the analysis of the relationships between the formal organization of high school systems and the informal communication structures within these systems. Unpublished doctoral dissertation, Univer. of Illinois, 1957.

Bernstein, Mildred R. H. A study of teachers' role-expectations and role-perceptions of a principal, superintendent and board of education, and the relationship between convergence and divergence of role-expectation and role-perception and teacher morale. Unpublished doctoral dissertation, New York Univer., 1959.

Betts, G. L., Frazier, B. W., & Gamble, G. C. *Selected bibliography on the education of teachers*. Washington, D.C.: U.S. Dept. of the Interior, Office of Education, Bull. 1933, No. 10, Vol. 1.

Bey, D. R. A further study in school organization. *Phi Delta Kappan*, 1956, **37**, 217–221.

Biddle, B. J., Rosencranz, H. A., & Rankin, E. F. *Studies in the role of the public school teacher*. Columbia: Soc. Psychol. Lab., Univer. of Missouri, 1961.

Bidwell, C. E. The administrative role and satisfaction in teaching. *J. educ. Sociol.*, 1955, **29**, 41–47.

────── Some effects of administrative behavior: A study in role theory. *Admin. sci. Quart.*, 1957, **2**, 163–181.

Bowman, E. W. A comparison of teachers' and administrators' opinions on personnel administration practices. *J. educ. Res.*, 1955, **49**, 229–233.

Boyan, N. J. A study of the formal and informal organization of a school faculty. Unpublished doctoral dissertation, Harvard Univer., 1951.

Bradford, L. P., & Lippitt, R. Building a democratic work group. *Personnel*, 1945, **22**, 142–152.

Brameld, T., & Sullivan, E. B. Anthropology and education. *Rev. educ. Res.*, 1961, **31**, 70–79.

Brayfield, A. H., & Crockett, W. H. Employee attitudes and employee production. *Psychol. Bull.*, 1955, **52**, 396–424.

Brookover, W. B. The relation of social factors to teaching ability. *J. exp. Educ.*, 1945, **13**, 191–205.

────── Teachers and the stratification of American society. *Harvard educ. Rev.*, 1953, **23**, 257–267.

────── Research on teacher and administrator roles. *J. educ. Sociol.*, 1955, **29**, 2–13. (a)

────── *A sociology of education*. New York: American Book Co., 1955. (b)

Butts, R. F. *A cultural history of education*, New York: McGraw-Hill, 1947.

Callaway, A. B. Some environmental factors and community influences that are brought to bear upon the personal lives of Missouri teachers and administrators. Unpublished doctoral dissertation, Univer. of Missouri, 1951.

Callis, R. Change in teacher-pupil attitudes related to training and experience. *Educ. psychol. Measmt*, 1950, **10**, 718–727.

Cameron, N. A. *The psychology of behavior disorders*, Boston: Houghton Mifflin, 1947.

Campbell, M. V. Self-role conflict among teachers and its relationship to satisfaction, effectiveness, and confidence in leadership. Unpublished doctoral dissertation, Univer. of Chicago, 1958.

Caplow, T. *The sociology of work*. Minneapolis: Univer. of Minnesota Press, 1954.

Centers, R. *The psychology of social classes*. Princeton, N.J.: Princeton Univer. Press, 1949.

Chansky, N. M. The self-concept and the perception of values of teachers. *Human Relations*, 1959, **7**, 358–366.

Charters, W. W., Jr. What causes teacher turnover? *Sch. Rev.*, 1956, **64**, 294–299.

────── The communication structure of school staffs. Paper read at Amer. Sociol. Soc., Washington, D.C., August, 1957.

Chase, F. S. The teacher and policy making. *Admin. Notebook*, 1952, **1**(1), 1–4.

Clark, E. F. Teacher reactions toward objectionable pupil behavior. *Elem. sch. J.*, 1951, **51**, 446–449.

Clifton, D. E. Dominative and socially integrative behavior of twenty-five second grade teachers. Unpublished doctoral dissertation, Univer. of Illinois, 1944.

Coffman, L. D. The social composition of the teaching population. *Teach. Coll. Contr. Educ.*, 1911, No. 41.

Coleman, J. S. *Social climates in high schools.* Washington, D.C.: U.S. Dept. of Health, Education, and Welfare, Office of Education, Coop. Res. Monogr. No. 4, 1961.

Congreve, W. J. Administrative behavior and staff relations. *Admin. Notebook*, 1957, **6**(2), 1–4.

Conrad, R. The administrative role: A sociological study of leadership in a public school system. Unpublished doctoral dissertation, Stanford Univer., 1951.

────── A sociological approach to public school administration. *Educ. Admin. Superv.*, 1952, **38**, 385–392.

Cook, L. A. *Community backgrounds of education.* New York: McGraw-Hill, 1938.

────── & Almack, R. B. The community participation of 2,870 Ohio teachers. *Educ. Admin. Superv.*, 1939, **25**, 107–119.

────── & Cook, Elaine F. *A sociological approach to education.* (2nd ed.) New York: McGraw-Hill, 1950.

────── & Greenhoe, Florence. Community contacts of 9,122 teachers. *Soc. Forces*, 1940, **19**, 63–72.

────── Almack, R. B., & Greenhoe, Florence. Teacher and community relations. *Amer. sociol. Rev.*, 1938, **3**, 167–174.

Cook, W. W., & Hoyt, C. J. Procedure for determining number and nature of norm groups for the Minnesota Teacher Attitude Inventory. *Educ. psychol. Measmt*, 1952, **12**, 562–573.

────── Hoyt, C. J., & Eikaas, A. Studies of predictive validity of the Minnesota Teacher Attitude Inventory. *J. teacher Educ.*, 1956, **7**, 167–172.

Cornell, F. G. Some aspects of teacher participation in administrative decision-making. Paper read at Amer. Educ. Res. Ass., Atlantic City, N.J., February, 1954. (a)

────── When should teachers share in making administrative decisions? *Nation's Sch.*, 1954, **53**(5), 43–45. (b)

────── Socially perceptive administration. *Phi Delta Kappan*, 1955, **36**, 219–223.

Counts, G. S. The social status of occupations. *Sch. Rev.*, 1925, **33**, 20–21.

Coutu, W. The relative prestige of twenty professions as judged by three groups of professional students. *Soc. Forces*, 1936, **14**, 522–529.

Cronbach, L. J. Stereotypes and college sororities. *J. higher Educ.*, 1944, **15**, 214–216.

────── Correlation between persons as a research tool. In O. H. Mowrer (Ed.), *Psychotherapy: Theory and research.* New York: Ronald Press, 1953. Pp. 376–389.

────── Processes affecting scores on "understanding of others" and "assumed similarity." *Psychol. Bull.*, 1955, **52**, 177–194.

────── Proposals leading to analytic treatment of social perception scores. In R. Tagiuri & L. Petrullo (Eds.), *Person perception and interpersonal behavior.* Stanford, Calif.: Stanford Univer. Press, 1958. Pp. 353–379.

Dahlke, H. O. *Values in culture and classroom.* New York: Harper, 1958.

Davie, J. S. Social class factors and school attendance. *Harvard educ. Rev.*, 1953. 23, 175–185.

Davies, A. F. Prestige of occupations. *Brit. J. Sociol.*, 1952, **3**, 134–147.

Davis, A., & Dollard, J. *Children of bondage.* Washington, D.C.: American Council on Education, 1940.

Day, H. P. Attitude changes of beginning teachers after initial teaching experience. *J. teacher Educ.*, 1959, **10**, 326–328.

Deeg, M. E., & Paterson, D. G. Changes in the social status of occupations. *Occupations*, 1947, **25**, 205–208.

DeGood, K. C. Can superintendents perceive community viewpoints? *Admin. Notebook*, 1959, **8**(3), 1–4.

DeGroat, A. F., & Thompson, G. G. A study of the distribution of teacher approval and disapproval among sixth-grade pupils. *J. exp. Educ.*, 1949, **18**, 57–75.

Dewey, R. The rural-urban continuum: Real but relatively unimportant. *Amer. J. Sociol.*, 1960, **66**, 60–66.

Dixon, N. R. Social class and education: An annotated bibliography. *Harvard educ. Rev.*, 1953, **23**, 330–338.

Douvan, Elizabeth, & Adelson, J. The psychodynamics of social mobility in adolescent boys. *J. abnorm. soc. Psychol.*, 1958, **56**, 31–44.

Doyle, L. A. A study of the expectancies which elementary teachers, school administrators, board members and parents have of the elementary teachers' role. Unpublished doctoral dissertation, Michigan State Univer., 1956.

Drews, Elizabeth M., & Teahan, J. E. Parental attitudes and academic achievement. *J. clin. Psychol.*, 1957, **13**, 328–332.

Dubin, R. Human relations in formal organizations. *Rev. educ. Res.*, 1959, **29**, 357–366.

Elsbree, W. S. *The American teacher*. New York: American Book Co., 1939.

Eson, M. E. The Minnesota Teacher Attitude Inventory in evaluating the teaching of educational psychology. *J. educ. Psychol.*, 1956, **47**, 271–275.

Evenden, E. S., Gamble, G. C., & Blue, H. G. *Teacher personnel in the United States*. Washington, D.C.: U.S. Dept. of the Interior, Office of Education, Bull. 1933, No. 10, Vol. 2.

Ferneau, E. Role-expectations in consultations. Unpublished doctoral dissertation, Univer. of Chicago, 1954.

Fiedler, F. E. *Leader attitudes and group effectiveness*. Urbana: Univer. of Illinois Press, 1958.

Fishburn, C. E. Teacher role perception in the secondary schools of one community. Unpublished doctoral dissertation, Stanford Univer., 1955.

Gage, N. L., & Cronbach, L. J. Conceptual and methodological problems in interpersonal perception. *Psychol. Rev.*, 1955, **62**, 411–423.

——— Leavitt, G. S., & Stone, G. C. The intermediary key in the analysis of interpersonal perception. *Psychol. Bull.*, 1956, **53**, 258–266.

Getzels, J. W. Changing values challenge the schools. *Sch. Rev.*, 1957, **65**, 92–102.

——— Administration as a social process. In A. W. Halpin (Ed.), *Administrative theory in education*. Chicago: Midwest Administration Center, Univer. of Chicago, 1958. Pp. 150–165.

——— & Guba, E. G. The structure of roles and role conflict in the teaching situation. *J. educ. Sociol.*, 1955, **29**, 30–40.

——— & Guba, E. G. Social behavior and the administrative process. *Sch. Rev.*, 1957, **65**, 423–441.

——— & Thelen, H. A. The classroom as a unique social system. *Yearb. nat. Soc. Stud. Educ.*, 1960, **59**, Part II, 53–82.

Gilbert, G. M. Stereotype persistence and change among college students. *J. abnorm. soc. Psychol.*, 1951, **46**, 245–254.

Gillin, J. The school in the context of the community. In G. D. Spindler (Ed.), *Education and anthropology*. Stanford, Calif.: Stanford Univer. Press, 1955. Pp. 62–72.

Girard, A., & Bastide, H. Orientation et selection scolaires: Une enquète sur les enfants à la sortie de l'école primaire. *Population*, 1955, **10**, 605–626.

Glidewell, J. C., Gildea, Margaret, C. L., Domke, H. R., & Kantor, Mildred B. Behavior symptoms in children and adjustment in public school. *Human Organization*, 1959, **18**, 123–130.

Gordon, C. W. The role of the teacher in the social structure of the high school. *J. educ. Sociol.*, 1955, **29**, 21–29.

―――― *The social system of the high school.* Glencoe, Ill.: Free Press, 1957. (a)

―――― The sociology of education. In J. B. Gittler (Ed.), *Review of sociology: Analysis of a decade.* New York: Wiley, 1957. Pp. 500–519. (b)

Grambs, Jean D. Teachers as a minority group. *J. educ. Sociol.*, 1949, **22**, 400–405.

―――― The sociology of the "born teacher". *J. educ. Sociol.*, 1952, **25**, 532–541.

Greene, E. J., & Staton, T. F. Predictive value of various tests of emotionality and adjustment in a guidance program for prospective teachers. *J. educ. Res.*, 1939, **32**, 653–659.

Greenhoe, Florence. The community contacts and participation of 9,122 public-school teachers selected as a national sample. *Sch. & Soc.*, 1939, **50**, 510–512.

―――― Community contacts of public-school teachers. *Elem. sch. J.*, 1940, **40**, 497–506.

―――― *Community contacts and participation of teachers.* Washington, D.C.: American Council on Public Affairs, 1941.

Griffin, J. F. Community relationships of business teachers in the high schools of Illinois (excluding Chicago). Unpublished doctoral dissertation, Northwestern Univer., 1953.

Griffiths, D. E. An evaluation of the leadership of the school superintendent. Unpublished doctoral dissertation, Yale Univer., 1952.

―――― *Human relations in school administration.* New York: Appleton-Century-Crofts, 1956.

Grobman, Hulda G., & Hines, V. A. Private life of the teacher. In L. J. Stiles (Ed.), *The teacher's role in American society.* New York: Harper, 1957. Pp. 132–145.

Gross, N., Mason, W. S., & McEachern, A. W. *Explorations in role analysis: Studies of the school superintendency role.* New York: Wiley, 1958.

Guba, E. G. Morale and satisfaction: A study in past-future time perspective. *Admin. sci. Quart.*, 1958, **3**, 195–209.

―――― & Bidwell, C. E. *Administrative relationships.* Chicago: Midwest Administration Center, Univer. of Chicago, 1957.

Gummere, R. M., Jr. Prestige and the teacher. *Sch. & Soc.*, 1960, **88**, 117–118.

Hall, R. K., Hans, N., & Lauwerys, J. A. (Eds.) *The yearbook of education 1953.* Yonkers, N.Y.: World Book Co., 1953.

Halpin, A. W. *The leadership behavior of school superintendents.* Columbus: School-Community Development Study Monogr. Series, No. 4, Ohio State Univer., 1956.

―――― A paradigm for research on administrator behavior. In R. F. Campbell & R. T. Gregg (Eds.), *Administrative behavior in education.* New York: Harper, 1957. Pp. 155–159.

―――― & Winer, B. J. *The leadership behavior of the airplane commander.* Columbus: Ohio State Univer. Res. Found., 1952.

Harding, J., Kutner, B., Proshansky, H., & Chein, I. Prejudice and ethnic relations. In G. Lindzey (Ed.), *Handbook of social psychology.* Cambridge, Mass.: Addison-Wesley, 1954. Pp. 1021–1061.

Hart, C. W. M. Contrasts between prepubertal and postpubertal education. In G. D. Spindler (Ed.), *Education and anthropology.* Stanford, Calif.: Stanford Univer. Press, 1955. Pp. 127–145.

Hartmann, G. W. The prestige of occupations. *Personnel J.,* 1934, **13,** 144–152.

Hatt, P. K. Occupation and social stratification. *Amer. J. Sociol.,* 1950, **55,** 533–543.

Havighurst, R. J., & Neugarten, Bernice L. *Society and education.* Boston: Allyn & Bacon, 1957.

Heider, F. *The psychology of interpersonal relations.* New York: Wiley, 1958.

Hemphill, J. K., & Coons, A. E. *Leader behavior description.* Columbus: Personnel Res. Bd., Ohio State Univer., 1950.

Henry, J. Culture, education, and communications theory. In G. D. Spindler (Ed.), *Education and anthropology.* Stanford, Calif.: Stanford Univer. Press, 1955. Pp. 188–207. (a)

———— Docility, or giving teacher what she wants. *J. soc. Issues,* 1955, **11**(2), 33–41. (b)

———— Attitude organization in elementary school classrooms. *Amer. J. Orthopsychiat.,* 1957, **27,** 117–133.

———— A cross-cultural outline of education. *Curr. Anthropol.,* 1960, **1,** 267–304.

Herda, F. J. Some aspects of the relative instructional efficiency of men and women teachers. *J. educ. Res.,* 1935, **29,** 196–203.

Hieronymus, A. N. Study of social class motivation: Relationship between anxiety for education and certain socio-economic and intellectual variables. *J. educ. Psychol.,* 1951, **42,** 193–205.

Hiller, E. T. *Social relations and structures.* New York: Harper, 1947.

Hines, V. A. and F. Scale, GAMIN, and public school principal behavior. *J. educ. Psychol.,* 1956, **47,** 321–328.

———— & Grobman, Hulda G. What a principal does, matters. *Phi Delta Kappan,* 1956, **37,** 308–310.

Hoehn, A. J. A study of social status differentiation in the classroom behavior of nineteen third grade teachers. *J. soc. Psychol.,* 1954, **39,** 269–292.

Hollingshead, A. B. *Elmtown's youth.* New York: Wiley, 1949.

Hughes, E. C. *Men and their work.* Glencoe, Ill.: Free Press, 1958.

Hunter, O. N. Relationship between school size and discrepancy in perception of the superintendent's behavior. Unpublished doctoral dissertation, Washington Univer., 1959.

Hyman, H. H. The value systems of different classes: A social psychological contribution to the analysis of stratification. In R. Bendix & S. M. Lipset (Eds.), *Class, status, and power.* Glencoe, Ill.: Free Press, 1953. Pp. 426–442.

Iannaccone, L. The social system of an elementary school staff. Unpublished doctoral dissertation, Teachers Coll., Columbia Univer., 1958.

Inabnit, D. J. Characteristics of teacher participation in decision-making functions of public school administration. Unpublished doctoral dissertation, Univer. of Illinois, 1954.

Inkeles, A., & Rossi, P. H. National comparisons of occupational prestige. *Amer. J. Sociol.,* 1956, **61,** 329–339.

Jackson, D. M. Administrative procedure in curriculum revision. *Admin. Notebook,* 1957, **5**(6), 1–4.

Jackson, P. W., & Guba, E. G. The need structure of in-service teachers: An occupational analysis. *Sch. Rev.,* 1957, **65,** 176–192.

Jaynes, B. L. Public attitudes in the State of Washington on important characteristics and salaries and personal practices of public school teachers as related to certain socio-economic factors. Unpublished doctoral dissertation, Washington State Coll., 1951.

Jenkins, D. H., & Lippitt, R. *Interpersonal perceptions of teachers, students, and parents.* Washington, D.C.: Division of Adult Education Services, National Educational Association, 1951.

Jensen, G. E. The school as a social system. *Educ. res. Bull.,* 1954, **33**, 38–46.

Jenson, T. J., & Staub, W. F. School-community relations. *Rev. educ. Res.,* 1961, **31**, 406–416.

Jones, H. E. Some aspects of an occupational stereotype: The American public school teacher. Unpublished doctoral dissertation, Claremont Graduate School, 1957.

Kahl, J. A. Educational and occupational aspirations of "common man" boys. *Harvard educ. Rev.,* 1953, **23**, 186–203.

Kandel, I. L. *The new era in education: A comparative study.* Boston: Houghton Mifflin, 1955.

Kaplan, L. The annoyances of elementary school teachers. *J. educ. Res.,* 1952, **45**, 649–665.

Katz, D., & Braly, K. W. Verbal stereotypes and racial prejudice. In Eleanor E. Maccoby, T. M. Newcomb, & E. L. Hartley (Eds.), *Readings in social psychology.* (3rd ed.) New York: Holt, 1958. Pp. 40–46.

Kiely, Margaret. Comparison of students of teachers colleges and students of liberal arts colleges. *Teach. Coll. Contr. Educ.,* 1931, No. 440.

Kluckhohn, C. *Mirror for man.* New York: McGraw-Hill, 1949.

——— & Kluckhohn, Florence R. American culture: Generalized orientations and class patterns. In L. Bryson, L. Finkelstein, & R. M. MacIver (Eds.), *Conflicts of power in modern culture.* New York: Harper, 1947. Pp. 106–128.

Kluckhohn, Florence R. Dominant and variant value orientations. In C. Kluckhohn & H. A. Murray, & D. M. Schneider (Eds.), *Personality in nature, society, and culture.* (2nd ed.) New York: Knopf, 1953. Pp. 342–357.

Knox, W. B. A study of the relationships of certain environmental factors to teaching success. *J. exp. Educ.,* 1956, **25**, 95–151.

Krech, D., & Crutchfield, R. S. *Theory and problems of social psychology.* New York: McGraw-Hill, 1948.

Lambert, P. Interaction between authoritarian and non-authoritarian principals and teachers. Unpublished doctoral dissertation, Univer. of California, 1955.

Levin, H., Hilton, T. L., & Leiderman, Gloria F. Studies of teacher behavior. *J. exp. Educ.,* 1957, **26**, 81–91.

Lewin, K. *A dynamic theory of personality.* New York: McGraw-Hill, 1935.

Lichliter, Mary. Social obligations and restrictions placed on women teachers. *Sch. Rev.,* 1946, **54**, 14–23.

Lieberman, M. *Education as a profession.* Englewood Cliffs, N.J.: Prentice-Hall, 1956.

Linton, R. *The cultural background of personality.* New York: Appleton-Century, 1945.

Lippmann, W. *Public opinion.* New York: Harcourt, Brace, 1922.

Lortie, D. C. Laymen to lawmen: Law school, careers, and professional socialization. *Harvard educ. Rev.,* 1959, **29**, 352–369.

MacIver, R. M. *Society: A textbook of sociology.* New York: Farrar & Rinehart, 1937.

Manwiller, L. V. Expectations regarding teachers. *J. exp. Educ.,* 1958, **26**, 315–354.

March, J. G., & Simon, H. A. *Organizations.* New York: Wiley, 1958.

Martindale, E. F. Situational factors in teacher placement and success. *J. exp. Educ.*, 1951, **20**, 121–177.

Mason, W. S., & Bain, R. K. *Teacher turnover in the public schools, 1957–58.* Washington, D.C.: U.S. Dept. of Health, Education, and Welfare, Office of Education, Circular No. 608, 1959.

—— Dressel, R. J., & Bain, R. K. *The beginning teacher.* Washington, D.C.: U.S. Dept. of Health, Education, and Welfare, Office of Education, Circular No. 510, 1958.

Mayer, K. The theory of social classes. *Harvard educ. Rev.*, 1953, **23**, 149–167.

McCleary, L. E. A study of interpersonal influence within a school staff: The development and trial of a method of analyzing influence within established networks of communication. Unpublished doctoral dissertation, Univer. of Illinois, 1957.

McGee, H. M. Measurement of authoritarianism and its relation to teachers' classroom behavior. *Genet. Psychol. Monogr.*, 1955, **52**, 89–146.

McGill, K. H. The school-teacher stereotype. *J. educ. Sociol.*, 1931, **4**, 642–650.

McGuire, C., & White, G. D. Social origins of teachers—in Texas. In L. J. Stiles (Ed.), *The teacher's role in American society.* New York: Harper, 1957. Pp. 23–41.

McPhee, R. F. Individual values, educational viewpoint, and local school approval. *Admin. Notebook*, 1959, **7**(8), 1–4.

Mead, Margaret. An anthropologist looks at the teacher's role. *Educ. Method*, 1942, **21**, 219–223.

—— Our educational emphasis in primitive perspective. *Amer. J. Sociol.*, 1943, **48**, 633–639.

—— Teachers' place in American society. *J. Amer. ass. univer. Women*, 1946, **40**, 3–5.

—— *The school in American culture.* Cambridge, Mass.: Harvard Univer. Press, 1951.

Menger, Clara. The social status of occupations for women. *Teachers Coll. Rec.*, 1932, **33**, 696–704.

Merton, R. K. *Social theory and social structure.* (Rev. ed.) Glencoe, Ill.: Free Press, 1957.

—— Reader, G. G., & Kendall, Patricia L. (Eds.) *The student physician: Introductory studies in the sociology of medical education.* Cambridge, Mass.: Harvard Univer. Press, 1957.

Meyer, W. J., & Thompson, G. G. Sex difference in the distribution of teacher approval and disapproval among sixth-grade children. *J. educ. Pyschol.*, 1956, **47**, 385–396.

Miller, N. E., & Dollard, J. C. *Social learning and imitation.* New Haven, Conn.: Yale Univer. Press, 1941.

Miner, H. The folk-urban continuum. *Amer. sociol. Rev.*, 1952, **17**, 529–537.

Mitchell, J. C. A study of teachers' and mental hygienists' rating of certain behavior problems of children. *J. educ. Res.*, 1943, **36**, 292–307.

Moffett, Mary L. *The social background and activities of teachers college students.* New York: Bur. of Publs., Teachers Coll., Columbia Univer., 1929.

Moore, H. E., & Burke, J. E. Staff—economic status. In C. W. Harris (Ed.), *Encyclopedia of educational research.* (3rd ed.) New York: Macmillan, 1960. Pp. 1367–1374.

Morris, C. N. Career patterns of teachers. In L. J. Stiles (Ed.), *The teacher's role in American society.* New York: Harper, 1957. Pp. 247–263.

Morse, Nancy C. *Satisfactions in the white-collar job.* Ann Arbor: Survey Res. Center, Univer. of Michigan, 1953.

Mort, P. R. School and community relationships to school quality. *Teachers Coll. Rec.*, 1954, **55**, 210–214.

—— & Cornell, F. G. *American schools in transition.* New York: Teachers Coll., Columbia Univer., 1941.

Mort, P. R., & Furno, O. F. *Theory and synthesis of a sequential simplex.* New York: Inst. of Admin. Res., Teachers Coll., Columbia Univer., Study No. 12, 1960.

—— & Pierce, T. M. Measuring community adaptability. *Sch. Executive*, 1947, **66**, 35–36.

Moser, R. P. The leadership patterns of school superintendents and school principals. *Admin. Notebook*, 1957, **6**(1), 1–4.

Moyer, D. C. Teachers' attitudes toward leadership as they relate to teacher satisfaction. Unpublished doctoral dissertation, Univer. of Chicago, 1954.

—— Leadership that teachers want. *Admin. Notebook*, 1955, **3**(1), 1–4.

Naslund, R. A., & Brown, C. A. The school and the community. *Rev. educ. Res.*, 1958, **28**, 16–28.

National Education Association, Research Division. First-year teachers in 1954–55. *NEA res. Bull.*, 1956, 34, No. 1.

—— The status of the American public-school teacher. *NEA res. Bull.*, 1957, **35**, No. 1.

National Opinion Research Center. Jobs and occupations: A popular evaluation. In R. Bendix & S. M. Lipset (Eds.), *Class, status, and power.* Glencoe, Ill.: Free Press, 1953. Pp. 411–426.

Newcomb, T. M. Autistic hostility and social reality. *Human Relations*, 1947, **1**, 69–86.

—— *Social psychology.* New York: Dryden, 1950.

—— *The acquaintance process.* New York: Holt, Rinehart, & Winston, 1961.

Odell, W. C. Are teachers aware of propaganda in sponsored teaching aids? *J. educ. Res.*, 1957, **51**, 81–88.

Odenweller, A. L. Predicting the quality of teaching. *Teach. Coll. Contr. Educ.*, 1936, No. 676.

Ojemann, R. H., Levitt, E. E., Lyle, W. H., Jr., & Whiteside, Maxine F. The effects of a "causal" teacher-training program and certain curricular changes on grade school children. *J. exp. Educ.*, 1955, **24**, 95–114.

Oliver, W. A. Teachers' educational beliefs *versus* their classroom practices. *J. educ. Res.*, 1953, **47**, 47–55.

Pace, C. R. Five college environments. *Coll. Bd Rev.*, 1960, **41**, 24–28.

—— & Stern, G. G. An approach to the measurement of psychological characteristics of college environments. *J. educ. Psychol.*, 1958, **49**, 269–277.

Parsons, T. The school class as a social system: Some of its functions in American society. *Harvard educ. Rev.*, 1959, **29**, 297–318.

Pepper, J. N. Factors involved in the recruitment and retention of teachers in Michigan. Unpublished doctoral dissertation, Wayne State Univer., 1954.

Perkins, H. V., Jr. Teachers' and peers' perceptions of children's self-concepts. *Child Develpm.*, 1958, **29**, 203–220.

Peters, D. W. The status of the married woman teacher. *Teach. Coll. Contr. Educ.*, 1934, No. 603.

Phillips, B. N. Community control of teacher behavior. *J. teacher Educ.*, 1955, **6**, 293–300.

Phillips, W. S. An analysis of certain characteristics of active and potential teachers. *Peabody Coll. Contr. Educ.*, 1935.

Prince, R. Individual values and administrative effectiveness. *Admin. Notebook*, 1957, **6**(4), 1–4.

Rabinowitz, W., & Rosenbaum, I. Teaching experience and teachers' attitudes. *Elem. sch. J.*, 1960, **60**, 313–319.

Rettig, S., & Pasamanick, B. Status and job satisfaction of public school teachers. *Sch. & Soc.*, 1959, **87**, 113–116.

Richey, R. W. The United States. In R. K. Hall, N. Hans, & J. A. Lauwerys (Eds.), *The yearbook of education 1953*. Yonkers, N.Y.: World Book Co., 1953. Pp. 203–228.

—— Fox, W. H., & Fauset, C. E. Prestige rank of teaching. *Occupations*, 1951, **30**, 33–36.

Riesman, D. *The lonely crowd*. New Haven, Conn.: Yale Univer. Press, 1950.

Rogers, Dorothy. Implications of views concerning the "typical" school teacher. *J. educ. Sociol.*, 1950, **23**, 482–487.

Rollins, S. P. A study of the diffusion of information within secondary school staffs.Unpublished doctoral dissertation, Washington Univer., 1958.

Ross, D. H. (Ed.) *Administration for adaptability*. (2nd ed.) New York: Metropolitan School Study Council, 1958.

Ruml, B., & Tickton, S. G. *Teaching salaries then and now*. New York: Fund for the Advancement of Education, 1955.

Ryans, D. G. *Characteristics of teachers*. Washington, D.C.: American Council on Education, 1960.

Saltz, Joanne W. Teacher stereotype—Liability in recruiting? *Sch. Rev.*, 1960, **68**, 105–111.

Sandgren, D. L., & Schmidt, L. G. Does practice teaching change attitudes toward teaching? *J. educ. Res.*, 1956, **49**, 673–680.

Sanford, R. N. (Ed.) *The American college*. New York: Wiley, 1962.

Sarbin, T. R. Role theory. In G. Lindzey (Ed.), *Handbook of social psychology*. Cambridge, Mass.: Addison-Wesley, 1954. Pp. 223–258.

Schrupp, M. H., & Gjerde, C. M. Teacher growth in attitudes toward behavior problems of children. *J. educ. Psychol.*, 1953, **44**, 203–214.

Seeman, M. Role, conflict and ambivalence in leadership. *Amer. sociol. Rev.*, 1953, **18**, 373–380.

—— Social mobility and administrative behavior. *Amer. sociol. Rev.*, 1958, **23**, 633–642.

Selltiz, Claire, Jahoda, Marie, Deutsch, M., & Cook, S. W. *Research methods in social relations*. (2nd ed.) New York: Holt, 1959.

Sharma, C. L. Who should make what decisions? *Admin. Notebook*, 1955, **3**(8), 1–4.

Shils, E. A. The study of the primary group. In D. E. Lerner & H. D. Lasswell (Eds.), *The policy sciences*. Stanford, Calif.: Stanford Univer. Press, 1951. Pp. 44–69.

Sims, V. M. The social-class affiliations of a group of public school teachers. *Sch. Rev.*, 1951, **59**, 331–338.

Sorokin, P. A. *Society, culture, and personality: Their structure and dynamics*. New York: Harper, 1947.

Spindler, G. D. Education in a transforming American culture. *Harvard educ. Rev.*, 1955, **25**, 145–156.

Stanley, W. O., Smith, B. O., Benne, K. D., & Anderson, A. W. (Eds.), *Social foundations of education*. New York: Dryden, 1956.

Stern, G. G. Student values and their relationship to the college environment. In H. T. Sprague (Ed.), *Research on college students*. Boulder, Colo.: Western Interstate Commission for Higher Education, 1960. Pp. 67–104.

Stouffer, G. A. W., Jr. Behavior problems of children as viewed by teachers and mental hygienists. *Ment. Hyg., N.Y.*, 1952, **36**, 271–285.

Swanson, G. E., & Miller, D. R. *The changing American family*. New York: Wiley, 1958.

Sweitzer, R. E. The superintendent's role in improving instruction. *Admin. Notebook*, 1958, **6**(8), 1–4.

Terrien, F. W. Who thinks what about educators? *Amer. J. Sociol.*, 1953, **59**, 150–158.

—— The occupational roles of teachers. *J. educ. Sociol.*, 1955, **29**, 14–20.

Thomas, M. R. Extra-school community activities of high school teachers with implications for the community school. Unpublished doctoral dissertation, Univer. of Utah, 1954.

Toby, J. Orientation to education as a factor in the school maladjustment of lower-class children. *Soc. Forces*, 1957, **35**, 259–266.

U.S. Department of Commerce, Bureau of the Census. *Census of Population: 1950*. Vol. 1. *Number of Inhabitants*. Washington, D.C.: U.S. Government Printing Office, 1952.

Wagenschein, Miriam. "Reality shock:" A study of beginning elementary school teachers. Unpublished master's dissertation, Univer. of Chicago, 1950.

Waits, L. A. A study of the comparative efficiency of single and married women as teachers. *Educ. Admin. Superv.*, 1932, **18**, 630–633.

Walker, K. F. A study of occupational stereotypes. *J. appl. Psychol.*, 1958, **42**, 122–124.

Waller, W. *The sociology of teaching*. New York: Wiley, 1932.

Warner, W. L. *American life: Dream and reality*. Chicago: Univer. of Chicago Press, 1953.

—— et al. *Democracy in Jonesville*. New York: Harper, 1949.

—— Havighurst, R. J., & Loeb, M. B. *Who shall be educated?* New York: Harper, 1944.

—— Meeker, Marsha, & Eells, K. *Social class in America*. Chicago: Science Research Associates, 1949.

Washburne, C. The teacher in the authority system. *J. educ. Sociol.*, 1957, **30**, 390–394.

Watkins, M. H. The West African bush school. *Amer. J. Sociol.*, 1943, **48**, 666–675.

Wattenberg, W. Social origins of teachers and American education. In L. J. Stiles (Ed.), *The teacher's role in American society*. New York: Harper, 1957. Pp. 61–70. (a)

—— Social origins of teachers—A Northern industrial city. In L. J. Stiles (Ed.), *The teacher's role in American society*. New York: Harper, 1957. Pp. 13–22. (b)

Weber, C. A. Reactions of teachers to in-service education in their schools. *Sch. Rev.*, 1943, **51**, 234–240.

White, R. K., & Lippitt, R. *Autocracy and democracy: An experimental inquiry*. New York: Harper, 1960.

Whiteford, Emma M. B. Administrators' stereotype of the high school home economics teacher. Unpublished doctoral dissertation, Univer. of Illinois, 1955.

Whyte, W. H., Jr. *The organization man*. New York: Simon and Schuster, 1956.

Wickman, E. K. *Children's behavior and teachers' attitudes*. New York: Commonwealth Fund, 1928.

Wilcox, R. T. Authoritarianism and expectations of leadership. Unpublished doctoral dissertation, Univer. of California, 1957.

Wiles, K., & Grobman, Hulda G. The role of the principal in curriculum development. *Educ. Admin. Superv.*, 1958, **44,** 10–14.

Willard, Ruth A. A study of the relationship between the valued-behaviors of selected teachers and the learning experiences provided in their classrooms. *J. educ. Res.*, 1955, **49,** 45–51.

Winget, J. Teacher inter-school mobility aspirations of elementary teachers, Chicago Public School System, 1947–48. Unpublished doctoral dissertation, Univer. of Chicago, 1952.

Znaniecki, F. The scientific function of sociology of education. *Educ. Theory*, 1951, **1,** 69–78, 87.

# DEFEATISM IN GHETTO SCHOOLS

*Kenneth Clark*

As Haryou gathered data on the schools, it became increasingly clear that the attitude of the teachers toward their students was emerging as a most important factor in attempting to understand the massive retardation of these children. It was necessary to find out what they really felt, and so the schools were asked to recommend teachers to discuss the problems of teachers in slum schools. Interviews were held; group discussions were conducted; questionnaires were distributed. They tended to make clear what a crucial role the teachers really played in the success or failure of their students. The problems of identifying with children of different backgrounds—especially for persons from the white middle class—the problems of rejection of children deemed unappealing or alien, and the problems of achieving empathy are multiple. Courses in educational philosophy and psychology as presently taught do not prepare these teachers for the challenge of their job.

The pattern of teaching in Harlem is one of short tenure and inexperience. Many white teachers are afraid to work in Harlem; some Negroes consider a post outside of Harlem to be a sign of status. Discipline problems pervade a number of the schools, as students show contempt for teachers and principals they do not respect; and, in turn, the emphasis on "good discipline" displaces an emphasis on learning, both in evaluating a teacher's record and in a teacher's estimate of his own effectiveness. Apathy seems pervasive.

A pattern of violence expected from students and counterforce from

599

the teachers creates a brutalizing atmosphere in which any learning would be hard. One teacher reported: "The children are not taught anything; they are just slapped around and nobody bothers to do anything about it."

Some teachers say or imply that Harlem children expect to be beaten:

When I came to school "X," I had never seen anything like that school. I cried, they behaved so badly. I soon learned that the boys like to be beaten; like to be spoken to in the way in which they are accustomed, and when I learned to say things to them that, to me, would be absolutely insulting and to hit them when they needed it, I got along all right and they began to like me. Somehow that made them feel that I liked them. I talked to them in the terms and in the way to which they are accustomed, and they like it.

Another white teacher said:

Here, both the Negro and white teachers feel completely free to beat up the children, and the principal knows it. They know he knows it and that nothing will be done about it. The principal is prejudiced. Because he knows he is prejudiced, he covers it by giving the Negro teachers the best classes. The Negro teachers are the best teachers because they are more stable. Some colored and white teachers ask for the worst classes because they don't want to work. In the worst classes they don't have to work because whatever happens, they can just say, "It is the children." The white teachers are largely inexperienced—the principal does not expect very much from the teachers. He often says, openly, "Why did they put me here?" The Board of Education should have put an experienced principal there. There is a lot of brutality—brutal beatings, and nobody cares—nothing is done about it. The parents, the principal, and the teachers don't care.

One teacher told of a teacher who exploited his students:

The teacher should set a good example; not a teacher who comes to class to shave, clean his teeth, and sleep—as does one of the teachers in my school. Then, so that he will be free of responsibility, he tells one of the bullies of the class to strong-arm the class and keep order.

One teacher of some sensitivity commented on the reaction of Negro children to the often severe, even brutal punishment inflicted upon them:

A child won't respond to minor discipline and will more often only respond to a more brutal form of discipline. There is inconsistent discipline and a lot of brutality in the Harlem schools. Many children are immature and, therefore, are extremely hurt by being disciplined. I have had the experience of children running out of the room after they had been yelled at—there seems to be a very low frustration point at which they can take discipline.

It is only in a context of utter apathy that such behavior could be tolerated. If only *one* teacher could talk of children expecting to be beaten, this would be evidence of inhumanity. The fact is that in the ghetto schools many teachers believe that such discipline is necessary for children who come from ghetto homes. In such an atmosphere where the priority is not on superior teaching, it is not surprising to discover that nearly half of the school personnel report that they find their work in the ghetto "more demanding and less satisfying" than work in other parts of the city.

Negro teachers tended to feel that the Negroes in Harlem are better teachers than the whites, in part because they stayed longer and could keep better discipline. One Negro woman teacher said that a white male teacher constantly asked her to restore order in his class-room. Whites, in turn, often feel a Harlem post is a step down. A Negro teacher said Harlem schools are "a dumping ground for condemned white teachers." Some white teachers report that they feel uneasy with Negroes. One white teacher interviewed said, "When I walk through the streets here I feel conspicuous; I would like to be able to blend into the scenery." Yet there are a number of dedicated men and women for whom the job of teaching the many neglected children of Harlem brings satisfaction and reward.

White teachers who feel they are in hostile territory and Negro teachers who resent their presence can hardly be expected to work together without friction. Much of the feeling is repressed, however, and only emerges in depth interviews conducted in confidence. Negroes express the feeling that whites feel and act superior and "cold" even when they are less well educated. Many of the white teachers are Jewish; for some of them this fact brings a sense of identification with another oppressed minority; for others, an impatience with an ethnic group, unlike their own, where the tradition of eager learning has not yet been firmly established. One Negro teacher expressed her view on the subject in these words:

I find that the Jewish people, in particular, will protect their own and are protected by their own. In our school, this young teacher says that the children "just
can't be taught" and even when the method used to teach is not a good one, she
blames the children for not having the mentality to learn.

Unless she is a lackey, the Negro teacher has a hard road to travel. Mostly,
they are doing a good job, but I don't think that there are enough Negroes in the
teaching field with the guts to fight against the things that should not be. Negro
teachers are too often trying to placate and please the white teachers. Most of the
white teachers are Jewish. They respect the Negro who will fight, but if they
find that they will not fight, they will walk all over them.

Negro teachers generally prefer not to associate with white teachers. As one said:

I, by choice, try not to socialize with them because I get sick and tired of hearing
how our children will never amount to anything, our children are ignorant, the
homes they come from are so deprived, these children are nothing, and so forth,
and so on. I get tired of hearing this conversation even though I realize there is a
problem.

Another Negro implied that friendliness to white teachers was taboo, and would be frowned upon or punished by her Negro colleagues:

I am a person who has been around and I get tired of "Oh, you feel white today,
you're eating with the white teachers." "Oh, ha, she's joining their gang, she's

turning on us." I won't eat with any of them. You know what, I'd rather go down to the Harlem Embers and eat by myself.

The dominant and disturbing fact about the ghetto schools is that the teachers and the students regard each other as adversaries. Under these conditions the teachers are reluctant to teach and the students retaliate and resist learning.

Negroes seldom move up the ladder of promotion in urban school systems. There are only six Negroes out of more than 1,200 top-level administrators in New York City, and only three Negroes out of 800 are full principals. Practically all of the Negroes are to be found quite far down in the organizational hierarchy—a fact discouraging in the extreme to Negro teachers and indirectly damaging to the self-image of Negro children who rarely see Negroes in posts of authority.

In past attempts to obtain experienced and qualified teachers for the schools in deprived communities, the Board of Education of the City of New York has not used its statutory power to assign teachers to these schools. The implicit and explicit reasons for not doing so were based upon the assumption that, given the "teacher shortage," teachers would refuse to accept such assignments and would leave the New York City school system if the board insisted upon exercising its power to make such assignments. The board, therefore, sought "volunteers" for these schools and flirted with proposals for providing extra bonuses for teachers who sought assignments in them. These methods have not been successful. The Allen Report declared that:

A spurious "reward structure" exists within the staffing pattern of the New York schools. Through it, less experienced and less competent teachers are assigned to the least "desirable" yet professionally most demanding depressed area schools. As the teacher gains experience and demonstrated competence, his mobility upward usually means mobility away from the pupils with the greatest need for skilled help. The classrooms that most urgently need the best teachers are thus often deprived of them.

Schools in deprived communities have a disproportionately high number of substitute and unlicensed teachers. Some of the classes in these schools have as many as ten or more different teachers in a single school year. Although precise figures are unavailable, nearly half of the teachers answering a Haryou questionnaire said they had held their posts for three years or less—far more than the citywide average (20 per cent in present post three years or less).

The persistent failure on the part of the New York Board of Education to solve the problem of the adequate staffing of these schools points to the need for a new approach to this problem. It is suggested that teachers be selected for assignment in these schools in terms of their special qualifications, training, and human understanding. Rather than seek to entice, cajole, or bribe teachers into serving in such "hardship or ghetto outposts," the board should set up rather rigorous standards and qualifications for the teachers who would be invited or accepted for this type of service. These teachers should be motivated and recognized as *master teachers* or individuals working toward such professional recognition. Realistic professional and financial incentives must be provided if this professional status is to be other than perfunctory or nominal. Extra pay should be specifically tied to superior skill and more challenging responsibilities. A high-level professional atmosphere of competent and understanding supervision, a system of accountability—objective appraisal of professional performance—and a general atmosphere conducive to high-quality teaching and clear standards for differentiation of inferior, mediocre, and superior teaching with appropriate corrections and rewards must be maintained.

Excellent teaching can be obtained and sustained only under conditions of excellent supervision. The roles of field assistant superintendents, principals, and assistant principals must be re-examined. Those individuals who are assigned to schools in deprived communities must be selected in terms of special competence and in terms of the highest professional and personal standards. It should be understood that they would be judged primarily, if not exclusively, in terms of objective evidence.

### Evidence of Effective Learning

The schools in the ghetto have lost faith in the ability of their students to learn and the ghetto has lost faith in the ability of the schools to lead. There are two conflicting points of view—one, that the pupils do not learn because they cannot; the other, that they do not learn because they are not taught. The fact is they are not learning. The problem is to see that they do, and only when the attempt is made with enthusiasm and competence will the answer be clear. As the Haryou report said:

Children do enter school with individual differences in experience, skills, and attitudes which make teaching more or less difficult. It is not unreasonable to expect that some of these differences will stem from differences in cultural or economic background. What has not been demonstrated, however, is that these differences constitute a permanent barrier to learning.

How long does it take to learn the colors of the spectrum, or develop the manipulative skills needed in order to do first grade work?

The studies cited by school administrators are silent on this point. Further, the data here presented show that the major deterioration in learning takes place between the third and sixth grades, not in the first and second grades. This leads to the inference that underachievement is the result of an accumulation of deficiencies while in school, rather than the result of deficiencies prior to school.[1]

[1] *Youth in the Ghetto*, Harlem Youth Opportunities Unlimited, New York, 1964, pp. 239–240.

Given no evidence to the contrary, the assumption can be made that cultural and economic backgrounds of pupils do not constitute a barrier to the type of learning which can reasonably be expected of normal children in the elementary grades—however much of a barrier such backgrounds are in respect to social problems such as delinquency, emotional stability, and the like. Only when it is permitted to be a barrier does it become a cumulative deteriorating force.

What are the facts that are presently available that would substantiate this point of view? A few examples follow:

1. A "crash program" of remedial reading for one summer month starting in 1955 and continuing until the summer of 1964 (the data available, however, cover only 1955–1959) at Northside Center for Child Development in New York discovered that a child who has one month of extra daily instruction can gain on the average of almost one school year in reading. The children with the least retardation gained the most—those with I.Q.'s of above 110 gained more than two years in reading achievement, but the most retarded gained at least five months. The 104 children helped came eagerly and voluntarily to the program. Attendance never was less than 85 per cent. Those who came more learned more.

This study of large numbers of woefully retarded, economically inferior Negro and Puerto Rican students reveals that such children can learn if taught. Nothing was done to change their "cultural deprivation." The only thing that was done was that they were being taught to read by individuals who believed that they could learn to read and who related to them with warmth and acceptance. Under these conditions they learned. And what is more, they sustained what they had learned during the school year. It is ironic, however, that when they returned to school they sustained their summer gains but they did not advance further.

All studies of the problem of education in deprived communities agree in concluding that the central problem in ghetto schools is the fact that the children are woefully deficient in reading. It has been suggested by the remedial reading staff of Northside Center that as a necessary first step in the development of a program to attain educational excellence in the Harlem schools, the Board of Education drop its normal curriculum in these schools for a period of half a school year, or perhaps a full school year, and immediately mobilize all of its resources toward the goal of raising the reading level of all children in the Harlem schools, especially those from the third to the eighth grades. During this *Reading Mobilization Year* the total school program in these schools would be geared toward the improvement of reading. All other school work would be temporarily postponed for those children who are retarded until they are brought up to grade level.

There is general agreement also, supported by Haryou's research findings and by the Board of Education itself, that there is a desperate need for afterschool remedial centers. Space is available in churches, renovated store fronts and lofts, social agencies, and community centers. What is not agreed upon, however, is the most effective type of remedial program. There is serious question whether submitting the child who has already experienced defeat in school to the same teachers, techniques, classroom settings, and general atmosphere is likely to result in any great educational achievement. An effective remedial program would require a revised curriculum, advanced teaching techniques and materials, a stimulating atmosphere, and generally increased motivation.

2. "Culturally deprived" children have learned in those public schools in which they are expected to learn and in which they are taught. Children attending Harlem schools in the 1920s and 1930s had average academic achievement close to, if not equal to, the white norms. Klineberg's study of the performance of Negro children migrating from the South to the North and those already in Northern schools during the thirties can be used as evidence that at that time the discrepancy between norms of white students and those of Negro students was minimal compared with the present gap.[2] It would be difficult to argue and to prove the contention that Negroes at that time were less culturally deprived than they were in the 1950s or than they are now.

3. Junior High School 43 on the periphery of Harlem, like most Harlem schools, was holding largely a custodial program for the "culturally deprived." In 1956, before the pilot project began, the teachers felt helpless to teach. Their students seemed then to be hopeless, and considered themselves failures, their teachers as enemies. Then the school became a pilot demonstration guidance program and what looked like a miracle occurrred. Six times as many students went to college (25 per cent) than had earlier (4 per cent). The dropout rate fell one-half, from 50 per cent to 25 per cent. Eighty-one per cent were judged to have greater intellectual capacity than their earlier I.Q. and achievement scores would have predicted—their I.Q.'s in the eleventh grade went up an average of eight to nine points. In the more than two years during which the tests were made, the average student gained 4.3 years in reading scores compared with 1.7 years during a similar earlier period. When one studies this pilot project, one does not find any revolutionary educational methods. Most of the New York City schools had both curriculum and individual counseling, trips and programs for parents, as did JHS 43, prior to the project.

The "miracle" seemed due primarily to an implementation of the belief that such children can learn.

School personnel were told to adopt an affirmative view of their students and give up their earlier negative views. Therefore, certain educational methods previously considered questionable for lower-class children were now used. Those who had openly blocked changes before became less

[2] Otto Klineberg, *Negro Intelligence and Selective Migration*, New York, Columbia University Press, 1935.

influential in the wake of the prestige of the new project. Most of the emphasis on discipline was toned down. Teacher responsibility for maintaining order was relaxed. Students felt that they were "special," and that they were expected to achieve and learn. Teachers were evaluated more on their teaching skill than on their discipline. Because the school administration was eager for the success of the experiment, it opened many previously clogged channels of communication between itself and teachers, parents, and pupils. Originally this was meant to win their support, but also, the administration was unconsciously stimulated to solve some of the problems and attend to some of the grievances not necessarily related at all to the question of race. Teachers began to consider themselves competent and their students capable. Pupils were told that they were trustworthy and that their teachers were committed to helping them succeed. Parents were advised that they could help in their children's education and progress. There was no attempt, because the task was too formidable, to reverse the environment of cultural deprivation of the community's children.

The cyclic relationship between educational effectiveness and heightened morale is indicated by the fact that a serious program designed to increase educational effectiveness invariably heightens the morale of pupils, teachers, and supervisors; the heightened morale increases the chances of success of the educational program. Conversely, inferior education in a school decreases morale of teachers, pupils, and supervisors, and the decreased morale tends to reinforce the educational inefficiency.

4. The Banneker Project in St. Louis, Missouri, showed similar striking results.

In 1957, St. Louis high schools inaugurated a three-track system of ability grouping based upon standardized I.Q. and achievement scores. Students scoring high on both tests were placed in Track I and given college preparatory courses. Those scoring below average were placed in Track III and given vocational and technical courses. Average students fell into Track II.

The Banneker School District is one of five elementary school groups in St. Louis and is one of two having the largest proportion of Negroes. The neighborhood is characterized by old housing, slums, high crime rate, high unemployment, etc. Of the 16,000 pupils in the Banneker schools, 9,590 are Negro.

The initial test scores for students in the Banneker District showed that only 7 per cent had Track I scores, whereas 47 per cent went into Track III. The median scores for reading, arithmetic, and language achievement were consistently below grade level. Otis Intelligence Test scores for 1958–1959 showed Banneker children with an I.Q. median of 90.5, with 12.1 per cent below I.Q. 79.

The district director, Dr. Samuel Shepard, immediately moved to improve performance, suggesting that the children had not been properly prepared for the testing experience and for that reason did not measure up as well as they might have if well motivated. Shepard initiated a program designed to stimulate teachers to teach students to learn, and parents to facilitate learning. The initial scores were graphically and comparatively represented to teachers, principals, students, and parents. It was made quite clear, however, that the low standing of Banneker children relative to children in other parts of the city was not to be ignored or explained away as the inevitable consequence of underprivilege. Rather, it was to be used to bring about improvement.

Principals were asked to help teachers have a more positive attitude toward the children and their chances for success. Teachers were to visit the homes of their pupils to familiarize themselves with the social and familial situation. In addition, teachers were asked to ignore I.Q. scores and to treat all children as if they had superior ability. As a result of this intensive, yet inexpensive and relatively uncomplicated approach, eighth graders went from 7.7 years in reading to 8.8 in two and one-half years; from 7.6 in language to 9.1; and 7.9 to 8.7 in arithmetic. Children assigned to Track I increased from 7 per cent to 22 per cent, while Track III assignments fell from 47.1 per cent to 10.9 per cent. Attendance in one school reached an unprecedented 97.1 per cent. The median I.Q. was raised almost ten points.

In spite of the fact that there had been no drastic change in curriculum, instructional technique, or the basic "underprivileged" social situation, improvements were definitely evident. What had changed was the attitude and perspective of teachers which influenced the way in which the students were taught and learned.

5. Baltimore, Maryland, has tried another interesting program—this one a preschool year for sixty children of four years of age in two of the city's most depressed neighborhoods, both Negro, where crime and delinquency rates have been so high that teachers hesitated to make home visits alone or at night. Francis Keppel, U.S. Commissioner of Education, reports that the school administrator in charge, Mrs. Catherine Brunner, has found that: Every child who entered in 1963 began kindergarten the following year, a record their older brothers and sisters had not matched. In kindergarten they did as well as children from middle- or upper-class families. In first grade, they showed better use of language, superior understanding of ideas and problem solving than other children from the same depressed neighborhoods. In the first grade, two-thirds of the original sixty were in the top half of their class; ten in the top quarter. Keppel quotes one kindergarten teacher's "candid and heartwarming judgment" of the project:

I've always been in the habit of dividing my kindergarten classes into two sections—those who come from poor neighborhoods and lack much background for learning, and those who come from better homes and are accustomed to books and cultural experiences in their families. In a sense, this has also seemed a logical division between the dull children, the ones who need help, and the bright ones, who go along very quickly.

But what seemed so logical before the project started now doesn't seem logical to me today. The youngsters who have this new preschool experience, I'm finding, belong among the highest achieving children in my classes and this is where I place them. It makes me wonder now whether many of us in teaching haven't a great deal to learn ourselves.

Despite the evidence of the effectiveness of early childhood education for the growth and development of children, public schools have not made adequate provision for extensive preprimary education. For children who live in disadvantaged circumstances, well-organized centers for early childhood education can partially compensate for lack of opportunities for wholesome development in these formative years.

There are more than 12,000 children between three and six years of age in Harlem. All of the twenty elementary schools in the area have kindergartens which children may enter at the age of five, but there are at least 4,000 children under five who should have preschool education if community pathology is to be resisted. Haryou proposed that in each school zone, two preschool academies be established, each serving 100 children three through five years old. At first, preference would be given to the four- and five-year olds. But preschool experience, however desirable for its own sake, will not lead children to learn basic skills in the primary grades if, when they reach these grades, the schools react to them as though they cannot learn.

One variable held constant in each of these programs is the nature and extent of the cultural deprivation found in the particular group before the program began. The program's success then would have to be due either to the unlikely fact that the culturally deprived are particularly responsive to a program of education or that their deprivation is less important in their success than other factors—such as the faith of the teachers, the quality of the education. The common denominator in all these successful programs was more efficient teaching—these children can be taught if they are accepted and respected. But how does one transform an apathetic teacher into an emphatic, accepting, and enthusiastic one?

If it were assumed on the other hand that teachers could only teach children who came from homes where learning is respected and encouraged, it would be analogous to physicians asserting that they could only help patients who are not too ill, or who are not ill at all.

If the cultural deprivation theories are valid and relevant explanations of the widespread problem, then it would follow that the extent and degree of academic retardation would be constant, that is, the same, under different conditions and at varying periods of time as long as the social, economic, and cultural conditions of the Negro group remained the same. A related hypothesis would be that the degree of retardation would increase or decrease in proportion to similar changes in the status of the Negro. Any evidence showing constancy in the degree of retardation in spite of changes in the economic and social status of the Negro would seem to raise serious questions about the cultural deprivation theories, and it would then be necessary to seek explanations of the academic retardation of Negro children in terms of variables directly related to the educational processes: What is happening in the classroom? Are these children being taught or are they being ignored? What is the attitude of their teachers toward them? Are they seen as primitive, unmanageable discipline problems and burdens, rather than as modifiable human beings who will respond positively if they are reacted to positively? In short, are these children seen as essentially uneducable because they are racially or culturally inferior? In the 1930s, Otto Klineberg, as noted earlier, succeeded in demonstrating that the academic performance of Negro youngsters in the New York City public schools was nearly equal to that of whites. The economic conditions of Negroes at that time were significantly lower than today. To assume that Negro children are inherently inferior or that environmental inferiority is responsible for poor school performance is educationally irrelevant—and even false. The assumption of inferiority might be the controlling fact which restricts the educational responsiveness of children to the alleged educational experience. In this regard, racial inferiority and cultural inferiority have identical practical educational consequences. This might, therefore, be the chief obstacle—the subtle, insidious human obstacle—which must be overcome if lower-status children are to be educated up to a level of efficiency necessary to bring them within a useful and creative role in society.

There is considerable evidence that this can be done. It has been done. The resistance to accepting this evidence and implementing it, the insistence upon labeling these children with euphemistically derogatory terms, might be the key human and educational problems to be studied if our society is to obtain the benefits of the trained intelligence of these children.

This is not to say that a teacher's affirmative attitude toward children is the only relevant factor influencing the performance of children in ghetto schools and that overcrowded classrooms, inadequate plants and facilities, unimaginative curricula, and the like, are irrelevant. All of these influence a child's educational growth. The point is rather that these factors cannot be given equal importance; in the light of available evidence the controlling factor which determines the academic performance of pupils and which establishes the level of educational efficiency and the over-all quality of the schools is the competence of the teachers and their attitude of acceptance or rejection of their students. Competent teachers who have confidence in children strive to achieve the other dimensions of good education also. But without such competence and confidence, children do not learn even if the textbooks are new and the classes small. There are ghetto schools which are brand new. There are some ghetto schools with comparatively small classes and with adequate facilities. But there are few ghetto schools where the morale of teachers and pupils is high and where the teachers truly believe in the humanity and capacity of the children to learn. In those few schools the children learn.

The pilot experiments in St. Louis, New York, and elsewhere are encouraging evidence that children can learn when they are expected to learn. The Negro child, like the Negro teacher, must be held to the same high standards of academic performance as their white counterparts in white schools. Obviously some Negroes, like some whites, will not have the innate capacity to respond. But many will, and each deserves the chance. Negro students cannot be excused for shoddy performance *because* they are Negro. To do so makes more rigid and intolerable the pathology, injustices, and distinctions of racism. There can be no double standards in education, no easy alibi. Schools are institutions designed to compensate for "cultural deprivation." If this were not true there would be no need for schools.

The schools are crucial to any positive resolution of the problems of the ghetto. As long as these ghetto schools continue to turn out thousands and thousands of functional illiterates yearly, Negro youth will not be prepared for anything other than menial jobs or unemployment and dependency; they will continue the cycle of broken homes, unstable family life, and neglected and uneducated children. The tragic waste of human resources will go on unabated.

# References to Introductions

1. Allport, Gordon W., "Prejudice: A Problem in Psychological and Social Causation," Supplement Series **4,** November, 1950.
2. Anastasi, Anne, *Psychological Testing*, Second Ed., New York, The Macmillan Company, 1961.
3. ——— and Rita D'Angelo, "A Comparison of Negro and White Pre-school Children in Language and Goodenough Draw-a-Man I.Q.," *Journal of Genetic Psychology*, 1952, **82,** 147–165.
4. Anderson, Olin, W., "Infant Mortality and Social and Cultural Factors," in Jaco, E. Gartley (ed.), *Patients, Physicians and Illness*, New York, Free Press, 1958.
5. Bagdikian, Ben H., *In the Midst of Plenty: A New Report on the Poor in America*, New York, Signet Books, 1964.
6. Bloom, Benjamin S., Allison Davis, and Robert Hess, *Compensatory Education for Cultural Deprivation*, New York, Holt, Rinehart and Winston, 1965.
7. Breckenridge, Marian E. and E. L. Vincent, "Nutrition and Growth," in Seidman, J. M. (ed.), *The Adolescent: A Book of Readings*, New York, Holt, Rinehart and Winston, 1962.
8. Bridge Project, *Learning to Teach in Difficult Schools*, New York, Queens College, Department of Education, 1963.
9. Brown, F., "An Experimental and Critical Study of the Intelligence of Negro and White Kindergarten Children," *Journal of Genetic Psychology*, 1944, **65,** 161–175.
10. Clark, Kenneth B., "Color, Class, Personality and Juvenile Delinquency," *Journal of Negro Education*, **28,** 1959, 240–251.
11. ——— *Dark Ghetto*, New York, Harper and Row, 1965.
12. Clark, Margaret, *Health in the Mexican-American Culture*, Berkeley, University of California Press, 1959.
13. Clausen, J., M. Seidenfeld, and L. Deasy, "Parent Attitudes Toward Participation of Their Children In Polio Vaccine Trials," in Jaco, E. Gartley (ed.), *Patients, Physicians and Illness*, New York: Free Press, 1958.
14. Conant, James B., *Slums and Suburbs, A Commentary on Schools in Metropolitan Areas*, New York, McGraw-Hill, 1961.

611

15. Davidson, Helen H., Judith Greenberg, and Joan M. Gerner, "Character-
    istics of Successful School Achievers From a Severely Deprived Environ-
    ment." Unpublished manuscript, The City University of New York, 1962.
16. Davis, A. and R. J. Havighurst, "Social Class and Color Differences in
    Child Rearing," *American Sociological Review*, 1948, **11**, 698–710.
17. Deutsch, Martin P., "The Disadvantaged Child and the Learning Process,"
    in Passow, A. Harry (ed.), *Education in Depressed Areas*, New York,
    Bureau of Publications, Teachers College, Columbia University, 1963.
18. ——— "Minority Group and Class Status as Related to Social and Person-
    ality Factors in Scholastic Achievement," *Society for Applied Anthro-
    pology*, Monograph no. 2, 1960.
19. Ford, Clellan A. and Frank A. Beach, *Patterns of Sexual Behavior*, New
    York, Harper and Brothers, 1951.
20. Frazier, Franklin E., *The Negro in the United States*, New York, The Mac-
    millan Company, 1949, pp. 320–332.
21. Gage, N. L. (ed.), *Handbook of Research on Teaching*, Chicago, Rand
    McNally and Co., 1963.
22. Gans, Herbert J., *The Urban Villagers*, New York, Free Press, 1962.
23. Giles, Harry H., *The Integrated Classroom*, New York, Basic Books, Inc.,
    1959.
24. Gregory, Dick, *Nigger*, New York, E. P. Dutton and Co., Inc., 1964.
25. Guetzkow, H. S., and P. H. Bowman, *Men and Hunger: A Psychological
    Manual for Relief Workers*, Illinois, Brethren Press, 1964.
26. Guilford, J. P., "Three Faces of Intellect," *American Psychologist*, 1959, **14**,
    469–479.
27. Hammer, Richard, "Report from a Spanish Harlem Fortress," in Harry L.
    Miller and Marjorie B. Smiley (eds.), *Education and the Metropolis: A
    Book of Readings*, New York, Hunter College, 1964.
28. Handlin, Oscar, *The Newcomers*, New York, Doubleday and Company, 1959.
29. Harrington, Michael, *The Other America*, Baltimore, Penguin Books, 1963.
30. Haubrick, Vernon F., "Teachers for Big-City Schools," in Passow, A. Harry
    (ed.), *Education in Depressed Areas*, New York, Bureau of Publications,
    Teachers College, Columbia University, 1963.
31. Hunt, J. McV., "Implications of Piaget's Stages for Matching Circum-
    stances and Schemata." In *Intelligence and Experience*, New York,
    Ronald, 1961.
32. Keys, A., J. Brozek, A. Herschel, O. Mickelsen, and H. L. Taylor, *The
    Biology of Human Starvation*, Minneapolis, University of Minnesota
    Press, 1950.
33. Klineberg, Otto, "Life is Fun in a Smiling, Fair-Skinned World," *Saturday
    Review*, February 16, 1963, pp. 75–77.
34. ——— *Negro Intelligence and Selective Migration*, New York, Columbia
    University Press, 1935.
35. ——— "Negro-White Differences in Intelligence Test Performance: A New
    Look at an Old Problem," *American Psychologist*, April, 1963, **18**(4),
    198–203.
36. Langner, Thomas S. and Stanley T. Michael. *Life Stress and Mental Health*,
    London, Collier-Macmillan Ltd., Free Press, 1963.
37. Lerner, M. and O. Anderson, *Health Progress in the United States: 1900–
    1960*, Chicago, University of Chicago Press, 1963.
38. Linton, Ralph, "The Natural History of the Family," in Fried, Morton H.
    (ed.) *Readings in Anthropology*, II, New York, Crowell, 1959, pp. 200–
    244.

39. Lipset, S. M. and R. Bendix, *Social Mobility in Industrial Society*, Berkeley, University of California Press, 1959.
40. Maslow, A. H., *Motivation and Personality*, New York, Harper and Brothers, 1954.
41. Michael, Donald N., "Cybernation: The Silent Conquest." A Report to the Center for the Study of Democratic Institutions. California: Center for the Study of Democratic Institutions, 1962.
42. Miller, Henry P., *Rich Man, Poor Man*, New York, Crowell, 1964.
43. Moreland Commission Report. Prepared by Greenleigh Associates, Inc. *Public Welfare in the State of New York*, Executive Number, State Capital, Albany 1, New York, 1963.
44. Osborn, R. T., "Racial Differences in Mental Growth and School Achievement: A Longitudinal Study," *Psychological Reports*, 1960, **7**, 233–239.
45. Pettigrew, Thomas, "Negro-American Intelligence: A New Look at an Old Controversy," *Journal of Negro Education*, 1964, **33**, 6–25.
46. Piaget, J. and Barbel Inhelder, "Diagnosis of Mental Operations and Theory of Intelligence." *American Journal of Mental Deficiency*, 1947, **51**, 401–406.
47. *Project True: Teacher Resources for Urban Education*, research project. Unpublished field observations from urban slum schools, Hunter College, 1963.
48. Riessman, Frank, *The Culturally Deprived Child*, New York, Harper and Row, 1962.
49. "The Great Cities School Improvement Studies," Ford Foundation Project, mimeographed, 1960. (Quoted in Riessman, Frank, *The Culturally Deprived Child*, New York, Harper and Row, 1962) p. 1.
50. Schneider, Louis and Sverre Lysgaard, "The Deferred Gratification Pattern: A Preliminary Study," *American Sociological Review*, 1953, **18**, 142–149.
51. Schoor, Alice L., *Slums and Social Insecurity*, Washington, D.C.: U.S. Department of Health, Education and Welfare. Research Report No. 1.
52. Sears, R. R., E. Maccoby, and H. Levin, *Patterns of Child Rearing*, Illinois, Row, Peterson and Co., 1957.
53. Seeley, John R. R., Alexander Sim, and Elizabeth W. Loosley, *Crestwood Heights*, New York, John Wiley, 1963 (c. Basic Book, 1956).
54. Senior, Clarence, *Strangers, Then Neighbors*, New York, Freedom Books, 1961, pp. 16–17.
55. Sexton, Patricia, *Education and Income*, New York, The Viking Press, 1961.
56. ——— *Spanish Harlem*, New York, Harper and Row, 1965.
57. Silberman, Charles E., "The City and the Negro," *Fortune*, March, 1962.
58. Spinley, B. M., *The Deprived and the Privileged, Personality Development in English Society*, London, Routledge and Kegan Paul, 1953.
59. Spiro, Melford E., *Kibbutz*, New York, Schocken Books, 1956, pp. 110–139.
60. Tomlinson, H., "Differences between Preschool Negro Children and Their Older Siblings on the Stanford-Binet Scales," *Journal of Negro Education*, 1944, **13**, 474–479.
61. Thorndike, Robert L. and Elizabeth Hagen, *Measurement and Evaluation in Psychology and Education*, Second edition, New York, John Wiley and Sons, Inc., 1962.
62. World Health Organization, *Deprivation of Maternal Care, a Reassessment of its Effects*, Geneva, W. H. O. Public Health Paper No. 14, 1962.

# CONTRIBUTORS

*Arensberg, Conrad M.*, Ph.D.
Professor of Anthropology, Department of Anthropology, Columbia University, New York, New York.

*Ashton-Warner, Sylvia*
Elementary school teacher and novelist, New Zealand.

*Ausubel, David*, Ph.D.
Professor of Educational Psychology, Bureau of Educational Research, University of Illinois, Champaign, Illinois.

*Ausubel, Pearl*
Wife of David Ausubel and frequent assistant in his research work.

*Bagdikian, Benjamin H.*
Journalist and author, Washington, D.C.

*Bardach, Joan L.*, Ph.D.
Assistant Chief Psychologist, Institute of Physical Medicine and Rehabilitation, New York University, New York, New York.

*Bernstein, Basil*, Ph.D.
Sociologist, Institute of Education, University of London, London, England.

*Boll, Eleanor S.*, Ph.D.
Sociologist and Director, William T. Canter Foundation for Child Development, University of Pennsylvania, Philadelphia, Pennsylvania.

*Bossard, James H. S.*
Deceased. Formerly associated with the University of Pennsylvania, Philadelphia, Pennsylvania.

*Bowman, Paul H.*, Ph.D.
Director of the Department of Preventive Mental Health, Greater Kansas City Mental Health Foundation, Kansas City, Missouri.

*Bronfenbrenner, Urie*, Ph.D.
Professor of Psychology of Child Development and Family Relations, Cornell University, Ithaca, New York.

*Brown, Bert*, Ph.D.
Research Psychologist, Institute for Developmental Studies, School of Education, New York University, New York, New York.

*Carson, Arnold S.*, Ph.D.
Clinical Psychologist, Broadlawns Polk County Hospital, Des Moines, Iowa.

615

*Caudill, William*, Ph.D.
Chief, Section on Personality and Environment, Laboratory of Socio-Environmental Studies, National Institute of Mental Health, Bethesda, Maryland.

*Charters, W. W.*, Ph.D.
Professor, Graduate Institute of Education, Washington University, St. Louis, Missouri.

*Clark, Donald*, Ph.D.
Administrator, Educational Clinic and Professor, Hunter College, New York, New York.

*Clark, Kenneth*, Ph.D.
Professor of Psychology, City College of New York, and Research Director, Northside Center for Child Development, New York, New York.

*Cuber, John F.*, Ph.D.
Professor of Sociology and Anthropology, Ohio State University, Columbus, Ohio.

*Cutler, Rhoda*, M.A.
Research Psychologist, Institute for Developmental Studies, School of Education, New York University, New York, New York.

*Davidson, Helen H.*, Ph.D.
Professor of Psychology, City College of New York, New York, New York.

*Deutsch, Martin*, Ph.D.
Professor of Education and Director, Institute for Developmental Studies, School of Education, New York University, New York, New York.

*DeVos, George A.*, Ph.D.
Professor of Anthropology and of the School of Social Welfare, University of California, Berkeley, California.

*Douvan, Elizabeth*, Ph.D.
Research Associate, Survey Research Center, University of Michigan, Ann Arbor, Michigan.

*Durkin, Kathryn*
Department of Psychology, University of Colorado, Boulder, Colorado.

*Elam, Sophie L.*, Ph.D.
Professor of Education, City College of New York, New York, New York.

*Fifer, Gordon*, Ph.D.
Professor of Education, Hunter College, New York, New York.

*Havighurst, Robert J.*, Ph.D.
Professor of Education, University of Chicago, Chicago, Illinois.

*Kahl, Joseph A.*, Ph.D.
Professor of Sociology and Anthropology, Washington University, St. Louis, Missouri.

*Katz, Irwin*, Ph.D.
Professor of Psychology and Director, Research Center for Human Relations, New York University, New York, New York.

*Kenkel, William F.*
Professor of Sociology, Department of Economics and Sociology, Iowa State University, Ames, Iowa.

*Kimball, Solon T.*, Ph.D.
Professor of Anthropology, Department of Anthropology, University of Florida, Gainsville, Florida.

*Lang, Gerhard*, Ph.D.
Research Associate, Board of Examiners, New York City Board of Education, New York, New York.

*Langner, Thomas S.*, Ph.D.
Professor of Psychiatry (Sociology), Department of Psychiatry, New York University, New York, New York.

*Lee, Rose Hum*, Ph.D.
Professor of Sociology, Phoenix College, Phoenix, Arizona.

*Lesser, Gerald*, Ph.D.
Professor of Education and Developmental Psychology and Director, Laboratory of Human Development, Harvard University, Cambridge, Massachusetts.

*Lewis, Hylan*, Ph.D.
Director, Child Rearing Project, Health and Welfare Council of the National Capitol Area, Washington, D.C.

*Liddle, Gordon P.*, Ph.D.
Associate Director, Interprofessional Research Committee on Pupil Personnel Services, Bureau of Educational Research, University of Maryland, College Park, Maryland.

*Lott, Albert J.*, Ph.D.
Professor, Department of Psychology and Professor of Behavioral Science, Medical School, University of Kentucky, Lexington, Kentucky.

*Lott, Bernice E.*, Ph.D.
Professor of Psychology, Kentucky State College, Frankfort and Research Associate, University of Kentucky, Lexington, Kentucky.

*Matthews, Charles V.*, M.A.
Associate Professor and Director, Delinquency Training Center, Southern Illinois University, Edwardsville, Illinois.

*McCord, Joan*, Ph.D.
Professor of Sociology, Stanford University, Stanford, California.

*McCord, William*, Ph.D.
Professor of Sociology, Stanford University, Stanford, California.

*McGeoch, Dorothy M.*, Ed.D.
Professor of Education, Teachers College, Columbia University, New York, New York.

*McKinley, Donald G.*, Ph.D.
Sociologist and Professor of Education, Teachers College, Columbia University, New York, New York.

*Michael, Stanley T.*, M.D.
Research Associate in Psychiatry, Cornell University Medical College, Ithaca, New York.

*Miller, Daniel R.*, Ph.D.
Chairman, Doctoral Program in Social Psychology and Research Associate, Institute for Social Research, University of Michigan, Ann Arbor, Michigan.

*Murray, Walter*, Ph.D.
   Professor of Education and Administrator of Department of Education, Brooklyn College, New York, New York.
*Padilla, Elena*, Ph.D.
   Adjunct Professor, Government Department, New York University, New York, New York.
*Paul, Elaine*, B.A.
   Editor, Social Service Employees Union News, Department of Welfare, New York, New York.
*Pettigrew, Thomas F.*, Ph.D.
   Professor of Social Psychology, Department of Social Relations, Harvard University, Cambridge, Massachusetts.
*Pierce, James V.*, M.A.
   Research Associate, University of Chicago, Chicago, Illinois.
*Rabin, Albert I.*, Ph.D.
   Professor, Department of Psychology, Michigan State University, East Lansing, Michigan.
*Rosen, Bernard C.*, Ph.D.
   Visiting Professor, Department of Social Relations, Harvard University, Cambridge, Massachusetts.
*Rue, Rose*, M.S.W.
   Social Worker, Department of Psychiatry, New York Medical College, New York, New York.
*Sexton, Patricia*, Ph.D.
   Professor of Educational Sociology, New York University, New York, New York.
*Swanson, Guy E.*, Ph.D.
   Professor, Department of Sociology, University of Michigan, Ann Arbor, Michigan.
*Terrell, Glen*, Ph.D.
   Dean of Faculties, University of Illinois at Chicago Circle, Chicago, Illinois.
*Thurber, Emily*
   Sociology Department, Stanford University, Stanford, California.
*Torrance, E. Paul*, Ph.D.
   Professor of Psychology, University of Minnesota, Minneapolis, Minnesota.
*Warner, W. Lloyd*, M.A.
   Professor of Social Research, Michigan State University, East Lansing, Michigan.
*Weiner, Max*, Ph.D.
   Professor, Brooklyn College, New York, New York.
*Wiesley, Melvin*
   Assistant Superintendent for Elementary Education, Boulder Valley Public Schools, Boulder, Colorado.
*Wortis, Helen*, M.A.
   Social Worker, Division of Pediatric Psychiatry, Jewish Hospital of Brooklyn and Assistant Clinical Professor of Psychiatry (Research), New York Medical College, New York, New York.

# Index